Bicameral Politics

From the *New York Times*, October 23, 1977. Cartoon by Randy Jones. Copyright © 1977 by The New York Times Company. Reprinted by permission.

Bicameral Politics

Conference Committees in Congress

LAWRENCE D. LONGLEY *and*
WALTER J. OLESZEK

With a Foreword by
Richard F. Fenno, Jr.

Augsburg College
George Sverdrup Library
Minneapolis, MN 55454

Yale University Press
New Haven and London

Published with assistance from the Louis Stern Memorial Fund.

Copyright © 1989 by Yale University.
All rights reserved.
This book may not be reproduced, in whole or in part, including illustrations, in any form (beyond that copying permitted by Sections 107 and 108 of the U.S. Copyright Law and except by reviewers for the public press), without written permission from the publishers.

Designed by James J. Johnson and set in Times Roman types by the Composing Room of Michigan. Printed in the United States of America by Vail-Ballou Press, Binghamton, New York.

Library of Congress Cataloging-in-Publication Data

Longley, Lawrence D.
   Bicameral politics.

   Includes index.
   1. United States. Congress—Conference committees.
I. Oleszek, Walter J.   II. Title.
JK1111.L65 1989   328.73'07657   88–27760
ISBN 0–300–04317–1 (cloth)
     0–300–04544–1 (pap.)

The paper in this book meets the guidelines for permanence and durability of the Committee on Production Guidelines for Book Longevity of the Council on Library Resources.

10 9 8 7 6 5 4 3 2 1

Contents

Foreword by Richard F. Fenno, Jr.		vii
Preface		xi
1.	Bicameral Politics and Congressional Conference Committees	1
2.	The Evolution of Conference Committees and State Practice	27
3.	The Changing Character of Conference Committee Politics	46
4.	What Do We Know—and What Do We Need to Know—about Conference Committee Politics?	73
5.	The Institutional Context	91
6.	The Committee and Individual Contexts	108
7.	Conference Processes, Types, and Players	127
8.	The Preconference Process	153
9.	During the Conference	192
10.	The Postconference Process	216
11.	Conference Politics: Nine Mini-Case Studies	254
	A. Heptanoic Acid and Needy Children	256
	B. Higher Education: Personalities and Exhaustion	258
	C. Two "Hello and Good-Bye" Conferences of 1979	269
	D. The 1982 Tax Increase Conference	274
	E. A Typical Low-Intensity Appropriations Conference	282
	F. The Case of the Purloined Papers: South African Sanctions in 1985	286
	G. Dollars for Defense: Les Gets More Amidst 1985 House Turmoil	294
	H. The Gramm-Rudman Conferences of 1985	307
12.	Conference Committees and Bicameral Politics	336
Index		353

Foreword

In the second week of their existence, in April 1789, the U.S. Senate and the U.S. House of Representatives each adopted the following rule:

> Resolved, That, in every case of an amendment to a bill agreed to in one House and dissented to in the other, if either House shall request a conference, and appoint a committee for that purpose, and the other House shall also appoint a committee to confer, such committee shall, at a convenient time, to be agreed on by their chairman, meet in the conference chamber, and state to each other verbally, or in writing, as either shall choose, the reasons of their respective Houses for and against the amendment, and confer freely thereon.

By these words, the legislative institution known as the conference committee came to the United States Congress. Of necessity, it came early. For it was the essence of a bicameral legislature that two different viewpoints could be brought to bear on every legislative proposal. Yet unless such differences could be resolved into a single piece of legislation, nothing could be signed into law by the president. At the same time, therefore, that the great constitutional compromise created a distinctive House and Senate, it also created the need for an internal mechanism to promote compromise between them. The conference committee met that legislative need. After both chambers had acted, a few members from one chamber would meet with a few members of the other chamber to resolve their differences. This simple arrangement became, as the authors of this book describe it, "the linking mechanism of congressional bicameral politics."

The conference committee is a fascinating and unique institution. It grew out of British parliamentary procedure and was widely used in the bicameral colonial legislatures. So it was no stranger to the members of the First Congress. But two hundred years later, it has developed—as the Congress itself has developed—into a more complex, more institutionalized, more influential, and altogether more intriguing object of study. As a feature of our legislative landscape it is less conspicuous than it is commanding. It comes into play in only about 15 to 25 percent of all pieces of legislation. But included within that group are most all of the consequential and highly publicized legislative enactments. And when a conference decides, ninety-nine times out of a hundred its decision becomes the law. Because of its penultimate position in the legislative process, therefore, and because of the finality of its decisions, it has been described—in language reported herein—as "the third house of Congress," "the epitome of legislative politics," "the real world of legislation," and "the Supreme Court of legislation."

Surely an institution bearing such striking labels is worth careful study. But just as surely it has not received such study from political scientists. The main reason for our neglect is the sheer difficulty of gathering data. Until the mid-1970s, conference committee activity took place in secret, attended only by the participants, who deliberated informally and left no account of the proceedings. And in the dozen years since conferences have been opened to public view, access has remained problematic. They often convene in small rooms, at odd hours; and they transact much of their business informally or in private. Academics are not alone in their difficulty. Present-day conferences, explain the authors, "make for difficult print coverage and for dull TV." Journalists, therefore, have not found them a congenial setting from which to report legislative activity. Party leaders, too, still complain that conferees "work in mysterious ways." In sum, a large mismatch has persisted between the importance of this institution and our understanding of it.

But no longer. Lawrence Longley and Walter Oleszek know more about conference committees than any political scientists have yet known. And they have written a careful, richly detailed, multifaceted book about the subject. With their book, our knowledge gap has been substantially narrowed. Readers will find here a comprehensive, well-rounded treatment—one in which conference committees are viewed independently as "crucially important to policy outcomes" and dependently as "products of their environments." Both perspectives are copiously illustrated with dozens of concrete examples. Some are taken from the authors' wide-ranging research in the public record; some are informed by their personal firsthand observation on Capitol Hill. Their writing captures at once the complexity and the flavor of the institution.

"Let's face it, the conference committee is where it all happens," the authors quote one participant. And they approach their subject in the same spirit, as one that encompasses all the ingredients of legislative politics. First, they examine contextual variables that affect conference committee activity—the House and Senate as distinct and rival institutions, the differences in behavior patterns among the standing committees whose members become the major conference participants, the personal goals of the individual conferees. Next, the authors examine the decision-making sequence of which the conference committee is a part—preconference anticipation, conference negotiation, and postconference approval—all of which are enveloped in a set of intricately woven procedures. The result is a kaleidoscopic look at the context and the sequence "where it all happens." The authors turn their viewing instrument first one way and then another, so that all the elements of legislative politics can be seen, first in one pattern then in another. The sheer variety of conference-related activity—as expressed, finally, in their detailed case studies—becomes a pervasive theme.

The ultimate fascination with the context lies in the interplay of motivations, incentives, opportunities, and constraints that push the conferees to take independent action, and, at the same time, pull them into conformity with their respective chambers and committees. When confronted with the problem of reconciling the proverbial apples and oranges, will the results, as President Ronald Reagan suggests herein, "come out a pear"? Or, as Speaker Jim Wright says, will the conferees "make fruit salad"? The authors describe both outcomes—the "runaway conference" and the "faithful reflection"—and everything in-between. In so doing, they portray the participants as they decide among their "diverse loyalties to chamber, chairman, committee, constituency, interest, and personal preference" and as they work in an atmosphere of "emotion, inertia, pressure, ambition." Bits of conversation evoke the atmospherics: "I help you, you help me. That's what this is all about. All I'm asking for is a measley $3 million"; and "The idealists all stand over in the corner and posture and let us compromisers get things done for them"; and "You back me or you won't get on the bus"; and "We have to be men or we will be mice."

In such a colorful context, scholarly judgment could easily give way to hyperbole and hype. Longley and Oleszek resist the seduction. Their accounts and judgments are consistently sober. Bicameral agreement is more common than disagreement; irresponsible conferences are the exception, not the rule; committee judgments are rarely bypassed; individual preferences do not normally dominate; opening up the conference has had less effect than expected; wheeling and dealing is constrained. The bargaining process, with its "gambits," "ploys," "psychology," "trades and logrolls," and "threats and bluffs," remains intriguing. But negotiations over apples and oranges produce, in the end, more fruit salads than pears, more compromise than reconstruction.

In their discussion of sequence, the authors display the same blend of comprehension and care. They begin by steering our attention away from the conventional research question, Who wins? and toward the more revealing question, What goes on? Their answer produces a discussion of stages; and the discussion of stages focuses, in turn, on strategies for winning at each stage and across stages. While bargaining inside the committee remains the centerpiece of conference activity, the authors wisely direct us to the many strategic considerations involved in setting up a conference and securing the approval of its work. Who should participate? When should it be held? How should the legislation be packaged? What items should be included as "sweeteners," "bargaining chips," or "conference bait"? To what degree should true preferences be revealed? Which chamber should go first in approving conference decisions?

As they lead the reader from preconference to conference to postconference, they display an encyclopedic knowledge of the procedural intricacies that now encrust the simple rule of 1789. These procedures link conferees to their chamber and help to shape their strategies—differences between House and Senate rules, House difficulty with the Senate's germaneness rule, Senate difficulty with the House's Rules Committee, procedures for determining which chamber acts first on the conference report, rules for selecting and instructing conferees, rules that govern the packaging and the amending of legislation, rules that hasten or delay action. Every rule confers, potentially at least, strategic advantages or disadvantages in matters of timing, anticipation, positioning, bargaining, coalition-building, and ultimately, of course, outcomes. Indeed, no better evidence exists for the crucial effects of procedure on policy than their three-stage discussion of conference decision making.

For students of Congress, this book provides a new window on recent changes in the institution. "As Congress changes, so also does the conference committee," say the authors. And they examine the relationship throughout. They tell us, for example, that the weakening of legislative leadership has resulted in less control over the conference by party and/or committee leaders. They tell us also that increases in referral of bills to multiple committees and increases in the omnibus packaging of bills have resulted in larger, more complicated, more difficult conferences. A participant in conferences in the 1960s between the House Armed Services Committee chaired by Representative Carl Vinson and the Senate Armed Services Committee chaired by Senator Richard Russell described the proceedings as "two gentlemen from Georgia talking, arguing, laughing, and whispering in each other's ear." These conferences were, of course, closed. By contrast, consider the conference on the 1981 reconciliation bill. It had 184 House conferees and 72 Senate conferees conducting business in 58 separate subconferences and reconciling 300 matters in disagreement. And all of it was—in theory—open to public view. The two instances are extremes, but the distance between them helps us to measure twenty years of congressional change. Whether the conference committee is more consequential under one set of conditions than the other is one more intriguing question.

Which is, perhaps, the proper attitude with which readers should approach this book. It is hard to imagine a question about the conference committee that will not be illuminated by a reading of *Bicameral Politics*. It is altogether a thorough treatment of the subject and a signal contribution to the study of Congress. That does not mean that it has answered the multitude of questions it raises or that it has formulated all the generalizations we shall need to fully understand conference committee linkages, behavior, influence, and the conditions under which such things vary. But Longley and Oleszek have persuasively placed it in the correct context—as "the central element of bicameralism" and "the essence of bicameral politics." And they have covered most of the ground demanded by that premise. In so doing they have provided other students of Congress and of legislatures generally with sufficient knowledge and sufficient incentive to build on their premise and on their work. It is a great service to us all.

University of Rochester —RICHARD F. FENNO, JR.

Preface

The authors of this book came to their mutual interest in bicameral politics and conference committee interactions by different routes. One author is a close observer and sometimes participant in congressional politics from his vantage point at the Congressional Research Service of the Library of Congress. His responsibilities include responding to procedural inquiries from congressional offices—queries that often include questions about conference committee processes and possibilities.

While one of us finds himself engaged as a neutral, if not always omniscient, consultant on the day-to-day struggles of legislative politics, the other author came to his interest in conference committee politics from a more academic perspective. While teaching at Lawrence University over the past twenty-four years, he has had occasion to develop and utilize in his courses a variety of relatively small-scale simulations, including, in his class on congressional politics, a fascinating simulation of conference committee policy-making.[1] This teaching simulation includes a role-playing recreation of conference committee deliberations on hypothetical anticrime legislation previously passed by the House ("The Mobilization against Crime Act") and the Senate ("The Safe Streets Act"). Some nine or ten conferees, composite abstractions of real-world congressional types with names such as Representative Robert Simmons (R, N.Y.) and Senator Herbert Lewis (D, Cal.), interact for several hours while attempting to compromise differences between the bills passed by the two chambers.

Over the years, this particular simulation has been held perhaps twenty times. Of

---

1. This simulation is based on Leonard Stitelman and William D. Coplin, *Decision-Making by Congressional Committees* (Chicago: Science Research Associates, 1969).

this varied collection of interactions, one particular conference stands out in the author's mind:

The conferees were facing enormous difficulties and limited time to resolve their differences. The chairman of the Senate conferees, Senator Edward Wallers (D, Ark.), found himself in agreement with the head of the House delegation, Representative John Stevens (R, Colo.), that *some* sort of compromise bill *must* emerge from conference. The personal and political stakes for both the senator and the representative were considerable—each had committed himself to eventual conference success.

Chairman Wallers, however, was keeping a wary eye on his southern Democratic colleague, Senator Dwane Matthews (D, Ga.), an adamant opponent of the passage of *any* bill, who had publicly pledged that he would block any compromise. Senator Matthews, however, did not appear to have any obstructionist allies among the four Senate conferees, and likewise little support among the Representatives.

The first House-Senate difference came up for conference discussion. It was a minor dispute, and Senator Matthews suggested the Senate conferees "recede to" (or accept) the House position. This was quickly agreed to. The second issue was taken up. Senator Matthews again exhibited surprising accommodation and suggested the conference accept the House language. The bill supporters were relieved by the Senator's positive approach—he was not, after all, going to be an obstructionist.

Issues were taken up one after another, in the order they occurred in the legislation. The Senate receded on one question, the House on the next, the Senate on several more; much of the bill was quickly worked out. No one noticed (except perhaps one person) that the many issues agreed to were the less consequential ones, while major disagreements remained to be resolved, and that in the agreements reached, the Senate had given in to the House on many more issues than the reverse.

Finally, late in the bargaining session, an especially important provision was addressed, one on which House and Senate differences were especially marked and apparently unbridgeable. On this issue, the House position was particularly well established and backed up by an overwhelming chamber vote. Senator Matthews again took the lead and suggested that on this issue the House should recede to the Senate position. After all, the Senate had agreed to House provisions on issue after issue—in fact on many more matters than the House had given way to the Senate. Simple bicameral courtesy would dictate that the House now recede on this disagreement.

The House conferees were horrified. They had accepted the previous Senate concessions with pleasure, although many of them were of slight importance to them. This issue, however, was crucial and non-negotiable. They must have their way on it. The House had expressed its strong feelings on this specific issue, and the Senate record reflected no such deep commitment to its language. We just cannot recede on this matter.

Senator Matthew raised his voice, which took on a harsh edge: Do you mean that the House has so little regard for the necessities of interchamber cooperation and *respect* that it demands that it win on this issue *too?* This is an *affront* to the *dignity* of the *U.S. Senate* itself!

The other Senate conferees found themselves agreeing with Senator Matthews as he pounded the table. Yes, they had exhibited exemplary accommodation in conceding

PREFACE xiii

issue after issue to the House, and now, at the very conclusion of the conference, the House was demanding even more. Getting a bill certainly was important, but protecting the Senate from this type of abuse was even more important. The senators, one by one, seconded Senator Matthews' position.

The House conferees pleaded that without this provision they certainly could not go back to the House with a bill to recommend for passage. The senators retorted: Well, we certainly cannot be expected to report favorably to our chamber on a bill so inequitably weighted toward the House. Without House concession on this issue, the conference can only fail. Votes were taken. The senators voted as a bloc for their language; the representatives as a unified group for their provision. The conference collapsed on the verge of final agreement, with even the authors of the original bills denouncing the other chamber's conferees and readily exchanging legislative success for loyalty to their chamber. Senator Matthews just smiled.

Our different experiences with conference committee politics—both applied and academic—helped define our early interest in bicameral politics. We became fascinated by such questions as What is the range of tactical possibilities in conference committee politics? When and how can rules and procedures be used to one's disadvantage—or advantage? Under what circumstances may institutional loyalties come to dominate individual legislative preferences?

Such common interests in the role of conference committees in bicameral politics led us a few years ago to agree to pool our resources—to bring together a close scholarly knowledge of day to day congressional politics and a more detached and analytical academic perspective. The result is a book that combines the strengths of both applied and academic analysis to shed light on the politics and procedures of congressional conference committees.

A large number of institutions and individuals have contributed to this project over the period of its genesis. Valuable and much appreciated assistance to the research on which this book is based was received in the form of a research grant from the Dirksen Center for the Study of Congressional Leadership of Pekin, Illinois, and grants and other assistance from the Public Policy Program, the Office of Academic Dean, and the Government Department of Lawrence University. This institutional support is gratefully acknowledged. In no way, of course, does this book imply or reflect any official views of Lawrence University or the Congressional Research Service of the Library of Congress.

It is impossible to mention the names of all the individuals who have helped us appreciate and understand the complexities of conference politics. Certain individuals, however, deserve special thanks for their help, time, and insight, including Congressman Les Aspin, William Baer, William Bremer, Bill Cherkasky, Roger Davidson, Richard F. Fenno, Terence Finn, Louis Fisher, Chong-do Hah, Michael Hittle, John D. Lees, Tom Mann, Jeffrey Miller, Norman Ornstein, Larry Patten, Robert Poling, Mojmir Povolny, Cathy Rudder, Howard Shuman, and James Sundquist. In addition to the assistance of these scholars and congressional observers, a number of individuals additionally were kind enough to review specific chapters of this book in draft form and offer their valuable advice, insight, and criticisms. These individuals include Paul A. Anderson, Donald A. Gross, Dennis S. Ippolito, Malcolm E. Jewell, Robert Keith, Thomas J. Lonsway, David L. Paletz, Barry S. Rundquist, Steven S. Smith, David Vogler, and William D. Zaferos.

Special appreciation is due Richard F. Fenno, both for his thoughtful reading of the entire manuscript and for his willingness to contribute a foreword that sets the tone and context for the book. As with so much contemporary research on Congress, Fenno defined the path along which this investigation has moved and shaped the research agendas for both this book and the further research that will surely follow it.

One individual stands out for her considerable and valuable assistance. Judith H. Longley painstakingly copyedited the entire manuscript before it was turned over to the publisher, and—later in the production process—conceived the cover design and prepared its thorough index. Her participation in this project was indispensable.

Generalized but not less grateful appreciation should also be expressed to numerous associates at the Congressional Research Service and to various generations of Lawrence University students, especially those who have sat in Government 35, Congressional Politics, over the years while their teacher mused about bicameral politics. Special appreciation is due some of these undergraduates: Tracy G. Coombs, Michael Gamsky, David King, Andrew N. McLean, Kerry Smith, John R. Stoner, John Ulrich, and Tom Watson. Each helped in the evolution of our thinking about conference politics.

Finally, unique contributions materially assisting this project were made by two students, one an undergraduate and the other a graduate student. Therese A. Barry, by means of a senior independent studies project on the consequences of the opening of conference committees, enriched our analysis in this regard as well as provided a rich summary of the complex maneuverings during the 1972 Education Act Amendments conference. Tom Kephardt contributed a set of tables summarizing a variety of newly compiled data concerning conference committees. To Tom and Therese, and all the other students of conference committee politics, we once again express our deep gratitude.

We further note with deep appreciation the labors of our typists, Lila Johnson, Millie Wallace, Justine Mathewson, Marion Okon, and Vicki Koessl, who have struggled successfully over the years to turn illegible prose into beautiful copy, the sensitive copyediting of Lawrence Kenney, and especially the encouragement of our editor, Marian Neal Ash of Yale University Press, who has been supportive in every way throughout this project and who brings to all her editorial work unfailing professional standards. Finally, we note—even declare—our special gratitude to our wives and families, to Judith, Rebecca, and Susan, and to Janet, Mark, and Eric, for their patient support of their husbands and fathers, for years fascinated and lost in the intricacies of conference committee politics. Their recurrent question still echoes: "Trying to write a book, huh?"

Egg Harbor, Wisconsin   LDL
Fairfax, Virginia   WJO

Bicameral Politics

1

Bicameral Politics and Congressional Conference Committees

> In the legislative process, all roads lead to the conference committee.
> —John Manley[1]

> You know, if an orange and an apple went into conference consultations, it might come out a pear.
> —President Ronald Reagan[2]

"If politics is the art of the possible and the essence of the legislative process is compromise," write two legislative scholars, "then the conference committee is the epitome of legislative pol-

---

1. John Manley, *The Politics of Finance: The House Committee on Ways and Means* (Boston: Little, Brown, 1970), p. 239.
   Some of the material in this chapter, as well as portions of other chapters, earlier appeared in quite different and greatly abbreviated form in Lawrence D. Longley and Walter J. Oleszek, "The Three Contexts of Congressional Conference Committee Politics: Bicameral Politics Overviewed," paper presented at the 1983 Annual Meeting of the American Political Science Association, Chicago, Illinois, September 1–4, 1983; Lawrence D. Longley and Walter J. Oleszek, "Bicameralism and House-Senate Intercameral Politics," paper presented at the 1985 Annual Meeting of the American Politics Group, Political Studies Association, Exeter (England), January 3–5, 1985; Lawrence D. Longley, "The Politics of Bicameralism: Congressional Conference Committee Interactions," paper presented at the 1985 Annual Meeting of the Political Studies Association of the United Kingdom, Manchester (England), April 16–18, 1985; Lawrence D. Longley, "Contemporary Legislative Bicameralism," paper presented at the Thirteenth World Congress of the International Political Science Association, Paris, July 15–20, 1985; and Lawrence D. Longley, "Why Bicameralism?" *Legislative Studies Section Newsletter*, Legislative Studies Section, American Political Science Association, vol. 9, no. 1 (November 1985), pp. 83–89.
2. President Ronald Reagan, in a radio interview, Dec. 17, 1982, as reported in Francis X. Clines, "President Invites Deal in Congress for Jobs," *New York Times,* Dec. 18, 1982, p. 1.

itics."[3] The congressional conference committee is that point in the bicameral legislative process where the separate actions of the House and Senate on similar measures are reconciled. House and Senate members (the conferees) are chosen to sit on an ad hoc joint congressional committee (the conference committee) for the purpose of working out differences on legislation passed in different form by the two houses.[4]

To be enacted into law, measures must ultimately be adopted by both House and Senate in identical form prior to being sent to the White House. The conference committee provides a means of reaching this necessary bicameral reconciliation, and while doing so, reflects all aspects of congressional politics. The bicameral politics of the conference committee are a crucial and vigorous manifestation of the legislative politics of Congress. As one widely respected Congressman expressed it, what goes on in conference is "the real world of legislation."[5]

Three important hallmarks of conference committees are worth noting at the outset: they are crucially important to policy outcomes; they are "the epitome of legislative politics" in terms of such processes as negotiation, bargaining, and compromise; and the state of knowledge concerning the dynamics of conference committees is spotty and limited. More than three decades ago, congressional observer George Galloway noted that this "third House of Congress" is "comparatively unknown except to the few who are familiar with the mysteries of the legislative process," and it is "the most unique and powerful legislative institution in America, . . . one that has received all too little attention."[6] Today, more than thirty years later, it is fair to describe the conference committee as still the most significant aspect of the congressional legislative process about which we know least.

It is to increase understanding of the congressional conference committee and the politics that permeate it that this book was written. Our fundamental objective is to shed light on this unique institution and, concurrently, to stimulate additional interest in and analysis of these bicameral units. Toward these ends, this chapter will provide an overview of the importance of conference committees, assess some of the issues involving these entities, touch on some of their complexities, and, finally, consider the functions of conference committees in both cross-national and national contexts.

---

3. Malcolm E. Jewell and Samuel C. Patterson, *The Legislative Process in the United States*, 4th ed. (New York: Random House, 1986), p. 169. Jewell and Patterson go on to say, "Nowhere in the legislative process are congressional skills—skills born of experience, knowledge and patient attention to the specialized demands of committee work—put to a greater test." Ibid.

4. This lends itself to a formal definition of a congressional conference committee: an ad hoc joint congressional committee composed of House members and senators selected by each chamber for the purpose of resolving differences on legislation passed by each chamber in differing form.

5. Rep. Barber Conable (R, N.Y.), "What Happens in Conference?" *Roll Call,* June 21, 1984, p. 4. Some years earlier another congressman, Rep. Clem Miller of California, concluded that "the conference committee is the essential core of the power [of the House]." This power center, Representative Miller argued, does not operate neutrally; rather "the conference committee is the ultimate flowering of the power of seniority" (John W. Baker, *Member of the House: Letters of a Congressman by Clem Miller* [New York: Scribners, 1962], p. 114).

6. George Galloway, "The Third House of Congress," *Congressional Record,* 84th Cong., 1st sess., March 8, 1955, p. 2556.

The Importance of Conference Committees

> When I came to Congress I had no comprehension of the importance of the conference committees which actually write legislation. We all know that important laws are drafted there, but I don't think one person in a million has any appreciation of their importance and the process by which they work.
> —An experienced congressman[7]

> Let's face it, the conference committee is where it all happens.
> —Rep. Norman D. Dicks (D, Wash.)[8]

The importance of congressional conference committees derives from the two main objectives they fulfill. First, the conference committee is the mechanism that allows a bicameral legislative body such as the U.S. Congress to operate. It is the bargaining unit between the House and the Senate. It is the place where Congress gets together to fashion the identical legislation required by the Constitution for a bill to become law. In short, *congressional conference committees are the central element of bicameralism and conference politics the essence of bicameral politics.*[9]

A second feature of conference committees is equally noteworthy: their power consequences. House versus Senate, committee chairman versus committee chairman, party versus party, chamber leadership versus committee leadership, faction versus faction—these are some of the divisions of Congress that are repeatedly represented in the politics of conference committees. *Congressional conference committees are an arena of power.* They are a means by which senators and representatives seek to enhance their influence over legislation and their power within the chamber.[10] It is from these dual functions of conference committees—as constitutionally necessary institution and as politically central arenas of power—that these bicameral entities gain their importance in the legislative process.

Not every bill in the legislative process goes to conference; many bills are enacted

---

7. Quoted in Charles L. Clapp, *The Congressman: His Work As He Sees It* (Washington, D.C.: Brookings Institution, 1963), p. 276. Concerning this lack of full awareness of the importance of conference committees, Clapp further notes that "although political scientists have long written about the impact of conference committees on legislation, members of Congress believe that even many students of government do not really understand their significance" (Ibid).

Even more striking than this lack of appreciation by political scientists of the crucial role of conference committees is the modesty of their efforts to assess conference politics. David J. Vogler, in one of the few works focusing on congressional conference committees, noted, "There remains a gap . . . between recognition of the importance of conference committees and their systematic study" (David J. Vogler, *The Third House: Conference Committees in the United States Congress* [Evanston: Northwestern University Press, 1971], p. 11). For a detailed assessment, see chapter 4 below.

8. Quoted in Janet Hook, "In Conference: New Hurdles, Hard Bargaining," *Congressional Quarterly Weekly Report*, Sept. 6, 1986, p. 2082.

9. These ideas are further developed in a later section of this chapter, "A Bicameral Perspective."

10. For further elaboration of these themes, see chapters 5 and 6 below, which analyze three contexts of conference committee politics: institutional, committee, and individual.

into law by one chamber accepting the version passed by the other.[11] Only about 15 to 25 percent of all public bills passed by Congress move through the conference committee process; these measures, however, compose the vast majority of controversial and important measures.[12] Significant measures avoid the conference process only infrequently, and many controversial bills are modified or die in this stage of the legislative process.

The utility of conference committees may extend as far as allowing Congress to maintain indecisiveness even while passing legislation. In June 1983, only days after the U.S. Supreme Court declared the legislative veto unconstitutional (in *Immigration and Naturalization Service* v. *Chadha*, 462 U.S. 919 [1983]), the House adopted a bill to reorganize the Consumer Product Safety Commission (CPSC). Two House amendments were hastily attached to the legislation in light of the Supreme Court decision—one required each proposed CPSC rule to be approved by both House and Senate and signed by the president *before* going into effect; the other allowed CPSC rules to go into effect *unless* disapproved by action of House, Senate, and president. The apparent purpose of House adoption of such curiously inconsistent legislation including two specifically contradictory procedures was to "let a House-Senate conference committee choose between them."[13] Sometimes conference committees are important in legislative policymaking because the House or Senate is unable to decide on an issue and is eager to send the unresolved matter to the conference.[14] Conference committees can also be used to rectify mistakes made by one or both chambers when they passed the original legislation.

Conference committees are more important today than ever in reconciling bicameral differences on legislation. This remains true despite changes in the mid-1970s in both the House and Senate designed to open conference proceedings to public view.[15] This continuing—even increasing—significance of conference committees has several causes. First, unlike most of the twentieth century, the 1980s witnessed six consecutive

---

11. Such chamber deference to the other house's bill may have various explanations, ranging from the minor character of intercameral differences to political necessity resulting from the scheduling crunch at the end of the legislative session. For further discussion, see chapter 8 below.

12. This estimate that about 15 to 25 percent of all public bills passed by Congress go to conference is a generally cited observation—see, for example, David J. Vogler, *The Politics of Congress*, 5th ed. (Boston: Allyn and Bacon, 1988), p. 211. A detailed review of various published estimates of the frequency with which conference is used in the legislative process can be found in chapter 8 below. Also reported in chapter 8 are new, original data concerning this question. Based on a previously unpublished actual count of all legislation in the 98th Congress (1983–84), it is there reported that between 11 and nearly 19 percent of all House- and Senate-passed acts went to conference, and 12 percent of all legislation finally enacted as public law in those two years had gone the conference route.

13. Steven Pressman, "Congress Considers Choices in Legislative Veto Aftermath," *Congressional Quarterly Weekly Report*, July 2, 1983, p. 1327.

14. In chapter 11 we present a case study of 1982 tax increase legislation that involved a conference in which the House and Senate met on a Senate-passed tax bill in the absence of any House-passed—or even House-considered—substantial legislation.

15. The opening of conference committees is discussed in detail, and the consequences of this change are evaluated, in chapter 3 below. Likewise, in that chapter the other changes briefly mentioned here—the partisan division of Congress, the utilization of omnibus legislation, and the diffusion of power in Congress—are further discussed in terms of their impact on conference committees.

years of divided party control of the House and Senate. While "institutional rivalry" is a constant in bicameral relations, there is no denying that split chamber control significantly shapes House-Senate actions and relationships. During that period, conference committees reconciled not only bicameral policy differences but partisan disagreements as well.

Second, a major new instrument of national policymaking has emerged on Capitol Hill: omnibus bills of massive size and scope. These "packages" cut across numerous policy areas (omnibus trade bills, for example) but are most prominent in the budgetary field in the form of continuing resolutions, reconciliation bills, tax legislation, and concurrent budget resolutions. The result for conference committees is that the final content of many of these comprehensive measures is frequently determined during conference negotiations. In some cases, for example, the Gramm-Rudman deficit reduction plan (see chapter 11 for a case study of this initiative, alternatively known as the Gramm-Rudman-Hollings plan), the conference committee, not the House and Senate as a whole, actually ends up writing the law.

Finally, lawmaking today is often characterized by "participatory democracy," including the selection of quite junior legislators as conferees (nearly unheard of in previous decades). The growth of subcommittee government, "juniority" rather than seniority, and individualism as well as the increasing numbers of staff aides, lobbyists, and multiple referrals combine, along with other developments, to make it harder for Congress to get its policy-making act together. The result is that today more members, many of whom are brighter and more aggressive than the people they replaced, understand that lawmaking is a "continuous flow"—what happens early in the decision making, such as committee markups, can shape later conference outcomes. Preparation for House-Senate conferences assumes greater significance because of anticipated consequences. Further, these bicameral units can act as centralizing forces in a Congress known for its heightened diffusion of authority and fragmented decision making.

Conference committees are important, then, for many reasons. They are the essence of bicameralism; they are central arenas of legislative power; they are major workshops of congressional lawmaking; they often determine bill content and sometimes even write original legislation; and they may serve as crucial consensus and support-building mechanisms for legislation. On occasion, conference committees are also noteworthy for their independence of action. It is to the "creative"—or runaway—conference that we next turn.

The Irresponsible Conference

> It is here, in secret meetings often not even announced until the last minute, that a few men can sit down and undo in one hour the most painstaking work of months of effort by several standing committees and the full membership of both houses.
>
> —Senator Albert Gore, Sr.[16]

16. Albert Gore, "The Conference Committee: Congress' Final Filter," *Washington Monthly*, June 1970, p. 43.

Conference committees have long been significant in the eyes of reformers and critics of congressional procedures who have seen conference committees as irresponsible yet crucial determinants of legislation. Senator Gore has had much company over the years. Senator George Norris (R, Neb.) spent much of his congressional career (which lasted from 1913 to 1943) crusading against the abuses of conference committees and personally popularized the pejorative description of them as the "third house" of Congress. "The members of this 'house' are not elected by the people," he argued in 1934. "The people have no voice as to who [the conferees] shall be. . . . No constituent has any definite knowledge as to how members of this conference committee vote, and there is no record to prove the attitude of any member of the conference committee."[17] Noteworthy, indeed, is that Norris helped reorganize the state legislature of Nebraska (also in 1934) by eliminating its second chamber. Nebraska to this day is the only state with a unicameral legislature and consequently having no need for any bicameral reconciling mechanism.[18]

A somewhat more recent but scarcely less negative assessment of the role of conference committees in lawmaking was provided by Senator J. William Fulbright (D, Ark.) in a biting floor speech:

> I submit, Mr. President, in all sincerity that there is no need whatever for the ordinary, lay member of Congress to come back to Washington for a special session. It is clearly evident, Mr. President, that to save the world and the people of this country from disaster, all that is needed is to reconvene, preferably in secret, only those incomparable sages, the conferees of the Appropriations Committee. From their deliberations the same results would be achieved and without the expense and trouble to everyone that is involved in going through the archaic ritual of pretended legislation. It is quite clear that regardless of what the common members of this body may wish, the conferees make the decision.[19]

This sardonic perspective on the role of conference committees was echoed some years later by Minnesota Democratic senator (and subsequent presidential candidate) Eugene McCarthy, who declared, "At least when we go to conference, we ought to walk slowly on the way . . . and very slowly on the way back, so at least one hour would elapse from the time we send conferees to negotiate for a settlement and the time they come back to the Senate to tell us that they could not do anything against the firm stand of the House of Representatives.[20]

    17. Quoted in Congressional Quarterly, *Inside Congress*, 2d ed. (Washington, D.C.: Congressional Quarterly, 1979), p. 67.
    18. Ibid. The varieties of reconciliation mechanisms used in the forty-nine bicameral states are discussed in chapter 2 below, in the section "Bicameral State Politics."
    19. In this sentiment, Senator Fulbright was somewhat elaborating on an earlier, tongue-in-cheek suggestion of Sen. Joel Bennett "Champ" Clark (D, Mo.), who once introduced a congressional resolution that "all bills and resolutions shall be read twice and, without debate, referred to conference" (Congressional Quarterly, *Guide to Congress*, 3d ed. [Washington, D.C.: Congressional Quarterly, 1982], p. 434).
    20. *Congressional Record*, 87th Cong., 2d sess., vol. 108, part 44, p. A2390, quoted in Vogler, *The Third House*, pp. 43–44.

This thesis of conference irresponsibility rests on the belief that frequently the views of conferees are at variance with the policy preferences expressed by their chamber. Bertram M. Gross, in his classic work *The Legislative Struggle* (1953), rather glibly wrote, "If one wanted to stretch the point a little, one might whimsically claim that any similarity between the views of the House or the Senate and those of the conferees is purely coincidental."[21]

Examples of conferees' disloyalty to their chamber's position abound. An extreme case, a conference on congressional redistricting legislation in 1967, found Senator Sam J. Ervin rejecting the Senate's measure and arguing for the House-passed bill, and Congressman Emanuel Celler, chairman of the House conferees, opposing the House position and fighting for the Senate legislation.[22]

Another fascinating example of conference committee independence from chamber preference came during the highly contentious conference on the supersonic transport (SST) in 1970. The House had voted $270 million for development of the SST; the Senate had voted for no funds at all. When the Senate conferees were announced, it was noted that a majority of them had opposed the crucial Senate-passed floor amendment that had deleted all SST funds. SST opponent William Proxmire (D, Wis.) objected vehemently, noting that "four of the [seven] conferees were Senators who were in favor of the SST, although the Senate had voted against the SST. . . . This is in direct violation of the Senate rules."[23] Despite Senator Proxmire's opposition, the seven proposed Senate conferees were confirmed and represented the Senate in conference.[24] After a total of three hours of deliberations (three times Senator McCarthy's suggested minimum time appropriate to sell out chamber interests), the Senate delegation reached an accommodation with the House and agreed that a fair compromise between a $290 million dollar House appropriation and a Senate zero dollar appropriation was $210 million. Senate conferee John O. Pastore (D, R.I.) reported to the Senate on this curious bargain: "If we stayed there until the cows came home, the answer would have been the same. . . . The fact is that the House was adamant, but the Senate did try."[25]

SST opponents were scarcely satisfied by these declarations of diligence and effort on the part of the Senate negotiators and promptly launched a filibuster against the

---

21. Bertram M. Gross, *The Legislative Struggle: A Study in Social Combat* (New York: McGraw-Hill, 1953), p. 241. The process of conferee selection is extensively discussed in chapter 8 below; the diverse loyalties of individual conferees are analyzed in chapter 6.

22. Vogler, *The Third House*, p. 44. For a detailed study of this conference, see David L. Paletz, "Influence in Congress: An Analysis of the Nature and Effects of Conference Committees" (Ph.D. diss., University of California at Los Angeles, 1970), esp. chap. 6.

23. *Congressional Record*, Dec. 17, 1970, p. S20413. The rules, official as well as unofficial, concerning conferee selection are described and analyzed in chapter 8 below.

24. Sen. Warren Magnuson (D, Wa.) defended the composition of the Senate delegation, contending somewhat ingenuously, "Conferees on the Department of Transportation appropriations bill are not appointed simply on the basis of their position on the SST. This is only one minor part of the bill" (*Congressional Record*, vol. 116, Dec. 19, 1970, p. 42703).

25. Congressional Quarterly, *Guide to Congress*, 2d ed. (Washington, D.C.: Congressional Quarterly, 1976), p. 356.

acceptance of the conference report.[26] The Senate became entangled in this controversy to the extent that final adjournment was delayed. Eventually, a face-saving agreement was reached involving temporary funding for the SST with long-term funding to be decided by the next Congress. By the time the new Ninety-second Congress convened, opinion had shifted significantly against the SST, and both the House and Senate voted to kill SST funding.[27] In short, despite the apparent willingness of Senate conferees to recede from their chamber's position, strong opposition to SST funding in the Senate was able to block adoption of the initial conference report and, over the long term, was able to prevail.

The Irresponsibility Thesis Reconsidered

The preceding example suggests some important modifications to the irresponsibility thesis. Despite the relative freedom of conferees either to stand fast for or quickly to concede chamber preferences, there are both subtle and not so subtle constraints that limit their choices. For one, the conferees are usually senior members of the committee or subcommittee that wrote the bill which passed their house. As the "movers and shakers" behind the legislation, their loyalty to chamber preferences often comes easily.

Further, conferees are bound to chamber position by clearly understood expectations, procedural rules, and sometimes even by formally expressed instructions.[28] Committee and chamber decisions usually set the limits of policy discretion for conferees. Consequently, the impact of conference committees on policy choices is often not as great as that of the original subject matter committees.[29] These conference constraints from either chamber or committee are illustrated in an account of conference staff negotiations:

> The overwhelming majority of both the Senate and House staff present opposed the Broyhill . . . [House] amendment and its Byrd Senate counterpart. Unfortunately there seemed little the staff or the conferees for that matter could accomplish. Formally, at least, they were obliged to accept those parts of the amendment which appeared in both bills or else risk a point of order on the floor on the grounds of exceeding authority. Thus, the staff agreed to accept the mildest possible language which was the first part of the Senate bill and omit all provisions not in both bills.[30]

To be sure, conference deviations from chamber position may result from ambiguities about intent or simple legislative necessity. The key issue in one contentious

---

26. The House, on the other hand, had little difficulty in agreeing to the conference report and speedily adopted it. Ibid.

27. Congressional Quarterly, *Guide to Congress,* 2d ed., p. 356. See also Congressional Quarterly, *Congress and the Nation, 1968–72,* vol. 3 (Washington, D.C.: Congressional Quarterly, 1973), pp. 158, 167; and *Congressional Quarterly Weekly Report,* Feb. 8, 1975, p. 293.

28. Choices among diverse loyalties available to the individual conferee are discussed in detail in chapter 6 below; the politics of instructing conferees is examined in chapter 8.

29. Richard F. Fenno, Jr., *The Power of the Purse: Appropriations Politics in Congress* (Boston: Little, Brown, 1966), p. 678.

30. Paletz, "Influence in Congress," p. 177.

transportation conference, for instance, included the "diversion of some Highway Trust Fund money to mass transit—which the Senate strongly favored and the House adamantly opposed."[31] The differences were seen as absolute and unbridgeable, but an artful compromise, which faithfully reflected the views of neither chamber, was eventually reached. Under this plan, some Highway Trust Fund money could be spent starting in the first year for "highway-related urban mass transport—such as bus purchases," and in the second year for nonhighway related transportation needs, including rail transportation.[32] Forging this compromise was an impressive achievement: "The conferees took a situation that looked very bleak and—by writing legislative language that appeared in neither the House nor the Senate bill—produced a winning compromise in three months."[33]

Similarly, tax reform conferees in late 1986 went beyond the bounds of the House- and Senate-passed legislation in order to protect an important constituency—as well as to protect the political interests of the tax reform bill itself. Both chambers' tax measures allowed elderly taxpayers an additional standard deduction of $600, but in conference the standard deduction was hiked to $750 for elderly taxpayers who were single. Political necessity produced an instance of conference "irresponsibility"—an agreement that exceeded both chambers' initial position. This conference irresponsibility, however, enhanced the prospect of the conference report's being accepted by both chambers.[34]

The tendency of most scholars—and the perspective we accept—is to see the conference committee, while sometimes at variance with chamber preferences, as more often a vital and indispensable reconciler of House and Senate preferences. The runaway conference, because of its colorful and celebrated nature, may oversuggest its frequency of occurrence. Gilbert Y. Steiner, for example, examined fifty-six major conferences from the Seventieth to the Eightieth congresses and found only three clear cases in which conferees either deleted material agreed to by both houses or included new material considered by neither. "The conference committee has not been a consistently irresponsible 'third house' of Congress," he concluded. "The conference committee is both a practical and satisfactory device to achieve [bicameral] accommodation."[35] Further, there appears to be general congressional acceptance of the necessity and usefulness of the conference committee as a reconciling agent.[36] Should a conference-negotiated product prove to be politically unpalatable, chamber rejection of the conferees' handiwork always remains as the ultimate check on an irresponsible conference.[37]

---

31. Michael J. Malbin, "Transportation Report: Long Deadlock Ends in Compromise Opening Highway Trust Fund for Mass Transit," *National Journal,* Aug. 11, 1973, p. 1163.

32. Ibid.

33. Randall B. Ripley, *Congress: Process and Policy,* 4d ed. (New York: Norton, 1988), p. 178.

34. David E. Rosenbaum, "Tax Bill Could Die with Vote on Rule," *New York Times,* Sept. 5, 1986, p. 12.

35. Gilbert Y. Steiner, *The Congressional Conference Committee: Seventieth to Eightieth Congresses* (Urbana: University of Illinois Press, 1951), pp. 173–74.

36. David Paletz, for example, notes in his study of conference committees a general lack of congressional dissatisfaction with the conference process. This he attributed to the useful role the conference committee plays in bicameral reconciliation. Paletz, "Influence in Congress," pp. 463–67.

37. The process and politics of acceptance or rejection of a conference report are further discussed in chapter 10 below.

Complex Bargaining Units

Conference committees are complex bargaining units that often face daunting tasks in terms of the range of issues requiring resolution, length of meeting time, and number of conference participants. The conference committee appointed to deal with the National Defense Authorization Act of 1987, for example, was faced with the need ultimately to resolve a total of 2,003 differences between the House and Senate versions of the bill—a task requiring many days of conference negotiations.[38] Lengthy meetings held over sustained periods of time can sap the patience and good will of any conferee. One ultimately successful education conference, for example, met twenty-one times for a total of approximately eighty hours of meetings over a period of two months.[39] The monumental energy legislation of 1978 involved dozens of public conference sessions extending over many months—meetings recurrently marked by an "atmosphere of disorder, frustration, confusion, and bad temper."[40]

Even more complex—especially in number of participants and diversity of issues in disagreement—was the historic budget reconciliation conference of 1981. "Over 250 Senators and Congressmen met in 58 separate conferences to consider nearly 300 individual issues; from magnetic fusion to small business loans, from dairy price supports to strategic mineral stockpiles, and from rural water programs to urban mass transit,"[41] noted Senate Majority Leader Howard H. Baker (R, Tenn.). This particular conference, the largest thus far in the history of Congress, was broken down into fifty-eight individual subconference committees charged with working out agreements on the more than $130 billion in spending cuts over three years sought by President Reagan—a goal eventually (and painfully) achieved.

The large conference committee, seen in its classic form in 1981, may well become habitual, particularly on complex multitopic legislation. The 1984 budget reconciliation bill, for example, was handled by a conference committee made up of 32 senators (just under one-third of the entire body) drawn from six different Senate committees and 90 representatives selected from twelve House panels. For the purpose of considering specific aspects of the comprehensive bill, the conferees divided themselves into twelve different subgroups. Exceeding even this in size was the conference in December 1985 on the fiscal 1986 reconciliation (or deficit reduction) bill, which involved a grand total of 242 conferees from the House and Senate (over 45 percent of the entire combined membership of Congress!) meeting in thirty-one subgroups over a period of two

---

38. *New York Times*, Nov. 5, 1986, p. 12.

39. Lawrence Gladieux and Thomas Wolanin, *Congress and the Colleges: The National Politics of Higher Education* (Lexington, Mass.: D. C. Heath, 1976), p. 163.

40. Diane Granat, "The Big Conference: Getting to be Old Hat," *Congressional Quarterly Weekly Report*, June 2, 1984, p. 1298.

41. Senate Majority Leader Howard H. Baker, in the *Congressional Record*, 97th Cong. 1st sess., July 29, 1981, p. S8711. Senator Baker, in his quoted floor remarks, was in fact understanding the size of the 1981 reconciliation conference. During that summer marathon, 256 members of the House and Senate—over 48 percent of Congress's combined membership—met at one point or another in conference to work out differences between the two chambers.

BICAMERAL POLITICS AND CONFERENCE COMMITTEES 11

weeks.[42] Although massive House-Senate conferences were once unusual, *Congressional Quarterly* notes that "they have become fairly routine as Congress bundles more legislation into omnibus bills."[43]

Conference committees are more than huge assemblies of representatives and senators. They can also be marathons testing the endurance of members. Apparently basing his remarks on personal observation, political scientist Charles O. Jones described a Budget Conference meeting held in May 1980:

> It was 90 degrees outside, and with the air conditioning reduced to save energy it was evident that the room would soon be hot and stuffy. Photographers and television camera crews moved around the table. One had to strain to hear the members. A House member shouted, "Let's get a mike that works." Conferees from both sides frequently asked for order in the room. At one point a rumbling was heard in the hallway making it impossible to hear anyone. A large hand cart filled with glasses finally worked its way down the cavernous hallway. . . .
> [By late afternoon] the room was still packed, and the members were trying to negotiate despite the noise and movement all around them. By this time, all members were in shirt sleeves. It was sweltering inside, and the place smelled like a locker room. All the windows were open, surely making the air conditioning work as hard as if it had been turned up.[44]

Lawrence Gladieux and Thomas Wolanin provide a somewhat similar account of a key education conference in 1972:

> The sequence of . . . offers and counteroffers continued into the early hours of the morning. At about midnight, two higher education lobbyists who had been keeping a vigil in the hall, went out and returned with a large tray of coffee and cookies from a local carry-out. These were eagerly consumed. The smokers' supplies of cigarettes were exhausted. The room became hot and stuffy as the air conditioning

---

42. Hook, "In Conference," p. 2082; Stephen Gettinger, "Deficit-Reduction Bill's Torturous Journey Ends," *Congressional Quarterly Weekly Report*, April 5, 1986, pp. 752–53. The "torturous journey" this article refers to was not the conference deliberations themselves, but the unprecedented series of back-and-forth maneuvers between the chambers involving the approval of the conference report. Between the time conference agreement was reached on December 19, 1985, and March 20 the following year, the deficit reduction bill "ping-ponged" between the House and Senate a total of nine times before winning final congressional approval. " 'I know the recording clerks were awfully glad to see the last of it,' said one clerk, noting the two-foot-high stack of documents that had to be lugged through the Capitol corridors every time one chamber acted on it" (ibid., p. 751).

43. Granat, "The Big Conference," p. 1298. The more usual size of conference committees is analyzed and discussed, using data especially compiled for this book, in chapter 6 below. The increasing use of omnibus legislation resulting in huge conferences is further discussed in chapters 3 and 8 below.

44. Charles O. Jones, *The United States Congress: People, Place, and Policy* (Homewood, Ill.: Dorsey Press, 1982), pp. 333–34. Jones abstracts a typical conference as "a room with a long table stacked with files and documents, a staff hovering over the members (more evident on the Senate than House side), and a large number of persons observing the proceedings, some attentive, others not. The noise level is typically quite high, the ventilation poor, and klieg lights may be switched on and off" (p. 333).

turned off automatically at 10 p.m. Jackets came off, sleeves were rolled up and ties were loosened. Fatigue began to wear on everyone as the long hours of debate dragged on, and the members continued to talk in a half-shout to make themselves heard in the cavernous chamber. Some of the exchanges became acrimonious. . . . The House Parliamentarian was roused out of bed at about midnight to give an opinion about one of the . . . proposals. Congressman Pucinski missed a plane for Illinois where he was to make an appearance in his campaign for the Senate. . . . The Senate and House delegations caucused without either one making much headway. The situation began to look grim. Some began thinking what before had been unthinkable—what if the conference failed to reach an agreement? . . . But gradually, through a combination of reasoned argument, pragmatic compromise, sheer exhaustion and stubborn unwillingness to let months of effort go to waste, a consensus began to emerge.[45]

This consensus, which started to appear only after agonizing hours of conference sessions, was ultimately to prove successful and would lead to the enactment of the Education Amendments Act of 1972, landmark higher education legislation. How was it that intercameral and personal conflict was transformed in this case into legislative agreement? Gladieux and Wolanin suggest that three factors explain "how this unusually difficult conference was brought to a successful conclusion. First, the choice of the conference members enabled two majority coalitions to be formed that agreed on the key issues; second, a process for decision making was established that facilitated agreement; and third, the key leaders, [Representative Carl] Perkins and [Senator Claiborne] Pell, were steadfastly committed to getting a bill and had the political skill required to achieve that objective."[46]

Part of the political skill of Chairman Perkins included knowing how to wear down the energy of everyone involved in the conference until exhaustion and hunger facilitated compromise. One conference participant recalls this marathon experience well, even after eleven years:

> The conference was long, arduous, and difficult. Tough issues were on the table. We had met off and on since mid-March in more than 20 conference sessions in all areas of the Capitol, but no accord could be reached. Finally, Chairman Carl Perkins called a meeting for 2 p.m. on May 16. . . .
>
> We all figured this was another stab in the dark and after pulling and hauling and arguing and pounding, we'd break about suppertime and come back to try again. But suppertime came and passed and we worked on, firing, then falling back to regroup. It was a fascinating study in human behavior. Hard bargaining was raised to an art form. There were offers, counter offers, grudging compromise and "aces up the sleeve". . . . But damn, was I hungry about 9 p.m.!
>
> Still, Mr. Perkins—not exactly a kid even in those days—kept the train on the

---

45. Gladieux and Wolanin, *Congress and the Colleges*, pp. 192–93. This 1972 higher education conference is further examined as a separate case study in chapter 11 below.
46. Ibid., p. 163.

track and kept pushing ahead determined to get an agreement. Soon the heads—even of the younger members—were nodding and their eyes glazing over. Still, Mr. Perkins forged ahead. He wanted an agreement and by darn, an agreement he'd get.

Finally, in one burst of energy—augmented by a large dash of "I don't give a damn anymore. I'm dead tired and nothing is worth this kind of pain"—the conferees agreed. The final differences were reconciled, hands—now limp and numb—were shaken all around, and the conference broke up shortly after 5 a.m. . . .

I learned a valuable lesson from Mr. Perkins that night, a lesson which has helped me in my career on The Hill and in my life: the race (or the conference) is not always won by the fleetest and most nimble (of foot or head) but by the most persistent, the most dogged, and the most determined.[47]

Clearly, conference committees are crucial, complex, and sometimes exhausting. They are also central to the adjustment necessary in a bicameral Congress between the actions of the two legislative halves. Legislative bicameralism requires a means of intercameral reconciliation, and in the U.S. Congress this is provided by the conference committee. The existence of the conference process, however, gives rise to larger questions such as Why congressional bicameralism? What are the benefits and justifications advanced for this legislative arrangement? and How does a bicameral perspective help us understand the nature of contemporary congressional interactions between House and Senate?

A Bicameral Perspective

> If we think in the context of bicameralism, we are forced to look at the Senate and the House of Representatives at the same time; and if we look at the two bodies simultaneously, we are forced to see them in relation to each other. . . .
>
> The idea of two legislative institutions acting separately and sequentially and thereby having an effect on each other is another ingredient of a bicameral perspective.
>
> —Richard F. Fenno, Jr.[48]

To understand better the bicameral nature of Congress, we will consider legislative bicameralism first as a cross-national phenomenon and then as it has evolved and operates today in the American system. Such a bicameral perspective facilitates greater understanding of the role of the conference committee as the linking mechanism of congressional bicameral politics.

47. Rep. Romano L. Mazzoli (D, Ky), "My Favorite Story," *Roll Call*, June 2, 1983, p. 5.
48. Richard F. Fenno, Jr., *The United States Senate: A Bicameral Perspective* (Washington, D.C.: AEI, 1982), pp. vii, 5.

Bicameralism—the separation of a legislature into two parallel but separate political bodies which must act in agreement for legislation to be enacted into law—is a feature of many legislative systems today. (The term itself combines two Latin words: *bi,* which means "two," and *camera,* "chamber"). Despite a structural arrangement that might seem inherently duplicative and inefficient, legislative bicameralism has been advocated and defended on a number of diverse grounds, both historically and contemporarily.

Major Justifications for Bicameralism

A classic justification for legislative bicameralism is that institutional dualism is necessary in order *to reflect class or other deep cleavages evident in the society of the day.* The British Parliament, for example, evolved from a class distinction between what became the British House of Lords and what emerged as the "Lower House" of the British Parliament—the House of Commons. Similarly, the colonial legislatures of America developed a bicameral form, with one house particularly reflecting the interests of the Crown and the aristocracy. After the Revolutionary War, most of the new states retained these bicameral arrangements, with the upper house continuing to favor the views of landed interests through property qualifications for both voting and membership, and a lower house reflecting somewhat more populist values.[49]

The U.S. Congress itself was the result of conflicting interests between Constitutional Convention delegates who fervently believed the new national legislature must be based on the equal representation of states, thus preserving the power of the smaller states, and those delegates who with equal vigor fought for legislative representation based on population, thus favoring the largest states. The Great Compromise resolved this large state–small state issue by the expedient of a bicameral Congress, with one chamber comprised of two senators representing each state regardless of its population, and the other made up of a variable number of representatives from each state depending on its size.

A second argument for bicameralism has been that this structural arrangement allows for the *simultaneous representation of aggregate national views as well as the special outlook of geographical components such as regions or states.* The West German Parliament, for example, comprises a popularly determined lower chamber, the Bundestag, of 518 members, 496 of whom are elected directly by voters in the various states, and an upper chamber, the Bundesrat, of 41 voting members selected by the ten state governments. Bundesrat members must be officials of their state government. Representation of state interests in the Bundesrat is further heightened by the practice of bloc voting by each state delegation.[50]

---

49. Gerhard Loewenberg and Samuel C. Patterson, *Comparing Legislatures* (Boston: Little, Brown, 1979), p. 121. Four of the five justifications for bicameralism discussed in the following paragraphs are adapted and modified from the excellent analysis contained in Loewenberg and Patterson, pp. 120–25. For a fuller discussion of the evolution of American legislative bicameralism in the colonial and post–Revolutionary War eras, see chapter 2 below and the sources cited there.

50. Ibid., p. 122. Such efforts to ensure an adequate reflection of distinctive state interests within national legislatures are common in contemporary federal systems, frequently taking the form of equal

This example suggests that bicameralism is particularly suitable to a federal political system; in fact, cross-national data show a strong association between the institutional arrangements of federalism and bicameralism: of eighty-three nations surveyed in one study, all but one of the seventeen federal systems had a bicameral legislature, while fifty-four of the sixty-six unitary governments utilized a unicameral legislative structure instead.[51] Another recent cross-national study of twenty-two democratic regimes found that the sixteen unitary governments considered divided evenly with regard to their legislative form: the national legislatures of eight were bicameral, while eight were unicameral. In striking contrast, all six of the federal systems examined had bicameral national legislatures. The study's author, Arend Lijphart, cited this and other evidence in finding "a clear connection between strong bicameralism and federalism," and forcefully concluded, "Strong federalism spells a strong federal chamber and hence strong bicameralism".[52]

A third justification for bicameral arrangements rests on the belief that *two legislative bodies will provide a check on each other's actions and avoid legislative excess and ill-conceived or hasty decisions*. This view was evident in 1787 during the deliberations

---

representation of states within an upper legislative house. Examples of such arrangements reflecting the U.S. "Great Compromise" can be found in the national legislatures of Argentina, Australia, Brazil, Mexico, and Switzerland (Inter-Parliamentary Union, *Parliaments of the World: A Comparative Reference Compendium*, 2d ed. [New York and Oxford, England: Facts on File, 1986], p. 15).

Arend Lijphart has argued that one of the inherent "characteristics of federalism is a second chamber which serves as a safeguard for the members of the federation." Arend Lijphart, *Democracies: Patterns of Majoritarian and Consensus Government in Twenty-one Countries* (New Haven: Yale University Press, 1984), p. 104.

Loewenberg and Patterson also point out (*Comparing Legislatures*, p. 125) that any bicameral institutional arrangement in which one chamber is based on a geographical rather than popular basis is inherently undemocratic; presumably in these cases the benefits of special attention being paid to regional or local views are seen as sufficient to outweigh this liability. This position, of course, is similar to arguments made in the United States during the 1960s in favor of one house of bicameral state legislatures being apportioned on the basis of nonpopulation factors such as the representation of counties, rural, or other geographically scattered populations. The U.S. Supreme Court, in a series of landmark decisions, most notably *Reynolds* v. *Sims*, 377 U.S. 533 (1964), struck down these justifications in holding that insofar as practicable, *both* houses of a bicameral state legislature must be apportioned on the sole principle of "one man, one vote."

51. Inter-Parliamentary Union, *Parliaments of the World*, p. 14. The unicameral exception among the federal systems is the tiny island state of Comoros, off southeast Africa. Overall, the Inter-Parliamentary Union found that fifty-five of the eighty-three sovereign states it surveyed had unicameral national legislatures, although five of these fifty-five single-chamber legislatures nevertheless could be said to "exhibit certain features of bicameralism." The tendency toward unicameralism, the Inter-Parliamentary Union concluded, was most pronounced in small, unitary, socialist, Scandinavian, and recently independent and politically evolving countries (p. 13).

52. Lijphart, *Democracies*, pp. 171, 104. A particularly outstanding analysis of the contemporary occurrence and forms of national legislative bicameralism is to be found in chapter 6 of this work, "Parliaments: Concentration vs. Sharing of Legislative Power." To the aforementioned factors, Lijphart further adds *size*. He finds national size to be strongly related to the existence of legislative bicameralism: all of the eleven larger democratic regimes studied had bicameral legislatures while only three of the eleven smaller countries were so constituted (pp. 93–94, 100–01). See also the discussion of country size and legislative bicameralism in Inter-Parliamentary Union, *Parliaments of the World*, pp. 16–18.

of the framers of the U.S. Constitution. The Philadelphia delegates, in brief, deliberately sought to create institutional differences between the House and Senate as part of their system of checks and balances, with legislative bicameralism providing division and restraint additional to the separation between executive and legislature. Similarly, in many cross-national instances, the checking of popular passions is seen as one of the inherent virtues of legislative bicameralism.

Bicameralism is sometimes advocated on the grounds that *two different legislative bodies can provide valuable diversity of outlook on matters* quite independent of any special functional role either of the houses may have in representing distinctive economic class interests or geographical areas, or any conception of bicameralism as part of a system of checks and balances. This view holds that political leaders, pivotal personalities, and legislative factions will inherently act differently in two parallel legislative bodies. This diversity of legislative politics is thought to be a considerable virtue. An example of such a perspective is the experience of the American states following the massive state legislative reapportionments of the 1960s and 1970s. As a result of federal court decisions, upper legislative chambers could no longer base their representation on nonpopulation factors. Thus, some commentators questioned the desirability of retaining two state legislative chambers, both based solely on population. No state, however, has changed—or come close to changing—from a bicameral to a unicameral legislature since. No doubt tradition and inertia (discussed next), combined with perceived benefits arising from two different sets of participants in the legislative process, preserved American state bicameralism even after one major customary justification for it—diversity of representation—had been removed.[53]

A final defense for bicameralism is not so much a justification as an explanation: sometimes bicameral arrangements persist due to a mixture of *political inertia and legislative adaptability*. Any effort to move from a two-chamber legislature to a one-chamber body necessitates at best enormous political effort. Further, jobs, political careers, and entrenched interests may well be threatened by such transformation. In almost all cases, constitutional change is necessary to move to a unicameral legislature. Combine personal and political interests in preserving the status quo with the usual difficulties (extraordinary majorities and lengthy processes, for example) in securing constitutional change[54] and you have powerful forces favoring the preservation of bi-

53. Forty-nine of the fifty American states have bicameral state legislatures; Nebraska, which has a unicameral legislature, is the sole exception. For an assessment of what we know about bicameral politics in the American states, see chapter 2 below, esp. its final section, "Bicameral State Politics."

54. On the political difficulties of constitutional reform politics, see Keith C. Banting and Richard Simeon, *Redesigning the State: The Politics of Constitutional Change in Industrial Nations* (Toronto: University of Toronto Press, 1985; also published in London by Macmillan in 1985 as *The Politics of Constitutional Change in Industrial Nations*), esp. the essay by Banting and Simeon entitled "The Politics of Constitutional Change" and that by Daniel J. Elazar, "Constitution-Making: The Preeminently Political act."

For other perspectives on constitutional change politics, see Lawrence D. Longley and David M. Olson, eds., *Two Into One: The Politics and Processes of National Legislative Bicameral/Unicameral Change* (forthcoming); Lawrence D. Longley and Alan G. Braun, *The Politics of Electoral College Reform*, 2d ed. (New Haven: Yale University Press, 1975); and Lawrence D. Longley, *Changing the System: Electoral Reform Politics in Great Britain and the United States* (Oxford, England, and Elmsford, N.Y.: Pergamon Press, forthcoming).

cameralism—even when the above-mentioned justifications for this arrangement have disappeared.[55]

Bicameralism may be maintained not only by inertia and vested interests, but also by the adaptability of the legislative arrangements themselves. The British Parliament continues today formally as a bicameral body in part because proponents of change cannot agree on an alternative arrangement. Beyond this, however, the heredity-dominated House of Lords has been adapted—and has adapted itself—to the modern era. The formerly exclusively aristocratic nature of the Lords has been modified by the appointment of life peers, and it has further accepted a systematic curtailing of its legislative powers. Simultaneously, the House of Lords has also developed a useful and distinctive legislative role for itself: scrutinizing (and sometimes modifying or even briefly delaying) proposals of the popular-based House of Commons.[56]

---

55. Despite these barriers to change, three Western developed countries have, since World War Two, changed from bicameral to unicameral legislatures: New Zealand in 1950, Denmark in 1953, and Sweden in 1971. Another country, South Africa, for reasons unique to itself, abolished its Senate in the early 1980s, and then, in 1984, replaced its short-lived unicameral legislature with a tricameral legislature, but one that excluded black representation from all three of its legislative chambers (telephone interview with South African Embassy, Washington, D.C., Nov. 16, 1987, and personal letter to authors from Arend Lijphart, April 13, 1988).

While an assessment of the politics of such cross-national institutional change is beyond the scope of our discussion here, such an analysis offers a most interesting comparative opportunity to consider the conditions and politics of legislative bicameral-unicameral choice. Such an analysis of legislative institutional change is, in fact, under way and, while focusing on the cases of New Zealand's, Sweden's, and Denmark's constitutional change from bicameral to unicameral national legislatures, also considers larger aspects of the comparative examination of institutional change and retention. Further information concerning this research is available from Professor Lawrence D. Longley, Department of Government, Lawrence University, Appleton, WI. 54912, U.S.A.; Professor David M. Olson, Department of Political Science, University of North Carolina at Greensboro, Greensboro, N.C. 27412, U.S.A.; Dr. David Arter, Senior Lecturer, Department of European Business, Leeds Polytechnic, Caedmon Hall, Beckett Park, Leeds LS6 3QS, England; Professor Keith Jackson, Department of Political Science, University of Canterbury, Christchurch 1, New Zealand; or Dr. Björn von Sydow, Statsrådsberedningen, Office of the Prime Minister, S-103 33, Stockholm, Sweden. The results of this collaborative inquiry into the politics and processes of national legislative bicameral/unicameral change are forthcoming in Longley and Olson, *Two Into One*.

56. See, for example, "Up the Nobility," *The Economist*, June 16, 1984, p. 18. For views of the contemporary changing relations between the British House of Lords and House of Commons, see the essays contained in Philip Norton, ed., *Parliament in the 1980's*, (Oxford, England: Blackwell, 1985); Philip Norton, *Parliament in Perspective* (Hull, England: Hull University Press, 1987); Donald Shell, "The Evolving House of Lords," *Social Studies Review* 1, no. 2 (Nov. 1985): 17–22; and Israel Shenker, "Lording It Over England," *New York Times Magazine*, May 8, 1988, pp. 34–36 ff.

Shell notes some 80 defeats for Conservative Governments in the House of Lords between 1979 and 1985, along with a dramatic increase in oral and written questions of the government and a growth in the Lords' hours of sitting and daily attendance (pp. 17–18), and stresses that "The House [of Lords] is not merely a body correcting errors and making technical improvements to bills" (p. 20). The Shenker article finds during the Thatcher years a total of 122 defeats of her government in the House of Lords on legislative clauses and amendments, in contrast with just 2 such losses in the House of Commons (p. 34).

These developments give new meaning to the classic epigram that the House of Lords "represents nobody but itself, and therefore enjoys the full confidence of its constituents" (quoted in Carl J. Friedrich, *Constitutional Government and Democracy: Theory and Practice in Europe and America*, 4th ed. [Waltram, Mass.: Blaisdell, 1968], p. 316).

Legislative bicameralism, then, has been justified and maintained cross-nationally for a number of reasons: to reflect class or deep cleavages of the society; to allow for the simultaneous representation of aggregate or national views as well as the special outlook of geographical components such as regions or states; to provide through twin legislative bodies a check on ill-conceived or hasty actions; and to ensure diversity of legislative outlook and response. Further, legislative bicameralism—even when these factors have failed to retain their former relevance—has survived because of political inertia and vested interest mixed with legislative adaptability.

Bicameralism Takes Many Forms

Bicameralism is a feature of many legislative bodies today, even though in some instances the constitutional form implies an equality between the two chambers that political reality denies. In other cases, constitutions prescribe relationships between the chambers based not on equality but on one chamber's playing a dominant or decisive role. Finally, even when bicameral institutions are constitutionally and politically equal and further separated by different electoral or political bases, the separation may itself be largely illusionary. A dominant agency external to the legislative branches, such as a ruling political party, a cohesive, integrated elite, the military, a legislatively dominant national leader, or a governing cabinet, may determine and coordinate the separate actions of the two chambers. In short, contemporary legislative bicameralism takes many forms and has many realities.

Both the West German and British parliaments, for example, consist of two chambers, but neither the German Bundesrat nor British House of Lords shares equal power with its lower chamber. The Bundesrat does have special powers coming close to equality on bills that directly affect the states, but on all other legislation it has at most only a "suspensive veto" subject to being overruled by the Bundestag.[57] The powers of the British House of Lords are limited by precedent and the Parliamentary Acts of 1911 and 1949 to those only of revising legislation passed by the House of Commons, introducing largely legal and noncontroversial bills, and, in extraordinary cases, delaying the enactment of legislation for up to one year. Money bills cannot be delayed by the House of Lords at all.[58] Such is the imbalance between the two chambers that the delaying power of the House of Lords on nonappropriations bills is widely viewed as theoretical

---

57. Loewenberg and Patterson, *Comparing Legislatures*, pp. 157–58. Such inequality between bicameral legislative halves is not unusual. Based on its analysis of twenty-seven bicameral national legislatures, the Inter-Parliamentary Union found that in about half of the instances even formal legislative powers were not shared equally between the chambers. A number of specific examples of bicameral inequalities are cited in its compilation, *Parliaments of the World*, pp. 881–85, esp. p. 881.

58. Loewenberg and Patterson, *Comparing Legislatures*, pp. 157–58. Bicameral inequality is most frequently found in the case of financial legislation: bills concerning taxes, budgets, and appropriations. It is not at all unusual to find upper houses severely limited on these matters; a number of examples of such formal inequalities of bicameral powers on financial legislation are provided in the Inter-Parliamentary Union's survey *Parliaments of the World*, pp. 884–85. When there is a distinction between the chambers, it is inevitably the upper house that is at the disadvantage and "always the popular House which has the decisive position in budgetary and financial matters" (p. 885).

rather than effective. Should the House of Lords attempt, other than infrequently, to assert its formal power to impede legislation favored by a parliamentary and party majority in the House of Commons, that action might well speed the demise of the House of Lords itself. Like the *Tarantula* spider, it would sting once and then die.

Clearly such imbalance in legislative equality makes bicameral accommodation easy: the weaker body eventually, albeit sometimes painfully, adjusts to the determined position of the stronger. The institutional form such bicameral adjustment takes is of little interest, for if one body has the power always to win, any process or procedure of reconciliation will work. One chamber will always defer to the other.

Bicameral reconciliation may also be accomplished by means of a dominant external entity. The British system is an example not only of bicameral inequality, but also of cabinet and party dominance of legislative choice and bicameral reconciliation.[59] The existence of such linkages provides an effective, if not always democratic, means of ensuring interchamber coordination and negates the need for a formal intralegislature mechanism for the purpose, such as a conference committee.[60]

The Congressional Experience: Conflict and Cooperation

> To avoid deadlock in a bicameral system, there must be some locus for final decisions, some group charged with reconciling differences. In Congress, this is the part played by the conference committee.
> —Malcolm E. Jewell and Samuel C. Patterson.[61]

The U.S. Congress is distinctive among national legislatures because the House and Senate share roughly equal and codeterminant powers.[62] No external force determines

---

59. Galloway, "Third House of Congress," p. 2558, and Ada C. McCown, *The Congressional Conference Committee* (New York: Columbia University Press, 1927), p. 229. Galloway notes that the conference committee system in England began to lose its significance with the development of cabinet government in the eighteenth century and, by the nineteenth century, had died out altogether (p. 2554).

For historical reviews of diverse methods of adjusting bicameralism, see H. W. V. Temperley, *Senates and Upper Chambers* (London: Chapman and Hall, 1910); H. B. Lees-Smith, *Second Chambers in Theory and Practice* (London, 1923); J. A. R. Marriott, *Second Chambers* (London: Oxford University Press, 1927); and Lord Campion, "Second Chambers in Theory and Practice", in Sydney D. Bailey, ed., *The Future of the House of Lords* (London: Hansard Society, 1954), p. 24.

60. For discussion of various ways by which bicameral legislatures reconcile their differences, see the analysis of "Agreement Between Both Houses," in Inter-Parliamentary Union, *Parliaments: A Comparative Study on the Structure and Functioning of Representative Institutions in Forty-One Countries* (New York: Praeger, 1961), pp. 185–89; and, more recently and incorporating 1985 information, Inter-Parliamentary Union, *Parliaments of the World*, pp. 882–907, esp. p. 883.

61. Jewell and Patterson, *Legislative Process in the United States*, p. 168.

62. David M. Olson, *The Legislative Process: A Comparative Approach* (New York: Harper and Row, 1980), p. 23. British political scientist David Butler stresses this unique feature of bicameral equality, noting that "only in the United States . . . is the upper chamber as important as the lower chamber" (David Butler, "Electoral Systems," in David Butler, Howard R. Pennman, and Austin Ranney, eds., *Democracy at the Polls* [Washington, D.C.: AEI, 1981], p. 8). In a similar vein, two

their actions.⁶³ Further, a key institutional mechanism for working out interchamber disagreements has evolved over the history of the Republic as a means of bicameral accommodation. It is to a consideration of legislative bicameralism specifically in the American context, and the conference committee as the mechanism for bicameral adjustment, that we next turn.

In creating a bicameral Congress, the delegates at the American Constitutional Convention in 1787 were acting with both purpose and intent. The founders understood the need for a strong and effective legislative authority to guard against possible abuses of power by the executive. They were, however, also aware of the dangers of legislative excesses and sought to protect against this by providing for a legislature itself divided. As they had structured a government balanced between national and state components and incorporating a separation of powers among the new national institutions, they likewise created a Congress made up of two institutionally distinct chambers.⁶⁴ "Bicameralism was a bedrock element of the constitutional arrangements of 1787," writes Richard F. Fenno. The delegates "argued not about the wisdom of bicameralism but about the appropriate relationship between the Senate and the House within the bicameral framework"⁶⁵

The framers of the Constitution in 1787 created a Congress composed of a House and Senate. Each would be constitutionally unique in size, term of office, and constituency. Somewhat different responsibilities were assigned by the Constitution to each chamber: initiating revenue measures for the House and advising and consenting to treaties and nominations for the Senate. Additionally, the two chambers have evolved their own rules, precedents, traditions, and customs. These distinctions are enduring. "Institutional differences between the House and Senate," wrote one scholar, "are real

---

American scholars suggest that "it is the prominence of the upper house that gives our bicameralism special significance" (Edward G. Carmines and Lawrence C. Dodd, "Bicameralism in Congress: The Changing Partnership," in Lawrence C. Dodd and Bruce I. Oppenheimer, eds., *Congress Reconsidered*, 3d ed. [Washington, D.C.: CQ Press, 1985], p. 414).

Whether the United States is truly unique in its coequal bicameralism has been questioned by one prominent scholar, who cites as an additional example the Swiss federal legislature, and possibly also formally coequal legislative chambers in Belgium and Italy (personal letter to authors from Arend Lijphart, April 13, 1988). Certainly, the question of whether legislative cameral equality in the United States is unique is debatable, but its prominence as an example of a coequal bicameral system is undisputable.

63. The contemporary American presidency might appear as an agency providing this coordinating role for House and Senate, and undoubtedly to an extent it does. As countless presidents have found to their dismay, however, a president does not determine the actions of House and Senate, but is better described as a stimulant of and influence on their decisions. Public opinion, too, affects legislative decisions but cannot guarantee them.

64. See the discussion of this point in chapter 5 below; see also Thomas H. Hammond and Gary J. Miller, "The Core of the Constitution," *American Political Science Review* 81, no. 4 (Dec. 1987). The idea of two coequal legislative bodies was not unknown to the Constitution makers. The English Parliament comprised both a House of Commons and a House of Lords, and likewise ten of the thirteen states had bicameral legislatures. Although the Continental Congress of the Articles of Confederation had been unicameral, there was an overwhelming acceptance at the Constitutional Convention of the idea that the new Congress should be bicameral.

65. Fenno, *The United States Senate,* pp. 1, vii.

and important in and of themselves, whether or not exacerbated by differences in policy approaches or partisan control."⁶⁶

Over the decades, these bicameral differences have spawned rivalry, conflict, and competition between House and Senate. For example, during floor debate in 1983, Senator Robert Dole (R, Kan.) declared, "I suggest that my colleagues in the House recognize that the U.S. Senate is part of the Congress, that we are not here to serve the House Ways and Means Committee or the House itself, that we have a right under the Constitution to amend revenue bills, and we intend to exercise that right."⁶⁷ Representative Silvio Conte (R, Mass.), ranking member of the Appropriations Committee, expressed a comparable House sentiment on another occasion: "I have been on the [Appropriations] Committee for 24 years, Mr. Speaker, and I have never seen the House treated so shabbily [by the Senate] as we have been this year, not only on this, but on certain other personal matters. I hope that it will stop here. I hope that the House will stand up for its rights and stand up for what it believes in."⁶⁸

Intercameral tension is sometimes carried into conference committee proceedings, especially on matters close to the hearts of representatives and senators. The Ninety-seventh Congress in 1982, considered legislation regulating outside earned income for congressmen. Quite different bills had passed the House and Senate, and a conference was necessary. When House members attempted to impose the same 30 percent limit on outside earned income on senators that the representatives operated under, there was strong bicameral reaction: the "conference committee meeting exploded into hostile shouting and cursing."⁶⁹

Countless other examples could be cited to highlight House-Senate conflict. Suffice it to say there is good reason why precedents in both houses forbid representatives and senators from speaking discourteously of one another and require members to refer to "the other body" and not name it directly during floor debate. (As of the 100th Congress, however, the House has permitted its members to utter the *S* word.)⁷⁰

 66. Stanley Bach, "Bicameral Conflict and Accommodation in Congressional Procedure," paper presented at the 1981 Annual Meeting of the American Political Science Association, p. 2. The impact of the divided partisan control of House and Senate between 1981 and 1986 is discussed in detail in chapter 3 below. For further discussion of institutional differences between House and Senate, see chapter 5 below.
 67. *Congressional Record*, 98th Cong., 1st sess., May 25, 1983, pp. S7493–94.
 68. *Congressional Record*, 97th Cong. 2d sess., July 13, 1982, p. H4039.
 69. *Washington Times*, June 11, 1982, p. 34.
 70. It is interesting to note that Senator Dole was at odds with this tradition in his heated comments quoted above. On the precedent of referring to the opposing chamber as "the other body," see Stanley Bach, "Rules and Bicameral Relations in the U.S. Congress," *Legislative Studies Quarterly* 7, no. 3 (Aug. 1982): 341, and the detailed references contained in note 1 of Bach, "Bicameral Conflict and Accommodation."
 This tradition itself is in a state of evolution. In December 1986, the House of Representatives adopted a new rule that permits representatives to utter the *S* word. The rule change allows House floor references to the other body by name and further permits representatives to mention Senate actions. Still prohibited, however, are "references to individual members of the Senate, expressions of opinion concerning Senate action, or quotations from Senate proceedings" (Janet Hook, "No More Talk of the 'Other Body,' " *Congressional Quarterly Weekly Report*, Nov. 29, 1986, p. 2985; idem, "House Leadership Elections: Wright Era Begins," *Congressional Quarterly Weekly Report*, Dec. 13, 1986, p. 3072).

Despite such institutional disagreements and rivalry, cooperation rather than conflict typically characterizes intercameral relations. The many volumes of the *Statutes at Large* attest to this cooperative spirit. Without bicameral compromise, no legislative proposal could be forwarded to the president. There are many ties that bind the two chambers together: partisan, individual, strategic, and structural-procedural, to name a few.

At the partisan level, House and Senate party leaders frequently consult about legislative priorities. This pattern of cooperative relations occurs even when both houses are controlled by different parties. "The inescapable necessity of bicameral cooperation" necessitates such interchamber cooperation: "The President and the public may attempt to set policy directions and goals for the Congress, but the institutional problems of bicameralism remain for the House and Senate themselves to resolve."[71] During the early 1980s, for instance, there was arguably more bipartisanship between Democratic Speaker Thomas P. O'Neill of Massachusetts and Republican Senate Majority Leader Howard H. Baker of Tennessee than between Congress and the White House. "Congress may still save the [budget] process over the President's objections," declared Speaker O'Neill at one point in 1983. "If we do it, it will be because of bipartisan cooperation."[72] When the Democrats took control of both chambers after the 1986 election, new House Speaker Jim Wright (D, Tex.) and Senate Majority Leader Robert C. Byrd (D, W.Va.) worked together to facilitate bicameral cooperation, a task now further made easier by their partisan common bond.

Individually, senators and representatives work together to pass or defeat legislation. During the Ninety-seventh and Ninety-eighth congresses, for instance, Senator Alan Simpson (R, Wy.) and Representative Romano Mazzoli (D, Ky.) sponsored legislation to revise the nation's immigration laws. As chairmen of Judiciary subcommittees with jurisdiction over this issue, Simpson and Mazzoli were well positioned to advance immigration reform legislation. The two members in effect worked as a bipartisan and bicameral team to mobilize support for their measure, which eventually became law during the Ninety-ninth Congress.[73]

Strategically, members of each chamber are mindful that the success or failure of their policy proposals can hinge on how well they involve the other body in their lawmaking plans. Representatives who find their bill stymied in the House may turn to

---

71. Bach, "Bicameral Conflict and Accommodation," pp. 40, 42. Bach concludes that "as a general matter, the two chambers have approached their bicameral relations by adopting a policy of noninterference whenever possible and by defending their individual prerogatives and procedures whenever necessary" (p. 3).

72. *Christian Science Monitor*, June 7, 1983, p. 4. Also see Richard E. Cohen, "Budget Process—and a Tax Increase—Are at Stake in Battle Over '84 Budget," *National Journal*, June 4, 1983, pp. 1162–64.

73. The team approach of Senator Simpson and Representative Mazzoli extended even to the point of agreeing upon identical initial bills to be introduced into both the House and Senate. They recognized that legislative realities would cause each bill to be changed as it moved through each chamber, but they reasoned that by starting with identical bills, such differences might be minimized, thus making subsequent conference deliberations easier. Harris N. Miller, "'The Right Thing to Do': A History of Simpson-Mazzoli," *Journal of Contemporary Studies* (Fall 1984): 68.

sympathetic senators to promote it in that chamber. Or members of one chamber might maneuver to avoid having their proposal sent to an unfavorable panel in the other body.

On one occasion, Senator Robert C. Byrd (D, W.Va.) persuaded the Senate to support a strip mining measure. When the bill was sent to the House, it was referred to the House Interior Committee; Morris Udall (D, Ariz.), chairman of that panel, opposed Senator Byrd's bill and successfully prevented any action on it. The next year, however, Senator Byrd managed to bypass Udall's House committee. He attached the strip mining proposal in the Senate as an amendment to a noncontroversial House-passed bill initially reported by the House Merchant Marine Committee. When the measure was returned to the House, the Merchant Marine Committee, not the less friendly Interior panel, assumed jurisdiction over the Byrd proposal.[74]

Legislative strategists must, therefore, be mindful of the personalities, structures, and biases of the other body as they bear on a particular bill. Sometimes compromises can be made in one chamber with confidence that the other legislative body will restore the lost provisions. On the other hand, if the other chamber is thought to be hostile to a policy initiative, a broader bill might be pressed to provide a stronger position for subsequent conference negotiations. Sometimes a bill of questionable merit is pushed in anticipation (unrealized at times) that the other chamber will kill it. In sum, the expected stance of the other body is anticipated by members and their actions planned accordingly.[75]

Finally, before any measure can become law, it must pass both chambers in absolutely identical form. "What the Constitution has divided, it also demands be united," writes Charles O. Jones.[76] Two parliamentary methods are employed to achieve bicameral reconciliation: motions and conference committees.[77] Under the first, the House and Senate can motion, or "ping-pong," measures back and forth between them until their disagreements are resolved. Congressional rules, however, limit each chamber to "two shots" at perfecting the legislation in observance of the parliamentary principle that forbids amendments in the third degree.[78] One chamber, to be sure, can simply adopt the other's bill verbatim and obviate the motion or conference route.

74. The House, however, refused to act on the Byrd proposal. See *1980 CQ Almanac* (Washington, D.C.: Congressional Quarterly, 1981), pp. 611–12.

75. This theme of anticipation of the other chamber's actions is further developed in chapters 5 and 8 below.

76. Jones, *United States Congress*, p. 351.

77. See chap. 8. A useful discussion of these alternatives is provided in Stanley Bach, "Resolving Legislative Differences in Congress: Conference Committees and Amendments between the Houses," Congressional Research Service Report no. 84. 214, Dec. 31, 1984.

78. This technique of "motioning" measures between the chambers is, of course, a means of *avoiding* conference, in contrast with somewhat similar ping-pong activity that sometimes occurs between House and Senate over approval of a conference report resulting *from* conference committee deliberations. Note 42 above mentions back-and-forth actions in 1986 concerning the conference report on the fiscal 1986 reconciliation (or deficit reduction) bill, which involved an astonishing total of nine passes of the report between the chambers. Congressional rules may technically limit each body to but two efforts to reconcile legislation in the absence of a conference, but no such limitation applies to conference reports, which presumably could wander endlessly (actually for up to two years) the Capitol hallways back and forth between House and Senate.

Members and staff aides from each chamber often consult in advance to facilitate the compromise-making process. These consultations sometimes result in one chamber accepting the other's legislative version. In 1981, for example, the House passed a measure involving agencies' internal accounting and administrative control systems. It was sent to the Senate, where the legislation was amended and then returned to the House. Representative Jack Brooks (D, Tex.), chairman of the House committee that reported the measure, asked unanimous consent that the House concur in the Senate amendment to H.R. 1526. He explained, "Mr. Speaker, we have worked with the Senate on the language of their amendment and I can assure my colleagues that the Senate amendment is consistent with the original intent of the bill as passed by the House."[79] The House granted the unanimous consent request. This action completed Congress's lawmaking steps, and the measure was transmitted to the president for his consideration.

The other major device for resolving interchamber differences on legislation is the conference committee—"a device well-suited to the purpose [of interchamber reconciliation] because it permits free discussion and negotiation in a relatively informal setting, in comparison with formal floor action by one chamber on the amendments of the other."[80] Composed of members from each chamber, typically from the committees that originally reported the legislation, conference committees are ad hoc bargaining units whose fundamental task is twofold: first, to negotiate an agreement that a majority of the conferees from each chamber can support, and, second, to report an agreement acceptable to a majority of both the House and Senate.[81] This task gives rise to an "inherent tension central to the conference process, [for] producing an acceptable compromise bill necessarily means each house must to some extent yield on their chamber's position."[82] The process of reaching such an agreement involves a complex mix of many forces, including institutional, committee, and individual. Their interactions shape significantly the character and content of the national policies that emerge from conference and define interchamber and conference committee politics.

The Plan of the Book

In the next several chapters, we focus in more detail and depth on the history, contexts, politics, and procedures of conference committees. Specific chapters will be devoted to a

---

79. *Congressional Record,* 97th Cong. 2d Sess., Aug. 19, 1982, p. H6650.
80. Bach, "Bicameral Conflict and Accommodation," p. 10.
81. Richard Fenno identifies this as the "two masters problem": conference negotiators must simultaneously satisfy the demands of their parent chamber while also meeting to an appropriate degree the expectations of the other chamber's conferees (Fenno, *The Power of the Purse,* p. 615). He concludes: "Conference committee activity can be described in terms of these twin problems of adaptation and the balance of independent and dependent behavior which arises from attempts to solve them" (p. 617).
82. Therese A. Barry, "Conference Committees and Institutional Adaptability" (1984 Senior Independent Studies Thesis, Lawrence University), p. 12.

discussion of these principal themes. In addition, nine minicase studies will be presented in chapter 11. Their objective is to spotlight different types of conferences, the negotiating process in practice, and conditions associated with floor action on bicameral agreements. Finally, the last chapter will outline the summary judgments that flow from all that has gone before.

A crowded House-Senate conference committee discusses a 1980 appropriations bill. (From the *Washington Post*. Photograph by James K. W. Atherton. Copyright © by The Washington Post Company. Reprinted by permission.)

2

The Evolution of Conference Committees and State Practice

> If one house in a bicameral system is so constituted as to be able to have its way in any event, then, perforce, almost any system of adjusting differences will work.
> —Ada McCown[1]

> American legislatures stand alone among modern bicameral legislative bodies in providing a formal method for adjusting differences between them.
> —George Galloway[2]

The bicameral U.S. Congress is distinctive among democratic legislative assemblies for three reasons: its bicameral chambers are effectively equals, there is no dominant external agency that determines and coordinates their actions, and an institutionalized conference committee mechanism exists for the purpose of reconciling the separate actions of each body. In this chapter, we shall first trace the origins of the conference committee in the United States and its English parliamentary and American colonial roots. Next, we shall briefly review its evolution over the history of Congress and its emergence as the central coordinating mechanism of bicameral politics. Finally, in counterpoint, we shall look at the bicameral accommodation practices of the American states as all but one (Nebraska) of the fifty subnational political systems deal with the problems of working out intercameral differences.

---

1. Ada C. McCown, *The Congressional Conference Committee* (New York: Columbia University Press, 1927), p. 229.
2. George Galloway, "The Third House of Congress," *Congressional Record,* March 8, 1955, p. 2556.

English and Colonial Antecedents of Conference Committees

The congressional conference committee was not an innovation created for the American constitutional system and its new national Congress. Rather, it was a well-established procedure for accommodating bicameral differences in both English parliamentary and early American colonial and state legislative practice.

The English Legacy

The origins of the conference committee in the United States can be traced back to fourteenth-century England and the emerging Parliament of the time. To favor their own social and economic class interests, the prelates and higher nobility joined to form the Upper House, or what became known as the House of Lords, while leaving the lesser nobility, knights, and burgesses to form the Lower House, or the House of Commons.[3] Early on it became customary for several of the lords to confer with members of Commons on the answer to be given to the king's request for money. Unfortunately, journals and records of the House of Commons do not begin until the middle of the sixteenth century (1547), so the extent and form of the conferences that took place until then will never be known.[4]

Interesting descriptions of early parliamentary conferences are provided in the House of Commons' journals. Delegations to the conferences customarily consisted of twice as many members from the House of Commons as from the Lords. In the conference of 1604, for example, the Lords named thirty members and the House of

---

3. William Stubbs, *Constitutional History of England* (Oxford: Oxford University Press, 1880), vol. 2, p. 645, quoted in McCown, *The Conference Committee*, p. 23. This and the following text paragraph contain points and language originally suggested by Lawrence University undergraduate John R. Stoner. Appreciation is expressed to him for these ideas.

Representation of the communities, or "Commons," evolved over a considerable period of time, appearing in Parliament as early as 1275, but usually only on occasions when support for taxation measures was needed. By the middle of the fourteenth century, however, the Commons came to be a regular element of the English Parliament. The separation of Parliament into two separate elements that would subsequently come to be known as the House of Commons and the House of Lords occurred by degrees between 1311 and 1340. "Early Origins of the English Parliament," in *The Scott Foresman Roberts' Rules of Order, Newly Revised* (Glenview, Ill.: Scott, Foresman, 1981), p. xxx.

For additional discussion of the early roots of English bicameralism, see R. W. Perceval, "The Origin and Development of the House of Lords," and Lord Campion, "Second Chambers in Theory and Practice," both in Bailey, ed., *The Future of the House of Lords;* Vernon Bogdanor, ed., *The Blackwell Encyclopaedia of Political Institutions* (New York and Oxford, England: Blackwell, 1987); and Inter-Parliamentary Union, *Parliaments of the World: A Comparative Research Compendium*, 2d ed. (New York and Oxford, England: Facts on File, 1986), esp. p. 13.

4. McCown, *The Conference Committee*, p. 23. The Journal of the House of Commons was started at the initiative of the clerk of the House in 1547, but was not utilized as a source of precedent on procedural matters until 1580 or 1581. It first received status as an official Commons document in about 1623. These early parliamentary records are not very illuminating as to either inter- or intrachamber procedures; as Thomas Jefferson would note some 450 years later (in the opening of his classic *Manual of Parliamentary Practice*, published in 1801), "The proceedings of Parliament in ancient times, and for a long time while, were crude, multiform, and embarrassing" ("Early Origins of the English Parliament," pp. xxx, xxxiv).

Commons sixty. "The time and place, usually the Painted Chamber, always were appointed by the Lords. The Lords came in body expecting the Commoners to await them. They sat with their hats on while the Commoners stood with their hats off."[5]

In addition to the size of conference delegations and patterns of interchamber deference, early English Parliaments grappled with other central issues such as which chamber should ask for a conference, what ought to be the conference's authority, and how issues should be considered and resolved. The rise of cabinet government in England eventually sent the conference committee into eclipse; yet it was in the heyday of the English conference committee, during the seventeenth century, that "the American colonial legislatures developed their systems of procedure."[6]

Colonial and Early State Experience

The legislative process in the United States inherited many features from the British parliamentary system. One of these inheritances was the bicameral legislature, predominate first in the colonies and the states and later the arrangement created for the new national Congress.[7] Along with the idea of two legislative chambers came also the practice of employing the conference committee as a means of interhouse reconciliation.[8]

There was extensive colonial and precolonial experience with conference committees. The Massachusetts Bay Colony, in fact, held the first recorded conference committee in the New World as early as 1645 on the curious issue of registering ships to do battle in the harbor. The novelty of this issue was not matched, however, by a uniqueness of the procedure, for over time "the conference was a regular institution in Massachusetts Bay . . . [where] it was used much as in England."[9]

The conference committee was used also as the means of working out differences between the branches of colonial legislatures, differences often exacerbated by interchamber conflict arising because the lower legislative house in many colonies repre-

---

   5. Sir Erskine May, *Parliamentary Practice* (London; 1924), p. 591, quoted in McCown, *The Conference Committee*, p. 25.
   6. McCown, *The Conference Committee*, p. 33.
   7. At the time of the Constitutional Convention in 1787, as we noted earlier, ten of the thirteen states had bicameral state legislatures; these state constitutional arrangements in almost all cases reflected previous colonial institutional practice.
   8. Thomas Jefferson in his *Manual of Parliamentary Practice* relied almost exclusively on English parliamentary practice for his discussion of conference committee procedures (Ralph Nader Congress Project, *Ruling Congress* [New York: Penguin Books, 1977], pp. 165–66). For a detailed discussion of the English parliamentary basis of the conference system, see McCown, *The Conference Committee*, chap. 2, "The Origin and Pre-Congressional Development of the Conference Committee." McCown makes a distinction between "simple conferences," in which each chamber's representatives limit themselves to stating their position without any discussion or negotiations ensuing, and "free conferences," in which discussion and compromise settle interchamber differences. Simple conferences were the predominant pattern in English parliamentary practice, while free conferences were the variant adopted in America (McCown, *The Conference Committee*, pp. 13–14).
   9. McCown, *The Conference Committee*, p. 33.

sented colonial or popular interests, while the upper house represented the views of the colony's owners or those of the king of England.[10] McCown noted that in "records of many of the colonies may be found evidence to show the general employment of the conference committee as a means of reconciling differences between the two Houses," for example in Maryland, Massachusetts, New Jersey, Virginia, and North Carolina.[11] New York provided for public conferences even in its initial state constitution of 1777: the Assembly and Senate of New York were to select their conferees by ballot, after which they would meet in the presence of both bodies.

This broad experience with conference committees in the colonies—and subsequently in the early years of the new states—lay the groundwork for the subsequent development of the conference committee in the U.S. Congress. By the time of the creation of the new Constitution (which is completely silent about conference committees), the conference committee as the means of reconciling the views of divided legislative institutions was well established in American legislative experience.

The Early Congresses

This legacy of English, colonial, and state experience helps explain the ready acceptance of conference committees at the outset of the history of the House of Representatives and Senate. "It is not surprising," writes a congressional historian, "that the system was taken for granted from the very beginning of the bicameral Federal Congress."[12]

Almost immediately upon the convening of the first session of the First Congress in 1789, the Senate and the House considered rules providing for conferences between the two chambers. On April 7, 1789, the first day following the initial securing of a quorum allowing the Senate to meet, the Senate appointed a five-member committee "to prepare rules for the government of the two houses in cases of conference."[13] The House soon named a panel of its own to confer with the Senate. Eight days after the senators were appointed, the Senate adopted rules governing conferences between the chambers:

> Resolved, That, in every case of an amendment to a bill agreed to in one House and dissented to in the other, if either House shall request a conference, and appoint a committee for that purpose, and the other House shall also appoint a committee to confer, such committee shall, at a convenient time, to be agreed on by their chair-

---

10. Ibid., p. 34. Reports of colonial conferences in New York State, for example, are analyzed by Mary Clarke in her study of parliamentary politics in colonial America (Mary P. Clarke, *Parliamentary Privilege in the American Colonies* [New Haven: Yale University Press, 1943], esp. p. 73). For further discussion of the colonial experience with bicameral relations, see Thomas F. Moran, *The Rise and Development of the Bicameral System in America* (Baltimore, 1898).

11. McCown, *The Conference Committee*, p. 33. For further details of the colonial experience with conference committees, see McCown, chap. 2.

12. Roy Swanstrom, *The United States Senate, 1787–1801*, Senate Doc. no. 64, 87th Cong., 1st sess. (1961), p. 232. McCown puts it similarly: "From the very beginning of our Congressional history, the conference committee was the accepted method of adjusting differences between the House of Representatives and the Senate" (*The Conference Committee*, p. 38).

13. *Annals*, 1st Cong., 1st sess., April 7, 1789, p. 18.

man, meet in the conference chamber, and state to each other verbally, or in writing, as either shall choose, the reasons of their respective Houses for and against the amendment, and confer freely thereon.[14]

On April 17, 1789, the House agreed to an identical resolution,[15] and initial procedures for bicameral reconciliation between the two houses of Congress were in place.[16]

The First Conferences

The first conference committee met in the next month, on May 14, 1789, to resolve not a substantive legislative matter but an issue of congressional etiquette: how was the president of the United States to be addressed by Congress? The Senate preferred to use honorific or laudatory terms in referring to the president; the House opposed using any such title, presumably because it sounded too royalistic. This curious interchamber disagreement resulted in the first chamber "win" in congressional conference committee history: the Senate finally agreed to accept the views of the House and use no laudatory titles.[17]

The first major issue to be decided by Congress arose shortly thereafter and concerned the question of how revenue was to be raised in order to meet the needs of the new nation. On April 8, 1789, Representative James Madison introduced two revenue-raising bills. One levied duties on imports; the other involved a tax on the tonnage of vessels bringing goods into the United States. On May 16, the House passed this first revenue bill. The Clerk of the House notified the Senate of the bill's passage and requested it to concur.

The Senate began debate on the import tax measure and passed it on June 11 but added several amendments. The Senate-amended version was returned to the House. On June 15 and 16, the House again debated the bill and agreed to accept several of the Senate's amendments but opposed the rest. Informed of the House's actions, the Senate resumed consideration of the House amendments to the Senate amendments. It "insisted" on certain of its original amendments to the House-passed bill but "receded" from others. The secretary of the Senate delivered this result to the House on June 19. For the third time, the House took up the issue. Refusing to concur in several of the Senate's amendments, the House asked to meet in conference with the Senate and appointed three representatives as conferees, including Madison.

14. Ibid., April 15, 1789, p. 19.
15. Ibid., April 17, 1789, p. 174.
16. David J. Vogler, *The Third House: Conference Committees in the United States Congress* (Evanston: Northwestern University Press, 1971), p. 4; and McCown, *The Conference Committee*, p. 38. These initial formal rules proved to be noteworthy for their singularity; as McCown notes, "Except for the first joint rule in the first Congress, providing for conferences between the two Houses, the Conference Committee System [has] grown up without particular definite rules governing it in either House" (p. 75). Some definite rules regulating conference committee operations, however, have been adopted in the House and Senate since McCown wrote in 1927; these are discussed in chapters 3 and 7–10 below.
17. McCown, *The Conference Committee*, p. 41.

The tonnage bill, meanwhile, had passed the House on May 29 and the Senate on June 17, although in each case in different versions. Seven days later the Senate received a written request from the House asking for a conference on both the import duty and tonnage measures. In addition to the written request, the House sent the Senate the original bills plus the Senate amendments to each (these documents are called the papers). On June 25, the Senate agreed to a conference on both measures and appointed three conferees.

On June 26, 1789, the first congressional conference on a substantive matter convened on the Impost (the term then for imports) and Tonnage Bill. It was, interestingly, an "open conference," open to any interested party. There was so much member interest in this conference that the Senate had to adjourn for lack of a quorum.[18] A similar problem occurred in the House; the entry for the record of events in the House for that day reads: "A number of the members attending the interesting conference which to-day took place with the Senate on the impost and tonnage bills, no business was done in this House." Records are not clear as to what occurred during this public conference, but it is worthy of note that this first conference proved also to be the last open conference that would be held for 122 years. (The next open conference meeting would not occur until 1911, when Senator Robert M. LaFollette of Wisconsin opened a single one-day tariff conference to the press and public as a short-lived experiment.)[19] The conferees did manage, however, to resolve their differences in one day; this was accomplished by resorting to a classic bicameral compromise: the House conferees accepted all the Senate amendments to the Impost Bill "which related to [tonnage] discrimination," and the Senate representatives "receded from its other amendments."[20]

The next day (June 27) both chambers planned to act on the conference report (a written document that embodied the negotiated agreement). When the Senate conferees made their presentation on the results of the conference, several senators wanted to vote immediately to adopt the conference report. The papers (bills and amendments of the conference), however, were in possession of the House. Some senators argued that a mistake had been made and sought unsuccessfully to obtain the papers from the House conferees. The result was that it was established that a conference report could be voted upon only by that chamber in possession of the papers. Senators "could not reconcile themselves to act without the bills," explained Senator William Maclay of Pennsylvania.[21]

Interestingly, the House acted first on the conference report, contrary to the principle evident even then that the chamber which asks for a conference votes last on the report. The jockeying going on between the legislative bodies, explained Senator Maclay, involved "a jealousy between the two Houses [over] who should act first, as the one which acted last would reject the bill, or at least have the blame of rejection if the bill was

18. Galloway, "The Third House," p. 2558; McCown, *The Conference Committee*, pp. 41–44.
19. McCown, *The Conference Committee*, pp. 43, 177–78. The later opening of nearly all conference committees in 1975 is discussed in chapter 3 below.
20. Ibid., p. 44.
21. The material regarding Sen. William Maclay (Pa.) was obtained from *The Journal of William Maclay* (New York: Albert and Charles Boni, 1927), pp. 87–89.

lost." Both chambers, however, eventually approved the conference report, and with it the import and tonnage legislation.[22]

Because the first formal rules regarding conferences were sketchy, assertions and assumptions more than rules influenced the initial development of conference procedure. There are some practices of the first conference, however, that still guide conference activity today. For example, to request a conference or to vote on the conference report, a chamber must be in charge of the papers. Each house, too, may appoint any number of conferees, although three was the usual number for many years.

During the First Congress, conferences were held to work out House-Senate differences on a wide variety of legislation. Besides the issues of etiquette and the Impost Bill, conferences were also held on a Salary of Members Bill, the amendments to the Constitution we now know as the Bill of Rights, the Judiciary Act of 1789, which established the federal court system, and a Post Office Bill.[23] The Salary of Members Bill, for one, provoked ferocious debate over whether representatives and senators should receive equal compensation for their services. Institutional conflict over the status and respect due each chamber was present even in the First Congress and in its first conferences.[24]

Another conference during the First Congress merits mention, for it illustrates both early conference independence from chamber preferences, and the responsiveness of conferees to executive or outside suggestions. As part of a measure providing the "means of intercourse between the United States and foreign nations," both the House and the Senate voted specifically that American ministers to foreign countries should be paid $30,000 for their expenses. The conference, however, eventually reported an agreement setting $40,000 for ministerial expense compensation. The conferees defended their action on the grounds that consultations with the secretary of foreign affairs had convinced them that the higher figure was necessary.[25]

This conference report, certainly a clear case if ever there was one of conferees exceeding their mandate to negotiate House-Senate *differences,* was accepted by both the House and the Senate, early initiating a tradition of latitude for conference committee action. By the conclusion of the First Congress, we find the conference committee, with its Engligh parliamentary roots and its colonial experience, well established as the mechanism for bicameral adjustment.

---

22. Original information on the first conference was derived from three sources: *Annals,* 1st Cong., 1st sess.; *Journal of the First Session of the Senate* (Washington, D.C.: Gales and Seaton, 1820); and *Journal of the House of Representatives,* 1st sess. of the 1st Cong., vol. 1 (Washington, D.C.: Gales and Seaton, 1826).

23. McCown, *The Conference Committee,* p. 39.

24. Stanley Bach, "Germaneness Rules and Bicameral Relations in the U.S. Congress," *Legislative Studies Quarterly* 7, no. 3 (Aug. 1982): 356, n. 1. See also William Maclay, *Sketches of Debate in the First Senate of the United States, in 1789-90-91,* ed. George W. Harris (Harrisburg, Pa.: Lane S. Hart, 1880), and Louis Fisher, "History of Pay Adjustments for Members of Congress," in Robert W. Hartman and Arnold R. Weber, eds., *The Rewards of Public Service* (Washington, D.C.: Brookings Institution, 1980).

25. McCown, The Conference Committee, p. 46-47.

Benchmarks of Conference Committee Evolution

> Inherited from England the conference committee system is an evolutionary product whose principal threads were woven on the loom of congressional practice into a unified pattern by the middle of the 19th century.
> —George Galloway[26]

Providing a comprehensive overview of conference committee activity over the nearly two-hundred-year span of history from 1790 to the present is unrealistic as well as quite undesirable from the point of view both of the reader and the authors. Suffice it here to note the existence of two detailed summaries of this history for the scholar who wishes to probe further into the history of the conference committee.[27]

Our objective is to discuss several important benchmarks or highlights of conference committee evolution. These developments include such conference procedural matters as the request for a conference, the selection of conferees, limitations on the authority of conferees, and floor consideration of conference reports. Any history of conference committees can never be complete or definitive simply because too many conferences have been held over too many Congresses. Still, it is useful to present some of the major practices associated with conference development. Like many things associated with Congress, they reveal that the understandings and procedures that govern conference activity were accepted gradually rather than instantly.

The Request for a Conference

Various traditions are associated with the request for a conference. Early on, as noted above, the House and Senate accepted the custom that a chamber must be in possession of the papers before the conference request can be made. It was also regular practice in the early 1800s for the chamber that disagreed to the amendments of the other House to its bill to wait for the amending chamber to request the conference. As Representative Daniel Webster of Massachusetts explained,

> This House had sent an important bill to the Senate—the Senate had passed it, with an amendment; and this House had disagreed to that amendment. The usual course was . . . that that House which proposed the amendment, if it did not see fit to recede from it, voted to insist on it, and proposed a conference on the disagreeing votes of the two Houses.[28]

By the end of the nineteenth century, however, both houses came to utilize the simplified procedure that is followed today: the House or Senate immediately requests a conference as soon as either passes with amendments a measure previously adopted by the other chamber. When "time is of great consequence," said Senator Aaron

---

26. Galloway, "The Third House," p. 2554.
27. McCown, *The Conference Committee*, published in 1927; Galloway, "The Third House," published in 1955.
28. *Register of Debates*, 19th Cong., 1st sess., May 4, 1826, p. 2601.

Sargent of California in 1876, "we have got into the habit, when non-concurring with [the other chamber's] amendments, of asking for a conference."[29]

What is central here is that both chambers must pass what is legislatively defined as the same bill before a conference can meet to adjust differences. What determines sameness sometimes is passage of legislation with the identical bill number, for example, H.R. 1 or S. 1. For instance, the Senate may take a House-passed measure, strike everything after what is called the enacting clause ("Be it enacted by the Senate and House of Representatives . . . "), and amend the House bill with a completely new policy proposal of its own. Technically, the parliamentary principle of sameness has been met and either can then request a conference on the legislation even though the enacted measure may reflect dramatic interchamber differences.

The Selection of Conferees

From the beginning, the Speaker named conferees from the House; in the Senate, this responsibility was similarly assigned to whomever was serving at the time as the presiding officer. No rules or precedents guided these leaders in deciding such matters as how many conferees to name, whether they should come solely from the committee that had considered the legislation, or whether identical conferees should be named if two or more successive conferences were required on the same measure.

For most of congressional history, the size of conference delegations ranged from three to around a dozen members. (The 1980s, by comparison, have seen instances when the House and Senate together have appointed more than 250 conferees!)[30] Changes resulting from the rise of standing committees came to influence conferee selection. In 1888, for example, the presiding officer of the Senate noted, in regard to an Army appropriations measure, that conferees "have been uniformly [drawn from] the subcommittees of the Committee on Appropriations having in charge the particular bill."[31] As standing committees came to exercise major policy-making influence in both houses, their leaders began to exercise a larger role in the choice of conferees and their members came almost exclusively to compose the conference delegations.

During much of the 1800s, conferees had not been uniformly chosen from the committee that had reviewed the measure. In 1857, for instance, four successive conferences were held on a deficiency appropriations bill. New conferees were chosen for each conference. Significantly, only one conferee of all those appointed by the House was a member of the panel that had jurisdiction over the measure.[32] By the 1880s, however, it became common for conferees to come from the committee of jurisdiction and to be in reality selected by the chairman of that standing committee. "The Chair will state that, in theory, the managers of a conference on the part of the Senate are appointed by the Chair," said one presiding officer in 1888. "In fact, they are designated by

29. *Congressional Record*, 44th Cong., 1st sess., April 25, 1876, pp. 2732–33.
30. For a discussion of the growth of the size of conference delegations in recent years, see chapter 1 above as well as chapter 3.
31. *Congressional Record*, 50th Cong., 1st sess., Aug. 3, 1888, p. 7224.
32. *Hinds' Precedents*, vol. 5, sec. 6345.

friends of the measure," that is, the panel that had reported the legislation and especially its chairman.[33]

Limitations on Conferees

An issue that has vexed the House and Senate from the beginning is how to control the actions of the conference to insure that it does not usurp the lawmaking authority of the full House and Senate. Some of the practices and procedures that have been developed include instructing conferees, limiting conferences only to those matters in disagreement between the houses, raising points of order against conference reports in violation of this restriction, recommitting conference reports to conference, and prohibiting the inclusion of new matter in conference reports. To discuss the evolution of each constraint, however, would require more space than is available.[34] Instead, we shall examine one—restricting conferees to the matters in disagreement—to illuminate how complexities can abound in practical application. In addition, we shall briefly discuss the evolution of the custom that conferees are expected to uphold their chamber's position in conference and not their own or that of their committee.[35]

Parliamentary principles state that the text to which both houses have agreed is not open to change by the conferees. Further, conferees are not to add new matter not included in either chamber's bill to their negotiated agreement. As early as 1812, Speaker Henry Clay ruled out of order a conference report on a military matter on the precise grounds that the "conferees had discussed and proposed amendments which had not been committed to them by either of the Houses."[36]

Despite numerous restricting precedents of this kind in both chambers, conference committees frequently have changed the text of measures to which both chambers had previously agreed, and the House and Senate have gone along with these transgressions. Several factors account for such acceptance: the absence of any point of order raised against the conference report (congressional rules, for the most part, are not self-enforcing), recognition by the members of each chamber that the transgressions were necessary to reach an agreement or were otherwise politically useful, or the use of devices such as unanimous consent to waive the precedents.

On July 5, 1888, for example, Senator Preston Plumb of Kansas presented a conference report to the Senate. Senator George Edmunds of Vermont raised a point of

---

33. *Congressional Record,* 50th Cong., 1st sess., Aug. 3, 1888, p. 7224.

34. For a fuller discussion of these tactics in the contemporary Congress, see chapters 8 and 10 below.

35. For a fuller discussion of the question of conferee loyalties today, see chapter 6 below. Runaway conferees are also treated in chapter 1. A relatively minor but fascinating conference "compromise" was reached during the Civil War years. An 1864 conference report recommended legislation imposing a revenue tax of $1.50 a gallon on whiskey. What was noteworthy was that the House legislation has called for a $1.00 a gallon tax, and the Senate-passed bill had set the tax at only $1.25 a gallon (McCown, *The Conference Committee,* p. 90). Creative conferences (or runaway conferences, as some would describe them) are not just a twentieth-century phenomenon but have been present throughout the history of Congress, including, as noted earlier in this chapter, even the very first Congress.

36. *Annals,* 12th Cong., 1st sess., June 23, 1812, p. 1532.

order against it, claiming that the report was "irregular" because it changed the text of a clause that both houses had agreed to when they first passed the legislation. Plumb responded that he knew the report was subject to a point of order, but he intended to ask the unanimous consent of the Senate to adopt the report despite the violation.

The chair initially concurred with Senator Edmunds's point of order. In an interesting development, however, Edmunds immediately asked the Senate to waive his point of order, and the conference report was then agreed to. Edmunds said he favored passage of the report but wanted it clearly understood that it was contrary to parliamentary precedents.[37]

By the 1860s, it became far harder to assess whether a previously agreed to text of legislation had been changed by the conferees. Both chambers by then had initiated a new development in lawmaking: the amendment in the nature of a substitute, the functional equivalent of a whole new bill. Here one chamber takes the other's bill, strikes all after the introductory enacting clause, and substitutes an entirely new bill. Technically, this change represents only one amendment. The conference then has before it the original bill as passed by one chamber and the complete substitute of the other. There are no discrete amendments in disagreement between the bodies. As a result, the conferees have greater latitude to propose new matter or even change the text that both houses accepted when the original bill and the complete substitute originally passed the House or Senate.

In February 1865, for example, the House passed a bill that established a Bureau of Freedmen's Affairs. The Senate then struck all after the enacting clause and substituted a proposal of its own. When the conference report was presented to the House, Representative William Holman of Indiana objected. He argued that the conference presents "an entire [new proposal] for both the original bill and the substitute adopted by the Senate, and it establishes a department unprovided for by either of the other bills." Speaker Schuyler Colfax of Indiana overruled the point of order and established a precedent that is still applicable today:

> If the two Houses had agreed upon any particular language or any part of a section, the committee of conference could not change that; but the Senate having stricken out the bill of the House and inserted another one, the committee of conference have the right to strike out that and report a substitute in its stead. Two separate bills have been referred to the conference committee, and they can take either one of them, or a new bill entirely, or a bill embracing parts of either. They have a right to report any bill that is germane to the bills referred to them.[38]

Whether something is germane (or relevant), of course, is a guideline replete with ambiguities.

Precedents in both chambers stipulate that conferees are to uphold the position of their respective chambers. "The theory . . . of these conference committees," said Senator William Allison of Iowa in 1888, "is that the members of the committee on the

---

37. *Congressional Record,* 50th Cong., 1st sess., July 5, 1888, pp. 5900–02.
38. *Congressional Globe,* 38th Cong., 2d sess., March 3, 1865, p. 1402.

part of the Senate shall represent the Senate, and not the views of the persons comprising the committee."[39] This standard, however, has been difficult to enforce throughout Congress's history. One way enforcement can occur is to challenge the choice of conferees in the Senate, an infrequent event. (There is no effective way to challenge the Speaker's choice of conferees in the House.)

In 1925, the Senate passed the Muscle Shoals Bill, and similar legislation was approved by the House. Senator George Norris of Nebraska, chairman of the Committee on Agriculture and Forestry, which originated the measure, along with Senator Charles McNary of Oregon, the second ranking majority member of the panel, were among those chosen to represent the Senate in conference on this measure. Senator Norris, however, had been the author of an alternative version of the legislation that had been defeated by the Senate. The Senate bill that had been adopted was based on a competing bill written by Senator Oscar Underwood of Alabama and opposed by both Senators Norris and McNary. Senator Underwood expressed concern that Senators Norris and McNary would not represent adequately the Senate's preferences on this issue and moved that they be replaced as conferees by senators who supported his measure.

In the grand tradition of conference committees, the result of this controversy was once again compromise. Senators Norris and McNary were chosen as conferees, thus honoring tradition and committee seniority. Then the two senators resigned from the conference, saying that they were not able to advocate the Senate-approved Underwood Bill, thus ensuring chamber representativeness of the Senate conference delegation.[40]

Floor Consideration of Conference Reports

Of the many topics associated with floor action on conference reports, two are especially worth reviewing: when can conference reports reach the floor of the House and Senate, and are they then open to amendment? During the first several Congresses, conference reports were not considered "privileged" business in either chamber. In other words, conference agreements could not be immediately brought to the floor for consideration ahead of other business. As the volume of legislative business grew and conferences became more frequent, by the mid-1800s both chambers began to accord these documents privileged status. They could be brought to the floor of either chamber for action before most other pending business. The parliamentary theory was that because conference committees settle differences between the chambers, their reports should have precedence over new legislation.

The principle that conference reports are unamendable also took several decades to develop. When the issue was first raised in the House, on February 3, 1804, Representative Joseph Varnum of Massachusetts voiced objection to a particular provision in a conference report. He proposed an amendment to eliminate the "repugnant" provision. Immediately a point of order was raised against Varnum's action.

39. *Congressional Record,* 50th Cong., 1st sess., Aug. 3, 1888, p. 7224.
40. McCown, *The Conference Committee,* pp. 158–62.

Speaker Nathaniel Macon stated that he knew of no precedents that could give him guidance in ruling on the parliamentary objection. He then asked whether any member could recollect any precedents. No member responded to the query. Speaker Macon then ruled in order the amendment to the conference report. Representative Joseph Nicholson of Maryland declared that the "point appeared to be a new one" and appealed the Speaker's ruling. The House adjourned before the appeal was voted upon.

The House resumed consideration of the appeal on February 6. Speaker Macon informed the House about several House precedents on the issue in question that he apparently had recalled (or found) over the weekend. He again stated that Varnum's amendment was in order based on these earlier precedents. Persuaded by the Speaker's declarations, Nicholson withdrew his appeal, whereupon Varnum's amendment to the conference report was agreed to.[41]

Speaker Macon's decision was reversed two decades later. On May 20, 1826, a House member again proposed an amendment to a conference report. On this occasion, Speaker John Taylor ruled that a conference report could *not* be amended. There was no discussion whatsoever on Taylor's decision.[42] This and similar rulings by subsequent Speakers finally and firmly established the House prohibition on amendments to conference reports.

The Senate took a bit longer to arrive at a similar result.[43] In 1852, the presiding officer ruled that the Senate could not "take a part of the report and agree to that, and disagree to the residue. The report is one entire thing." Several senators objected to the ruling and cited for the chair instances in the past when conference reports had been divided and amended. The presiding officer replied that "whatever may have been done heretofore, this is the only correct course. If a different course has ever been pursued, it was informal, and incorrect."[44]

The prohibition against amending conference reports rests on the notion that inordinate and perhaps interminable delays would result if conference reports were amendable. There must be some place in the lawmaking process where finality is achieved. Moreover, the addition of amendments might cause the entire conference report to be killed. Finally, it is discourteous to the other house to amend a joint product of each chamber's conferees.

---

41. *Annals*, 8th Cong., 1st sess., Feb. 4 and 6, 1804, pp. 975-78.

42. McCown, *The Conference Committee*, p. 255.

43. This twenty-six-year gap between Senate and House action is not at all unusual in the evolution of the conference committee; as McCown puts it, "These practices seem to have originated independently and at intervals of years" (ibid., p. 256).

44. *Congressional Globe*, 32d Cong., 1st sess., Aug. 31, 1852, pp. 2487-88. The chair in this instance had a very early precedent in his favor. In 1796, an effort to amend a conference report in the Senate had been ruled out of order on the grounds that a conference report must be considered as a whole (McCown, *The Conference Committee*, p. 255). This and other precedents in the Senate (and also the House) were not considered for some years as absolutely binding, and it was only by the middle of the nineteenth century that "conference reports [were] treated in both houses as indivisible, unamendable, and capable only of acceptance or rejection" (ibid., pp. 55, 52).

Transforming Precedents into Rules

Countless other examples of conference committee politics and procedures could be provided from the lengthy history of that institution. The preceding instances suffice to establish both the evolutionary pattern of conference activity and the recurring nature of many of the issues that surround these bicameral entities. By the end of the nineteenth century, the major features of conference procedure had taken shape.[45] These features were almost entirely based on understandings, rulings, and tradition until the end of the 1800s, when some of the informal practices were formalized into rules.

In 1880, for example, the House passed its first definite rule (as opposed to precedent) establishing the priority of conference reports over other House business.[46] The House adopted another rule in 1902 that required that conference reports be printed in the *Congressional Record* along with an "accompanying statement of explanation." In 1918, following a particularly sharp controversy over new provisions inserted in the War Revenue Bill of 1917, the Senate unanimously approved a rule making explicit the traditional but often ignored prohibition against the including of new material in conference reports.[47]

To conduct a thorough and complete history of conference committees is no easy task, for so much has developed through unwritten practices and slowly developing traditions. In the next chapter, we shall focus on conference committee change in recent decades and shall show how contemporary conference committee politics has adapted to change in Congress itself. But before we conclude this chapter's review of conference committee evolution, it is useful to examine state interchamber adjustment practices in the forty-nine American states with bicameral legislatures.

---

45. The national tensions of the decades preceding the Civil War, well represented in Congress, provided a major impetus for the institutionalization of the conference committee. During these years, the major features of modern conference procedure took shape. These include the uniformity of House and Senate conference reports to each chamber, the special parliamentary privileged consideration these reports enjoy in both House and Senate, and the earlier development of the unamendable conference report, conference latitude, and the concept of interchamber compromise as the basis of conference decision. Other modern features of conference committees institutionalized during this period were the secrecy of conference deliberations (actually in effect since 1789), the right of conference committees to report legislation as late as the closing hours of the legislative session, and the choosing, as conferees, of legislators exclusively drawn not only from the committee that had considered the measure, but also from among the senior members of that committee. By late in the nineteenth century, then, the modern conference committee, largely as it exists today, had evolved (ibid., pp. 254–55, 49–50). It should be noted, however, that two of these features, the absolute nondivisibility of conference reports and the secrecy of conference proceedings, have undergone substantial change in recent years. See chapter 3 below.

46. Ibid., p. 101.

47. Ibid., pp. 172–73. Explicitness, however, does not necessarily mean uniformity of enforcement. This prohibition is surely honored as much by the exception as in the letter or the spirit of the rule. The House further provided, in 1920, for limitations on the power of conference committees to accept Senate amendments, especially nongermane Senate amendments, to House-originated appropriations bills (ibid., p. 173). This issue of Senate nongermane amendments has proved to be a recurrent one; for further discussion, see chapters 9 and 10.

Bicameral State Politics[48]

> Very few state legislators have reason to lie awake nights lamenting the power of conference committees or their immoderate use, for as a rule they are neither very powerful nor used very often. Their influence occupies a threshold well below that of congressional conference committees.
> —William J. Keefe and Morris S. Ogul[49]

> Whether legislators lie awake at night lamenting the power of conference committees depends upon the state. Where they are used, their influence is significant. Important questions of policy that divide chambers are settled in these committees.
> —Jeanie Mather and Glenn Abney[50]

What stands out about interchamber reconciliation procedures in the forty-nine bicameral states is their enormous variety.[51] Some states follow no established pro-

---

48. An earlier version of the discussion in this section was published as Lawrence D. Longley, "Bicameral Politics in the American States," *Legislative Studies Section Newsletter,* Legislative Studies Section, American Political Science Association, vol. 9, no. 2 (April 1986), pp. 60–64.

49. William J. Keefe and Morris S. Ogul, *The American Legislative Process: Congress and the States,* 5th ed. (Englewood Cliffs: Prentice-Hall, 1981), p. 175.

50. Jeanie Mather and Glenn Abney, "The Role of Conference Committees in State Legislatures," paper prepared for delivery at the 1981 Annual Meeting of the Southern Political Science Association, Memphis, Nov. 2–4, 1981, p. 17.

51. As we noted earlier, Nebraska is the unique exception to the universality of state legislative bicameralism in the United States. Due to the determined efforts of reformers, most notably Sen. George Norris (R, Neb.), the state eliminated its second chamber in 1934 and thus created what is still today the nation's only unicameral state legislature. The change was widely debated at the time as being a crucial legislative reform. See, for example, John P. Senning, *The One-House Legislature* (New York: McGraw-Hill, 1937); Alvin W. Johnson, *The Unicameral Legislature* (Minneapolis: University of Minnesota Press, 1938), and Thomas A. Rousse, *Bicameralism vs. Unicameralism* (New York: Thomas Nelson, 1937).

Despite the extensive discussion of the matter in the late 1930s, there has been little concerted effort in recent decades to advocate unicameralism, and the great debate of the 1930s has largely faded from most people's political agendas. A noteworthy exception, however, was the 1971 advocacy by Jess Unruh, the former Speaker and master of the California state assembly, of unicameralism as "the wave of the future." He wrote, "I favor unicameralism because I believe that it would improve the legislature's competitive position with respect to other branches of government. A shift to unicameral legislatures is at the heart of legislative reform" (Jess Unruh, "Unicameralism—The Wave of the Future," in Donald C. Herzberg and Alan Rosenthal, eds, *Strengthening the States: Essays on Legislative Reform* [Garden City: Doubleday, 1971], pp. 87, 94. The quotation is on p. 92. Of course, we might add, unicameralism would also make the task of legislative leadership easier. A powerful chamber leader, as Jess Unruh was for many years, would not find his leadership checked by an independently acting second chamber with its own leadership.

For further information concerning state bicameral and unicameral arrangements, see the sources cited in Lawrence D. Longley, "Legislative Bicameralism and Unicameralism in the American States: A Research Bibliography," *Legislative Studies Section Newsletter,* Legislative Studies Section, American Political Science Association, vol. 10, no. 1 (Nov. 1986), pp. 82–85.

cedure, with one chamber or the other just deciding to accept the legislation as passed by its counterpart. In other states, intercameral adjustment is usually performed through informal negotiations on the part of the legislative leadership. And in many states differences between the chambers are worked out by some form of conference committee.[52]

An early 1980s mail survey of presiding officers and committee chairmen in all forty-nine bicameral states found that twenty-eight states principally rely on leadership consultation to work out interchamber differences. Conference committees were primarily used in twelve states. In four states, both methods were viewed as being of roughly equal importance. Conference committees were not used at all in three states, with these and two others relying on a variety of alternative methods, including chamber deference, standing joint legislative committees, party caucuses, and informal consultations involving bill sponsors and committee chairmen.[53]

States that utilize the conference committee vary widely both in the significance of the conference and the frequency of its use. Alan Rosenthal reports that "in a number of states—Wisconsin and Texas for example—the major decisions are almost always made in conference."[54] Jewell and Patterson found that "conference committees are used much more frequently in some state legislatures than in others, but the reasons for these variations are obscure, and little research has been done on conference committees."[55]

Scholars have embarked on efforts to examine the conditions that determine when state conference committees will play a significant policy-making role. Based on a forty-nine-state survey, Mather and Abney found that "states having the greatest degree of

52. Malcolm E. Jewell and Samuel C. Patterson, *The Legislative Process in the United States,* 3d ed. (New York: Random House, 1977), p. 440, and Donald A. Gross, "House-Senate Conference Committees: A Comparative-State Perspective," *American Journal of Political Science* 24 (Nov. 1980): 769. An earlier version of this article was given as a paper at the 1979 Annual Meeting of the American Political Science Association in Washington, D.C., Aug. 31–Sept. 3, 1979, under the title, "House-Senate Conference Committees and the Politics of Appropriations: A Comparative State Perspective." All references here are to the published version.

Concerning state reconciliation practices, see also *Lawmaking in the West* (San Francisco: Council of State Governments, 1967), and *Legislative Openness* (Kansas City: Citizens' Conference on State Legislatures, 1974). For a counterpart examination of the unicameral alternative, see John W. Manning, *Unicameral Legislation in the States* (Lexington: University of Kentucky Bureau of Government Research, 1938); and Robert Sittig, "The Nebraska Unicameral after Fifty Years," paper prepared for delivery at the Hendricks Symposium on State Legislature Reform, University of Nebraska—Lincoln, April 2–4, 1986. The latter retrospective review includes a useful, although undocumented, account of the adoption of the unicameral legislature in Nebraska (affectionately known in the state as "The Unicameral"), an account that stresses the role of constitutional convention, petition-initiative, and George Norris in Nebraska's movement to unicameralism.

53. Mather and Abney, "The Role of Conference Committees," p. 3. This mail survey was sent to ten presiding officers and committee chairmen in each of the forty-nine bicameral states and had a 48 percent response rate (ibid., p. 2). On the number of states not using conference committees, Jewell and Patterson reported a 1975 estimate of seven states in contrast with the Mather-Abney figure of three.

54. Alan Rosenthal, *Legislative Life: People, Process and Performance in the States* (New York: Harper and Row, 1981), p. 294.

55. Jewell and Patterson, *The Legislative Process,* p. 440.

Methods of Interchamber Reconciliation
Used in the American States

Predominant Methods	*Number of States*
Leadership consultation	28
Conference committee	12
Both leadership consultation and conference committee	4
Alternative methods (including chamber deference, standing joint legislative committee, party caucus, and informal consultation of key legislators)	5
	49 = N

SOURCE: Jeanie Mather and Glenn Abney, "The Role of Conference Committees in State Legislatures," paper prepared for delivery at the 1981 Annual Meeting of the Southern Political Science Association, Memphis, Tenn., Nov. 2–4, 1981, p. 3.

conflict are those where conference committees are the most common mechanism of conflict resolution. . . . Where differences between the two chambers become intense, the conference committee is needed to resolve differences; in these situations the informality of consultations between legislative leaders does not appear to work as well."[56]

Jewell and Patterson offer somewhat complementary hypotheses linking the utilization of conference committees to issue significance and legislative conflict. They suggest that "appropriations measures," presumably because of their importance,[57] "are sent to conference committees more often" than other substantive measures.[58] Further, "in states where the committees play a decisive part in the decision-making process, conference committees are likely to be used, at least on the most important and controversial legislation in a session."[59]

In a later reformulation, Jewell and Patterson added partisan factors to their analysis: "Conference committees play a more important role in resolving conflicts between

---

56. Mather and Abney, "The Role of Conference Committees," p. 4.

57. The quantitative nature of most aspects of appropriations legislation may also lend itself especially well to the compromise style of conference. Certainly, it is easier to split the difference on dollar amounts of appropriations than to bargain on qualitative questions in chamber disagreement such as the creation of a new program or the structure of a new state government agency. These latter questions might well be seen as requiring the utilization of alternative intercameral reconciliatory devices, such as leadership consultations or informal negotiations between bill authors or managers.

58. Jewell and Patterson, *The Legislative Process*, pp. 400–41. In a 1986 revision, Jewell and Patterson added the observation that in thirty-seven states, major appropriations legislation routinely goes the conference committee route (Malcolm E. Jewell and Samuel C. Patterson, *The Legislative Process in the United States*, 4th ed. [New York: Random House, 1986], p. 170; referring to information derived from the Council of State Governments, *American State Legislatures: Their Structures and Procedures* [Lexington, Ky.: Council of State Governments, 1977], p. 69).

59. Jewell and Patterson, *The Legislative Process* (1977), pp. 440–41.

the chambers in those states where committees are more powerful and where party organizations and leadership are less strong."[60] This promising hypothesis, partially suggested by the analysis of Abney and Mather but identified and proposed by Jewell and Patterson, awaits further investigation.

Other perspectives on conference committee politics in the states include a study by Donald A. Gross. He explored the level of interchamber disagreement on appropriation items in ten state legislatures through the use of nine "structure/institutional" or "political/partisanship" variables. Not surprisingly, he concludes that where chamber partisan differences are greatest, interchamber disagreements are also greatest.[61] In other research, Mather and Abney, in their survey of state conference committees, suggest that conferees can be categorized in terms of four representative types: the representative of one's chamber's position, the representative of one's own views, the representative of the view of one's constituents, and the negotiator of compromises.[62] An analysis by Eugene Declerq points out the importance of recognizing interhouse differences in understanding state bicameral politics. He finds the most substantial differences between legislative chambers involve neither committee autonomy nor partisan balances, but the formal powers of the chamber's leadership, and concludes that "inter-house variance should be viewed as an empirical question."[63]

Finally, in his study of conference committees in the states, Donald A. Gross also addressed the perennial question Which chamber wins? His analysis of bicameral appropriations politics in ten states leads him to conclude that the upper chamber wins approximately 60 percent of the time; however, the chamber that acts second, whether upper or lower, wins 67 percent of the time.[64] In these respects, Gross's findings are compatible with the "structural-process hypothesis" advanced to explain "who wins" in Con-

---

60. Ibid. (1986), p. 170. One reason why conference committee use could be related to the presence of a strong committee system would be that usually conference committees are dominated by leaders of the chamber committees that originally considered the legislation. Certainly, these committee chairmen or senior committee members would see the conference committee as a forum more susceptible to their influence than an alternative reconciliation process involving others in central roles, such as consultations between legislative leaders, the involvement of a standing joint committee, or the use of party caucuses.

Jewell and Patterson also speculated in their 1977 analysis concerning a relationship between powerful party leadership and conference committee significance: "In states where there is strong party leadership, the conference committee may simply ratify the decisions made by these leaders; on other occasions, the party leaders or the governor may be unwilling to delegate (even formally) the settlement of controversies to a conference committee" (p. 441).

61. Donald A. Gross, "Conference Committees and Levels of Inter-Chamber Disagreement: A Comparative State Perspective," *State and Local Government Review*, 1983. Another particularly interesting article by the same author applies formal theory and the theory of sophisticated voting to conference committee politics: "Bicameralism and the Theory of Voting," *Western Political Quarterly* 35, no. 4 (Dec. 1982): 511–26.

62. Mather and Abney, "The Role of Conference Committees," p. 14. For a different analysis of conference loyalties, see chapter 6 below.

63. Eugene Declerq, "Inter-House Differences in American State Legislatures," *Journal of Politics* 39 (1977): 774–85. The conclusions and quotations are from page 784.

64. Gross, "House-Senate Conference Committees," p. 773.

gress—a theory that holds that the sequence of chamber voting is the major determinant of chamber prevalence.[65] Gross further extends his conclusions to incorporate interchamber partisan contrasts, arguing that "the greater the partisan difference between the two chambers, the more likely are conferees from the second-acting chamber to win."[66] It is worth noting in this regard that Mather and Abney report that, based on responses from 238 state legislators, "for most of our respondents the essential focus is not which chamber wins, for many have other concerns."[67] In conclusion, it is fair to conclude, as do Jewell and Patterson in 1986, that "the workings of conference committees at the state level remains an area about which we know relatively little."[68]

Summary

Our examination of state conference committees has shown them to be a major but not universal means of legislative reconciliation. They tend to flourish under conditions of sharp policy and interchamber conflict.

Our earlier evaluation of congressional conference committees highlighted how several of their procedural features evolved and took root in both chambers. In the next chapter, we examine how the modern conference committee continues to adapt to changing circumstances.

---

65. The leading example of this approach is Gerald S. Strom and Barry S. Rundquist, "A Revised Theory of Winning in House-Senate Conferences," *American Political Science Review* 71 (June 1977): 448–53. For an evaluation of this and other approaches to the question Who wins? in interchamber negotiations, see chapter 4 below.
66. Gross, "House-Senate Conference Committees," p. 776.
67. Mather and Abney, "The Role of Conference Committees," p. 14.
68. Jewell and Patterson, *The Legislative Process,* 1986, p. 170.

3

The Changing Character of Conference Committee Politics

The history of bicameralism is one of change.
—Edward G. Carmines and Lawrence C. Dodd[1]

When we started the openness thing we found it more and more difficult to get something agreed to in the conferences; it seemed to take forever. So what did we do? . . . We would break up into smaller groups and then we would ask our chairman . . . to see if he could find his opposite number on the House side and discuss this matter and come back and tell us what the chances would be of working out various and sundry possibilities.
—Senator Russell B. Long (D, La.)[2]

Change is the most durable iron law of legislative politics. Conference committees are products of their political environments; as pressures have built for such objectives as legislative openness or democratization of power in the House and Senate, conference committees have likewise undergone adaptation both in their formal rules and in their informal procedures and operations.

Later sections of this chapter will trace the events and consequences of congressional decisions to open conferences to public observation, and the impact—on conference

---

1. Edward G. Carmines and Lawrence C. Dodd, "Bicameralism in Congress: The Changing Partnership," in Lawrence C. Dodd and Bruce I. Oppenheimer eds., *Congress Reconsidered,* 3d ed. (Washington, D.C.: CQ Press, 1985), p. 432.
2. *Congressional Record,* Feb. 20, 1986, p. S1463.

committee operations—of such changes in Congress as the weakening of chamber and committee leadership, the growing role of subcommittees, the increase in multiple referral of bills to committee, the development of massive omnibus bills and unusual legislative procedures, and the division of partisan control over Congress. In each instance, a significant change in congressional politics has had a corresponding impact on the politics and procedures of conference committees.

Before discussing these major developments, we shall first mention briefly several less sweeping changes that largely occurred in the period 1965–75. These include a modification (made in 1965) in how the House goes to conference, procedural revisions contained in the Legislative Reorganization Act of 1970, and changes resulting from the Congressional Budget and Impoundment Control Act of 1974 and the Gramm-Rudman legislation of 1985. Following that discussion, we shall examine how the traditional secrecy of conference committee meetings was transformed, and the significance of this development. Finally, we shall consider the impact of a variety of other changes in congressional politics, including the decentralization of power in the House and Senate, upon conference committees. The contemporary conference committee is indeed an evolving institution—one that responds both to developments integral to conference committees and to forces arising from the changing congressional environment.

Procedural Changes

Many cases of comparatively small procedural revision arouse major political controversy because the change shifts the distribution of political power. This was the case for a 1965 change in the means by which the House could agree to a conference. Prior to that year, if any representative objected to a unanimous consent request for a conference, a special rule (a simple resolution that sets the terms for dealing with a bill on the floor) that would allow the House "to go to conference" had to be obtained from the Rules Committee. This rule gave that committee, at the time justly known as the graveyard of liberal legislation, enormous power over legislation, even *after* House passage. This "postpassage" power complemented Rules' crucial control over committee-reported bills needing a special rule for *initial* floor consideration. In 1960, for example, the House passed landmark general aid to education legislation that contained only modest provisions for primary and secondary school construction. The Senate likewise approved a similar bill but added several amendments providing for more extensive school construction aid. Following Senate passage, the legislation was returned to the originating chamber—the House. There a motion was made to go to conference with the Senate, but objection was made, and the matter was referred to the House Rules Committee for a special rule. By a vote of 5–7, however, the committee refused to grant the needed rule, and the measure died in the closing days of the session.[3]

---

3. Lewis A. Froman, *The Congressional Process* (Boston: Little, Brown, 1967), p. 143; Robert Bendiner, *Obstacle Course on Capitol Hill: What Happens to a Bill in Congress* (New York: McGraw-Hill, 1964), pp. 168–71; and Spark M. Matsunaga and Ping Chen, *Rulemakers of the House* (Urbana: University of Illinois Press, 1976), p. 26. Froman provides a number of examples of the Rules Committee's denial of conferences—see pp. 145–53.

The defeat of the 1960 education bill by unilateral action of the House Rules Committee was exceptionally controversial and proved to be one of the major catalysts for the attack in 1961 on the procedural prerogatives of the Rules Committee by the combined forces of the newly elected Democratic president, John F. Kennedy, and House Speaker Sam Rayburn. Their challenge took the form of a plan to enlarge the size of the committee "temporarily" from twelve to fifteen members. The new appointees presumably would be sympathetic to Kennedy's New Frontier program. This expansion was eventually adopted by the House by a vote of 217–211, and the increased size of the committee was made permanent in 1963.[4]

This change was not sufficient, however, to bring the House Rules Committee under majority leadership control; further, it did nothing to weaken the stranglehold the committee had over the convening of conferences. Consequently, in 1965, the House, by a vote of 224–201, adopted a new rule providing for an alternative means, one not involving the Rules Committee, for the House to go to conference. Under this procedure, the Speaker, at his discretion, could recognize a member of the standing committee that had originally reported the legislation to move that the House request a conference on a bill.[5] Thus, the House Rules Committee's absolute veto power over the convening of conference committees was eliminated, and an alternative means of calling a conference was lodged with the Speaker and a majority of the House.[6]

---

4. See Matsunaga and Chen, *Rulemakers of the House;* James A. Robinson, *The House Rules Committee* (Indianapolis: Bobbs-Merrill, 1963); Milton C. Cummings, Jr., and Robert L. Peabody, "The Decision to Enlarge the Committee on Rules: An Analysis of the 1961 Vote," in Robert L. Peabody and Nelson W. Polsby, eds., *New Perspectives on the House of Representatives* (Chicago: Rand McNally, 1963), chap. 7; and Hugh Douglas Price, "Race, Religion, and the Rules Committee: The Kennedy Aid-to-Education Bills," in Alan F. Westin, ed., *The Uses of Power* (New York: Harcourt, Brace & World, 1962), pp. 1–71.

5. Froman, *The Congressional Process,* p. 144, and Congressional Quarterly, *Guide to Congress,* 3d ed., (Washington, D.C.: Congressional Quarterly, 1982), p. 469. On the contemporary Rules Committee, see "Rules Committee No Longer Impenetrable Barrier," *Congressional Quarterly Weekly Report,* Nov. 12, 1965, pp. 2323–25; "House Rules Committee Regains Image of Independence," *Congressional Quarterly Weekly Report,* March 30, 1974, pp. 804–10; Bruce I. Oppenheimer, "The Rules Committee: New Arm of Leadership in a Decentralized House," in Lawrence C. Dodd and Bruce I. Oppenheimer, *Congress Reconsidered* (New York: Praeger, 1977), pp. 96–116; and Andy Plattner, "New Rules Committee Head Expected to Carry Forward in Tradition of Rep. Bolling," *Congressional Quarterly Weekly Report,* Nov. 9, 1982, p. 2801.

6. The House Rules Committee continues to have an important power concerning conference committees: it may issue a special rule for a conference providing for a general waiver of all points of order against a conference committee report (Matsunaga and Chen, *Rulemakers of the House,* p. 28). For additional detailed discussion of the process of seeking a conference, see chapter 8 below; for analysis of the process by which conference reports are adopted, see chapter 10.

The process of seeking a conference in the Senate usually involves a unanimous consent request. In theory this procedure could be far more vulnerable to minority obstruction than the House Rules Committee-dominated process of the pre-1965 era. Informal senatorial norms of comity and accommodation, however, have allowed the Senate process of obtaining a conference to operate without the controversy the House experienced in the early 1960s.

Later changes in conference committee procedures were somewhat less controversial. The Legislative Reorganization Act of 1970, for example, required that conference reports to the House and Senate be accompanied by a statement explaining specific changes made by the conference. The act further required the statement to be prepared jointly by the conferees of both houses so that the explanation of what was decided upon would not be different in the two chambers and thus subject to differing interpretations.[7]

Another issue addressed in the 1970 Legislative Reorganization Act was a recurring one: the question of how the House should handle nongermane (that is, not on the same topic) Senate amendments to House-originated bills. The House, with its strict germaneness requirements, had long opposed Senate amendments of this kind, contending that they undercut the role of House committees, enabled important and controversial measures to be adopted with minimum consideration (House rules permit only one hour of debate on conference reports), and forced the House to accept Senate provisions that were inconsistent with House rules prohibiting nongermane legislation. Frequently, the House was faced with a take it or leave it proposition—accept the nongermane Senate amendments or lose the bill in its entirety, including, of course, House-passed provisions. Many members of the House were frustrated by this recurring dilemma. "I have chafed for years," declared Rules Committee Chairman William Colmer (D, Miss.) in 1970, "about the other body violating the rules of this House by placing entirely foreign, extraneous, and non-germane matters in House-passed bills."[8] As a result, the House finally acted against the Senate practice during the 1970s by taking several procedural steps, including language in the Legislative Reorganization Act of 1970 and two other (1972 and 1974) rules changes permitting separate House votes on the nongermane parts of conference reports.[9]

One effect of these House procedural changes has been to strengthen the bargaining leverage of the House in conference. Representatives are now able to demand during conference negotiations that Senate nongermane amendments be dropped on the grounds that otherwise they will be voted down in the House. These rules may even have the effect of reducing on occasion the introduction of nongermane amendments on the Senate floor. Finally, this change has meant that conference committee reports can be viewed at times as less than indivisible wholes. Under some circumstances, the House will vote to exorcise parts of a conference report ruled as containing nongermane Senate

---

7. For a fuller discussion, see Walter J. Oleszek, "Conference Committee Procedure and Reform," paper prepared for the Select Committee on the Operation of the Senate Committee System, in *Appendix to the Second Report, with Recommendations* (Washington, D.C.: U.S. Government Printing Office, 1977), p. 42.

8. *Congressional Record,* 91st Cong., 2d sess., Sept. 15, 1970, p. 31842.

9. For a fuller discussion, see Stanley Bach, "Germaneness Rules and Bicameral Relations in the U.S. Congress," *Legislative Studies Quarterly* 7, no. 3 (Aug. 1982): 345 ff. Bach analyzes this procedural change in terms of bicameral adjustment: the House had to find a way of adapting its rules *prohibiting* non-germane legislation to Senate rules that *tolerate* nongermane amendments. This adaptation was made easier, Bach argues, since the procedure was also useful for the House majority leadership.

language and deal separately with the remaining matter—or alternatively will decide, by majority vote, to retain nongermane material in the conference report.[10]

Another noteworthy change in conference committee procedure occurred when Congress revised its budgetary process in the early 1970s. With enactment of the Congressional Budget and Impoundment Control Act of 1974 and the Gramm-Rudman deficit reduction legislation of 1985 (see chapter 11), the congressional budgetary process now imposes spending limits on all congressional committees, including conference committees. For example, in the wake of the stock market crash of 1987 and fiscal summitry between White House and Congress, the Senate rejected a housing conference report because it exceeded expenditure limitations set forth in the budget previously adopted by Congress. The conference report, said Senator Pete Domenici (R, N.M.), is "an absolute budget buster in the midst of a budget crisis in the name of housing reform."[11] As the revised budgetary process has imposed a degree of centralized direction on standing committees, it likewise has added constraints on conference committees.

Thus far, we have been discussing a variety of specific changes affecting conference committees that, while procedurally significant, neither individually nor collectively have had a fundamental impact on conference committee deliberations. A change adopted in 1975, however, had far-reaching implications. This change was the decision of both the Senate and House to open conference committees to public observation.

The Opening of Congressional Conference Committees

> Secrecy is an important shield for conferees against pressures from outside.
> —Jeffrey L. Pressman[12]

---

10. House procedures for handling nongermane provisions are discussed further in chapter 10 below.

In reciprocal fashion, the Senate, in late 1985, instituted a new procedure for its handling of nongermane material originating in the House and coming to the Senate as part of a reconciliation bill or conference report. S.Res. 286, adopted on December 19, 1985, provided that a point of order may be raised in the Senate concerning such extraneous material, which, if upheld, would strike out the offending language. The purpose of this change, as its author, William Roth (R, Del.), explained, would be to give the Senate the ability "to request further conference or to insist on its disagreement or to recede and concur in the House amendment [bill] with an amendment incorporating the remainder of the text of the conference report or any other permissible variation which does not revive the provision deemed stricken by the successful point of order" (*Congressional Record*, Dec. 19, 1985, p. S18255).

The effect of this Senate rules change was to strengthen the Senate's position in postconference intercameral politics—and it may also enhance the position of Senate conferees during the conference, allowing them to oppose the inclusion of extraneous House provisions in the conference report on the grounds that they will be stricken from the legislation in the Senate on a point of order.

11. *Congressional Record*, Nov. 17, 1987, p. S16360. See also *Washington Post*, Nov. 23, 1987, p. A15.

12. Jeffrey L. Pressman, *House vs. Senate* (New Haven: Yale University Press, 1966), p. 56.

> When conferences were in executive [closed] session, members didn't have to pound the table and make speeches they hope will be reported back home. They could sit there and say, "You know where I sit and I know where you sit so we've got to compromise." We do the same thing now but it takes much longer because we have to give all of our speeches first.
> —Senator Mark Hatfield (R, Ore.)[13]

From the First Congress in 1789 until 1974, conference committee meetings—with but two exceptions[14]—invariably had been closed to the public and press. This is not to say that the only persons present at conferences were the conferees themselves. Committee staff, congressional aides, and executive branch officials certainly observed (and sometimes participated actively in) conferences over the years.[15] Sometimes members of the House and Senate who were not officially members of the conference but had a personal interest in the legislation would "drop by" conference meetings and even express their views on the legislation. A conference would on occasion bring in outside experts to advise it on complex policy questions,[16] and lobbyists were never very far away—either politically or physically.[17] Finally, representatives of the president often would be invited to observe or participate in so-called closed conference sessions out of a realization that any compromise would still be, after congressional enactment, subject to presidential review and possible veto. Those whom the closed conference committee *did* exclude were representatives of interests not favored by conference leaders, the press that might write uncomplimentary stories about the wheeling and dealing of conference committee bargaining, and members of the general public, who could only wonder what happened to chamber-passed legislation in conference.

During the closed years, conference committee interactions were marked by political candor that included explicit threats, cajoling, and bargaining often resembling

---

13. Quoted in *Los Angeles Times*, Dec. 22, 1979, p. 6.

14. An open conference had been held in 1911 on the Tariff Bill of that year and was chaired by Sen. Robert La Follette of Wisconsin. Senator La Follette's Progressive Party stood for openness of all political and legislative activity; consequently he pushed the novel idea of opening conference deliberations to public scrutiny. As a trial, a one-day conference committee meeting on August 11, 1911, was opened to all comers. This experiment elicited considerable interest and detailed press commentary, but it would not be repeated until 1974. A detailed account of this open conference may be found in the *New York Times*, Aug. 12, 1911, p. 2; a briefer summary in Ada C. McCown, *The Congressional Conference Committee* (New York: Columbia University Press, 1927), pp. 177–78. For discussion of the only other pre-1974 open conference, that of 1789, see chapter 2 above.

15. For a discussion of the role of congressional staff and executive branch personnel in conference committee proceedings, see chapter 7 below. Among the other conference "players" there discussed are the president, agencies, the press, interest groups, and other congressmen.

16. Bertram M. Gross, *The Legislative Struggle: A Study in Social Combat* (New York: McGraw-Hill, 1953), p. 323.

17. Despite closed conference committees, as Rep. Morris Udall (D, Ariz.) put it, "The lobbyist always knew what was going on" (quoted in Adam Clymer, "A Congress Spectacular: Energy Bill," *New York Times*, Oct. 17, 1977).

simple horse trading.[18] After the battle was over, however, the only public records of conference deliberations were the unrevealing official conference report together with often self-serving informational statements made to each chamber by the conferees. No printed or written records were publicly available, and conference bargaining and negotiations were revealed only to the extent desired by the participants.[19] The conference committee was a mysterious black box into which the House and Senate placed their adopted bills to be transformed into new "compromise" conference legislation.

The fog began to lift in the mid-1970s. Early in that decade, there was increasing pressure from change-minded members and groups such as Common Cause to open House and Senate proceedings to the press and public. In 1974, as an experiment, twelve conferences voluntarily chose to open their sessions. The first of these was on a particularly contentious strip mine regulatory bill and, as the first open conference in sixty-three years, understandably attracted considerable press and public attendance. In order to get into the conference room, "Members had to carve their way through a wall of human flesh," one conferee ruefully reported.[20]

Despite such congestion, conference participants were generally pleased by the experience with openness—it proved to many that public conference meetings "would not disrupt the conference process."[21] Among those seeing benefits in open meetings were lobbyists on both sides of the initial strip mining conference. One mining industry representative pointed out that the open conference "benefits both sides . . . [since] you have a better idea of what's happening on a day-to-day, hour-by-hour basis." John McCormick, a lobbyist representing the opposing Coalition Against Strip Mining, argued that "openness was an assurance that we weren't going to lose anything major" during the bicameral deliberations. In support of this view, McCormick cited an instance when his organization was able to change the position of one conferee by informing

---

18. Charles L. Clapp, *The Congressman: His Work as He Sees It* (Washington, D.C.: Brookings Institution, 1963), p. 284. One political scientist recounted his surprise upon gaining access some years ago to the preopening conference minutes and files of the House Government Operations Committee. They were, he reported, "utterly explicit" in terms of deals and negotiations; presumably this candor was due to the presumption that the documents were absolutely confidential and for internal use only. Audience discussion at Congressional Politics Panel held at the Annual Meeting of the American Political Science Association, Chicago, Sept. 1, 1983.

19. As part of the actions taken in 1975 by the House and Senate to open conference committees, rules were also adopted that year requiring that a transcript or electronic recording be made of all conference committee proceedings—unless conferees should specifically vote otherwise. Even this "requirement," however, is commonly ignored by conference committees or honored only to the minimum degree of keeping exceedingly sketchy conference minutes noting only formal motions. Further, these records, where they exist, are usually only accessible at committee offices to those who can convince committee staff both of the reasonableness of their inquiry and of the existence of these fugitive records.

20. Rep. John F. Seiberling (D, Ohio), quoted in Congressional Quarterly, *Guide to Congress*, 2d ed. (Washington, D.C.: Congressional Quarterly, 1976), p. 354.

21. "Conference Committees Opened to Public" in Congressional Quarterly, *Inside Congress*, 2d ed. (Washington, D.C.: Congressional Quarterly, 1979), p. 67. An earlier version of this piece was published as "Reform Penetrates Conference Committees," *Congressional Quarterly Weekly Report*, Feb. 8, 1976, pp. 290–94.

constituents of his conference stance.[22] The general acceptance that the twelve open conferences of 1974 received paved the way for Congress to act the next year to open all conferences.[23]

In January 1975, a rules change was proposed in the House that would require all conferences to hold open sessions unless a majority of House conferees voted in public session to close a particular meeting. Such a vote would apply only to that single session of the conference committee; closing any subsequent meeting would require separate public votes each day. The proposed rules change drew some mixed reactions from representatives and lobbyists. Longtime congressional reformer Richard Bolling (D, Mo.) surprisingly exhibited considerable caution about this reform: "Sunshine laws kid the public. They imply a total openness and there never will be." Bolling pointed out that while openness was desirable, legislative compromises and accommodations must also be provided for, and these require privacy. "If we have to meet in our wives' boudoirs—if they still have such things—we will."[24] Responded another veteran reformer, Congressman Abner Mikva (D, Ill.): "[Representative Al] Ullman and [Senator Russell] Long still will go out to lunch together—as they did last Monday—and trade Park Place for Boardwalk, but that's no excuse for not opening up conference meetings."[25] A lobbyist for the U.S. Chamber of Commerce cautioned that open conference sessions could disrupt needed negotiations: "Compromise could be a little more difficult to come by. If you put a flock of Ralph Naders, John Gardners, or Sierra Clubbers in a conference room . . . it will make some conferees sweat."[26] This prospect, however, rather appealed to David Cohen of Common Cause, who expressed the view that public conference sessions would benefit public interest groups like his by making it easier to compete effectively with other interests traditionally well established in Congress.[27]

The open conference committee rule was adopted by the House on January 14, 1975, as House Rule 28. A similar rules change was proposed in the Senate at about the same time, although it was not approved in that chamber until November 4. As a consequence, by the end of 1975, both houses had acted decisively to change one fundamental and traditional aspect of conference committees—their secrecy.[28]

22. Ibid., pp. 67–68. McCormick also speculated, according to CQ, "that open conferences might cut down the number of nongermane and special interest amendments added to the legislation in the Senate. Many of those amendments are accepted on the floor with the clear understanding that they will be quietly dropped in conference. The member benefits, however, because he can tell his constituents that he had the amendment approved on the floor." (p. 68)

23. Congressional Quarterly, *Congressional Quarterly Almanac, 1974* (Washington, D.C.: Congressional Quarterly, 1975), pp. 961–62. A list of the twelve open conferences of 1974 can be found on page 962 of this work.

24. "Conference Committees Opened to Public," p. 68.

25. Quoted in *Chicago Tribune,* March 31, 1975.

26. "Conference Committees Opened to Public," p. 68.

27. Ibid. See also the discussion, later in this chapter, of the consequences to various interest groups of open conference sessions.

28. On the 1975 rules change, see "Conference Committees Opened to Public," pp. 67–71; Congressional Quarterly, *Guide to Congress,* 3d ed., pp. 435, 455; idem, *Congressional Quarterly Almanac, 1975* (Washington, D.C.: Congressional Quarterly, 1976), pp. 39–40, 931; idem, *Congress and the Nation: 1973–1976,* vol. 4 (Washington, D.C.: Congressional Quarterly, 1977), pp. 767, 770, 773.

One further modification of congressional rules concerning open conference proceedings occurred two years later. In December 1977, the House amended its rules additionally to require that all conference sessions be open unless the *full House* voted for a closed conference meeting.[29] As a result of this additional strengthening of the House's general prohibition against closed conference meetings, virtually all conference committees, except those dealing with national security issues or involving the Intelligence committees, are today officially open.[30] However, as we shall see, most public conferences still involve private conferences.

The Consequences of Open Conference Committees

> Instead of waiting in uncomfortable corridors, lobbyists and reporters . . . now wait in uncomfortable committee rooms, mostly small old ones in the Capitol designed for private meetings.
> —Adam Clymer[31]

> It is my absolute conviction that the meetings that have been transpiring are not meetings of the conference but are informal expressions between members on both sides in an effort to advance—I will concede—in an effort to advance the business of the conference.
> —Representative Thomas I. Ashley[32]

Because conference committee sessions are now open does not mean that the public can easily observe conference proceedings. Unlike hearings and other meetings of regular standing committees, which are usually held in large hearing rooms in the House or Senate office buildings, most conference committees meet in tiny, exceedingly cramped cubbyhole rooms, often in the Capitol building itself. Meeting close to both chambers reflects a bicameral geographical fairness and enables conferees to reach their chamber quickly for floor votes or quorum calls. The predilection for conference locations in the Capitol building, however, creates special problems for nonconferees. On November 4, 1981, for example, a House-Senate appropriations conference convened in Room S-126

---

29. As a result of this 1977 action, House Rule 28 now reads: "Each conference committee between the House and Senate shall be open to the public except when the House, in open session, has determined by a roll-call vote of a majority of those members voting that all or part of the meeting shall be closed to the public." No formal comparable action was taken by the Senate in 1977 or in the following years, but in practice Senate conferees have accepted the House prohibition against closed meetings without explicit chamber approval (Congressional Quarterly, *Guide to Congress,* 3d ed., p. 455). As far as we know, there has been no conflict between the chambers on this point, with the House wishing to close conference sessions and the Senate urging open meetings (or vice versa).

30. Ibid.

31. Adam Clymer, "A Congress Spectacular: Energy Bill," *New York Times,* Oct. 18, 1977.

32. Rep. Thomas I. Ashley (D, Ohio), chairman of the House Ad Hoc Committee on Energy and cochairman of the 1978 Energy Conference (quoted in Richard Corrigan, "The Sunshine in Room S-334," *National Journal,* April 29, 1978, p. 681).

of the Capitol promptly at 8 A.M. The only problem was that the Capitol building is not open to the public at that hour, and unless one had staff or press credentials it was impossible to gain access either to the Capitol or to the conference.

The size of conference meeting rooms frequently poses additional problems for observers.[33] In many cases, there just is not space in the conference room for more than a handful of the general public after staff and journalists have crowded in to join the conferees. In another 1981 appropriations conference, on an agriculture funding bill, dozens of high-powered agricultural lobbyists and interested observers were left for hours standing in a dark corridor outside Capitol Room S-146 while the conference conducted its business. A grand total of two persons from the long line of those waiting were ever able to gain admittance to the conference, while everyone else, including many who had lined up two hours or more before the scheduled time for the conference, were denied access. While waiting in the dark shadows of the hall, one could only speculate on the per-hourly fees the three-piece wool-suited lawyers and industry representatives were receiving for leaning against cold marble corridor walls.[34]

Not only well-tailored suits are in ample evidence outside conference rooms, but also fine footwear. At one point in the course of the 1982 tax increase conference (discussed in detail in chapter 11), an aide to Senate Finance Chairman Robert J. Dole (R, Kan.) peeked into the hall and reported the now-legendary assessment, "There's wall-to-wall Guccis out there!"[35]

33. These access problems are most severe for the general public and for many—but not all—lobbyists. Journalists usually enjoy preferred access ahead of others, and congressional staff, especially key committee staff, and sometimes personal staff, gain entry to conference committees almost automatically.

34. Seeing this talent cooling its heels outside the conference room brings to mind the observation Sen. Pete Domenici (R, N.M.) made in 1976 on a similar occasion of observing a long line of lobbyists unable to get into the conference: "There's more real knowledge of this bill out there than in here" (Bernard Asbell, *The Senate Nobody Knows* [Garden City: Doubleday, 1978] p. 436).

35. Dale Russakoff, "No More Wall-to-Wall Guccis: Tax Lobbyists Have Been Exiled from the Room," *Washington Post National Weekly Edition*, April 28, 1986, p. 15. This article referred to a novel experiment made in 1986 by the Senate Finance Committee during markup sessions on that year's far-reaching tax bill. Instead of having lobbyists overflowing the conference room and adjacent corridors, it was decided to pipe its proceedings two floors down into a large auditorium. There, interested parties could hear the conference discussions "while enjoying new freedom to smoke, drink coffee, curse the Senators under their breath and, when the going gets dull, read newspapers." The innovation was favorably received by many lobbyists who otherwise would have had to fight for a handful of seats within the conference room or spend hours standing in halls outside. "This is the most civilized markup we've had in years," reported Standard Oil lobbyist Dave Franasiak (ibid.).

The Gucci image continued throughout the 1980s to be a key aspect of references to lobbyists intensely interested in conference negotiations. The lobbyist corridor gathering place outside conference rooms was known as Gucci Gulch; the lobbyist with a weak legislative case "doesn't have a Gucci to stand on." The Gucci rhetoric, according to Capitol Hill lobbyist Lawrence F. O'Brien, "is a surrogate for the $500 suit, or variation on that theme." Even hallway repairs were blamed on the wall-to-wall Guccis: when it was necessary at one point to repaint a second-floor Dirksen Senate Office Building corridor, then-Senate Finance Committee Chairman Robert Dole asserted that the scuff marks resulted from waiting lobbyists "with their Guccis." A few years later, during the landmark tax reform conference in 1986, Senator Dole offered the observation that the Gucci-footed lobbyists would soon (after

The virtual exclusion of the public and some lobbyists from many conferences might appear to be nothing more than the unfortunate consequence of inadequate centrally located meeting space, except that, as pointed out by Representative Les Aspin (D, Wis.), it is a "tactic of Congress . . . to hold conferences in rooms that are too small to hold visitors."[36] Many congressmen see small meetings rooms as a real assistance to conference committee proceedings. "You keep out a lot of the pirates," one aide to House Ways and Means Chairman Dan Rostenkowski (D, Ill.) explained in 1981. "The physics of a small room gets the job done faster."[37] Congressman Leon Panetta (D, Cal.) turned this idea into an equation: "The tighter the room, the quicker the resolution."[38] If using small Capitol meeting rooms provides both useful conference "physics" and the exclusion of "pirates," so much the better. There are few incentives for conferees to seek meeting space more adequate to the spirit of openness, and many reasons that small meeting rooms appear convenient, cozy, and desirable.

The openness of conference committee proceedings is also seriously limited through the growing tendency for preconference and during-the-conference informal caucuses and meetings. A major conference in 1979 between the House Ways and Means Committee and the Senate Finance Committee was announced, and the huge (in

---

passage of the tax legislation) be barefooted. Seldom if ever has so much political consequence been attributed to one brand of soft-leather loafers. Robin Tower, "Fear and Shoe Leather Among the Lobbyists," *New York Times,* July 31, 1986, p. 10.

For additional analysis of the Gucci gang, especially as regards their presence and activity during conference consideration of the landmark tax reform bill of 1986, see Jeffrey H. Birnbaum and Alan S. Murray, *Showdown at Gucci Gulch: Lawmakers, Lobbyists, and the Unlikely Triumph of Tax Reform* (New York: Random House, 1987).

36. Rep. Les Aspin (D, Wis.), letter to Therese A. Barry, Feb. 1, 1984. This correspondence was at the initiative of Barry as part of her 1984 Senior Independent Studies Thesis at Lawrence University, "Conference Committees and Institutional Adaptability." Members of the House Appropriations Committee jokingly refer to what they call "closed open meetings." These sessions, although officially open, are deliberately held in rooms too small to accommodate more than a few observers and reporters. Further, no documents are available concerning decisions made until days after the meeting, thus further hindering any effort by outsiders to monitor the action. Appropriations Committee Chairman Jamie L. Whitten defended the withholding of written reports on the grounds that often "something unexpected needs to be corrected" (Jacqueline Calmes, "Few Complaints are Voiced as Doors Close on Capitol Hill," *Congressional Quarterly Weekly Report,* May 23, 1987, p. 1060).

37. Quoted in *Boston Globe,* Aug. 7, 1981, p. 8. This idea of "keeping out the pirates" somewhat echoes a complaint made in 1975 by Rep. Wayne L. Hayes (D, Ohio) that "the most insidious part of open conferences is seeing lobbyists passing notes to members in conferences" (quoted in Congressional Quarterly, *Congress Quarterly Almanac, 1975,* p. 930).

A contention of many members is that closed meetings barred to lobbyists facilitate tough decisions on controversial legislation. Observed Representative Don J. Pease (D, Ohio), a former newspaper editor, "In a closed meeting, you can come out and say, 'I fought like a tiger for you in there, but I lost' " (Calmes, "Few Complaints are Voiced," p. 1059).

38. Quoted in *Congressional Insight,* July 24, 1981, p. 2. The pressure on the limited number of Capitol rooms for conference space was so great during the 1981 budget reconciliation process, which involved fifty-eight separate subconferences, that almost every Capitol meeting space was used. "One secretary in a secluded GOP leadership office was shocked when members marched into the small room and announced a conference committee meeting" (ibid.).

THE CHANGING CHARACTER OF CONFERENCE POLITICS 57

this case) Ways and Means Hearing Room was packed with hundreds of observers and intensely interested parties. The senators entered the room and sat down at the huge table. The House members also seated themselves. House Ways and Means Chairman Al Ullman (D, Ore.) spoke: "Before we formally convene this conference, the House members will caucus in the chairman's office; the Senate conferees will meet in Room _____." The conference members then retired to their informal caucuses in the privacy of members' offices while the public speculated about what deals were being struck. Hours later, when the conferees had failed to reappear in the hearing room, most of the observers had melted away, in many cases to make their own private soundings about emerging compromises.[39]

Similar accounts abound concerning informal private discussions replacing, or at least supplementing, the formal and public conference committee sessions. The conference on the 1976 Clean Air Act, for example, was preceded at 10 A.M. by a meeting of Senate conferees to work out strategy.[40] Similarly, a 1978 energy conference was announced for Capitol Room H-328 but was preceded by lengthy meetings of the entire conference in S-334, the Capitol hideaway office of Senator Henry Jackson (D, Wa.). This location was so inaccessible as to defy discovery by even the most knowledgeable Capitol Hill journalist—to say nothing about any public citizen.[41] (These preliminary meetings were the "informal expressions between members on both sides" referred to by House conferee Thomas I. Ashley in the quotation introducing this section.)

In a classic instance of backroom discussions replacing open conference negotiations, a 1985 conference committee on that year's Farm Bill was quickly adjourned after an initial session to allow for informal conferee meetings. The initial conference meeting had been extremely difficult, so tense in fact that Senate Majority Leader Robert Dole publicly reported, "We're just shooting each other in there."[42] Unofficial meetings among conferees, staff, or both, it was felt, would better serve conference progress on this contentious legislation.

In some instances, preconference informal discussions may serve as the forum for major negotiations and the working out of compromises. When this occurs, the subsequent conference meeting may well be staged almost along the lines of a script, with conferees for one House proposing an alternative that is quickly agreed to, followed by the other conferees making a proposal that is likewise concurred with, and so forth. Bargaining and compromise may be formally represented in the conference, but only as an agreed-upon reflection of preconference agreements.[43]

Sometimes informal meetings are necessary during the conference deliberations themselves. One legendary Capitol Hill story concerning the major energy conference of 1976 has Congressman John Dingell (D, Mich.) and Senator Henry Jackson (D, Wash.)

---

39. The preceding paragraph is based on the personal observation of one of the authors.
40. Asbell, *The Senate Nobody Knows*, pp. 432–33.
41. Corrigan, "Sunshine in Room S-334," p. 681.
42. *Congressional Quarterly Weekly Report*, Dec. 7, 1985, p. 2555.
43. These types of prearranged conferences we later term Hello and Good-Bye conferences. They are discussed further in chapter 7 below and illustrated by two brief examples in chapter 11.

desperately needing to negotiate a key point but being unable to confer directly in the crush of the conference. They finally had to retreat to the john, where they cut the crucial deal. Necessity is indeed the mother of invention—in this case of an innovative meeting place in order to limit conference openness.[44] And, of course, such highly informal meetings as the Dingell-Jackson summit and the other unofficial gatherings we have discussed do not include other private deals made over the phone, in one-on-one discussions in offices, or in the corridors of the Capitol.[45]

Finally, "nonconference" negotiations can occur near the end of a conference in order to conclude unresolved matters in an expeditious manner. These final questions may be minor housekeeping matters, but often they involve substantial and contentious differences. Longtime House conference negotiator Representative Barber Conable (R, N.Y.) described this final stage as follows:

> Usually, the non-controversial things are quickly disposed of, but the tough ones are saved for last, and involve separate caucuses of the delegations from the two Houses, with staff members sashaying back and forth with messages and offers. . . . The caucuses constitute forums for frank discussions and privacy. In short, openness in joint meetings does not mean we are always open.[46]

There are other consequences of open conference committees besides the development of means of limiting openness. As suggested by the statement of Senator Mark Hatfield quoted earlier in this chapter, things may take longer because conferees feel the need to give their speeches first. Daniel Dreyfus, staff director of the Senate Energy Committee, echoed Senator Hatfield's remarks in commenting, "Since we opened up the doors, there has been a lot of time wasted in conferences. In the old days, someone would say, 'I know I'm going to lose on this item, so let's just go ahead.' Now, with a gallery there, they hold on for weeks trying to show they're hanging tough."[47]

The result is that under the watchful eye of lobbyists, conferees tend to fight harder for provisions they might have dropped quietly in the interests of bicameral agreement. This is illustrated by an early open conference committee in which a tendency toward

---

44. One account in the Capitol Hill newspaper *Roll Call* neatly characterized several of the ploys we have discussed for limiting the openness of committee meetings: *the squeeze play*—purposely using too small a meeting room in order to keep out most lobbyists, members of the public, and some journalists; *the committee caucus*—meeting in a back room to work out a compromise; and *shuttle diplomacy*—sending staff back and forth between chamber caucuses with compromise proposals. This article, however, also described one additional, truly innovative "sneak play," which it labeled *the football huddle*: "Popularized by former Rep. Richard Bolling (D, Mo.), when he headed the Rules Committee, lawmakers group head-to-head at the center or perimeters of a committee room, conducting business in inaudible whispers but in full view of the public" (Barbara Rosewiez, "The Sunshine Slowly Fades," *Roll Call*, Oct. 20, 1983, p. 4).

45. "Conference Committees Opened to Public," p. 70.

46. Rep. Barber Conable, "What Happens in Conference?" *Roll Call*, June 21, 1984, p. 4.

47. Quoted in *Wall Street Journal*, March 4, 1980, p. 12. Similar posturing was found in a study of a 1980 conference on a continuing authorization for the Federal Trade Commission. This lengthy conference was characterized by "months of political game-playing and maneuvering" (David King, "In the Hands of a Chosen Few: The Federal Trade Commission's Struggle for Authorization" [Undergraduate research paper, Lawrence University, 1982], p. 20).

conference speech making was found to be linked to a tendency toward secret meetings. During these energy conference negotiations in 1975, it was observed that "several Senators and Representatives tend to give long-winded speeches and members from both sides find the need to meet regularly in private to plot strategy for the public sessions."[48]

Anticipated Versus Actual Consequences

Many changes in conference committee proceedings were predicted to result from their opening. Among these were decreased efficiency in reaching agreements, an increased tendency for conference members to grandstand and play to the press, a wider use of secret meetings and caucuses to work out compromises awkward to negotiate in public view, and a greater tendency for conferees to argue for external interests and constituency concerns.[49] Any conclusions as to the extent these expectations have been fulfilled can only be tentative; however, we have cited some evidence supporting two of these three predictions: that open conferences have often tended toward speech making and posturing, and that informal and private "consultations" frequently supplement formal and open conference committee meetings. Now we note similar limited evidence to suggest shifts in conferee loyalties and behavior resulting from the opening of conference committees.[50]

The presence of lobbyists in the conference room may cause subtle changes in the political context of conference decision making.[51] Of course, in many cases before open conference committees, lobbyists were able to gain entry to a conference or be nearby. Face-to-face contact between conferee and lobbyist during a conference session, however, is considerably easier with open meetings. In 1981, for example, a key farm lobbyist was credited with influencing the agricultural conference "just by sitting in the front row." His presence was significant because "members know that he will report back to the sugar growers telling them who their friends are, and his mere presence reminds the lawmakers how the game is played."[52] With lobbyists able to scrutinize

48. David E. Rosenbaum, "Senate and House Conferees Approve Separate Bills on Energy," *New York Times,* Nov. 6, 1975, p. 24. Rosenbaum goes on to describe the conference environment as follows: "This morning, the conference met in a room in the Capitol that is only slightly larger than a tennis court. More than 50 Senators, Representatives and their assistants were crammed together in the front of the room around tables placed in a circle while scores of lobbyists and reporters sat and stood elbow-to-elbow in the back."

49. These expectations of the likely consequences of opening conference committees are adapted from two tutorial papers prepared by Lawrence University undergraduates Andrew N. McLean, "A Comparison of Environmental Influencing Agents on Appropriations and Labor Conference Committees," 1979, and John R. Stoner, "A Summary of What Is Known about Congressional Conference Politics and Bargaining," 1981.

50. The diverse loyalties of conferees are further examined in chapter 6 below.

51. The analysis in this and the following four paragraphs is adapted from and influenced by a 1984 undergraduate Senior Independent Studies Thesis at Lawrence University by Therese A. Barry, "Conference Committees and Institutional Adaptability." Appreciation is expressed to Barry for insights and analysis incorporated into the following discussion.

52. Steven V. Roberts, "Conferences are Site of Legislative Showdowns," *New York Times,* Nov. 20, 1981.

proceedings in person, conferees may feel bound to maintain positions that they might otherwise quickly abandon in order to facilitate conference compromise. In an open meeting, the lobbyist knows "who does what, says what, and stands for what." The conferee's decision is there for all to see, and "promise-making includes promise-keeping."[53]

Besides pressures on conferees arising from lobbyists' presence, open conference sessions give lobbyists and other interested parties the ability to know more precisely and accurately what is going on. When conferences were closed, a lobbyist's knowledge of the proceedings was less certain because he generally could monitor the conferences only through information supplied him by conferees who favored his viewpoint. Allies are not always perfect information sources, especially if they have modified or wavered in their initial views and positions. Now, having more complete and direct information through personal observation of conference negotiations, lobbyists can better ensure that their influence and persuasive efforts bear fruit.

In another way, open conferences also multiply interest group pressures by providing better access to a new type of lobbyist. Representatives of public interest groups usually had great difficulty knowing what was happening behind closed conference room doors. By contrast, clientele-type organizations, well represented in congressional districts, often would be accorded "courtesy" entry into a conference room or be given full briefings on the committee's activity. Such courtesies were seldom available to those groups advocating innovation or change in traditional practices and benefits. With the opening of conference committees, these new groups or their representatives are now able to compete more effectively and equally with entrenched, clientele-oriented groups.[54]

---

53. Telephone interview with Ward Sinclair, congressional reporter, *Washington Post,* March 1, 1984. This interview was at the initiation of Therese A. Barry as part of her Senior Independent Studies Thesis.

54. An early anticipation of this leveling impact of open conference committees can be found in "Reform Penetrates Conference Committees," *Congressional Quarterly Weekly Report,* Feb. 8, 1975, p. 291. For a more recent assessment of the implications of this change for interest groups, see Gary W. Copeland, "The Opening of Conference Committees: A New Arena for Interest Groups," paper prepared for delivery at the 1985 Annual Meeting of the American Political Science Association, New Orleans, Aug. 27–Sept. 1, 1985.

Closed meetings inherently advantage well-connected veteran lobbyists over less experienced individuals. AFL-CIO lobbyist Calvin P. Johnson, certainly one of the former, observes:

> A lot of lobbyists really complain about closed meetings. It tends to be less the men or women who are on the Hill every day working than the folks from the law firms and the accounting firms who come up here to take notes and go back and write up a newsletter and charge their clients $250 an hour. They scream and yell like crazy because they don't know what's going on. They have fewer contacts and they don't feel comfortable with grabbing members as they go in and out and asking them what in the world is going on.

In contrast, Johnson notes, "We can find out. I can find out who rolled me and let them know that we weren't pleased with that. And when they come around to us for funds or for support or something, we can let them know, 'you banged me on that one, don't look to us on this'" (Calmes, "Few Complaints are Voiced," p. 1060).

A final consequence of open conferences is that journalists are able to attend at least the official conference committee meetings. This change had been anticipated as having great significance: government in the sunshine would produce greater public accountability of government. Whether these objectives have been achieved is difficult to say, in part because the proliferation of unofficial meetings has clouded over government in the sunshine. It is undeniably true that at times press, media, and editorial commentary can influence support or opposition to conference compromises.[55] Journalistic and media coverage of conference committees, however, is limited and usually deals only with the most dramatic and important conferences in which conference positions and political maneuvers are generally well known. Coverage of less prominent conferences is so minimal as to limit significant public accountability. In short, the "third branch of Congress" continues as a generally obscure arena of power, but today more because of spotty journalistic coverage than because of exclusion.

The story of the impact of open conference sessions on bicameral politics is largely one of institutional and individual adaptability. Some posturing and speech making are inevitable with open conferences, so stands are stated and speeches are given. Following this, the conference proceeds to work. "The fears [that posturing and long-winded speeches would impede the serious business of the conference] have never been realized," writes Representative Morris Udall (D, Ariz.). "Members do not waste the time of the committee. Nor is there much obstructionism."[56] It was anticipated that open conferences might make negotiation and deal making politically difficult, so unofficial, closed meetings have developed to facilitate these activities. In short, "Congress itself has been able to adapt to the reform [of open conference committees] in such a way that clearly diminishes any impact it may have had."[57] Rather than being the catalyst for sweeping transformation of conference committee politics and processes, the opening of conference committees has had far more subtle and modest consequences than either its proponents or opponents expected.

The Impact of External Change on Conference Committees

The conference committee, like Congress itself, is shaped by and responsive to the political environment of which it is a part. While bargaining and compromise remain fundamental and stable elements of the conference process, they take place within a

---

55. For an example, see David Rapp, "Budget Conferees Fail to Reach Accord," *Congressional Quarterly Weekly Report,* May 21, 1988, p. 1355.

56. Rep. Morris Udall (D, Ariz.), letter to Therese A. Barry, March 21, 1984, p. 2. This correspondence was at the initiative of Barry as part of her 1984 thesis. Representative Udall's deemphasis on the impact of openness on conference work is seconded by Frank A. Aukofer, Washington bureau chief, the *Milwaukee Journal.* In a telephone interview on March 13, 1984, conducted by Therese A. Barry, he stressed that following the opening of conference committees, all that was involved was members getting used to being in the public eye.

57. Barry, "Conference Committees," p. 106. As Jacqueline Calmes of Congressional Quarterly observes, "Both miniskirts and 'sunshine in government' reforms were fashionable in the early 1970's. Then the skirts were tossed out as inconvenient and too revealing" (Calmes, "Few Complaints are Voiced," p. 1059). As skirts have been lengthened, conference committees have been closed.

contemporary setting that differs in many ways from the recent past. For instance, today's committee and party leaders no longer wield the kind of authority their predecessors did in the 1950s, legislation is often reviewed by several committees simultaneously, omnibus bills or "package legislation" dominate much legislative decision making, and divided party control of Congress during six years of the 1980s added an intense partisan dimension to conference politics. As Congress changes, so also does the conference committee.

Weakening of Party and Committee Leadership

One of the most significant changes in Congress in recent years is the general weakening both of party leadership in the House and Senate and of the powers of committee chairmen. In the past, the conference committee was described as "the ultimate flowering of the power of seniority."[58] Today, the power of senior leaders of the chamber and of committees in conference decisions is much less certain and often more circumscribed.

Leadership in the House and Senate, in brief, is not what it used to be. Prior to the last two or three decades, the Senate majority leader and Speaker of the House often asserted an important role in significant conference negotiations. In the late 1950s, for example, there was a regular pattern of intervention by the Speaker in appropriations conferences:

> Annually Speaker [Sam] Rayburn importuned an embattled [House Appropriations Committee Chairman] Clarence Cannon to yield his conference position for the sake of a year-end bill. . . . Cannon had to "deliver" under external pressure of this sort. From general exhortations through telephone calls from the Speaker, the conferees are subjected to environmental influences and they do make decisions which are directly responsive to these influences.[59]

Today, the personal intervention of the majority leader or Speaker in conference politics is more occasional. In the tax increase conference of 1982, for example (recounted in chapter 11), the major players were the conferees, not the House and Senate leaders. The historically unprecedented conference in 1981 on the budget reconciliation bill, which included 58 separate subconferences and over 250 senators and congressmen, was coordinated in the House not by Speaker Thomas P. O'Neill but by a relatively junior member of the Budget Committee, Leon E. Panetta (D, Cal.), who at the time had served in the House for only four years. Direct leadership involvement, to be sure, is still evident in conferences dealing with issues of the highest substantial and

---

58. John W. Baker, *Member of the House: Letters of a Congressman by Clem Miller* (New York: Scribners, 1962), p. 114.

59. Richard F. Fenno, Jr., *The Power of the Purse: Appropriations Politics in Congress* (Boston: Little, Brown, 1966), p. 647. These interventions by House Speaker Sam Rayburn may have been particularly characteristic of appropriations legislation and the relationship between Speaker Rayburn and Appropriations Chairman Cannon. It is not certain how customary such involvements by the Speaker in conference negotiations were prior to the 1920s; it *is* clear—as noted in the next paragraph—that any such interventions are much rarer today.

political priority, such as tax, budget, trade, and deficit reduction measures. Such intervention today, however, seems much more selective and occasional than the usual pattern of leadership involvement in the past.

Committee chairmen, too, have lost some control over conference committees. One way this has occurred is through the development of autonomous subcommittees within their full committees—subcommittees chaired by bright and aggressive members eager to take on floor or conference management responsibilities for legislation. This rise of subcommittee independence, labeled subcommittee government by some observers, has been widely commented upon in terms of such consequences as policy fragmentation, lack of legislative coordination, and the emergence of decision-making units with even greater interest imbalance than the parent committees.[60] A major consequence of subcommittee government is that inherently it involves the shifting of power from the committee chairman to the subcommittee leader and a sharing of intracommittee authority.[61]

One way this shift of power may be measured is in terms of bill management responsibilities. One scholar has charted this change in terms of floor management of legislation, finding that in the case of the House, "most bills are now managed by subcommitte chairs whereas in the 1960's most bills were managed by House full committee chairs."[62] (House Democratic Caucus rules in fact now require full committee chairmen to allow subcommittee chairmen, if they wish, to floor manage legislation reported from their subcommittee.)

By contrast, subcommittee government has not been duplicated in the Senate. For instance, floor management by Senate subcommittee chairs *declined* somewhat between the Eighty-sixth and Ninety-fifth Congresses (from 1959–61 to 1977–78), from 31 percent of all bills to 22 percent. Full committee chairman management during the same period stayed at virtually the same level—between 14 and 15 percent.[63]

While these data are subject to diverse interpretations and speculation, what is interesting for our purposes is the evidence that subcommittee government has devel-

---

60. See, for example, Roger Davidson, "Subcommittee Government: New Channels for Policy," in Tom E. Mann and Norman J. Ornstein, eds., *The New Congress* (Washington, D.C.: AEI, 1981); and Christopher J. Deering, "Subcommittee Government in the U.S. House: An Analysis of Bill Management," *Legislative Studies Quarterly* 7, no. 4 (Nov. 1982): 533–46.

61. See Roger H. Davidson, "Congressional Committees as Moving Targets," *Legislative Studies Quarterly* 11, no. 1 (Feb. 1986): 19–33.

62. Deering, "Subcommittee Government," p. 541. In subsequent research in which Deering was joined by Steven S. Smith, it was found that whereas in the 86th Congress (1959–60), 30 percent of all legislation was floor-managed in the House by subcommittee chairmen, by the 95th Congress (1977–78) this figure had more than doubled to 67 percent. Floor management by the full committee chairman had sharply declined during the same period from 54 percent of all bills to 28 percent. Sixteen percent of all House bills were floor-managed by "others" in the 86th Congress, and 5 percent by others in the 95th. Christopher J. Deering and Steven S. Smith, "Subcommittee Government?" paper prepared for presentation at the Annual Meeting of the American Political Science Association, Chicago, Sep. 1–4, 1983, p. 19.

63. What dramatically increased during this eighteen-year period was the assumption of floor management duties by the Senate majority leader—from 13 percent of all bills in the 86th Congress to 45 percent in the 95th. Forty-one percent of all Senate bills were floor-managed by others in the 80th Congress, and 19 percent in the 95th. Deering and Smith, "Subcommittee Government?" p. 19.

oped rather differently in the House and Senate. The House has witnessed a significant shift of legislative management responsibility from full committee to subcommittee leaders; the Senate, on the other hand, "continues to be a highly individualistic body—perhaps the ultimate form of decentralization."[64] As in so many other matters the House and Senate are indeed quite different institutions.[65]

A conclusion drawn from this comparison pertains to the composition of conference delegations. Now committee chairmen (and even party leaders) have less freedom of choice in determining conferees. Particularly in the House, where the flowering of subcommittee government is more advanced than in the Senate, committee chairmen are virtually obligated to recommend (that is, select) their subcommittee leaders as conferees. These members, in effect, are preselected as conferees. The rules of the House Education and Labor Committee, for example, even stipulate that the "Chairman shall recommend to the Speaker as conferees the names of those members of the subcommittee which handled the legislation in order of their seniority upon such subcommittee." Such practices help ensure that conference delegations reflect diverse committee viewpoints.

Even when the full committee chairman today retains some latitude in the exercise of his power to name conferees (with his selection being subsequently ratified by appointment by the Speaker or Senate presiding officer), certainly the chairman cannot ignore the subcommittee chairman and other leading members who have floor managed the legislation during chamber consideration. As early as 1979, House and Senate committee chairmen had begun "to choose as conferees members of the subcommittee that originated the legislation."[66] This pattern reflected the tradition of both chambers' Appropriations Committees, which long have had quite autonomous subcommittees with special bill management and conference roles.[67] In short, the increasing independence of subcommittees in legislative origination and management means that full committee chairmen have less freedom of choice in determining conferees and, consequently, less influence over the conference committee itself.[68]

    64. Ibid., p. 12.
    65. For an elaboration of institutional contrasts between House and Senate, see chapter 5 below.
    66. "Conference Committees Opened to Public," p. 69. This development is clearly of fairly recent vintage. George Galloway writes that as of 1955, "a tradition has not yet developed as to whether subcommittee members deserve a preferred place on the conference committee over ranking members of the full committee" (George Galloway, "The Third House of Congress," *Congressional Record*, March 8, 1955, pp. 2555). By the 1980s, however, this tradition *had* developed.
    67. In 1969, for example, three senators chosen as conferees on the Legislative Branch Appropriations Bill were the three lowest-ranking Democrats on the full Appropriations Committee, but were selected because their subcommittee had had the initial responsibilities for the legislation ("Closed Conferences Often Wield Legislative Power," *Congressional Quarterly Weekly Report*, Dec. 12, 1969, p. 2573).
    68. For a fuller discussion of conferee selection procedures, see chapter 8 below. Among the intriguing questions raised by the growing importance of subcommittees are to what degree a subcommittee chairman may serve as the *informal* leader of chamber conferees, and how often a subcommittee chairman may end up chairing a chamber delegation or even the entire conference itself. Appreciation is expressed to Steven S. Smith of the University of Minnesota for suggesting these future avenues of research.

Additionally, this development of subcommittee autonomy has an impact on chamber leadership power. In the past, discretion in who was to be a conference member provided considerable choice for both the full committee chairman and in many cases the chamber leader (working through and in negotiation with the chairman); to the degree this freedom of choice is diminished, both chairman and chamber leader lose influence over the composition and balance of the conference delegation.

Multiple Referral of Legislation

Another congressional development has had an impact on the power of committee chairmen. As the complexity of legislation has grown in recent years, there has been an increasing trend in the House toward the multiple referral of bills to committees. Many contemporary issues embrace the concerns of numerous committees. Recognition of this accounted in part for the House's adoption of a rule in 1975 formally permitting the Speaker to assign a measure to two or more committees simultaneously. As a result, it is today quite common for bills to move through several different House committees.

Since the adoption of the House rule in 1975, over six thousand bills and resolutions have been referred to multiple House committees. In one representative Congress, the Ninety-ninth (1985–86), such multiple referrals constituted over 25 percent of the total House committee workload.[69] The Senate, on the other hand, has long permitted the multiple referral of legislation by unanimous consent of the full membership, a practice anticipating the more recent House development. Multiple referral, however, is used less in the Senate (party leaders there strongly prefer that measures be assigned to only one panel); in 1983–84, for example, about 10 percent of the committee workload of the Senate consisted of bills and resolutions considered by more than one committee.[70]

The consequence, in terms of conference, of multiple referral of legislation in House and Senate is that conferees often come from various panels in each chamber rather than from just one committee. It has become standard practice, on multireferred measures, for conferees to be named from all the several committees that had charge of the legislation. The Carter energy proposals of 1977, for example, were considered by two different, uncoordinated committees in the Senate. Five committees in the House considered parts of Carter's plan before their efforts were coordinated and synthesized by a specially created ad hoc Committee on Energy. The resulting conference commit-

---

69. Roger H. Davidson, Walter J. Oleszek, and Thomas Kephart, "One Bill, Many Committees: Multiple Referrals in the U.S. House of Representatives," *Legislative Studies Quarterly* 13, no. 1 (Feb. 1988): 3. See also Roger H. Davidson, "The Legislative Work of Congress," paper prepared for delivery at the 1986 Annual Meeting of the American Political Science Association, Washington, D.C., August 28–31, 1986; and Roger H. Davidson and Walter J. Oleszek, "From Monopoly to Interaction: Changing Patterns in Committee Management of Legislation in the House," paper prepared for delivery at the 1987 Annual Meeting of the Midwest Political Science Association, Chicago, April 9–11, 1987.

70. Davidson, "The Legislative Work of Congress," p. 15. An earlier analysis found that a total of 236 multiple committee referrals occurred in the Senate during the 95th Congress (1977–78) alone, many just to two committees, but some to as many as four. The referrals varied in type—some were simultaneous, others were sequential, and others were split, with parts of the proposed bill being sent to different committees (Davidson, "Subcommittee Government," pp. 120–21).

tee, drawing members from all eight of the involved committees, was highly diverse: twenty-eight senators met at different times and in widely different combinations with twenty-five representatives.[71]

Multiple referrals affect conference committees in several other ways. First, there has been a gradual shift toward larger conference delegations.[72] It is mainly a matter of arithmetic. As a rule, the more committees that review a measure, the larger the conference delegation. More committees means more members with a reasonable claim for being selected as a conferee. The 1975 Energy Bill, for example, was considered by only one House committee, and seven conferees later represented the House in conference. On the other hand, in the Senate the legislation was referred to three committees, and twenty-five senators (one-fourth of the entire Senate) were selected as Senate conferees.[73]

The number of conferees per committee is commonly worked out informally by the principals and generally reflects each committee's proportionate involvement with the legislation going to conference. Particularly with omnibus or controversial legislation, the designation of conferees can be quite a complex task, involving not only how many conferees are allotted each committee, but also the scope of involvement of different groups of conferees. For example, conferees can be named to deal only with certain sections or titles of the legislation. As a result, not only do committees sometimes disagree over their "fair share" of the conference delegation, but diverse committee representation and differing conferee authority and involvement mean that conferees may not reflect common perspectives and values or function in a cohesive manner.[74]

Second, the more committees that select conferees, the longer it takes to iron out bicameral differences. Intradelegational feuds erupt on some occasions. While the controversial bicameral issues in disagreement remain the critical factor prolonging the compromise-making process, large and diverse conferences are likely to complicate the effort.

Multiple committee representation in conference can also affect the mechanics of

---

71. Charles O. Jones, *The United States Congress: People, Place, and Policy* (Homewood, Ill.: Dorsey Press, 1982), p. 330. The consideration of energy legislation in 1977–78 by a total of six House committees was by no means unique. The House record for multireferrals was a measure that was dealt with by fifteen different House committees! Several other bills have moved through as many as nine standing committees. On the average, however, 80 percent of all multireferred measures go to only two committees. Davidson, "The Legislative Work of Congress," pp. 17, 18.

72. The tendency for conference committees to become larger because of multiple referral of legislation is a trend suggested by the specific examples cited in the text. In chapter 6, we report tabulations made especially for this book about conference size for three selected Congresses. These data demonstrate the wide variety of sizes of conference committees in different issue areas but do not themselves, however, reveal an overall systematic growth in conference size over time.

73. *Washington Post,* Nov. 9, 1975, p. A3. It is important to recall that the number of House or Senate conferees is of no importance in determining chamber success in conference. All conference committee votes are by chamber, with a majority of each chamber's conferees (no matter how many there are) needed for an agreement.

74. The impact of standing committees upon conferees is discussed in chapter 6 below. The increase in conference size and in the diversity of composition may have the consequence not only of making bargaining more difficult but also of making grandstanding more likely.

decision making. The conference itself, for instance, may subdivide into smaller groups, so-called subconferences. There may be *general* conferees to coordinate the activities of the *special* conferees assigned to various subconferences. For example, during the omnibus trade conference of the 100th Congress (1987–88), conferees were chosen from twenty-three House and Senate committees. One hundred and fifty-five House conferees and forty-four Senate conferees convened in seventeen subconferences, with some subconferences even forming subgroups ("sub-subconference") of their own. Interestingly, House conferees were selected to consider only issues that fell within their committee's jurisdiction. As a result, the decisions reached by any House subconference were binding on all House conferees. The Senate conferees, however, operated under informal procedures that permitted the entire group to review and override decisions reached by their senatorial colleagues on the respective subconferences.

Multiple referral further makes unclear who will chair the chamber delegation or even the entire conference. In the case of a single referral, the chairman of the full committee handling the legislation is normally accorded the role of delegation chairman. When a number of committees are involved in considering a measure, the question of who will lead the chamber's conferees—and the influence of that person as delegation chairman—can be a source of conflict subject to varying political and personal considerations.

Floor consideration of conference reports on multireferred measures may be more complicated than for singly referred legislation. This is particularly true in the House, which has stricter rules of procedure than the Senate. Conference reports are commonly called up in the House by the floor manager, debated for one hour, and then voted upon. On complex bicameral agreements involving multiple committees, it may be necessary for the House Rules Committee to establish special procedures for debating the conference report. For instance, the synthetic fuels conference report of 1980, which was hammered out by conferees from four House committees, came to the House floor under an unusual rule from the Rules Committee permitting four hours of debate. In short, multiple committee involvement in chamber consideration of legislation often adds to the length and complexities of subsequent postconference committee proceedings.

Omnibus Measures and "Fast Track" Procedures

During the 1980s, Congress and the White House developed a rather novel way of legislating. Instead of single-focused legislative measures, Congress's annual agenda became dominated by action on huge "packages," or omnibus bills, touching on multiple legislative matters. Tax, budget, trade, spending, and social security legislation are prominent examples of this approach. The Omnibus Reconciliation Act of 1981, a centerpiece of President Reagan's first-term economic agenda, for example, affected some three hundred different issues and, when enacted, repealed or changed more than four hundred laws. Omnibus bills may also be massive just in terms of sheer size: the House Trade and International Policy Act of 1986 ran nearly five hundred pages long, the Senate version of the 1986 tax reform bill totaled some fifteen hundred pages in length, and the Omnibus Trade Act of 1987 ran over two thousand pages.

These massive legislative initiatives have led to similarly massive conferences. This was the case with the budget reconciliation bill of 1981, the equally large 1984 budget bill, the 1986 reconciliation bill, and the 1987 trade bill. The conference on each of these measures included as conferees hundreds of senators and representatives. Occasionally bicameral negotiations involving such massive conference delegations are further slowed down because key conferees must be absent to attend to other important legislative business.

The packaging concept has come to be used in part to overcome institutional inertia and to protect members from the importunings of special interest groups. By packaging scores of issues into one bill, legislators can argue that they had to support the comprehensive measure both because of party leadership pressure and because any change in the package could cause it to unravel. "As long as special interests dominate the political scene in Washington, D.C.," noted Representative Mike Synar (D, Okla.), "the only way to fight them off is by packaging the legislation."[75]

The recurrent utilization of omnibus, multitopic bills requiring bicameral reconciliation in conference means that conference committees increasingly serve as the center playing fields of legislative politics and policymaking. Many packages in fact are not subject to significant floor amendments in either chamber. An antiamendment strategy, for instance, helped to propel the 1986 tax simplification bill through the Senate. A fundamental objective of Senate leaders and the White House was to get the Senate bill, with its attractive lower rates and virtual wipe-out of tax deductions, to the conference stage intact. There the conferees, not the rank-and-file representatives and senators, would write the final compromise bill. (Not surprisingly, the two tax-writing chairmen— Representative Dan Rostenkowski [D, Ill.] and Senator Bob Packwood [R, Ore.]—devoted considerable effort to insuring that their strongest allies were selected as conferees.)[76] Such massive legislative initiatives centering on the conference process involve a significant shift of legislative political centrality from the chamber floor to conference committee.

Some of the packages also short-circuit the normal legislative process of lengthy committee consideration and floor action in both chambers. There is increasing use of what has been called the legislative fast track for complex contentious legislation— shortcut methods including such techniques as rules from the House Rules Committee that restrict floor amendments, expedited procedures prescribed by statutes that limit both floor debate and amendments, the adding of substantive legislative riders to appropriations bills, and even the passage of bills that had never been considered by committee.[77] In the 1982 tax increase conference (see case study in chapter 11), the delibera-

75. *New York Times,* Feb. 21, 1983, p. B6.
76. Conferee selection on the 1986 Tax Bill is discussed further in chapter 8 below. See also Birnbaum and Murray, *Showdown at Gucci Gulch,* for a full account of these and other conference considerations concerning the 1986 legislation.
77. John F. Hoadley, "Easy Riders: Gramm-Rudman-Hollings and the Legislative Fast Track," *PS* 19, no. 1 (Winter 1986): 30–36; and Louis Fisher, "Across-the-Board Cuts and Behind-the-Scene Fixes," *Legislative Studies Section Newsletter,* Legislative Studies Section, American Political Science Association, vol. 9, no. 2 (April 1986), p. 58.

tions in conference were on a detailed tax bill as passed by the Senate and a phantom House bill existing in name only that reflected no House position on the issues to be discussed in conference. Another case study, in chapter 11, "The Gramm-Rudman Conferences of 1985," similarly reveals passage of major legislation that had received little subcommittee, full committee, or floor consideration in *either* House or Senate:

> The passage of Gramm-Rudman-Hollings marks the approval of major legislation affecting macroeconomic policy, the fate of numerous government programs, and congressional budget procedures, without public hearings, without debate of any standing committee of the House or of the Senate, and without any debate on the House floor (other than on motions on whether to seek a conference or on a motion to approve the final conference report).[78]

The recent trend toward fast track consideration of important but controversial bills is notable. "In fact," according to one scholar, "one can argue that most major legislation of the past five years has gone through fast track procedures. . . . In the new legislative obstacle course, the major difficulty is finding the right fast-tracked vehicle for your rider."[79] Further, the utility of such expedited procedures has an effect on legislation moving on more usual paths: legislative vehicles on the fast track "crowd out free-standing measures, or at least encourage other issues to hitch rides on the major measures."[80]

The significance of curtailed committee consideration and speeded-up chamber consideration of legislation is to enhance the significance and power of the conference committee. When a bill—either because of the pressures of time or as part of an effort to avoid divisive chamber conflict—moves through the House or Senate stages without full and detailed consideration of its provisions, then it is the conference committee that will end up not only adjusting intercameral differences, but even crafting the final legislation itself. As with the 1985 Gramm-Rudman plan and the 1986 tax reform legislation, the chamber may provide the canvas, but it is in the conference committee that the colors are defined and the picture is painted.

Divided Party Control of Congress

Thus far, we have been examining a series of changes in Congress involving the weakening, compared with some earlier eras, of the legislative primacy of chamber leadership and committee chairmen. One final congressional change should be noted, one not internal to either House or Senate but resulting from differences between them. This is the split in partisan control of Congress that arose from the election of 1980 and that continued through 1986. The last time the two houses of Congress had been divided

---

78. Hoadley, "Easy Riders," p. 31.
79. Ibid., pp. 33, 35.
80. Roger H. Davidson, "'Grambo, or First Blood, Part Two': The New Improved Budget Process," *Legislative Studies Section Newsletter,* Legislative Studies Section, American Political Science Association, vol. 9, no. 2 (April 1986), p. 57. This hitching of riders onto a bill has given rise to another striking motorcycle analogy: the legislative easy rider.

between the parties was fifty years earlier, in the days of Herbert Hoover, when the Seventy-second Congress (1931–33) had—by the narrowest of margins—a Republican Senate and a Democratic House.[81] In the early 1980s, conference committee politics occurred in a most unfamiliar situation: the natural rivalry of House versus Senate was accentuated by the natural partisan divisiveness of Republican versus Democrat.

"As a result," Steven V. Roberts of the *New York Times* observed in 1985, "many of the conflicts dominating political debate [in Congress] today eventually get funneled into a conference for final disposition."[82] The resulting conference committee politics reflected not only interchamber tensions but also partisan conflict. As Kirk O'Donnell, counsel to House Speaker Thomas P. O'Neill, Jr., put it, "Conferences [in the early 1980s] are not just reconciling the differences between two houses of Congress, they are reconciling the differences between two political parties."[83]

Partisan differences between Senate and House also dictated different attitudes toward presidential preferences, with the Senate Republican majority generally tending to support their Republican president and the House Democratic majority frequently disagreeing with his goals. The result was that while the House played a largely defensive role, the Senate came to act both as a legislative gatekeeper and as a legislative facilitator (or, at times, referee) among the three political branches. As described in the *Congressional Quarterly Weekly Report,* "The Senate leadership generally has been able and willing to close the gate on measures the House has passed against Reagan's wishes. And since 1981 it often has fallen to the Senate leadership to find and open the door to compromise when confrontation between Reagan and the House threatens to disrupt the government's business."[84]

An additional factor complicating any effort to facilitate conference agreement is the impact of budget austerity. In the past, the increasing of spending levels was a common tactic used to buy off competing interests and thereby meet the legislative interests of both House and Senate. With budgetary cutbacks taking place throughout the 1980s, this tool is less available to conference negotiators. As John E. Dean, former House Education and Labor Committee aide, put it, "In the old days, it was not a zero-sum game. You could come up with a package that gave the House and Senate everything they wanted."[85] Given the politics of fiscal austerity of the 1980s, conference negotiations are now more typically zero-sum situations with a resulting heightening of

---

81. Stanley Bach notes that "since 1881, there have been only seven Congresses in which party control of the House and Senate was divided" (Stanley Bach, "Bicameral Conflict and Accommodation in Congressional Procedure," paper prepared for presentation at the 1981 Annual Meeting of the American Political Science Association, note 2). In the twentieth century, there have been but two instances prior to 1981: the 62d Congress, 1911–13, and the 72d Congress, 1931–33.

82. Steven V. Roberts, "The Nitty-Gritty of the Conference," *New York Times,* July 17, 1985, p. A18.

83. Quoted in ibid.

84. "GOP Senate Plays Gatekeeper Role in 1983," *Congressional Quarterly Weekly Report,* Dec. 3, 1983, p. 2548.

85. Hook, "In Conference," p. 2080.

interchamber conflict and conference difficulty. In short, contemporary conference committees tend to be fraught with conflict and uncertainty.

Greater bicameral partisan disagreement is suggested by a sharp decline in the number of bills that went to conference in the first two years of divided partisan control of Congress—from 1981 through 1982. From 1947 through 1982, the average number of bills in conference during each two-year Congress was 139: the lowest number previous to 1981 during that thirty-six-year span was 110 (in 1959–60). In 1981–82, however, only 82 bills went to conference, a historic and sharp low.[86] Other factors unique to the Ninety-seventh Congress also played a contributing role in this sharp break—factors such as the difficulties in any new and innovating administration in coming up to full speed on legislation, a relative disinclination on the part of the Reagan administration to advocate new domestic legislation in contrast with letting old laws and policies expire, a wish not to load up Congress's agenda with scores of suggested new laws, and the aforementioned bundling of multiple legislative matters into comprehensive bills. Nevertheless, the sharp decline in measures going to conference in 1981 and 1982 did reflect the tensions of partisan bicameral differences. Anticipation of likely conference conflict and difficulties often led sponsors of bills to attempt to work out House-Senate differences by other, nonconference means, such as adopting floor amendments designed to create identical bills and faster bicameral policy coordination from the legislation's inception.[87] In short, divided partisan control of Congress encouraged partisan conflict in conference committees; it also heightened the tendency to seek ways to avoid conferences.

The practical and political consequences of the bipartisan party split played out differently on diverse bills; partisan disunity was often—in specific instances—overshadowed by bipartisan cooperation on major legislation. At other times, the partisan minority members of one chamber might make common cause with the majority members of the other to further their ends. In the past the majority Democrats in the Senate and House could, as a Democratic Senate aide at the time said, "work things out" between them when necessary. With divided partisan control of Congress, it is different; but we can still do an "end run appeal" to the Democratic majority of the House.[88] A Republican House committee aide similarly saw intercameral strategies as compensating for chamber partisan weakness:

> Because we have a Republican Senate, [the Democratic House committee majority] has come to recognize the value of getting the minority on board. . . . If they tick off the Republicans totally, what we will usually do . . . is get to the Senate people and say "we need to kill this bill." That unspoken threat—the realization that the Republicans control the Senate and the White House—has been very impor-

---

86. These data were specially tabulated for this book by Tom Kephardt.
87. For an example of such bipartisan and bicameral cooperation, see the discussion in chapter 1, p. 22, concerning the immigration reform bill efforts of the 97th and 98th congresses.
88. Washington interview, Nov. 4, 1981.

tant. . . . During the Carter administration, you found that [committee Democrats] were much less willing to accommodate Republican concerns.[89]

The politics of divided partisan bicameral lawmaking from 1981 through 1986 was fascinating to watch as each chamber adjusted to the changing context of intercameral partisan differences. If nothing else, it underscored for political scientists and other commentators the reality of bicameralism—that textbook verity all too often glossed over.

---

89. Quoted in Richard L. Hall, "Participation in Committees: An Exploration," paper presented at the 1984 Annual Meeting of the American Political Science Association, Aug. 30–Sept. 2, 1984, p. 21.

4

What Do We Know—and What Do We Need to Know—about Conference Committee Politics?

In the preceding chapters, we outlined some of the essential characteristics of congressional conference committees, including their evolution over time and the contemporary changes they have undergone. Before we continue in the next chapters of this book to analyze three contexts within which conference committees operate, it would be useful to pause in order to consider what is presently known about conference committee politics and what still needs to be determined.

What Is Known?

What is known about a key congressional process such as conference committee interactions is often very different in the professional literature from what is known on Capitol Hill.[1] Veteran lawmakers, congressional staff, and other Capitol Hill insiders commonly feel they have acquired through experience an understanding of the patterns and possibilities of conference committee politics that allows them to make rather definite statements about how it all works. Political scientists, on the other hand, frequently find these conclusions to be particularistic and personal in perspective and in need of further systematic evaluation before they can be accepted as valid general statements about conference politics.

The approach we have followed in this book is to meld these academic and insider perspectives. In our examination of conference committee politics we attempt to com-

---

1. Appreciation is expressed to Terence Finn, both a political scientist and an experienced Capitol Hill observer, for suggesting this point.

bine the understandings of conference politics of the close observer of Capitol Hill with the more detached, analytical point of view of the academic scholar. Throughout the book, and especially in reporting the observations and statements of congressmen and other Capitol Hill sources, we reflect "what is known" by those who regularly involve themselves in conference activities or have occasion to observe them closely. Similarly, throughout the book, we have also sought to utilize the best available political science scholarship wherever possible as a means of examining and understanding systematically the political processes under way. In this chapter, we focus on this body of professional writing to determine "what is known" in the published professional literature concerning conference committee politics.

What Has Been Written?

The existing literature dealing with conference committee politics is strikingly limited and spotty. Only three books on the congressional conference committee have been published in the twentieth century: one by Ada C. McCown in 1927, another by Gilbert Y. Steiner in 1951, and a third by David J. Vogler in 1971.[2] The first two of these mix useful detailed histories of conference committees over extended time spans with formalistic accounts of conference committee rules and procedures as used in particular areas. Steiner and Vogler further combine their descriptive material with discussions that try to determine whether, in the conferences studied, the House or the Senate was dominant.

The published work touching on conference committee politics, of course, is not limited to these three books. It also encompasses a wide variety of articles, chapters, papers, and the like. Overall, the literature on conference committees can be grouped into six broad categories: generalized descriptions, case studies, and studies of who wins, conferee perceptions, strategic choices, and power consequences.

Generalized Descriptions of Conference Procedures

Virtually every textbook on Congress contains general accounts of conference committees, usually stressing their importance in the legislative process as well as how little is really known about them. Examples include the standard textbooks by Malcolm E. Jewell and Samuel C. Patterson, William J. Keefe and Morris S. Ogul, Roger H. Davidson and Walter J. Oleszek, Randall B. Ripley, and David J. Vogler,[3] and well-

2. Ada C. McCown, *The Congressional Conference Committee* (New York: Columbia University Press, 1927); Gilbert Y. Steiner, *The Congressional Conference Committee: Seventieth to Eightieth Congresses* (Urbana: University of Illinois Press, 1951); and David J. Vogler, *The Third House: Conference Committees in the United States Congress* (Evanston: Northwestern University Press, 1971).

3. Malcolm E. Jewell and Samuel C. Patterson, *The Legislative Process in the United States*, 4th ed. (New York: Random House, 1986); William J. Keefe and Morris S. Ogul, *The American Legislative Process*, 6th ed. (Englewood Cliffs: Prentice-Hall, 1984); Roger H. Davidson and Walter J. Oleszek, *Congress and Its Members*, 2d ed. (Washington, D.C.: CQ Press, 1985); Randall B. Ripley, *Congress: Process and Policy*, 4th ed. (New York: Norton, 1988); and David J. Vogler, *The Politics of Congress*, 5th ed. (Boston: Allyn and Bacon, 1988).

known classic descriptive studies such as those by W. F. Willoughby, George B. Galloway, Ernest S. Griffith, Ada C. McCown, Lewis A. Froman, and Walter J. Oleszek.[4] This descriptive literature sometimes contains a sharply critical or reformist perspective, such as in works by Senator Albert Gore, Sr., and Bertram Gross.[5]

Case Studies of the Legislative Process that Explicitly Include Conference Committee Politics

Works by Stephen K. Bailey, David L. Paletz, John A. Ferejohn, Michael J. Malbin, Lawrence Gladieux and Thomas Wolanin, William I. Bacchus, and Jeffrey H. Birnbaum and Alan S. Murray are examples of the case study literature that contain chapters or sections recounting conference committee actions concerning a particular bill or set of bills.[6] These case studies, although often rich in detail, usually do not

---

4. W. F. Willoughby, *Principles of Legislative Organization and Administration* (Washington, D.C.: Brookings Institution, 1934); George B. Galloway, *The Legislative Process in Congress* (New York: Crowell, 1953); Ernest S. Griffith, *Congress: Its Contemporary Role,* 3d ed. (New York: New York University Press, 1961); McCown, *The Congressional Conference Committee;* Lewis A. Froman, *The Congressional Process* (Boston: Little, Brown, 1967); and Walter J. Oleszek, *Congressional Procedures and the Policy Process,* 3d ed. (Washington, D.C.: CQ Press, 1989).

5. Albert Gore, "The Conference Committee: Congress' Final Filter," *Washington Monthly,* June 1970, pp. 43–48; see also the assessment by Senator Gore quoted earlier in chapter 1. Bertram Gross, in *The Legislative Struggle: A Study in Social Combat* (New York: McGraw Hill, 1953), similarly writes, "If one wanted to stretch the point a little one might whimsically claim that any similarity between the views of the House and the Senate and those of the conferees is purely coincidental" (p. 321).

6. These seven case study examples are as follows:

Stephen K. Bailey, *Congress Makes a Law* (New York: Columbia University Press, 1950), esp. chap. 11, "Conference and Compromise," pp. 220–34.

David L. Paletz, "Influence in Congress: An Analysis of the Nature and Effects of Conference Committees" (Ph.D. diss., University of California at Los Angeles, 1970), esp. chap. 4–6, "1966 Amendments to the Economic Opportunity Act of 1964," "Traffic Safety Act of 1966," and "Congressional Redistricting," pp. 84–355. A portion of this dissertation was delivered as a professional paper with the same title at the Annual Meeting of the American Political Science Association, September 1970. All subsequent references here, however, are to the dissertation.

John A. Ferejohn, *Pork Barrel Politics: Rivers and Harbors Legislation* (Stanford: Stanford University Press, 1974), esp. chap. 7, "The Conference Committee," pp. 116–26.

Malbin actually has written two very valuable case studies: one on the 1973 highway trust fund dispute, Michael J. Malbin, "Long Deadlock Ends in Compromise Opening Highway Trust Fund for Mass Transit," *National Journal,* Aug. 11, 1973, pp. 1163–71, and one on a "phantom conference" on GI legislation, Michael J. Malbin, *Unelected Representatives: Congressional Staff and the Future of Representative Government* (New York: Basic Books, 1980), esp. chap. 5, "Detailed Negotiations: The Phantom Conference on the GI Bill," pp. 73–93.

Lawrence Gladieux and Thomas Wolanin, *Congress and the Colleges: The National Politics of Higher Education* Lexington, Mass.: D. C. Heath, 1976), esp. chap. 8, "The Conference Committee," pp. 161–205.

William I. Bacchus, *Inside the Legislative Process: The Passage of the Foreign Service Act of 1980* (Boulder, Col.: Westview Press, 1984), esp. the chapter entitled "Conference."

Jeffrey H. Birnbaum and Alan S. Murray, *Showdown at Gucci Gulch: Lawmakers, Lobbyists, and the Unlikely Triumph of Tax Reform* (New York: Random House, 1987), esp. chap. 11.

develop generalizations about the conference process but settle for telling the who, what, when, where, and how concerning the specific events of the controversy.

Who Wins in Conference: House or Senate?

This has been by far the overriding question traditionally posed about conference committees, and thus will be considered in depth separately. Representative works that dwell upon this question include those of Gilbert Y. Steiner, Richard F. Fenno, Jr., David J. Vogler, John A. Ferejohn, and Gerald S. Strom and Barry S. Rundquist.[7] The various conclusions of these works, as we shall see later in this chapter, have been somewhat contradictory and are also, perhaps, inherently inconclusive.

Studies of the Perceptions of Conference Committee Members

Books written by Charles L. Clapp, John Manley, and Richard F. Fenno, Jr.,[8] provide the best consideration of the ways individual conferees perceive their roles and responsibilities in the conference committee process. This particularly interesting line of inquiry, however, has not been to date extensively pursued.

What Strategies are Followed in Conference under What Circumstances?

The question What strategies are followed in conference under what circumstances? is crucial in understanding conference politics; earlier scholars have, however, touched on it only parenthetically, usually in the context of case studies (see above, most notably the excellent case studies of conference committees provided by Lawrence Gladieux and Thomas Wolanin, John A. Ferejohn, Michael J. Malbin, and David L. Paletz).[9] Works that raise questions explicitly concerning conference strategies include studies by Richard F. Fenno, Jr., Walter J. Oleszek, Lewis A. Froman, Jeffrey L. Pressman, and David J. Vogler.[10] A major work not specifically on conference commit-

---

7. Steiner, *The Congressional Conference Committee;* Richard F. Fenno, Jr., *The Power of the Purse: Appropriations Politics in Congress* (Boston: Little, Brown, 1966), esp. chap. 12, "The House and the Senate: The Conference Committee," pp. 616–78; Vogler, *The Third House;* and David J. Vogler, "Patterns of One-House Dominance in Congressional Conference Committees," *Midwest Journal of Political Science* 14 (May 1970): 303–20. Also Ferejohn, *Pork Barrel Politics;* John A. Ferejohn, "Who Wins in Conference Committee?" *The Journal of Politics* 37 (Nov. 1975): 1033–46; and Gerald S. Strom and Barry S. Rundquist, "A Revised Theory of Winning in House-Senate Conferences," *American Political Science Review* 71 (June 1977): 448–53.

8. Charles L. Clapp, *The Congressman: His Work As He Sees It* (Washington, D.C.: Brookings Institution, 1963); John Manley, *The Politics of Finance: The House Committee on Ways and Means* (Boston: Little, Brown, 1970), esp. chap. 6, "The Committee and the Senate," pp. 248–321; and Fenno, *The Power of the Purse.*

9. Gladieux and Wolanin, *Congress and the Colleges;* Ferejohn, *Pork Barrel Politics;* Malbin, "Long Deadlock Ends" and *Unelected Representatives;* and Paletz, "Influence in Congress."

10. Fenno, *The Power of the Purse;* Oleszek, *Congressional Procedures;* Froman, *The Congressional Process;* Jeffrey L. Pressman, *House vs. Senate* (New Haven: Yale University Press, 1966); and Vogler, *The Third House.*

tees but that nevertheless integrates committee member goals, environmental constraints, strategic premises, and decision-making processes is the widely noted book by Richard F. Fenno, Jr., *Congressmen in Committees*.[11]

What Are the Consequences of Conference Committees upon Power within Each Chamber?

The consequences of conference commmittees upon power within each chamber is a particularly important issue that has been largely ignored in previous work. Paletz, however, focuses on this key question in his writings and attempts to relate the existence and politics of the conference committee to the nature and distribution of influence within Congress.[12] This promising initiative by Paletz, unfortunately, has not been followed up by subsequent scholars.

In short, the existing literature relevant to conference committees is generally focused on questions *other* than the politics of conference committees. Questions of which chamber wins have been far overrated at the cost of necessary inquiry into more important considerations concerning congressional conference committees. *What is needed is an understanding of the processes and politics that determine policy and power outcomes in congressional conference committees.*

The Recurrent Question: Who Wins—House or Senate?

> The central question of conference committee decision-making is, "Who wins?" It must be answered before the other important questions of "how" and "why" can be broached.
> —Richard F. Fenno, Jr.[13]

> A committee's conference scorecard . . . is hardly a reliable indicator of inter-chamber dominance or leadership; indeed, legislative boldness probably makes for a reduced rate of success in conference.
> —David E. Price[14]

The central question in the scholarly literature on conference committees has indeed been: who wins—House or Senate? Work after work has examined the relative success of each chamber in particular sets of conferences with, however, somewhat contradicto-

---

11. Richard F. Fenno, Jr. *Congressmen in Committees* (Boston: Little, Brown, 1973).
12. Paletz, "Influence in Congress."
13. Fenno, *The Power of the Purse,* p. 661.
14. David E. Price, "Policy-Making in Congressional Committees: The Impact of 'Environmental' Factors" (working paper, Center for Policy Analysis, Institute of Policy Science and Public Affairs, Duke University, 1976), p. 55. An abridged version of this paper was subsequently published under the same title in the *American Political Science Review* 72 (June 1978): 548–74.

ry results. One early study, for example, concluded that over a twenty-year period there was a general pattern of House dominance in conference interactions; subsequent investigations found a general tendency for the Senate to win, but for diverse reasons; yet another work concluded that who wins really depends not on chamber strength or skills, but on the usual sequence of intercameral voting.

We have already suggested that the preoccupation of scholarly research with House and Senate success scores has been at the cost of needed investigation into the *political and policy consequences of conference committees*. Consider the classic observation of Richard F. Fenno quoted just above: "The central question of conference committee decision-making is, 'Who wins?'" In the context in which Fenno was writing, he was speaking of interchamber wins. His statement, however, can be expanded to include all factional and individual conflicts. The question Who wins? then truly does become central to conference committee politics, but in far broader terms than just chamber victories.

The scholarly literature to date, however, has tended not to see conference committees in these larger terms of political conflict and consequence. Rather, it has generally concentrated on determining the relative proportion of House and Senate victories in conference disputes. While we doubt the enduring significance of this preoccupation with chamber success scores, its pervasiveness requires that we summarize briefly the literature's findings, its strengths, and its weaknesses.

Two Contradictory Initial Studies

One of the first efforts to determine whether the House or Senate wins in conference committee interactions was made by Gilbert Y. Steiner in *The Congressional Conference Committee: Seventieth to Eightieth Congresses (1951)*.[15] Steiner studied in detail 56 major conferences drawn from ten different subject matter areas over a twenty-year span and concluded that in 32 of these, the House position prevailed, in 15 the Senate views dominated, and in 9 there was no clear winner. The House won, then, in 57 percent of the conferences studied, the Senate in 27 percent, and neither chamber in 16 percent. Eliminating the cases in which there was no clear chamber winner resulted in a finding that the House won in 68 percent of the cases and the Senate in 32 percent. (The findings of Steiner and those of the other studies subsequently discussed are summarized in the table on page 85.). Steiner concluded that these data suggest "the generalization that at a point of disagreement between Senate and House on a question of legislative policy, the viewpoint of the House is more likely to prevail in conference committee."[16]

Steiner's conclusion of House advantage in conference committee interactions was challenged in 1966 with the publication of Richard F. Fenno's monumental study of congressional appropriations politics, *The Power of the Purse*. Analyzing a large set of House-Senate interactions on appropriations bills, Fenno found that in 331 appropriations conferences held between 1947 and 1965, the Senate won in 187 of them, or 56.5

15. Steiner, *The Congressional Conference Committee*, esp. pp. 170–72.
16. Ibid., p. 172.

percent of the total. The House prevailed in 101, or 30.5 percent, and the House and Senate "split the difference" in 43 cases, or 13 percent. Exclusion of the latter category (when there was no chamber win) resulted in a finding of 65 percent Senate wins in contrast with 35 percent House victories.[17]

Fenno was not content, however, just to record these findings, but also attempted to account for them. One explanation he considered for the Senate's appropriations conference committee dominance was simply that it tended to be the "high" chamber in appropriations conferences—in other words, it supported the higher dollar figure most often. In conference negotiations it is presumably easier politically to add to than to take away appropriation monies in order to arrive at a compromise. If the Senate persistently favored higher figures, and if these figures tended to prevail in bicameral negotiations, then the pattern of Senate wins could be a reflection of these patterns rather than evidence of chamber influence or success.[18]

Initially, Fenno found support for this line of reasoning. Eliminating the forty-three instances in which neither chamber had prevailed, Fenno found that in the remaining conferences,

> the conferees supporting the higher appropriations figure won 170 (59.2%) times and the conferees supporting the lower appropriations figure won 117 (40.8%) times. Furthermore, as one might expect, the conferees supporting the higher figure normally came from the Senate, and the conferees supporting the lower figure normally came from the House. The Senate was the high house 82.6% of the time—or, in 237 out of 287 conferences. The Senate won and the high house won.[19]

This might well seem to support the idea that the Senate wins *because* it is the high house. Fenno, however, went on to ask if the reverse was also true: does the Senate lose when it favors the lower figure? This, he found, was not the case. While the Senate won 64.6 percent of the time when it favored the higher appropriations, it actually prevailed in 66 percent of the instances when it supported the lower figure in conference.[20] Thus, there was not an automatic linkage between the Senate's being the high chamber and its winning. Its success depends on something other than the level of appropriations favored.

This something else, Fenno concluded, was the nature of the Senate itself and the relation of appropriations conference delegations to it: "*The Senate is stronger in conference,*" Fenno argued, "*because the Senate Committee and its conferees draw more directly and more completely upon the support of their parent chamber than do the House Committee and its conferees.*"[21] The Senate conferees derive valuable political support for their position from this political linkage:

17. Fenno, *The Power of the Purse*, p. 663.
18. Ibid., pp. 666–67.
19. Ibid., p. 667. The conferences actually considered totaled 287 rather than 288 as noted earlier because one conference was later excluded from the analysis for technical reasons. See ibid., p. 667*n*, for an explanation of this anomaly.
20. Ibid.
21. Ibid., pp. 668–69 (italics in original).

> When the Senate conferees go to the conference room, they not only represent the Senate—they are the Senate. The position they defend will have been worked out with a maximum of participation by Senate members and will enjoy a maximum of support in that body. . . . The bill will be defended in conference by men who are the leaders not just of the Committee, but of the Senate.[22]

It is this chamber support for Senate conference position, Fenno argued, not chamber preference for higher or lower figures or some advantage inherent in one chamber, that really explains why the Senate tends to win in conference committee interactions. The Senate backs up its conferees and by doing so allows them to prevail in appropriations negotiations.

Fenno Supported

Four years after the publication of Fenno's book, a companion study, *The Politics of Finance: The House Committee on Ways and Means* by John Manley, was published. As Fenno had assessed interchamber success in the appropriations area, Manley now considered who wins in the case of tax legislation. Studying a smaller number of legislative acts, twenty major tax bills drawn from the years 1947 to 1966, Manley also found an overall pattern of Senate success: the Senate prevailed in 56 percent of the overall legislative outcomes, and in 70 percent of the instances where there was a chamber victory.[23] The explanation that Manley gave for Senate success was somewhat similar to the theory advanced by Fenno, but differed in one fundamental respect, its emphasis on conferee rapport with external participants rather than with their chamber:

> The reason the Senate does better in cases of conflict with the [House] Ways and Means Committee is because politically Senate decisions are more in line with the demands of interest groups, lobbyists, and constituents than House decisions. Ways and Means decisions, made under the closed rule, tend to be less popular with relevant publics than Senate decisions.[24]

A fourth evaluation of Who wins? was offered in 1970 and 1971 by David J. Vogler. Two hundred and ninety-seven conferences drawn from five Congresses were categorized by means of *Congressional Quarterly* coverage into three classes: Senate wins—59 percent, House wins—32 percent, and split compromises—9 percent. Eliminating the latter category resulted in Vogler's conclusion that in instances where one chamber prevailed over the other, the Senate won 65 percent of the time.[25] This figure, strikingly enough, is identical to that found earlier by Fenno for his equally large set of appropriations bills.

The explanation Vogler advanced to explain this Senate domination stressed neither chamber linkage nor external rapport, but rather committee status differences: "House conferees drawn from committees with lower prestige than that of the Senate committees

---

22. Ibid., p. 669.
23. Manley, *The Politics of Finance*, pp. 269–94, esp. pp. 276–77.
24. Ibid., p. 279.
25. Vogler, *The Third House*, pp. 55–56, 110–11. The 1970 work by Vogler was his "Patterns of One-House Dominance."

involved in conference were generally more successful than were House conferees from committees with prestige rankings above those of their Senate counterparts."[26] This curious finding that committees with lower status are more successful in conference negotiations than committees with greater chamber prestige initially may seem to violate common sense, but it must be stressed that chamber status is not the same thing as chamber support. As John A. Ferejohn later put it while interpreting Vogler's data, "The less prestigious House committees may be more permeable to influence from the House as a whole than the prestige committees, which are expected to control some natural excesses of the House. Thus conferees from low prestige House committees enjoy more floor support than do conferees of the prestige committees."[27] In this regard, Vogler's finding of greater success for conferees drawn from lower status committees may be viewed essentially as an extension of Fenno's thesis that the most successful conference delegations are those that enjoy greatest chamber rapport and linkage.

Other Evaluations of Who Wins?

Several other studies of the 1970s touching on the question of who wins should also be noted. Arnold Kanter, in an examination of congressional activity concerning the defense budget between 1960 and 1970, found that in 161 conference decisions, the House accepted the Senate position on specific defense budgetary items 57 percent of the time, while the Senate accepted the House preferences in only 23 percent.[28] The exclusion of 20 percent of the cases in which no chamber victor could be determined resulted in 71 percent of the Senate positions prevailing, against 29 percent of the House stands. Kanter suggested that although "the dollar amount recommended in the conference report was equal to the Senate appropriations about three and a half times as often as to the House figure," these Senate victories were not necessarily on the most important items. "The preponderance of Senate victories in conference," Kanter notes, "is, to some degree, inversely related to the importance of the budget category."[29]

Kanter's observation points out a rather significant limitation of interchamber victory scorecards: the assumption inherent in such tabulations that each issue has equal importance. Obviously, some issues are more important than others, and a conference delegation may be quite content to win on a lesser number of these while losing on a greater number of marginal matters. One further possibility exists: the chambers may differ in the degree that their chamber-passed bills are laden with less important matters that may be freely given up or "lost" in order to win on a few key, basic goals. The question of House-Senate political differences along these lines will be examined in the

26. Vogler, "Patterns of One-House Dominance," pp. 303–20.
27. Ferejohn, *Pork Barrel Politics*, p. 118n. In a letter to the authors, Vogler has emphasized that he viewed committee status differences not as a separate variable, but rather as a way of measuring chamber linkage. (Personal letter to authors from David J. Vogler, November 18, 1983. See also Vogler, *The Third House*, p. 74.) In this case, Vogler's argument became essentially identical to the interpretation of his data advanced by John A. Ferejohn, as discussed in the text.
28. Arnold Kanter, "Congress and the Defense Budget: 1960–1970," *American Political Science Review* 66 (March 1972): 129–43, esp. p. 142.
29. Ibid., pp. 140–41.

next chapter, "The Institutional Context," but the findings of Kanter suggest at least the possibility that such chamber political differences may account for the particular pattern he notes of Senate wins on less significant defense budgetary items.

Three other studies have looked at chamber success in specific domestic policy areas: rivers and harbors bills, higher education legislation, and budget resolutions. John A. Ferejohn reported in 1974 and 1975 publications that "with respect to Corps of Engineers appropriations, the House does somewhat better at getting what it wants in the conference than the Senate."[30] Specifically, Ferejohn found two somewhat contradictory patterns: on 452 rivers and harbors appropriations proposed cuts over seventeen years, the House view prevailed in about 60 percent of the instances, but on a larger category of 1,309 chamber disagreements on specific provisions of rivers and harbors appropriations bills over a sixteen-year period, the Senate won 65.5 percent of the time.[31]

Ferejohn took care to stress, however, that these various findings concerning chamber success were less significant than the general pattern of mutual interest and accommodation that prevails on rivers and harbors legislation: "on . . . items of overlapping interest, both bodies are able to obtain what they want most of the time."[32] He also declared considerable reservation about the entire enterprise of determining chamber dominance, expressing "some doubt on whether the measures presented in studies of the conference can be unambiguously interpreted as measures of 'who wins.' Instead, the conference committee can more usefully be seen as an arena in which the two bodies try to attain partly incompatible goals. And to a certain extent both may be fairly successful."[33]

Lawrence Gladieux and Thomas Wolanin's study *Congress and the Colleges: The National Politics of Higher Education* examined in detail the legislative politics surrounding the enactment of the Higher Education Act of 1972, which included particularly complex and multifaceted conference negotiations. In reflecting on chamber success on the various issues addressed, they exhibited considerable reluctance to arrive at simplistic judgments of House or Senate success:

> It can be argued that in every successful conference both sides won, in the sense that at least a majority from each house finds the agreements acceptable. . . . [In addition], simply counting the number of differences settled by adopting the position of each house and the number that were compromised overlooks the relative importance of the issues.[34]

Despite these caveats, Gladieux and Wolanin did note that in terms of the final conference agreement, "on the major higher education issues, student aid and institutional aid, the Senate won. On the hundreds of additional differences between the two bills, both sides won about an equal number, and a large number of issues were settled by compromises that could not be characterized as a victory for either."[35]

---

30. John A. Ferejohn, "Who Wins in Conference Committee?" p. 1043. See also Ferejohn, *Pork Barrel Politics*, esp. pp. 116–26.
31. Ferejohn, "Who Wins in Conference Committee?" pp. 1042–44.
32. Ibid., p. 1044.
33. Ibid., p. 1045.
34. Gladieux and Wolanin, *Congress and the Colleges*, p. 204.
35. Ibid.

A third work examined the particular case of conferences on budget resolutions over five years. Dennis S. Ippolito found no clear pattern of chamber dominance in this legislative area; rather, he concluded that "the Senate's statistical edge [of 55 percent wins] is largely, though not entirely, balanced by the House's substantial success with the more important type of conference decisions."[36] Here Ippolito, like Ferejohn and Gladieux and Wolanin before him, recognized the limitations inherent in evaluating qualitative political compromises in quantitive terms as House or Senate wins.

A New Explanation for Conventional Findings

One final work should be discussed. It evaluated chamber wins in conference interactions but presented a substantially different explanation for its findings. The initial conclusions of Gerald S. Strom and Barry S. Rundquist in their article "A Revised Theory of Winning in House-Senate Conferences" do not seem particularly surprising in light of the previously discussed body of literature. Examining 136 conference decisions during the Ninety-second Congress, they found that the Senate won in 46 percent of the instances and the House 30 percent, with 24 percent of the outcomes not favoring either chamber. When only conference decisions in which one chamber won were considered, the Senate was found to have won in 60 percent of the cases, the House in 40 percent.[37] These findings are in striking correspondence with almost all of the Who wins? research covering three decades that we have reviewed. (See the accompanying table for a summary of this literature.) Only Steiner in 1951 and Ferejohn in a limited subset of rivers and harbors appropriations actions found a pattern of House interchamber dominance. All other studies concluded either that the Senate was the dominant chamber or that the question of who wins was unclear or undeterminable. The conclusion of Strom and Rundquist that the Senate won in 60 percent of the cases studied dovetails with the findings of those several scholars who had found patterns of Senate victories in conference negotiations.[38]

36. Dennis S. Ippolito, "House and Senate Influence on Budget Conference Committees," paper prepared for delivery at the Annual Meeting of the Southern Political Science Association, Memphis, Tenn., Nov. 5–7, 1981, pp. 19, 6–8. A considerably revised version of this paper was later published as Dennis S. Ippolito, "House-Senate Budget Conferences—Institutional and Strategic Advantages," *American Politics Quarterly* 11, no. 1 (January 1983): 71–90. Some of this material was also incorporated into Dennis S. Ippolito, *Congressional Spending: A Twentieth Century Fund Report* (Ithaca, N.Y.: Cornell University Press, 1981).

37. Strom and Rundquist, "A Revised Theory of Winning," p. 448.

38. This scholarly consensus on Senate domination of conference committees is at striking variance with the belief of some knowledgeable Capitol Hill sources that usually the House prevails. Howard E. Shuman, long-time Senate legislative aide, observes that generally House conferees are better informed than senators about legislation. Further, House conference delegations often find the time for preconference strategy meetings; this is seldom the case for Senate conferees. The greater legislative and political demands on senators also acts as a distraction and leads to a tendency for senators to leave legislative details to Senate staffers. This additionally weakens the conference positions of senators who are less prepared to argue over legislative specifics than legislative specialist House members. Finally, House conferees, because of self-perceived interchamber status inferiority, often tend in conference to compensate by being intransigent. (Howard E. Shuman, *Politics and the Budget: The Struggle between the President and the Congress* 2d ed. [Englewood Cliffs: Prentice-Hall, 1988], pp. 79–80).

These assessments by Howard Shuman were echoed in 1986 by Senator Max Baucus (D, Mont.),

What was new about Strom and Rundquist's research, however, was the explanation they advanced for this chamber advantage. Strom and Rundquist did not attempt to account for chamber success by means of an institutional or political support explanation based on factors such as committee prestige, group acceptance, or legislative chamber support for conferees. Rather they advanced a boldly innovative strategic hypothesis[39] to explain who wins: *The chamber that acts second in considering legislation tends to prevail in conference interactions.*

In order to test this hypothesis, they reexamined 103 conference decisions during the Ninety-second Congress in which one chamber could be said to have won. Of these, the House had acted first in 75 instances, while the Senate had been the initiating chamber 28 times. The relationship between acting first and the *other* chamber winning was striking:[40]

	Senate wins	*House wins*
House acts first	72%	28%
Senate acts first	29%	71%

who argued that because senators were spread so thin, they are less successful in conference: "All things being equal, the House tends to prevail over the Senate. . . . They simply know the bill better" (quoted in David E. Rosenbaum, "Why the Two Houses Behave the Way They Do," *New York Times,* March 6, 1986).

Such perceptions by one set of negotiators that the other side usually wins is not, of course, unusual in any bargaining situation. What is striking, however, in both Howard Shuman's and Sen. Baucus's conclusions is, first, the clear perception by one chamber's conferees of the nature of the other chamber's conferees (this theme is explored further in the next chapter); and, second, the sharp variance of their conclusions with scholarly consensus. As we noted at the outset of this chapter, what is known on Capitol Hill is often quite different from what is known in the scholarly literature. Who wins? is at best a highly subjective question subject to widely varying personal judgment.

39. The distinction made here between institutional and strategic explanations was suggested by Dennis S. Ippolito in his paper, "House and Senate Influence on Budget Conference Committees," p. 2. Donald A. Gross has alternatively characterized this distinction as one between political support and structural-process hypotheses (Donald A. Gross, "House-Senate Conference Committees: A Comparative-State Perspective," *American Journal of Political Science* 24 [Nov. 1980]: 769–78). Rundquist and Strom themselves have more recently termed their bill construction and sequence approach "entrepreneurial sequence theory" (Rundquist and Strom, "Influence and Sequence in Legislative Processes," paper presented at the Annual Meeting of the Western Political Science Association, Las Vegas, March 28–30, 1985, p. 14).

Strom and Rundquist were not entirely original in suggesting their strategic hypothesis. Other scholars before them, most notably John Manley in *The Politics of Finance,* had mentioned the possibility that chamber success might be related to acting second. What was significant about the work of Strom and Rundquist, however, was that this strategic hypothesis was considered by them not as a passing reflection, but as the central element of the explanation offered, and this hypothesis was systematically tested, with solid evidence being found in support of it.

40. Adapted from Strom and Rundquist, "A Revised Theory of Winning," p. 451. In earlier research reported but never published the same two scholars examined in a similar manner a larger category of 603 conferences drawn from six different Congresses in which there was a chamber winner. In this analysis, they found that the second-acting chamber won in 412, or 68.3 percent, of the instances, while the initiating chamber prevailed in only 191, or 31.7 percent (Barry S. Rundquist and Gerald S. Strom, "House-Senate Conferences and the Legislative Process," revised version of paper presented at the 1976 Annual Meeting of the Midwest Political Science Association, Chicago, p. 4). Their subse-

Who Wins? A Summary of Findings

Study	Conferences Considered	Dominant Chamber	Percentage of Wins for Each Chamber
Steiner (1951)	56 major conferences over 20 years	House	68—House 32—Senate
Fenno (1966)	331 appropriations conferences over 18 years	Senate	65—Senate 35—House
Manley (1970)	20 major tax conferences over 19 years	Senate	70—Senate 30—House
Vogler (1970 & 1971)	297 conferences over 20 years	Senate	65—Senate 35—House
Kanter (1972)	161 defense budgetary conference decisions over 10 years	Senate, but often on the less significant matters	71—Senate 29—House
Ferejohn (1974 & 1975)	452 rivers and harbors appropriations proposed cuts over 17 years	House	60—House 40—Senate
(same)	1,309 specific chamber disagreements on provisions of rivers and harbors appropriations bills over 16 years	Senate	65.5—Senate 34.5—House
Gladieux and Wolanin (1976)	Various aspects of the Higher Education Act of 1972	Senate somewhat	not specified
Ippolito (1981 & 1983)	480 budgetary resolution issues over 5 years	Unclear—Senate has statistical edge while House has advantage on substance	statistical edge: 55—Senate 45—House
Strom and Rundquist (1976 & 1977)	136 conference decisions during the 92nd Congress	Senate	60—Senate 40—House

The conclusion appeared inescapable: the finding that the Senate tends to win in conference results not from some inherent institutional strength or characteristic, but rather from the fact that the Senate generally acts second on legislation, especially in that large category of revenue-raising measures for which the Constitution specifies House origination.[41] As a generalization, Strom and Rundquist proposed that "conferences are best

quently published *APSA* article, however, was based only on the smaller set of cases discussed in the text. (Personal letter from Barry S. Rundquist to authors, October 14, 1983.)

41. For useful summaries of this point, see Ripley, *Congress*, p. 175; and Vogler, *The Politics of Congress*, p. 213. An instance in which the Constitutional requirement for the House to act first on tax bills was honored only remotely—even in form—is discussed in the chapter 11 case study "The 1982 Tax Increase Conference."

understood as contexts in which conferees from the first chamber bargain for the support of the conferees from the second acting chamber, rather than as 'the third House' in which the forces that lead to legislative victories are similar to those that lead to legislative victories at earlier stages of the legislative process."[42]

In assessing this strategic argument, it is important to recognize that winning in interchamber negotiations is not the same thing as having the greatest influence over legislation. The initiating chamber (the so-called weaker one) has, in many cases, set the priorities and agenda for the legislative initiative, and the role of the chamber acting second may be little more than one of modifying or reacting to the ideas originated by the first chamber. Of course, in this case, the second chamber may seem to win on many of these modifications, but on more marginal matters.

The lesser number of such victories for the initiating chamber belies its major role in setting the basic course of policy deliberation and choice. Strom and Rundquist were sensitive to this distinction, noting that "the conferees from the first acting chamber have an incentive to exchange marginal amendments in the bill with conferees from the second acting chamber to obtain the latter's support for the major aspects of the bill their chamber has passed."[43] Their awareness of this important difference between chamber win and legislative influence led Strom and Rundquist to a curious and striking conclusion that despite their earlier findings, the House may well be the dominant chamber *on legislation:*

> The evidence that the Senate usually wins in conference, does not mean that the Senate's version of a bill usually predominates. Just the opposite is true: the House has more influence on the content of the bill because it acts first. . . .
>
> If we are correct that acting first allows a chamber to have greater impact on the content of legislation, then clearly the House has more legislative impact than the Senate.[44]

The research of Strom and Rundquist, then, provides further evidence that, in terms of the traditional question of who wins, the Senate tends to prevail in conference interactions. It also advances a new and intriguing strategic or sequence explanation for this chamber success.[45] In the course of doing so, however, Strom and Rundquist also

   42. Strom and Rundquist, "A Revised Theory of Winning," p. 452.
   43. Ibid.
   44. Ibid., pp. 451, 453. For an elaboration of this argument, see Gross, "House-Senate Conference Committees," p. 772; and Allen Schick, *Congress and Money: Budgeting, Spending, and Taxing* (Washington, D.C.: Urban Institute, 1980). Schick similarly suggests that in the case of joint budgetary resolutions, "an early budget mark can have more influence on the outcome than a later Senate action" (p. 539).
   45. A subsequent interesting use of sequence theory has concluded that a major basis of committee power in House and Senate lies in the fact that in conference key committee members "get a second chance [to deal with legislation] after their chamber has worked its will." These "ex-post adjustment powers wielded by committees in conference" accord congressional committees a special institutional power over bills—a sort of "ex-post veto" (Kenneth A. Shepsle and Barry R. Weingast, "The Institutional Foundations of Committee Power," *American Political Science Review*, 81, no. 1 [March 1987]: 85–104, esp. 85, 86). (For additional discussion of this approach, see also chapter 6, note 6, below.)
   This argument has been forcefully criticized by Keith Krehbiel on the grounds that "congressional committees have, in fact, never possessed an uncircumventable ex-post veto and are very much con-

provide us with even stronger evidence that the recurrently posed question Who wins—House or Senate? may be of little relevance to the actual politics of legislation and to the more significant questions of which political and legislative interests prevail. Who wins in conference committee politics? is a significant question, but not when expressed in terms of chamber success scores or statistical counts. Who wins? should be addressed in terms of other questions—questions concerning interest and individual advantages rather than chamber wins.

What We Need to Know

> A comparison of the conference report on a bill with the House and Senate versions of the bill may reveal the number of instances in which each chamber acceded to the position of the other (if the differences are discrete), but it cannot reveal the relative importance of each matter in disagreement, nor the number of items taken to conference either in order to expedite initial floor action and increase support for initial passage of the bill or to offer greater latitude in conference negotiations. A Senate floor manager, for instance, may accept another Senator's floor amendment, whether germane or not, to avoid prolonged debate and to attract the latter's support for the bill, but without any intention of insisting on the amendment in conference. The floor manager also may accept one or more amendments for the purpose of increasing the Senate's bargaining opportunities and leverage in conference.
>
> —Stanley Bach[46]

> [One should] consider some of the *strategies* used by the participants to gain their preferred ends.
>
> —Jeffrey L. Pressman[47]

---

strained by their parent chambers'' (Keith Krehbiel, ''Why Are Congressional Committees Powerful?'' *American Political Science Review* 81, no. 3 [Sept. 1987]: 929–35, esp. 929). Shepsle and Weingast provide a rejoinder to the Krehbiel criticism of their original analysis in the same issue of the *American Political Science Review*, pp. 935–45.

These utilizations of sequential concepts are quite different from Strom and Rundquist's explanation for intercameral wins, but they stand as intriguing extensions of a theoretical focus on sequence and its significance in legislative politics.

46. Stanley Bach, ''Bicameral Conflict and Accommodation in Congressional Procedure,'' paper presented at the 1981 Annual Meeting of the American Political Science Association, p. 11.

47. Pressman, *House vs. Senate*, p. 63 (italics in original). A more recent call for consideration of strategic factors in conference interactions, rather than which chamber has won, can be found in Joe A. Theissen, ''Congressional Conference Committees: New Avenues for Research,'' paper prepared for delivery at the 1985 Annual Meeting of the Southern Political Science Association, Nashville, Nov. 1985.

Another study of conference committees suggests a recent shift away from Senate dominance of conference decisions, especially since 1976, but couples this tentative conclusion with an emphasis on

We have argued that research focusing on which chamber prevails in conference interactions is at best an uncertain enterprise with probably inherently undeterminable results. We have also suggested that statistical counts of wins as the basis of determining chamber successes are themselves an unsatisfactory means of determining legislative influence. As Stanley Bach points out in the above quotation, such quantitative scorecards inevitably will fail to measure the relative significance of different provisions—or the differing perceived importance of such items to participants.

Certainly the determination of victory is particularly difficult when chamber differences are expressed in qualitative terms: chamber A prefers a program with certain specified policy dimensions, while chamber B supports an alternative approach with different policy aspects. On the other hand, the determination of chamber success seems far more certain when chamber differences are essentially quantitative. If one chamber approved an appropriation for a particular program at the $100 million level, while the other chamber supported an appropriation for the same program of $150 million, and the conference compromise reports an appropriation of $140 million, then it might appear easy to conclude that the second chamber's wishes prevailed. However, even in this clear instance of interchamber negotiations over dollar figures, simple measures may disguise political realities. Richard Fenno sensitively recognized the severe limitations of quantitative measures of political victory:

> If, for example, one group is willing to give up an item costing $50 million to get some especially valued item costing $10 million, then dollars and cents measures will be inadequate to define "winning." Or, a key point at issue may be a matter of language providing for the distribution of money, in which one side may yield entirely on the monetary amount in order to get the language provisions it desires. Any empirical measure which uses only monetary data will miss the outcome of this bargain entirely.[48]

Other problems exist with the simple comparison of chamber bills with the conference report beyond differing weights conferees may give to different provisions, or the possible mix of quantitative and qualitative issues in conference bargaining.[49] Cham-

---

the need for careful examination of the significance of committee factors in conference committee politics. It is argued that "it is primarily the relationship between standing committees and their parent chamber that influences their conference performance" (John J. Carter and John R. Baker, "Chamber Dominance in House-Senate Conferences: Who Wins, Who Loses, and What Difference Does It Make?" paper presented at the Annual Meeting of the Southwestern Political Science Association, Houston, March 20–23, 1985, p. 28). The committee context of conference committee politics is examined in chapter 6 below.

48. Fenno, *The Power of the Purse*, p. 661.

49. A particularly vivid example of conference negotiations on a varied mix of quantitative and qualitative questions occurred in the 1984 conference on the 1985 Defense Authorization Bill. Conferees not only had to resolve House-Senate quantitative differences on funding levels, but also the fate of highly contentious programs such as the MX missile, antisatellite missile testing, and broad policy questions, including U.S. policy in Central America—especially concerning the possible use of U.S. combat troops. These complex and qualitative issues are not ones that can be settled by numerical compromise; as Pat Towell put it in connection with the defense conference, "The conferees will not be

bers may also differ in the extent that their bills are bare-bones expressions of their preferences, or instead have thick icing made up of less substantive sweeteners added during legislative passage either to satisfy personal preferences or to anticipate the upcoming need to "compromise" during conference.[50] In short, winning in conference, when measured in statistical terms, has little empirical or substantive meaning.

What questions concerning conference committee politics, then, should be posed? We suggest that a more useful perspective is one that emphasizes *what goes on* in congressional conference committee interactions and *how the processes and politics of this central manifestation of bicameral politics determine congressional power and policy*. Appropriate questions include: How are chamber interests represented? To what extent are congressional committee preferences—or the special concerns of their chairman—articulated? In what manner do the individual interests of conferees appear as significant factors? What strategies are utilized by conference participants? Under what circumstances are some strategies more useful than others? What patterns of conference bargaining are prevalent, and under what circumstances do these patterns differ? What effect does conference politics have on the power of different interests and individuals? How do these characteristics of congressional bicameral politics affect final policy decisions?

These kinds of questions, we suggest, are truly important for an understanding of bicameral conference committee politics, and they are the type of inquiries we pursue in the remaining chapters of this book. In the next two chapters, we shall examine three different contexts within which conference committee interactions occur: the institutional, the committee, and the individual. Then we shall discuss conference committee politics as a policy process, considering initially different types of conferences and varieties of participants. That is followed by a detailed study of the sequence of actions that comprise the conference process. Throughout these chapters we will be emphasizing the strategic possibilities available at every stage of conference committee activities as well as the patterns of bargaining and compromise that tend to appear at each point. Finally, in a series of case studies of conference committee politics, we illustrate these dimensions of bicameral politics by detailed accounts of actual conferences. What goes on? is indeed the crucial question in conference committee politics, and in the coming pages we propose to describe what does go on in the process of House-Senate bicameral politics.

---

able to resolve those issues by simply splitting the difference" (Pat Towell, "Difficult Conference Looms on Defense Issues," *Congressional Quarterly Weekly Report,* June 23, 1984, p. 1479). Conferences with varied elements such as this defy simple judgments as to chamber wins, either on the entire conference, or on individual components of what will be necessarily an interconnected set of conference final decisions.

50. For a consideration of chamber differences in anticipating conference, see chapters 5 and 8 below.

Senator Daniel Patrick Moynihan (*left*) conferring with J. Roger Mentz, assistant secretary of the Treasury for tax policy, prior to a closed 1986 tax conference. (From the *New York Times,* August 3, 1986. Photograph by Paul Hosefros. Copyright © 1986 by The New York Times Company. Reprinted by permission.)

5

The Institutional Context

The House and Senate, it has been said, have only three things in common: their members are elected, they both pass legislation, and they share the same building.
—David C. Kozak and John D. Macartney[1]

It is further from the House to the Senate than from Capitol Hill to the White House.
—Old Capitol Hill saying

Thus far we have shown the legislative importance of congressional conference committees and have placed them in the context of bicameral politics. We have traced the evolution of the conference committee system, considered bicameral reconciliation practices in the states, and analyzed the changing character of congressional conference committee politics resulting from internal and external forces. Finally, we have described and categorized the scholarly literature dealing with conference committees and suggested some important questions that should be addressed in the study of conference committee politics.

Now we should make explicit what is implicit in the preceding chapters—a conception of conference committee politics as shaped by three different contexts: institutional, committee, and individual. First of all, conference committees are where the institutions of the House and Senate confront each other in terms of divergent personalities, norms, styles, power relationships, rules and procedures. Besides this *institutional context,* conference committees also involve interactions between groups of conferees typically drawn from matched House and Senate committees. Each chamber's conferees reflect

---

1. David C. Kozak and John D. Macartney, *Congress and Public Policy: A Source Book of Documents and Readings* (Homewood, Ill.: Dorsey Press, 1982), p. 52.

this *committee context* in their bargaining behavior, including both the nature of their parent committee and their conceptions of the other chamber's committee.

In addition to the institutional and committee context of conference committee politics, there is also an *individual context*. Conference committees are made up of individuals who are concerned with using the conference as a means to achieve at least two divergent ends: influence over legislation and influence for the self. This "play of power" is a central dynamic of conference committees. Individual conferees seek to shape legislation in accord with their goals and to act during the conference committee process to enhance their political standing among diverse entities, including chamber, committee, faction, constituency, press, party, interest group, and administration.

To further highlight the institutional context of conference committees, we will consider in this chapter four themes: face-to-face chamber meetings, the creation of two separate chambers, the contemporary partnership, and bicameral interactions and conflict. This discussion is designed to illuminate important institutional factors that recurrently affect House-Senate conference negotiations.

The Chambers Meet

It was late in the afternoon of a contentious 1978 conference on an appropriation bill. The small conference room, S128, was jammed with lobbyists, press, and observers crowded elbow to elbow around a long table. On one side of the table sat the Senate delegation headed by Senator Warren Magnuson (D, Wash.), chairman of the Senate Appropriations Committee. On the other side sat the House conferees, led by the chairman of the House Appropriations Subcommittee on Labor, Health and Human Welfare, Daniel Flood, (D, Penn.). The conference was engaged in a line-by-line review of the legislation.

One of the House conferees inquired about the fiscal implications of a specific item included in the Senate bill. Senator Magnuson replied with a mutter inaudible even across the narrow table. The representative repeated the question. The senator spoke, only slightly more distinctly now: "It's all right, let it be." The House conferee was not to be put off so easily. After all, he represented the House and felt it important to understand provisions to which the House was being asked to agree. The representative asked again: What does this language do?

Senator Magnuson raised his head, his face turning red, and spoke quite clearly now: "*I said*—It's all right—*Let it be!*"

This vignette, personally observed by one of the authors, whose body was jammed up against the left ear of the representative engaged in this House-Senate confrontation, catches well one context of bicameral politics: conferences involve direct, face-to-face meetings between the House and the Senate. The representative was in fact no more than reflecting the traditional House value of craftsmanship and expert knowledge in legislative decision making. Senator Magnuson, on the other hand, was not in the habit of having his judgment questioned by anyone. As the dean of the Senate (the majority senator with the longest service), his judgment that "it's all right" was customarily accepted with little question in that chamber.

In short, this conference exchange reflects the clash of the values and power relations of the two chambers inherent in conference deliberations. "Conference committee activity," notes Richard F. Fenno, "must be understood in terms of a conflict between two on-going political subsystems whose permanent differences are more deeply rooted than any single dollars and cents controversy."[2]

The conference committee is the only regular, formal meeting place of House and Senate with legislative significance. When the two chambers meet in conference, institutional contrasts and distinctions easily breed tension and clashes. This is probably inevitable, for inherent in these bicameral interactions is a tendency for interinstitutional conflict. This recurrent tendency, however, gives rise to the question Why *is* Congress constitutionally divided into two bodies? As Congress commences its third century of bicameral existence, it is appropriate to examine the historical roots of congressional bicameralism to determine why the legislative system for the new United States government was deliberately separated, in the new U.S. Constitution, into two contrasting and potentially conflicting halves.

Two Separate Chambers

> All legislative Powers herein granted shall be vested in a Congress of the United States, which shall consist of a Senate and House of Representatives.
> —The Constitution of the United States, Art. 1, Sec. 1

It is perhaps especially fitting that legislative bicameralism is specified in the First Section of the First Article of the U.S. Constitution, for it is a central feature of one of the major institutions of government established by that document—the new Congress of the United States. This national legislature was divided in the Constitution into two separate chambers both to accommodate competing interests vigorously represented at the Constitutional Convention in Philadelphia in 1787 and to act as a check upon legislative power and possible excesses. The former reason is well known and is captured by the classic concept of "the Great Compromise." In short, the delegates in Philadelphia were torn by bitter dissent over the question of whether the national legislature should be apportioned on the basis of equal state representation (which would preserve the power of even the smallest states) or on the basis of population (which would greatly enhance the importance of the largest, most populous states at the cost of the small states).

After much dispute, numerous proposals, and threatened deadlock, the Constitutional Convention delegates finally agreed on a critical political compromise: a two-house Congress in which one chamber would be structured along equal state lines and the other on population representation principles. This bicameral legislative arrangement was itself not difficult for the delegates to understand, for legislative bicameralism had

---

2. Richard F. Fenno, Jr., *The Power of the Purse: Appropriations Politics in Congress* (Boston: Little, Brown, 1966), p. 635.

been part of the new nation's British heritage and had predominated in America's colonial and state government experience.³ Most important, however, was the fact that legislative bicameralism accorded the Constitutional Convention delegates the means of reconciling competing interests and thus overcoming a major stumbling block in their immensely difficult task of constitution making. As Peter Woll puts it, "Bicameralism provided a way for the large and small states to reach agreement."⁴ James Sundquist adds a valuable coda: "When that great compromise saved the Constitution, it riveted the principle of bicameralism into the Constitution."⁵

The establishment of two separate legislative chambers, however, was also seen as having an additional highly desirable result: it provided the means of checking and controlling any abuse of legislative power that might otherwise arise. This benefit was extolled most explicitly in the newspaper essays published in New York City in behalf of the ratification of the draft Constitution that have come to be known as the *Federalist Papers*.⁶ In these writings, which served both as expositions upon and defenses of the new Constitution, Alexander Hamilton, James Madison, and John Jay discussed at length the institutional arrangements that made up the proposed national government, including its bicameral Congress. *Federalist Papers* nos. 51 to 66, in particular, defended the divided structure of Congress as a necessary check upon any legislative abuse of power. This goal, it was argued, could best be accomplished by dividing the legislative institution itself.⁷

    3. The historical antecedents for American bicameralism are discussed further in chapter 2 above in the section "The English Legacy." Chapter 2 also discusses the colonial and early national experience with conference committees, complementing this chapter's focus on the bicameral basis of institutional interactions.
    4. Peter Woll, *Congress* (Boston: Little, Brown, 1985), p. 16. If only a single unicameral legislature had been under consideration, one side or the other by necessity would have won—at the cost of bitter opposition to any such arrangement by the other. As James Sundquist puts it, "Bicameralism did turn out to be the magic solvent for that great dispute that had threatened to destroy the convention" (James L. Sundquist, *Constitutional Reform and Effective Government* [Washington, D.C.: Brookings Institution, 1986], p. 24).
    5. Sundquist, *Constitutional Reform*, p. 24. See also Thomas H. Hammond and Gary J. Miller, "The Core of the Constitution," *American Political Science Review* 81, no. 4 (Dec. 1987): 1155–74.
    6. The most frequently cited edition of these essays is the New American Library edition of 1961: Alexander Hamilton, James Madison, and John Jay, *The Federalist Papers* (New York: New American Library, 1961) (hereinafter cited as *Federalist Papers*).
    7. Benjamin I. Page, for example, has argued that the Founding Fathers saw "as the major benefit of bicameralism the prevention of error through a slowing of the legislative process and provision for expertise, and in particular through resistance to temporary passions or fluctuations in popular opinion" (Benjamin I. Page, "Cooling the Legislative Tea," in Walter Dean Burnham and Martha Wagner Weinberg, eds., *American Politics and Public Policy* [Cambridge: MIT Press, 1978], p. 172).
    This conception of bicameralism as an essential check on legislative power was particularly well developed in *Federalist Papers* nos. 51 and 62. James Madison in Federalist 62, for example, wrote that a restraining upper house was needed because of "the propensity of all single and numerous assemblies to yield to the impulse of sudden and violent passions, and to be seduced by factious leaders into intemperate and pernicious resolutions" (*Federalist Papers*, p. 379). Because of this inevitable tendency of single-chamber legislatures, bicameralism was seen as "an important mechanism for checking ill-considered popular action" (Woll, *Congress*, p. 35).

The delegates at the Constitutional Convention had structured a government balanced between national and state components and incorporating a separation of powers among the new national institutions; they likewise had created a Congress made up of two distinct legislative bodies.[8] As delegate James Wilson of Pennsylvania had said, "If the Legislative authority be not restrained, there can be neither liberty nor stability; and it can only be restrained by dividing it within itself into distinct and independent branches."[9] In the *Federalist Papers,* James Madison similarly made the case:

> In republican government, the legislative authority necessarily predominates. The remedy for this inconveniency is to divide the legislature into different branches; and to render them by different modes of election and different principles of action, as little connected with each other as the nature of their common functions and their common dependence on the society will admit.[10]

To accomplish these goals, the Congress had been constituted as two quite separate institutions, each constitutionally unique in size, term of office, and constituency. James Madison suggested that this was essential as "the improbability of sinister combinations will be in proportion to the dissimilarities in the genius of the two bodies."[11] For this reason, "the Framers deliberately established 'dissimilar modes' of constituting the House and Senate to 'permanently nourish different propensities and inclinations.' "[12] Different constitutional responsibilities were also assigned to each chamber: initiating

---

8. Edward G. Carmines and Lawrence C. Dodd, "Bicameralism in Congress: The Changing Partnership," in Lawrence C. Dodd and Bruce I. Oppenheimer, eds., *Congress Reconsidered,* 3d ed. (Washington, D.C.: CQ Press, 1985), p. 415. Madison caught well this idea of controlling power by dividing it when he wrote in *Federalist Paper* no. 51 that the Constitution was constructed on the principle of "contriving the interior structure of the government as that its several constituent parts may, by their mutual relations, be the means of keeping each other in their proper places" (*Federalist Papers,* p. 320).

9. James Madison, *Notes of the Debates in the Federal Convention of 1787* (New York: Norton, 1969), pp. 126–27. This statement by James Wilson was quoted by Chief Justice Warren Burger in his opinion for the Court in the June 1983 legislative veto case, *INS* v. *Chadha* (462 U.S. 919). Chief Justice Burger went on to cite Hamilton's warning in Federalist no. 22 that should there be only one legislative organ, "we shall finally accumulate in a single body all the most important prerogatives of sovereignty, and thus entail upon our posterity one of the most execrable forms of government that human infatuation ever contrived. Thus we should create in reality that very tyranny which the adversaries of the new Constitution either are, or affect to be, solicitious to avert" (*Federalist Papers,* p. 152). The Court was reviewing the Constitutional basis of bicameralism as part of its justification for striking down the "one-house" legislative veto—a disapproval of administrative action by vote of only one chamber. Other sections of the Court opinion went on to expand on the unconstitutionality also of the "two-house" legislative veto because it likewise did not involve the president.

10. *Federalist Papers,* p. 322. This quotation is from *Federalist Paper* no. 51.

11. *Federalist Papers,* p. 379. This quotation is from *Federalist Paper* no. 62. In this essay Madison stressed the need for real institutional differences between the two chambers: "It must be politic to distinguish them from each other by every circumstance which will consist with a dual harmony in all proper measures, and with the genuine principles of republican government" (*Federalist Papers,* p. 379).

12. Henry B. Dawson, ed., *The Federalist* (New York: Scribner, 1876), p. 418. The words quoted within the passage are from *Federalist Paper* no. 59.

revenue measures to the House, and advising and consenting to treaties and nominations to the Senate. Additionally, the two chambers would evolve their own rules, precedents, traditions, and customs. These distinctions would be enduring differences,[13] necessary as a safeguard against legislative tyranny. The two legislative chambers would provide "two different bodies of men who might watch and check each other."[14] In order to provide this watching and checking function, however, the two bodies had to be constituted as different as possible from each other.

The House of Representatives was to be first and foremost a representative body directly elected by the people—"the grand repository of the democratic principles of the government."[15] The Senate, initially elected indirectly by the state legislatures until ratification of the Seventeenth Amendment in 1913, was expected to operate with "more coolness, with more system and with more wisdom than the popular branch."[16] The classic anecdote concerning the Senate[17] catches well the distinctive features seen for that chamber in the legislative process. Thomas Jefferson at one point asked George Washington why the new Constitution provided for a second legislative chamber, the Senate: " 'Why,' asked Washington, 'did you pour that coffee into your saucer?' 'To

---

13. This enduring bicameral heritage is stressed by Carmines and Dodd, who suggest that Congress throughout its history must be viewed against the backdrop of bicameralism: "two distinct independent chambers with different sizes, terms of office, constitutional responsibilities, and constituencies" (Carmines and Dodd, "Bicameralism in Congress," p. 417).

14. Madison, *Notes of the Debates,* p. 193.

15. George Mason of Virginia, quoted in Max Farrand, ed., *The Records of the Federal Convention,* 4 vols. rev. ed. (New Haven: Yale University Press, 1937), 1:48.

16. Madison, *Notes of the Debates,* p. 83. Similarly, Madison is said to have referred to the Senate in conversation with Jefferson, as "the great anchor of the government." More recently, political scientist Richard F. Fenno, Jr., has characterized this prevailing view of the Senate as "a restraining, stabilizing counterweight, . . . the source of a more deliberate, more knowledgeable longer-run view of good public policy" (Richard F. Fenno, Jr., *The United States Senate: A Bicameral Perspective* [Washington, D.C.: AEI, 1982], p. 3).

Another view of the Senate was that of George Mason of Virginia, a sometimes Antifederalist, who found comfort in the Constitutional provisions for the selection of senators by the state legislatures: "The states would have the power through the Senate to defend themselves against encroachment by the federal government just as the presidential veto enables the executive branch to defend itself against the legislature" (Sundquist, *Constitutional Reform,* pp. 23–24, based on Farrand, *Records,* 1:155–56, 407). With the popular elections of senators mandated by the adoption of the 17th amendment in 1913, this safeguard, so treasured by George Mason, was removed.

17. This exchange between Washington and Jefferson has indeed become legendary and is recurrently cited for many different purposes. For example, during Senate debate in 1986 over allowing television coverage of the Senate (an issue undoubtedly neither Washington nor Jefferson foresaw), the cooling saucer analogy was repeatedly utilized by senators to support their views: "It is important to the institution and to this nation for the Senate to play the role of the saucer where the political passions of the nation are cooled" (Sen. Charles McC. Mathias [R, Md.], quoted in Alan Ehrenhalt, "The Senate: World's Least Effective 'Saucer'," *Congressional Quarterly Weekly Report,* March 8, 1986, p. 583); and—in strong opposition to Senate television—"The public will never understand why it's important to this institution and to the nation for the Senate to play the role of the saucer" (Sen. J. Bennett Johnson [D, La.], quoted in Jacqueline Calmes, "Senate Agrees to Test of Radio, TV Coverage," *Congressional Quarterly Weekly Report,* March 1, 1986, p. 521).

cool it,' said Jefferson. 'Even so,' replied Washington, 'we pour legislation into the senatorial saucer to cool it.' "[18]

The adoption of bicameralism did not occur merely as a result of tradition or by accident. The bicameral structure of Congress was "an integral element of the theory of government articulated at the Convention and outlined in the *Federalist Papers*."[19] This theory embraced the concept that the best way to prevent excesses of government was to provide for varieties of institutions and balances of authority. The new government would be a democratically constituted one, but it would also be one with appropriate safeguards. Noted James Madison in the *Federalist Papers*, "A dependence on the people is, no doubt, the primary control on the government; but experience has taught mankind the necessity of auxiliary precautions."[20]

Legislative bicameralism for the new Congress was seen as one of the most important of these "auxiliary precautions." The adoption of a bicameral structure for the Congress, then, provided both the means for success at the Constitutional Convention and the promise of controlling legislative power. As the Constitution had checked national governmental power by dividing it, so also it provided for the limitation of congressional power by dividing that institution itself into two separate chambers.

The Contemporary Partnership

> The root institutional differences between Senate and House are those of size, procedure, constituency and tenure. They, in turn, combine to produce very different decision making structures in the two chambers.
> —Richard F. Fenno, Jr.[21]

> The House and Senate are naturally unlike.
> —Woodrow Wilson[22]

The precise roles of House and Senate as legislative percolating or cooling mechanisms change over time. At points, the Senate may well be the innovative institution and the House the restraining agent; at other times the reverse is true. The bicameral necessity

---

18. Farrand, *Records*, 3:359. The purpose of such institutional contrast, of course, was to improve the legislative product. Political scientist Benjamin I. Page catches this concept well (even if his recollection of Jefferson's drink is a bit off) when he writes that it is in "the furtherance of deliberation, the production of evidence, and the revealing of error that bicameralism probably had its greatest effects.... While American bicameralism no doubt sometimes keeps us from drinking any tea at all, it may often improve legislative tea which was at the outset excessively hot, or ill-brewed" (Page, "Cooling the Tea," p. 186).

19. Carmines and Dodd, "Bicameralism in Congress," p. 415.

20. *Federalist Papers*, p. 322. The quotation is from *Federalist Paper* no. 51.

21. Richard F. Fenno, Jr., *Congressmen in Committees* (Boston: Little, Brown, 1973), pp. 145–46.

22. Woodrow Wilson, *Constitutional Government in the United States* (New York: Columbia University Press, 1911), p. 87.

remains, however, for the two quite different institutions to interact for the purpose of agreeing on common legislation.

The contemporary House and Senate are two distinctive institutions separated by a variety of enduring factors. Among these bicameral contrasts are differing terms of office, the size and nature of constituencies, chamber size, special constitutional responsibilities assigned to each body, as well as rules, procedures, customs, and traditions that have developed differently in each chamber.[23] These factors ensure fundamental and enduring differences between House and Senate that transcend short-term evolutional changes.[24] How do these institutional differences manifest themselves specifically in conference committee interactions?

One consequence of these institutional distinctions is that each chamber delegation approaches conference deliberations with different expectations. "House conferees come to the bargaining table to uphold bills fashioned in committee workshops," notes one scholar. "Senate conferees come to make sure that individual senators' provisions to help certain segments of the public are not dropped from the final bill."[25] These intercameral distinctions, of course, reflect fundamental chamber differences—most notably that the legislative process in the House is much more of a committee-dominated process than in the Senate,[26] while in the Senate, principles of comity and reciprocal favor-doing prevail—a form of "politics by consensus."[27]

These differences in purpose even influence the preparation of each chamber's

---

23. Walter J. Oleszek, "House-Senate Relationships: Comity and Conflict," *Annals of the American Academy of Political and Social Science* 411 (Jan. 1974): 75.

24. Norman J. Ornstein has argued that the classic institutional distinctions between House and Senate have, in recent years, begun to break down: "The House has become less identified with legislative carpentry and more noted for grappling with the larger issues in policy debate. The Senate has moved away from its focus on debate and deliberation, and toward a preoccupation with the legislative nitty-gritty." The result, he suggests, "has been to make the House more like the Senate and the Senate more like the House. As a result, the unique policy roles . . . ascribed to the two chambers have been blurred—leading to less consistent and more erratic policy outcomes." Ornstein goes on to argue, however, that the impact of these evolutions has not been to diminish bicameral conflict, for neither chamber is entirely satisfied or comfortable with these changes, and each is uneasy and uncertain about its new legislative roles. Such *intra*chamber discomfort and unease breeds potential *inter*chamber tension. Norman J. Ornstein, "The House and the Senate in a New Congress," in Thomas E. Mann and Norman J. Ornstein, eds. *The New Congress* (Washington, D.C.: AEI, 1981), pp. 371, 366, 371.

Despite these changes—transitory or enduring as they may be—the two houses remain institutionally distinct, a distinction maintained by those factors enunciated in the preceding text paragraph. The changes in style and outlook that Ornstein considers certainly are significant, at least in the short run. The enduring factors cited in the text, however, ensure that the House and Senate will always maintain that institutional separateness sought after so emphatically by the Framers of the Constitution. (The changing relationship of the House and Senate is further thoughtfully examined in the essay "Bicameralism in Congress" by Carmines and Dodd.)

25. David J. Vogler, *The Politics of Congress*, 5th ed. (Boston: Allyn and Bacon, 1988), p. 213.

26. Fenno, *Congressmen in Committees*, p. 147. Concerning committee power differences between the two chambers, Fenno suggests two generalizations: "Senators do not specialize as intensively or as exclusively in their committee work as House members do" and "Senate committee chairmen have less potential for influence inside their committees than House chairmen" (p. 172).

27. Lawrence Gladieux and Thomas Wolanin, *Congress and the Colleges: The National Politics of Higher Education* (Lexington, Mass.: D. C. Heath, 1976), p. 193.

representatives for conference;[28] as one observer argues, "House conferees have usually spent more time studying the legislation and probably know the details better than the Senators, who after all, have more demands on their time than House members."[29] On the other hand, while the representatives may know the substantive details of the bill far better, the senators, as noted in the preceding chapter, are likely to have developed chamber political support for their legislation more thoroughly.[30]

These differences of political environment and preparation are exacerbated by intercameral perceptions. House conferees view themselves as legislative craftsmen compared to the individualistic and mutually self-serving Senate conferees. One House member expressed his disdain for senators in conference in the following words:

> The fifty members of the House Appropriations Committee are experts. They sift evidence and studiously tackle appropriations. The Senate knows nothing. They have little time and do not go into the evidence. In conferences, they don't contribute much. You have all those prima donnas in the Senate. On the House side, the Appropriations Committee is the salt mine of the Congress. But Senators are interested in flashy issues like foreign policy and the House has to do the grub work on appropriations.[31]

---

28. One interesting bicameral difference in preparation for conference is a tendency, noted by one observant Senate aide, for House conferees to meet far more often than Senate conferees in preconference delegation caucuses to work out chamber position. (Washington interview, Nov. 4, 1981.) (A similar observation by Howard E. Shuman was cited in chapter 4, note 38.) Along this line, one of the authors, while observing an Appropriations Agriculture Subcommittee conference later that day, Nov. 4, 1981, noticed that the House conferees arrived at 3 P.M. in a wave, accompanied by staff. The Senate conferees trickled in individually over some time.

29. John Manley, *The Politics of Finance: The House Committee on Ways and Means* (Boston: Little, Brown, 1970), p. 293.

Gladieux and Wolanin note, based on their close observation of the complex 1972 Higher Education conference, a major difference between House and Senate conferees: "The average House conferee was more expert and informed on the substantive issues than his Senate counterparts because House members serve on fewer committees and sub-committees and can specialize more intensely" (p. 201). Similarly, Paletz concluded his lengthy, detailed study of three conferences by observing, "Burdened by more committees, more subcommittees, ordinarily larger constituencies, greater demands from the news media, and other conference committee responsibilities, Senators are frequently less diligent in their attendance, less informed, and less involved in a conference than Representatives" (David L. Paletz, "Influence in Congress: An Analysis of the Nature and Effects of Conference Committees" [Ph.D. diss., University of California at Los Angeles, 1970], p. 441). Fenno also similarly concludes that in conference negotiations, "House conferees are better prepared, better organized, better informed, more single-minded in their interest, and employ a more belligerent bargaining style" (Fenno, *The Power of the Purse*, p. 668).

30. For a fuller discussion of the political support thesis for explaining interchamber power differences, see in chapter 4 the section "The Recurrent Question: Who Wins—House or Senate?" In that discussion, we quote Fenno's classic explanation for why the Senate appears to prevail in House-Senate negotiations: "When the Senate conferees go to the conference room, they not only represent the Senate—they are the Senate. The position they defend will have been worked out with a maximum of participation by Senate members and will enjoy a maximum of support in that body. . . . The bill will be defended in conference by men who are the leaders not just of the Committee, but of the Senate" (Fenno, *The Power of the Purse*, p. 669).

31. Jeffrey L. Pressman, *House vs. Senate* (New Haven: Yale University Press, 1966), p. 10.

In a study conducted in 1983 similar examples were given of negative assessments by representatives of the Senate and of senators:

> The Senate is a zoo. I have no interest in the Senate. . . . The Senate is all personality dependent.

> I've never liked Senators. Those folks don't know much, and they're not very competent.

> There is an aura about the Senate that I don't like. I was on a panel recently with three Senators. I was the only House member speaking before the group. There is no edge to them. . . . They are spread so thin that they can't hold a candle to House members in terms of substance. Their egos are very big. . . . The House is the institution closest to the people, and we do have a legitimate claim to having performed the representative burden better than our colleagues in the Senate.[32]

By comparison, there is little public information concerning Senate conceptions of the House as an institution.[33] Senators tend to focus on their chamber and its individualistic politics, rather than on the huge and seemingly anonymous mass of representatives. The Senate perceptions of the House that do exist seem to be focused more on its committees than on the entire institution.[34] In the case of appropriations politics, for example, senators were found in the mid-1960s to believe that the House Appropriations Committee frequently plays an economizing game—slashing proposed appropriations severely in committee in anticipation that in conference many of those cuts will have to be restored in order to have a compromise bill.[35] In other cases, however, senators are

---

32. Three members of the House of Representatives, quoted in John F. Bibby, ed.. *Congress Off the Record: The Candid Analyses of Seven Members* (Washington, D.C.: AEI, 1983), pp. 51–52. These statements of House members should be viewed in part in a context of self-conscious assertiveness of House superiority to the more prestigious Senate. As Fenno notes, "The perception of the Senate as the 'upper body' dominates House thinking" (Fenno, *The Power of the Purse*, p. 627).

33. This may be less the case for senators who formerly were House members and still recall their negative view of the Senate held while serving in the House. One colorful illustration of this occurred early in 1985 in the course of a Republican House-Senate leadership private luncheon. Referring to his Senate colleagues, Sen. Robert Dole (R, Kan.) told the House members, "There are six of us on this side of the table and I want you to know that there are four of us who started our careers as House members. We all know that you all think we are jerks" (quoted in David Shribman and David Rogers, "Party Divisions: Relationship is Tense Between Republicans in House and Senate," *Wall Street Journal*, May 1, 1985, p. 1).

34. For a fuller discussion of interchamber *committee* conceptions, see chapter 6 below.

35. Fenno, *Power of the Purse*, p. 633. The Senate perceptions of House conferees were paralleled by House perceptions of themselves "as the responsible guardians of the federal Treasury and . . . their Senate counterparts as being excessively profligate with the public money" (p. 626). This economizing role for the House Appropriations Committee was probably an artifact of the times; in the 1980s, such an economizing role is more often played by the Senate and the Senate Appropriations Committee. Similarly, the House Appropriations Committee has undergone profound changes over the past decade. See, for example, Diane Granat, "Special Report: House Appropriations Committee," *Congressional Quarterly Weekly Report*, June 18, 1983, pp. 1209–21.

Writing in 1981, Allen Schick observed, "Over the years, the House and Senate have developed reciprocal expectations concerning each other's behavior on revenue and spending measures. . . . In

profoundly indifferent about House activities. One senator, a member of the Finance Committee, expressed his lack of interest in the other chamber's counterpart committee in observing, "We don't pay any attention to what the Ways and Means Committee is doing, other than reading it in the papers. It's a totally separate process."[36]

House members, on the other hand, seem to have a clearer, more accurate conception of the Senate's institutional and committee processes concerning bills coming to conference. "To some degree, House managers believe, Senate bills are 'loaded for compromise.' Many items go into the bill so that a few can be taken out in conference."[37] This loading up of legislation is directly due to the highly individualistic nature of the Senate. The Senate is "more likely to proceed on the basis of mutual noninterference in the interests of one's colleagues, which is supported by the realization that in many cases logroll amendments will be 'taken to conference' and dropped."[38] In other words, politics *within* the individualistic Senate often leads to legislation containing provisions added to further chamber passage.

---

dealing with appropriations, the House has traditionally acted more as a guardian of the treasury, the Senate more as a program advocate." Schick goes on to suggest, however, in comments somewhat echoing Ornstein's more general chamber observations (cited in note 24 above) that these traditional roles have undergone significant evolution: "The two chambers appear to be becoming more alike in their budgetary dispositions, with the House more an advocate than it once was and the Senate more a guardian. . . . The relationship between the two bodies is undergoing change" (Allen Schick, *Reconciliation and the Congressional Budget Process* [Washington, D.C.: AEI, 1981], pp. 40, 41).

36. Quoted in Manley, *Politics of Finance,* p. 269. This "indifference theme" should not be pressed too far. Both bodies are often keenly interested in the *legislative* activities of the other, despite declarations to the contrary. The range of House-Senate policy interactions is too extensive to catalog in detail, but a brief listing will highlight how the two chambers influence each other. Floor leaders in one chamber may try to pass a bill by a large margin in their house in the hopes that this will build momentum for its consideration by the other body. Representatives often will argue in their chamber that certain House amendments should be rejected because they would be likely to provoke a Senate filibuster (extended debate) by opponents there. Senators will at times filibuster measures in order to provide time for their House allies to plan strategy for dealing with the legislation when it arrives in their chamber. One body will sometimes pass a bill in the expectation that the other will kill it. One chamber will even occasionally wait for the other to act first on certain matters. "If the Senate passes" campaign reform legislation, said Speaker Jim Wright (D, Tex.) in mid-1987, then the House "will take it up" but not until and unless the other body acts favorably (Jeremy Gaunt, "Partisan Standoff in Senate Stalls Campaign-Finance Bill," *Congressional Quarterly Weekly Report,* June 20, 1987, p. 1332). In short, the Senate House and Senate may be relatively indifferent toward each other as institutions with distinctive values, procedures, and pivotal personalities. They are, however, necessarily interconnected in terms of legislative interests and sequences of actions.

37. Fenno, *The Power of the Purse,* p. 627. An amusing reflection of this House perception of Senate bills being loaded with expendable provisions occurred at the opening of the 1984 Tax Bill conference. House Ways and Means Chairman Dan Rostenkowski (D, Ill.) read to the conference an April 12 statement "by an important Senator" concerning Senate amendments that had been added to the House-originated tax legislation: "99 percent of these amendments will not survive the conference." Then Rep. Rostenkowski presented a framed poster of these words to their author, Sen. Robert Dole (R, Kan.) as a public reminder that House conferees intended to fulfill his prediction. Senator Dole ruefully accepted this presentation and even attempted to hang the poster on the curtain behind the dais, from which it repeatedly dropped (*Congressional Quarterly Weekly Report,* June 9, 1984, p. 1348, and *New York Times,* June 12, 1984).

38. Manley, *Politics of Finance,* p. 268.

What about in conference? Are these superfluous amendments readily abandoned there by Senate conferees in order to enhance bicameral accommodation? Sometimes they are, but Senate conferees may resist giving up such items—even provisions openly acknowledged as being of particular interest to one senator only. Lamented one House Ways and Means conferee, "All the Senators are interested in is getting their amendments into these tax bills, when we come to conference. They make no bones about it, they're very open. They'll sit down for God's sake and say, 'Now let's see, whose amendment was this? Oh yes, it's _____ and I told him I would support it. We are going to stand firm on that.'"[39]

Such resistance to negotiation—especially on items not central to the chamber-passed bills—rankles the House contingent of subject matter specialists. They want to work out a compromise conference bill, but the senators seem to be more interested in protecting their own and their colleagues' interests than in negotiating on a bill.[40] During lengthy and complex conference meetings on the 1972 Higher Education Act, for example, House members chafed under the insistence by Senate delegation head Claiborne Pell (D, R.I.) that "issues of special interest to individual Senate conferees not be dealt with in their absence. This resulted on several occasions in juggling the agenda to accommodate a Senator, while House Members were only rarely accorded the same privilege."[41] In addition to these irritants arising from seeming differences in purpose, House members also believe (quite accurately in many cases) that "they know much more about the subject than the men who sit on the other side of the conference table."[42] These interchamber perceptions breed resentment that transcends disagreements over

---

39. Quoted in ibid., p. 269. Similarly, Fenno writes, "When brought face to face with Senators, House members are most impressed by the frequency with which Senate conferees defend items in their bill on the grounds that these items represent the identifiable desire of an individual Senator. As House conferees see it, an individualistic style of decision making has produced the Senate bill and continues to dominate the bargaining in conference" (Fenno, *Congressmen in Committees*, p. 146).

40. Charles L. Clapp, *The Congressman: His Work As He Sees It* (Washington, D.C.: Brookings Institution, 1963), p. 285. Fenno also expresses this point: "According to House [Appropriations] Committee perceptions, a guiding principle of the behavior of Senate Appropriations Committee members is their willingness to vote appropriations for their fellow Senators on a personal basis" (Fenno, *The Power of the Purse*, p. 627).

Of course, special interests of members may appear in the House as well as in the Senate, and sometimes even lead to bicameral deals. A late 1986 example concerning higher education legislation will suffice to illustrate this point:

> A last-minute obstacle to agreement arose when Senate negotiators initially refused to accept House provisions for funding projects at colleges in the districts of several House conferees and other key members. The projects were included after conferees agreed to provide an equal sum for projects sought by Senators.
>
> House conferees agreed to the deal, 16-4, despite the objections of Rep. Steve Gunderson, R-Wis., to what he called educational "pork-barrel" [Janet Hook, "Conferees Reach Agreement on Higher Education Measure, *Congressional Quarterly Weekly Report*, Sept. 13, 1986, p. 2124].

41. Gladieux and Wolanin, *Congress and the Colleges*, p. 261.
42. Fenno, *The Power of the Purse*, p. 628.

the substantive issues themselves.[43] Interchamber conflicts, comments one scholar, "are often of greater symbolic than substantive importance."[44]

In summary, conference committees are the essence of bicameralism, and the bicameral nature of Congress is amply reflected in institutional conference conflict. Liberal or conservative policy biases may change over time in light of partisan or ideological surges,[45] but the "inescapable necessity of bicameral cooperation" remains.[46] This inescapable necessity is inherent in the congressional bicameral legislative system: "The framers did not so much create one precipitate chamber and one stabilizing chamber as they did force decision making to move across two separate chambers, however those chambers might be constituted. The strategic maneuverings necessitated by such a process become a subject for empirical investigation."[47] It is these strategic maneuverings of bicameral politics upon which we focus, both in this chapter on the institutional context, and in a larger sense throughout this book.

Institutional Interactions

> The Conference Committee can be seen as an arena in which the two bodies try to attain partly incompatible goals
> —John A. Ferejohn[48]

> Reconciling House-Senate differences over policy is necessarily a ticklish business, if only because each

---

43. Ibid., p. 631. Fenno provides an extensive discussion entitled "Shared and Different Perceptions and Attitudes: House and Senate," ibid., pp. 624–41. Different political balances and resulting opposing policy preferences between the chambers can also have a direct impact on conference interactions. As Bibby and Davidson noted in the late 1960s, "the increasingly liberal complexion of the Senate [in the 1960s] produced strains in interhouse comity since agreement by House-Senate conferees on different versions of bills passed by the two houses became more difficult to achieve" (John Bibby and Roger Davidson, *On Capitol Hill: Studies in the Legislative Process* [New York: Holt, Rinehart and Winston, 1967], p. 155).

44. Paletz, "Influence in Congress," p. 39.

45. Bicameral tensions may exist even within a political party. In 1985, for example, it was reported that an exceptional degree of conflict had developed between House and Senate Republicans, in contrast with four years earlier when Republicans in both chambers worked closely together to support President Reagan's far-reaching 1981 budgetary proposals. In contrast, in 1985, "tension between House and Senate Republicans is one of the strongest underlying currents of the session. 'You can hear it, you can see it, you can smell it,' says Charles Mathias of Maryland. 'It's all around here'" (Shribman and Rogers, "Party Divisions," p. 1). For a consideration of different patterns of partisanship in House and Senate, see David E. Rosenbaum, "Do's and Don'ts of Party Cooperation," *New York Times*, Oct. 27, 1987.

46. Stanley Bach, "Bicameral Conflict and Accommodation in Congressional Procedure," paper presented at the 1981 Annual Meeting of the American Political Science Association, p. 40.

47. Fenno, *The United States Senate*, p. 5.

48. John A. Ferejohn, "Who Wins in Conference Committee?" *The Journal of Politics* 37 (Nov. 1975): 1045.

> chamber, cherishing its autonomy, must accept the coequal status of the other. Each chamber must sacrifice preferred positions or face the prospect of stalemate. The conference committee is a device well-suited to the purpose because it permits free discussion and negotiation in a relatively informal setting, in which positions can be explored, options can be presented, and trade-offs can be proposed without foreclosing other possible compromises until full agreement or deadlock is reached.
>
> —Stanley Bach[49]

When the House and Senate meet, they are faced with the need, if legislation is to be finally enacted into law, to reconcile their differences. This legislative reconciliation, moreover, must occur in the face of institutional pride and defensiveness. "The prestige of each house is regarded as being at issue," remarks one scholar. "It sometimes seems that it is fully as important to many members to demonstrate the power of the House or Senate as to retain or delete features of a bill on which the body has expressed itself."[50]

How to find a balance between institutional and substantive interests is a recurrent backdrop to conference negotiations. Conferees, to be sure, are not always dedicated to the protection of legislation as it passed their chamber. A major amendment added during floor consideration, for example, may be opposed by that body's conferees. Or a majority of the conferees from a chamber may oppose the entire legislative proposal as it passed their body. As one observer notes, "Many members come to a conference committee eager to defend the views represented in the bill passed by the other house or to strike out provisions inserted in their own house."[51]

During the early 1970s, for example, liberal House committees often found themselves agreeing more with legislation passed by the Senate than with the bills eventually adopted by their own chamber. The House Education and Labor Committee often reported out legislation more liberal than what the full House would accept, and closer to the Senate's preferences. After the House had modified the committee proposal, almost always in a conservative direction, the chamber-amended bills would go to conference. The House conferees, appointed from the Committee on Education and Labor, would be dominated by representatives more attuned to the Senate- rather than the House-passed legislation. When the conferees met, these conferences resembled more a gathering of like-minded legislators who shared similar ideas and values than one group of unified chamber antagonists pitted against another. Of course, when conference "compromises" were worked out, the House conferees were often criticized by minority Republican conferees and by members on the floor of the House itself. As one House

---

49. Stanley Bach, "Germaneness Rules and Bicameral Relations in the U.S. Congress," *Legislative Studies Quarterly* 7, no. 3 (Aug. 1982): 354–55.

50. Clapp, *The Congressman*, p. 280.

51. Bertram M. Gross, *The Legislative Struggle: A Study in Social Combat* (New York: McGraw-Hill, 1953), pp. 321–22.

THE INSTITUTIONAL CONTEXT

Republican at the time put it, "Nine times out of ten, they [the Education and Labor conferees] go there committed to sell out the position of the House."[52] What was actually occurring was not so much an intercameral "sell out" as a deliberate decision by the House conference majority to further their policy preferences in conference at the cost of pure institutional representation.[53]

Institutional Conflict

> The conference collapsed on the verge of final agreement, with even the authors of the original bills denouncing the other chamber's conferees and readily exchanging legislative success for loyalty to their chamber.
> —From the account of a conference committee simulation contained in the Preface
>
> [Capitol room] EF-100 remains as a monument to the difficulties of bicameralism.
> —Former Congressman Abner J. Mikva and Patti B. Saris[54]

Many times institutional representation and substantive preferences are not merely choices, but rather are mutually incompatible forces. In these instances, "the process of policy accommodation can become the subject of institutional conflict."[55] Sometimes institutional loyalty may come to dominate conference politics, even at the cost of the proposed legislation. In the Preface we recounted an example of conference committee politics (drawn from a simulation) in which institutional rights and pride became dominant. Even the authors of the legislation and others with a strong interest in passing the bill joined bill opponents in preferring to see the legislation die rather than give in to what was seen, by conferees from each chamber, as unreasonable demands from the other house.

Institutional protectiveness may be intertwined not only with policy preferences, but also with personal status issues. One of the best publicized conference disputes ever was the battle in 1962 between the House and Senate Appropriations Committees. The conflict resulted in conference paralysis for over three months and stymied the activities of many governmental departments awaiting needed appropriations.

The struggle was expressed in institutional terms but to a significant degree had its basis in the fiercely determined stances of the two octogenarian Appropriations chairmen: Representative Clarence Cannon (D, Mo.), eighty-three years old, and Sen-

---

52. *Congressional Record,* March 8, 1972, p. H1844.
53. The preceding material is adapted from Oleszek, "House-Senate Relationships," p. 79. For further discussion of individual conferee choices between such factors as individual preferences and chamber representation, see chapter 6 below.
54. Abner J. Mikva and Patti B. Saris, *The American Congress: The First Branch* (New York: Franklin Watts, 1983), p. 241.
55. Bach, "Bicameral Conflict and Accommodation," p. 79.

ator Carl Hayden (D, Ariz.), eighty-four years old. Neither of these powerful congressmen was accustomed to brooking dissent in his legislative domain, and each chairman was determined in this dispute to fight simultaneously for personal and chamber perogatives.

The institutional issues were several in number, and they were significant. They included: (1) Did the Senate have the Constitutional power to initiate appropriations bills on its own? (2) Could the Senate add funds for proposals not considered by the House to House-passed appropriations bills? (3) Where would appropriations conferences be held, and who should chair them?[56] Traditionally, the House Appropriations Committee had asserted its sole power to originate all general appropriations measures, and, likewise traditionally, senators had chaired appropriations conferences, most of which were held on the Senate side of the Capitol.

In April 1962, House Appropriations Chairman Cannon proposed that meeting sites for appropriations conferences should alternate between the Senate and House wings. Senate Appropriations Chairman Hayden countered by suggesting that the Senate should originate half of all appropriations measures; Hayden finally agreed to hold appropriations conferences temporarily in the old Supreme Court chamber, which lies halfway between the two chambers in the middle of the Capitol. Cannon then demanded that House members (in effect himself) should chair conferences half of the time. Hayden rejected this idea, and no further Appropriations conferences were held for the next three months, from April 10 to July 18. Extensive peacemaking efforts by other members of the two committees eventually worked out a temporary solution. The chairmanship of appropriations conferences would be decided by agreement, or in the likely case that agreement was not reached by a coin flip; the conference would continue to meet in physically neutral territory; and an ad hoc committee would "study" the remaining unresolved issues.[57]

These agreements ended the conference deadlock of 1962, although flashes of the feud reappeared from time to time in the months following. Physical testimony to this dispute appeared when the East Front of the Capitol building was expanded in 1963: a special conference chamber (Capitol Room EF-100) was built straddling the line between the House and Senate wings. EF-100 is the only room in the entire Capitol complex that contains duplicate sets of voting lights and bells—one for the Senate and one for the House.[58] The institutional conflict of the preceding year had led to a physical adaptation of space to the necessities of bicameral cooperation.

56. Adapted from Pressman, *House vs. Senate,* p. 2. This book provides a detailed study of this particular dispute and is the leading source on it. Other useful discussions of the 1962 conflict can be found in "Closed Conferences Often Wield Legislative Power," *Congressional Quarterly Weekly Report,* Dec. 12, 1969, p. 2576; Fenno, *The Power of the Purse,* pp. 635–41; Bach, "Bicameral Conflict and Accommodation," n. 22; Stephen Horn, *Unused Power: The Work of the Senate Committee on Appropriations* (Washington, D.C.: Brookings Institution, 1970), pp. 165–72; and Charles O. Jones, *The United States Congress: People, Place, and Policy,* (Homewood, Ill.: Dorsey Press, 1982), p. 331.

57. "Closed Conferences Often Wield Legislative Power," p. 2576.

58. Mikva and Saris, *American Congress,* p. 241; Robert L. Peabody, Jeffrey M. Berry, William G. Frasure, and Jerry Goldman, *To Enact a Law: Congress and Campaign Financing* (New York: Praeger, 1972), p. 157; and Adam Clymer, "A Congress Spectacular: Energy Bill," *New York Times,* Oct. 18, 1977.

Conclusions

The House and Senate are flexible and adaptable entities that change over time and in their relations with each other. They are, paradoxically, separate yet interlocked institutions. While bicameralism can lead to the defeat or delay of legislation, it can also produce better legislation or prevent unwise policies from becoming law. House-Senate conflict is one of the contexts in which bicameral negotiations play themselves out. The other two contexts of bicameral politics and policymaking are the committee and individual dimensions. We turn to them in the next chapter.

6

The Committee and Individual Contexts

> The conferees are usually old colleagues. The subcommittee chairmen have been bargaining and trying to persuade one another sometimes for a decade or more. While a conference is ad hoc, it is also in a very real sense a continuing institution. In the short run the issues may change; the participants seldom do. If a group of conferees is unsuccessful this year, there is always next year.
>
> —Stephen Horn[1]

It is in the congressional conference committee that the two institutions of House and Senate confront each other. Conference is also where "old colleagues" get together—conferees drawn from matched House and Senate committees who reflect the values and traditions of their home committee, and conferees who also see the conference as an opportunity to advance their individual goals and purposes. In the preceding chapter, we examined the institutional context; here we similarly describe the committee and individual contexts of conference committee politics.

The Committee Context

The basic structural feature of a conference committee is two groups whose individual members have stronger ties

---

1. Stephen Horn, *Unused Power: The Work of the Senate Committee on Appropriations* (Washington, D.C.: Brookings Institution, 1970), p. 155.

to their own committee than to the conference as a whole.

—Richard F. Fenno[2]

When the House and Senate go to conference, the members of each chamber delegation are traditionally drawn almost entirely from a single substantive committee of that house.[3] Conferees reflect the general outlook and internal power relations of their parent committee. Conference committees are not only intercameral mechanisms whose interactions are shaped by chamber institutional characteristics, but also "intercommittee bargaining structures,"[4] whose interactions are influenced by House and Senate committee characteristics. Seventy-five years ago Woodrow Wilson offered the classic observation that "Congress in its committee-rooms is Congress at work."[5] The reciprocal is also true: Congress at work in conference is Congress in its committee rooms. To a significant degree "conference committees must be viewed as an extension of the standing committee system."[6]

---

2. Richard F. Fenno, Jr., *The Power of the Purse: Appropriations Politics in Congress* (Boston: Little, Brown, 1966), p. 642.

3. In chapter 3, we discussed in some detail the recent tendency for Congress to refer legislation to multiple committees and to rely upon omnibus package legislation touching upon multiple topics. In these instances, of course, resulting conferences will *not* be made up of conferees from single House and Senate committees. Rather, conferees will be drawn from a variety of different committees in each chamber which handled the legislation or have policy jurisdiction over matters incorporated into an omnibus bill.

The committee context, as examined in this chapter, primarily pertains to the more normal conference—still the vast majority of instances—when the legislation in conference is topically focused and the conference, as a result, is almost entirely made up of members of matched congressional committees. This traditional conference is still overwhelmingly predominate, although multireferred or omnibus legislation—when it occurs—may deal with highly contentious and far-reaching measures.

In these chapters, we examine the more usual conference committee as it exists in three contexts: institutional, committee, and individual. The occasional, but very important multireferred or omnibus legislative conference essentially operates in two of these contexts—institutional and individual. Because of the diversity of committees from which conferees are drawn in the case of multireferred or omnibus legislation, the distinctive and homogeneous *committee* outlook of chamber conferees, as described in this chapter, may be largely absent (except perhaps at the subconference level). Rather, chamber conferees will bring to their conference duties varying committee values and traditions. The result is that conferences on multireferred or omnibus legislation are more likely to be marked by significant *intra*delegation conflict in contrast with *inter*delegation conflict more typical of the traditional conference. Tensions and disputes within the chamber delegation, in the case of these conferences, are heightened by the lack of common committee context. In the case of the traditional conference, chamber delegation members tend to be united by their common committee experience, and conference conflict is more likely to be bicameral than intrachamber in character.

4. David J. Vogler, "Patterns of One-House Dominance in Congressional Conference Committees," *Midwest Journal of Political Science* 14 (May 1970): 310–11. See also David J. Vogler, *The Third House: Conference Committees in the United States Congress* (Evanston: Northwestern University Press, 1971), p. 64.

5. Woodrow Wilson, *Congressional Government* (Boston: Houghton Mifflin, 1912), p. 79.

6. Bertram M. Gross, *The Legislative Struggle: A Study in Social Combat* (New York: McGraw-Hill, 1953), p. 317. A recent study of the institutional foundations of the power of standing committees concludes that a central element of the legislative influence of committees lies precisely in their con-

Not only are conferees who represent a chamber usually drawn from a particular committee, but in instance after instance they face representatives from the other chamber who are drawn from a matching standing committee. Conferees from Senate Armed Services repeatedly interact with members from the House Armed Services Committee; House Ways and Means members will deal time after time with senators drawn from Senate Finance; Senate Agriculture and House Agriculture Committee members will inevitably compose conferences on farm bills. (An argument sometimes heard from Senate floor managers is, "Don't offer that nongermane amendment to this bill because its adoption will encourage the other body to name conferees from other standing committees and complicate conference negotiations.") A basic parallelism exists in the structure of House and Senate standing committees, not from some grand design but from the fact that they have similar substantive pressures and constituency interests.[7] This committee parallelism (which, of course, is not perfect) means that conference committees are most often made up of conferees with a substantial experience of interactions with the counterpart committee and with many of the same individuals from that committee. These long-term "intercommittee relationships" between matched House

---

ference roles (see also discussion in chapter 4, note 45, above). This substantive power may be exercised in conference itself, but it also has an anticipated impact upon committees within their own chambers; "the deference given committees on the floor," for example, "is a natural consequence of the ex post adjustment powers wielded by committees in conference." In short, because conference habitually accords committee key members a second "bite of the apple," such opportunities for "ex post enforcement confer power on committees" (Kenneth A. Shepsle and Barry R. Weingast, "The Institutional Foundations of Committee Power," *American Political Science Review* 81, no. 1 [March 1987]: 85–104; quoted passages from pp. 86, 102).

The Shepsle-Weingast thesis, however, has been soundly criticized by one scholar as overstating the degree to which a congressional committee possesses such an ex-post veto free of constraints from its parent chamber. See Keith Krehbiel, "Why Are Congressional Committees Powerful?" *American Political Science Review* 81, no. 3 (Sept. 1987): 929–35. (Shepsle and Weingast restate and defend their original thesis in a rejoinder in the same journal issue, at 935–45.) Similarly, another scholar concluded his examination of the ex-post veto by finding that although it is "an important source of leverage for committees," it is not a determinant basis of committee power; rather, "there are many bases of [committee] power in Congress" (Steven S. Smith, "An Essay on Sequence, Position, Goals, and Committee Power," *Legislative Studies Quarterly* 13 no. 2 [May 1988]: 151, 175).

The analysis of Shepsle and Weingast is extended and applied to House procedures for conferee selection in Jonathan Nagler, "Strategic Implications of Conferee Selection in the House of Representatives: 'It Ain't Over Till It's Over,' " paper prepared for delivery at the 1987 Annual Meeting of the Southern Political Science Association, Charlotte, North Carolina; and Jonathan Nagler, "Conferee Selection for Appropriations Legislation: 1973–1980," paper prepared for delivery at the 1988 Annual Meeting of the American Political Science Association, Washington, D.C., Sept. 1–4, 1988.

7. Stanley Bach, "Germaneness Rules and Bicameral Relations in the U.S. Congress," *Legislative Studies Quarterly* 7, no. 3 (Aug. 1982): 354. See also Walter J. Oleszek, "House-Senate Relationships: Comity and Conflict," *Annals of the American Academy of Political and Social Science* 411 (Jan. 1974): 75–86. Hinckley finds this committee parallelism the basis of "strong House-Senate intercorrelations of committees dealing with the same subject matter" (Barbara Hinckley, "Policy Content, Committee Membership, and Behavior," *American Journal of Political Science* 19 [August 1975]: 543). In effect, bicameral committee parallelism not only is the *result* of similar policy concerns, it also itself *creates* comparable political environments within counterpart committees.

and Senate committees is a central feature of conference committee interactions.[8]

The House and Senate practice of usually appointing the most senior members of the standing committee as conferees further strengthens this legacy of intercommittee experience. The typical conference will be made up largely of senior members of one specialist committee meeting once again old combatants from the corresponding committee of the other chamber.[9] This recurrent pattern has distinct consequences in terms of conference committee interaction—the conferees know what to expect from the other delegation. As Paletz puts it, "[In] conferences in which many of the same individuals meet year after year on the same specific topic . . . attitudes, objectives, and sensibilities are likely to become common knowledge and therefore predictable prior to conference."[10] The stability of personnel and position is a source of continuity and stability in conference committee interactions; it allows conferees to "establish procedural routines, adjust to one another's personal idiosyncrasies, anticipate one another's desires, become friendly enemies, and, in general, develop an important degree of institutional stability."[11] In short, the recurrent meeting of many of the same individuals in conference after conference not only provides a degree of predictability of behavior, but also facilitates the development of stable interpersonal relationships, which furthers the process of bicameral reconciliation.

---

8. The significance of "intercommittee relationships" is stressed in the context of recent multiple referral developments in the House, in Roger H. Davidson, Walter J. Oleszek, and Thomas Kephart, "One Bill, Many Committees: Multiple Referrals in the U.S. House of Representatives," *Legislative Studies Quarterly* 13, no. 1 (Feb. 1988): 3–28, esp. p. 4. Such intercommittee relationships, we stress, are equally important in bicameral politics.

9. The exposure of representatives and senators to conferences, however, varies between the two bodies. Senior members of committees in both houses will usually have extensive conference experience, but overall the members of the two chambers differ dramatically in the extent of their conference participation. David Paletz found that, on the average, in a two-year Congress "approximately fifty percent of House members participated in no conference," while, in the case of the Senate, "more than fifty percent of the members of the Senate participated in six or more conferences each [year's] session" (David Paletz, "Influence in Congress: An Analysis of the Nature and Effects of Conference Committees" [Ph.D. diss., University of California at Los Angeles, 1970], pp. 51–52, 69).

The result of the relatively limited House opportunities for conference participation, Fenno notes, is that "for most House committee members, their one conference each year is a matter of paramount concern." Fenno, *The Power of the Purse*, p. 631. The weakening of the powers of seniority in recent decades in both House and Senate has some effect on the depth of intercameral experience. Junior congressmen who are issue specialists or authors of major amendments now often join senior committee members as conferees; they will, however, lack the depth of conference committee experience of longtime committee members. Further, in a more general sense, both Senate and House are becoming more junior as, in recent years, the average length of legislative service has declined. This means that committee members, even comparatively senior ones, may not have the same extent of interchamber and intercommittee bargaining experience as their counterparts decades ago. For a detailed discussion of the practices used in appointing conferees, see chapter 8 below; for a discussion of various aspects of the changing character of Congress and the impact of these changes on conference committee politics, see chapter 3.

10. Paletz, "Influence in Congress," p. 425.

11. Fenno, *The Power of the Purse*, p. 643.

Committee Interactions

> The conference is the place of interaction between the two committees and the point at which conflict becomes apparent.
> —Jeffrey L. Pressman[12]

> Conference committee members are called upon to play different roles in settling interchamber disputes than they are in dealing with legislation in their respective standing committee bailiwicks.
> —David J. Vogler[13]

When a conference meets, the conferees are typically drawn from two very different committee worlds—that of the Senate and that of the House committee. It is important to recognize that, as Richard Fenno put it in his classic study *Congressmen in Committees,* "Senate committees, as a class, differ from House committees as a class." These fundamental differences have their root in the differing roles that congressional committees play in each chamber: "Senate committees are less important as a source of chamber influence, less preoccupied with success on the chamber floor, less autonomous within the chamber, less personally expert, less strongly led, and more individualistic in decision making than are House committees."[14]

Conferees reflect in their behavior both institutional differences (as discussed in the preceding chapter) and committee contrasts. In short, conflict in the conference process has as its basis not only "a power struggle between the two houses of Congress, . . . [but also] patterns of socialization in each committee which lead to group ideologies hostile to the opposite committee [and] differences in constituency, committee structure, procedure, and method of subcommittee assignment."[15]

In some committees, values of intracommittee harmony and helpfulness are stressed, in others the prevailing ethos is one of deference to senior members, and in yet others, the standard is one of securing specific benefits for one's constituents. These different norms and attitudes carry over to conference. Conferees reflect the values of their parent committee as they attempt to work out bicameral accommodations. In the case of the Appropriations Committees of the early 1960s, for example, Pressman argues that "we can see the conference as the place of bargaining between the House committee, representing the interests of thrift and economy in society, and the Senate commit-

---

12. Jeffrey L. Pressman, *House vs. Senate* (New Haven: Yale University Press, 1966), p. 54.
13. David J. Vogler, *The Politics of Congress*, 3d ed. (Boston: Allyn and Bacon, 1980), p. 240.
14. Richard F. Fenno, Jr., *Congressmen in Committees* (Boston: Little, Brown, 1973), pp. 190–91.
15. Pressman, *House vs. Senate,* p. 90. Allen Schick has suggested that in the process of bicameral accommodation, "Congressional committees usually are brought together by their similarities rather than by their differences. To achieve these common objectives, they must overcome differences in the legislation emanating from the House and Senate. With common program interests, they are predisposed toward reconciliation of the matters on which they disagree" (Allen Schick, *Congress and Money: Budgeting, Spending, and Taxing* [Washington, D.C.: Urban Institute, 1980], p. 299).

tee, representing the various governmental agencies and their constituents."[16] Conference committee politics are shaped not only by substantive policy disputes but also by committee purposive differences.

These committee distinctions are further sharpened by intercommittee perceptions—"the images that members of each house have of themselves and each other."[17] Pressman notes that, in the case of Appropriations, "the 'images' of the House and Senate Appropriations Committees, the shared ideologies of each committee, are in conflict with each other."[18] Similarly, Manley, in his study of the tax-writing panels, stresses the importance of "how the members of the House Ways and Means Committee perceive the 'other body.'"[19] He finds that Ways and Means members see themselves as responsible legislators, while they perceive their Senate Finance counterparts as prone to engage irresponsibly in logrolling.[20]

House-Senate images may provide some source of stability in conference relations by providing clear conceptions of counterparts[21]—but conflicting substantive images can also be the basis of resentment and conflict. House Appropriations Committee members "complain that they often have to trudge back to the House two or three times to answer roll calls during a conference. They say they go over in a body to work, while Senators flit in and out. . . . The House Appropriations Committee feels that it does all the hard work listening to witnesses for months on each bill, only to have the Senate committee sit as a court of appeals and, with little more than a cursory glance, restore most of the funds cut."[22] One House Appropriations veteran rather bitterly remarked,

> Someone on the other side will say, "Senator so-and-so wants this project," or, "Senator so-and-so is interested in this item." That Senator isn't even on the Committee and hasn't attended the hearings, but he wants something and the rest look out for him. He isn't even in the conference room, but he's in there just the same. It's a club and they are trying to help him out. Maybe he just spoke to the Chairman or the clerk and said, "I want this in," and they'll fight for him in conference.[23]

---

16. Pressman, *House vs. Senate*, p. 78. The House-Senate Appropriation Committees purposive relationships have obviously changed since the early 1960s. For a discussion of some of these changes, see, in the preceding chapter, note 35.

17. Charles O. Jones, *The United States Congress: People, Place, and Policy* (Homewood, Ill.: Dorsey Press, 1982), p. 33.

18. Pressman, *House vs. Senate*, p. 85. See Fenno, *Congressmen in Committees*, p. 241, for further discussion of intercommittee perceptions.

19. John Manley, *The Politics of Finance: The House Committee on Ways and Means* (Boston: Little, Brown, 1970), p. 249.

20. Ibid., p. 250. Manley provides extensive material on Ways and Means perceptions of the Senate and the Senate Finance Committee in his chapter 6, "The Committee and the Senate."

21. Fenno, *The Power of the Purse*, p. 635.

22. *Washington Post*, April 24, 1962, p. 1. Quoted in Richard F. Fenno, Jr., "The House Appropriations Committee as a Political System: The Problem of Integration," *American Political Science Review* 56 (1962): 310–24.

23. Quoted in Fenno, *Congressmen in Committees*, p. 146.

Senate committee members, on the other hand, also have conceptions of the recurrent tendencies of the House Appropriations Committee. One senator, for example, explained that "on appropriations you always appropriate above the House figure in the knowledge that [in conference] you are going to cut it in half."[24] Senator Mark Hatfield (R, Ore.), upon becoming chairman of the Senate Appropriations Committee following the 1980 election, expressed his concern that during conference, the Senate generally "gets taken to the cleaners." He suggested that there should be more preconference caucus meetings of Senate Appropriations members, paralleling those traditionally held by House committee members, to work out chamber positions. "I think we have to have a little more strategy when we go into conference—this is something that has not been given attention in the past."[25] Such strategic sensitivity, presumably, would help keep the Senate committee from being "taken to the cleaners" by House conferees prone to carefully preparing their conference positions and plans.

Committee Contrasts

> Each committee's internal decision-making processes are shaped by its members' goals, by the constraints placed upon the members by interested outside groups, and by the strategic premises that members adopt in order to accommodate their personal goals to environmental constraints.
>
> —Richard F. Fenno[26]

Congressmen in conference are Congressmen from committees. The political environments of parent committees shape the behavior of conferees. In the preceding section, we outlined some of the norms and attitudes present in committees and suggested that these distinctions may be magnified by sharply held intercommittee perceptions. Now we return to the theme of committee contrasts and suggest some ways that parent committee differences may shape conference committee politics.

Congressional committees differ one from another, not just in subject matter jurisdiction, but in more fundamental political terms. Some congressional committees exhibit a high degree of internal cohesion—they are "integrated" in the sense that "the parts of a committee (that is, the individuals and, to a lesser extent, the subcommittees) mesh as the committee operates from day to day."[27] A list of well-integrated committees usually includes the House Appropriations Committee[28] and the House Ways and Means

---

24. Quoted in Randall B. Ripley, *Power in the Senate* (New York: St. Martin's Press, 1969), p. 128.

25. Quoted in *Congressional Quarterly Weekly Report*, Nov. 8, 1980, p. 3307.

26. Fenno, *Congressmen in Committees*, p. 137.

27. Randall B. Ripley, *Congress: Process and Policy*, 4d ed. (New York: Norton, 1988), p. 166.

28. Pressman suggests that "consensus, careful recruitment, the nature of the work, and committee attractiveness help to explain the integration of the [House Appropriations] Committee" (Pressman, *House vs. Senate*, p. 36).

Committee (until 1975), while the House Committee on Education and Labor is often cited as an example of a committee that lacks internal integration.[29]

What is the significance of the extent of parent committee integration when conferees from a committee go to conference? Are members from well-integrated committees, for example, more successful in defending committee preferences in conference? The evidence on this question is, unfortunately, rather spotty and inconclusive. Committee unity has been found to be related to committee success concerning floor amendments *within* the chamber,[30] but no studies explicitly relate committee integration to conference success. If we assume some correlation, however, between chamber prestige and committee integration (on the grounds that a high status committee will probably tend also to be a well-integrated committee and vice versa), then some findings can be identified. In chapter 4, we discussed evidence showing that less prestigious chamber committees tend to be more successful in conference since such committees, because of their lack of stature and political independence, "draw more directly and more completely upon the support of their parent chamber."[31] According to this argument, when conferees from well-integrated committees meet conferees from less integrated committees *that have well-established links to their parent chamber,* the latter will tend to prevail.[32]

Of course, it is conceivable that in some instances weakly integrated committees might not enjoy particularly strong chamber support: perhaps the committee jurisdiction is thought to be minor and uninteresting or the committee is widely viewed in the chamber as being irresponsible or lacking leadership. In this case, there is no reason to assume that conferees from that committee would do especially well in conference.

Another situation is that in which both sets of conferees come from relatively unified parent committees that substantially agree on the committees' goals. In another scenario—as in conferences between the House Education and Labor and the Senate Labor and Human Resources committees—there may be significant disagreement within each committee and within each conference delegation as to the committee's purpose. In these two cases, the degree of committee integration will have its effect not in one set of conferees having an advantage over the other but in the degree of intradelegational harmony or conflict.

When both parent committees are well integrated, and especially when each committee is committed to the enactment of legislation, conference bargaining may reflect a mutual assumption that although each chamber will fight for its bill's provisions, compromise is better than having no bill at all.[33] On the other hand, when both parent

---

29. Ripley, *Congress,* pp. 166–69.
30. For example, Richard Fleisher and Jon R. Bond, "Beyond Committee Control: Committee and Party Leader Influence on Floor Amendments in Congress," *American Politics Quarterly* 11, no. 2 (April 1983): 131–61.
31. Fenno, *The Power of the Purse,* pp. 668–69.
32. See also Vogler, *The Third House,* p. 73. Vogler concludes, "The findings here suggest rejection of the general hypothesis that high committee prestige is positively related to success of that committee's representatives in conference."
33. Fenno, *The Power of the Purse,* p. 617.

committees are fragmented in outlook, bargaining in conference may be difficult and uncertain. Perhaps a conference coalition cutting across chamber lines will be forged in favor of a particular approach or compromise, but generally fragmented delegations are more likely to lead to conference deadlock and legislative failure. As Senate Majority Leader Robert Dole (R, Kan.) observed in mid-1986, "It is difficult enough to bridge the gap between House and Senate—without differences among House Members."[34] Differences in *both* House and Senate conference delegations, of course, make the task of bridge building even more formidable. Interdelegation conflict can even overshadow interchamber differences and preempt efforts to achieve conference agreement. "There was not much traditional us-vs.-them. There were lots of us-es and lots of thems," noted one House member in describing the bitter disputes within the House and Senate conference delegations in 1986 on superfund legislation.[35] When chamber delegations are deeply divided, achieving bicameral accommodation is immensely more difficult.

Besides subject matter and integration differences, congressional committees also differ in internal values. Some committees are dominated by a desire to make good policy, others by an interest in committee work as it influences power relations within the chamber, and others by divisible benefits that are available for committee members to confer upon their constituents and favored interests.[36] Often, like-minded committees meet in conference; at times, however, conferees from a good policy committee find themselves in conference with conferees drawn from a committee whose prevalent value is the distribution of benefits. In this instance, *conference* integration would be very low, and conferees might find it exceedingly difficult to find points of agreement—or even to talk the same political language.

Committees themselves can change in terms of dominant values. John Ferejohn suggests that such a transformation occurred in the middle 1950s in the Subcommittee for Public Works of the House Appropriations Committee. Prior to that time, the prevailing subcommittee value was that of "defender of the economy." In conference, this value clashed severely with the Senate committee's interest in mutual satisfaction of individual senatorial wishes. After 1955, however, the subcommittee gradually took on a "constituency service" orientation. The result was a facilitating of conference bargaining, as "logrolling became the primary mode of decision-making in the conferences."[37]

Finally, let us consider certainly the most noted and broadest analysis of differences between congressional committees. Richard F. Fenno, in *Congressmen in Committees*,

---

34. *Congressional Record,* May 12, 1986, p. S5745.

35. Janet Hook, "In Conference: New Hurdles, Hard Bargaining," *Congressional Quarterly Weekly Report,* Sept. 7, 1986, p. 2081.

36. This is an adaptation of a typology proposed by Fenno to explain member goals in committees. For a fuller discussion of these motivations, see Fenno, *Congressmen in Committees.* A valuable assessment of changes in congressional committees in the "post-Fenno period" (since the early 1970s) is provided in Roger H. Davidson, "Congressional Committees as Moving Targets," *Legislative Studies Quarterly* 11, no. 1 (Feb. 1986): 19–33.

37. John A. Ferejohn, *Pork Barrel Politics: Rivers and Harbors Legislation* (Stanford: Stanford University Press, 1974), p. 125.

suggests that differences between committees are systematic and can be defined in terms of five major variables: member goals, environmental constraints, strategic premises, decision-making processes, and decisions made.[38] Basing his conclusions on a close study of six House committees—Appropriations, Ways and Means, Foreign Affairs, Education and Labor, Post Office and Civil Service, and Interior and Insular Affairs—Fenno argues that these variables constitute a framework for analysis and comparison of congressional committees.

Likewise, these five variables can be used to analyze conference committees. Let us briefly sketch such an analysis, using Fenno's five variables:

1. *Member Goals*—Conference participants seek to implement the goals that led them originally to seek membership on their parent committee. Among these are making good policy, pursuing influence in the chamber, and enhancing reelection prospects by constituency service. In conference, additional goals may be present, such as protecting chamber interests, defending the handiwork of the committee, proving loyalty to the committee chairman, and protecting a particular interest or cause. (These individual member goals will be discussed in detail in the next section of this chapter.)

2. *Environmental Constraints*—Conference committees are influenced by such factors as the parent chamber's expectations and the manner and degree to which these expectations are expressed. Other environmental constraints are key clientele group or presidential wishes and priorities and the compatibility of these demands with chamber expectations.

3. *Strategic Premises*—The immediate result of member goals and environmental constraints is a set of strategic premises (or decision rules, as Fenno alternatively terms them) unique to each conference situation. Among the recurrently evident strategic premises of conference are the following: compromise quantitative controversies by splitting the difference, negotiate qualitative disagreements through sequential bargaining ("We'll recede on provision A if you give us provision B"), and craft compromises in light of what can pass both houses.

4. *Decision-Making Processes*—The goals of members and the political environment of the conference determine the strategic premises of conference interactions, and these three factors together determine the process of decision making. In some conferences partisanship is muted, in others it is highly articulated. In some instances, chamber loyalty will be a strongly stressed value, whereas in other cases the prevailing focus will be on working out legislative differences.

   Conference differences arising from the first three variables influence the processes of decision making that are utilized, such as whether chamber representatives put forth preemptory demands and positions or whether conferees deal with legislative disagreements from the point of view of adjusting differences so each chamber's goals and major interests are reasonably satisfied.

5. *Decisions Made*—The legislative output is a dependent variable also deter-

---

38. Fenno, *Congressmen in Committees*, p. xi.

mined by the first three independent variables. What sort of compromises are reached, or if any agreement at all is possible, will be determined by these previously discussed factors. In some cases, the decisions made may reflect bicameral compromise; in other instances success by one chamber or set of interests will be at the cost of others, and occasionally the decision reached will be to have no bill come out of conference at all.

Fenno's typology for contrasting congressional committees has been used to suggest some of the ways that conference committees may differ from each other. Much as parent congressional committees from which conferees are drawn differ, so conference committees are different one from another. In this discussion, we have emphasized the differences among congressional committees, and how conferences, made up of members selected generally from matched pairs of standing committees, reflect these differences. Next, we will consider the individual context within which conference committee interactions occur.

The Individual Context

> It is my impression that conferences always start out with all Senators of both parties supporting the Senate's position. But, if the conference drags on, the individual attitudes of the various members begin to show.
> —A senior member of the U.S. Senate[39]

> Conference committees are the ultimate high for legislators. They are the Supreme Court of legislation. If you don't get it here, there's no other place to go.
> —Representative Dennis E. Eckhart (D, Oh.)[40]

Conference committees are collections of individuals who bring to their participation in conference diverse personal goals and loyalties. This dimension of conference interactions is our third and final context of conference committee politics—one that now focuses on the individual conferee.

Individual interests are writ especially large in conference committee politics. A congressman is only one of 100 or 435 individuals in his chamber, and only one of perhaps 20 or 30 members in his parent committee. In conference, however, he is usually one of only 20 or so conferees and one of perhaps 10 or 12 representatives of his own chamber. (The typical size of conferences as well as of House and Senate delegations is examined by means of new data especially prepared for this volume in an appendix to this chapter.)

The conference committee is where the individual congressman can wield the greatest influence over legislation. One House member underscored the importance of the solitary conferee, arguing, "There is more opportunity for an individual to dominate a conference committee than a standing committee. It is important to note that fewer

---

39. Quoted in Ripley, *Power in the Senate,* p. 128.
40. Quoted in Hook, "In Conference," p. 2080.

people are involved in giving consent there than in any other step in the legislative process. A powerful person who knows the bill and what he is trying to accomplish can dominate in that situation."[41]

The individual conferee is especially important on the Senate side of conference committee delegations because Senate conferees have many other committee duties and demands on their time. As a result, Senate negotiations will often be left to one or two senators who have particular knowledge of or interest in the legislation. In one remarkable instance during 1986 conference deliberations on higher education legislation, Senator Robert T. Stafford (R, Vt.) found himself acting as the sole representative of the Senate. After hearing a House compromise proposal, he responded, "I'm caucusing with myself. Can you give me a couple of minutes to complete the arguments?"[42]

Another congressman emphasized the opportunity that conferences committees provide conferees—and especially chairmen--to pursue their own preferences:

> I think it depends on the chairman of our conferees. Take _____ committee matters. The House generally goes beyond the views of the committee chairman in passing bills relating to the committee's work. Yet he acts as chairman of our conferees when these matters go to conference. Since he is not favorable to the action of the House, he doesn't defend it very long, and you usually get a different result in conference.[43]

Conferences provide opportunities for the advancement of the interests of any of the conferees, but the leaders of committees are particularly well situated to benefit from conference interactions. "The committee chairmen are frequently the major beneficiaries" of conference, observes one scholar. Through their dominance of who is going to be a conferee, chairmen "can generally ensure that a majority of their chamber's conferees are sympathetic to their legislative and political objectives."[44]

The conference committee, then, is not just a mechanism for reconciling bicameral legislative differences. It is also a means by which individuals—especially committee leaders—can pursue their personal goals and interests and enhance their legislative power. The conference committee is an arena of politics; it is also a means to personal power.

Conferee Goals

> Each member of each committee wants his committee service to bring him some benefit in terms of goals he holds as an individual Congressman.
> —Richard F. Fenno[45]

---

41. Quoted in Charles L. Clapp, *The Congressman: His Work As He Sees It* (Washington, D.C.: Brookings Institution, 1963), p. 279.
42. Hook, "In Conference," p. 2081.
43. Quoted in Clapp, *The Congressman*, p. 278.
44. David L. Paletz, "Comments on Vogler's Article Concerning Congressional Seniority," *Polity* III (Spring 1971): 457.
45. Fenno, *Congressmen in Committees*, p. 1.

Conferees approach their responsibilities as members of a conference committee in terms of various alternative and overlapping roles. Some congressmen see themselves essentially as legislative craftsmen who attempt to bridge interchamber differences with carefully worded compromises.[46] Others view themselves more as political facilitators who concern themselves with creating and maintaining a productive conference process that will enhance political bargaining and issue adjustment.[47] Alternatively, some conferees see their role as obstructionists opposed to conference agreement. Still others operate as neutral issue specialists, partisan or ideological advocates, or manipulators of the conference for personal ends. In short, individuals bring to their positions as conferees a wide variety of potential roles that shape their behavior as conferees. How may this smorgasbord of alternative roles be sorted out?

We suggest that the variety of conferee roles may be grouped into two broad categories: Those based on a desire to influence legislation and those designed to gain power and influence for the conferee within chamber and committee.[48] These two groupings of purpose, and their mix in specific instances, broadly determine individual conferee behavior in conference.

The first of these goals, the influencing of legislation, is easy to understand. Some members strongly favor the bill as it passed their chamber; they may have even been its author or its floor manager during chamber adoption. Their political future may be heavily dependent upn the success of conference committee deliberations. In contrast, some conferees have goals that likewise focus on the fate of the legislation, but in this case they desire its defeat. Like the bill's supporters, these obstructionists believe that

---

46. Lawrence Gladieux and Thomas Wolanin, *Congress and the Colleges: The National Politics of Higher Education* (Lexington, Mass.: D. C. Heath, 1976), p. 200. Gladieux and Wolanin describe this role in their case study of the Higher Education Act of 1972 as follows:

> The legislative craftsmen were in the thick of the debate on the issue, arguing and exploring alternatives. Words of legislative art to take care of potential problems are their stock in trade. These conferees had the ability to read the original language of the two bills, read the language of a proposed compromise, listen to the compromise being explained by its sponsor, assimilate whispered comments from the staff man at their elbow, lean over and converse with a colleague, draft their own compromise language, and be prepared to present and defend their alternative, all practically simultaneously. This role involves the political skill of formulating, packaging, negotiating, and compromising on the issues [ibid.].

47. Ibid. Gladieux and Wolanin describe the political facilitators as being "less concerned with substantive content." Rather, "they were more interested in structuring the process so the legislative craftsmen could operate effectively. Opening lines of communication, getting the right people together, avoiding unproductive personality clashes and fruitless deadlocks, timing the pace of activities and, in general, greasing the wheels were their speciality." An alternative typology of conferee roles has been provided by David L. Paletz, including the *energizer,* "who prods the group to action," the *initiator-contributor,* "who proposes new ideas or . . . problem solutions," the *information giver,* "who provides data relevant to problem solving," and the *harmonizer,* "who mediates . . . disagreements" (Paletz, "Influence in Congress," p. 416).

48. This distinction between the conferee goals of power over legislation and power inside Congress was originally suggested by Richard Fenno in a conversation with the authors (Washington discussion, November 2, 1981). Fenno stressed the need to consider what each member of a conference committee wishes to get from the conference, in effect to "look over the shoulder of the member."

their political power and status will be measured by their ability to use the conference to achieve their legislative objectives. Interestingly, we find here a partial linking of legislative and power goals, for while these legislators are devoted to the substantive ends of legislative passage or defeat, these goals—whether achieved or stymied—will also have a major effect on their political standing in chamber and committee.

Legislative goals may take another form. Besides showing general support for or opposition to the legislation, a conferee is sometimes intensely interested in securing approval of some provision that is of special interest to him or his district. Two examples, both from 1979, illustrate this type of legislative goal. In the course of conference consideration of the Endangered Species Act of 1979, Representative (now Senator) John B. Breaux of Louisiana expressed great concern that the act as drafted might make difficult the export of alligators, an issue of concern in Louisiana. At his repeated urging, the draft language authorizing an Endangered Species Scientific Authority was modified to ensure that alligator exports would not be banned. The same year, a conference dealing with the Department of Education heard pleas from one conferee, Representative Don Fuqua (D, Fla.), concerning a junior college in his congressional district. This school also administered the affairs of a college in the Panama Canal Zone, an administrative arrangement that might have been threatened by language in the proposed act. The conference responded to the congressman's concern and added a provision to the conference report to ensure that the junior college would be able to continue this relationship.[49] In these two instances, substantive goals were linked to personal concerns. Each congressman was fighting for a specific legislative cause, but he was doing so out of a wish to serve an interest of his constituency—and also to enhance his reelection prospects.

Legislative goals are not motivated solely by extralegislative considerations. Often a conferee will fight for or against some specific legislative provision or work in support of or opposition to an overall bill simply because he thinks it represents good or bad policy. In other instances, conferees' legislative and political goals are intertwined.

Let us now turn our focus to the second category of goals—the use of conference by the individual conferee to enhance his influence within the legislative process.[50] A conferee's personal power status can be boosted by conference events in several ways. A member's behavior and activity in conference may bring praise—or scorn—from fellow conferees and may foster an image of him as a skilled parliamentarian—or as a dogmatic ideologue. The ability to secure specific conference concessions for constituents or other interests (as illustrated above) may further the conferee's reputation and political standing. Finally, the overall success or failure of conference negotiations on important

---

49. These examples are drawn from an unpublished paper by a Lawrence University undergraduate based on fieldwork and conference committee observations in Washington, D.C.: John R. Stoner, "The Congressional Conference Committee as a Center in Determining Legislative Outcomes," esp. pp. 23–24. They are more fully described in the two case studies in chapter 11 called "Two 'Hello and Good-Bye' Conferences of 1979."

50. Gross, *Legislative Struggle,* p. 319. See also Paletz, "Influence in Congress," for a general discussion of this theme.

legislation may make or impair the political reputations of prominent conferees closely linked to the fate of those bills.[51]

When conferees go to conference, they may be concerned with making good legislation. Wrapped up with that goal, however, is often another important component: enhancing one's political status. These two goals are often intertwined and mutually supportive but can also be separately identified. In short, individual conferees act during conference for purposes transcending purely legislative ends.

Conferee Loyalties

> "I think you go over there with the idea you are representing the House view and not necessarily your own."
>
> "That may be, but you don't have to stand there and die fighting for a position you really don't believe in."
>
> —Discussion between two representatives[52]

Another aspect of individual conferee behavior has to do with loyalties. Formally, individual conferees are expected to defend the legislation as it passed their chamber. Even though conferees may have the best of intentions, however, that standard is not always easy to uphold. Measures become the repository of a variety of interests in each house as they head toward conference.[53] Sometimes, amendments are agreed to by voice vote or after minimal chamber consideration. Plainly, the breadth or depth of the chamber's interest in such proposals is unclear. Some amendments may even run counter to the spirit or purpose of other provisions of the legislation. The bill, too, may have been enacted by a coalition of unlikely groups. Conferees, indeed, confront great uncertainties in trying to determine chamber interests and wishes from such a tangled legislative history.

Chamber representatives may also face issues not considered in any fashion by either house. One chamber may have taken a policy direction quite different from the other, forcing conferees to consider the relative merits of apples and oranges. On one

---

51. Along this line, Clapp notes that "House-Senate conference committee negotiations are often regarded as contests, as tests of the skills of the principal negotiators of each body" (Clapp, *The Congressman*, p. 280).

For a contemporary account of the personal power stakes of Senate Finance Committee Chairman Robert Packwood (R, Ore.) and House Ways and Means Committee Chairman Dan Rostenkowski (D, Ill.) in the successful conclusion of the 1986 tax reform conference, see Jeffrey H. Birnbaum and Alan S. Murray, *Showdown at Gucci Gulch: Lawmakers, Lobbyists, and the Unlikely Triumph of Tax Reform* (New York: Random House, 1987), esp. chap. 11.

52. Quoted in Clapp, *The Congressman*, p. 278.

53. Palétz, "Influence in Congress," pp. 25–26. Palétz extends this line of argument and concludes that "with rare exceptions, then, it is difficult to define a bill that passes a chamber and enters conference as representing the will of that chamber" (Ibid., p. 26). Whether chamber intent is determinable or not, what is important, of course, is that the bill or amendment *did* pass the chamber.

occasion the Senate completely rewrote a House-passed bill concerning emergency price controls and adopted a version incorporating entirely new ideas. The conferees faced a difficult task of reconciling the vastly different fruits of the two chambers' labors. After intense negotiations, they emerged with a conference compromise bill innovatingly combining elements of both chambers' bills. The conference negotiations, however, were then roundly criticized in both houses for abandoning chamber preferences and adopting provisions not considered by their chamber. One representative, for example, said, "The House conferees in all honor and honesty, and I am sure that they are honorable men, will have to admit that they do not know what the House thinks about the issues involved, and they are simply expressing their own personal opinions."[54]

Besides this primary loyalty to chamber preferences—as far as they can be ascertained—the individual conferee has a variety of other loyalties from which to choose. These include loyalty to his committee chairman or to the parent committee as a whole, loyalty to factional, constituency, party, interest group or administration wishes, or loyalty simply and directly to personal preferences. These alternatives are not necessarily mutually exclusive. A conferee may find that favoring the wishes of his committee chairman is compatible with supporting the view of a political interest that he personally favors, or that in fighting for his personal legislative preferences he is likewise reflecting the majority viewpoint of his parent congressional committee or chamber.

What is noteworthy, however, is that conferees may find themselves selecting one of these loyalties at the cost of upholding their chamber's views. Let us consider some simple examples. If one chamber has adopted a bill providing for a $100-million authorization for a particular program while the other body approved a $200-million amount, we might naturally assume that conference bargaining on this issue would occur near the middle point between $100 and $200 million. The conferees from the first chamber would push for as low a figure as possible, while the conferees from the other would favor a higher figure. Chamber preferences would determine the conferees' stand.

Things may not be that simple, however, for the individual conferee. His parent committee chairman may have fought strongly in committee or on the chamber floor for a substantially higher authorization figure than that approved by the chamber. While the chamber approved only $100 million, the chairman may have sought a $180-million authorization. The individual conferee may well feel a personal loyalty to his chairman—after all, the chairman selected him to be a conferee. Moreover, the chairman is a person with whom the individual conferee must deal politically and personally for many more years. In such cases, the individual conferee may believe it appropriate (even necessary) to join his chairman in supporting a conference "compromise" closer to the higher figure favored by the *other* chamber than to the lower figure approved by his own body.

Loyalty to the chamber's position can also be strained by committee ties. Let us assume the committee had originally reported out a bill with an authorization figure substantially different from the amount subsequently adopted by the chamber. An individual conferee drawn from that same committee might view the chamber vote as

54. Quoted in Vogler, *The Third House,* p. 89.

misguided and certainly not based on the more specialized and expert knowledge and deliberations of the subject matter committee. The conference committee can offer such committee loyalists an opportunity to redress the shortsightedness of their chamber in favor of the committee's original position. Individual conferees, then, may believe it appropriate in some instances to leaven chamber loyalty with an ample dose of support for their committee's or chairman's preferences.

Conferees' articulation of these options is limited by the official expectation that they will be loyal to their chamber. In the course of conference bargaining, however, there is ample opportunity for interests such as constituency concerns, both general and specific (as in the alligator and junior college examples above), to be pursued. Similarly, loyalties to a legislative or ideological faction, to a particular external interest or cause, to the White House, or to a personal policy preference can appear during conference interactions. Conferees can provide a "court of last resort" for a particular cause, preference, or interest—constituency, ideological or personal—otherwise unsuccessful in the legislative process, and an individual conferee may be drawn to conduct "one last fight" in conference for these concerns. The conference committee is an arena of politics and a means to power; it is also a legislative-determining institution. The pressures on the individual conferee are consequently great to use his position in conference for purposive ends.

In conclusion, the individual conferee serves as a representative and defender of his chamber's interests. He may also, however, respond to other loyalties—loyalties that sometimes lead him to support positions at considerable variance from chamber preferences. Conferees must strike a personal balance among these diverse loyalties to chamber, chairman, committee, constituency, external interest, and personal preferences and respond in their own individual fashion to the choices inherent in conference interactions. This is the individual context of conference committee politics—the individual conferee's weighing of different roles and diverse loyalties as a member of a congressional conference committee. These individual conferee choices, together with the influences of committee and chamber discussed above, constitute the three contexts—institutional, committee, and individual—within which conference committee politics exist.

Appendix

Conference and Delegation Size

The size of conference delegations varies considerably, both by chamber and by subject matter area.[55] A tabulation of the average number of House and Senate conferees by legislative issue areas in three selected Congresses—the Ninety-fourth (1975–76), the Ninety-sixth (1979–80), and the Ninety-seventh (1981–82)—was prepared especially for this book. These data show that the average number of House *and* Senate conferees in those years ranged from a low of thirteen (in 1979–80 on both environmental-energy-water power and transportation issues) to thirty-three (on agriculture bills in 1981–82). The average number of House conferees ran from a low of seven (on transportation legislation in 1979–80) to a high of twenty-four (on agriculture issues in 1981–82). Comparable Senate averages ranged from five (on environmental-energy-water power legislation in 1979–80) to a high average of sixteen Senate conferees (in 1981–82 on agriculture issues).

The average number of House conferees exceeded the average Senate number in eighteen of the twenty-four areas over the three Congresses considered; only on appropriations bills was there a general tendency for the number of senators in a conference to be greater than the number of representatives. This likely reflects the House tradition of handling appropriations legislation almost exclusively by autonomous subcommittees of the parent appropriations committee. Consequently, House appropriations conferees are almost always drawn from a relatively small subcommittee, while Senate conferees are drawn from the larger full Senate Appropriations Committee.

In conclusion, it is found that the number of House conferees generally exceeds the number of Senate delegates, except on appropriations bills. Conferences typically involve roughly between nine and about fifteen House members and somewhere between six and about thirteen senators. Appropriations conferences tend to be the largest conferences, with a three-Congress average of twenty-seven members (about thirteen representatives and fourteen senators); in contrast, environmental-energy-water power and transportation bills usually involve the smallest conferences, averaging about sixteen members (about nine representatives and seven senators).

---

55. The tabulations reported in this Appendix were carried out by Tom Kephardt especially for this book. Appreciation is expressed to him for the laborious research involved in the analysis of 270 individual conferences in the 94th Congress (1975–76), the 96th Congress (1979–80), and the 97th Congress (1981–82), as well as for a confirming larger analysis also carried out by him of conference size over the thirty-six-year span covering the eighteen Congresses from 1947 to 1982 involving well over 2,000 conferences.

Conference proceedings, both large and small. (*Top*) A crowded 1986 conference committee session dealing with higher education reauthorization legislation. (*Bottom*) Private, chairman-to-chairman negotiations between Representative Dan Rostenkowski (D, Ill.) (*left*) and Senator Bob Packwood (R, Ore.) during a key 1986 tax reform conference meeting. (From *Congressional Quarterly Weekly Report,* September 6, 1986. Photograph (top) by Bruce Katz; photograph (bottom) by Teresa Zafala. Both photographs copyright © by Congressional Quarterly, Inc. Reprinted by permission.)

7

Conference Processes, Types, and Players

Conference politics comprise a policy process. There are many different types of conference committees. A variety of individuals beyond the conferees themselves regularly participate in conference committee processes. These three statements constitute the foci of this chapter.

Initially, we present a sequential conceptualization of conference committee politics centered around three stages through which conference politics moves. Simultaneously, we establish the conference process as a central component of the larger legislative process by which ideas are transformed (in some cases) into law.

Second, we distinguish among different types of conference committees. Some conferences are simple, straightforward proceedings devoid of significant drama and uncertainty. Others are marathon events that test the endurance and determination of participants and obscure the prospects for eventual success. Despite their common purpose of achieving bicameral reconciliation, conference committees do not come in one form or with common dynamics; they vary as much as human interactions themselves.

Finally, we discuss the different groups of players who regularly are involved in conference politics. Beyond the official conferees, these include such auxiliary participants as nonconferee members of Congress, Capitol Hill staffers, the president, representatives of governmental agencies, interest group spokesmen, and the press. A conference committee may officially comprise a defined number of conferees, yet many other participants with stakes in the policy outcome have both motive and means to influence conference decision making.

Conference Politics and Processes

Conference politics comprise a particularly significant element of the lawmaking process. Before a measure is enacted into law, it must first be introduced by a representative or senator, referred to one (or more) appropriate standing committee of the House or Senate,[1] secure the approval of that committee (or committees), obtain floor consideration by the full chamber, and win majority support from that body. Not only is this preconference set of activities complex and multiphased, it must also be largely duplicated in the other chamber. Legislative proposals move through dual bicameral channels—sometimes more or less simultaneously, other times more or less sequentially—prior to the formal commencement of bicameral reconciliation processes.

This is not to say that the separate lawmaking processes of the House and Senate occur with participants unaware of subsequent bicameral adjustment necessities. Conference committee bargaining is commonly anticipated even while the House or Senate is putting its distinctive imprint on legislation. The preconference process (as discussed in chapter 8) is frequently marked by an awareness of upcoming conference interactions—sometimes through what is included in the bill (perhaps as "bargaining chips" to use in conference negotiations), or by what is left out of the legislation (again as a bargaining ploy). Sometimes deep divisions or uncertainties within the House or Senate are papered over by a deliberate decision to "wait for the conference" to resolve what the chamber could not. In short, conference politics does not start only after the two bodies have completed their initial legislative work. Rather, the expectation of conference politics colors and influences each chamber's initial activities.

Once the House and Senate have completed their bill-passing work, the events of the formal conference processes can begin. These complex, multiphased processes can best be divided chronologically into three elements: *the preconference process, activities during the conference,* and *the postconference process.* In each of these stages, certain typical and important actions occur.

The Preconference Process

The preconference process often begins—even while the legislation is originally before the House and Senate—with efforts to *load a bill* with disposable provisions or *unload a bill,* that is, deliberately omit provisions preparatory to conference bargaining. Additionally, chamber and legislative leaders may find themselves *counting on the conference* to work out matters left unresolved or "messy" during the chamber's con-

---

[1]. The growing congressional tendency for the referral of legislation to more than one standing committee is discussed and assessed in terms of its significance to conference committees in chapter 3 above. The growth of multiple committee referral of legislation in the House since 1975 is specifically documented and analyzed in Roger H. Davidson and Walter J. Oleszek, "From Monopoly to Interaction: Changing Patterns in Committee Management of Legislation in the House," paper presented at the Annual Meeting of the Midwest Political Science Association, Chicago, April 9–11, 1987; and Roger H. Davidson, Walter J. Oleszek, and Thomas Kephart, "One Bill, Many Committees: Multiple Referrals in the U.S. House of Representatives," *Legislative Studies Quarterly* 13, no. 1 (Feb. 1988):3–28.

sideration of the bill. Besides these two early aspects of the preconference process, three additional actions deserve mention.

The first of these is *deciding to have a conference*. Although almost all major and controversial legislation ends up going to conference, such a step is not inevitable. Bicameral reconciliation can also be accomplished by one chamber deferring to the legislative version of a bill adopted by the other. Alternatively, adjustments between House and Senate bills can occur by shuttling proposed changes and amendments between the chambers.[2] Finally, it is also possible that, following a debilitating struggle over chamber passage of an especially controversial measure, political will and effort to persevere may be exhausted, and the legislation may be allowed to die. Usually, however, the forces that proved sufficiently strong to see a bill through both the House and Senate are also sufficiently determined to attempt to see the legislation also through the shoals of bicameral reconciliation politics—and that means, most often, through conference.

The second element of the preconference process (besides the decision to go to conference) concerns the *selection of conferees*. This is a major topic that we shall discuss in some detail in chapter 8. It is sufficient here to say that one of the most important determinants of the dynamics of conference committee politics is the decision about who will be there participating as a voting conferee.

The final concern of the preconference process has to do with *instructing conferees*, an action by which the House or Senate seeks to provide guidance for its conference representatives. Exerting the most control over the actions of a chamber's delegation, of course, are the actual provisions of the legislation as adopted by the parent body.[3] Instructions provide an additional means of highlighting and emphasizing policy provisions and goals that the chamber delegation is "instructed" to favor or defend. While conferees generally have considerable latitude in interpreting their mandate during bicameral bargaining,[4] instructions attempt to limit this latitude by a formal expression of chamber expectations and wishes.

In sum, then, there are five key aspects of the preconference process (all of which, of course, will be discussed in the next chapter): loading or unloading a bill in anticipation of conference bargaining, counting on the conference to work out matters unresolved during chamber action, deciding to have a conference, selecting conferees, and instructing conferees.

Activities during the Conference

Activities during the conference vary widely according to such factors as the size of the conference, the diversity of the subject matter at stake, the differences between initial chamber positions, time pressures on the negotiators, and the political skills of con-

   2. These alternatives to conference are discussed further in chapter 1 above.
   3. For a consideration of additional determinants of conferee actions during conference, see chapter 6 above.
   4. An extreme instance of such conferee latitude, the so-called runaway conference, is discussed in chapter 1 above.

ference leaders. While each set of conference activities has a unique quality to it, six elements are present in virtually every instance. To avoid undue anticipation of the analysis of politics "During the Conference" that constitutes chapter 9, we will just mention now those six constant elements.

Every conference first has to take account of and follow (at least to some degree) *official rules* of the House and Senate that are relevant to conference actions. A failure to conform to such restrictions might lead later to a point of order in one of the chambers, damaging or even proving fatal to hours of conference work. Chamber rules shape conference interactions by making risky or even precluding some potential policy decisions.

A matter of special significance that is persistently controversial is *the germaneness issue*. This arises because House and Senate chamber rules and traditions are fundamentally different in their toleration (in the Senate) or prohibition (in the House) of nongermane, or nonrelevant, amendments and additions to an original bill. Consequently, these institutional differences[5] have over the years led to recurrent difficulties as House and Senate meet in conference to adjust legislative efforts arising from vastly contrasting traditions. (While this problem manifests itself during conference interactions, substantial resolution of the controversy has come about through the adjustment of chamber rules for handling conference reports. As a result, and in order to maintain topic unity, this issue will be discussed almost entirely in chapter 10, "The Postconference Process.")

Another area of procedure is also recurrently of substantive significance. This is the question of *the custody of the papers*. At any given time, there exists a set of official legislative documents: an enrolled (or parchment) print of each chamber's bill, the official request for a conference, and the like. In short, whichever chamber or conference delegation has momentary "custody of the papers" has special opportunities for requesting a conference and voting first on a conference report. Custody of the papers at first sounds like a particularly arcane aspect of the conference process, but its significance runs throughout conference interactions. (Although we consider it here as an element of activities during the conference, we should also note that its significance during this stage, although real, derives from its importance during preconference and postconference processes.)

The fourth aspect of conference proceedings is less codified and definite than the official chamber rules we discussed above. *Unofficial rules and understandings* comprise a wide variety of "customary" conference arrangements and procedures ranging from who is likely to become the chairman of the conference committee to how conference bargaining is expected to be carried out. While not official, these understandings give continuity to conference activity and conferee interactions.

The fifth element of conference interactions is likewise a broad category. *Strategies* refer to the wide variety of means by which conferees try to achieve their goals during

---

5. The broad topic of institutional differences between House and Senate, especially as they impact on conference committee interactions between representatives of the two chambers, is examined in chapter 5 above.

conference. These range from posturing and ultimatum-giving on one hand to efforts to build a sense of progress and momentum in the conference by keeping the conference's attention initially focused on easy-to-resolve provisions.[6] A skilled and effective use of strategic choices is one hallmark of the successful conferee, both those seeking to foster conference success and those opposed to conference agreement.[7]

The final element of activity during conference is essentially a particular conference strategy, yet because of its significance, it should be treated separately. As a strategic ploy during conference interactions, leaders of one delegation may threaten to (or actually) break off conference negotiations for good or for the purpose of *seeking chamber reinstructions*. The purpose of the latter step officially is to determine chamber wishes on a proposed concession or amendment. As a conference strategy, it also usefully serves to tie the conferees' hands—to prevent them (as they may well wish) from being able to agree to a proposal being pressed upon them by the other chamber's conference delegation.

In short, we have suggested that six elements are recurrently significant *during the conference:* official rules, the germaneness issue, the custody of the papers, unofficial rules and understandings, strategies, and the seeking of chamber reinstructions.

The Postconference Process

The events of the postconference process are substantially shaped by those that transpire earlier. If a conference adopts a report despite significant and well-entrenched dissent, then these conference divisions are likely to be mirrored during each chamber's consideration of the conference accord. Alternatively, if the conference was remarkably successful in forging consensus and unity—especially both bipartisan and bicameral accord—then ratification of a conference agreement is likely to move relatively smoothly. The major determinant of postconference politics, then, is the nature of those interactions that precede and lead to the conference agreement.

Nevertheless, despite this essential dependency, there are three elements (or stages) inherent in the postconference process. The first of these is *preparing the conference report* (and also the accompanying joint explanatory statement and unofficial statements by conferees to their chamber). This activity is more than technical in character and leads into and overlaps with the second element (or stage): *selling the report to the House and Senate*.

Winning chamber agreement for the bicameral accord involves a wide variety of diverse actions and procedures, which are dealt with in chapter 10. Suffice it to say that conference politics in no way stops with the reaching of House-Senate agreement, but rather is carried on through campaigns in both chambers on behalf of the conference report.

---

6. A particularly clear example of this latter strategy in practice is provided in the chapter 11 case study "Higher Education: Personalities and Exhaustion."

7. For an intriguing illustration of how conference strategy may prove useful to an opponent of bicameral agreement, see the example drawn from a conference simulation in the Preface.

Throughout both the conference and the postconference period, a third concern is also present—one that becomes particularly urgent during the postconference process. This is *securing presidential approval* for the conference compromise. At many points during the legislative and conference processes, the president will find occasion to indicate his opinions and reactions to legislative developments.[8] It is at the conclusion of the conference process, and following the acceptance of the conference agreement by the House and Senate, that the opportunity finally arises for the president to cast his vote on the conferees' handiwork by vetoing or accepting it.

The presidential decision to approve or to disapprove of legislation essentially falls into a category of the congressional process beyond the conference stages as we have described them here; to be sure, the president's decision is influenced by a variety of considerations, including the nature of the bicameral accord as worked out in conference and subsequently accepted by House and Senate. Similarly, those final events of the legislative process that follow after such a presidential decision—possible congressional attempts to override the presidential veto, and bureaucratic and administrative implementation of laws resulting from either an initial presidential signature or a successful congressional veto-override effort—have as their basis the events and political developments of earlier stages, especially key conference actions.

Types of Conferences

Conferences differ considerably. Some are large, others are small; some face enormously complex issues, others need resolve only relatively minor bicameral differences. In some conferences, heavy pressures come from outside the conference itself and influence what goes on during negotiations. In others, the conference performs its tasks essentially free of such constraints. Some conferences are ultimately successful in their efforts, whereas others fail—during the conference itself, in securing chamber approval, or in obtaining presidential acceptance of the conference-crafted legislation. To impose some order on the many differences among conferences, we organize them collectively into four broad categories.

Size and Deliberative Differences

An important structural-physical difference among conferences is their *size*. Most conferences, as we noted in chapter 6, involve roughly between 9 and about 15 House members and somewhere between 6 and about 13 senators; many conferences, however, vary widely from these norms. This is especially true in the case of conferences handling omnibus legislation, a recent congressional trend. Several examples are provided in chapters 1 and 3 of conference committees running into hundreds of members, usually meeting in numerous subconferences. An omnibus budget reconciliation conference in

---

8. See the discussion that follows in this chapter of the president as an important participant in conference committee politics.

1986, for example, included as conferees 242 representatives and senators—over 45 percent of the entire membership of Congress!

On the other hand, some conferences are relatively cozy events. In chapter 11, a case study account is given of an appropriations conference in 1979 in which seven House members met with a solitary representative of the Senate to work out bicameral differences.

Conferences also differ markedly concerning the *length of conference proceedings*. Particularly on contentious or multifaceted legislation, lengthy conferences are not uncommon. Omnibus bills customarily require elongated processes. The historic conference on the 1981 budget reconciliation bill, which incorporated in one package many of the numerous policy objectives initially sought by the Reagan administration, took much of the summer of 1981 to complete its deliberations. The conference on President Carter's energy package took a year before agreement was reached between the houses on its multitude of issues in 1978. The 1972 higher education bill (see the case study "Higher Education: Personalities and Exhaustion" in chapter 11), although focused on a single policy, still required fourteen weeks of long, exhaustive conference meetings in order to resolve a total of 383 differences in the bills that had passed the House and Senate.

In striking contrast are conference meetings that might be called Hello and Good-Bye conferences. These are bicameral proceedings that are exceedingly short (sometimes only minutes in duration). Social pleasantries and personal greetings are often more evident than hard bicameral bargaining. These conferences may be so short that the greetings of conferees upon arrival seem to blend with their good-byes upon departure.

Two examples of Hello and Good-Bye conferences are given in chapter 11. In one instance, the entire conference proceedings ran no more than fifteen minutes; in the other, conference negotiations on far more complex legislation required only a single conference session of about two hours.

These instances suggest two circumstances under which such extraordinarily swift conference proceedings are likely to be found: when there is in fact very little to resolve (in the first instance the only matter the conference had to decide was how to respond to a particular concern of one conferee) or when substantive interchamber differences have been resolved through preconference negotiations (as in the other case). The Hello and Good-Bye conference usually occurs when conferees meet to clear up minor bicameral differences of little general interest or when they convene to ratify agreements and understandings previously reached through informal discussions among conferees and staff.

Problems and Problem Solving

A second set of differences among conferences has to do with the nature of the problems facing the conference. An initial distinction has to do with *the complexity and familiarity of the issues before the conference*. Some legislative topics are recurrent matters on which conferees have well-developed attitudes and routines, such as MX missile funding, veterans' benefits, or agricultural price support levels. On these issues, the political and policy landscape is familiar and well trod, and this familiarity fosters relatively predictable and stable conference reconciliation processes (even though conflict may suffuse and permeate conference negotiations).

At other times conferees find themselves dealing with legislation that is either extraordinarily complex or innovative. An example of the former is the 1977–78 conference on President Carter's package of energy proposals, the complexity of which required negotiations extending over many months, the appointment of ad hoc committees, direct presidential intervention, and numerous behind-the-scenes negotiations. An example of conferences dealing with innovative legislation is the Gramm-Rudman deficit reduction conferences (note the plural) of 1985. (These are described in detail in chapter 11.)

Another distinction related to the problems facing conferences has to do with *the differences between the chambers.* Sometimes these differences are slight, allowing for quite abbreviated conference discussions. At other times, they are so enormous and all-encompassing as to make eventual conference agreement difficult to achieve.

Bicameral differences are not all of one type. *Quantitative differences* between the chambers concerning the level of funding for a program, or how many of something to approve, lend themselves to bicameral reconciliation by such familiar means as "splitting the difference." *Qualitative differences,* however, usually pose more difficult bargaining situations. The structure of a new governmental program or a definition of permissible conditions for government-funded abortions is not amenable to settlement at a midway point. Rather, conference resolution of such matters more likely will involve either a substantive concession by one chamber's representatives to the views of the other, some sort of sequential process of alternating bicameral concessions on different provisions of the legislation, or the artful use of language that enables both chambers to claim that their views were upheld.

Besides quantitative-qualitative differences, another aspect of chamber differences also influences conferences. This is *the extent to which the positions of House and Senate have been emphasized,* either by the margin of the vote in a chamber for particular provisions or on final passage or by special instructions given to the conference delegation that emphasize non-negotiable items or items that may be conceded. When floor votes are one-sided or chamber wishes on legislation are reinforced by specially adopted instructions to its conferees, bicameral agreement on significant differences is sometimes made more difficult.

A third difference among conferences, involving how a conference deals with the substantive problems facing it, may be termed *problem-solving perceptions.* Conference committees differ, first, according to *the degree of conferee-shared perceptions,* both among each chamber delegation and among the conference members as a whole.[9] A common outlook among conferees—either within the delegation or in the overall conference—fosters effective bargaining; those negotiating will be speaking the same lan-

---

9. These two distinctions among conference committees are based on an idea suggested by Richard F. Fenno, Jr., in a Washington discussion on Nov. 2, 1981. Appreciation is expressed to him for his insight.

guage as they discuss their differences and consider various means for resolving them.

Conferences also differ in *the extent of conferees' previous experience.* Today it is not uncommon for conferees to be drawn from diverse committees and to include less senior and experienced legislators.[10] Lack of conference negotiating experience and of shared outlook can produce obstacles in reaching House-Senator agreement.

A final aspect of conference problem-solving concerns the use of *special bargaining techniques and procedures. Unofficial meetings* before and during the conference are the most frequent of such techniques. Meetings may be held by a chamber delegation, a partisan component of that delegation, or key conferees and staff from either or from both chambers. Sometimes the key conference decisions will be worked out in meetings directly between the two *committee chairmen.*[11] In other cases, crucial bargaining will be carried out by a series of *ad hoc conferee groups.*[12] And finally, in still other cases, key understandings will be established through lengthy *staff negotiations* that occur either prior to the conference's initial convening[13] or during the conference deliberations themselves.

Not all conferences resort to small-group negotiations as a means of paving the way for full conference agreement. Serious and substantive bargaining goes on in the conference committee itself.[14] The key point is that, in many conferences, unofficial bargaining units supplement or even supplant regular conference negotiations.

Outside Pressures

Another important element that distinguishes one conference from another is *the extent and source of external pressures.* Some conferences have few such influences with which to deal (an example is the low-intensity appropriations conference on the funding of the Washington, D.C., government considered in chapter 11). In these instances, the conferees are relatively free to perform their tasks without having to look

10. Recent modifications in the traditional practice of conferee selection from matched pairs of House and Senate standing committees, and of the most senior members of those committees, are discussed in chapters 3 and 6 above.

11. A classic example of chairman-to-chairman negotiations occurred during the final difficult conference bargaining over sweeping tax reform legislation in November and December 1986. Lengthy discussions between Senate Finance Chairman Robert Packwood (R, Ore.) and House Ways and Means Chairman Dan Rostenkowski (D, Ill.) were crucial in hammering out the final conference agreement. For a detailed account of these events, see chapter 11 of Jeffrey H. Birnbaum and Alan S. Murray, *Showdown at Gucci Gulch: Lawmakers, Lobbyists, and the Unlikely Triumph of Tax Reform* (New York: Random House, 1987).

12. Informal conference groups were instrumental in the conference accord eventually reached by the second Gramm-Rudman conference in late 1985. See the case study in chapter 11 below for an account of these complex proceedings.

13. For an example, see the chapter 11 case study of the Department of Education Organization Act, the second of "Two 'Hello and Good-Bye' Conferences of 1979."

14. It is possible, however, that there has been some lessening of the use of the official conference sessions as the arena for bargaining as a result of the opening up of most conference sessions to interest groups, press, and public. This change is discussed in detail in chapter 3 above.

over their shoulders to get the reactions or approval of deeply interested nonconferee participants.

In many cases, however, there is little political isolation for the conferees. Instead, external participants (discussed below) such as the president, representatives of governmental agencies, and interest groups have intense interest and impact on the conference deliberations. "This is not a conference between the two houses," remarked Senator John Danforth (R, Mo.) in 1988 about the omnibus trade conference of the 100th Congress. "It's a conference between Congress and the administration."[15] Some conferences, in brief, operate in relative isolation; others are deeply immersed in politically volatile webs of interest and pressure.

Conference Success (or Failure)

Our final distinction among conferences is the most obvious of all: whether they succeed or fail. Even this simple distinction has its subtleties. For example, a conference may be a rousing success in achieving the reconciliation of differences, but the resulting conference agreement fail to pass either chamber or to secure presidential approval and signature.

How, when, and why conferences fail is one means of distinguishing among them. Conversely, successful conferences can be analyzed in terms of how, when, and why conditions developed that led to their eventual success. Conference success and failure, then, provides yet another and final set of differences among conferences.

In conclusion, we have identified a wide number of conference differences. These included distinctions such as large versus small, lengthy versus quick, complex versus simple, familiar versus unconventional topical material, modest versus major chamber differences, conferences composed of conferees with shared perspectives versus those with conferees with diverse perspectives, conferences with more experienced versus less experienced conferees, conferences forced to react to intense external pressure versus conferences more politically isolated, and conference success versus conference failure. Indeed, conferences are not all the same, but come in a wide diversity of types.

Varieties of Players

Thus far in this chapter, we have examined conference politics as a policy process and discussed the many different types of conference committees. Now, in this third and final section of the chapter, we turn to a consideration of the variety of individuals beyond the conferees themselves who regularly participate in conference deliberations.

Clearly, the most central participants in conference interactions are the officially appointed conferees. They have the formal duty of reconciling bills passed by House and Senate, they are the conference participants with the right to vote on proposed measures, and, of course, only they exercise the official powers of conference members in agreeing

15. Elizabeth Wehr, "Negotiations on Trade Bill Gain Momentum," *Congressional Quarterly Weekly Report,*" March 19, 1988, p. 732.

on and reporting to the House and Senate a final bicameral accord. The conferees, however, are usually not the only participants in conference politics.[16] Recurrently, other players, at the physical (but not political) periphery of the conference, let their opinions and judgments be known and, by doing so, seek to influence conference outcomes. These additional major participants are *nonconferee members of Congress, Capitol Hill staffers, the president, representatives of governmental agencies, interest group spokesmen,* and *the press.*

Nonconferee Congressmen

Many members of the House and Senate besides the conferees themselves may have an interest in conference committee deliberations. Typically, these congressmen include the leaders of each chamber, authors of major amendments, important nonconferee members of the parent committees, and any other congressmen with some personal interest, expertise, or stake in the legislation. These nonconferees may follow proceedings from a distance or dispatch a staff aide to monitor the conference's actions. Nonconferees will sit in at various points (or sometimes for entire days) during conference activities and even argue for or against matters that are in disagreement between the houses.

Admittance to conference is a courtesy extended almost automatically to any member of the House or Senate. A few House and Senate committees have even worked out informal arrangements for participating in each other's conferences. Leaders of the House Armed Services Committee, for instance, sit in as ex-officio conferees during defense appropriations conferences, just as members of the House Defense Appropriations Subcommittee participate in military authorization conferences. The ex-officio members may debate matters but have no right to vote.

It is not unusual to observe at conference sessions a few congressmen sitting directly behind the conferees or settled in the front rows of the meeting room. In the case of the initial conference on the highly controversial Gramm-Rudman legislation in 1985, for example, all three of its principal authors were excluded (for various reasons, as noted in chapter 11) from service as Senate conferees; nevertheless, all three—Senator Phil Gramm (R, Tex.) most noticeably—observed the conference negotiations closely. A 1984 tax conference similarly was marked by the intense interest of one House member, James R. Jones (D, Okla.). The Senate bill had placed a 3 percent excise tax on, among countless other things, fish-finding devices. The House version did not tax such items. The interest of the representative in this very specific matter arose because a major manufacturer of fish-finders, Lowrance Electronics, happened to be in his district.

---

16. There are exceptions, as we have noted earlier in this chapter, when conferences are able to perform their tasks with a minimum of outside pressure—or even interest. Most typically this occurs on noncontroversial legislation, bills that essentially continue the policy status quo, or bills whose House- and Senate-adopted versions are essentially in agreement. In these instances, policy battles will be viewed as having been already waged—either in the past or during chamber adoption of essentially similar legislation—and the conference will be seen as a technical reconciling rather than a policy formulating or modifying institution.

Although Representative Jones's legislative concerns usually were far broader in scope due to his responsibilities as chairman of the House Budget Committee, in this case they were quite narrowly focused. He was observed pacing around the conference room until finally his concerns were relieved by a late conference amendment that specifically excluded fish-finders from the excise tax.[17]

Sometimes the presence of nonconferee legislators can itself become an issue. In June 1976, a conference committee on military procurement legislation was holding a closed session (presumably because classified matters would be discussed). Two junior House Armed Services Committee members, Bob Carr (D, Mich.) and Patricia Schroeder (D, Col.), were concerned, however, that the real reason for the conference session being closed was to allow conferees a convenient and discreet occasion to drop a number of liberal House amendments—including two they had authored and successfully navigated through the House over the opposition of senior Armed Services Committee members. The two representatives chose to attend the closed conference meeting and declined to leave when requested to by conference leaders (including the same senior members of Armed Services whom they had earlier defeated). The House sergeant-at-arms was called, but he indicated he could not act because the conference was meeting in the Senate wing of the Capitol. Next, the Senate sergeant-at-arms was contacted, but he likewise demurred on the grounds that he had no authority over members of the House. Representatives Carr and Schroeder remained and were able to witness the defeat in conference of their amendments.[18] (The following year, when the House strengthened its openness rule by requiring a majority vote of the entire House to close conference meetings, the Speaker ruled that the motion to close conference sessions to the public could explicitly permit sitting members to attend the closed sessions.)

Nonconference congressional interest is not always reflected in conference attendance. Sometimes concerns are expressed at a distance in the form of threats or warnings on the chamber floor. "I hope the Senate realizes that there is no way the House will accept a conference report that walks away completely from this issue," declared a House member in 1984.[19]

Chairmen and members of committees other than those formally represented in conference may have a special stake in conference outcomes. The House and Senate Budget committees, for example, are responsible for tracking the spending and revenue-raising recommendations of all committees, including conference committees. Con-

17. *New York Times,* June 12, 1984.
18. *Washington Star,* May 24, 1977, p. A2. Representative Carr, it seems, runs into problems with conference committees. Three years after these events, he arrived ten minutes late at another conference committee meeting (which was, this time, entirely open). His tardiness was unfortunate; in these few minutes the House delegation had quickly agreed to drop a key amendment that Carr had sponsored and the House had passed. Even more striking was that this concession of the House conferees to the Senate position occurred despite a House delegation meeting only minutes prior at which Carr was present during which House conferees had pledged to uphold the House (and Carr's) amendment. (For a lively discussion of these events, see *Congressional Record,* 96th Cong., 1st sess., Dec. 19, 1979, pp. H12262–63.)
19. *Washington Post,* April 13, 1984, p. F6.

ference decisions are required to be consistent with the revenue and expenditure targets adopted by Congress, and are so monitored by the budget panels. Conference reports that fail to conform to overall budgetary guidelines are subject to attack on the House or Senate floor on those grounds.[20] During conference proceedings, leaders of the Budget committees may offer public warnings that certain conference actions would likely trigger parliamentary objections on the floor.

It is fitting that there is also reciprocal watchfulness by committee leaders over conference decisions made by members of the House and Senate Budget committees. When Robert Dole (R, Kan.) chaired the Senate Finance Committee, he once advised budget conferees that if they recommended large tax increases and marginal spending cuts as the way to achieve deficit reductions, there would be little likelihood of any such tax bill being reported from his committee: "A budget conference that calls for huge tax increases will give the tax-writing committees an impossible job. If the [budget] conferees press for unrealistically high taxes, the result may be no revenue increase at all."[21] Heeding Senator Dole's warning, the budget conference reversed itself and agreed to only modest tax hikes.

Finally, House and Senate leaders are frequently important nonconferee participants. Chamber leaders, for instance, can influence the composition of their body's conference delegation; they can serve as conferees; they can prod, cajole, or broker compromises; they can dispatch their aides to assist in negotiations; they can set deadlines for completing actions; they can bargain behind the scenes with conferees and other actors; and they can work out strategic arrangements for debating the conference report on the House or Senate floor. "Leadership involvement at the conference stage," a scholar on the topic has explained, "is most frequently aimed at facilitating an agreement so that a bill will emerge and at influencing the form of the compromise."[22] Chamber leaders (and individual members too) may also make floor speeches, propose "sense of the House (or Senate)" resolutions, write letters to conferees, threaten to lead floor fights against the conference report, or engage in other tactics, all designed to influence conference decision making.[23]

Capitol Hill Staffers

Capitol Hill staffers are additional nonconferee players who are highly visible in and around conference committees. Wherever one sees representatives and senators on

---

20. For a detailed discussion of conference report ratification politics, see chapter 10 below.
21. *New York Times*, June 2, 1983, p. D20.
22. Barbara Sinclair, *Majority Leadership in the U.S. House* (Baltimore: Johns Hopkins University Press, 1983), p. 172.
23. Despite the multitude of ways in which congressional leaders *may* influence conference interactions, see also the related discussion in chapter 3 above, especially the section "Weakening of Party and Committee Leadership." There we argue that despite these various opportunities for influence, "today, the personal intervention of the Senate Majority Leader or Speaker in conference politics is more occasional" and likely to be most "evident in conferences dealing with issues of the highest substantial and political priority" (pp. 62–63).

Capitol Hill, one will also find congressional staffers—and this is certainly true concerning conference committees. Further, the influence of staff members over conference decisions is not minor, and sometimes even seems to rival that of the conference members themselves. Senator Edward M. Kennedy (D, Mass.) was reported to have asked, upon surveying a conference room overrun with congressional staff, "Can we [the conferees] sit in while they make the decisions?"[24]

Capitol Hill staffers come in a number of varieties, of which the most noticeable during conferences are the standing committee staffs loyal to each committee's leaders, and the personal staffs of individual conferees.[25] Additionally present are the personal staffs of congressmen who are not conferees and—on important issues—staffers serving the House or Senate leaders. The functions of these staff members are to observe and report on conference activity and sometimes to represent their patron's views. Other Capitol Hill staffers occasionally seen include experts on particular matters from Capitol Hill institutions such as the Congressional Budget Office, the Office of Legislative Counsel, and the Congressional Research Service of the Library of Congress.

The importance of congressional staff to the work of conference committees is hard to overemphasize, for they are the individuals who frequently hammer out detailed agreements[26] and identify major questions of disagreement on which the conference itself will focus. Congressional staff act as channels of communication among conferees, executive branch aides, and lobbyists, facilitating compromise and coalition formation.[27]

Capitol Hill staff members influence policymaking in many ways.[28] In specific terms of their conference responsibilities, House and Senate staffers play at least four key roles. First, they are *educators*. They provide information and analyses of the proposals in bicameral dispute, develop alternative recommendations, and evaluate the implications, political and technical, of various policy options.[29]

Second, staff aides are *negotiators*. Even before conferences formally convene, House and Senate aides meet to consider agendas, set meeting times and places, prepare

---

24. Martin Tolchin, "Staff Takes Leading Role at Conference on Budget," *New York Times*, July 23, 1981, p. A19.

25. In the case of a crowded conference room, it is possible that not all staffers will be able to fit; in that instance, committee staff members generally have priority over a conferee's personal staff. It has been suggested by one scholar and longtime Capitol Hill observer, Catherine Rudder, that this is one significant (and not unanticipated) consequence of small conference rooms—a shift of power to the committee staffs and consequently also to the committee chairmen who direct them.

26. For an example, see the chapter 11 case study "The Department of Education Organization Act," the second of "Two 'Hello and Good-bye' Conferences of 1979."

27. For an example, see the chapter 11 case study "Higher Education: Personalities and Exhaustion."

28. A leading study of the political and policy importance of congressional staff is Michael J. Malbin, *Unelected Representatives* (New York: Basic Books, 1980).

29. For a classic instance of a congressional staff member serving as an information source, see in the chapter 11 case study "The Gramm-Rudman Conferences of 1985" the key role of Stephen E. Bell, staff director of the Senate Budget Committee, as explainer of the meaning of specific provisions of the Gramm-Rudman legislation.

working documents,[30] and establish ways to iron out differences. "Agendas are often worked out in advance by staff," the Senate Labor staff director pointed out in late 1983. "If [the House and Senate Labor staff] couldn't agree, it could have been a waste of time for the conferees to meet."[31] Sometimes these preconference staff meetings are occasions for more than agenda-setting, and major areas of bicameral disagreement are settled. (Chapter 11 provides an extreme example of such staff negotiations, which in this instance resulted in a complete accord being worked out before the conference officially met. Once it did, the conference proceedings went smoothly and swiftly, almost as if by a script.)[32]

When the hard bargaining begins in conference, staffers continue to have important roles. After one difficult snag had arisen during budget reconciliation activity in 1981, Senator Orrin G. Hatch (R, Utah), chairman of the Labor and Human Resources Committee, suggested to his House counterpart, "Let's get our staffs together and narrow these issues."[33] The results of these staff meetings were truly astonishing and greatly facilitated conference action:

> In one relatively brief session, the conference ratified staff agreements on financing for the Department of the Interior; an American Indian health program; a Navajo and Hopi relocation problem; a newly created office of Federal inspector of the Alaska pipeline; the Pennsylvania Avenue Development Corporation in Washington; a holocaust memorial council; and an advisory council for historical preservation.[34]

This resort to staff to work things out is commonplace. At the opening of a mammoth conference in 1977 on energy legislation, Senator Henry M. Jackson (D, Wash.) surveyed the three hundred pages of legislative provisions and concluded, "We're simply not going to be able to go through it section by section." Instead, he suggested the conference review it topically, and then "rely on the staff to work out the language, rather than have the on stage cast debating punctuation."[35] An account of a defense appropriations conference in 1983 similarly noted staff roles in the dealings: "The dollar figures in the huge piece of legislation are so immense that House-Senate conferees . . .

---

30. An awkward staff error occurred in 1966 in the course of the preparation of working documents for one conference. Senate committee staffers wrote two analyses for the use of Senate conferees—one outlining the Senate's initial position and a second summarizing delegation discussions of what the Senate conferees would be willing to accept. To the dismay of everyone involved, both documents were inadvertently circulated to the House conferees, revealing fully Senate negotiating plans and fallback positions. David L. Paletz, "Influence in Congress: An Analysis of the Nature and Effects of Conference Committees" (Ph.D. diss., University of California at Los Angeles, 1970), p. 183.

31. *Washington Post,* Nov. 19, 1983, p. A13. For a discussion of staff roles in preconference negotiations, see also Richard F. Fenno, Jr., *The Power of the Purse: Appropriations Politics in Congress* (Boston: Little, Brown, 1966), p. 648.

32. See the chapter 11 case study of "The Department of Education Organization Act," the second of "Two 'Hello and Good-bye' Conferences of 1979."

33. Tolchin, "Staff Takes Leading Role," p. A19.

34. Ibid.

35. Adam Clymer, "A Congress Spectacular: Energy Bill," *New York Times,* Oct. 17, 1977.

relegated almost every item less than $100 million [in bicameral disagreement] to staff aides on the grounds that the members themselves did not have time to deal with such items, which Sen. Ted Stevens (R, Alaska) called 'small potatoes.' "[36] The use of congressional staff for such negotiations has been heartily defended as necessary and proper. For example, the executive director of the House Budget Committee stressed, in connection with the 1981 budget reconciliation conference, that "the role of the staff has been not only to explore where there may be areas of agreement but also to make the deal. How else are you going to get hundreds of issues resolved in a couple of weeks unless you give the staff some kind of license?"[37]

Third, staff members are *strategists*. Working with conferees, lobbyists, executive branch officials, and others, they suggest ways to forge agreement among conferees on their side and to frustrate those on the other side in terms of policy objectives. They use a multiplicity of devices—calculated delays, mobilization of outside pressure, the introduction of cleverly drafted initiatives, and the like—to achieve results that maximize the attainment of conference goals. In addition, staff assume further important responsibilities even after the conference in helping to oversee passage of the conference report in their chamber.[38]

Finally, staffers are also *drafters*. They write the conference report (the conference agreement) and the joint explanatory statement that must accompany the report. The preparation of the report and the accompanying statement, in which intent is clarified, can sometimes be an arduous process as staff struggle to find the language that reflects conference agreements.

The deep involvement of congressional staff members in conference committee activities sometimes gives rise to controversy. Few would criticize their technical support activities, such as the preparation of documents (called "spread sheets") summarizing the major points of difference in the chamber-passed bills,[39] or their preparation of the final conference report and joint explanatory statement. What *is* controversial concerns the central roles that staffers recurrently play in conference bargaining and the setting of strategic moves for conference members. (House conferees sometimes lament that during conference meetings they negotiate more with Senate staff aides than with senators.)

At times, staffers seem to act almost as House and Senate members themselves. Late in the summer of 1986, for example, bicameral disputes over reauthorization legislation for the Export-Import Bank threatened the bill's future. The two chambers were in summer recess at the time, so committee aides from the House and Senate Banking committees took the opportunity to hold what amounted to a "shadow conference" to work out an entirely new bill. These bicameral staff meetings left at least one key representative "somewhat stunned" at this demonstration of staff primacy. He

---

36. *Washington Post,* Nov. 20, 1983, p. A13.
37. Tolchin, "Staff Takes Leading Role," p. A19.
38. See chapter 10 below.
39. Rep. Barber Conable (R, N.Y.), "What Happens in Conference?" *Roll Call,* June 21, 1984, p. 4.

promised, however, not to let his opinion be prejudiced until he had the opportunity to review the new, staff-generated bicameral agreement.[40]

A particularly colorful instance of staff involvement in bicameral reconciliation proceedings came in what has been termed "The Phantom Conference on the GI Bill."[41] What happened in this case was a total replacing of the usual conference committee by staff negotiations:

> Conferees never were appointed and the leading members [of the standing committees in each chamber] met only once over an informal breakfast. . . . The leaders of the two veterans' committees used the calendar as their excuse for letting the staff do the work of a conference committee. Key staff people simply sat down for three days in late October and early November and resolved the differences between the two bills.[42]

These bicameral staff negotiations were not over minor or technical questions, but involved major substantive issues of policy. The resulting "staff level compromise was no simple split-the-difference" matter, but involved rather "imaginative new formulations significantly changing existing law . . . some of which had never been discussed in either chamber."[43] An official conference committee never met; instead, the staff agreement was informally accepted by key committee members and subsequently was passed by both the Senate and House with almost no debate and with unanimous votes in both chambers.

The President

The participants in conference committee interactions whom we have discussed thus far—conferees, nonconferee congressmen, and Capitol Hill staffers—are all internal to Congress. Besides these, there are four other conference participants that merit mention, each of which is essentially external to Congress.[44] The most noteworthy is certainly the best-known player in national policymaking: the president.

The influence of the president on the legislative process is always pervasive—but not determinate. The president proposes legislative measures and supports them during

---

40. Steven Pressman, " 'Shadow Conference' Meets on Ex-Im Bank Authorization," *Congressional Quarterly Weekly Report*, Aug. 30, 1986, p. 2040. The August congressional recess, when members of the House and Senate customarily flee Washington, accords staff special responsibilities— and opportunities. A conference on major housing legislation convened in 1987 shortly prior to the August break. Before the conference members dispersed, "the conferees instructed their staffs to resolve as many conflicts as possible over the August recess" (Ronald D. Elving, "Conferees Open Negotiations Over Omnibus Housing Bill," *Congressional Quarterly Weekly Report*, Aug. 8, 1987, p. 1810).

41. A spirited account is given in Malbin, *Unelected Representatives*, pp. 75–93. Readers are referred to this telling to catch the full flavor of these events.

42. Ibid., p. 76.

43. Ibid.

44. The importance of a careful consideration of these external participants was especially usefully stressed in a Washington conversation with Louis Fisher on Oct. 20, 1981. Appreciation is expressed to him for his suggestion.

the congressional process by means of public activities and private deeds. Similarly, conference committee processes are influenced in many ways by presidential views and actions.

It was an exceedingly difficult conference, complained one senator in reporting on a conference agreement unfavorable to the Senate. "We were pitted against both the House conferees and the administration as they pressed for figures that were much lower than ours."[45] It is indeed difficult, as the senator had found, to buck both the other chamber and the president. Given our interconnected system of shared powers, it is not surprising that often one finds presidential preferences meshing during conferences with those of the House or Senate. Presidential involvement in conference negotiations is recurrent and inevitable. During conferences it occurs in two broad and overlapping ways: individually and collectively.

Presidents (often working through executive branch senior officials) seek first of all to shape the negotiating views of individual conferees. The director of the Office of Management and Budget, cabinet secretaries and sometimes even the president himself will lobby (by letter, telephone, or in person) specific conferees. Further, presidents may invite selected conferees to the White House to attempt to enlist their support for key administration positions. This occurred in the course of a conference in 1981 on a supplemental appropriations bill. "Late in the afternoon, the conferees recessed and a delegation of Republicans, led by Senator Howard H. Baker, Republican of Tennessee, the Majority Leader, went downtown to the White House."[46] Similarly, a 1980 conference on appropriations for the Federal Trade Commission (FTC) was floundering over issues involving the legislative veto (declared unconstitutional in 1983). In order to get conference negotiations started again, President Carter met with FTC staff members on April 22, 1980, to review strategy and then convened the entire conference committee at the White House itself on April 24 for additional discussions.[47]

Conferees try in turn to reshape White House thinking on issues or urge presidential support for certain conference compromises. Senator Orrin Hatch (R, Utah), for example, chairman of a key health conference in 1981, refused to support a conference agreement on family planning until he had received formal White House approval. "I just wanted them [the White House officials] to stand up and share the burden. They reluctantly agreed with what had to be done," he said. "They don't like family planning, but they understand we don't have the votes in either the House or Senate" to pass the conference report unless it contains the family planning provision. What was needed, Hatch determined, was clear presidential support for this step.[48]

Presidents are well positioned to win the votes of individual conferees through the skillful use of executive bargaining chips, such as White House promises to back federal

45. *Congressional Record,* 92d Cong., 2d sess., May 18, 1972, p. S8119.
46. Steven V. Roberts, "Congress Presses Talks on Spending Beyond Deadline," *New York Times,* Nov. 22, 1981.
47. Washington interview with William Baer, former staff aide and lobbyist for the Federal Trade Commission, Nov. 3, 1981.
48. *Congressional Quarterly Almanac, 1981* (Washington, D.C.: Congressional Quarterly, 1982), p. 487.

projects in conferees' states or districts, or pledges to aid members in passing other legislation dear to their political hearts. The White House can also encourage conferees to add or drop provisions in order to help build winning coalitions on other measures. At times, this may even resemble a form of political blackmail. To win House Republican support for a 1982 tax bill, for example, a simultaneously occurring military authorization conference dropped, at the White House's request, a military plane that was being built in the districts of several Republican House members. Representative Norman Lent (R, N.Y.), whose district manufactured portions of the aircraft, bitterly commented on his resulting coerced decision to back the tax measure:

> Was the A-10 [military plane] a factor in my consideration of the tax bill? The answer is yes. We've been trying for more than a year to assure the continued manufacture of the plane. This is a constant concern. One of the issues that was openly discussed by the White House lobbyist, but not the determining factor, was the A-10. Just as important [it was stressed] was that the tax bill would be terrific for New York State.[49]

Presidential stands may also influence the *collective* decisions of conferences in numerous ways. White House representatives are regularly in attendance at or near these bicameral meetings and participate informally or formally in rendering advice and counsel on proposed agreements. On occasion, Office of Management and Budget and other senior White House officials appear in person to indicate the acceptability of conference compromises.[50] The leaders and staffs of the standing committees represented in conference in addition regularly consult the White House directly about issues, agendas, and compromises.

Obtaining White House input during conference deliberations, especially on important bills, is not difficult—advice is almost always near at hand. At the outset of

49. *New York Times,* Oct. 7, 1982, p. A19.
50. *New York Times,* Aug. 3, 1977, p. 43. An example of this occurred in 1982 during the tax conference of that year: "For hours this afternoon, the House and Senate negotiators met separately on opposite sides of the Capitol, searching for a solution, the Chairmen and top staff members communicating occasionally on the telephone. Secretary [of the Treasury James] Baker sat in with the Senators" (David E. Rosenbaum, "Conferees Strive for Final Accord on Tax Overhaul," *New York Times,* Aug. 17, 1982, p. 18). For a detailed account of the events of this conference, see the chapter 11 case study "The 1982 Tax Increase Conference."

In another instance, at various times in the course of the 1981 Farm Bill conference, Secretary of Agriculture John R. Block joined conferees to assist their deliberations (*New York Times,* Dec. 9, 1981). At difficult moments during this conference, "an effort was made . . . to have ranking conferees meet [one-on-one] with Block to get a clearer line on what the administration will accept" (*Washington Post,* Dec. 9, 1981, p. A4).

Sometimes the number of senior administration officials present can become a bit overwhelming. During final stages of a 1972 debt ceiling conference, the secretary of the Treasury, the deputy under secretary of the Treasury, and the director of the Office of Management and Budget all joined in the conference at the same time. Even more striking was that this session of the conference—like almost all conferences prior to the mid-1970s—was *closed,* nominally limited to conferees and staff only! (Walter J. Oleszek, "House-Senate Relationships: Comity and Conflict," *Annals of the American Academy of Political and Social Science,* 411 [Jan. 1974]:81).

conference negotiations in 1986 on landmark tax reform legislation, the Reagan administration "mobilized an army of tax lawyers, economists, and computers" to assist conference decision making:

> Seated a few feet in front of the conferees as they began work . . . was an entourage of Treasury Department officials who plan to assert White House positions on every one of about 300 provisions that will be incorporated in the final bill. . . .
>
> [This entourage's] mission is to instantly appraise conference proposals, recommend compromise solutions, negotiate with Congressional aides, help draft the legislation and otherwise exert some control over Mr. Reagan's initiative in this last and most important struggle.[51]

These White House representatives were not left to their own resources in assessing conference developments. Backing up this frontline presidential defense were the 130 members of the Office of Tax Policy of the Treasury Department, the same group that had earlier generated the original presidential tax overhaul bill that had led to this conference. Also available to the administration lobbyists were the elaborate computer facilities of the Department of the Treasury, which were ready to estimate the revenue consequences of each amendment proposed and considered by the conferees:

> The Treasury, using sophisticated computer models of the economy and taxpayer behavior, makes its own revenue estimates as a cross-check on those made by the Congressional Joint Committee on Taxation for the conferees. If quick estimates are needed in the middle of a [conference] debate, a projection can often be made in a few minutes. . . .[52]

Besides these instrumental ways, there are several other broad methods presidents may use to influence conference outcomes. First, they can attempt to mobilize public pressure on conference committees, especially by means of presidential statements and addresses. President Jimmy Carter, for example, went on nationwide television to outline in detail what he expected from the 1977–78 energy conference. Second, presidents can threaten to use their veto power unless conferees reach an acceptable compromise. It was Woodrow Wilson who once wrote that by means of the veto, the president "acts not as the executive but as a third branch of the legislature."[53] Just the threat of a veto was sufficient to convince a 1983 conference to reduce spending levels contained in an emerging conference accord. Senator Mark O. Hatfield (R, Ore.) echoed presidential warnings in telling the conferees that "we're looking a veto square in the face unless we bring this bill down." With the August recess near at hand and few prospects of Con-

---

51. Gary Klott, "Calling All the President's Tax Experts," *New York Times,* July 19, 1986.

52. Ibid. These 1986 administration assessments constituted an institutionalized extension of the more personal services earlier offered conferees by then-OMB Director David Stockman. In the course of a complex 1981 appropriations conference, for example, Stockman, Max Friederdorf, the president's chief congressional lobbyist, and other White House officials were deeply involved in every phase of the negotiations, with Stockman readily providing numbers as needed. "Conferees would periodically ask him what certain decisions would mean for the budget. Stockman would tap away [on his calculator], then provide answers" (*Time,* Dec. 7, 1981, p. 17).

53. Woodrow Wilson, *Congressional Government* (Boston: Houghton Mifflin Co., 1885), p. 52.

gress being able to override a veto, the conferees relented and reluctantly accepted deep spending cuts in the measure.[54]

Conferees, to be sure, will frequently work to reduce the possibility of a veto. As Senator Jake Garn (R, Utah) proudly noted at the conclusion of a 1983 conference,

> I am pleased to report that the conference agreement on the first of the regular appropriations bills . . . was completed . . . and that the resulting bill is acceptable to the administration. On the day of the conference, the conference received a letter from [Office of Management and Budget Director David Stockman] . . . stating that he would recommend the bill be signed if the conferees satisfactorily addressed four issues. Each of these issues was, indeed, resolved to the administration's satisfaction in conference.[55]

On the other hand, heavy-handed threats of a presidential veto may irritate the conferees and be counterproductive. They may pay such threats little heed or even determine to call the president's bluff either by adopting an agreement that would stand a good chance of winning the necessary two-thirds vote in each house to override a veto or by adding provisions that the president dislikes to "must" legislation. Because of the potential of presidential vetoes, multiple conferences are sometimes convened on what is essentially the same legislation: an omnibus bill and smaller parts of it that are embodied in separate legislation. A president who vetoes the omnibus conference report may still accept all or some of its less controversial parts in separately enacted legislation.

Finally, presidential influence can be exercised indirectly—although no less strongly—through intermediaries, most often House or Senate leaders of the president's own party. In mid-1986, for example, President Reagan was concerned over the direction that a major budget conference was taking. Discussions ensued between White House Chief of Staff Donald T. Regan and Senate Majority Leader Robert J. Dole (R, Kan.). The result was a strong public commitment by Senator Dole: "We pledged we would break up the conference if we had to unless we worked out something agreeable to the White House on defense."[56]

Representatives of Governmental Agencies

The next category of participants in conference politics are a hybrid. In one sense, representatives of governmental agencies are part of the presidency; in another sense, they are akin to interest group spokesmen (to be discussed next). In fact, while something of each, they are uniquely distinctive.[57]

---

54. Judy Savasohn, "Conferees Accept Deep Cuts in Supplemental Funding Bill," *Congressional Quarterly Weekly Report,* June 23, 1983, p. 1525.
55. *Congressional Record,* 98th Cong., 1st sess., June 29, 1983, p. S9430.
56. *Washington Post,* May 9, 1986, p. A6.
57. The significance of agency representatives in conference politics was stressed in conversations held in Washington with Louis Fisher on Oct. 20, 1981, and William Baer, former staff aide and lobbyist for the Federal Trade Commission on Nov. 3, 1981, and in a conversation with Terence T. Finn of NASA in Chicago on Sept. 1, 1983. Appreciation is expressed to these longtime Capitol Hill observers for their suggestions.

Certainly, agency representatives, as part of the executive branch, are not about to lobby openly in opposition to presidential positions. In fact, much of their conference activity is explicitly in support of broad presidential policy. When House and Senate conferees during the 100th Congress finished their work on a major expansion of Medicare, they broke into applause for Health and Human Services Secretary Otis Bowen, who had worked diligently to push the issue of catastrophic medical costs onto the president's agenda. Secretary Bowen was an important participant during the Medicare conference's deliberations.[58]

At other times, representatives of governmental agencies are concerned with more parochial issues. These matters may be substantially independent of presidential priorities and can include such issues as appropriations levels for specific programs or the enactment of legislation facilitating the agency's mission. When agency representatives are advocating agency-dependent legislative goals, their conference role will be less that of presidential policy advocate than representative of a particular interest—their governmental agency.

Representatives of governmental agencies are a rather special type of interest spokesmen. As part of the administration, they may be able to clothe their appeals vaguely as being compatible with the president's program. As directors of a sector of governmental policy, they may be able to find common cause with key conferees who have a strong personal or constituency commitment to established or evolving agency programs. And, as administrators dealing with ongoing governmental problems and programs, they have a special responsibility (eagerly accepted in most cases) to share their experiences and appraisals with Congress. It is indicative of their special relationship with congressmen and conferees that representatives of governmental agencies have a privileged place (along with officials speaking directly for the president) in conference meetings and negotiations—even those gatherings officially closed to outside participants.

An example from an agriculture conference held in 1984 illustrates the involvement of agency representatives in bicameral negotiations, especially in establishing bargaining limits as to what their agency will or will not accept. Agency leverage of this sort, of course, requires firm backing from House or Senate conferees. This was the case in this instance. Senate Agriculture Chairman Jesse Helms (R, N.C.) held the proxies of enough Senate conferees to give him a solid majority on the Senate conference delegation for his agricultural views, which also enjoyed the strong support of the Department of Agriculture. With the rapid approach of the spring planting season, the legislative alliance of Helms and the department was able to "call the shots" in conference. As House Democratic conferee Berkeley Bedell of Iowa subsequently explained to the House,

---

58. Julie Rovner, "Catastrophic-Costs Bill Ready for Final Action," *Congressional Quarterly Weekly Report,* May 28, 1988, pp. 1448–49. The various instances of the involvement of personnel from the Treasury Department in conference deliberations that we cited in the last section constitute additional examples. In working in support of the 1986 tax reform bill, for instance, the Treasury forces were very much lobbying on behalf of the president.

> For those who were not at the conference committee, let me tell you how it worked. The way it worked, we Members on the House side brought up several proposals in order to improve this legislation. Each time the Senate side asked the Department of Agriculture whether they would agree to our proposal or whether they would not. They did not agree and the Senate then, which was controlled by a majority of Republicans, simply said, "No, we cannot accept it," and it was turned down.[59]

The House believed it necessary to go along with the Senate and the Agriculture Department to avoid taking the blame for delaying the conference and upsetting farmers during an election year. Thus, representatives of a governmental agency, working in conjunction and cooperation with the majority of one chamber's conferees, were able, in this case, to dominate conference deliberations.

Interest Group Spokesmen

Lobbyists are an integral part of the legislative process, including at the conference stage. They provide expertise, analysis, and advice to conferees and often act as brokers and coordinators among various conference participants. Their clout in conference depends on a variety of factors such as an adroit application of the broad arsenal of persuasive techniques (from direct to indirect methods), the cohesiveness of the group, its capacity to form coalitions with like-minded associations, and the nature and visibility of the issues it advocates.

At various places in this book, we have considered the roles of interest groups in conference interactions, especially in terms of the changes resulting (or only partially resulting) from the opening of conference committees to lobbyists on an equal basis in the mid-1970s.[60] Without repeating these discussions, we note again the constant presence and influence of interest group representatives at every point in the conference process, from the decision to have a conference and the selection of conferees, through the meetings of the conference committee itself, to the ratification politics of the conference report.

An example of the pervasiveness of interest representation concerns the extensive interest group activity that permeated every stage of the legislative history of the 1986 tax reform bill. On one particularly oppressive Saturday in early August, for instance, dozens of lobbyists and reporters were "huddled around the closed doors of a Capitol meeting room where the [conference] lawmakers were working."

> To the casual observer, it is hard to figure out why scores of lobbyists need to spend time hanging around the Capitol on [an August] weekend. Congress has been working on tax reform for more than a year, so they've already had plenty of time to make their pitches.
>
> But lobbyists still have some ways to try to prevent damaging provisions from being written into the law.

59. *Congressional Record,* 98th Cong., 2d sess., April 3, 1984, p. H2183.
60. For a detailed discussion of the consequences of the opening of conference sessions, see chapter 3 above.

Suppose, for instance, that lawmakers start discussing limits on the deductibility of charitable contributions and come up with a compromise. As long as they know lobbyists from non-profit groups—who have been vigorously fighting to preserve such deductions—are just a few steps away, they can easily dispatch an aide to find out whether the compromise is acceptable. If the lawmakers learn that it isn't, they may decide to come up with a new approach—possibly one suggested by the lobbyists. Or they may choose to take the heat of making a decision that they know will be unpopular in certain quarters.[61]

Interest group activity may also take less dramatic and visible form. Representative Bill Alexander (D, Ark.) recalls what a lobbyist once told him: "Conference is where the dirty work gets done. A strategically placed phrase in a conference report can carry more weight [for the lobbyist's cause] than a whole year of hearings."[62]

One way that interest group representatives develop access to and favorable relations with conferees is through their extensive and detailed knowledge of the technical aspects of policy questions and legislative language. At times, this resource can be immensely helpful to conferees. Representative Thomas S. Foley (D, Wash.) points out the importance of this knowledge: "I've seen lobbyists save conferees from making technical mistakes."[63]

Clearly, any time an interest group can join forces with other participants—be they key conferee groups, representatives of governmental agencies, or other interest groups—it will be in a particularly strong position. Coalitions in interest group politics may transform narrow, selfish goals into what are instead perceived as expressions of the public interest. This is why interest group spokesmen will so readily cooperate with others who have allied goals. In 1981, representatives of sixteen major farm organizations quickly responded to a presidential request to meet at the White House to chart a common strategy; they agreed upon common goals concerning an agricultural conference that was agonizing its way through what would be twenty-seven marathon sessions.[64]

Compromise is the essence of interest group politics—compromise among groups attempting to form a lobbying alliance, compromise by conferees seeking to placate interest group demands, and compromise—always—among conferees attempting to reach bicameral agreement on a contentious bill. Not all legislative matters, however, lend themselves to easy compromise. Differences of conscience or principle are frequently difficult to resolve. Abortion is a classic example.

Throughout the 1970s the House and Senate frequently locked horns over federal funding for abortions. Both chambers struggled to define antiabortion language that each could accept. The House generally opposed any federal funding except when the life of

---

61. Stacy E. Palmer, "College Lobbyists Stand Guard as Tax-Reform Compromise is Forged," *Chronicle of Higher Education*, Aug. 6, 1986, p. 10. See also the comprehensive account of this legislative initiative contained in Birnbaum and Murray, *Showdown at Gucci Gulch*.

62. Steven V. Roberts, "Conferences are Site of Legislative Showdowns," *New York Times*, Nov. 20, 1981.

63. Ibid.

64. Ward Sinclair, "Reagan Adds to Pressure on Farm Bill Conferees," *Washington Post*, Dec. 3, 1981.

the mother was endangered, while the Senate tended to insist on broader exceptions for abortion aid. Pro-life and pro-choice organizations mobilized public sentiment in members' states and districts, and individual lobbyists were active participants in day-to-day conference negotiations. One such interest group spokesman, Mark Gallagher, represented the right-to-life position of the nation's Roman Catholic bishops and was a particularly significant actor at the conference bargaining table. "Every time the Senate conferees make a compromise offer, Mr. Gallagher quietly walks to the conference table to tell a staff aide to the 11 House conferees whether the proposal is acceptable to the bishops," one account noted. "His recommendations invariably are followed."[65]

Because of the intense viewpoints associated with this issue, conference compromises were seen as only temporary decisions, subject to periodic debate and revision in subsequent bicameral negotiating sessions. Groups opposed to current federal abortion aid policies could be counted on to spark new efforts to secure future language more acceptable to their preferences. The dilemma for conferees, noted one representative, is that no matter what was done concerning the Senate or House legislative language, "All we do is assure that every year we will have the same fight."[66] Policy questions of this type reverberate from year to year.

Congressional conferences have been termed "the court of last resort for affected interests."[67] Along with the interests of the presidency and governmental agencies, one also finds well represented in conference politics the vigorously articulated interests of private organizations of every variety.

The Press

The last of our participants in conference committees purports to be not a participant but an observer. Press coverage of conference deliberations and deal making, however, seldom is neutral in its impact. Particularly with the opening of conference committee sessions generally to press scrutiny, the reporting of conference negotiations and potential compromises can have significant impact on the processes of bargaining and negotiations. Yet, as discussed earlier,[68] journalistic coverage of conference interactions is highly spotty and uneven. The usual tendency of the media is to cover the outcome of conferences rather than to inquire into the internal dynamics of who and what determined the result. The result is that this important element of the legislative process seldom receives the journalistic coverage accorded other more prominent stages of the lawmaking process—such as a showy committee hearing featuring celebrity witnesses.[69]

65. *New York Times,* Nov. 27, 1977, p. 4E.
66. Mary Eisner Eccles, "Conferees Inch Toward Abortion Agreement," *Congressional Quarterly Weekly Report,* Oct. 1, 1977, p. 2084.
67. Randall B. Ripley, *Congress: Process and Policy,* 2d ed. (New York: Norton, 1978), p. 85.
68. The recurrent tendency of journalists to neglect conference negotiations is discussed in chapter 3 above.
69. Noteworthy exceptions to this generalization include the excellent, ongoing Capitol Hill journalism of the *New York Times,* the *Wall Street Journal,* and the *Washington Post,* and most of all, the superb in-depth accounts of conference committee politics regularly contained in the *Congressional Quarterly Weekly Report* and yearly *Congressional Quarterly Almanac.*

The central problem is that conference deliberations—even when reporters, or less likely television camera crews, can shove into a hopelessly overcrowded conference room—can be dull and messy events. They are not easy to summarize in reasonably brief written form, and even less suitable for mass TV viewer comprehension. No glamorous witnesses dramatize issues and causes and very few clear-cut votes occur. Many provisions are agreed to on a nod or a mumble, and even more have been privately worked out and may not even be put to a formal vote. In short, conferences make for difficult print coverage and for dull TV.

Despite these constraints, the media do on occasion affect conference interactions, especially as potential deals are reported and communicated to affected interests beyond the conference. Reactions resulting from media coverage of conference activity may have considerable impact on what the conference does—or does not do. At times, then, the media can have real consequence in conference committee politics; in this sense the media can be viewed as another player in conference committee interactions.

We close this chapter on conference processes, types, and participants with a final, ambiguous scene. It is June 12, 1984, and House and Senate conferees (along with hundreds of interested additional congressmen, staffers, and journalists together with representatives of interest groups, governmental agencies, and the president) are jammed into one of the largest Capitol Hill committee rooms waiting for the official opening of what is expected to be a difficult conference on tax legislation. Everyone who has managed to fit into the meeting room, and those who crowd the corridor outside, wait impatiently for the proceedings to begin. The official hour for the convening of the conference comes—and passes.

The reason for the delay is quite simple. Senator Robert Dole (R, Kan.), chairman of the Senate Finance Committee and also chairman of the conference, has urgent business in the corridor outside the conference room. He has a date with a TV camera crew from Wichita, Kansas, and they are late in arriving. As he stands in the hallway reflecting both on the long conference process about to start and on the power of the media that has held everything up, he remarks ambiguously in words referring possibly to the process ahead, to deals already made, or even to the microphone now snapped onto his necktie, "We've got this wired."[70]

---

70. *New York Times*, June 12, 1984.

8

The Preconference Process

"Things almost always turn out otherwise than one anticipates": this is an aphorism that members of Congress well appreciate. Congressional policymaking, after all, commonly occurs in an atmosphere replete with emotion, inertia, pressure, ambition, and scores of other forces that make any prediction unsure. Still, congressmen seek to shape and direct legislative outcomes in an attempt to reduce this uncertainty. Particularly on major, controversial legislation, senators and representatives, their staff aides, and many others are constantly assessing the options, strategies, and procedures they can employ to accomplish their goals. Far better to prepare purposefully for objectives than to rely on fate or the mood of the moment to dictate what happens to cherished legislative initiatives.

In the expectation that measures will end up in conference, senators and representatives regularly employ particular tactics and strategies to enhance their chamber's negotiating leverage with the other body. These strategic and tactical actions during the preconference process can be roughly classified into two broad types: chamber-passing and conference-asking. The first deals with the multiple elements associated with moving a bill through the House and Senate; they include introduction, committee, and floor phases. The second category refers to the procedural and policy considerations that permeate the process of requesting and agreeing to a conference. Such issues as which chamber first asks for or—in response—agrees to a conference, and how each request or acceptance is actually accomplished, can shape when or whether the chambers go to conference and what policy outcomes result from the House-Senate deliberations. Preconference strategies, in short, are significant features of congressional decision making and are important determinants of the conference committee interactions that follow.

The Chamber-Passing Stage

Pushing a law through Congress is a continuous, arduous, and interconnected process. Congressmen regularly organize and plan their activities during one lawmaking phase to advance their interests in another. Rather than attempt an exhaustive review of preconference strategies, we examine only the most noteworthy in this chapter. In short, members regularly anticipate House-Senate conferences throughout the chamber-passing stage.

Introduction of Legislation

To fashion a bill with a conference in mind is an enterprise fraught with uncertainty. Unless members (such as committee chairmen) are strategically placed as to be decisive in moving bills, lawmaking for most legislators is too unpredictable to permit worrying about later conferences during such early stages as bill drafting. Their immediate initial priority is to get a measure through committee, onto the House or Senate floor, and passed by that legislative body. Even at the introductory stage of lawmaking, however, there are at least five considerations that can shape a subsequent House-Senate conference.

First, *who* introduces a bill, *why*, and *when* can be critical to its fate. Only members of the House or Senate may introduce a bill, although they may introduce a measure for scores of different reasons, including to stimulate public debate, influence agency decision making, attract constituent and interest group support, and sometimes even to try to enact a law. *Who* sponsors legislation, however, can influence whether a bill ever reaches conference. House Judiciary Chairman Peter Rodino (D, N.J.), for example, is a key figure on civil rights issues. "You want him on board originally as a cosponsor [of a civil rights bill]," stressed a lobbyist. "Rodino is a legendary figure and carries great weight with the House, and to have him joining [as a sponsor] . . . is a very critical part of the strategy" of winning approval for such a measure in committee, on the House floor, and in conference with the Senate.[1]

Timing, too, can affect policy outcomes. A controversial measure must be introduced early enough in a session of Congress to provide sufficient time to overcome anticipated obstacles to its passage. Proponents of the legislation must allow time for lengthy conference deliberations followed by further consideration of the conference report in the House and Senate. During the Ninety-fourth Congress, for instance, the Senate failed to adopt a conference report involving major revisions of the Clean Air Act. When the report finally reached the Senate, late in the Congress, only a few days remained before the Senate's final adjournment and there was insufficient time to defeat a filibuster against the conference report. Frustration was evident in the remarks of Senator Edmund Muskie (D, Me.), the principal author and advocate of the conference accord. "My point, Mr. President," declared Senator Muskie, "is this: when a major

---

1. Nadine Cohodas, "Special Report: Peter Rodino," *Congressional Quarterly Weekly Report*, May 12, 1984, p. 1102.

Senate priority such as the Clean Air Act, which has consumed two years of intensive work, reaches the last two or three days of a session, it should not be possible for a handful of Senators to frustrate the will of the Senate, and to block even a *vote* on that major measure."[2]

Second, the content of bills is governed by what congressmen (or agency officials and lobbyists if they are parties to the legislation's development) want included in the measure. The "wordsmithing" process can greatly affect later conference activities. For one thing, members may deliberately include in a bill scores of ambitious proposals on the theory that many will be lost, modified, or traded away during floor and conference deliberations. By "asking for the moon" initially, legislators hope that they will be able to achieve a satisfactory result in the end.

As an example, late in 1985 the Senate approved a defense appropriations measure totaling $288 billion, almost $12 billion greater than the House-enacted figure. The strategy behind this action was simple: "Senate Republicans figure that by starting off with a bigger budget, when they go to reconcile the two bills [in conference] they'll end up with a higher figure than they would otherwise."[3] A member of the House Ways and Means Committee once described a similar strategy followed by then-Chairman Wilbur Mills (D, Ark.): "[He] will say, 'Maybe we can live with 10 percent, but if we send it over there [to the Senate] they'll make it 15 and we'll have to live with 12. So let's make it 8.' You say O.K. and go along."[4]

To be sure, bills can also be "sweetened"—made particularly acceptable for members of the other body. Projects wanted by key senators, for instance, can be included in the House bill with the expectation that these inclusions will lead the interested senators to galvanize their chamber into action on the House legislation. Alternatively, matters favored by senators may deliberately be left out of House legislation to enhance representatives' bargaining leverage with conferees from the other body.

It must be kept in mind that the breadth of subjects addressed in a bill can affect the number of committees that are parties to its consideration. Quite often a measure that seeks comprehensively to resolve a public problem will be referred simultaneously or sequentially to several committees. House and Senate rules permit measures that crosscut the jurisdictions of several committees to be assigned to each panel, even if serious delay is the consequence. An additional consequence of this practice is that a number of different committees may end up sending conferees to the conference committee.

In general, the more committees involved with a bill, the longer it takes for consensus to evolve. A 1979 synthetic fuels bill, for example, was reviewed by several House committees before it eventually reached conference; conferees were drawn from each of these committees. House conferee John Dingell (D, Mich.) characterized the resulting

2. Bernard Asbell, *The Senate Nobody Knows* (Garden City: Doubleday, 1978), p. 445.
3. Tim Carrington, "Senate Defense Bill has Over $2 Billion for Items the Pentagon Never Requested," *Wall Street Journal,* Nov. 11, 1985, p. 50. Ensuing conference events are examined in chapter 11 below in the case study "Dollars for Defense: Les Gets More Amidst 1985 House Turmoil."
4. John Manley, *The Politics of Finance: The House Committee on Ways and Means* (Boston: Little, Brown, 1970), p. 264.

conference as being "like a meeting of the U.N."—in other words, bedlam.[5] In consequence, members may purposively draft bills narrowly to maximize the chances for a solitary referral, or if that is not feasible, at least seek to limit the number of sections of their bill that might be within another panel's purview.

Third, members may introduce bills to send "signals" to the other body. In 1984, for example, the Senate passed the president's "down payment" deficit reduction package in statutory form. The counterpart House plan, however, had been expressed in the form of a nonbinding resolution. "Senate Republican leaders pushed for actual legislation . . . as a bargaining device," Senate aides reported. "By approving separate, legislated limits for military and nonmilitary spending, Senate leaders hoped to display the chamber's resolve in conference."[6]

Legislation is also introduced to counter proposals being considered by the other body. Senate Banking Chairman Jake Garn (R, Utah) advocated legislation in 1984 to deregulate the banking industry and prepared a bill to that effect. In the House, meanwhile, Banking Chairman Fernand St. Germain (D, R.I.) was advocating *more* rather than *less* regulation of banks. Commentators suggested that Representative St. Germain's remarks were made with an eye toward a later legislative conference with the Senate. "I'm not pushing any bill at the moment," said St. Germain. "But if the Senate wants a bill, we'll have something to offer, too."[7]

Fourth, House and Senate members may work together to introduce companion legislation. These bills, virtual identical twins, are often introduced in each chamber at about the same time. The sponsors in each chamber work in conjunction to move the legislation through the various lawmaking stages of each body, compare notes and strategies with each other, and seek generally to facilitate bicameral progress on the legislation. During this process, one of the companion bills might be reshaped to accommodate the particular concerns of its chamber, but the legislation's basic objections are likely to remain constant. As a result, during conference, conferees will be able to address points that are in disagreement without needing to question the main thrust of the legislation.

Finally, members of the House and Senate may introduce a single omnibus bill and also introduce as separate bills each major part of the comprehensive legislation. The strategic calculation behind this maneuver is that the omnibus bill will be assigned to several committees and each specific measure to one panel. If stalemate should occur on the major bill, one of the narrower measures might still reach conference. Then, if the votes are there, the whole package might be reassembled in conference and presented to the respective chambers. This is a high-risk strategy because House and Senate committees are jealous guardians of their jurisdictional turf and are likely to mobilize against a conference-reconstituted omnibus conference report that has bypassed their committee.

   5. *Washington Post,* Dec. 8, 1979, p. A6.
   6. *Wall Street Journal,* May 18, 1984, p. 4.
   7. Jacqueline Calmes, "Banking Bill May Emerge: Interstate Forays by Big Banks Revive Interest in Legislation," *Congressional Quarterly Weekly Report,* May 5, 1984, p. 1026. See also *Washington Post,* May 25, 1984, p. D9. Chairman St. Germain soon introduced legislation to ban so-called nonbank banks.

The Committee Stage

In the early 1970s, a noted congressional scholar made a simple but fundamental observation about House and Senate committees: they are all different.[8] Committees differ in their authority, decision-making styles, membership characteristics, staff organization, and in numerous other ways. Committees also vary in their interactions with their counterpart panels from the other body.[9] Some House and Senate committees (the tax and appropriations committees, for example) meet frequently in conference. Others, such as the House and Senate veterans committees, rarely convene in conference. Instead, intercameral differences on veterans' legislation are typically resolved through behind-the-scenes negotiations among the members and staff aides of the two panels.

Unsurprisingly, differences among committees affect the choice of preconference strategies. Panels that infrequently or rarely go to conference generally operate without the sensitivity to preconference strategies that characterizes committees who regularly consider issues of a "conferenceable" nature. Committees that review major, controversial, and visible issues understand that bicameral differences will usually be settled in conference; hence, preconference considerations will permeate the three main stages of committee decision making: the hearings, the markups, and the reporting phase.

1. THE HEARINGS. Congressional hearings are an integral part of lawmaking and serve a variety of overlapping purposes. Among other things, hearings can be used to gather information, review the administration of laws, and investigate public problems. They may also be employed to stall or defeat legislation through interminable interrogations or, alternatively, by means of compressed or minimal hearings, seek to expedite a bill through the legislative labyrinth.

These and other objectives of hearings can affect subsequent conference deliberations. For instance, members who have advocated positions at public hearings, perhaps in committee rooms overflowing with lobbyists, may be reluctant to compromise those views later in conference without first putting up a good fight for the benefit of their special interest supporters.[10] Hearings may also be used to develop a public record for or against issues that are sure to be in contention at the conference stage (conversely, issues may not survive in conference if they have bypassed the hearing stage; conferees can argue that without a hearing record they are lawmaking in the dark). House committees sometimes even invite senators to testify before House committees to put them and their support for the legislation on the record for the Senate and later for the conference.

An example will illustrate the impact of committee hearings on conference decision making. In mid-1980, a House critic of defense cost overruns opposed the temporary suspension of a law that permitted the federal government to reclaim excess profits from defense contractors. The suspension, agreed to in conference, had not been part of the House bill on defense procurement; it had been, however, included in the Senate

---

8. Richard F. Fenno, Jr., *Congressmen in Committees* (Boston: Little, Brown, 1973).

9. For an extended discussion of these matters, see the first section of chapter 6 above, "The Committee Context."

10. See chapter 3 above for a consideration of the necessity of such posturing resulting from the opening of conference committees in the mid-1970s.

bill. Representative Joseph Minish (D, Pa.) charged that a brief hearing on the suspension issue held just prior to the conference by the House Armed Services Committee was designed solely to enable the House conferees (chosen from the military panel and not including Representative Minish) to justify their ready conference acceptance of the Senate suspension provision. "It's all wired," claimed Representative Minish. "They hold this quickie hearing, and then the House guys use that to go along with the Senate bill in conference."[11] When the House subsequently considered the conference report, criticism of House conferee acceptance of the suspension provision was rebuffed by Armed Services conferee Samuel Stratton (D, N.Y.). The final version of the suspension provision, he proudly stated, "is the version that I recommended [to the House-Senate conferees] on the basis of our hearing and which the conference unanimously accepted."[12]

2. THE MARKUPS. Committee markups occur sometime after the hearings—if they take place at all. At the markup sessions committee members determine the final committee product by deciding whether the legislation as originally introduced should be revised, either in whole or in part. Numerous markup decisions have implications for conferences, but three broad considerations merit special discussion.

First, the decision as to which "vehicle" to use for markup—the measure as introduced, a bill written or backed by the administration, a staff proposal, or a draft prepared by the chairman—can be instrumental in shaping conference outcomes. Tactically, it is far easier to retain something already in a bill than to add or strike language from the measure during committee, floor, or conference deliberations. "Everybody knows," observed Senator John Tower (R, Tex.), "that if you believe strongly in something, it is best to get it in the committee bill because it is much more difficult to get something out of a committee bill than it is to put something into the committee bill."[13]

Second, committee members can employ a variety of markup strategies to maximize the achievement of policy objectives in conference. Among the most notable are:

- keeping something out of a bill that the other chamber favors so leverage can be obtained with the other body;[14] or, alternatively, putting proposals in the bill that

---

11. *Washington Post*, June 25, 1980, p. A14. See also *Congressional Record*, 96th Cong., 2d sess., Aug. 26, 1980, p. 23120.

12. *Congressional Record*, 96th Cong., 2d sess., Aug. 26, 1980, pp. 23120–21. For a related example, see Ronald Brownstein, "Sun, Sand and Eurobonds," *National Journal*, April 18, 1984, p. 830.

13. *Congressional Record*, 98th Cong., 1st sess., July 20, 1983, p. S10430.

14. As a Senate aide put it: "We often zero-out items we know they [the House] want" (Washington interview with Larry Patten, Nov. 4, 1981). An interesting example of this tactic comes from the other chamber, the House. In 1980 a House subcommittee deliberately acted to end special revenue sharing benefits for Louisiana sheriffs, in effect since 1976, in anticipation of an upcoming conference with the Senate. Central among the Senate conferees would be Sen. Russell B. Long (D, La.), the author and proponent of the special arrangement for the sheriffs of his state. "It's pretty simple," one strategist put it. "The subcommittee knew Russell Long would hit the roof when he got wind of this. Now they'll have something to trade with him when the bill goes to conference" (Ward Sinclair, "Dealing Sheriffs Out," *Washington Post*, July 1, 1980, p. A1; and Washington interview with Rep. Les Aspin (D, Wis.), Oct. 28, 1981. As Representative Aspin put it during this interview, "We leave the funds for the Louisiana sheriffs out so we can get favors during the conference to put them back in."

the other body wants in order to encourage that chamber to act and thus improve the measure's chances of reaching the conference stage;
- adding numerous politically palatable provisions that can be used as bargaining chips with conferees from the other body;[15]
- weakening or otherwise changing a bill in committee so that it stands a better chance of winning majority support on the floor. Supporters can then try to persuade conferees to strengthen the measure in conference;
- providing guidelines or directives for decision making in conference;[16] or
- crafting a bill that includes the priority proposals of targeted leaders and factions in the other body.

Finally, committee markups affect the "scope" (more on this in chapter 10) or range of issues and programs addressed in legislation. *Scope* is a technical term laden with policy implications, but its meaning is easily understood by means of an example from 1984:

> The Senate rejected a very expensive version of a new GI Bill, estimated by the Congressional Budget Office to cost eventually more than $1 billion per year. It chose instead a relatively austere plan proposed by Sen. John Glenn, which is estimated to cost about $20 million per year. The House had earlier passed a much more generous version, which ultimately would top $750 million per year. . . . The choice confronting legislators going to conference on the defense authorization bill this week is how much to spend on a new GI Bill.[17]

Under precedents that are expected to guide conference decision making, House and Senate conferees are to remain within the scope or range of differences committed to them. In the example above, House-Senate conferees were bound neither to go above the

---

15. An additional benefit of such "Christmas Tree" legislation can come during chamber consideration. A floor manager for the bill may be quite willing to accept a wide variety of amendments sought by individual members (thus winning their support for chamber acceptance of the bill) because he knows they can be disposed of later in conference. Washington interview with William Cherkasky, former longtime Senate aide, Nov. 3, 1981.

One senator, a member of the Senate Appropriations Committee, explained this action as follows: "'The Committee will try to help a fellow out by putting a project in the bill as long as he understands it will not be pushed in conference. When you get the real money—the big money—you have to have merit'" (Steven Horn, *Unused Power: The Work of the Senate Committee on Appropriations* [Washington, D.C.: Brookings Institution, 1970], p. 91).

Another Senate aide explained that "comity" usually results in the inclusion without controversy of the pet projects and proposals of the committee chairman and chamber leaders: "If they only cost $10 to $30 million, there is no problem" (Washington interview with Larry Patten, Senate staff aide, Nov. 4, 1981).

16. As an example, the Senate Finance Committee included a provision in a 1983 general revenue sharing measure that increased the availability of funds for certain local governments. However, those increases would take effect "only if House members in a conference on the measure insist on increasing the size of the program." A majority of Senate Finance members voted for the triggering proviso with the foreknowledge that the House had already voted to increase the size of the program (Richard Whittle, "Finance Panel Votes Changes in Revenue Sharing Formula," *Congressional Quarterly Weekly Report*, July 2, 1983, p. 1360).

17. *Washington Post*, June 18, 1984, p. A23.

House-passed figure of $750 million nor below the Senate-passed figure of $20 million, and certainly would be prohibited from embracing the original $1 billion plan the Senate considered but rejected. To be sure, complexities abound in determining the dimensions of scope when words rather than figures are in bicameral disagreement.

Committees that know what the other body has enacted can also make decisions designed to diminish or enhance the chances for conference agreement. If the House passes a tax bill, for example, the Senate Finance Committee could adopt many of the House provisions during its markup sessions and thus minimize the number of matters in bicameral disagreement. Sometimes committees will deliberately wait until the other body (either its committee or the floor) acts on legislation so they can better calculate what needs to go in their own bill—either to ensure as much harmony as possible between the versions or to collect some ammunition for later bipartisan negotiations. After a House Public Works subcommittee in 1984 included thirty-one new projects in a highway bill, numerous senators urged their transportation subcommittee to authorize yet additional projects. "When we get into that conference," declared Senator Lloyd Bentsen (D, Tex.), "we're going to have some trading material."[18]

3. THE REPORTING PHASE. Once committees conclude their markup, they next vote on reporting the bill out of committee. (House and Senate rules require a committee majority to be present for this purpose.) This vote can be critical for what it might portend for conference negotiations. Bills voted out of committee unanimously or with broad majorities stand better chances both on the floor and in conference than measures reported with narrow committee majorities. Legislation adopted by a united committee, in brief, is advantaged in conference from a bargaining standpoint compared to one adopted by a committee rent with sharp divisions.

Another consideration is the option chosen by committees in reporting their own measure or legislation that has previously passed the other chamber. Committees may opt to report such measures without any change, with a series of amendments to different parts of the bill, or with an "amendment in the nature of a substitute." The latter is the functional equivalent of a new bill. It recommends new language for the *entire* bill. This option also grants House-Senate conferees the greatest latitude in negotiating bicameral compromises.

When the House enacts a committee-reported amendment in the nature of a substitute (ANS), what typically happens next is that the House will take the comparable Senate-passed measure, strike all the language after the enacting clause ("Be it enacted by the Senate and House of Representatives . . .") and insert its own legislation in the form of an ANS. This procedure is important for subsequent conference deliberations, because House-Senate conferees may later, during conference negotiations, take the two chamber-passed bills (with identical bill numbers and enacting clauses but quite different texts) and substitute a third version of the legislation. The main constraint on the conferees' action is that the substitute must be a germane (or relevant) modification of the two chambers' products. However, what constitutes a germane modification in this case

18. Robert Rothman "Scramble On to Add Pork to Road Bill," *Congressional Quarterly Weekly Report,* May 5, 1984, p. 1070.

is often difficult to interpret; hence the conferees' discretion is large despite the germaneness constraint.[19]

By contrast, when House-Senate conferees consider a series of discrete amendments in bicameral disagreement, they operate under tighter negotiating restrictions. According to the House and Senate parliamentarians,

> If there are multiple amendments by the Senate to a House-passed version of a bill, the conferees under the rules are allowed to deal only with the language inserted in the House-passed bill by the Senate amendments or any language of the House-passed bill stricken out by Senate amendments—this is all that is in conference for compromise; the language of the bill approved by both Houses is not in conference and may not be touched by the conferees.[20]

Finally, a standing committee sometimes will reconvene to draft alternative proposals if their originally reported bills stir up strong opposition from the other chamber, the White House, or lobbyists. "Knowing that its original committee-reported bill faced stiff opposition from the administration and the Senate," wrote a journalist in 1980, "the House Merchant Marine and Fisheries Committee offered a committee-approved substitute on the [House] floor."[21] Such a substitute can enhance the prospects for a bill's passage in the other body and smooth the way for conference decision making.

Floor Decision Making

Floor action on bills is somewhat comparable to committee markups with one exception: while the House or Senate *makes* revisions to measures, formally their committees only *recommend* amendments to legislation for subsequent chamber acceptance. During floor consideration of bills, senators and representatives use a variety of devices that are designed to enhance their bargaining leverage with the other body. They can be categorized as debating, amending, voting, and passing strategies.

1. DEBATE. Talk is crucial to legislative decision making. It is commonly employed to send signals to various "listeners," such as potential conferees, the other body, executive branch officials, and lobbyists. Explained Senate Majority Leader Howard Baker (R, Tenn.) in 1982:

---

19. For detailed discussion of germaneness rule differences between House and Senate and their impact on conference processes, see chapter 10 below.

20. Floyd M. Riddick [parliamentarian emeritus of the Senate] and William Holmes Brown [parliamentarian of the House], "Conferences and Conference Reports: STAFF Introduction to the Rules," *STAFF*, issue 15 (Sept. 1978), p. 1. Some committees regularly employ the multiple amendment option when reporting legislation; the Senate Appropriations Committee is a prime example. By custom, the House initiates appropriations measures, and the multiple amendment option obviates concern on the part of the House that the Senate is intruding on its initiatory prerogatives by proposing a new bill in the form of a substitute amendment. On major bills, the other House and Senate committees typically report an amendment in the nature of a substitute.

21. Kathy Koch, "Congress Clears Legislation to Revamp Federal Program for Managing Coastal Zone," *Congressional Quarterly Weekly Report*, Oct. 4, 1980, p. 2934.

Let me say to my friend [Senator Mark Andrews (R, N.D.)], who served in the House of Representatives so long, that he knows even better than I do that in advance of a House-Senate conference it is not unusual for the respective parties to stake out positions for themselves and even to utter statements about their absolute intransigence, that sometimes does not always prevail when the conference convenes.[22]

Floor debates and speeches, in short, are commonly made with conference objectives in mind, such as highlighting bicameral differences (or agreements) on issues, attempting to weaken the resolve of the other body by firing verbal salvos at it, or encouraging conferees to take certain positions. "I urge my colleagues who will be Senate conferees on this most vital legislation," said Senator Carl Levin (D, Mich.) in 1984, "to accede to the House and accept . . . the U.S. Policy Towards South Africa Act."[23]

2. AMENDMENTS. The floor-amending process is a crucial decision-making stage in the House and Senate, for amendments permit each chamber to put its policy stamp on legislation. Sometimes amendments become more important or controversial than the bill themselves.[24] Amendments, too, can be artfully employed to influence House-Senate conferences. In brief, amendments often serve combined purposes such as building winning floor coalitions and providing bargaining chips for conference. Members responsible for shepherding bills to final passage (called floor managers) commonly accept amendments from colleagues both to give them a stake in passage of the bill and to obtain trading material for conference.

In 1984, for example, the Senate amended a revenue bill to include a variety of tax relief amendments. Finance Chairman Robert Dole (R, Kan.), who opposed many of these proposals, nevertheless recognized that their adoption would give the senatorial sponsors a vested interest in the measure and win their vote for the bill's final passage. "This is the grease that smoothes the path" of Senate passage and gets the measure to conference, he acknowledged.[25] Besides "grease," these amendments were also dubbed by the *Wall Street Journal* "conference bait"—provisions to be traded away as needed during conference.[26] Over the years a master of the addition of such amendments was Senator Russell B. Long (D, La.), who was noted for what was called "corn shucking": "He would sit quietly while the Senate passed dozens of amendments. Then, in conference with the House, he would throw the amendments away, like the husk on an ear of corn, until he reached the legislative kernels he wanted to retain."[27]

    22. *Congressional Record*, 97th Cong., 2d sess., Dec. 20, 1982, p. S15757.
    23. *Congressional Record*, 98th Cong., 2d sess., March 1, 1984, p. S2140.
    24. See, for example, the amendment to routine debt ceiling legislation in 1985 that came to be known as the Gramm-Rudman plan. A case study in chapter 11 below examines the legislative and conference history of this noted and controversial floor amendment.
    25. *New York Times*, April 27, 1984, p. A16.
    26. *Wall Street Journal*, April 16, 1984, p. 4.
    27. David E. Rosenbaum, "Senators Expect Approval in '86 of Tax Changes," *New York Times*, Jan. 27, 1986, p. A19. See also Daniel J. Balz, "When the Man from Louisiana's There, It's a Long, Long Road to Tax Reform," *National Journal*, May 23, 1976, p. 694.
    Upon Senator Long's retirement from the U.S. Senate, he was lauded by President Ronald Reagan as "the one legislator who had his mind on the conference . . . when the others were worrying about the floor debate" ("Remarks of President Ronald Reagan at a Dinner Honoring Senator Russell B. Long of

Three points about amendments as bargaining chips require discussion. First, the Senate's emphasis on individualism and its lack of a general germaneness (or relevance) rule means that it is easier for senators than representatives to add scores of floor amendments to legislation (the House has a strict germaneness requirement for amendments).[28] The Senate's ability to add trading material is, however, a two-edged sword. On the one hand, Senate conferees often will adopt amendments for conference trading purposes. On the other hand, Senate bills can become so cluttered with unrelated amendments that they prevent the legislation from ever reaching conference—or even strengthen the hand of House conferees later in bicameral negotiations. For example, a banking bill to which the Senate has added an important agriculture amendment is unlikely, for jurisdictional and policy reasons, to be accepted by House conferees largely or entirely chosen from the House Banking Committee. They will likely agree to accept the Senate's amendment only in exchange for significant concessions from their Senate counterparts on key banking provisions important to the House conferees.

Second, senators understand that when legislative managers say on the floor of their chamber, "I will take the amendment to conference," that is often little more than a death knell for that amendment.[29] Senator Howard Metzenbaum (D, Ohio), for example, inquired of Senator Dole in 1984 if certain Senate amendments were destined to be dropped in conference. In a typically tongue-in-cheek response, Senator Dole replied, "I would rather say 'disposed of in conference.' I have indicated to the Senator from Ohio that we will certainly consider these carefully in conference before they are disposed of."[30]

Third, some bargaining chips are more equal than others. Amendments sponsored by influential legislators may not be dropped—or dropped only after careful consideration of the implications of offending such important members, even if retention of the provisions might jeopardize conference agreement or chamber passage of the conference report. Members, too, may "not fight as hard against objectionable [floor] amendments if they know that the person who proposed the amendment will not be represented in conference."[31] Absent an advocate, such amendments will probably be quickly and easily disposed of in conference.

Louisana Upon His Retirement, Oct. 16, 1985," *Weekly Compilation of Presidential Documents*, Oct. 16, 1985, p. 1260).

28. Germaneness as an issue in conference report consideration is considered in chapter 10 below. For a general discussion of House and Senate rules and their policy implications, see Walter J. Oleszek, *Congressional Procedures and the Policy Process*, 3d ed. (Washington, D.C.: Congressional Quarterly Press, 1989).

29. Sen. Kenneth Keating (R, N.Y.) once expressed a hope, concerning an amendment of his, "that the words 'taken to conference' do not have a sinister connotation and that it will emerge from conference as well as being taken there" (*Congressional Record*, 88th Cong., 2d sess., 1984, vol. 110, pt. 2, p. 2372, quoted in Randall B. Ripley, *Power in the Senate* [New York: St. Martin's Press, 1969], p. 129).

30. *Congressional Record*, 98th Cong., 2d sess., May 17, 1984, p. S5969. With open conferences, conferees may put up harder fights before certain amendments are dropped because campaign-supporting lobbyists are now watching the proceedings in person. See chapter 3 above.

31. Abner J. Mikva and Patti B. Saris, *The American Congress* (New York: Franklin Watts, 1983), p. 243.

A further example of preconference maneuvering is that floor managers will sometimes tell members not to worry about a particularly muddled or unfortunate provision of a proposal on the floor because in conference "we will clean it up" by clarifying the language or rectifying the oversight. In 1985, for example, House backers of legislation limiting textile imports resisted a potential flood of floor amendments seeking to protect other industries by indicating that substantial changes in the legislation would be considered during conference: "There's a lot of legislating to do until we get a bill to the President's desk," observed James T. Broyhill (R, N.C.), the chief proponent of the bill in the House.[32] Sometimes postponing important legislative matters to conference appears less noble. To somewhat modify one representative's observation, "The phrase 'the conference will fix it up' is the moral equivalent of 'I'll respect you in the morning.'"[33]

The amendment process can affect conference deliberations in other ways. Opponents of legislation, for example, might "add as many [floor] amendments as possible," particularly if the bill faces a deadline, to ensure a "lengthy and complex conference process."[34] Amendments can also be employed to either broaden or narrow the scope of issues in bicameral disagreement. As Senator Ted Stevens (R, Alaska) pointed out during Senate consideration of a defense appropriations bill,

> These are items we have examined. What they do is increase the Senate's position as we go into conference. These are items we had discussed before. For instance, there is the EP-3 aircraft item of $70 million. The House committee had zeroed that out and we had not provided any moneys also. It is a matter that is of interest to Members of the Senate to have that item in conference. We are willing to take it to conference. That is the basis, as the Senator from Michigan stated, that this amendment increases the amount that is stated in the bill for the purpose of conference as we approach negotiations with the House.[35]

Members who are frustrated in offering or winning support for amendments in their chamber may look for assistance to the other body. For instance, in 1984 a House member who had been unsuccessful in his efforts to add an amendment to a foreign aid measure was encouraged by the legislation's House floor manager to "work" the Senate. He promised that if the member "is successful in getting the matter added in the other body, then I, for one, will be very happy to accept both the amount and the theory and the purpose of the amendment" when the foreign aid bill reaches conference.[36]

Similarly, a Senate Democratic Committee aide explained in late 1980, following the loss of Democratic control of the Senate, "We're going to follow events in the House a lot more closely from now on. Before, we were pretty self-possessed here [in the Senate], but if we can't get our way as the minority, we may persuade our House contacts

---

32. Harrison Donnelly, "Congress Mulling Options on Textile Quotas," *Congressional Quarterly Weekly Report,* Oct. 5, 1985, p. 2017.
33. Adapted from an observation about a bill by Rep. Bill Frenzel (R, Minn.) concerning the House's tendency to count on the Senate to "fix it up." Quoted in *New York Times,* Dec. 4, 1985, p. D2.
34. Mikva and Saris, *The American Congress,* p. 243.
35. *Congressional Record,* 98th Cong., 1st sess., Nov. 8, 1983, p. S15663.
36. *Congressional Record,* 98th Cong., 2d sess., May 9, 1984, p. H3573.

THE PRECONFERENCE PROCESS 165

to put certain features into their bills and then fight for them when the measure comes to conference."37

3. VOTES. Voting is one of the more important actions that congressmen take. It is a public expression of their position on an amendment or measure. It is also a key feature of preconference strategy on legislation. One strategy on behalf of a bill is to roll up a huge chamber vote in its favor in an attempt thus to enhance its prospects for reaching and surviving conference. As Senator Packwood noted in mid-1986 during debate on the landmark overhaul of the internal revenue code,

> I think when the bill passes the Senate, and it is clear that it will pass, that momentum will carry though the Congress to the House. . . . This momentum grows daily, and I think it might peak just about the time we are at conference. If it passes here 100 to nothing or even if it passes 75 to 25 . . . I think the chances are pretty good for the bulk of the substance of this bill being adopted in conference.38

Member's reasons for voting for matters are not always clear-cut. They may vote for an amendment in the deliberate expectation (and often hope) that the conference will kill it. Sometimes congressmen will even vote on both sides of an issue—agreeing to the bill but later opposing the conference report or vice versa, in order to get at least one vote of theirs on the record in a politically useful direction.

Suffice it to say that the range of circumstances that influence particular votes is broad and complex. One decision, however, is important as regards later conference deliberations: whether or not to have a recorded vote. In brief, the decision to subject floor amendments or bills to recorded votes can affect their fate in conference. For example, a Senate floor manager in the late 1970s sought a recorded vote on a colleague's amendment he opposed: "Culver's idea is to beat the amendment, and beat it good, burying the issue in the Senate once and for all, and also putting him in a position to tell a Senate-House conference on the bill that the proposal was resoundingly defeated in the Senate."39

Recorded votes, in short, are part of the arsenal of devices employed to promote a chamber's bargaining position with the other body. As a House conferee told his Senate counterparts in 1984, "The House has voted twice to stop the war in Nicaragua. This is not negotiable."40 It is also important above all to avoid a negative recorded vote. "If you get your amendment brought up in the Senate, and it loses 80-20," noted a lobbyist in 1986, "it sure ruins your clout in the conference committee."41

  37. William J. Lanouette, "Don't Look for Quick Policy Shifts from the GOP Senate's Committees," *National Journal,* Jan. 3, 1981, p. 16.
  38. *Congressional Record,* 99th Cong., 2d sess., June 10, 1986, p. S7157.
  39. Elizabeth Drew, *Senator* (New York: Simon and Schuster, 1979), p. 174.
  40. *New York Times,* May 17, 1984, p. A14.
  41. Eileen Shanahan, "New, Diverse Coalition Works to Pass Tax Bill," *Congressional Quarterly Weekly Report,* May 24, 1986, p. 1147. For a particularly vivid instance of a legislative supporter avoiding a possibly negative chamber roll call vote on his amendment, see *Congressional Record,* 80th Cong., 2d sess. (1948), p. 6900. For an example of a legislative *opponent* similarly avoiding a likely *favorable* chamber vote on an amendment he opposed (this vote was finally avoided only by the strategist's reluctant acceptance of the proviso as part of the bill going to conference), see *Congressional Record,* 79th Cong., 2d sess. (1946), p. 6093. Both of these examples are drawn from Bertram M. Gross, *The Legislative Struggle: A Study in Social Combat* (New York: McGraw-Hill, 1953), pp. 318–19.

Very often an opponent of an amendment will seek to avoid a recorded vote so as to allow conferees leeway to interpret their chamber's views any way they want. At one point in 1984, Senator Dole was leading the opposition to an amendment backed by Senator Russell Long (D, La.). He prevailed upon Senator Long to accept a chamber vote on his amendment by voice vote rather than by roll call. The absence of a recorded vote on the amendment was later important to Senator Dole during the conference: it "had the political effect of strengthening Senator Dole's hand in trying to kill the Long provision in conference, which is precisely what Sen. Dole did."[42]

There are occasions, to be sure, when support for an amendment or for the bill itself is so strong that a recorded vote is thought to be unnecessary for conference purposes. Noted Senator Long in this instance,

> In view of the fact that the Chairman and, I am sure, the Democratic Members strongly support this, and in light of the fact that some of the Republican Members of the conference are cosponsors of the amendment—in light of the fact that I believe it will have very strong support on the Senate side, I am persuaded by the distinguished Chairman that a roll call vote could not put us in any stronger position than we are in already. Therefore I am not going to ask for a roll call vote.[43]

In his assumption that support for his amendment was sufficiently strong to insulate it from being dropped in conference Senator Long was, as events demonstrated, wrong.

4. FLOOR PASSAGE. Senators and representatives maneuver to win passage of legislation whose overall design can serve as the point of departure for conference bargaining. Measures may be deliberately fashioned, for instance, to be polar opposites from those passed by the other body. They might also be designed—in contrast with the other body's version—to be broad or narrow, flexible or restrictive, complex or simple, centrist or extremist. We know "what the Senate will be bringing to the conference table," declared a representative in 1982, and it is "critical that everyone factor in what the Senate-passed resolution contains." It is necessary that the House "go into conference with a more centrist budget resolution" than the Senate's.[44] Then, during conference, he concluded, House conferees would have the opportunity to pull their counterparts back toward the House's view of the center.

Another approach is for one chamber to pepper the other with several versions of the same bill. This strategy permits the other body to pick and choose among the alternatives, generating momentum for the legislation by accommodating the desires and concerns of diverse members. In 1978, for instance, Congress enacted a massive bill creating over one hundred parks in forty-four states. The major force behind the legisla-

---

42. *Wall Street Journal,* May 25, 1984, p. 25. A general rule of thumb is that floor managers will avoid recorded votes on those amendments that they are willing to accept during chamber consideration but may later wish to dispose of in conference. Conversely, sponsors of such amendments will usually wish to have the chamber go on record by means of a formal vote on each amendment in order to strengthen its prospects of surviving conference negotiations. Washington interview with Howard E. Shuman, longtime Senate aide, Nov. 2, 1981.

43. *Congressional Record,* 98th Cong., 2d sess., May 17, 1984, p. S5961.

44. *Congressional Record,* 97th Cong., 2d sess., May 25, 1982, p. H2783.

tion was Representative Philip Burton (D, Cal.), who in the closing days of the Ninety-fifth Congress "had the House pass three versions of the bill" to "accommodate Senators and to speed passage of the measure."[45] The political adjustments possible in this approach can sometimes smooth conference deliberations.

A final point: broad political and electoral considerations are also ever-present in bicameral positioning for conference. In 1983, the Democratic House and Republican Senate differed over both expenditures for defense and general revenue increases. Declared a White House aide, "It's important to get a Republican budget resolution through the Senate to establish that Republicans are higher on defense spending and lower on the revenue side than the Democrats. It puts more onus on the Democrats to push for tax increases."[46] If this strategy were successful, then the "tax, tax, tax" label could be pinned on congressional Democrats by the Republicans (particularly if the chambers deadlocked in conference) and be usefully exploited by President Reagan during the upcoming national election. Both legislative and partisan considerations, in short, may underlie preparation for conference maneuverings.

The Conference-Asking Stage

Following these chamber-passing activities come conference-asking processes, the selection of conferees, and—in some instances—the adoption of instructions to guide the chamber's conferees. These steps, of course, presuppose that a conference will, in fact, be the next step in the legislative process. Not all legislation, however, goes the conference route; in chapter 1 we cited the frequent observation that only about 15 to 25 percent of all congressionally passed public bills move through conference committees. (For a further examination of the overall frequency with which legislation goes to conference, see the Appendix to this chapter, "The Use of Conference"). Almost all significant and controversial bills, however, do end up in conference, for the institution of the conference committee is particularly well suited as an agency of bicameral compromise.

What of those bills that do not go to conference? One alternative to seeking a conference is, of course, to let the measure die, but a more positive response is for one chamber to adopt the other body's version of the bill.[47] Sometimes a conference is avoided because of the weakness of or loss of support for a proposal already passed in differing form by both chambers. The votes may not be there for adoption of a conference report, even if they had been there by narrow margins for the passage of the

---

45. Ann Pelham, "Three Versions: Congress Clears Measure Creating Parks in 44 States," *Congressional Quarterly Weekly Report*, Oct. 28, 1978, p. 3147.
46. *New York Times*, May 11, 1983, p. B6.
47. Such was the case in 1986 when the Senate floor manager for eased gun control legislation decided to accept House amendments to the Senate-passed bill "to avoid sending the bill to a legislative conference committee where it might 'run into a dead-on-arrival syndrome that would kill it' " (*The Los Angeles Times,* May 7, 1986, part I, p. 26). See also Nadine Cohodas, "House Committee Votes 35-0 for Controversial Gun Bill," *Congressional Quarterly Weekly Report,* March 15, 1986, p. 598.

original measure.[48] Alternatively, time at the end of a congressional session may be too brief to allow for a difficult conference; it may seem better to adopt the other chamber's bill, especially if differences are only technical or minor, than to attempt to undertake the time-consuming uncertainties of a conference.[49] At times, then, conferences on major, controversial legislation may be avoided. The more usual case concerning contentious legislation, however, is to convene a conference committee as the means for working out House and Senate differences. The first step in this move to conference is for one chamber to ask for a conference.

A variety of political and procedural issues influence the means by which a conference is requested. Politically, there are questions such as when to ask for or agree to a conference, whether it is possible to "logroll" on a conference request (such as refusing to meet in conference until another matter is resolved), and how best to package the bill to be used as the vehicle for conference. Procedurally, there are concerns about control of the papers (the "engrossed" bill, which includes the changes made on the floor together with the amendments of the other body) and House-Senate distinctive approaches to reaching the conference stage. In short, what appears at first blush to be a simple matter—Which chamber should ask for (or agree to) a conference with the other body?—actually involves a complex mix of political and procedural elements. These political and procedural conditions, despite their interconnections, can be best illuminated by addressing each in turn.

Political Considerations

1. TIMING. A careful planning of actions to accommodate or exploit circumstances is standard operating procedure on Capitol Hill. "Everything in politics is timing," former House Speaker Thomas P. O'Neill, Jr. (D, Mass.) frequently pointed out. Similarly, attempts to convene conferences are shaped by a wide constellation of congressional events, moods, and pressures. Three examples illustrate the point.

Central to the Carter administration's energy program were presidential and legislative efforts to reduce America's dependence on foreign oil and to promote energy

---

48. In 1985, senators faced a preconference House ultimatum on highway funds—"This is it. It's not negotiable at all," stated House Chairman James T. Howard (D, N.J.)—and eventually backed down and accepted the House bill with its lower funding. Conference prospects were viewed as highly uncertain, and, as Sen. Quentin N. Burdick (D, N.D.) explained, "By going with the House bill, [Senate] committee members decided that a bird in the hand was worth much more than two in a bush" (Stephen Gettinger, "Senate, House Pass Different Highway Measures," *Congressional Quarterly Weekly Report,* March 2, 1985, p. 380; and idem, "Senate Clears Bill Freeing States' Road Funds, *Congressional Quarterly Weekly Report,* March 9, 1985, p. 463).

49. A classic instance of changed circumstances occurred concerning Alaska lands legislation in the postelection session of the 96th Congress, following the 1980 election. "Democratic sponsors of the House-passed bill, facing the political realities of the Republican election landslide that November [which had elected a Republican-controlled Senate soon to take office], grudgingly accepted the less environmentally protective Senate version rather than risk a conference version or perhaps no bill at all" (Congressional Quarterly, *Guide to Congress,* 3d ed. [Washington, D.C.: Congressional Quarterly, 1982], p. 434.

conservation. To accomplish these objectives, the president threatened in 1978 to impose quotas on oil imports. A bipartisan Senate group, however, successfully added an amendment to a pending appropriations bill that specifically forbade President Carter from imposing such quotas. The president was incensed over the Senate action, especially as it occurred on the eve of a major international economic meeting. As reported in the *Congressional Quarterly Weekly Report,*

> The Senate slap at Carter came less than three weeks before the President's economic summit conference with Western allies starting July 16 in Bonn. Carter has been criticized by Western leaders for failing to cut U.S. oil imports. Carter allies feared the Senate vote would further weaken the President in dealing with foreign governments.[50]

Earlier, the House had passed the appropriations bill without the restrictive language added in the Senate. House-Senate passage of appropriations legislation normally triggers a conference to resolve disagreements, including bicameral differences such as the oil import Senate amendment. In this instance, however, the House, at the administration's request, delayed "sending the bill to conference to avoid a needless fight on import fees just before the summit," thus embarrassing the president.[51]

Second, interest groups, too, may have an interest in the convening—or nonconvening—of conference committees. Dairy lobbyists, for example, successfully persuaded leaders of the House Agriculture Committee in 1983 to push for an immediate conference with the Senate on a House bill to which the Senate had added, among other things, a major new dairy program. The dairy program, which directed the national government to pay dairy farmers for reducing milk production, had been agreed to by the House committee but had never been either debated or passed by the full House. Despite heavy lobbying by the dairy industry, many representatives objected both to the proposal's substance (dubbed "loafing payments" by the House Republican leader) and the procedural methods being used to bypass House debate on it. As a result of these considerations, the House rejected the Agriculture Committee chairman's request for an immediate conference with the Senate on the dairy issue. Subsequently, the House separately debated and enacted its own version of the program; following this the two chambers then agreed to meet in conference.[52]

Finally, the political mood of the moment can be exploited to advance legislation to the conference stage. With unemployment soaring in late 1982, the leaders of the House and Senate viewed the just-concluded November elections as a mandate for Congress's lame duck session to do something about jobs. House and Senate bills to finance and repair highways, which had not received floor consideration during the regular session, suddenly became priority legislation. Recast now as "jobs legislation," these bills had

---

50. Bob Rankin, "Defeat for Carter: Oil Import Fees, Quotas Blocked by Senate Vote," *Congressional Quarterly Weekly Report,* July 1, 1978, p. 1659.

51. *Washington Post,* July 12, 1978, p. A9.

52. See *Congressional Record,* 98th Cong., 1st sess., Oct. 18, 1983, pp. H8284–95, and Nov. 4, 1983, pp. H9218–22.

new political life. Both chambers passed versions of the highway legislation and then quickly agreed to meet in conference. "Despite members' growing impatience to go home for the Christmas holiday," noted one account, "negotiations on the Senate and House version of the legislation took all day, Dec. 21, before a compromise was reported."[53] With time rapidly running out, the conference compromise was agreed to by both houses.

    2. LOGROLLING. To build winning coalitions for legislation, many different forms of bargaining are used, including what is termed logrolling. This practice involves an exchange by members of voting support on different bills. It takes the simple but effective form "I'll vote for your bill if you vote for mine." Logrolling can be employed to convene conferences; it may also involve even the White House.

    During the Ninety-seventh Congress in the early 1980s, House Interior Chairman Morris K. Udall (D, Ariz.) successfully pushed through Congress a minor bill that settled Indian water rights of the Papago tribe in Arizona. President Reagan, however, vetoed the legislation on the ground that the settlement would cost the federal government too much money. Also moving through Congress at this same time was controversial and important legislation involving farm use of water from federal reclamation projects.

    Both chambers passed the reclamation legislation, which President Reagan also supported, but the House refused to go to conference with the Senate to work out relatively minor bicameral differences. Explained Senate Energy Chairman James McClure, (R, Idaho), whose committee had reported the reclamation bill:

> The Senate . . . asked for conference [on July 16]. As of this date, the House has not agreed to the requested conference on H.R. 5539 [the Reclamation Reform Act]. I believe it is general knowledge that the House has not acted because of the continued negotiations between the administration and members of the House Interior and Insular Affairs Committee regarding the Papago Indian Water bill, H.R. 5518, which was vetoed by the President on June 1, 1982. Further action by the House on the reclamation reform bill has been delayed pending successful resolution of the Papago Indian water issue.[54]

In effect, the important reclamation legislation was being held hostage by the House (and Representative Udall) until the president changed his mind on the minor Indian water bill. Eventually, a resolution between the House and the president was achieved, and a single conference was held that involved both the Papago and the reclamation measures. The two matters subsequently each became public law.

    3. PACKAGING. At times, bills that have powerful enemies can be joined to bills that have powerful friends. This technique is commonly used on Capitol Hill to move controversial legislation through the House and Senate. Congress also employs this device in dealing with the White House; a House chairman once described it as "co-

---

    53. *Congressional Quarterly Almanac, 1982* (Washington, D.C.: Congressional Quarterly, 1983), p. 329.
    54. *Congressional Record*, 97th Cong., 1st sess., Aug. 20, 1982, p. S11057.

ercing the President to approve a bill that he does not want by coupling it with one that is necessary or highly desirable.[55] Similar packaging strategies can also influence the convening of conference committees.

During the Ninety-eighth Congress from 1983 to 1985, the House, the Senate, and the White House were all involved in a lengthy, three-way struggle over two particularly controversial proposals: an $8.4 billion loan to the International Monetary Fund (IMF) and a $15.6 billion housing program. The president wanted the IMF bill but not the housing program; the Senate similarly favored IMF but not housing; and the House supported both proposals. Both chambers passed the IMF bill, but the Senate balked on the housing legislation. The House, however, had passed the controversial IMF bill (condemned by some as a "bailout for big banks" that had made bad loans to nations plagued by huge debts) by only six votes; support there for that legislation seemed quite weak and fragile.

Subsequent to House passage of the IMF measure, the Republican Congressional Campaign Committee sought to make partisan hay on the issue by launching a public relations attack against twenty Democratic representatives who, although voting for the IMF, had also opposed an amendment that would have prohibited the lending agency from making loans to communist countries. Radio advertisements in these members' districts began, "What do you call a congressman who votes to give loans to Communist countries?"[56] Incensed by the Republican attack, the "Democratic leadership in the House . . . refused to let a conference committee meet to sort out the differences until the President apologizes for the attacks on the 20 Democrats by the Republican campaign committee."[57] President Reagan did send a note to these members thanking them for their IMF support, but the Democrats were still angry.

Meanwhile, House Banking Committee Chairman Fernand St. Germain (D, R.I.), whose committee had jurisdiction over both issues, repackaged the two proposals—the IMF loan and the housing program—into one measure. "If the White House will switch on the green light on a housing-I.M.F. package, I am convinced the houses can solve their remaining differences quickly," noted Chairman St. Germain.[58] He and other members reasoned that neither proposal would pass if considered separately by the House or Senate, but packaged together they might survive. This step appeared necessary because otherwise the housing legislation would be filibustered in the Senate, and the IMF loan (because of the controversial Republican political attacks) appeared to be dead in the House. In the end, this composite legislative package was agreed to by Congress, but as part of an omnibus supplemental appropriations conference report. It was signed into law by the president.

A variation on the packaging theme is for one chamber to tack a proposal that is unwanted by the other house onto other legislation heading to conference. House oppo-

---

55. *Congressional Record,* 82d Cong., 2d sess., Feb. 25, 1952, p. A1152. See also T. R. Reid, *Congressional Odyssey* (San Francisco: Freeman, 1980), p. 10.
56. *Los Angeles Times,* Nov. 14, 1983, part 1, p. 3.
57. *New York Times,* Oct. 24, 1983, p. D7.
58. Ibid.

nents of noise control legislation in 1979, for instance, had been able successfully to prevent House consideration of it through their arguments that the bill would actually permit more noise, not less. The Senate, however, had passed similar legislation and wanted further bicameral progress on it. The chairman of the Senate committee that had reported the noise control bill consequently took a House-passed airport development bill and amended it to include the Senate-passed and House-neglected noise control legislation. The House's airport bill, with the noise control addition, was then returned to that chamber. Despite the ire of many representatives, who pointed out that the House had never debated the noise control proposal, a majority of the House agreed to accept the Senate's request for a conference, in part to expedite the airport development legislation that had been languishing for some time.[59]

Procedural Considerations

1. ASKING, AGREEING AND "THE PAPERS." It is common practice in both houses to request a conference after the second chamber has amended and passed legislation coming from the first. For instance, after the Senate amends and passes a House-originated bill, it typically asks for a conference with the House on the differences between them. (Technically, only the matters in *disagreement* between the two versions are subject to conference resolution.) Alternatively, the Senate could return the House bill with Senate amendments to the other body in the hope that the House might agree to the Senate's revisions. Should the House not wish to so agree, the House could instead ask for a conference with the Senate. In either case, the chamber that requests a conference must be at that moment in possession of the "papers."

The significance of the papers is twofold. First, the House or Senate must be in possession of the papers before a conference can be requested with the other body. For example, in 1980, the Senate defeated a higher education conference report. When unanimous consent was then asked that the Senate meet in renewed conference with the House, the presiding officer stated, "Before a conference can be requested, the papers would have to be at the desk."[60] The problem was that they were not at the desk, or indeed anywhere in the Senate. Instead, for various reasons, the papers were in transit to the House; this procedural fact prevented further Senate action at that time.

Second, it is usual practice for the chamber that *asks* for the conference to act *last* on the conference report. The chamber that *agrees* to the request for a conference, consequently, acts *first* on the conference report. In either case, a chamber must possess the papers before the conference report can be taken up. Sometimes possession is deliberately manipulated in conference to permit one chamber to act before another regardless of which body had actually asked for or agreed to the conference. This might be done to maximize the likelihood of passage of the conference report or to accommodate a chamber that wants to act first.[61]

59. Judy Sarasohn, "Senate Maneuver Revives Plane Noise Issue," *Congressional Quarterly Weekly Report,* Oct. 27, 1979, pp. 2406–08.
60. *Congressional Record,* 96th Cong., 2d sess., Sept. 4, 1980, p. S12101.
61. For additional discussion of custody of the papers as it can influence adoption of a conference report, see chapter 10 below.

For example, the Senate asked for a conference with the House on President Reagan's massive three-year tax cut of 1981. The House agreed to the Senate's conference request. Under normal practice the Senate would act last on the conference report; instead, it acted first. With Congress's August recess near, explained Senate Finance Chairman Robert Dole (R, Kan.), the chairman of the House Ways and Means Committee "was kind enough to give us the papers so we could act on [the conference report] first" and thus oblige senators who wanted "to finish the conference report because they had travel plans."[62] (This maneuver also, it should be noted, assisted the legislation's prospects by putting the chamber most strongly in favor of the legislation first.)

Strategically, too, whether one house acts first or last can be important later to passage of the conference report. This is the case because the first-acting house typically has only three choices: to accept, to reject, or to recommit the report to conference. Passage of the report in the initial chamber disbands the conference committee; hence, the chamber that acts last can only accept or reject the conference report.

Particularly where passage in one house is uncertain, making that chamber act last subjects it to a combination of factors that may facilitate enactment of the report. This combination includes the momentum generated by the first chamber's passage of the report, the limitation of voting options left to the second house, and the attention and pressure that the second-acting chamber receives from lobbyists, executive branch officials, journalists, and media commentators as an important bill approaches the final step in the process of congressional enactment.

During creation of the Department of Education in 1979, for example, House Government Operations Chairman Jack Brooks (D, Tex.) initiated the request for conference with the Senate. As a result of ensuring that the House would act last on the resulting conference report, Chairman Brooks limited the options of opponents of the legislation in the House, who otherwise would have sought to recommit the bill to conference.

> House opponents of the Education Department, who were only four votes short of killing it on the floor, had been looking to action on the conference report as the last chance to stop the bill. Now, having lost on the motion to ask for a conference, they will have only the option of trying to kill it outright, without a chance to force a new version out of the conference committee.[63]

Faced with the choices of either killing or adopting it, combined with intense lobbying by presidential agents and interest groups, the House approved the conference report on the Education Department.

2. HOUSE-SENATE METHODS FOR REACHING CONFERENCE. Unsurprisingly, the House and Senate have different methods for reaching conference. In short, the smaller and operationally less complex Senate has simpler procedures than the House. In vir-

---

62. *Congressional Record,* 97th Cong., 1st sess., Aug. 1, 1981, S9029.
63. "Education Department Ploy," *Congressional Quarterly Weekly Report,* July 21, 1979, p. 1462. The events of this conference are examined further in the chapter 11 case study "The Department of Education Organization Act," the second of "Two 'Hello and Good-Bye' Conferences of 1979."

tually every instance, the Senate uses a standard motion to go to conference with the other body: "Mr. President, I move that the Senate insist on its amendments, request a conference with the House on the disagreeing votes thereon, and that the Chair be authorized to appoint conferees." This triple motion rolled into one—to *insist* (an alternative form is to "disagree to the House amendments" to the Senate-passed bill), *request,* and *appoint*—is rarely divided, filibustered, or defeated.[64] The House, by contrast, has four different routes to reach conference. These bicameral dissimilarities result, in part, from how the chambers treat amendments of the other body to its legislation.

(i) *Senate.* If a Senate-passed bill has been amended by the House and returned to the Senate for its consideration, the House amendments are held at the Senate presiding officer's desk for subsequent disposition. The form of that disposition can affect conference deliberations, and it is worth noting how it can occur.

Unlike the House, the Senate considers amendments added by the other body to its legislation as being "privileged" matter. This means that the Senate can easily take up and deal with the House's amendments. Any senator can offer one of four motions to dispose of the amendments of the House. In order of precedence, the motions are *to refer to committee, to amend, to agree,* or *to disagree.* The first motion occurs infrequently; the second is discussed below; the third enacts the bill and clears it for presidential action; and the fourth is usually the first part of the aforementioned triple motion.

In terms of the motion to amend, the Senate, under its rules, is free to amend some or all of the House's amendments. For purposes of conference, a key consideration in amending involves the effect of this action on the "scope" of issues subject to conference deliberation. Anytime the Senate concurs in (or agrees with) a House amendment, the issue reflected in that amendment is no longer "conferenceable" because it is no longer in bicameral dispute. Any changes in the House amendments, however, will be subject to conference negotiations—and possible conference change.[65]

For example, when the Senate began consideration in 1944 of several House amendments to a Senate-passed bill providing for absentee ballots for military personnel, one senator suggested that his colleagues accept the House amendments. The Senate Democratic leader, however, advised against that approach, arguing that "the effect of agreeing to a motion to concur is to limit the scope of the conference. In contrast, the effect of agreeing to a motion to disagree is to extend the scope of the conference and the

---

64. "Insist on its amendments" is used when the Senate amends a House bill; "Disagree to the House amendments" is used when the House amends a Senate bill. Any senator can demand that the triple motion be divided into two parts for sequential consideration: a motion to insist and request and a motion to authorize the chair to appoint conferees. Rarely is the motion to go to conference itself divided, and then only when senators want to delay or stymie action on legislation.

65. The Senate's amendments to the House amendments will be returned to the other body, usually with a request for a conference. However, the House may ignore this conference request and instead agree to the Senate changes, thus concluding the legislative process, or amend all or some of the Senate's changes. It is at this point that the "ping-pong" process usually stops. A conference must now be convened, or some other approach taken to resolve the bicameral disagreement—such as the introduction of new, consensus legislation.

authority of the conferees."[66] In other words, his goal was to maintain bicameral disagreement so as to preserve maximum conference flexibility.

The Democratic leader's alternative plan was to amend one of the House amendments with a major Senate substitute, disagree to the other House amendments, and then ask for a conference with the other body. His objective was to insure that the Senate's conferees had the "widest possible latitude" in dealing with the whole subject. He explained,

> Personally I see no objection to amendments numbered 1 and 2, but, in order that the entire subject may be in conference we ought to disagree to them and have the entire subject in conference, if it is to go to conference, which I hope it will, and I think probably it will. Therefore, as the separate [House] amendments are reached, I hope the Senate will disagree to them so that we may have the entire subject for the conferees to deal with when they reach that point.[67]

In the end, the Senate adopted this basic approach and thus permitted the whole subject to be open to conference consideration.

(ii) *House.* When the Senate amends a House-passed bill and returns it to the other body, the Senate's amendments, along with the House bill, are assigned to the Speaker's table. There they stay until a representative takes some action on them. How to bring the other chamber's amendments to the floor, however, is not as easy as in the Senate. They lack privilege (ready access to the floor) and other motions (to amend, agree, disagree, or send to conference) cannot under House rules be easily employed.[68] In effect, House members can bring the Senate amendments to the floor only under four procedures: unanimous consent, suspension of the rules, a "rule" from the Rules Committee, or what is called Rule XX procedure.

In most instances the House considers Senate amendments by means of *unanimous consent.* Typically, the following motion is made: "Mr. Speaker, I ask unanimous consent to take from the Speaker's table the bill H.R. 1234 with the Senate amendments thereto, disagree to the amendments of the Senate and ask for a conference with the Senate." However, an objection from any single representative negates this request, which is the fundamental shortcoming of the procedure.

The House can also *suspend its rules.* It requires, however, a two-thirds vote to adopt this motion, which takes the following form: "Mr. Speaker, I move to suspend the rules and take from the Speaker's table the bill H.R. 1234 with the Senate amendments

---

66. *Congressional Record,* 78th Cong., 2d sess., Feb. 7, 1944, p. 1293.
67. Ibid.
68. Technically, at this point the House has not voted itself into a formal stage of disagreement with the Senate. Thus motions to perfect the Senate amendments take precedence over motions to go to conference. The parliamentary dilemma, however, is how to perfect the Senate amendments when they lack privilege and cannot reach the floor except under the four procedures noted here. Once the House votes to disagree with the other body, the Senate's amendments are privileged, but now they are on their way to conference. In practice, the privilege concept comes into play (in terms of the precedence of motions) after a conference has met without success. Senate amendments may also be introduced as new legislation, and the Speaker may refer them to the appropriate standing committee.

thereto, disagree to the amendments of the Senate and ask for a conference with the Senate." Attracting two-thirds support can also be difficult, especially on controversial legislation.

The third procedure involves seeking *a special rule from the Rules Committee*. This panel has enormous and unique powers concerning both nonconference and conference reconciliation processes. In regard to the former, the Rules Committee may report (or may refuse to report) a unique rule by means of a simple resolution permitting any matter—including Senate amendments—to reach the House floor, even when they otherwise lack privilege.[69] Concerning a conference, a majority of the committee can block a request for a rule to permit the House to meet in conference with the Senate. Until 1965, the Rules Committee's refusal to grant such a rule would keep a measure from reaching conference.[70]

Frustration over such enormous and often negatively exercised power being concentrated in the Rules Committee led in 1965 to an important change in the rules of the House providing for an alternative route to conference. No longer does a single objection to a unanimous consent request, the existence of significant opposition to a suspension of the rules motion, or the intransigence of the House Rules Committee prevent bills from reaching conference. Instead, representatives can invoke the so-called *Rule XX procedure*. This procedure permits measures to reach conference by a simple majority vote of the House *if* a member of the committee of jurisdiction, usually the chairman, is authorized by his panel to offer the motion to go to conference. Quite often, a chairman will come to the floor armed with such authorization and alert the Speaker of this fact. Then, if a member objects to a unanimous consent request for conference, the chairman will be immediately recognized by the Speaker to offer the Rule XX motion.

The application of House procedures is seldom independent of the policy, personalities, and circumstances of the moment. Rule XX, for instance, might be appropriate for some situations but not others, such as bills that are multiply referred to several committees. In this latter case, House practice requires *all* committees with a claim on the legislation to agree to the Rule XX procedure. Refusal by any one committee can block or delay the convening of a conference. That situation, however, can still be circumvented by the Rules Committee. In one such instance, a Rules Committee member explained why a special rule was needed for a controversial multiple-referred measure:

> Mr. Speaker, generally after passage of a House bill which is in disagreement with the companion passed bill in the Senate, the chairman or chairmen of the committee or committees involved will ask the House to request a conference. This is usually

---

69. There are occasions when a rule from the House Rules Committee expedites the convening of a conference by providing a "Senate hookup." If the House passes its bill, the hookup rule permits the companion Senate-passed version to be immediately called up and the House-passed version inserted after the Senate's number. Technically, the House and Senate have passed the same numbered measure; in practice the conference will consider both versions.

70. For further consideration of controversies over the conference powers of the House Rules Committee, especially concerning the controversial demise of a major 1959 education bill, see the opening pages of chapter 3 above.

done by unanimous consent so as not to take up the valuable time of the House.

However, last week on a motion to send [the measure] to conference an objection was raised by an opponent of the measure. In this instance it would require the four committees who have jurisdiction over this bill to meet and vote on whether to direct the chairmen of these respective committees to offer a motion on the floor to request a conference. Unfortunately, such a procedure would require a significant amount of time and would have delayed further consideration of this bill.[71]

Following this explanation, the House adopted the rule that sent to conference the House-passed bill and accompanying Senate amendments.

Under certain circumstances, the Speaker can, if he wishes, obviate the Rule XX procedure by referring nongermane Senate amendments to standing House committees. Under House precedents, the Speaker may so act, although this authority is only infrequently exercised; when it is, this referral takes precedence over the Rule XX motion. Such a referral might undermine a bill's chances of ever reaching conference.

An example of this relatively unusual step occurred in 1984. Speaker Thomas P. O'Neill (D, Mass.) exercised his referral option to prevent House Education and Labor Chairman Carl Perkins (D, Ky.) from sending a popular but controversial measure to conference. The Senate had attached to a House-passed measure to improve mathematics and science education a nongermane provision establishing the right of student religious groups to use public schools for meetings during extracurricular periods. When the Senate returned the math-science bill with its school access rider to the House, Chairman Perkins expected that his request to go to conference would be quickly approved. When he offered the conference request, however, Speaker O'Neill told Perkins he could not be recognized for that purpose because the chair had already referred the school access nongermane amendment to both the Committees on Education and Labor and the Judiciary for careful study.

Chairman Perkins was infuriated at this decision because the Judiciary Committee was filled with hostile opponents of the school access proposal and would be unlikely to ever report the amendment. "I do not want this bill sent to a burial committee," declared Perkins. "I know this referral is not justified . . . to the Committee on the Judiciary."[72] Nevertheless, it was to the Judiciary Committee (along with the House Committee on Education and Labor) that the Senate school access amendment went. In summary, the decision to go to conference usually occurs without controversy or conflict. Significant legislation sometimes becomes enmeshed in a web of procedures, personalities, and pressures that block it from reaching conference. Senators and representatives, however, are normally reluctant to let House- and Senate-passed bills die for lack of an effort to compromise bicameral differences.

71. *Congressional Record*, 96th Cong., 1st sess., July 30, 1979, p. H6848.

72. *Congressional Record*, 98th Cong., 2d sess., June 28, 1984, p. H7238. See also *New York Times*, June 29, 1984, p. B6. Earlier, during House floor action, Perkins had drafted a school access proviso of his own to avoid any referral to the Judiciary Committee. The measure nearly passed the House under a suspension of the rules procedure, falling only eleven votes short of the two-thirds requirement.

Selection of Conferees

The selection of House and Senate conferees (or managers, as they are frequently termed) is important because the decision of who is to represent each chamber affects both the type of conference deliberations and the policy decisions adopted by the conference. Whether "compromising" or adamant, dig-in-the-heels types are chosen as managers, for example, can affect whether bicameral differences are successfully resolved—or a conference deadlock results. The conferee selection process is guided by two general considerations: formal rules and political considerations.

Formal Rules and Practices

1. HOUSE. Two rules and practices of the House of Representatives, one concerning *who makes the selection,* the other dealing with the case of *conferees with uncertain loyalties to the House position,* govern the selection of conferees. First, although House rules simply declare that the "Speaker shall appoint . . . conference committees,"[73] in practice, the Speaker names conferees from lists submitted to him in advance by the chairman of the standing committee (or committees) that reported the legislation heading to conference.[74] (On bills that have been multiply referred, the proportion of conferees from each panel is subject to negotiation among the respective chairmen.)[75]

Informal yet significant constraints guide a committee chairman in determining his conferee list for the Speaker. First, Democratic Caucus rules obligate chairmen to insure that party ratios on conference delegations reflect the distribution of majority and minority members on the full committee. Further, custom and courtesy require that the naming of minority political party conferees be in consultation with (and usually effectively at the choice of) the ranking minority party leader of the committee.[76] The chairman does not have a free hand even concerning the selection of majority party conferees. Some committees, for example, have their own rules or well-entrenched customs dictating

---

73. The full text of House Rule X, sec. 6, pt. f, which provides for the selection of conferees, is:

The Speaker shall appoint all select and conference committees which shall be ordered by the House from time to time. In appointing members to conference committees, the Speaker shall appoint no less than a majority of members who generally supported the House position as determined by the Speaker. The Speaker shall name members who are primarily responsible for the legislation and shall, to the fullest extent feasible, include the principal proponents of the major provisions of the bill as it passed the House.

74. The significance to committee power and chamber deference of the key role of standing committee chairmen in the selection of House conferees is stressed in Jonathan Nagler, "Strategic Implications of Conferee Selection in the House of Representatives: 'It Ain't Over Till It's Over,' " paper prepared for delivery at the 1987 Annual Meeting of the Southern Political Science Association, Charlotte, N.C.; and Jonathan Nagler, "Conferee Selection for Appropriations Legislation: 1973–1980," paper prepared for the 1988 meeting of the American Political Science Association, Washington, D.C., Sept. 1–4, 1988.

75. For additional discussion of the conference consequences of the growing congressional tendency for the multiple committee referral of legislation, see chapter 3 above.

76. Congressional Quarterly, *Guide to Congress,* p. 435.

conferee selection, such as the virtually automatic inclusion as conferees of members of the subcommittee that handled the bill or committee members who were instrumental in markup or in proposing important amendments in committee. In addition, sometimes a committee chairman will be loath to omit from a conference delegation a particularly prominent or outspoken committee member. To leave such a person off the conferee list might offend him—and certainly give him the freedom to engineer possible chamber opposition to a conference agreement. Inclusion of such a committee member in some cases may provide a means of neutralizing someone who might be otherwise a dangerous opponent.

House Speakers, in ratifying a committee chairman's choices as conferees, are not, however, merely rubber stamps. Depending on the Speaker and his relationship with the chairman, he may choose conferees in addition to those the chairman has proposed, or even veto some who offend his personal or political sensibilities. To be sure, extensive changes in the conference delegation happen relatively infrequently; more usually Speakers simply appoint as conferees the list of proposed members submitted to them by the committee chairman (who uniformly has selected members only of his own panel), or limit their intervention to, at most, perhaps a modest addition or two.

Second, House rules and precedents require that the Speaker select a conference delegation, at least a majority of which generally support the House position on the legislation, "as determined by the Speaker." House rules further stipulate that the Speaker shall name as conferees members "who are primarily responsible for the legislation" as well as try to include the "principal proponents of the major provisions of the bill as it passed the House." In strict application, these requirements could have the potential of giving rise to serious problems. A standing committee chairman who was on the losing side of a floor fight would certainly be unenthusiastic about recommending to the Speaker a conference delegation made up of those he had unsuccessfully opposed. Further, few if any of the principals in the successful floor fight may be members of the standing committee; selection of a number of these representatives (probably at the initiative of the Speaker) could lead to a conference delegation that had few ties to the committee of the House responsible for the policy area.[77]

Fortunately for the Speaker, such clear-cut situations seldom arise. The very fuzziness of the "generally support" standard in actual practice allows the Speaker considerable latitude in selecting conferees, and he is generally free to interpret this standard in a manner allowing him to accept almost entirely the committee chairman's recommendations. Often, it is not clear what actually constitutes the majority House viewpoint. Usually reference is made to a member's vote on final passage as a measure of agreement with the majority position. It is also common that the chamber vote on a critical amendment may have been far more legislatively significant—and far more revealing of a member's true position on the legislation. This vexing issue of standards (which also provides welcome leeway) is left to the Speaker to resolve.

77. House rules expressly require the Speaker to name as conferees "the principal proponents of the major provisions of the bill as it passed the House." This provision alone ensures that, on occasion, noncommittee members will be appointed as conferees.

Clearly, the Speaker has both discretionary authority in the implementation of these rules and a responsibility to insure that the "fox is not put in charge of the chickens."[78] In reality, discretion usually prevails over a concern with foxes. A Republican member in late 1977, for example, challenged the conferees selected for a labor bill as being out of step with the majority House position. In the course of raising a point of order, he said,

> Mr. Speaker . . . , [there are] three items in contention between this body and the other body. . . . Every one of the majority Members, with the exception of the gentleman from Pennsylvania, did not support the House position during the consideration of the bill on the floor.
>
> I will admit, Mr. Speaker, that all of the Members who were present did vote for the [final] passage of the bill. The passage of the bill is not in contention. Those items that are in contention . . . are the three items that I have mentioned, and the majority of the conferees named by the Speaker are not among those Members who supported the majority position in the House.[79]

After some general discussion by the chairman of the Education and Labor Committee (one of the proposed conferees) about the need for the House to "look at this picture as a whole" and reminders that numerous other House-adopted amendments had been supported by the conferees, Speaker Thomas P. O'Neill, Jr. (D, Mass.) ruled that the naming of conferees was his responsibility "which the Chair feels he has properly exercised."[80] Indicative of the Speaker's control over this responsibility is the fact that the House has never overturned a Speaker's choice of conferees (which also effectively means in most cases the selection of almost all conferees by the standing committee chairman; moreover, there is no formal procedure for this purpose.

2. SENATE. In the smaller, more flexible Senate, no formal rules govern the selection of conferees. Instead, practice and precedent provide that managers be named by the presiding officer in response to a motion adopted by the Senate; the presiding officer simply exercises a nondiscretionary ministerial duty. As in the House, the real choice of conferees is made essentially by the committee chairman and the ranking minority member (sometimes party leaders also have a say in the selections). The chairman selects from the majority members of his committee a majority of the Senate's conference delegation, and the ranking minority member picks from the committee a lesser number of conferees of his party. These names are then given to the presiding officer, who appoints them as conferees when authorized by the Senate.

Various criteria shape conference selection by the committee chairman and ranking minority member. Among the most noteworthy are seniority on the committee; membership on the specific subcommittee that handled the measure; special knowledge or familiarity with the subject matter; the particular importance of the measure to a commit-

---

78. Jefferson's Manual (a guide to congressional procedure originally written by Thomas Jefferson) puts the same idea differently in quoting an English parliamentarian that "the child is not to be put to a nurse that cares not for it." See also *Congressional Record*, 86th Cong., 1st sess., May 12, 1959, p. 7975.
79. *Congressional Record*, 95th Cong., 1st session, Oct. 12, 1977, pp. H10818–19.
80. Ibid., p. H10819.

tee member's state; support of the senator for the majority position of the Senate; and the personal and political relationship between the member and the committee chairman. Given the contemporary influx of many new members into the Senate, seniority alone is less significant today as a criterion of selection, and the other factors correspondingly more important relatively than a few decades ago.

Senate conferees, like those from the House, are expected to support the Senate's position in conference. In a classic expression of this undertaking, Senator Richard Russell (D, Ga.) once declared, "When I go to a conference as a representative of the Senate, I represent the Senate viewpoint as vigorously as possible, even though it may not be in accord with the vote or votes I cast on the floor of the Senate. I conceive that to be the duty of the conferee."[81] Reality does not always comport with theory. Sometimes the positions of the Senate delegation can be at striking variance with the Senate position. "The fact is," said a senator in criticizing actions of a 1983 conference, "that when the Senate votes by 3 to 1 in favor of something, we do not expect the Senate conferees to vote 1 to 3 the other way."[82]

Unlike the House, which lacks any effective means to challenge the Speaker's selection of conferees, Senate procedures provide for the full Senate membership to elect conferees. A senator, for instance, can offer a substitute motion listing a different set of conferees at the time conferees are to be named by the presiding officer. Senators, too, can mount filibusters or prolonged debates in an attempt to persuade colleagues that new or different conferees should be appointed. Senators can also challenge the conferees at the time they are formally named by offering a motion to reconsider their appointment. If that motion should be successful, the Senate would then consider a motion selecting different conferees. Despite such procedural possibilities, they are in fact rarely used, in large part because of the Senate's tradition of comity and trust among members. The procedural options outlined above inherently and fundamentally question senators' integrity and devotion to chamber representational duty; their utilization consequently would violate these underlying values.[83]

Political Estimations

Political considerations surround conferee selection. Because they permeate both chambers, we will discuss House and Senate factors jointly. Among the important

---

81. *Congressional Record,* 86th Cong., 2d sess., Aug. 26, 1960, p. 17831. For a discussion of other possible conferee loyalties, see the second half of chapter 6 above, "The Individual Context."
On a 1943 tax bill, Senator Bob La Follette (Prog., Wis.) announced to the Senate that he could not serve as a conferee; he was "so out of sympathy with the action taken by the Senate" in passing the bill that he must ask "to be relieved from service on the conference committee." *Congressional Record,* 78th Cong., 1st sess., May 14, 1943, p. 4458.

82. *Congressional Record,* 98th Cong., 1st sess., March 22, 1983, p. S3637. For additional discussion of what are sometimes called runaway conferences, see chapter 1 above.

83. For an example in which these traditions failed to deter a senator, see the discussion in chapter 1 above of Sen. William Proxmire's forceful opposition to Senate conferees named for the supersonic transport (SST) conference in 1970.

political calculations involved in the selection of conferees are *when, who,* and *how many* conferees should be appointed.

1. TIMING. Normally conferees are designated immediately after the adoption of the motion to go to (or agree to) a conference. There are occasions when it suits one or both chambers (or their leaders) to delay conferee selection. A House chairman, for example, might refuse for a while to name conferees to signal his displeasure with the other body's amendments and to soften up their conferees by this early expression of intransigence in anticipation of when the two chambers actually convene in conference. Sometimes delays in conference selection are necessary to work out problems; at other times, delays are promoted by the legislation's opponents to weaken the measure's prospects by running down the clock near the end of a Congress. Delay in conferee selection can also be intended just to provide potential conferees with political and substantive breathing room.

During the Ninety-eighth Congress, for instance, the House and Senate passed controversial immigration reform legislation. The chief Senate sponsor of the legislation, Alan K. Simpson (R, Wyo.) deliberately delayed in having conferees selected "until after the [1984] Republican convention to avoid pressure from Hispanic groups on the Republican members named" as managers.[84] Many Hispanic groups strongly opposed the bill and presumably would have vigorously lobbied conferees had their identity been certain. Meanwhile, in the House, Speaker O'Neill delayed two months before designating House conferees, in part because the immigration bill sharply divided the Democratic party as it entered the national election of 1984.

2. WHO IS SELECTED. Numerous factors affect conferee selection, including committee ranking, personal characteristics, geography, and political loyalty. In 1986, Senate Finance Committee Chairman Bob Packwood (R, Ore.) went to great lengths to find a way of including on the tax bill conferee list *Democratic* Senator Bill Bradley of New Jersey—"the Senate's leading and most tenacious advocate of tax reform, even though the chairman technically can pick only conferees of his own party."[85] Senator Bradley, known as the godfather of tax overhaul, had been a principal actor in both chambers in winning enactment of the landmark legislation. Thus, despite his lack of committee seniority (seventh of nine committee Democrats), Finance Committee leaders of both parties were determined to have Bradley on the conference committee and ignored seniority to accomplish this.

Similarly, House Ways and Means Chairman Dan Rostenkowski (D, Ill.) initially delayed naming conferees in order to reexamine the statements and positions of committee Democrats on tax issues and bill provisions. Loyalty to the chairman's viewpoints and responsiveness to his leadership were of utmost concern to Rostenkowski. He "will pick whatever he needs to have control," observed one Ways and Means Democrat. "The one thing you have to know about Danny: He knows how to count." Chairman

---

84. Nadine Cohodas, "Caught in Swirling Political Currents: Immigration Reform Measure Now 'Hanging by a Thread,'" *Congressional Quarterly Weekly Report,* July 28, 1984, p. 1839.

85. Eileen Shanahan, "Tax Bill Wins Senate Approval; Post-Recess Conference Next," *Congressional Quarterly Weekly Report,* June 28, 1986, p. 1452. See also David E. Rosenbaum, "Big Changes Loom in Final Tax Bill, Lawmakers Agree," *New York Times,* May 26, 1986, p. 31.

Rostenkowski also ignored seniority and selected as a conferee Richard Gephardt (D, Mo.), who had been coauthor with Bradley of the original tax overhaul plan, to insure that the Democratic party received full political credit for overhauling the internal revenue code.[86]

A number of elements were evident in the choice of conferees in 1979 for legislation concerning the creation of a national energy mobilization board. Senate leaders wanted Pete Domenici (R, N.M.) appointed to the conference because he "attends meetings, works at compromises, and lobbies his fellow Republicans."[87] However, three other Republican senators were senior to Domenici on the Energy Committee. In order to reach Domenici, the three more senior Republicans were also named to the conference. (Such decisions, to be sure, also affect the size of conference delegations—see the discussion of this below.)

The selection of House conferees for this bill was also marked by interesting maneuvers. The mobilization board bill had been referred jointly to the House Energy and Interior Committees. The Energy Committee chairman flatly refused to name three particular committee members as conferees because they opposed a controversial provision favored by the chairman. Their omission from the committee conferee list was striking because they had more seniority than other committee members who were named to the conference. One of the representatives, however, was able later to win an Interior Committee conferee slot, where he was also a member, and another successfully appealed to Speaker O'Neill for appointment as a conferee.[88]

Geography, too, plays a role in conferee selection. On a 1979 bill creating a synthetic fuels corporation, fourteen New England House Democrats protested to Speaker O'Neill of Massachusetts that their energy-consuming region lacked representation on the synfuels conference while a number of conferees represented the energy-producing states. In response, the Speaker added Toby Moffett (D, Conn.) as a conferee. Interestingly, House Majority Leader Jim Wright (D, Tex.), who was not a member of any of the committees with jurisdiction over the synfuels bill but who was a strong supporter of the program, was also named a conferee. Complained one member, the leaders have "arranged it so nobody who is against a massive government corporation for synfuels is on [the conference]."[89]

The "stacking" of conferences is sometimes merely the inevitable result of overwhelming committee support for a legislative proposal. The House Banking Committee, which had primary responsibility for the synfuels proposal (in large part because it was carefully drafted in such a way as to fall under that panel's jurisdiction), had favorably reported the legislation by a 39 to 1 vote. Ample conference committee representation of

---

86. *New York Times*, May 26, 1986, p. 31. See also the full account of these events contained in Jeffrey H. Birnbaum and Alan S. Murray, *Showdown at Gucci Gulch: Lawmakers, Lobbyists, and the Unlikely Triumph of Tax Reform* (New York: Random House, 1987), esp. chap. 11.

87. Ann Pelham, "Mobilization Board Conferees Face Off Soon," *Congressional Quarterly Weekly Report*, Dec. 1, 1979, p. 2712.

88. *Washington Post*, Dec. 8, 1979, p. A6.

89. Pelham, "Mobilization Board," p. 2712.

the standing committee that had handled the legislation would in this case inherently ensure an unbalanced delegation.

There are other occasions when committee and party leaders deliberately skew the selection process. In 1981, for example, Speaker O'Neill "chose liberal conferees for the conference on President Reagan's tax package specifically because they were unrepresentative of the rank-and-file membership that had supported a more conservative proposal."[90] Presumably, these conferees were representative of something other than rank-and-file House views, namely, the preferences and goals of the House Democratic leadership.

Finally, there are times when party loyalty is especially critical in conferee selection. A classic example involved Representative Phil Gramm, now a Republican senator from Texas. In 1981, Gramm was a *Democratic* House member and a member also of the House Budget Committee. Despite his Democratic party affiliation, Gramm worked secretly with David Stockman, President Reagan's director of the Office of Management and Budget, to formulate the major Reagan administration domestic spending reduction measure that was ultimately passed in place of a Democratic budget alternative. Known informally as the Gramm-Latta proposal (after Gramm and Republican Representative Delbert Latta of Ohio), both the measure and Gramm personally received wide national publicity. Not surprisingly, Representative Gramm was not selected as a Democratic conferee on this measure and had to sit out the conference on the official sidelines.[91] He was widely perceived by House Democrats as a renegade; as House Budget Chairman Jim Jones of Oklahoma acidly put it in explaining Gramm's omission as a conferee on "Gramm-Latta," "He really didn't have anything to do with the bill. He was last in line in seniority. And we couldn't appoint Stockman, so. . . ."[92]

3. NUMBER OF CONFEREES. The number of conferees is affected by whom committee or party leaders want on the conference (as in the case cited earlier concerning the efforts to include Senator Domenici as a conferee) and by the number of committees that considered the original legislation. The 1981 conference on the Gramm-Latta bill, the largest in congressional history, had over 250 House and Senate conferees. Fifteen House and fourteen Senate committees sent conferees to the proceedings. By comparison, the important immigration reform measure of 1984 was handled by only one Senate committee and four House panels. The result was an exceedingly small conference for so controversial a bill—a total of 7 Senate conferees and 29 House managers.[93]

Pressures from both standing committees and rank and file may produce increases

---

90. Mikva and Saris, *American Congress*, p. 241.

91. A similar fate befell now-Senator Gramm concerning the first conference committee on his Gramm-Rudman deficit control legislation in 1985. Not being a conferee, however, did not keep Senator Gramm from the conference room—see the chapter 11 case study "The Gramm-Rudman Conferences of 1985."

92. *Washington Star*, July 15, 1981, p. A6.

93. In chapter 11, the case study "A Typical Low-Intensity Appropriations Conference" describes how seven House members met with but one senator (more had been appointed as conferees but did not attend the conference) to work out bicameral differences.

in conference size. "I intend that the Committee on Agriculture be represented in any conference which may be held," declared the House Agriculture chairman in 1984.[94] (His assertion is commonplace for House and Senate chairmen, who jealously protect their committee's jurisdiction.) While I "do not object to [the wilderness bill] being taken up on the floor of the House without consideration by my Committee," asserted the chairman, "the Agriculture Committee must appoint conferees on the measure."[95]

In another House measure in 1982, Representative Patricia Schroeder (D, Col.) strongly objected to informal ground rules worked out by party and committee leaders that permitted only five conferees to be named from each of the *nine* committees that had considered the 1982 reconciliation bill. Fearful that some more senior Post Office Committee members might not sufficiently strive to protect the interests of federal government retirees, Representative Schroeder wanted herself and another Postal Committee colleague to be additionally named as conferees. Rebuffed in her effort, Representative Schroeder could only serve notice that "I will scream bloody murder if the budget reconciliation conference ends up reducing Federal retirees'" cost of living adjustments.[96]

Several points about size merit discussion. Initially, one must keep in mind that the size of one chamber delegation in relation to the other is itself without political significance concerning the bicameral balance on the conference committee. Each delegation votes in conference on all matters as a unit; a majority of *both* the House conferees (be they five or fifty) and the Senate delegation (of whatever size) is necessary for any matter to be agreed upon in conference. As a consequence, whether a given chamber sends few or many conferees to conference does not by itself tilt the balance between House and Senate. The size of the conference does have consequences, but of a different kind.

First, the more conferees, the more time and effort is invariably required to resolve bicameral differences. The controversiality of the issues in disagreement, to be sure, is a primary factor affecting the complexity and length of the compromise-making process, but large conferences typically complicate the effort. "You are dealing with so many pieces and so many authorizing committees [that] to suddenly make it all happen, and make it all come together, is a challenge," remarked a key conferee, Representative Leon Panetta (D, Cal.), about the colossal 1981 conference.[97]

In addition, size affects the mechanics of decision making. Large conferences regularly and by necessity subdivide into smaller groups. Conferences on reconciliation legislation—usually massive affairs—ordinarily are broken down into what are termed subconferences:

> A subconference consists of the House and Senate conferees appointed for particular elements of the reconciliation legislation. For example, if the legislative change involved the Food Stamp program then the conferees from the House and Senate

94. *Congressional Record*, 98th Cong., 2d sess., April 2, 1984, p. H2149.
95. Ibid.
96. *Congressional Record*, 97th Cong., 2d sess., Aug. 11, 1982, p. H5748.
97. Diane Granat, "The Big Conference: Getting to be Old Hat," *Congressional Quarterly Weekly Report*, June 2, 1984, p. 1298.

Committees on Agriculture and the House and Senate Committees on the Budget would resolve those issues within the parameters of a subconference. In cases of joint committee jurisdiction over a program a subconference could involve many committees.[98]

Size, too, can affect the pace of conference decision making. The involvement of key legislators in more than one subconference, for example, can inhibit the scheduling of simultaneous bicameral meetings and generally slow conference progress down.

In short, large conferences usually require greater time and effort to achieve bicameral reconciliation, often utilize decision-making subgroups, and can suffer delay because of scheduling difficulties. Good reasons indeed why chamber and committee leaders often prefer small conferee delegations; political and procedural considerations often make such goals unfeasible and result instead in large bicameral meetings.[99]

Instruction of Conferees

Instructions are akin to "free advice" given to conferees by their chambers. Conferees are not bound by such instructions and may choose to follow or ignore the proffered advice.[100] On one occasion late in 1977, Senator Russell Long (D, La.) asked the presiding officer of the Senate for a formal parliamentary ruling on whether Senate instructions are in fact binding on its conferees. Replied the presiding officer, "[The instruction] is not binding on the conferees, and, as Vice President Barkely used to say, it falls within the category of a pious hope."[101] Conference reports may not be ruled out of order in either chamber on the grounds that conferees disregarded their instructions; the underlying theory is that House and Senate conferees must be free to negotiate differences and either chamber is free to vote to reject the product of such negotiations, the conference report.

98. *A Review of the Reconciliation Process,* House Committee on the Budget, Oct. 1984, Serial no. CP-9, p. 59.

99. Data concerning conference and delegation size for three Congresses are presented and discussed in the Appendix to Chapter 6 above.

100. For example, Sen. Bob Packwood (R, Ore.), chairman of the Senate Finance Committee, opposed the adoption of Senate instructions concerning the 1986 tax conference and further indicated that he would not feel constrained by any such specific instructions: "We're going to conference on 100 to 200 issues and we'll end up with a package. For me to single out one issue and say how I would handle it would be irresponsible" (Eileen Shanahan, "Senate Nears Tax Bill Passage, Adheres to No-Change Rule," *Congressional Quarterly Weekly Report,* June 14, 1986, p. 1311).

101. *Congressional Record,* 95th Cong., 1st sess., Oct. 29, 1977, p. S18151. The nonbinding quality of chamber instructions is also illustrated by a 1972 conference exchange between Representatives Romano Mazzoli (D, Ky.) and Carl Perkins (D, Ky.): "Mazzoli, a freshman Democrat from Kentucky, rather innocently asked Chairman Perkins, 'What is the impact of the House instructions?' Perkins responded, 'Well, we'll try to follow the spirit of it.' A roar of laughter swept the room. Perkins quickly amended his statement saying, 'We'll try to follow the spirit and the letter of it.' Mrs. Green then dryly observed, 'I think we should follow the letter since the spirit is weak.' " (Lawrence Gladieux and Thomas Wolanin, *Congress and the Colleges: The National Politics of Higher Education* (Lexington, Mass.: C. C. Heath, 1976), p. 192). This conference is examined in chapter 11 in the case study "Higher Education: Personalities and Exhaustion."

Instructions, on the other hand, are more than mere advisory opinions. They serve important political and strategic purposes. Politically, instructions can be important because of the message they convey to conferees and to the other chamber. In general, they place additional political and moral pressure on the conferees and may even strengthen the conferees' hand and determination in bicameral bargaining.[102] As one House member put it in support of a motion to instruct conferees, "We need to give the House conferees some backbone to stand up to the Senate on this issue."[103] The instructing of conferees has the advantage of making more likely, but not certain, the conference delegation's insistence on its chamber's version of the legislation—but at the danger of increasing the probability of conference deadlock and failure.

Strategically, instructions enjoy the virtue of being flexible. They can be employed at any point—before, during, or after a conference. Despite this flexibility, there is a general reluctance in both chambers—but especially in the Senate—to adopt conferee instructions because of the implied insult to conferees and violation of the value of bicameral compromise.[104] From 1980 through 1986, for example, the Senate considered instructions only five times compared to nearly twenty such efforts by the House. Further, conferees and potential conferees especially dislike instructions because they imply a lack of confidence in their fidelity and impose constraints on their bargaining freedom;[105] yet they sometimes maneuver to introduce mild instructions to head off

---

102. See the discussion of this point in chapter 9 below. Jeffrey L. Pressman put this argument particularly succinctly: by instructions, "one side may increase its bargaining power by *depriving* itself of the power to act [contrary to instructions]" (Jeffrey L. Pressman, *House vs. Senate* [New Haven: Yale University Press, 1966], p. 66). Of course, since conferees from both sides also understand that instructions are suggestive rather than controlling, any bargaining power consequences from instructions can only be relative.

103. *Congressional Record*, 98th Cong., 1st sess., June 23, 1983, p. H4435. The "backbone" description of conference instructions often is used by congressmen. In 1981, for example, Rep. Norman Dicks (D, Wash.) supported instructing House conferees on the Defense Department Authorization Act, explaining, "What we are trying to do here today is to stiffen the spine, the resolve of the conferees." One of the conferees, Rep. William Dickinson (R, Ala.), somewhat defensively replied, "I did not think I was in need of strengthening my backbone on this thing" (*Congressional Record*, 97th Cong., 1st sess., Oct. 29, 1981, pp. H7890–91).

104. See Richard F. Fenno, Jr., *The Power of the Purse: Appropriations Politics in Congress* (Boston: Little, Brown, 1966), pp. 657 ff.; David L. Paletz, "Influence in Congress: An Analysis of the Nature and Effects of Conference Committees" (Ph.D. diss., University of California at Los Angeles, 1970), pp. 9, 11; and David J. Vogler, *The Third House: Conference Committees in the United States Congress* (Evanston: Northwestern University Press, 1971), pp. 94 ff.

105. Conferees often oppose instructions—especially to accept a provision favored by the other body—because such directives make it more difficult to demand a reciprocal favor from that chamber for the concession. Such was openly argued on the floor of the House in an exchange concerning an upcoming conference on defense legislation. Rep. Pat Schroeder (D, Colo.) sought to have the House conferees instructed to accept a Senate provision sponsored by Sen. Sam Nunn (D, Ga.). House Armed Services member Sonny Montgomery (D, Miss.) indicated that he and other House conferees did not oppose the Nunn amendment, but pleaded with the House not to *instruct* them to accept it. "Give us bargaining freedom," he argued. "We can accept it [the Nunn amendment], but let us get something in conference in return for it" (personal observation by one of the authors of House of Representatives floor debate of Oct. 29, 1981).

stronger versions. In both houses, rules provide that only one successful motion to instruct is in order prior to the start of a conference; it must be offered immediately after a chamber agrees to the conference but before it formally names the conferees. This provides the opportunity for preemptive moves to preclude other, more limiting preconference instructions.

For example, House Republicans made strenuous efforts in 1983 to avoid having instructions given to House defense appropriations conferees on nerve gas production. The House version of the defense appropriations bill had contained no funds for this purpose, while the Republican-controlled Senate had passed defense appropriations legislation containing nerve gas production funds. House opponents of nerve gas production sought to instruct their conferees to refuse to accept the Senate's position.

A senior Republican House Appropriations member (the minority party under House precedents is accorded priority of recognition for instruction motions) attempted to short circuit this Democratic effort. He proposed instead that House conferees be instructed to oppose experimentation on animals. This motion was denounced by nerve gas opponents as "simply a smoke screen to prevent us from getting to the issue that . . . is most paramount in this bill, and that is whether this House is going to allow its conferees to go uninstructed on the question of resuming chemical weapons production."[106] The Democratic majority of the House then rejected the animal experimentation instructions and instead came up with an intriguing compromise set of instructions: House conferees were instructed to oppose *both* nerve gas production and animal experimentation.

House rules permit that chamber to adopt additional instructions if, after twenty days, House conferees have not reached agreement with their Senate counterparts. In the case of the Senate, it may, by resolution, instruct its conferees at any point while the bill is in conference. For both chambers, instructions during a conference occur far less frequently than at the beginning of the bicameral process—only twice in the House and but once in the Senate in the years between 1972 to 1985. Still, a conferee threat to seek instructions during a conference can sometimes be a useful bargaining ploy. An example from the early 1960s graphically illustrates this:

> Last year there was a difference of about $400 million between the House and Senate versions of the foreign aid appropriation. The Chairman of the House delegation in the conference took a very firm position that we had to end up with slightly less than 50 percent of the difference as a matter of prestige. It was the day we were to adjourn. We were in conference until about 10:30 p.m., and the Senate wouldn't give in. I think the difference between conferees was only five or ten million dollars. The Senate was fighting for its prestige, and our Chairman for his. At 10:30 he started to close his book and got up saying he would get instructions from the House. All the rest of our conferees did the same. That prospect was too much for the Senators. They capitulated.[107]

106. *Congressional Record,* 98th Cong., 1st sess., Nov. 15, 1983, p. H9866.
107. Charles L. Clapp, *The Congressman: His Work As He Sees It* (Washington, D.C.: Brookings Institution, 1963), p. 249.

Finally, conferees may be instructed even after they have produced an agreement, but then only by the chamber that is in the position to act first on the conference report. (As noted earlier, the chamber that agrees to the conference acts first on the conference report.) The first-acting chamber has three main options: to accept, to reject, or to recommit the report to the House-Senate conference. Under the latter option, instructions may be included in the recommittal motion, such as urging the chamber's conferees to concur in a position taken by the other body. On the other hand, if the first-acting chamber agrees to the conference report, its action technically disbands the conference, leaving the second-acting house with only two choices: to accept or reject the report, and instructions are no longer an option.

There are many occasions, to be sure, when members will offer their "instructions" informally to conferees, either in groups or individually.[108] In addition, floor statements may be made or pointed questions asked of prospective conferees regarding their policy intentions. These devices are often used because members are uncertain whether they have the votes to carry a formal instruction motion. A defeat of attempted conference instructions not only fails to constrain conferees, it even confirms the conferees' bargaining leeway and thus can be risky for those contemplating instructions. Whether instructions occur formally or informally, they are one important part of the preliminary moves intended to shape conference negotiations—along with conferee selection, conference-asking, and chamber-passing activities.

Conclusions

To move legislation through the maze of lawmaking steps requires political and procedural skill and fortitude. Members take advantage of the arsenal of preconference strategies in attempting either to develop and maintain momentum for legislation or to stymie and sidetrack it entirely. The outcome often depends on the extent to which members plan and organize their parliamentary efforts and strategies. Doing nothing and relying on political fate to take care of things is a risky strategy—especially for bill supporters. Thus it is no surprise that early in their preparation for conference, members maneuver to join strategy with substance to keep bills alive and moving toward conference and final passage.

---

108. Fenno, for example, speaks of "a variety of less authoritative yet persuasive methods [beyond instructions]—from statements on the floor to roll-call votes—whereby the House or Senate expresses its sentiments to the managers and thereby influences the outcome of the conference" (Fenno, *The Power of the Purse*, p. 624).

Appendix

The Use of Conference

With what frequency are conferences used in the legislative process? In chapter 1, we noted the generally cited observation that about 15 to 25 percent of all congressionally passed public bills go to conference.[109] There is, however, actually considerable diversity in the estimates provided by various scholars and observers. One early writer on the history of the conference committee concluded in 1927 (without providing any quantitative specifics) that "on the average, one-tenth of the bills and resolutions that pass through Congress are agreed to by conference committees. . . . In this one-tenth of all bills and resolutions are included practically all important bills."[110] Somewhat differing estimates of the proportion of bills going to conference are provided by *Congressional Quarterly,* depending on definition and time: "About 8 percent of all public and private bills passed by either house [during the Eighty-eighth Congress] are sent to conference";[111] "About 10% of all bills passed by both houses require action by a House-Senate conference committee";[112] "Over one-quarter of all public bills enacted during the 96th Congress—including all of the annual appropriations bills—were products of conference deliberations. Many other bills that were not enacted also ended up in conference committees";[113] and, "Approximately one-third of all the bills enacted into public law in the 93rd Congress, including all regular appropriations bills, were products of conference committees."[114] With estimates ranging from 8 percent to 10 percent to 25 percent to approximately 33 percent, obviously there is considerable variation in the available literature. This is due not only to changes from Congress to Congress but also to differences among such definitions as "all public and private bills," "all public bills," "passed by either house," "passed by both houses," and "enacted into public law."

In the most recent and comprehensive determination of the utilization of conference committees in the legislative process, Congressional Research Service Analyst Ilona B. Nickels has found that of the 623 public laws enacted in the course of the Ninety-eighth Congress (1983 and 1984), 75 (or 12 percent) either resulted from conference committee action or were the product of both conference negotiations and interchamber amendments. In contrast, 391 laws (63 percent) were enacted when one house accepted, without change, the other chamber's version, and a further 157 (25 percent) resulted

---

109. See, for example, David J. Vogler, *The Politics of Congress,* 5th ed. (Boston: Allyn and Bacon, 1988), p. 241.

110. Ada C. McCown, *The Congressional Conference Committee* (New York: Columbia University Press, 1927), p. 11.

111. "Closed Conferences Often Wield Legislative Power," *Congressional Quarterly Weekly Report,* Dec. 12, 1969, p. 2573.

112. Congressional Quarterly, *Research Manual for Congressional Quarterly's Seminar: Congress and the Legislative Process* (Washington, D.C.: Congressional Quarterly, 1981), p. 51.

113. Congressional Quarterly, *Guide to Congress,* 3d ed., p. 434.

114. Congressional Quarterly, Inc., *Guide to Congress,* 2d ed., (Washington, D.C.: Congressional Quarterly, 1976), p. 353.

from another nonconference process of one chamber agreeing to amendments proposed by the other.

In addition to these 623 successful public laws, Nickels reports that another 52 (less than 8 percent of the total) public bills and joint resolutions passed both House and Senate in the course of this two-year period, but failed to be enacted as public law either because of subsequent conference failure or—in a relatively few cases—because of presidential veto. These data would bring the proportion of House- and Senate-passed legislation (as distinct from public laws enacted) that went to conference in 1983–84 to some unspecified figure falling between 11.1 and 18.8 percent.[115]
Senate-passed bills went to conference, and 12 percent of all legislation finally enacted as public law in those two years went the conference route.

---

115. Ilona B. Nickels, "Guiding a Bill Through the Legislative Process: Considerations for Legislative Staff," unpublished Congressional Research Service study, March 1, 1986, p. CRS-35.

9

During the Conference

> The overriding ethic of the conference committee is one of bargaining, give-and-take, compromise, swapping, horse-trading, conciliation, and malleability of all concerned. Firm positions are always taken, and always changed. Deadlocks rarely occur to the degree that the bill is killed. Someone gives a little, perhaps after an impressive holdout, in return for a little; compromise is the cardinal rule of conference committees. Small wonder that each side claims victory; because almost everyone does win—something, somehow, sometime.
> —John Manley[1]

Members "work in mysterious ways" to resolve bicameral differences, once noted House Republican Leader Bob Michel of Illinois.[2] The mysterious ways of the conference committee and its procedures of bicameral reconciliation are indeed curious and at times baffling—sometimes to members of Congress, and often to those outside it. The objective of this chapter is to peel away some layers of these mysteries by describing what happens in conference, why it happens, and with what effect.

To comprehend this legislative entity that so often has the final word on the form and content of crucial legislation, one must pay attention to certain features of its operation. These center around the central purpose and dynamic of the conference committee—the process and politics of bicameral compromise-making. In short, our focus will be on the strategies, rules, activities, and pressures that surround efforts to reach conference compromise and agreement. Understanding how this unique joint institution of House and Senate works will clarify both the nature of conference pol-

---

1. John Manley, *The Politics of Finance: The House Committee on Ways and Means* (Boston: Little, Brown, 1970), p. 271.
2. *Congressional Record*, 98th Cong., 1st sess., Nov. 1, 1983, p. H8927.

icymaking, and the place of the conference committee in the larger legislative process.

Sections of this chapter will consider how conferences are organized and conduct their affairs. In addition, standard negotiating strategies recurrently utilized during conference deliberations will also be examined, starting with the most basic conference activity—bargaining.

Bargaining in Conference

> The essence of bargaining is the communication of intent, the perception of intent, the manipulation of expectations about what one will accept or refuse, the issuance of threats, offers and assurances, the display of resolve and evidence of capabilities, the communication of constraints on what one can do, the search for compromise and jointly desirable exchanges, the creation of sanctions to enforce understandings and agreements, genuine efforts to persuade and inform, and the creation of hostility, friendliness, mutual respect, or rules of etiquette. The actual talk, especially the formal talk, is only a part of this, often a small part.
> —Thomas C. Schelling[3]

This classic description of bargaining was originally derived from analyses of relations between nations, but it applies equally well to conference interactions between House and Senate. Conference intent, and the perceptions by the other chamber's conferees of this intent, is communicated by such preconference actions as the instructing of conferees and floor declarations of determination to achieve certain goals in conference. An anticipation of a "difficult" conference, in which final agreement is expected to be elusive or even impossible to achieve, may be confessed by delegation leaders as a means of softening up conferees who are dedicated to conference and legislative success. Threats, offers, and assurances sometimes are stated prior to the conference's first meeting, or at other appropriate times during the negotiations. The resolve of a chamber's representatives to insist on a key provision can be backed up by an impressive show of delegation unanimity or by citation of an overwhelming chamber vote on the amendment.[4]

The search for conference solutions occurs in light of these kinds of conditioning factors and can be successful only through the development of understandings and trust among the conferees and an awareness of common interests in facilitating bargaining

---

3. Thomas C. Schelling, *Arms and Influence* (New Haven: Yale University Press, 1966), p. 136.

4. One means of demonstrating chamber resolve on an issue, although a step more often threatened than actually utilized, is the seeking of reinstruction from the delegation's parent body. When used, this maneuver can be a most potent tool. As Richard F. Fenno concluded about appropriations conference interactions, "Inside the conference rooms, the threat of one group to seek instructions from the parent chamber is considered the ultimate weapon" (Richard F. Fenno, Jr., *The Power of the Purse: Appropriations Politics in Congress* [Boston: Little, Brown, 1966], p. 658).

processes. Compromise—that key to bicameral agreement—comes about through the skillful utilization of developing personal ties and relationships among the conference negotiators and agreed-upon means and processes of defining and implementing ongoing adjustments and agreements between opposing positions.

Bargaining in conference, then, like bargaining between nations, is a process based on a carefully planned prepositioning of the parties, a skilled use of resources and opportunities during conference interactions themselves, and the development of personal bonds and mutual interests among the parties involved in the conference. "It is maybe a government of laws and not men," said Senator Alan K. Simpson (R, Wy.), "but I have found it is more a government of men and women and their personal relationships with each other as you move the tough pieces of legislation."[5]

Bargaining in conference has other noteworthy features. First, conference committees function in an "agreement-oriented" context. Their raison d'etre is the reconciliation of bicameral differences between the House and Senate: "In most conferences, . . . one criterion of success is reporting out a bill. If a conference report is not filed, then the conference is a failure, and if the conference is a failure, it is difficult for the conferees to avoid the feeling that they too have failed."[6]

Conferees, moreover, are professional politicians accustomed to the personal posturing, trade-offs, bargains, and accommodations that characterize congressional negotiations. That conferences sometimes deadlock over issues of principle, policy, or politics in no way diminishes their basic operational norm: to reach an accord. There are even instances when House and Senate members convene in "informal conference" to expedite the compromise-making process. Even before the Senate took up the 1987 Defense Authorization measure, which was being filibustered by Republicans, Senate Armed Service Democrats met with their partisan House counterparts in a "rump conference" to hammer out an accord on the basic features of the legislation. On some measures, such as "must" bills that fund the government or raise the national debt ceiling, it is a virtual certainty that conferees will eventually, somehow, reach final agreement.

Three major objectives overlie the work of conferees. First, they are mandated to support the majority position of their chamber; second, they must fashion an agreement that a majority of the conferees of each chamber will be willing to sign; finally, they have to create compromise legislation that can attract majority support in each chamber. Conflicts are inherent among these diverse responsibilities: "On the one hand, a conferee is expected to act as a representative of his house and to defend its version of the bill. On the other hand, he is expected to reach an agreement, which necessarily involves compromise. Thus conferees are almost always vulnerable to the charge that they failed adequately to protect their house's position."[7]

---

5. *Congressional Record*, 99th Cong., 2d sess. June 25, 1986, p. S8402.

6. David L. Paletz, "Influence in Congress: An Analysis of the Nature and Effects of Conference Committees," (Ph.D. diss., University of California at Los Angeles, 1970), p. 400.

7. Lawrence E. Gladieux and Thomas R. Wolanin, *Congress and the Colleges: The National Politics of Higher Education,* (Lexington, Mass.: D. C. Heath, 1976), p. 200.

Further, success in reaching conference agreement is no sure thing. Intense partisan, personal, bicameral, committee, or delegational conflicts can produce irreconcilable differences and negotiating deadlocks. "I think we've had enough," declared House conferee Glenn Anderson (D, Cal.) in 1984 after receiving the Senate conferees' final counteroffer on highway demonstration legislation. "I don't think you want a conference," he told his Senate counterparts. He then gathered up his notes and stalked out of the meeting room. The other House conferees followed suit and that ended for good conference negotiation on that bill—and the legislation's prospects for enactment.[8]

House and Senate conferees, however, infrequently walk out of conference committees—except as a bargaining tactic (a most vivid form of bargaining "threat"). Instead, they usually reach some form of conference agreement, in large measure because the central processes of the conference function to promote negotiating success. To discuss in more detail how conference committees work in this regard, we next provide an overview of the main features of conference bargaining followed by an account of the basis of organizing the conference and an examination of the standard reconciliation strategies used in conference negotiations.

General Features of Conference Bargaining[9]

Conference committees can best be viewed as *multilateral* rather than *bilateral* affairs. Although nominally constituted in terms of House versus Senate bargaining teams, conference negotiations usually involve more than just House and Senate interactions. Numerous other parties, such as interest groups and executive branch officials, recurrently have a hand and intense interest in the deliberative process.[10] Even minor or noncontroversial conferences, such as appropriations for the government operations of the District of Columbia, involve not only members from the appropriate House and Senate committees, but also district and national government officials.[11] In the case of complex and highly contentious legislation such as defense appropriations measures or

---

8. Stephen Gettinger, "Highway Bill Conferees Stalemated," *Congressional Quarterly Weekly Report*, Oct. 13, 1984, p. 2670.

9. A variety of theoretical perspectives could be used to examine bargaining in conference. Some of these would include systems theory (viewing conference committees as subunits of the larger congressional system); public choice theory (emphasizing rationality and the maximization of self-interest during conference interactions); game theory (stressing who wins and who loses); and organizational theory (focusing on the political and analytic devices that can reduce conference conflict). See David J. Vogler, *The Third House: Conference Committees in the United States Congress* (Evanston, Ill.: Northwestern University Press, 1971), chap. 5. Our analysis incorporates aspects of a number of these different approaches to conference bargaining, but we posit no single theory to predict or explain conference performance. Instead, our objective is to illuminate the diverse but regular bargaining patterns that influence the strategy of choice in conferences.

10. The various nonconferee participants in conference committee politics are discussed in some detail in chapter 7 above. Six particular players beyond the conferees themselves are considered there: nonconferee Congressmen, Capitol Hill staffers, the president, representatives of governmental agencies, interest group spokesmen, and the press.

11. See the chapter 11 case study "A Typical Low-Intensity Appropriations Conference."

deficit limitation initiatives, the number of additional participants besides House and Senate conferees multiplies.[12] Instead of two-way compromises, then, we commonly find in conference negotiations among three or more sides, with various participants pursuing their own special objectives.

Conference bargaining can be further distinguished in terms of several different yet somewhat overlapping styles of negotiation processes. Based on personal observation, they can be roughly classified as traditional, offer-counteroffer, subconference, and pro forma. *Traditional conferences* are those in which the participants meet face-to-face, haggle among themselves about the items in disagreement, and then reach an accord. The bulk of conferences are of this type. *Offer-counteroffer conferences,* often used by the tax-writing panels, involve meetings where one side suggests a compromise proposal, the other delegation recesses to discuss it in private, and then returns to present a counteroffer. *Subconference* refers to the utilization of special negotiating units and frequently occurs on omnibus bills, when there are numerous conferees. To facilitate negotiations, such a large conference usually breaks into small units to reconcile particular matters or to deal with special topics or sticking points. (At times, as noted in chapter 7 and illustrated in the case studies of chapter 11, these bargaining units may be as small as just the two standing committee chairman.)[13] *Pro forma conferences* are those in which issues are resolved informally—by preconference negotiations between conference leaders or even by staff—even before the conference first meets. The conference itself simply ratifies the earlier decisions.[14]

Third, conference bargaining is profoundly influenced both by what has gone on before and expectations about what will come after. In this sense, conference committees are examples of what have been termed "repetitive games"—recurrent situations

---

12. See, for example, the chapter 11 case studies "Dollars for Defense: Les Gets More Amidst 1985 House Turmoil" and "The Gramm-Rudman Conferences of 1985."

13. Such was the case concerning key conference negotiations in 1986 on massive tax reform legislation. The two chairmen involved, Rep. Dan Rostenkowski (D, Ill.) and Sen. Robert Packwood (R, Ore.), engaged in extensive personal negotiations in order to work out the final successful conference accord: "Over four days, the two men, both proud of their stamina and bargaining ability, spent more than 30 hours in Mr. Rostenkowski's office, swearing, arguing and, according to Mr. Packwood, at one point coming close to crying. By dawn Saturday, they were within a hairbreadth of accord" (David E. Rosenbaum, "Bipartisan Leaders Predict Passage of Tax Bill in Fall," *New York Times,* Aug. 18, 1986, p. 14).

The extent to which conference negotiations in this instance were delegated to the two chairmen was most unusual. Noted one account, "While behind-the-scenes, chairman-to-chairman negotiations are not uncommon on major bills, no one could remember a precedent for conferees formally instructing their chairmen to resolve the differences the conference committee as a whole had been unable to" (Eileen Shanahan, "Tax Bill Negotiators Optimistic Despite Setback Over Revenue," *Congressional Quarterly Weekly Report,* Aug. 16, 1986, p. 1864). This delegation of negotiating responsibilities to the chairmen largely came about because conference negotiations had become increasingly tense and abrasive. The *New York Times* reported, "After the conference dissolved into a shouting match on August 19 [1986], the conferees instructed Packwood and Rostenkowski to try to work out compromises in man-to-man negotiations" (*New York Times,* Aug. 17, 1986, p. 1).

14. For an example, see in chapter 11 the case study "The Department of Education Organization Act," the second of "Two 'Hello and Good-Bye' Conferences of 1979."

"in which participants interact over a period of time to produce a number of decisions, each of which has its own outcome and an impact on subsequent play."[15]

The interactions of a given conference committee do not happen in a political vacuum but are instead the current manifestation of an ongoing series of interactions between conferees usually drawn from matched pairs of House and Senate committees.[16] The legacy of yesterday's conference negotiations on earlier bills has an impact on today's conference, and the anticipation of conferences to come has additional influence on what happens now. For example, conferees may feel the need today to attempt to redress the imbalance of past agreements, or alternatively to take a forceful stand on today's matters to avoid future assumptions of negotiating weakness.

Important similarities, however, tend to promote accord rather than conflict between House and Senate conferees. Congressional committees, after all, are not neutral entities but to some degree serve as advocates for the agencies and programs that fall within their jurisdiction. The House and Senate Agriculture committees, for instance, are filled with members who are strongly supportive of farm interests and programs. Therefore, when conferees from these two panels meet, their compatible outlook predisposes them to work out their differences on specific legislation.

Finally, conference bargaining is not static. It changes in close synchronization with developments in Congress itself. During the era of powerful standing committee chairmen (roughly the 1920s through the early 1970s), House-Senate conference negotiations were substantially controlled by these committee leaders. When the House and Senate Armed Services committees met in conference, for instance, the respective Armed Services chairmen—Representative Carl Vinson (D, Ga.) and Senator Richard Russell (D, Ga.)—dominated the secret, closed-door proceedings. This gave vivid reality to the characterization by one congressman of Armed Services conferences as "two gentlemen from Georgia, talking, arguing, laughing, and whispering in each other's ears."[17] During this era, there was a general pattern of each chamber's delegation deferring to its chairman.

Today, the congressional trend toward participatory democracy permeates conference deliberations. The contemporary diffusion of authority in the House and Senate, the considerable increases in personal staff assistance, the influx of aggressive, media-oriented junior members into the U.S. Congress, the general opening of legislative proceedings in both chambers, and the numerous means by which junior members may assume legislatively significant congressional roles mean that now any conferee—de-

---

15. Barbara Hinckley, *Coalitions and Politics* (New York: Harcourt, Brace, 1981), p. 81. Such "repetitive games" lend themselves particularly well to the use of "simplifying techniques," a number of which we identify and discuss in the next pages. For a general discussion of simplifying techniques in complex negotiations, see Peter F. Nardulli, Roy B. Flemming, and James Eisenstein, "Unraveling the Complexities of Decision Making in Face-to-Face Groups: A Contextual Analysis of Plea-Bargaining Sentences," *American Political Science Review* 77 (Dec. 1984): 912-28.

16. For further discussion of this point, see chapter 6 above.

17. Congressman Otis Pike (D, N.Y.), "Legislator is Taught How Congress Works," quoted in *Washington Star*, March 12, 1964, p. 1.

pending on personal skill and determination—can have the opportunity to affect conference outcomes.[18]

In summary, we have identified five important general but distinctive features of conference bargaining: it is multilateral and effectively carried out by various participants beyond just representatives of the House and Senate; it takes a variety of different forms in the conference quest for compromise and agreement; it is shaped by past and anticipated bargaining experiences; it is facilitated by underlying common interests among conferee negotiators; and it changes as a process as does Congress itself. Now we turn more explicitly to the specifics of conference activity—namely, to how the conference is organized.

Organizing the Conference

Rules and Organization

Conference committees are informal, unfettered units. During conference, "the arch, buttoned-up style of most congressional deliberations melts away. Suit jackets come off and sleeves roll up. References to 'distinguished' and 'honorable' colleagues get junked in favor of first-name banter."[19] The conferees are well aware of and appreciate the heightened informality of the conference. Observed Representative (and now House Speaker) Jim Wright in 1981 of the greater ease of bargaining in conference over deal making in standing committees: "It's cozier, and the trades can be done more blatantly. One doesn't have to go through the theatrics, the snake dance of bringing in witnesses before a full committee."[20]

Conference committees operate virtually free of the formal rules and chamber precedents that regulate the organization and operation of House and Senate standing committees. There are, for example, no general conference rules governing quorum, proxy, amendment, or voting procedures.[21] House and Senate rules require only that

18. See the discussion in chapter 3 of the changing character of conference committee politics for a consideration of these and other changes affecting conference processes.

19. Steven V. Roberts, "Conferences Are Site of Legislative Showdown," *New York Times,* Nov. 20, 1981.

20. Ibid. The informality of the conference can also allow for a distinctive style of humor. Observed Sen. Robert Dole (R, Kan.) of a $1 billion conference request for new funds for the Social Security system, "I'm sure we can work it out. It's only money" (ibid.).

Another 1981 conference was similarly marked by whimsy. After some conference confusion, Rep. E. "Kiki" de la Garza, chairman of the House Agriculture Committee, responded with, "I move to do whatever it was we just decided to do" ("Washington Notes," *New York Times.* Nov. 18, 1981). Negotiations at this 1981 agricultural conference later took an amusing turn when a provision came up providing funds for goat research. "Goat research?" asked Senator Jesse Helms (R, N.C.), an opponent of governmental waste. "Where is this goat research to be carried out?" Helms inquired. "In Texas," replied Representative de la Garza, whose district includes Prairie View A&M University, the locale of the study. "Senate recedes," Senator Helms replied instantly (ibid.).

21. On this point, see also Stanley Bach, "Resolving Legislative Differences in Congress: Conference Committees and Amendments between the Houses," Congressional Research Service Report no. 84-214, Dec. 31, 1984, esp. pp. 47–51, "Conference Procedures and Reports."

conferences be officially open to the public (except for national security and certain other sensitive affairs)[22]; no other formal rules prescribe their decision-making processes.

Only when the conferees present their report to the House or Senate does their handiwork become subject to the constraints of formal chamber rules. Conference reports, for instance, may be ruled out of order in either chamber if it is shown that the conferees met in secret, contrary to House and Senate rules, added new subject matter not considered by either chamber, changed the text to which both houses had agreed, or exceeded their authority in other ways. Even in these cases, though, conference reports can be protected from the application of these formal rules by their waiver or by other means. (These matters will be addressed in chapter 10.)

House and Senate conferees informally observe many of the rules and practices that apply to debate in their respective chambers or committees. "I think it is only natural," observed one senator, "that, since the conference [Senate delegation] is made up of members of the Energy and Natural Resources Committee, the manner in which business had been conducted in committee is the manner in which it would be conducted in the conference."[23] Sometimes, however, the absence of formal rules may produce conference controversy as, for instance, in the case of proxy votes. Challenges are at times raised in conference as to the validity or accuracy of proxy votes cast by conferees on behalf of absent colleagues.[24] Still, the lack of formal rules contributes significantly to successful conference outcomes, because it affords conferees maximum flexibility in the means they use for reconciling their disagreements.

There are occasions, to be sure, when the members of a particular conference will, out of necessity, develop their own informal rules. This happened, for instance, prior to the largest conference in congressional history, that on the Omnibus Reconciliation Act of 1981, which provided for $130 billion cuts in domestic social programs. With 256 conferees (184 from the House and 72 from the Senate) drawn from scores of standing committees, this huge gathering required members of the House and Senate Budget committees and each chamber's party leaders to take the lead in developing informal rules and guidelines for the conference's operations. The fundamental objective of these procedural understandings was to encourage both chambers, which were at the time controlled by different parties, to reconcile their numerous and deeply controversial disagreements. This wish was reflected in one of the guidelines, which simply stated, "The leadership of both Houses will make every effort to get conference agreement on all issues, as quickly as possible."[25] In fact, despite the conference's enormous size and formidable task, an accord on the reconciliation legislation was eventually reached—after much effort.

22. The adoption of this open conference requirement and the consequences attributed to this change are discussed in the first half of chapter 3 above.
23. *Congressional Record,* 95th Cong., 1st sess., July 20, 1977, p. S12434.
24. Ibid. See also *Washington Post,* April 18, 1973, p. A6. At times, proxy disputes may concern the appropriateness of conference proxy votes cast by *staff members* representing absent members. Usually such disputes are resolved by reference to the rules and traditions of the parent chamber committee. Washington interview with Larry Patten, Senate staff aide, Nov. 4, 1981.
25. *Congressional Record,* 98th Cong., 1st sess., July 16, 1981, p. H4420.

Selection of Conference Chairman

One important matter that requires initial resolution for each conference is the question of who is to chair the proceedings. The delegation sent to conference by each chamber is led by the most senior majority member (in practice almost always the chairman) of the committee that reported the original legislation.[26] In addition, the conference itself selects an overall chairman. This decision is sometimes made in a casual way, sometimes in prearranged fashion. For example, if parallel House and Senate committees meet frequently in conference, the post is often determined on the basis of alternation between the chambers. At times, the chairman of one delegation may be intensely interested in the legislation and therefore wish to be conference chairman; in these instances the other body may willingly oblige the legislator.[27] Rarely are there significant disputes in the choice of conference chairman, even though the post at times can be crucial to the outcome of a conference.[28] Two brief examples, however, illustrate occasions when the conference chairmanship *was* a matter of concern to one or both chambers, and how the question was resolved.

In recent congressional history the classic instance of a bitter dispute over who was to be conference chairman involved the struggle in 1962 between the two octogenarian chairmen of the House and Senate Appropriations committees, Representative Clarence Cannon (D, Mo.) and Senator Carl Hayden (D, Ariz.). This dispute, as discussed in chapter 5, was finally resolved after months of deadlock by an agreement alternating the chairmanship between the two chamber committees and eventually by meeting in a room (EF-100) designated especially for conference meetings, located exactly midway between the House and Senate wings of the Capitol.[29]

26. At times, as noted in the preceding chapter, things are not quite so simple as this. The most common complicating factor arises from the possibility that the conference-bound legislation may have undergone multiple referral to various committees. (For a discussion of the impact on conference of this growing congressional practice, see chapters 8 and 3 above.) In these cases, the delegation leadership may be open to some negotiation but usually will be assumed by the chairman of the committee that provided the majority of chamber conferees.

27. At times, a wish to be conference chairman is based on more than just personal legislative interest—or even sentiment. In 1979, House and Senate versions of the Federal Trade Commission Improvement Act were sent to conference for reconciliation. According to intercommittee custom, it was the Senate's turn to provide the conference chair. The problem was that both the chairman and ranking majority member of the Senate committee involved were personally opposed to the legislation and appeared disinclined to do much to further its conference prospects. House Chairman Harley Staggers (D, W.Va.)—a bill supporter—was prevailed upon to request that he be allowed to chair the conference since he would be retiring from Congress soon. This sentimental request, motivated, however, by underlying substantial reasons, was readily agreed to by the Senate delegation (Washington interview with William Baer, former lobbyist for the Federal Trade Commission, March 12, 1981).

28. A useful summary of the potential influence of the conference chairman is provided by David L. Paletz: "Conference chairman is not a role endowed with much authority, yet it is often important. A sensitive chairman can represent the majority of the conferees (from both chambers), guide the discussion, summarize points of view, keep the meeting under control, sense when one or another side is willing to compromise or capitulate on an issue, and, therefore, judge when to pass over a subject because it is still deadlocked or to call for a vote" (Paletz, "Influence in Congress," p. 168).

29. For the story behind this struggle, see Jeffrey L. Pressman, *House vs. Senate* (New Haven: Yale University Press, 1966), as well as the fuller discussion of these events in chapter 5 above.

More recently, the House Ways and Means and Senate Finance committees engaged in maneuvers that involved a key conference chairmanship. The tax committees traditionally have rotated the conference leadership post between their chairmen. In early 1984, the House passed legislation raising the national debt ceiling. When the bill went to the Senate, then-Finance Chairman Robert Dole (R, Kan.) won Senate approval to substitute a slightly different termination date for the one in the House-passed bill. The measure was then returned to the House and a conference on this seemingly inconsequential matter appeared likely. House members complained that the change of date by the Senate was really a subterfuge concerning a dispute between Dole and House Ways and Means Chairman Dan Rostenkowski (D, Ill.). The real issue between the chairmen concerned who would chair an important and controversial upcoming conference on tax reform legislation, which was proceeding through Congress at the same time as the relatively minor debt ceiling legislation. The two issues were intertwined because it was "Rostenkowski's turn to chair a conference, but if there was a debt conference before the tax conference, Dole would wind up chairing the tax session."[30] Ultimately, Representative Rostenkowski chaired the tax conference because he was successful in persuading the House to accept the Senate's debt ceiling date change, eliminating the necessity for a prior conference on that matter. (There was a repeat performance in 1986 when Ways and Means Chairman Rostenkowski and Senate Finance Chairman Bob Packwood (R, Ore.) each maneuvered to head the conference on the massive tax reform bill of that year. Rostenkowski prevailed in this instance, too.)[31]

Jockeying for the conference chairmanship is, at times, motivated by a desire for publicity and attention, but usually has underlying causes more substantial than headline seeking alone. Members understand that a conference chairman is strategically positioned to set the conference agenda, schedule negotiating sessions, and shape the tone and pace of the proceedings. These powers are especially real given the general absence of rules and precedents limiting a conference chairman's choices. An artful use of these informal powers can be critical to conference success; if exercised carelessly, they may make more likely conference tension, problems, or even failure. Agenda control, for instance, can serve multiple policy making purposes. By starting the conference with the noncontroversial rather than the controversial matters in bicameral disagreement, the chairman can establish a cooperative and conciliatory atmosphere, accustom the conferees to working together, prevent the conference from bogging down, and give conferees a cumulative stake in reaching agreement with every successful reconciliation. This process can produce an "accommodating spirit" sufficient later in the negotiations to facilitate the resolution of the more controversial House-Senate disagreements.[32]

Scheduling meetings and determining their length are other prerogatives of the chair. In chapter 1, we recounted the story of how Carl Perkins (D, Ky.), chairman of the

---

30. *Washington Post,* May 25, 1984, p. A4.
31. For a full account of these maneuvers, see Jeffrey H. Birnbaum and Alan S. Murray, *Showdown at Gucci Gulch: Lawmakers, Lobbyists, and the Unlikely Triumph of Tax Reform* (New York: Random House, 1987), especially chap. 11.
32. For a particularly clear example of this strategy, see the chapter 11 case study "Higher Education: Personalities and Exhaustion."

House Education and Labor Committee and the conference chairman on a controversial and landmark higher education bill, kept conference negotiations going for fifteen straight hours until an accord was reached, in part because the conferees were numb with exhaustion. A similar strength of constitution was attributed by veteran legislative aide Christopher Matthews to Senator Ed Muskie (D, Me.) as chairman of the Budget Committee: "Muskie's great strength was that he never left the [conference] room. I mean he *never* went to the bathroom. He'd go in at nine o'clock and stay until one. Everybody else was getting hungry. . . . Muskie would stay—right? That's a great strength. . . . He's there to get the bill passed—*his way!* And if you're hungry and he's not, all the better. He'll wait until one o'clock and if you want to go eat at twelve, fine, leave a proxy. He'll take your proxy, and he'll finish at one-thirty, and he'll have his resolution then."[33]

Meeting Locations

The decision on where to meet can sometimes shape policy outcomes. Occasionally, conference chairmen will schedule meetings in Capitol hideaways; or they may abruptly change the time and place of the meeting. These ploys are used gingerly, yet they can impede attendance by some conferees who might be able to block agreements that have the support of conference leaders. What such maneuvers *do* accomplish is to make difficult—if not impossible—the witnessing of conference negotiations by the general public, some interest group representatives and many members of the press. (Of course, favored individuals in the latter categories can always be given precise, updated information on the conference meeting).

Another consideration is the relationship between room size and the dynamics of deliberation (sometimes termed the architectural strategy). Although formal bicameral deliberations are now usually open to public observation, some conferences (as discussed in detail in chapter 3) manage simultaneously to meet in public and operate in secret. One way this occurs is by conferences being deliberately scheduled in rooms large enough to accommodate only the conferees themselves and a few others. The objective is to expedite decision making by excluding lobbyists, the press, and the public from attending and observing conference deal making. If hordes of lobbyists and others were watching the proceedings, it is reasoned, conferees might believe it necessary to fight harder and make longer speeches for provisions they might otherwise drop quietly in the interest of bicameral agreement. For example, the huge conference on one of President Reagan's economic centerpieces, the Economic Recovery Tax Act of 1981, not by accident met in a Capitol room measuring but sixteen by thirty feet; the relative

---

33. An account of the former events is contained in Gladieux and Wolanin, *Congress and the Colleges;* the story of conference chairman Perkins's strategy is told by Rep. Romano L. Mazzoli (D. Ky.) in "My Favorite Story," *Roll Call,* June 2, 1983, p. 5. This instance of conference committee politics is further examined in the chapter 11 case study "Higher Education: Personalities and Exhaustion." The Muskie story is drawn from Hedrick Smith, *The Power Game: How Washington Works* (New York: Random House, 1988), p. 62.

tininess of the room was seen as facilitating conference negotiations by providing a degree of privacy.

Conference Negotiations

General Considerations

Conference negotiations are marked by informal give-and-take. The one overriding official rule is that for a provision to be finally agreed to, a majority of House conferees and a majority of Senate conferees must both favor it. (This principle means that the size of each chamber's delegation conveys no numerical advantage to either side during bicameral negotiations and voting.) What do count are the composition of each chamber's delegation, the goals each conferee seeks, and how these compositional and goal factors shape conference negotiations.[34]

Conference actions are carried out by means of informal negotiations, most often in the form of "horse trading" among the conferees on various provisions. Logrolling is a frequent activity. As we noted above, it entails the trading of support on one measure for support for another. When chamber differences are expressed in quantitative terms, bargaining is often simplified and facilitated. Greater problems occur, as we have discussed, when the differences are not quantitative but qualitative. When such differences occur, splitting the difference is impractical, and sequential bargaining rather than quantitative adjustment may be the norm: "We'll recede on this provision, but we will expect a comparable consideration from you on some later matter of particular concern to us."

Various other strategies, as outlined next in this chapter, may be used during conference negotiations. Conferees may threaten to take the issue and dispute back to their chamber and "seek instructions," thereby deliberately tying their hands.[35] Conference negotiators may declare that unless the other chamber accepts a specific provision, they will be unable to support any conference bill. Individual conferees may threaten not only not to sign the conference report, but to lead opposition to its enactment on the floor of their chamber.[36]

In short, during the conference, interactions are marked by informality, give-and-take, and shifting prospects of conference deadlock and failure—or legislative success.

Standard Negotiating Strategies

Scores of strategies are employed during conference negotiations. Since it is possible neither to identify nor analyze them all, our objective is to focus on a wide array of

---

34. For an examination of conferee roles, see the second half of chapter 6 above.

35. The instructing of conferees prior to conference, however, occurs far more frequently than the reinstructing of the conference delegation during the conference. For this reason, these tactics are largely discussed together in chapter 8 above.

36. For a discussion of how conference actions influence subsequent conference report approval politics, see chapter 10 below.

conventional negotiating devices that in the aggregate present an overall perspective of the bicameral reconciliation process. These strategies are illustrated by instances of their use and are organized into three general categories: opening gambits, obtaining information, and giving-and-taking.[37]

OPENING GAMBITS. Bargaining is largely an art, and an artful use of various strategic openings can shape the course of negotiations. Ploys, procedures, and psychology are among the devices that conferees use to feel each other out in an attempt to gain preliminary advantage. Conferees, to be sure, are usually aware of the use of these sorts of devices because of previous conference experience and exposure to conferees who often are recurrent bicameral opposites. Seldom, therefore, are seasoned conferees really surprised by what the other side attempts. Still, conferees realize that such opening gambits are part of the conference preparatory homework and can promote negotiating climates that facilitate advantageous bicameral outcomes.

Ploys, for our purposes, mean opening proposals that are calculated to rebound to the offerer's advantage. There are two major variants of such opening moves, each with its own advantages and disadvantages. One approach is the bold or extreme approach. Bargainers knowingly ask for far more than is politically or practically reasonable to dramatize their position, provide subsequent trading options, demonstrate resolve, and set the tone and agenda for subsequent conference bargaining. The extreme opener can sometimes produce unexpected but welcome concessions from the other side; it also gives its initiators a reference point to use in claiming numerous concessions during the course of conference deliberations. Two major disadvantages adhere to the hard-line opening. It can backfire and lead to early negotiating deadlock, particularly if the other side counters with its own extreme, forcefully stated position. The tough opener can also be ineffective if it is quickly dismissed as entirely unrealistic—simply an aspect of legislative gamesmanship—and ignored by conferees from the other side.

An alternative major opener is the fair or reasonable approach. This involves an initial proposal formulated to take account of the different needs and objectives of the negotiators. The conference settlement of differences may well be greatly facilitated by this step because mutually advantageous compromises are attractively brought together in an initial package. One fundamental drawback of this approach is that conferees are likely to differ greatly in their interpretation of what is fair. Another is that determined counterpart negotiators may view the initial offering not as the basis for possible agreement, but as the starting point for further concessions.

Procedural considerations also permeate the opening round of conference deliberations. Some of these have already been discussed—who is to chair the conference and when and where it will meet, for instance. Another initial concern is the specific method

---

37. These three categories have a loose correspondence with the three stages of the process of negotiations identified by I. William Zartman and Maureen R. Berman. In their analysis, these stages are *diagnostic, formula,* and *detail.* The *diagnostic* stage is marked by participant efforts to define the situation and by initial efforts at negotiations—including opening gambits; the *formula* phase by the identification of a pattern or formula for agreement, and the *detail* period by the working out of the specifics needed to put the formula into effect (I. William Zartman and Maureen R. Berman, *The Practical Negotiator* [New Haven: Yale University Press, 1982]).

of resolving the items in dispute. Usually conferees work off documents that list side-by-side the House and Senate positions (and sometimes also White House views) on the matters in disagreement. That practice is not, however, invariably used. Alternatively, one chamber's bill or the other's may serve as the basis for negotiations, with changes and compromises being agreed to as amendments to that basic text. Such was the case during a conference on clean air legislation in 1977. The House agreed to work off the text of the Senate legislation and further, to drop provisions that were not present in some fashion in both bills. These decisions had several consequences: they expedited the bargaining process (the House bill had far more provisions than the Senate version); it strengthened the Senate's bargaining leverage because it is harder to add something to a measure than to take it out; and it caused considerable concern among House conferees that the deletion of so many House provisions would make difficult House approval of any compromise conference legislation. In the end, however, the House never got the chance to vote on the clean air conference report because it was rejected in the Senate.[38]

Psychological stratagems are also employed at the start of conference negotiations. They are designed to influence the behavioral actions of conferees who are, after all, subject to the same attributes of human nature as everyone else, including ambition, peer pressure, pride, and ego. Conferees, in brief, often try to play on the personal characteristics of their conference colleagues and negotiating counterparts. A vivid example of the use of psychology occurred in 1975 when the two tax committee chairmen, the seasoned senator Russell Long (D, La.) and Representative Al Ullman (D, Ore.)—who had just replaced Wilbur Mills (D, Ark.) as chairman—faced each other:

> [Long's] first tactic was to psyche out Al Ullman, the new Chairman of the Ways and Means Committee who was sitting in Wilbur Mills' old bargaining position on tax matters for the first time.
>
> Ullman had done something the day before that Mills would never have done; he tipped his hand on national television, saying that many of the amendments in Long's Senate bill bordered on being "irresponsible" and would have to be removed.
>
> All day Monday, according to one participant, Long and his fellow Senators unanimously rejected every compromise Ullman offered. Frequently they used the word "irresponsible."[39]

Thrown off balance by these and other psychological tactics, the House conferees eventually abandoned their support of the elimination of the tax depletion allowance and accepted Long's position, which provided only for its modification.

OBTAINING INFORMATION. Another negotiating strategy includes conferees' efforts to obtain information—both policy and political. Important in this regard is who provides the information and what kind it is. Providers are typically other congressmen,

---

38. Bernard Asbell, *The Senate Nobody Knows* (New York: Doubleday, 1978), pp. 431–47. See the additional discussion of this postconference failure in chapter 10.

39. *Congressional Record*, 94th Cong., 1st sess., April 14, 1975, p. S5911 (the discussion contained in the *Congressional Record* was drawn from an article that originally appeared in the *Washington Star*).

the president, executive branch officials, representatives of interest groups, committee and personal staff, and the media.[40] At times, these "third parties" and their information can be instrumental in the resolution of conference disputes. For example, at one point the Carter administration strongly opposed a tuition tax credit provision that had been added in the Senate to a measure increasing Social Security taxes. During conference, Senator William Roth (R, Del.), in an action supported by all the Senate conferees, at first refused to withdraw this provision despite an offer by the administration to study means by which college tuition costs could be eased for students and families. Eventually, the Senate conferees changed their stand and agreed to drop the tuition tax provision, paving the way for final conference agreement (to the administration's relief). This happened only after the chairman of the House Ways and Means Committee, himself not a conferee, promised to conduct hearings on the issue. This action by a committee chairman, and the communication to the conferees of his intent, proved to be the key in this instance to conference success.[41]

Conferees often seek technical and substantive information as well as political assessments concerning legislation before them. Members regularly find themselves addressing complex, technical topics (genetic engineering and surrogate motherhood, for example) that challenge both their understanding and their capacity to fashion workable compromises. The information initially available to them might be inadequate for determining effective policy choices or even whether various possible programs are administratively feasible. To reach agreement on such complex issues often requires conferees to obtain additional technical and scientific information from some outside source. Coincidental with on-going bicameral negotiations, the House and Senate committees participating in conference may even convene hearings to gather supplemental testimony from expert witnesses; this information will then be used by the committees' conferees to shape conference decisions.

Politically, conferees also seek information on such matters as who might benefit from different decisions and, more generally, the electoral and political ramifications of various choices. For instance, some conferees may be under considerable personal pressure to reach an accord on a conference matter because it will enhance their reelection prospects. One reason Senator Claiborne Pell (D, R.I.) was intensely interested in the successful resolution of a major 1972 higher education conference was because of his reelection worries. At the time, Pell was "rated a distinct underdog," in part because of what was seen as his skimpy record of legislative accomplishment. "Guiding the Education Amendments, with the 'Pell Grants' included," successfully through the Senate and conference, noted two observers, "would be an important achievement bolstering his

---

40. The various participants in conference committee activities are discussed in turn in chapter 7 above.

41. *Congressional Quarterly Almanac, 1977* (Washington, D.C.: Congressional Quarterly, 1978), p. 172, and *New York Times*, Dec. 11, 1977, p. 27. To be sure, the threat of a presidential veto of any conference-generated legislation retaining the tuition tax provision undoubtedly also encouraged the Senate to relent.

record."[42] The electoral necessities of one key conferee in this case were a significant factor in eventual conference legislative success.[43]

Sometimes conferees seek to generate outside pressures on conference decision making as a means of facilitating conference negotiations. Representative John Dingell (D, Mich.), a leader of the 1981 budget subconference charged with considering spending cuts in the health area, convened a subcommittee hearing of the House Energy and Commerce Committee (which he chairs) while the subconference was still meeting. He explained, "I am convening . . . [this] hearing . . . to assess the potential impact of these [proposed conference] cuts on child health and infant mortality so that conferees might be better able to weigh this impact during our conference discussions."[44] The information and media attention generated by the House hearings, it was hoped, would encourage the health subconference to act to restore the funding of these social programs.

The availability of new information or forecasts can facilitate—or sometimes alternatively threaten—conference agreement. The report of an improving economy generating unexpected revenues can make the negotiating burdens of budget, tax, or appropriations conferences easier, certainly far more than news of dismal economic conditions requiring the distribution of financial pain rather than gain. Control of information, too, can be a resource for conferees. If only a limited number of conferees and staff are privy to certain information, their knowledge is power that can be used to fashion outcomes favorable to their ends.

House-Senate Negotiating Differences

The profound institutional differences between House and Senate have a direct impact on many aspects of conference policy making and negotiations. House debate rules, for instance, are much stricter than the Senate's. Unlike the House, where nearly every second of debate time is regulated by rule or precedent, Senate rules and traditions permit unlimited debate and emphasize the protection of the rights of political or legislative minorities (be they the minority party, any group of senators, or even one senator). Conference decisions are influenced by these profound interchamber differences, at times even forcing conferees from one chamber to appeal to their conference counterparts for an understanding of the peculiar traits of their body. Such an instance arose during conference negotiations in late 1984 when Senator Orrin Hatch (R, Utah) "found himself in the unlikely position of asking House negotiators to limit the [House school]

---

42. Gladieux and Wolanin, *Congress and the Colleges*, p. 172. In these regards, Senator Pell was both legislatively and politically successful. For additional analysis of this conference, see the chapter 11 case study "Higher Education: Personalities and Exhaustion."

43. A similar motivation has been attributed to Sen. Robert Packwood (R, Ore.) to explain his late-blooming enthusiasm for major tax reform and determination to see a successful conclusion for the landmark 1986 tax conference. See Birnbaum and Murray, *Showdown at Gucci Gulch*, for an insightful analysis of Senator Packwood's conversion to tax reform.

44. *Congressional Record*, 97th Cong., 1st sess., July 23, 1981, p. H4829.

prayer language because he expected it would provoke a filibuster in the Senate."[45] The House conferees accommodated Senator Hatch's request. For its part, House negotiators commonly argue in conference that Senate provisions must be dropped because they are in violation of House rules and, if retained in the conference report, would be subject to parliamentary objections in the form of points of order on the House floor.[46]

Senate conferees, too, are generally more likely than their House counterparts to protect their colleagues' legislative and political interests should schedules require them to be absent from conference deliberations. This behavioral bicameral difference stems in large part from the Senate's smaller size and its stronger adherence to norms of comity and accommodation compared to the larger, more anonymous House. These chamber norms are buttressed by the formidable powers that Senate rules accord any senator. A failure of Senate conferees to protect the special interests of absent colleagues could provoke an outraged senator to launch a filibuster or other obstructionist steps against the conference report.

Interchamber differences occur in the policy realm, too. One house may, at times, be marked by majority views that are strikingly opposite to those of the other: pro- or antiabortion, for or against increases in defense expenditures, and so forth. Such strong bicameral policy differences can lead to sharp bicameral policy conflict or even deadlock in conference. More often, policy disagreements are settled through compromise agreements that neither side finds completely acceptable but that each recognizes as the best attainable. It is to this process of conference give-and-take that we next turn.

GIVING-AND-TAKING. One senator, a frequent conferee on appropriations legislation, caught well the concept of conference negotiations as involving giving-and-taking. During conference committee interactions, he observed, "basically it's a matter of settling a difference of opinion between two bills. It's a knockdown drag-out affair until you get agreement. It's a lot of fun if you like that sort of thing. You get in there and pinko pinko back and forth. . . . A conference on an appropriations bill is just horse trading. You've got a horse you want to trade and I've got a pony I want to trade. And you know you've got to have a bill."[47]

Horse trading and other forms of adjustment are essential to conference success. "A conference where there are no concessions will be a conference where there is no report," asserted Senator Sam Nunn (D, Ga.) in 1984.[48] Conference bargaining consists of more than just concessions. It also involves compromises, deadlocks, disputes, and even straight-out victories for either the House or Senate. The result—singly or in combination—depends on negotiations that commonly involve more than mere interactions between House and Senate delegations. The process of giving-and-taking may also occur between individual conferees, within chamber delegations, across party and

45. Janet Hook, "Silent Prayer Dropped from Final School Bill," *Congressional Quarterly Weekly Report*, Oct. 6, 1984, p. 2460.
46. The impact of interchamber differences on conference report approval politics in House and Senate is discussed in detail in chapter 10 below.
47. Fenno, *The Power of the Purse*, p. 625. See also the classic description of conference bargaining by John Manley quoted at the beginning of this chapter.
48. *Congressional Record*, 98th Cong., 2nd sess., Aug. 10, 1984, p. S10373.

chamber lines, and among numerous other combinations of conferees as well as nonconferee participants.

Amid this negotiating diversity is an equally wide range of bargaining devices that overlie the basic "unit rule" of conference decision making: that each chamber delegation makes decisions by majority vote of its members. Constructing the necessary "two majorities" of House and Senate conferees can be a complex and arduous process. Lawmakers regularly achieve positive results because they use an array of rather straightforward and widely understood bargaining approaches that apply to most conference situations. Among the most recurrent and noteworthy of these negotiating strategies are trades or logrolls, "splitting the difference," compromises, threats or bluffs, and simple utilization of negotiating skills.

Trades or logrolls involve exchanges of voting support on different issues by groups of conferees. At times, the initiation of a trade can be quite explicit. Exclaimed Representative Silvio O. Conte (R, Mass.) during one conference, "I help you, you help me. That's what this [conference negotiation] is all about. All I'm asking for is a lousy $3 million."[49]

In a trade or logroll, each side gets something in return for giving away something. For example, during a 1984 conference, liberal representative Henry Waxman (D, Cal.) sought Senate conferee support for an "orphan drug" program, which would utilize tax incentives to encourage the commercial development of drugs to treat rare diseases. Conservative Senator Orrin Hatch (R, Utah) wanted Waxman's backing for a program to aid Utah residents who acquired leukemia, apparently as a result of nuclear testing during the 1950s and 1960s. The representative and the senator were quick to forge a deal on these two unrelated matters and agreed to make common cause on behalf of both.[50]

In this instance, the two conferees were strongly committed to their own particular issue, and not especially opposed to the other. This absence of objection to either proposal facilitated the bipartisan and bicameral logroll. Once the trade was worked out between Senator Hatch and Representative Waxman, conference agreement on the arrangement followed easily. When leading and opposing conferees join forces in agreement on various provisions, others are prone to ratify the accord.

Trades are not always easy to arrange, and each side may require protracted periods to devise appropriate offers or counteroffers. Describing how a 1984 tax conference managed to resolve a grand total of 386 items in disagreement, Representative Donald Pease (D, Ohio) mentioned the frequent use of secret caucuses to plan strategy and to formulate trades, and further stressed the give-and-take of conference logrolling: "Typically on any group of 10 items, the House might yield to the Senate on three provisions,

---

49. John Fenton, "Foreign Aid Funding Bill Caught in Budget Crunch," *Congressional Quarterly Weekly Report,* March 8, 1980, p. 700. One study of conference decision making on defense appropriations concluded that "logrolling is the dominant form of conflict resolution in the conference [on defense issues]. The House either accepts the Senate position, or the Senate accepts the House position; very rarely do they fix on a figure which is neither. Conflict is resolved by trading concessions on separate individual decisions" (Arnold Kanter, "Congress and the Defense Budget: 1960–1970," *American Political Science Review* 66 [March 1972]:141).

50. *New York Times,* Sept. 14, 1984, p. A24.

the Senate might recede to the House on three items, and the conferees would agree to compromise language on the other four."[51]

Numerous subtleties abound in such trading processes. Sometimes members of one delegation will be quick to accept the other's position because it corresponds with their own policy preferences. Precedents that obligate conferees to fight for their chamber's views may be either ignored or lightly observed. (To avoid charges from the full membership that they "sold out" to the other side, conferees will later report to their chamber that they fought hard for their chamber's position, but they had no choice but to give in to the other side.) In these instances, conference negotiations do not really involve hard bargaining as much as consensus determination.

Another trading situation occurs when one side fights hard against provisions it is in fact only mildly opposed to, but that are important to conferees from the other body. Such initial opposition may be successful in winning concessions from opposing conferees in exchange for the cessation of this opposition. Alternatively, conferees from one chamber may readily concede to the other on a series of initial issues in order to build credit with their opposite numbers. This credit will be "cashed in" later for some item of fundamental importance to the agreeable conferees. One long-time conferee described this tactic graphically: "You recede graciously early on some not too important issue, then you cite it again and again as you rape them."[52]

Sometimes the items conceded by conferees were deliberately added to the conference-bound legislation during chamber consideration purposefully to be disposed of during conference negotiations.[53] As one House conferee observed about a tax conference, "[The Senate] came to the bargaining table with a goose that was full of goodies. Ours was much skinnier. [Senator Russell] Long kept talking about how much they had given up and what were we going to give up?"[54]

"Splitting the difference," as noted earlier, is a time-honored tradition of conference bargaining. Most often associated with bicameral disagreements that involve numbers, this conflict-resolving tactic was once described in 1984 by that master of conference bargaining Senator Long in the following terms: if the Senate legislation contains a number, "say it is 200, and the House has a number of 100, if we cannot get together, we would say, 'Let's make it 150. Let's split the difference.'"[55] While neither side necessarily will agree with the result, noted Senator Long, splitting the difference is reasonably acceptable to both sides because it means that if "you are wrong, you are only half wrong; and if we are wrong, we are only half wrong."[56]

At times, the process of splitting the difference can be a real accelerator of conference decision making—even at the cost of certainty as to what is being decided. Recalled one senator about a frequent House counterpart, "[Representative] Al Thomas

---

51. *Congressional Record*, 98th Cong., 2d sess., June 27, 1984, p. E3019.
52. Paletz, "Influence in Congress," p. 418.
53. The preconference loading of legislation with expendable provisions in anticipation of conference is discussed in chapter 8 above.
54. *Congressional Record*, 94th Cong., 1st sess., April 14, 1975, p. 10142.
55. *Congressional Record*, 98th Cong., 2d sess., Aug. 1, 1984, p. S9605.
56. Ibid.

is a great negotiator. He says—'split, split, split: House yields here, Senate yields there.' . . . Goes really fast. You have to say, 'Stop it, Al.' "[57]

On many occasions, to be sure, the numerical split may lean more to one side than the other. Time lags between the passage of the legislation by each chamber and the start of conference negotiations often account for this result. As a result, conferences are subject to agency reestimates, the availability of new information, and a host of other factors (including chamber prestige)[58] that may move conferences away from an even division of differences and more toward one chamber's figures because they reflect changing realities and understandings better.[59]

Other deviations from a middle point between the House and Senate figures can result from simple negotiation. In 1977, the Senate authorized $30 million for new "magnet" schools, and the House $7.5 million. Conference negotiations went like this:

Senator Edward Brooke (R, Mass.)—"We want $22 million."
Representative Daniel Flood (D, Pa.)—"Nineteen-five."
Senator Brooke (R, Mass.)—"Twenty million and we'll take it."[60]

Compromises are a variation of splitting the difference. They involve building winning coalitions in conference through negotiations over and adjustments in the content of legislation. Each side agrees to change the conference bill in a way that is more acceptable to the other. Unlike trades, in which conferees do not modify their policy objectives but exchange some goals for others, compromises require both sides to rework and adjust their original positions on countless if not nearly all provisions.

Congress is an institution that thrives on compromise; it is, therefore, not surprising that conferees readily recognize the value of reciprocal concessions as essential in

---

57. Pressman, *House vs. Senate*, p. 72.

58. As Pressman notes, "If the prestige of the two houses is at stake, it is possible that each side will seek to reach agreement at a place slightly on its own side of the 'middle point' " (ibid.).

59. Besides changing factual information, committee factors may also cause subsequential deviation from straight split-the-difference solutions. Writing about the House and Senate Budget committees, for example, Allen Schick found that "although both [Budget] committees want to reach agreement in conference, they have not resolved disputes by splitting the differences. . . . Virtually every contested functional allocation has been decided by tilting toward one side or the other. (In a few cases, the conference allocation was below or above the amounts set by the two Houses.)" These deviations, Schick argued, were largely due to committee-specific factors, especially the high turnover of membership on the House Budget Committee together with its being generally more out of tune with its chamber than the Senate committee (Allen Schick, *Congress and Money: Budgeting, Spending and Taxing* [Washington, D.C.: Urban Institute, 1980], p. 302).

60. James R. Dickenson, "When Hill Conferees Confer, The Talk Can Get Hot," *Washington Star*, July 22, 1977, p. C8. Even while figures are being bantered around, the split-the-difference figure is never totally forgotten. In the course of another 1977 conference on the funding of teacher training centers, conferees were trying to agree on a compromise figure between the House's $5 million amount and the Senate's $12.5 million level. House conferee Daniel Flood offered to increase the funding level above the House-approved level, saying, "We'll go up some." One senator quickly suggested, "Make it another $3 million, that'll look better." (The resulting amount would then total $8 million.) Another senator chimed in, "Make it $3,250,000 [closer to midpoint] that'll look even better" (ibid.). It is out of such auctionlike conference interactions that some legislation is formed.

conference negotiations. "You take strong people with strong views who work hard on issues," noted Senator Christopher Dodd (D, Conn.) in 1983, "and if you have any hope at all of moving forward in vital areas . . . it takes compromise."[61] The objective of compromise, in short, is to achieve conference agreement on legislation that, while not perfect, will enjoy sufficient support to be accepted by both houses. (Compromises, of course, are not worked out just between House and Senate conference delegations, but also within each delegation and among other concerned conferee groups and outside entities with a stake in conference decisions.)

Different techniques are employed in compromise making. In one instance, the leader of a conference delegation may ask his members to vote initially against compromises they actually support to demonstrate to their parent house that they stood firm for their chamber's views before they eventually had to reconsider and yield to a compromise agreement. (This approach may be useful later in selling the conference report to their chamber's full membership—see the discussion in chapter 10.) One chamber's conferees may also raise the specter of lengthy parliamentary floor battles against the conference report unless certain compromises are reached. At times, wavering conferees will be won over to a compromise if "clarifying" language is included in the official "explanatory statement" that accompanies the conference report to the House and Senate.

Issues that raise matters of conscience or principle, such as abortion, school prayer, or school busing, are always the most difficult to compromise. Conferences that consider such matters time after time become embroiled in emotional and protracted conference debate as national political passions swirl around the proceedings. The question for conferees in these circumstances may become whether an imperfect compromise on such highly contentious matters *is* in fact better than none at all. More typically, conferees are able to fashion acceptable conference accommodations, transforming abstract principles into tangible compromises. As representative and veteran conferee Barber Conable (R, N.Y.) once put it, "The idealists all stand over in the corner and posture, and let us compromisers get things done for them."[62]

Threats or bluffs are common pressure tactics in any negotiations. Their fundamental purpose is to weaken the resolve of the other side by suggesting undesirable consequences. Whether threats or bluffs succeed or instead simply produce counterthreats depends on a host of circumstances. Of these, one important factor is timing. Another concerns the strength of each side's bargaining position. A third involves the negotiating skill of the conferees.

Timing is an ever-present political consideration for conferees, particularly when they confront legislative and adjournment deadlines or upcoming congressional elections. The effect of deadlines can be dramatically seen when conference negotiations continue up to or near recess or adjournment dates, and threats of walkout or other forms of conference intransigence take on added political significance.

The anticipation of elections, too, is a common backdrop to many conferences. In

---

61. *Congressional Record*, 98th Cong., 1st sess., Nov. 17, 1983, p. S16505.
62. *New York Times*, Aug. 7, 1984, p. B6.

the summer of 1984, for instance, House and Senate conferees were locked in a tense conference on Pentagon spending. President Reagan and Republican Senate conferees sought increases in defense spending; Democratic House conferees were insistent on reductions to curb mushrooming governmental deficits and to encourage arms control. The conference became deeply bogged down over these issues, especially on the particular issue of the procurement of additional MX missiles. Stalemate, however, was not an unhappy prospect for everyone. "Absent an agreement," calculated Senator Richard Lugar (R, Ind.), chairman of the Republican Senatorial Campaign Committee, "[Republicans would] have a campaign issue we can take to the public."[63] Lugar and other Republicans looked forward to the possibility of portraying Democratic senators and candidates as being "soft on defense." Democrats, for their part, were anticipating being able to link Republican support for defense spending increases to the huge national deficit and to another arms race. In the end, the conference deadlock was broken, and each side got something it could support. Senate Republicans (and the White House) got more money for defense. House Democrats, on the other hand, won approval of a voting procedure, to take effect after the politically charged November elections, that would require as many as four separate affirmative votes (two in each chamber) before more MX missiles could be built.

While bargaining and accommodation are the essence of conference committee interactions, there are occasions when one side inherently has the stronger hand. In this case, it may be able to threaten the other chamber to "take it or leave it." The Senate enjoyed this position in 1983 on conference negotiations on legislation extending general revenue sharing.

The revenue sharing program expired September 30, while the extension legislation was still in conference. The House bill had authorized $5.02 billion annually for the program and the Senate legislation had provided $4.6 billion. Senate conferees, led by Robert Dole (R, Kan.), announced as soon as the conference convened that conference negotiations must end up at the senatorial figure (the amount originally requested by the White House)—or nothing at all. "It's going to be four-six [$4.6 billion] or zero, as far as the Senate is concerned," he declared.[64] Any other amount would be rejected either by the Senate conferees or by the Senate chamber or be vetoed by the president.

House conferees expressed profound shock at the Senate delegation's unyielding attitude. "I've never seen a situation where one side says, 'Take it or leave it,' " said Representative Ted Weiss (D, N.Y.), unofficial leader of the House conferees.[65] He proposed instead the traditional step of "splitting the difference" between the two spending figures. As promised, however, the Senate conference delegation rejected this compromise. Not very surprisingly, given the hardening of positions, conference negotiations broke down, with neither side willing to relent. Subsequently, the House conferees reconsidered their rejection of the Senate ultimatum as concern mounted about congressional failure to authorize continuation of the revenue sharing program and as

63. *New York Times,* July 29, 1984, p. E1.
64. Richard Whittle, "Conference Breaks Up: Funding Dispute Stymies Revenue Sharing," *Congressional Quarterly Weekly Report,* Nov. 12, 1983, p. 2354.
65. Ibid.

major recipients of funds under the program launched a drive to win continued funding for it. The conference was reconvened, and the House delegation reluctantly—even bitterly—accepted the Senate's $4.6 billion figure.

When the conference report was considered on the House floor, Representative Jack Brooks (D, Tex.), the official leader of his chamber's conferees, explained the House conference turnabout in terms as mild as possible under the circumstances: "In the face of insistence by the Senate conferees on their figure, the threat by President Reagan to veto any bill containing an amount higher than the current funding level, and simple economic reality, the conferees agreed to adopt the Senate figure."[66] In short, Senator Dole had strengthened the Senate's bargaining leverage by limiting the negotiating options to its figure or none. This all-or-nothing tactic rests, noted one of the foremost scholars of strategic bargaining, "on the paradox that the power to constrain an adversary may depend on the power to bind oneself."[67]

The *negotiating skills* of individual conferees can also produce desirable results for either chamber. Threats, bluffs, jokes, knowing when to hold firm or give way, and other devices are among personal bargaining devices with policy consequences. Certainly the adamant approach of Senator Dole helped win the day for the Senate on revenue sharing. A legislator noted for his bargaining tenacity is Representative John Dingell (D, Mich.), chairman of the House Energy and Commerce Committee. Dingell's negotiating prowess is legendary on Capitol Hill. "After a [conference] stalemate of several months," wrote one scholar about Dingell's insistence that his position prevail, "there seemed to be no other course than to capitulate to the adamant [congressman]."[68] Similarly, Representative Carl Perkins (D, Ky.) was famous for his legislative determination and personal skills during conference negotiations. Senator Alan K. Simpson (R, Wy.) observed of his frequent conference opponent, "When you get into a conference committee with Carl Perkins, you may end up not having any furniture left in your office. He's awesome."[69]

Stubbornness by individual or chamber conferees can sometimes produce desired outcomes, but at a cost. It may enhance a reputation for tenacity and skill that can be valuable in subsequent conferences. But victory today often means concessions tomorrow. Members and committees interact continuously throughout the lawmaking process,

---

66. *Congressional Record*, 98th Cong., 1st sess., Nov. 17, 1983, p. H10169.

67. Thomas C. Schelling, quoted in Vogler, *The Third House*, p. 93. The use of this "commitment strategy," the approach in which "one side paradoxically increases its bargaining power by depriving itself of the ability to act," is further discussed in relation to conference committees in Aaron Wildavsky, *The Politics of the Budgetary Process*, 4th ed. (Boston: Little, Brown, 1984), p. 101. See also Roger Fisher and William Ury, *Getting to Yes: Negotiating Agreement Without Giving In* (New York: Penguin, 1983), esp. their discussion of the "extreme commitment" tactic, pp. 145–46.

68. James Everett Katz, *Congress and National Energy Policy* (New Brunswick, N.J.: Transaction Books, 1984), p. 139. "Representative [John D.] Dingell]D, Mich.] is legendary not only for his negotiating skills, but also for his mastery of the strategic possibilities of rules and procedures. He once pithily observed, 'If you let me write procedures and I let you write substance, I'll screw you every time'" (Janet H. Hook, "Parliamentarians: Procedure and Pyrotechnics," *Congressional Quarterly Weekly Report,* Aug. 22, 1987, p. 1951).

69. *Los Angeles Times*, June 25, 1984, p. 14.

and congressmen understand that negotiations can never be for long "zero-sum games," in which one player wins everything and the other nothing. When the same (or many of the same) actors meet again in conference, the price for having been adamant earlier may be necessary flexibility or even conciliation in the future. Similarly, an awareness of past and future conference relationships will have an impact on current interactions. "Like a *history* of negotiations," writes one scholar, "the prospect of *future* negotiations can aid conferees in reaching an agreement in the present." One way this occurs is by "providing an opportunity for future repayment of present concessions."[70]

There are many instances, too, when one house or the other has little or no choice in how a specific issue is to be resolved. Threats, bluffs, jokes, or skillful ploys are of little or no use in these circumstances. When the Senate has enacted legislative language on a topic but the House bill is silent on the issue, the conference decision boils down to a compromise between "something or nothing." Some flexibility, to be sure, may exist even in this situation if both sides want to consider a germane (or relevant) modification of the Senate provision. But, if the House conferees decide to accept the Senate position as passed by that chamber, the Senate conferees cannot do a thing other than accept the House "concession." This occurred in 1982 in a tax increase conference following Senate passage of legislation doubling the excise tax on cigarettes.

The House had adopted no legislation at all on the topic. During the conference, Senate Finance Committee Chairman Robert Dole (R, Kan.) proposed that the cigarette tax be kept at the present level. The leader of the House conferees, Representative Dan Rostenkowski (D, Ill.) rejected Senator Dole's initiative, pointing out that since the House had no enacted position on this legislative question, "You are totally defenseless at this point, and certainly I realize that, because the House has the privilege of receding, and there is no action that the Senate can take."[71] By accepting the Senate-passed provision, House member Rostenkowski was able to force the Senate position upon that chamber's reluctant representatives in conference. This ironic situation is a fitting conclusion to our consideration of the multitude of strategic maneuvers and actions possible during the conference.

Conclusions

Conference bargaining is subject to an enormous range of strategies, deadlines, choices, and environmental pressures. The House and Senate may initially enter negotiations with the view that "what's mine is mine, and what's yours is negotiable," but each side typically changes its perspective, often numerous times, in the course of reaching bicameral accommodations. As conferees come closer to agreement, they become increasingly sensitive to how their package will be received by their parent chambers. We now turn to the procedural and political considerations that govern postconference action by the House and Senate on conference reports.

70. Pressman, *House vs. Senate*, pp. 71, 73.

71. *Congressional Record*, 97th Cong., 2d sess., Aug. 16, 1982, p. S10569. The events of this tax increase conference are more fully explored in the chapter 11 case study "The 1982 Tax Increase Conference."

10

The Postconference Process

House Speaker Jim Wright (D, Tex.) was once asked how a conference committee could reconcile disagreements as disparate as apples and oranges. "We'll make fruit salad," he replied.[1] Whether such composite agreements are perceived by the House and Senate as delectable morsels or as lemons is another question. The conference on President Reagan's 1981 tax cut bill, for instance, produced a "better bill (in the judgment of both sides) than either the House or Senate wrote on its own."[2] On the other hand, there are bicameral agreements that undo the substantive achievements of either or both chambers and produce indigestion for many members. In 1985, for example, House Democratic leaders were forced to postpone floor consideration of a defense authorization conference report because many House liberal colleagues were incensed at their own conferees for "selling out" to the Republican-controlled Senate. Angry at numerous specific concessions and the conferees' acceptance of the Senate's $302 billion budgetary total for defense rather than the House figure of $292 billion, these Democrats threatened to reject the conference report. The result was a delay of several weeks to cool the heated feelings. "Time is always a great curer," declared then-Speaker Thomas P. O'Neill (D, Mass.).[3]

Conferees strive to produce conference agreements that can win approval in the House and Senate (along with the backing of the president);[4] hence their care in calculat-

---

1. *Christian Science Monitor*, May 24, 1985, p. 1.
2. *Boston Globe*, Aug. 14, 1981, p. 2.
3. *Los Angeles Times*, July 31, 1985, p. 7. These events are recounted in greater detail in the chapter 11 case study "Dollars for Defense: Les Gets More Amidst 1985 House Turmoil."
4. For a discussion of the president as an indirect participant in conference politics, see chapter 7 below.

ing how negotiated settlements affect the vote-building process in their chambers. Amendments supported by numerous or powerful members and groups, for example, are unlikely (or only most reluctantly) to be dropped or gutted in conference. Such actions could jeopardize later passage of the conference report. The high floor approval rates for conference reports—they are rejected no more perhaps than once or twice a session[5]— underscore conferees' skill in mobilizing backing and counting votes for their handiwork.

Other considerations, too, explain why conference reports are difficult to defeat. Among them is the fact that conference reports are "privileged" business in each chamber, which means they can be brought to the floor at almost any time. Supporters choose propitious times for their consideration, sometimes even when key opponents are out of town. Further, conference reports generally cannot be amended; it is "take it or leave it" at this stage. There is even a way by which partial conference reports may be adopted, which then focuses House and Senate attention on a narrow set of remaining outstanding issues (see discussion below). Chamber action on conference reports, including which body should act first or last, can also be manipulated to promote the report's passage.

Finally, there are institutional and political incentives for the adoption rather than the rejection of conference work. Consideration of a conference report comes at the end of an extended legislative process. As one representative put it, "When the bill [in the form of a conference report] returns to the House and Senate, members feel they have already expressed themselves on it and ordinarily don't take too much interest."[6] Senators and representatives understand that the defeat of a conference report will likely subject the legislation to further arduous, lengthy lawmaking procedures. As another House member said in urging his colleagues to approve a conference report, "I think it is terribly important to remember that this is not a House bill coming from a committee to the floor. This is a conference report which, after months, has come through the mill, through the grinding mill of two very, very different institutions."[7]

These several topics will be addressed in appropriate sections of this chapter, which is organized in the following manner. First, we shall discuss some of the political considerations that precede floor action on conference reports. Then we shall focus on which chamber acts first or last and the voting consequences that flow from each sequence; House and Senate procedures for acting on these bicameral agreements,

---

5. Congressional Quarterly, *Guide to Congress*, 3d ed. (Washington, D. C.: Congressional Quarterly, 1982), p. 455. This estimate is supported by new tabulations (carried out especially for this book) of the occurrence of conference report recommital and rejection for the thirty-six-year period from 1947 to 1982. These data are contained in the Appendix to this chapter. There it is shown that in only five instances were as many as three conference reports rejected in a two-session Congress by either chamber, while there were five Congresses in which no conference reports were rejected by either house.

6. Quoted in Charles L. Clapp, *The Congressman: His Work As He Sees It* (Washington, D.C.: Brookings Institution, 1963), p. 279.

7. *Activity Report of the House Ad Hoc Committee on Energy*, H. Rept. 95-1820, 95th Cong., 2d sess., 1978, p. 78. For a valuable extended discussion of why few conference reports are defeated, see David L. Paletz, "Influence in Congress: An Analysis of the Nature and Effects of Conference Committees" (Ph.D. diss., University of California at Los Angeles, 1970), esp. pp. 395, 377.

including the parliamentary objections that can be leveled against conference reports; and the options that become available if conference reports are rejected or if conference committees report back to their chambers in disagreement.[8]

Political Considerations

An axiom of congressional politics is that one gets in front of an issue only by doing the painstaking backstage work that produces the winning margins necessary to pass legislation. It is far better for proponents to work at lining up sufficient commitments in advance of conference report consideration than to believe that potential opposition can be later dealt with on the House and Senate floor. Integral to these prefloor preparations are three crucial elements: timing, lobbying, and framing the issue.

Timing

The question of when to take action on a measure is central throughout the entire lawmaking process; little surprise, then, that this question surfaces also after the conference. The issue here involves how soon following a conference should the bicamerally negotiated agreement be brought up in the House and Senate. A variety of circumstances influences this decision.

One consideration involves the length of time it takes staff to draft the conference report and the joint explanatory statement (both are printed together in the same document). The conference report states in precise legal terminology the recommendations of the conferees on the issues committed to them. The joint explanatory statement provides additional information on and analyses of these recommendations. These two documents are illustrated below with excerpts from a Defense Authorization Report and Explanatory Statement:[9]

Conference Report	*Joint Explanatory Statement*
ELIGIBILITY FOR ADVANCED TRAINING IN SENIOR ROTC	Eligibility for advanced training in senior ROTC program (sec. 543).—The
SEC. 543. (a) Section 2104 of title 10, United States Code is amended—	House bill contained a provision (sec. 422) that would delete the requirement that
(1) by striking out "who have two academic years remaining at such	students have two years remaining in their degree programs in order to enroll in

---

8. The concern of this chapter is with the postconference *congressional* process, as distinguished from what happens after the conference report is approved—such as the presidential decision to sign or veto the legislation. As noted in chapter 7 above, conference committee politics ends with the acceptance or rejection of conference handiwork by the House and Senate; the legislative process goes on to encompass presidential veto/signature decisions, congressional attempts (following a veto) to override the presidential veto, and bureaucratic administrative implementation of resulting law. As we have necessarily limited our concern with the early stages of conference committee politics to those events directly leading up to conference and other efforts at bicameral reconciliation, so also our postconference concern will stop at the point of final congressional enactment of identical legislation.

9. *Department of Defense Authorization, 1985*, H. Rept. 98-1080, 98th Cong., 2d sess. (1984), pp. 41, 292.

educational institution" in subsection (a); and

(2) by striking out subsection (b)(6) and inserting in lieu thereof the following:

"(6) either—
"(A) complete successfully—
"(i) the first two years of a four-year Senior Reserve Officers' Training Corps course; or
"(ii) field training or a practice cruise of not less than six weeks duration which is prescribed by the Secretary concerned as a preliminary requirement for admission to the advanced course; or
"(B) at the discretion of the Secretary concerned agree in writing to complete field training or a practice cruise as prescribed by the Secretary concerned within two years after admission to the advanced course."

(b) The amendments made by subsection (a) do not constitute authority for the enactment of new budget authority for a fiscal year beginning before October 1, 1984.

advanced Reserve Officers' Training Corps (ROTC) training. This provision would not change the obligation to complete all the academic and field training requirements of advanced Reserve Officers' Training Corps training.

The section would also permit the service Secretaries to accept for advanced training persons who have not yet completed the first two years of the Senior Reserve Officers' Training Corps program or performed the six weeks field training or practice cruise so long as the enrollees agree to complete such field training or practice cruise.

The Senate amendment contained no similar provision.

The Senate recedes.

House and Senate staff aides are responsible for writing the conference report and the explanatory statement. Preparation of these documents can take several weeks, especially when the legislation is controversial, and may require intensive, round-the-clock work on measures that face tight deadlines. Draft conference language will usually circulate for approval among the conferees and other interested parties, including executive branch officials. The conference itself sometimes even reconvenes to insure that bicameral agreements have been interpreted accurately in the draft materials.

Agreement is reached on the conference report and statement when a majority of the House and Senate conferees affix their signatures to each document. Conferees who refuse to sign are barred by House and Senate precedents from including a section on "minority views" in either report or statement. They may, however, include their dissenting views on the conference report in the *Congressional Record* or use other means to convey their dissatisfaction with the final product.

Supplementing the conference report and explanatory statement will be the statements of conference leaders concerning the conference accord. These informal delegation reports customarily consist of carefully weighed assessments stressing themes appealing to the particular chamber. They emphasize how difficult it proved for the conference to reach final agreement, and how, nevertheless, the delegation ultimately was able to prevail on those provisions most important to the body. During conference, the chamber delegation had decried the great concessions it was making; in reporting to its parent body, the delegation usually will instead claim bicameral victory.

Each delegation will stress that their chamber's successes resulted from hard conference bargaining and conferee skills while simultaneously minimizing concessions made to the other body.[10] A selective presentation of information and detail is customary, and sweeping claims of success in the protection of chamber interests are prevalent. Two such contrasting assessments were offered concerning one budget resolution. The chairman of the Senate Budget Committee explained to the Senate, "Your conferees went into yesterday's negotiations determined to defend the Senate's positions and to arrive at a responsible spending plan. We accomplished both of these objectives." Meanwhile, the leader of the House conference delegation was reassuring his chamber, "The conference report is not much different from the bill that passed the House."[11]

On the occasions when it is necessary to acknowledge unsuccessful efforts to preserve chamber preferences, conferees will "report back to their respective bodies in tones of despair and fatigue, 'It was this bill or nothing.' "[12] One representative dramatically explained a politically awkward House concession in the following words: "We had a gun barrel at our heads. . . . It was either this compromise or nothing. . . . We did not raise any white flag; had it not been for the time element and immediate adjournment slapping us in the face, I would have hung the jury until Gabriel blew taps on his trumpet. I would never have compromised."[13]

Sometimes these statements by chamber representatives are more posture than reality. In 1981, Senate conferee efforts to defend a Senate-passed heating tax credit provision were proudly described by the Senate conferees as Herculean—although unsuccessful. The transcript of conference discussion of this amendment suggests a somewhat less impassioned and informed defense:

Senator Dole (R, Kan.)—"Do you have anything on this [amendment], Senator Long?"

---

10. Two examples of House and Senate delegations both claiming conference victory in statements to their chambers can be found in Richard F. Fenno, Jr., *The Power of the Purse: Appropriations Politics in Congress* (Boston: Little, Brown, 1966), pp. 618, 619.

11. *Congressional Record*, 1980, pp. S14576 and H11038, quoted in Dennis S. Ippolito, "House and Senate Influence on Budget Conference Committees," paper prepared for delivery at the Annual Meeting of the Southern Political Science Association, Memphis, Nov. 5-7, 1981, pp. 5-6. A somewhat similar instance of conference leaders describing a conference agreement to their chambers in terms that made the agreed-upon legislation sound like two very different bills occurred in 1965 in connection with excise tax reduction legislation. Ways and Means Chairman Wilbur Mills (D, Ark.) and Senate Finance Chairman Russell Long (D, La.) seemed to differ on almost every important aspect of the compromise agreement, generally in the direction of the preferences of their chamber. See John Manley, *The Politics of Finance: The House Committee on Ways and Means* (Boston: Little, Brown, 1970), p. 271.

12. Bertram M. Gross, *The Legislative Struggle: A Study in Social Combat* (New York: McGraw-Hill, 1953), p. 324.

13. *Congressional Record*, 80th Cong., 2d sess., June 18, 1948, p. 8859, quoted in ibid.

Senator Long (D, La.)—"I did not vote for it."
Senator Dole—"I did not vote for it either."[14]

The sponsors of amendments dropped in conference may lament the lack of forcefulness of their own conferees. "The Senate conferees receded from [my] amendment without debate and without a roll call vote," exclaimed Senator Charles Grassley (R, Iowa) in 1987. "I suppose, Mr. President, that the Senate conferees receded with just something of a smile or a snicker or a wink."[15]

Another timing consideration involves the House rule that requires a three-day waiting period between the time the report is filed (or formally introduced in the House) and its consideration by the representatives. The report and joint explanatory statement must also be printed and available to House members at least two hours prior to floor debate. Quick House action on conference reports generally is not feasible—unless these rules are waived.[16] The Senate does not have a layover rule,[17] and it lacked, until 1986, a requirement that reports be available before they are taken up.[18] The absence of such rules accords Senate floor managers greater latitude in that chamber in determining when conference reports will be debated.

Periodically, members lament the sloppy work that sometimes permeates conference reports prepared under severe deadline pressures and rushed to the floor. On the Chrysler loan guarantee issue, the Senate was "presented with an alleged conference report which in my judgment was about as unprofessional a document as could be imagined," lamented Senator William Armstrong (R, Col.). "Some may recall that the so-called report was covered with pencil lines; it had a great deal of material typed into the margin and referenced into the bill at various points."[19]

Mistakes in conference reports and required clarifications are typically corrected via later, follow-up legislation, usually in the form of concurrent resolutions. These "technical corrections" resolutions usually are designed to fix up the countless minor drafting errors that can appear in legislation as lengthy and complicated as, for example, the 1986 tax revision bill. The conference report on that landmark measure was contained in two volumes totaling 1,811 pages. Inevitably, minor problems appeared in the enacted legislation, including misspellings and wrong addresses and dates. New York City's Carnegie Hall, for example, was identified at an erroneous address. The legislative process cannot always wait, however, for such errors to be found and corrected. This

14. *Boston Globe,* Aug. 7, 1981, p. 8.
15. *Congressional Record,* 100th Cong., 1st sess. Sept. 23, 1987, p. S12550.
16. House rules also require that the Report and Statement be printed in the *Congressional Record* on the day those documents are filed. Neither this rule nor the three-day rule, however, apply during the last six days of a session.
17. Under the Budget and Impoundment Control Act of 1974 (P.L.93-344), however, conference reports on concurrent budget resolutions are in order for Senate floor consideration only on the third day after those reports are filed and available.
18. When the Senate in February 1986 authorized the televising of its floor sessions, it also amended its rules to require that conference reports be taken up only when a copy is available on each senator's desk.
19. *Congressional Record,* 97th Cong., 2d sess., April 15, 1982, p. S3577.

tax bill, errors and all, was signed into law by President Reagan on October 22, 1986.

A concurrent resolution incorporating most of the needed error corrections for the tax bill had actually been written before the president signed the bill, but it became bogged down in controversy. There was no opposition to correcting the glaring errors contained in the bill, but the concurrent resolution also incorporated a large number of "transition rules" for special parties, allowing for one-year tax breaks. These special provisions had been kept secret until the last moment, when they were sprung on the House and Senate. It was because of the controversial and substantive matters incorporated in what was to have been merely an error-correcting concurrent resolution that it was not passed prior to the enactment into law of the 1986 tax bill.[20]

The strength of potential opposition to conference reports also affects the timing calculus. On reports where leaders have scheduling discretion (some reports must be taken up almost immediately because failure to act could precipitate a crisis such as the shutdown of federal programs or agencies), it may be in their interest either to move quickly or alternatively to delay consideration. Speedy action may prevent the opposition from effectively mobilizing against a conference report. Delay, on the other hand, allows proponents more time to muster support.

The "mood" of the Congress, too, can affect action on conference reports. While this can be a nebulous condition to evaluate, experienced legislators typically have sensitive political antennae that can sense the optimal time for taking up conference reports. As a House member recounted in 1985 in explaining why he and other lawmakers failed in earlier attempts to revamp a governmental policy but succeeded later, "The mood wasn't there. The mood [then] was to give them what they want. The circumstances haven't changed, but the mood in Congress has."[21]

Lobbying

Practically every major corporation, trade association, and professional group has Washington lobbyists, and their ability to influence congressional policymaking is significant. Through the sophisticated application of standard pressure techniques—direct (face-to-face), grass-roots and alliance (multiple group)—interest groups can play important roles in insuring the passage or defeat of conference reports. For their part, conferees and staff members work diligently to enlist the support and endorsement of both colleagues and outside groups. To secure passage of a higher education conference report, for example, House Education and Labor Chairman Carl Perkins (D, Ky.) and his aides lobbied a wide variety of members and groups. Recalled one participant,

---

20. See Eileen Shanahan, "President Signs Sweeping Overhaul of Tax Law," *Congressional Quarterly Weekly Report*, Oct. 25, 1986, pp. 2669–70; and Stephen Gettinger, " 'Technical' Tax Corrections' Future Uncertain," *Congressional Quarterly Weekly Report*, Dec. 13, 1986, pp. 3055–56. The tortuous path of the tax bill's "technical corrections" legislation continued through 1987—see Stephen Gettinger, "Tax Writers Release Measure to Fix 1986 Tax Overhaul Bill; Timetable for Passage Uncertain," *Congressional Quarterly Weekly Report*, June 13, 1987, p. 1228.

21. *Washington Post*, June 26, 1985, p. A6.

After the conference concluded, we at the full committee level were working the colleges and universities and every interest in the nation. We were sending out poop sheets and summaries and analyses and countersummaries, and we were on the telephone with everyone we could think of. Perkins was talking to every Member on the floor and particularly cornering the southerners. He would call them up at home in the evening. He has a great knowledge of each of them as persons and knows their districts as well. So he could dwell on whatever piece of the bill was of most interest to them. We worked to match up the colleges and the congressional districts where they were and who knew the Members at that college in that district. . . . We were all over the country.[22]

Just as members lobby other members, and groups and staff lobby other staff and groups, presidents and executive branch officials also engage their lobbying skills and apparatus to win public backing for important conference reports. A classic instance occurred during the Carter administration. Soon after assuming office, President Carter went on national television and declared the "moral equivalent of war" on the energy problem. Part of this way involved the deregulation of natural gas prices—an issue of enormous controversy and complexity that periodically had confronted Congress during the previous forty years.

House and Senate conferees struggled for months during 1977 and into 1978 before they reached a compromise that called for the gradual decontrol of natural gas prices. Each chamber came to conference with divergent positions: the House wanted controls on gas prices to continue while the Senate opted for price decontrol. Once a rather shaky conference settlement was reached, numerous diverse opponents organized against the report.[23] Liberal organizations, including labor, consumer, and public interest groups, opposed the report in large part because prices for natural gas were expected to escalate dramatically; conservative groups, especially most segments of the oil and gas industry, rejected the compromise on the grounds that it would discourage gas exploration and lead to complex and heavy federal regulation of gas producers.

To overcome such formidable and vociferous opposition, Carter and his aides took the offensive to win interest group backing for the beleaguered gas compromise. Critics of the compromise—business leaders, bankers, state and local officials, and scores of others—were brought to the White House to hear the president and administration officials argue for the conference report. "Even executives of firms that have strongly attacked the bill," one account noted, "[indicated] they would 'take another look' at

---

22. Lawrence E. Gladieux and Thomas R. Wolanin, *Congress and the Colleges: The National Politics of Higher Education* (Lexington, Mass.: D. C. Heath, 1976), pp. 210–11. These events are recounted in greater detail in our chapter 11 case study "Higher Education: Personalities and Exhaustion."

23. The conference agreement was rather shaky because of deep divisions among both House and Senate conferees. The final compromise was backed by ten of the seventeen Senate conferees, and by only thirteen of the twenty-five House members. For a summary of the events surrounding the National Energy Act of 1978, see John H. Kessel, *Presidential Parties* (Homewood, Ill.: Dorsey Press, 1984), pp. 11–16.

their opposition'' to the conference report.[24] In the end, the skillful orchestration of presidential pressure on Congress helped to win approval of the 1978 natural gas conference compromise.[25]

Framing the Issue

Legislators who can adroitly frame the issue often can also frame the outcome. Policy struggles frequently revolve around which officials, groups, or institutions can shape and define the national debate on legislation. ''It is with words we govern men,'' Disraeli once wrote.[26] Language can persuade, provoke, energize, and create images behind which people can mobilize. Whether federal aid to the Chrysler Corporation was seen as a ''bailout'' or as an ''unemployment and national security matter'' was critical to the passage of that legislation. The politics of language, in short, can promote agreement or provoke disagreement.

A major influence on issue framing is the general climate or context of the times. Policy choices can be influenced by such considerations as whether the nation is in a period of economic boom or bust, legislative-executive conflict or cooperation, global calm or crisis, or energy abundance or shortage. For example, President Carter and congressional leaders were successful in 1978 in winning approval of the natural gas conference report in part because of national concern about long gasoline lines, oil embargoes, and energy price hikes. Congressional leaders stressed the adverse international repercussions that would flow from defeat of the conference agreement. Argued Senate Democratic Leader Robert C. Byrd of West Virginia, ''To reject the conference report would be to say to the OPEC countries, to our industrial and NATO allies, and to the world that the United States cannot discipline itself to deal with the energy problem at home, and, thus, is incapable of providing world leadership in dealing with a global problem.''[27]

The Sequence of Floor Decision Making

Which chamber acts first or last on conference reports is determined by both custom and politics. As noted earlier, the house that agrees to the other body's request for a conference usually acts first on the report, while the asking chamber moves last. This custom is not rigid, however. Either chamber can act first if it has custody of the papers[28]—the original House or Senate bill, the amendments thereto, interchamber messages, and (following the conference) the conference report. Typically, the chamber that agreed to

---

24. *Washington Post,* Sept. 1, 1978, p. A10. See also James Everett Katz, *Congress and National Energy Policy* (New Brunswick, N.J.: Transaction Books, 1984), and Kessel, *Presidential Parties,* chap. 1.

25. For discussion of presidential influence on conference deliberations, see chapter 7 above.

26. Quoted in Daniel Patrick Moynihan, ''Words and Foreign Policy,'' *Policy Review* (Fall 1978): 69.

27. *Congressional Record,* 95th Cong., 2d sess., Sept. 6, 1978, p. 27972.

28. Only the chamber in ''possession of the papers'' can request a conference.

the conference assumes control of the papers at the conclusion of a successful conference. Moreover, because the Constitution formally authorizes the House to initiate revenue-raising measures (a prerogative informally extended to appropriations bills as well), the House usually acts first on tax and appropriations conference reports. The Senate almost always asks for the conference on these measures so the House can maintain its initiatory role. (A noteworthy exception—for strategic reasons such as those noted next—was Senate action first on the conference report on the landmark Economic Recovery Tax Act of 1981.)

Strategic Implications

There are occasions when one chamber is deliberately placed in the position either of acting first or last on conference reports.

This is done in order to give the report what is thought to be a more advantageous parliamentary advantage. Translated, this means that the body where there is thought to be greater opposition to the report is made to act last so that the other body might first agree to it and discharge its conferees. Many believe that this forces the body acting last to choose between taking the report and killing the legislation since it is not in order to recommit a report to conference when the other body has discharged its conferees.[29]

These considerations permeated congressional debate on President Carter's request in 1979 for a new Department of Education. The Senate acted first on the original legislation and passed it by a wide margin (72 to 21). This large vote was a psychological and political plus for House supporters, who knew the proposal faced tough opposition there. Subsequently, the legislation barely managed to win House committee (20 to 19) and floor approval (210 to 206). Floor manager Jack Brooks (D, Tex.) maneuvered to ensure that the House asked for the conference. As a result, when the conference was complete, the Senate was able to act first and pass the report overwhelmingly. The House then faced the choice of either accepting or rejecting the report amid the glare of press and media attention and the aggressive (and successful) lobbying of President Carter and education groups.[30]

Other procedural and political factors can influence chamber sequence. President Carter's massive energy plan provides an example. The House passed the five main parts of the energy plan (natural gas, coal conversion, utility rate reform, energy conversion, and energy tax) as a single package. In contrast, the Senate divided the House's package into its five parts and considered and passed each separately. The resulting energy conference also produced five separate conference reports. The principal leaders of both

---

29. *Manual on Legislative Procedure in the United States House of Representatives*, 5th ed., 97th Cong. 2d sess., January 1982, p. 292. The *Manual* was prepared under the auspices of the House Republican leader.

30. *Congressional Quarterly Almanac, 1979* (Washington, D.C.: Congressional Quarterly, 1980), pp. 465–74. These events are recounted in greater detail in the chapter 11 case study "The Department of Education Organization Act," the second of "Two 'Hello and Good-Bye' Conferences of 1979."

chambers favored the Senate acting first and in a manner likely to enhance enactment. As described in one study, "Under an agreement between Senate Majority Leader Byrd and House Speaker O'Neill, the [conference reports were] to go first to the Senate, where each portion would be voted on separately, and then to the House, where [the five reports] would be voted on as a whole. This was in keeping with Byrd's preference for a multiple-bill strategy, and O'Neill's desire for a single-bill strategy."[31] O'Neill wanted to wait for Senate action on the separate reports so he would know which energy components to package together for subsequent House action. Forcing the House to act on a comprehensive energy plan in a single up-or-down vote, O'Neill believed, would increase its chances of passing. His packaging strategy eventually succeeded—but by a final margin of only one vote!

Leverage for Negotiations

Possession of the papers can give one chamber leverage over the other in the event of bicameral policy and political clashes. In 1981, President Reagan appeared on national television to defend Social Security even while he was supporting elimination of minimum benefits for needy retirees who had contributed only marginally to the program during their working years. Chagrined at Reagan's action, House Rules Committee Chairman Richard Bolling (D, Mo.), whose panel often plays a key role in clearing crucial conference reports for floor action, issued a warning to Reagan and the Republican-controlled Senate: restore the minimum benefits provision or else there would be no action on the omnibus reconciliation conference report pending in the House. That legislation, which included the Social Security cuts, made huge reductions totaling about $130 billion over three years in numerous social programs.

Then-Senate Majority Leader Howard Baker of Tennessee responded with an ultimatum of his own to House Democrats: take action on the reconciliation conference report or the Senate will accept the House-passed version of the reconciliation bill, which made even deeper cuts in social programs. Baker could deliver his threat because Senate conferees, anticipating prospective problems, had taken possession of the papers when the reconciliation conference ended, even though the House had agreed to the conference and by custom would be expected to act first on the report.

Senate control of these conference papers encouraged the House to reach an accommodation with the other body leading to quick action on the reconciliation conference report. Under this agreement, the Senate returned the papers to the House, which then acted first and adopted the conference report. Prior to that action, and also by agreement, the House enacted a separate bill to restore the Social Security benefits otherwise cut in the reconciliation conference report, legislation that eventually became law.[32]

31. Kessel, *Presidential Parties*, p. 13.
32. *Congressional Quarterly Almanac, 1981* (Washington, D.C.: Congressional Quarterly, 1982), pp. 117–20; *Wall Street Journal,* July 31, 1981, p. 3; and *Congressional Record,* 97th Cong., 1st sess., July 31, 1981, pp. H5731–44.

Debating Conference Reports: The House

Procedural Routes to the Floor

Conference reports, as noted earlier, are privileged, which means that they can be called up by the senior majority party conferee at almost any time during House proceedings without the necessity of first obtaining unanimous consent. In practice, however, conference reports are almost always scheduled for floor action by the majority party leadership; House Speakers, consequently, are rarely "surprised" when members move to take up conference reports. On the other hand, the average House member may receive little advance notice of floor consideration of these reports.

Three main procedural routes (besides unanimous consent) are available for taking up conference reports: invoking the one-hour rule, seeking a suspension of the rules, and obtaining a special "rule" from the Rules Committee. Which approach is used depends upon the contentiousness of the report and the goals of chamber and conference leaders. The choices, too, underscore the interplay between procedures and policymaking.

Most conference reports are considered under the *one-hour rule,* with the time typically divided equally between the majority and minority floor managers. In 1985, the House changed its rules to permit one-third of the time to be assigned to a member who opposes the conference report if both the Democratic and Republican managers support it.[33] On occasion, the time for debate is extended beyond one hour, either by unanimous consent or by a rule from the Rules Committee. Amendments to conference reports are not in order; therefore, once debate is concluded after the specified time of one hour (or more), the House votes directly on the report itself. Conference reports are most often considered under the one-hour rule both because it is customary and also because it is appropriate for the large majority of measures.

Suspension of the rules is seldom used for taking up conference reports because the procedure involves a severe requirement: a two-thirds rather than majority vote for adoption. Needless to say, attracting two-thirds support for procedural steps is not easy in the case of controversial reports. Debate on a motion to suspend normal House rules (such as the one-hour rule) and pass conference reports is also limited to forty minutes, equally divided between proponents and opponents.

Despite these constraints, this procedure is sometimes employed when circumstances offer little other recourse. Two situations are noteworthy. First, the suspension procedure protects conference reports from points of order (or parliamentary objections) that, if upheld by the chair, could result in the immediate rejection of the conference agreement. To obviate "killing" points of order, conference strategists may be forced to use the suspension procedure. Conferees will often know in advance that their reports violate House rules, either because they intentionally went beyond the rules to reach an accord or because they received informal warning from the House parliamentarian that

33. For an example of the early utilization of this new rule in the case of House final passage of the Gramm-Rudman deficit reduction legislation, see the chapter 11 case study "The Gramm-Rudman Conferences of 1985."

the report is vulnerable. In these instances, suspension of the rules may well be the only feasible option open to them.

The second circumstance under which the suspension procedure may be used involves the Rules Committee, which has the general authority to grant waivers of points of order. If a majority of the Rules Committee opposes the bicameral agreement, conference floor managers probably will find this route to the floor closed off. The suspension procedure, then, will become the only route left.[34] This option could prove particularly attractive when there is a compelling urgency for the conference report and broad support for it among chamber members and other interested parties.

Obtaining a "rule" from the Rules Committee is the final avenue to the floor for conference reports. This approach is typically used for controversial legislation to insure that the bicameral agreements are debated in timely and complete fashion by the full membership. The Rules Committee can achieve these results because of its unique scheduling prerogatives that distinguish this panel from any other congressional committee. Some brief mention of the panel's special powers would be helpful at this point.[35]

Very few major bills go directly from committee to the floor for initial House consideration because the vast majority are not eligible under the Standing Rules of the House to be called up for immediate debate. To acquire such privileged status for their legislation, committee members seek a "rule" (a simple House resolution) from the Rules Committee that, if agreed to by the majority of the House, grants their measure the right of immediate floor consideration. Further, rules from the Rules Committee determine the length of debate on bills, the extent to which they may be amended, and whether (and which) House rules are to be waived, thereby preventing members from raising troublesome or even fatal points of order.

Conference reports, to be sure, are automatically accorded privileged access to the floor under House rules, although they must still lay over three days before they enjoy that right. Still, conference floor managers may seek special rules largely to accomplish the two aforementioned objectives: to set aside the three-day layover requirement (either to meet deadlines or exploit propitious political circumstances) or to prevent points of order against their handiwork. In addition, the Rules Committee can promote the consideration of issues deemed especially important by key members, party leaders, or the White House by imaginatively crafting rules governing consideration of particular conference reports.

Conference reports cannot be amended when they are considered on the floor, and they may not be tabled or referred to standing committee. The only options before the House are to accept, reject, or recommit the report (the last option is available only if the Senate has not already acted on the accord). Nonetheless, there are ways to amend

---

34. To be sure, conferees could return to conference to delete the offending provisions, but this might jeopardize the entire agreement. Alternatively, the legislation's floor manager could bring the conference report up under the one-hour rule and hope that no member raises any points of order (House rules are not self-executing). Conference supporters could also attempt to pressure the majority leadership to use its influence to get a waiver, in the form of a special rule, from the House Rules Committee.

35. See also *A History of the Committee on Rules* (Washington, D.C.: U.S. Government Printing Office, 1983).

conference reports indirectly to ward off challenges that might defeat the agreements or in order to attract supporters and mollify critics. It is the Rules Committee that can authorize the procedures necessary to accomplish these various objectives. An example is the House's consideration on March 12, 1980, of two rules for a particularly controversial windfall profit tax conference report. First, a paragraph of background.

President Carter devoted considerable effort to promoting the nation's energy production and independence. To move in that direction, Carter successfully urged Congress to remove domestic price controls on oil. With the expected escalation of oil prices, energy corporations would reap huge profits but so would the federal government through a multibillion dollar "windfall" in new tax revenues. Carter wanted the new revenues (expected to be over $227 billion by 1990) to be used for two main purposes: to promote the development of synthetic fuels, thus cutting America's dependence on foreign oil imports, and to assist low-income families in meeting their home heating costs.

House and Senate conferees argued strenuously over the use of the extra, or windfall, government revenues. The conference report recommended in nonbinding language that most of the windfall (60 percent) go for tax cuts, with the remainder distributed between aid for low-income families in meeting fuel expenses (25 percent) and the development of new energy sources (15 percent). Subsequent legislation would determine the precise revenue distribution, but the conference report's guidelines would set the framework for these later statutory actions.

Two members of the House Ways and Means Committee, Joseph Fisher (D, Va.) and Richard Gephardt (D, Mo.), neither of whom had been chosen as a conferee on this measure, took issue with the conference proposal. They and their allies strongly favored using most of the windfall revenues for energy development rather than tax cuts. "It does seem very strange that we would go through long turmoil—agony, almost—to produce a bill," Fisher said, "[but] then at the end of it recommend not that energy be given the principal attention, but that tax reduction be given the principal attention."[36]

The Fisher-Gephardt forces successfully persuaded the Rules Committee to grant a rule bringing a nonbinding resolution to the floor that expressed the House's support for their distribution of revenue rather than that provided for in the conference report. This resolution came up prior to consideration of the conference report itself. Republican Rules member Trent Lott of Mississippi expressed anger at this unusual step: "As long as I have been here," Lott declared, "I have never seen this type of procedure where we attempt to amend the language of the conference report before we even take up such conference report."[37] By a narrow margin (201 to 215), the House, however, then rejected the Fisher-Gephardt resolution.

The chairman of the Rules Committee next called up a rule that made in order the windfall conference report itself. A rule was necessary because the report included new and nongermane matter that otherwise would open it to points of order. In addition, the report violated provisions of the Budget and Impoundment Control Act of 1974 prohibit-

36. *Congressional Record*, 96th Cong., 2d sess., March 12, 1980, p. 5375.
37. Ibid., p. 5374.

ing increases or decreases in revenue prior to the adoption of the first concurrent budget resolution. Besides legitimizing these irregularities, the proposed special rule also waived the three-day layover rule. While the special rule was eventually adopted, it provoked sharp objection from those who strongly opposed the conference report itself. In the end, the report was agreed to by the House but not before a final attempt was made to kill it by recommitting it to conference.[38]

Another controversial, indirect effort to amend a conference report occurred during the second session of the 100th Congress in mid-1988. In an attempt to woo blue-collar workers to their party's presidential nominee (Massachusetts Governor Michael Dukakis) and embarrass Republicans, House Democrats won passage of a concurrent resolution that authorized "technical" corrections in the formal printing of the trade conference bill to which both chambers had already agree. Among the technical corrections, as we shall see, was also a significant, substantial change. (We noted earlier that concurrent resolutions are usually adopted to make grammatical or other minor corrections in conference reports that have passed both houses. Once these technical changes have been made by the enrolling clerk, the corrected measure is then sent to the White House.)

The House's attempt to make a substantive change in the already-passed conference report was triggered by President Reagan's vow to veto the trade bill because it contained a provision requiring businesses with 100 or more employees to provide their workers with a 60-day plant closing notice. Republican strategists realized that to veto the trade bill on that ground alone would antagonize the average worker. Hence, they found another objectionable provision—a restriction on oil exports from Alaska—on which to base the planned presidential veto.

To counter this move, House Democrats passed the concurrent "correction" resolution which, besides making necessary technical changes, also directed the enrolling clerk to delete the Alaskan provision from the trade bill before sending it to the White House. If the President now vetoed the bill on the plant closing issue alone, Democratic lawmakers reasoned, then they would be able to exploit the issue during the Fall presidential campaign. (Public opinion polls revealed overwhelming support for advance notification of plant closings.) The Democratic maneuver succeeded in the House but, however, ultimately failed in the Senate.[39]

Action of the Floor

The conference floor managers, usually the senior majority conferees, are key actors in developing appropriate strategy for winning enactment of the bicameral accord. Consultations with party leaders, executive branch officials, and affected interest groups, among others, are standard elements of the coalition-building process both before and during floor deliberations. On the chamber floor itself, the floor managers'

38. For an overview of these events, see *Congressional Quarterly Almanac, 1980* (Washington, D.C.: Congressional Quarterly, 1981), pp. 473–82.

39. See Elizabeth Wehr, "House Strikes Alaska Oil Rules from Trade Bill," *Congressional Quarterly Weekly Report,* May 7, 1988, p. 1200.

primary concerns are threefold: (1) who should debate and when, (2) how to respond to points of order, and (3) how to ensure the votes are there to adopt the report. In the next pages, we shall examine in turn each of these concerns.

1. DEBATE. The effect of floor debate on policy outcomes is often disputed. Some members argue that debate rarely changes anyone's mind; others contend that talk can influence opinions and sway votes. Lawmaking, to be sure, contains ample dosages of logrolling, compromises, and power plays but also involves reasoned deliberation. Debate on conference reports is significant first and foremost because that, along with voting, is about all that is permitted on conference reports. For that reason, conference report managers and their allies give careful consideration to organizing and directing the floor discussion.

The debate surrounding conference reports will often focus on twin themes of national and constituency concerns. Supporters of the conference report, first of all, will explain and justify the agreements reached, rebut critics, and try to solidify support within a context of broad national interest. Appeals will be made for the agreement on the grounds that, even with its deficiencies, the accord meets national needs and represents the best that could be attained from people possessing different views of the public interest. As the House conference chairman declared during floor debate concerning the conference accord on the National Energy Policy Act of 1978 (notice the title), "This [conference report] is a product of the best efforts of many men and women of different minds and philosophies but who shared one common goal: persevere and do what is right for America."[40]

On another level, debate may also be designed to convince members that it is in their own and their constituents' interests to support the conference report. Arguments put forth in support of a conference agreement often are carefully calculated to appeal to constituency interests as broadly as possible—or alternatively to local interests and other concerns of special importance to key legislators. A well-known belief on Capitol Hill is that the best way to a congressman's heart is through his constituency; this strategy applies fully in the seeking of support for conference reports.

Tactical considerations permeate floor debate. Anticipating rancorous and emotional debate on a higher education conference report containing the issue of school busing, the floor managers "mapped out a floor strategy": "Decisions were reached on who should speak on the floor and how speakers in support should be paired with the speakers in opposition to maximize the impact of the former and minimize the impact of the latter. One pairing was suggested on the grounds, 'Let's match our best demagogue against their best demagogue.' "[41] Conference floor managers, in short, typically plan the order in which certain members should speak and even whom of the opposition they should precede or follow.

2. POINTS OF ORDER. Parliamentary objections in the form of points of order always have the potential to derail conference reports in the House unless the Rules Committee has granted a rule that waives them. If a point of order against a conference

---

40. *Congressional Record,* 95th Cong., 2d sess., Oct. 14, 1978, p. 38351.
41. Gladieux and Wolanin, *Congress and the Colleges,* p. 212.

report is upheld by the Speaker, then one of three results follows: the report is stalled or killed, another conference is convened, or the legislation returns to its preconference status with the offending matter excised from the legislation and the chambers in disagreement. Conference floor managers, to be sure, always are sensitive to the possibility of points of order and marshall their arguments and rebuttals in anticipation of such objections.

Two classes of points of order may be raised against legislative measures: those directed against their *consideration* and those aimed at their *content*. This distinction, however, is somewhat fuzzy in the case of conference reports because points of order in both classes must be made at the same time—during the interval when the conference report is called up but before debate has begun on it. Points of order may be raised against conference reports on many different grounds. For our purposes, it is best to limit the analysis here to the two major parliamentary objections most often lodged against conference reports: scope and nongermaneness.

Scope is a technical term difficult to define precisely. It fundamentally addresses the issue of whether conferees have exceeded their authority by, for example, including in the report matters or topics not committed to the conference committee. How to determine whether conferees have gone beyond proper bounds is, however, not easy. The precedents are complex and difficult to apply to practical cases. Reasoning from example or by illustration, however, provides probably the clearest means of grasping the term's meaning and application.

Scope can be viewed from both quantitative and qualitative perspectives. *Quantitatively,* House precedents state that "conferees may not go beyond the limits of the disagreements confided to them, and where the differences involve numbers, conferees are limited to the range between the highest figure proposed by one house and the lowest proposed by the other."[42] This precedent is easy to comprehend and often relatively easy to apply in practice. Its objective is to limit the discretionary authority of conferees. Yet, it is not uncommon for conferees to agree on a compromise figure that is higher or lower than that proposed by either chamber without a point of order being raised against the conference report. Sometimes such lack of objection reflects general consensus over the conference's work. At other times, there may be objection to the agreement, but such opposition is unable to take the form of a point of order because of a curious parliamentary quirk.

In 1982, for instance, the House and Senate passed defense authorization bills that recommended spending levels of $175.3 billion and $177.4 billion, respectively. The eventual conference report proposed $177.9 billion in military spending, greater than

---

42. Clarence Cannon, *Cannon's Precedents of the House of Representatives of the United States,* vol. 8 (Washington, D.C.: Government Printing Office, 1935), p. 748. A discussion of congressional rules as they limit the authority of conference committees to the matters in bicameral disagreement is provided in Stanley Bach, "The Nature of Congressional Rules," paper prepared for delivery at the 1987 Annual Meeting of the American Political Science Association, Chicago, Sept. 3–6, 1987, esp. pp. 20–26. For a 1986 example in which concerns over quantitative scope almost sank a landmark tax reform bill, see David E. Rosenbaum, "Tax Bill Could Die With Vote on Rule," *New York Times,* Sept. 5, 1986, p. 12.

either original figure. Nevertheless, the conference agreement was defended by conferee (and now Armed Services Committee chairman) Les Aspin (D, Wis.) as not subject to a point of order.[43] In fact, he was correct, because of an important interpretation given the aforementioned House precedent. Unless a specific overall dollar total (consisting of the total of the sums allocated to each line item in the legislation) is explicitly identified in a bill, then technically no total exists—even though the press and media may report on the overall cost. In the absence of such a statement of the total authorized outlay of House and Senate measures, there is no official way of recognizing that a later conference report falls outside the permissible quantitative limits. Representative Aspin described what may occur in conference when legislation is silent concerning the total dollar amount:

> What happens is that in the absence of totals the rule about staying within the limits of the House and Senate bills has been interpreted to apply only to the "line items," or the various, specific programs within the bill. The conferees then proceed to play a legislative version of a rigged poker game, the House caving in ("receding") on those items in which the Senate figure is higher, and the Senate receding to the House when the House is higher. . . . Certainly it is easy to see how this kind of wheeling and dealing can drive up the pot.[44]

Qualitative questions of scope are even more tricky because words are more difficult to judge than figures. Various "tests" based on precedents and prior rulings of the Speaker may help to pinpoint scope violations in some instances. The major tests for qualitative scope violations include actions that expand the meaning of a specific provision—such as adding new countries to lists that originally contained only two, inserting new substantial items not contained in either chamber's bill, and changing or dropping identical provisions contained in both chambers' legislation. While these tests might appear to establish some standards, their application to practical cases is often not clear.

For example, when a controversial conference report on outer continental shelf lands was brought to the House floor in 1976, Representative Hamilton Fish (R, N.Y.) raised seven consecutive points of order against its consideration based on scope.[45] In one instance, Representative Fish pointed out, the House and Senate versions of the legislation contained identical language requiring federal officials to "promulgate a complete set of safety regulations." He further explained, "The conference report gratuitously added the word 'new' in the middle of the quoted language. Since both versions were identical, this should have been handled in the statement of the managers. It is not in order to consider such a modification of identical language . . . and the conference report should be ruled out of order."[46] The floor manager of the conference

---

43. See *Congressional Record*, 97th Cong., 2d sess., Aug. 18, 1982, p. H6493.

44. Les Aspin, "Billion-Dollar Loophole," *The Progressive*, Jan. 1974, p. 36.

45. Another pertinent precedent was also noted by the Speaker in this instance: "The Chair must state that when more than one point of order is going to be made under a particular House rule, it is proper under the precedents for the Chair to require all such points of order to be stated and for the Chair then to make his decision on the separate points of order." *Congressional Record*, 94th Cong., 2d sess., Sept. 26, 1976, p. 33020.

46. Ibid., p. 33021.

report, John Murphy (D, N.Y.), responded to Fish's contentions, arguing that Fish misconstrued the intent of the quoted material. The Senate version, Murphy stressed, also used the word "repromulgate," which meant that existing regulations were to remain in effect until a new set was prepared. After listening to this rather arcane debate, the Speaker overruled Fish's parliamentary objection and ruled: "A careful reading of the Senate bill demonstrates that the two provisions were not identical, as the Senate bill contained the word 'repromulgate,' not contained in the House [version]. Therefore, the issue whether the regulations were to be new regulations or could be existing regulations was a matter before the conferees."[47]

Three other aspects of scope merit some mention. First, precedents state that it is permissible to change the phraseology of identical provisions in order to enhance clarity and consistency, provided those revisions do not go beyond the purposes of the original language. This, of course, always allows for challenge on the ground that such revisions in fact represent substantive modifications.

Second, where one chamber has addressed an issue and the other has not, then permissible compromise falls in a curious range between something and nothing. Similarly, when one house proposes to amend existing law and the other body does not address the issue at all (usually because it implicitly prefers the current statute), then allowable conference reconciliation involves the area between the existing law and the proposed modification of it.

Finally, whenever one chamber uses the parliamentary device of replacing the entire text of the other body's bill with what is called an "amendment in the nature of a substitute" (the functional equivalent of a new bill), then conferees have extremely broad latitude and may even propose a third version of the legislation. Language contained in both chambers' bills can be discarded and brand new text proposed. Even in this situation, conferees operate under some constraints: they are not to include new topics or issues; they may propose only changes that perfect and do not broaden the intent of both houses; and any substitute language (or third version) they recommend must be a germane, or relevant, modification of the two versions committed to conference. Unless there are obvious flagrant examples, however, it is often not easy to determine when these rules are transgressed, particularly in conference reports of massive size. It can be especially difficult during an end-of-session rush to adjourn to identify instances when new topics have been added or identical provisions expanded beyond their original intent.

The House and Senate are fundamentally unlike in their procedural methods of operation, especially concerning the issue of *germaneness*. In brief, because of the House's larger size it is a far more structured body than the Senate. The restraints imposed on representatives by rules and precedents are far more severe than those affecting senators. Whereas Senate rules maximize freedom of expression and amendment, House rules limit freedom of debate, and, among other things, impose a strict germaneness (or relevancy) requirement on floor amendments. These procedural difference frequently produce sharp policy disagreements because senators under their

---

47. Ibid., p. 33023.

rules can propose changes in House-passed bills that are out of order under House rules. Insofar as conference reports are concerned, procedural hassles between the House and Senate most often concern two specific areas: the addition of nongermane Senate amendments to House-passed bills and the inclusion of policy (or legislative) matters in general appropriations bills contrary to House (and even Senate) rules.

Senators have great latitude to offer nongermane floor amendments in the Senate. This latitude includes the right to add nongermane material to House-passed legislation. These amended bills then become conferenceable issues, even though they clearly violate House rules and have bypassed House committee review. The Senate, for instance, can take a one-title (or one-topic) House energy bill and add to it any number of relevant *or totally irrelevant* titles. Because House conferees may be unable or unwilling to drop the Senate's proposals, they can become part of the conference report (which must be subsequently approved by both chambers whole or not at all). The House in this situation faces a dilemma: accept the senatorial nongermane addenda or defeat the conference report, including what may be seen as very worthy and necessary original legislation.

Frustration with the Senate's practice has, over the years, mounted in the House. "We have to be either men or we are going to be mice," once declared a House committee chairman. "We have to stand up to this other body and say that if you want to amend, then amend according to [House] rules."[48] Such concern prompted the House to amend its rules in 1970, 1972, and 1974 to establish mechanisms for handling nongermane Senate amendments. The rules needed three successive revisions largely because of unforeseen consequences, including extremely hostile senatorial reaction to initial efforts.[49] After the 1970 change, for example, Senator Howard Baker (R, Tenn.) declared that the new House rule was unacceptable to the Senate because it thwarted the integrity of Senate internal and conference procedures. The House will have to make revisions, he asserted, "to end the intolerable restrictions placed on House-Senate conferees" by the House action.[50]

By 1974, a procedure generally satisfactory to both chambers had finally been devised to allow for House handling of nongermane Senate amendments. House rules now permit any member to raise a point of order stating that the conference report contains matter proposed by the Senate that is nongermane to the original House bill. If the Speaker sustains the point of order (and members under this procedure can raise successive points of order), then the member who raised the parliamentary objection offers a motion to reject and delete the offending matter from the conference report. The motion to reject is debated for a maximum of forty minutes, equally divided between the maker of the motion and the conference floor manager. The point to underscore here is that the House can now decide to *retain* the nongermane material, even if it would normally violate House rules. What is ostensibly a question of procedure is often resolved instead on the basis of substance.

48. *Congressional Record*, 91st Cong., 2d sess., Sept. 15, 1970, p. 31843.
49. For a review of the three House revisions, see Stanley Bach, "Germaneness Rules and Bicameral Relations in the U.S. Congress," *Legislative Studies Quarterly* 7, no. 3 (Aug. 1982): 341–57.
50. *Congressional Record*, 92d Cong., 1st sess., June 4, 1971, p. 18127.

For example, a House member successfully raised a germaneness point of order against a conference report on the Ethics in Government Act. The Senate, he pointed out, had tacked onto the ethics bill a "far-reaching" special prosecutor provision that was "different in form, different in purpose, different in all respects" from the original House bill.[51] During the following forty minutes of debate, however, representatives did not discuss how Senate conference insistence may have compelled the House conferees to accept something clearly nongermane under House rules. No member argued that House prerogatives needed to be defended against the Senate action; nor did anyone complain that the Senate's action bypassed the authority of the House committee system. Instead, the entire debate focused on the substantive importance of the special prosecutor provision and how it had in fact been considered and studied at great length by the House (although never formally adopted). The chairman of the Judiciary Committee, Peter Rodino (D, N.J.), whose panel exercises jurisdiction over both ethics and special prosecutor legislation, urged adoption of the conference report with the special prosecutor Senate amendment. This is a "very effective provision in this ethics [conference report] which will deal with a situation which has been crying out for a solution for a long period of time," he said.[52] In the end, the House voted overwhelmingly (344 to 49) against the rejection motion, accepting the nongermane Senate amendment despite the Speaker's earlier ruling that the special prosecutor provision violated House rules.

Of course, there are many instances when the House will vote to delete nongermane matter from the conference report.[53] The conference report is then considered also to be rejected. In this case, House rules provide for an automatic procedure: the conference floor manager is recognized to offer a motion that the House accept the remainder of the report—the original conference report minus the successfully challenged matter. If that motion is adopted by the House, the Senate then has the option of either accepting or rejecting what remains of the conference agreement. Alternatively, the Senate may choose to request that a new conference be convened, starting the conference process anew.[54]

3. VOTING ON CONFERENCE REPORTS. Critical both to making laws and keeping them from being made is voting on conference reports. While bicameral agreements are usually approved by each house for the reasons we have noted previously (favorable

51. *Congressional Record,* 95th Cong., 2d sess., Oct. 12, 1978, p. H12582.
52. Ibid.
53. For an example of such a successful motion, see *Congressional Record,* 97th Cong., 2d sess., Dec. 2, 1982, pp. H8802–26.
54. House rules provide an alternative procedure if the nongermane matter appeared in the original Senate bill. When the House takes the Senate measure up on the floor, it could delete the nongermane matter while amending other provisions of the Senate bill, and then request a conference with the Senate. The nongermane material, however, might still find its way into the conference report because of Senate conference insistence. The procedure described above would still apply: any Representative could raise a point of order against the report and then a majority of the House could vote to delete that material. However, parliamentary principles stipulate that the House cannot again modify its own amendment. As a result, in this situation, the conference floor manager will insist on the House's amendment (the deletion of the nongermane material). Then the Senate bill and House amendment will be returned to the Senate and that body could then either request another conference or adopt the House's amendment.

scheduling, their privileged status and indivisibility, and a recognition that rejection can mean repetition of the entire lawmaking process), there are occasions when conference reports are either defeated or recommitted to conference (an option, however, available only to the first-acting chamber).

Three reasons largely explain the occurrence of defeat or recommittal of conference reports. First and most obvious, the conferees may propose agreements that a majority of their chamber colleagues strongly oppose. Conferees necessarily and commonly drop provisions in conference that were adopted earlier by their chamber. Such actions may irritate and arouse the opposition of some members, but such deletions by themselves are unlikely to result in rejection of the conference report unless they are, individually or collectively, both significant and controversial. "The chamber has been sold out" is the charge leveled against the conferees in these cases. "The House [conferees'] collapse is too obvious a betrayal of instructions," declared one representative. "National security, common sense, and honor of the House demand the defeat of the conference report."[55]

Sometimes these criticisms can be headed off through adroit bicameral maneuvering. For example, the Senate acted first and approved an education conference report with school busing language stronger than that contained in the original Senate bill, but weaker than in the original House version. Several liberal senators strongly opposed and voted against the conference report both because of the busing provision and (it was suggested) to enhance the agreement's uncertain prospects in the House. Proponents of the conference accord in the House then were able to use the liberal senators' strenuous opposition to demonstrate that they had won a "meaningful curb on busing," even if it was weaker than what had originally been passed by the House.[56]

A second reason for chamber discord over conference ratification is that the issue itself may be divisive and difficult to resolve. Only eleven of twenty House conferees signed a 1980 conference report that proposed creation of a new Energy Mobilization Board. The narrowness of that eleven to nine delegation vote underscored the tenuousness of support for the proposition. The conference itself had "stalemated for months over the issue of whether the board could waive the substantive provisions of existing [state and local] laws that would hinder construction of a priority energy project."[57] In addition, interest groups split sharply; environmental groups and state and local government interests generally opposed the new board and industry associations for the most part backed it. Even the board's supporters in the House did not argue strongly for the proposal, in contrast with the intense opposition. On the day of the House conference report vote, members who opposed the conference report came onto the floor wearing buttons decrying "Even More Bureaucracy" (presumably resulting from the creation of the Energy Mobilization Board). In the end, the report was recommitted to conference and, in this case, killed.

55. *Congressional Record,* 96th Cong., lst sess., Sept. 20, 1979, p. H8250. For a similar example of a House sense of conference betrayal, see the chapter 11 case study "Dollars for Defense: Les Gets More Amidst 1985 House Turmoil."
56. Gladieux and Wolanin, *Congress and the Colleges,* p. 208.
57. *Congressional Quarterly Almanac, 1980* (Washington, D.C.: Congressional Quarterly, 1981), p. 483.

Recommittal, however, does not always mean the death of a conference agreement. In 1982, a budget reconciliation conference report was recommitted when representatives focused on a previously little-noticed provision for a congressional salary increase. Observed one representative, "Mr. Speaker, I simply want to say, I honor perhaps as much as anybody the work that has gone into this reconciliation. It is no easy job to cut billions and billions of dollars, particularly from the truly needy; but I do want to say how inappropriate I believe it is for the House to set in motion any mechanism which has to do with the pay level of Members of Congress without a separate recorded vote on that issue alone."[58] The conference quickly reconvened, dropped the offending material—a minor part of the whole legislation—and brought the revised bicameral accord back the next day to the House, where it was dutifully adopted.

Finally, as mentioned earlier, the "atmosphere" of the moment—the degree of trust between Congress and the White House, the extent of confusion about the issue, concern about cost, and much more—can lead to rejection of conference reports. During the rapid disintegration of the South Vietnamese government in the spring of 1975, the House was faced with a conference report that would have provided evacuation and humanitarian assistance to homeless Vietnamese citizens and authorized the use of American troops to evacuate U.S. citizens from South Vietnam. Events, however, would overtake the conference report.

The House considered the conference agreement two days after South Vietnam had fallen. During floor debate, representatives expressed two concerns about the conference legislation: it might be used to authorize the reintroduction of U.S. troops to Vietnam, and it could be seen as authorizing the expenditure of U.S. funds to aid the new communist-controlled government of South Vietnam. "This bill has become moot," declared a House member, in one of the milder assessments.[59] The House agreed and voted 162 to 246 against approving the conference report.

Even the defeat of a conference report does not automatically mean the end of the involved legislation. In the Vietnam case, for instance, many members supported humanitarian aid but opposed any proposal that permitted even the possibility that U.S. troops might be reintroduced into Vietnam. They urged that the conference report be defeated, so the House could return to the parliamentary situation that existed prior to conference. The House would then be able to strike the troop authorization provision while retaining the refugee humanitarian aid legislation. As the Speaker pointed out, "When the House disapproves a conference report, the matter is left in the position it was in before the conference was asked. . . . In other words, the conferees of the Senate have been discharged [that chamber acted first and passed the Vietnamese conference report]. The House would start all over with the House bill and the Senate amendments."[60] The House would thus be able to accept the Senate amendment or, alternatively, request another conference with the Senate on those portions of the legislation in bicameral disagreement.[61]

    58. *Congressional Record,* 97th Cong., 2d sess., Aug. 17, 1982, p. H6105.
    59. *Congressional Record,* 94th Cong., 1st sess., May 1, 1975, p. 12760.
    60. Ibid., p. 12761.
    61. For various reasons, this procedure was in fact not followed in this instance. Rather, Congress subsequently acted in separate legislation to provide aid to Vietnamese refugees.

Debating Conference Reports: The Senate

The House and Senate are vastly different legislative institutions.[62] Many of these differences flow fundamentally from size: the House is more than four times the measure of the Senate. It is no wonder the House imposes many kinds of procedural limitations and requirements on lawmaking. By contrast, the Senate is more personal and individualistic. It functions to a large extent by unanimous consent, in effect adjusting or disregarding its formal rules as it goes along. Similarly, there are enormous differences in the ways the two chambers take up, consider, and vote on conference reports. Whereas procedural complexities abound in the House, senatorial action on conference reports is typically characterized by relatively few parliamentary obstacles and formal requirements.

Procedural Routes to the Floor

Conference reports are called up for debate in the Senate in one of two ways: by unanimous consent or by formal motion. Most reports reach the floor by unanimous consent. Typically, the majority leader or the conference floor manager will state, "I submit a report of the committee of conference on S. 1234 and ask for its immediate consideration." The presiding officer responds, "Without objection, the Senate will proceed to the consideration of the conference report."

Any senator may say, "I object." Since a motion to proceed to a conference report is nondebatable, in that case the conference floor manager or majority leader will simply move to take up the report, which requires only a majority vote for approval. Motions to take up are approved almost automatically for three intertwined reasons: they are part of the majority leader's acknowledged scheduling prerogatives, they are procedural and not substantive in character (it is usually more difficult to organize opposition against process than policy questions), and they provide an opportunity to consider issues that most senators want to debate.

In sum, relatively little can prevent Senate consideration of conference reports given their privileged character and the concurrence of the majority leader and conference floor manager to take them up. There are, however, two formidable obstacles that merit some attention. Both are especially effective blocking actions near the end of a Congress: requiring that the conference report be read and threatening to filibuster it to death by "extended debate."

Rarely are conference reports read verbatim. However, any senator has the right to demand that a conference report be read in full if that request is made immediately after the request to take it up is made (either by unanimous consent or by motion) but before it is agreed to. One senator, in short, can effectively kill a lengthy conference report, particularly during the waning hours of a Congress, by requiring that it be read in full. It was in this fashion that the conference report on the Clean Air Act of 1976 was killed.[63]

---

62. For a discussion of the institutional distinctions between House and Senate, see chapter 5 above.

63. For a discussion, see Bernard Asbell, *The Senate Nobody Knows* (New York: Doubleday, 1978), pp. 440–47.

Of course, the norms and understandings of the Senate usually discourage frequent or wanton use of this weapon.

The other action that can prevent consideration of a conference report is the threat of a filibuster. While filibusters can be stopped by using the Senate's cloture rule (Rule XXII), it is not always easy to invoke (sixty votes are necessary), and cloture does not necessarily put an immediate stop to delaying actions. When Senator Alan Cranston (D, Cal.) called up a conference report late in the Ninety-sixth Congress, he was advised by Majority Leader Howard Baker of Tennessee that the "opposition is significant enough" that cloture would be required "to reach final passage on this measure."[64] Given the difficulties in terminating a filibuster so late in the congressional year, Senator Cranston withdrew the conference report.

Consideration of conference reports is sometimes regulated and expedited by the use of unanimous consent or time-limitation agreements. The fundamental objective of these informal arrangements is to control the time needed to dispose of measures in an institution noted for unlimited debate. Negotiated by party leaders, key senators, and staff aides, these agreements set aside the Senate's formal rules and consequently must be accepted by all senators. Once adopted, unanimous consent agreements are as binding on the Senate as any formal rule and can be set aside or modified only by other unanimous consent agreements.

Conference reports are in fact seldom filibustered,[65] yet any senator can choose to discuss these bicameral accords at great length—as well as any other debatable matter, including a motion to recommit a report to conference. Unanimous consent agreements, then, are framed to insure that senators have adequate time to debate conference reports without unnecessarily prolonging final action on them.

Action on the Floor

Conference reports in the Senate, as in the House, cannot be amended; they are indivisible products that are voted up or down in a single vote. Senate conferees, like their House counterparts, will frequently laud the bicameral accord in the hope of generating support for it. Conference floor manager Robert Dole (R, Kan.), in urging support for a 1984 trade conference report, noted,

> Mr. President, the agreement of the conferees on the trade bill, H.R. 3398, represents a remarkable achievement. The conferees faced substantial editorial opposition, threats of Presidential veto, strong expressions of opposition from many domestic groups and foreign governments, and extreme time pressure. Despite significant differences among the conferees on many issues, the result of 2 days of hard bargaining is a good bill by almost everyone's standards.[66]

---

64. *Congressional Record,* 96th Cong., 2d sess., Nov. 17, 1980, p. S14549.
65. Evidence of the rarity of conference report filibusters was provided by Democratic Majority Leader Robert C. Byrd of West Virginia, who stated in 1980 that "I do not recall a successful filibuster on a conference report since I have been in the Senate" (*Congressional Record,* 96th Cong., 2d sess., April 30, 1980, p. S4358). For an example of such a filibuster success, however, see the chapter 11 case study on South African sanctions legislation in 1985.
66. *Congressional Record,* 98th Cong., 2d sess., Oct. 9, 1984, p. S13969.

To be sure, a bill may not be seen as good by everyone. Senators whose amendments get dropped in conference may be irate and make their displeasure known during debate on the conference report.

Despite these bicameral similarities we have noted, there are also significant differences between the chambers in how they handle conference reports. In addition to the filibuster, there are two other distinctive senatorial practices: the disposing of conference reports and the raising of points of order.

Motions to Dispose of Conference Reports

Unlike the House, the Senate permits additional motions (other than to accept, reject, or recommit) that dispose of conference reports. These other means, while infrequently used, include motions to postpone, refer, and table. Any senator can propose at any time during floor debate on conference reports that final action be *postponed* for a limited period—or even indefinitely. For instance, upset that Senate conferees had eliminated a cherished amendment of his despite preconference assurances to the contrary, Senator Howard Metzenbaum (D, Ohio) moved in late 1985 to postpone consideration of a conference report to a later date. That date was calculated to come after Congress had enacted budget reconciliation legislation; the conference report then would be subject to a point of order under the 1974 Budget Act for causing an excessive deficit. While providing strategic benefit to conference report opponent Metzenbaum, the motion to postpone was justified by him on broader public interest grounds: "This will give the Finance Committee time to report back an amendment to the reconciliation measure that raises at least $115 million over the next three years."[67] Metzenbaum's motion, however, was overwhelmingly rejected (seven to ninty-one), testimony to the broad popularity of the conference report and the wish of the Senate majority not to jeopardize the report's approval by postponement.

Motions to *refer conference reports to a standing committee* are quite rare indeed. The only attempt in recent history, so far as we know, occurred in 1964 when Senate Foreign Relations Chairman William Fulbright (D, Ark.) made such a motion. He followed this course because he felt the Agriculture Committee had improperly trespassed on the jurisdictional prerogatives of his committee.

During a House-Senate conference on an agricultural measure, a House provision limiting the sale of agricultural products to Poland and Yugoslavia was adopted by the conferees. Neither the House nor the Senate Foreign Relations Committees had considered this issue, and Fulbright was incensed that his panel had been bypassed. He said, "I shall not sit idly by and have a foolish thing done in this manner and have the Committee on Agriculture and Forestry impose upon one of the most important aspects of our foreign relations. I think this is unacceptable procedure."[68] When Senator Fulbright moved that the conference report be referred to his committee, the Senate rejected the motion by a twenty-four to forty-six vote.[69] The defeat of the referral motion reflected in

---

67. *Congressional Record*, 99th Cong., 1st sess., Oct. 1, 1985, p. S12348.
68. *Congressional Record*, 88th Cong., 2d sess., Sept. 23, 1964, p. 22575.
69. *Congressional Record*, 88th Cong., 2d sess., Sept. 24, 1964, p. 22770.

part the recognition that even if the report was sent to the Foreign Relations Committee, it would be able only to hold hearings and make recommendations. Under Senate rules concerning the handling of conference reports, the committee would not have authority to modify or amend the conference report.

Motions to *table a conference report* are also unusual. An interesting instance occurred in 1974 during the Watergate investigation of President Nixon. The Senate took up a controversial conference report establishing a Legal Services Corporation. The most contentious issue in the report involved the proposed funding by the corporation of poverty law research centers, called back-up centers. Conservative legislators opposed the corporation in part because legal services attorneys, they held, aggressively pushed social activist policies.

Senatorial supporters of the conference report realized that they had no chance to override President Nixon's threatened veto of the legislation. Some senators believed that Nixon planned to use his veto to build support among conservatives before possible impeachment proceedings began. The plan conference report supporters devised was to table the report. The objective of this surprising step was to return the Senate to the legal services version it had originally enacted as a substitute for an earlier House-passed proposal. Once the Senate had its original bill back in front of it, the chamber would then insist on it and send the legislation back to the House, which was expected to drop the contentious poverty law centers provision. This approach would avoid another conference, "where pressure to change other provisions might be great," if the conference process had to start anew.[70] This strategy was carefully outlined by conference floor manager Gaylord Nelson (D, Wis.):

> Adoption of the motion to table the conference report would leave the legislation in the following status: The Senate would revert back to the point at which the Senate passed its version of the legislation as a substitute amendment to the House-passed bill. At that point, assuming adoption of the motion to table the pending conference report, I will then move that the Senate further insist upon its amendment to the text of the House bill.
>
> The purpose and effect of these motions will be to send the bill back to the House of Representatives where the managers of the bill will move to concur in the Senate amendment with a further amendment: to substitute the text of the conference agreement with the one exception that the authority for backup centers would be replaced by the language of the House-passed bill prohibiting grants and contracts for backup centers.
>
> Assuming the House takes such action, the revised conference agreement will then come back to the Senate for our concurrence, at which time the legislation would be cleared for the President's signature.[71]

With advance assurances from the president that he would sign the legislation if the provision for the backup centers was dropped, the strategy so candidly outlined by Senator Nelson was successful.

70. *Congressional Quarterly Almanac 1974* (Washington, D.C.: Congressional Quarterly, 1975), p. 494.

71. *Congressional Record,* 93d Cong., 2d sess., July 10, 1974, p. 22603.

Raising Points of Order

Unlike representatives, senators can raise points of order against conference reports any time during their consideration on the floor. There is no requirement for the timely (at a specific procedural stage) offering of points of order.[72] Further, there is no panel in the Senate comparable to the House Rules Committee with the power of proposing the waiver of points of order. The Senate does have a procedure for suspending its rules, but it is rarely used—virtually never for conference reports. Senate and House rules are somewhat comparable, however, in certain areas. Senate rules, like House rules, prohibit the inclusion of new matter in conference reports and the deletion of topics agreed to by both chambers. In the case of complete Senate substitutes for House bills, Senate conferees are likewise prohibited from going beyond the issues committed to them (in other words, from violating scope) and may make only germane modifications of the subjects in disagreement.

The Senate and House differ widely, however, in the application and interpretation of these rules. Parliamentary objections against conference reports are infrequently made in the Senate. The reasons are threefold. The Senate is an institution traditionally noted for comity, accommodation, and trust among senators; points of order appear to challenge the integrity of Senate colleagues. Further, it is not uncommon for rulings of the Senate's presiding officer to be overturned if they are appealed to the full Senate. (This is almost unheard of in the House.) "I do not intend to make the parliamentary point of order against the conference report," noted one senator in 1985, "because I feel confident that it would be overruled by a vote of the Senate."[73] Senators, in short, direct their attention to voting conference reports up or down rather than focusing on how these agreements can be sidetracked through parliamentary objections.

Perhaps most important, the Senate accords wide latitude to its conferees in reaching agreements with the other body. Despite the rulebook, the standards applied by the Senate presiding officer to judge those points of order that are raised are far more flexible than those used in the House. For example, one senator claimed in 1982 that a conference report was out of order because "it inserted new matter that had been approved at no time by either the Senate or the House." The presiding officer rejected the point of order, saying, "The conferees went to conference with a complete substitute, which gives them the maximum latitude allowable to conferees. The standard [applicable here] is that matter entirely irrelevant to the subject matter is not in order. That standard has not been breached."[74] "Entirely irrelevant," of course, is a standard broad enough to cover many Senate sins of omission or commission.

72. If a conference report is considered under a time-limitation agreement, points of order can be made after the expiration of the debate limitations or after the time has been yielded back to the chair. Debate time under a unanimous consent agreement is divided equally between the majority and minority party and not between supporters and opponents.

73. *Congressional Record,* 99th Cong., 1st sess., May 16, 1985, p. S6367. To be sure, there are instances when points of order are sustained against conference reports. See, for example, *Congressional Record,* 97th Cong., 2d sess., Aug. 12, 1982, pp. S10364–75. Senate rules provide that if a point of order is sustained and the House has not acted, the conference report is automatically recommitted to conference. Otherwise, the Senate's choices are to request another conference, propose amendments to the other body, start the lawmaking process over again, or do nothing.

74. *Congressional Record,* 97th Cong., 2d sess., Aug. 19, 1982, p. S10899.

Voting on Conference Reports

Putting together the votes to pass conference reports can be difficult or easy. Much depends on the nature of the report itself—its controversialness, visibility, or "must-pass" status—and the skill of conference floor managers and allies in winning colleagues' support. For example, the chairman of the Senate Environment and Public Works Committee expressed concern in 1981 that a defense conference report proposed "some very significant changes" in matters within the jurisdiction of his committee. The conference floor manager, the chairman of the Senate Armed Services Committee, assured his colleague that the military panel "will cooperate fully with the Senator's committee" to ensure that the provisions in question would be implemented in a manner consistent with the environment panel's responsibilities.[75] His concerns eased, the Environment Committee chairman then supported and voted for the conference report.

Test votes, too, can be used to demonstrate early support for conference reports, develop momentum for their passage, and sustain or mobilize outside backing for the bicameral accords. These elements were in play when Senator Lowell Weicker (R, Conn.) moved in 1985 to table a conference report, a motion usually made by an opponent of the accord. Weicker, however, strongly backed the conference report and wanted to show that the report had strong support in the Senate despite a filibuster threat that had postponed final action until after Congress returned from a month-long recess. As Senator Weicker explained, "It was my intention in moving to table the conference report to put the Senate on record on this issue before we recess. I regret that a small number of Senators have chosen to prevent final Senate action tonight, but as this vote indicates, there is overwhelming support for this conference agreement."[76] The motion to table was rejected by a zero to ninety-seven vote, with even the potential filibusterers voting against it to stymie Weicker's goal of singling them out as obstructionists.

On occasion the Senate defeats or recommits conference reports for many of the reasons cited previously for comparable House action. Typically, however, important substantive issues are involved when conference reports fail. The Senate, for instance, recommitted a conference report in 1974 that was designed to promote energy independence. The opposition was on substantive grounds; many senators believed that the accord actually threatened to undermine the 1970 Clean Air Act, foster more air pollution, and adversely affect the public's health.[77] When important values conflict, such as energy versus environment, the general tendency to support chamber conferees may evaporate in the heat of fundamental policy differences.

In another interesting case, the Senate first approved, then reconsidered that decision, and then finally rejected a contentious conference report early in 1980. A conference agreement involving small business had become embroiled in controversy over one issue. This specific provision had never been discussed in the Senate but had found its way into the report via a House floor amendment to the Senate-passed measure. The

---

75. *Congressional Record*, 97th Cong., 1st sess., Nov. 5, 1981, p. S13009.
76. *Congressional Record*, 99th Cong., 1st sess., Aug. 1, 1985, p. S10729.
77. *Congressional Quarterly Almanac 1974* (Washington, D.C.: Congressional Quarterly, 1975), pp. 728–32.

Senate Budget Committee chairman led the charge against the provision, holding that it was a backdoor device designed to circumvent the 1974 Budget Act and hide the true cost of a program run by the Small Business Administration. Despite these objections, the Senate initially approved the conference report by a fifty-five to twenty-seven vote.

However, when the conference floor manager made the customary motion to reconsider that decision (before a vote is considered final, both chambers permit its reconsideration within a limited period of time) followed by the also customary motion to table that request, the Senate by a thirty to fifty vote refused to table (or kill) the reconsideration motion. The conference floor manager understood well why the tabling motion had failed; while a substantial majority of the Senate favored the conference report, a majority also opposed the particular provision. Recognizing that the votes likely were there to kill the conference agreement, the floor manager recommended the following convoluted strategy: that the Senate first approve the motion to reconsider, then vote to reject the report, then agree to the conference report minus the offending provision (presented as an amendment to the House amendment to the Senate-originated bill), and finally send everything back to the House. The Senate agreed and successfully followed this complex course of action.[78]

Partial Conference Reports

Another practice that sometimes helps passage of bicameral agreements is adoption of what is called a partial conference report. It is common for some conferences (particularly on general appropriations bills) to reach agreement on most but not all the outstanding matters in disagreement: "In such a case, [the conferees] issue a conference report encompassing their areas of accord and report certain amendments in disagreement. It is required that before the amendments in disagreement can be reached, the conference report be adopted. Then, the amendments in disagreement are taken up one at a time."[79]

An example of this procedure occurred in late 1986. Conferees on a half-billion dollar omnibus appropriations bill reported their agreement on all but six provisions. This partial conference report was approved first by the House on October 15 and then by the Senate the next day. The six items still in bicameral disagreement were then subjected to a series of separate votes in both chambers over the following days. These steps eventually led to a negotiated compromise between the House and Senate that paved the way to final enactment into law of the spending measure.[80]

Several points are worth noting about this procedure. It applies only when conferees have before them a series of individual amendments in disagreement rather than one so-called amendment in the nature of a substitute (recall that this is the equivalent of a new

---

78. *Congressional Record,* 96th Cong., 2d sess., Jan. 24, 1980, pp. S331–59.

79. Martin B. Gold, *Senate Procedure and Practice: An Introductory Manual,* 2d ed., Office of the Senate Majority Leader, December 1983, p. 57. See also Floyd M. Riddick [parliamentarian emeritus of the Senate] and William Holmes Brown [parliamentarian of the House], "Conferences and Conference Reports: *STAFF* Introduction to the Rules," *STAFF,* issue 15 (Sept. 1978), pp. 1–3, esp. p. 3.

80. Elizabeth Wehr, "Congress Clears $576 Billion Spending Measure," *Congressional Quarterly Weekly Report,* Oct. 18, 1986, p. 2584.

bill). Conferees cannot report the sole amendment in disagreement because that technically is the entire matter before the conference. (An option in this case would be for the conferees to issue a conference report in total disagreement; see the section below on this strategy.)

If the two chambers cannot reconcile their differences on the various amendments reported in disagreement, another conference may be convened. The same conferees are usually reappointed, but they are now limited to resolving the remaining amendments in dispute. They cannot reopen consideration of issues already agreed to by both houses in the partial conference report. Measures cannot be finally enacted by Congress until both chambers reconcile all their differences, including each of the amendments reported in disagreement.

The practice of reporting amendments in disagreement provides considerable flexibility to the conferees in reconciling their differences. It also enables the conferees to follow the rules of their respective chambers that prohibit including topics in conference reports that violate House and Senate procedure. Additional complexities sometimes attach to this procedure because there are two types of such unsettled amendments: those that are technical and noncontroversial (known as amendments in technical disagreement) and those that raise controversial substantive issues (known as amendments in true disagreement).

Amendments in Technical Disagreement

It is not unusual for conferees knowingly to exceed their authority and develop compromises that are subject to later points of order. New information, requests from presidents, and other events typically account for such actions. Parliamentary objections in the House and Senate, however, apply against conference agreements and not amendments in disagreement. Conferees, in short, may work out compromises on some issues but not include them in the conference report to prevent points of order. These compromises are instead presented to the House and Senate, after the partial conference report is agreed to, as amendments in technical disagreement, to be considered separately and later, and in the favorable context of partial approval of the conference work. These later conditions may suffice to allow the more questionable conference compromises dealt with separately to survive possible points of order.

Interestingly, amendments in technical disagreement are routine for general appropriations measures. By custom, the House initiates these measures and the Senate offers a series of individual amendments (each amendment is numbered to avoid confusion) to various parts of the House-passed legislation. To maintain its initiatory role, as discussed previously, the House acts first on the agreed-upon portions of the conference report and then considers separately the numbered Senate amendments that are reported in technical disagreement.

These Senate amendments regularly violate House rules. House conferees, for instance, are forbidden to agree to certain kinds of Senate amendments, namely, those that permit the expenditure of funds for purposes not previously authorized by law and those that change existing law or policy.[81] (Such amendments, however, are common in the Senate because its rules are more flexible than those of the House.) To protect its prerogatives, House rules specifically state that its conferees cannot agree to such Senate amendments unless they receive advance approval from the House. That is not in fact how the House rules work in practice. Instead, after the partial conference report is adopted, the conference floor manager presents the Senate amendments to the full House. Thus, the House as a whole can decide whether the amendments are justified, even if they do formally contravene House rules.

These amendments are typically each approved in a minute or two, without objection or discussion. The form followed is that conference floor managers offer motions that ask the House to concur in Senate amendments reported in technical disagreement—even those not in conformity with the rules of the body. House rules are not self-enforcing, and if no representative raises points of order, the Senate amendments usually will be quickly accepted by the House. This is especially true for noncontroversial proposals. "We have several amendments [in technical disagreement] on which the conferees are in full agreement and which are not controversial," declared the chairman of the House Appropriations Committee concerning a 1984 appropriations measure. "I repeat, these amendments are noncontroversial," reiterated the chairman. "The conferees are in full agreement on them."[82] In such cases, the various amendments in technical disagreement may even be approved by unanimous consent *en bloc* (all together).

Amendments in True Disagreement

When conferees cannot agree on how to resolve substantive matters in disagreement, they submit amendments in "true" disagreement to their respective chambers. This practice focuses House and Senate attention on important issues left unresolved by the conference and isolates them for resolution without threatening defeat of the entire report. Conference floor managers often spotlight such amendments: "Amendment No. 14 comes back to the House in true disagreement," reported the Republican floor manager in regard to a bitterly disputed provision of the same appropriations measure.[83]

Amendment No. 14 was a controversial and important provision added by the Senate to the 1984 appropriations legislation that provided $21 million for "covert" Central Intelligence Agency aid to Nicaraguan rebels, or contras. By agreeing to disagree, the conference sent that highly contentious issue to the House and Senate floor for resolution. "This side of the table is not under any circumstances going to recede" on the contra aid issue, House conferee Edward Boland (D, Mass.) had asserted. For their

---

81. Points of order can also be made if the Senate amendments are nongermane to the House bill. Further, to protect the tax and tariff prerogatives of the Ways and Means Committee, any Senate amendment reported in technical disagreement to legislation that did not originate in the taxing panel is subject to points of order at any time during House consideration of the measure.

82. *Congressional Record*, 98th Cong., 2d sess., May 24, 1984, p. H4783.

83. Ibid., p. H4779.

part, Senate conferees voted five to three to insist on the contra aid proposal. "At this point, the Senate has spoken," noted Senate conferee Ted Stevens (R, Alaska). "We would like the House to address this issue."[84] Neither side, in short, wanted or felt able to retreat from its position.

When Amendment No. 14 "in true disagreement" was taken up in the House, Representative Boland offered an amendment to the Senate covert aid proposal that would prohibit the CIA from directly or indirectly supporting military or paramilitary operations in Nicaragua. This amendment was debatable by the House for one hour, with the time divided between supporters and opponents. The House then voted 241 to 177 to adopt the Boland amendment as an addition to the Senate provision. The House amendment was then transmitted to the Senate along with the other official conference papers.[85]

For the next month, House and Senate leaders and the Reagan administration negotiated over funding for the contras. Because other issues were involved in the conference-approved legislation, especially money for famine-striken Africans and summer jobs for American teenagers, pressure mounted for the House and Senate to resolve the contra aid issue. Finally, the Senate conference floor manager acted to strip the Senate amendment from the appropriations bill, and by an eighty-eight to one vote, the Senate agreed to drop the proposal.[86] The next day the House in turn deleted the Boland language, bringing the chamber measures finally into accord. "Since the funding [Amendment No. 14] is no longer in this measure," noted the House floor manager, "the language prohibition [the Boland amendment] is no longer required and it can now be deleted so that this bill may go to the President."[87] This 1984 case illustrates how bicameral disagreements can be resolved through a combination of processes: the adoption of partial conference reports, the sending of amendments back and forth between the chambers (mindful of the parliamentary "third degree" prohibition), the utilization of private negotiations, and even the potential convening of additional conferences.

Another procedural complexity in bicameral reconciliation of conference reports merits mention because it highlights the close tie that inherently exists between procedure and policy. Unlike the Senate, the House establishes priorities for motions that deal with amendments in disagreement. Which motion has priority over another depends upon whether the House has already formally agreed to go to conference; this period is

84. Robert Rothman, "Conferees on Supplemental Agree to Disagree," *Congressional Quarterly Weekly Report,* May 19, 1984, p. 1201.

85. *Congressional Record,* 98th Cong., 2d sess., May 24, 1984, p. H4806. Boland had two other options he might have followed instead of proposing an amendment to the Senate's covert aid provision. He could have insisted that the House remain adamant in its opposition to the Senate's proposal. (In response, the Senate could further insist on its amendment and request another conference.) Alternatively, Boland could have asked the House to accept the Senate amendment, a most unlikely step, however, in light of the views both of Boland and the House.

86. *Congressional Record,* 98th Cong., 2d sess., June 25, 1984, p. S8173. Other options available to the Senate floor manager would have included proposing to amend further the Boland amendment, to agree to it, to disagree to it and request another conference, to insist on amendment 14 as mentioned earlier, or to recede from amendment 14 (which has the same effect as a tabling motion).

87. *Congressional Record,* 98th Cong., 2d sess., June 26, 1984, p. H6834.

THE POSTCONFERENCE PROCESS

technically called the stage of disagreement. Prior to this stage, House motions that "perfect" by changing Senate amendments have preference over motions that bring the two chambers into agreement by means such as accepting the Senate's entire proposal. After the conference, however, the priority of motions is reversed. Motions that resolve bicameral conflict by concurring in the Senate version then have preference over those that keep the chambers apart.

This distinction is important because the House (unlike the Senate) allows the motion to "recede and concur with an amendment" to be split or divided in half upon a single member's request. Any representative can simply say, "Mr. Speaker, I demand that the question [the motion to recede and concur with an amendment] be divided." Because that motion contains two distinct elements (to recede and concur and to amend), it is divided automatically by the Speaker, and each part is subsequently debated and voted upon separately.

The point is that should the motion to recede be agreed to, the House then returns to the predisagreement stage, and members may then offer preferential motions to perfect the Senate amendments. Members and even conferees who are dissatisfied with agreements reached by the conference committee may thus be able to employ the division motion to change policy outcomes.[88] Alternatively, members who are upset with what the conferees have reported often will seek to defeat the motion to recede in order to demonstrate support for the House's original policy position. If the motion to recede is defeated, the only motion then in order is for the House to insist on its disagreement to the Senate amendment. By this action, the House is telling the Senate that it is determined to support the policy contained in the measure it originally agreed to, instead of either the Senate version or the compromise recommended by the conference committee. Then the Senate must decide whether to accept the original House provision or recede from its own amendment and propose yet another change in the House language.[89]

There are, to be sure, additional procedural intricacies. Suffice it to say that members who know the rules and who have sufficient backing from their colleagues can change conference recommendations. Despite the many twists and turns that can affect amendments in disagreement, the vast majority are resolved with a minimum of delay and confusion. The practice, in brief, serves the interest of both chambers.

Conference Reports in Disagreement

There are infrequent occasions when conferees cannot agree, either for real or technical reasons, and report that their efforts are in complete disagreement. This usually occurs when the conferees have before them an amendment in the nature of a substitute, which, while technically one amendment, is actually a complete new bill. In reporting to their respective chambers, conferees will review their body's original positions and state that they were able to resolve, say, 110 of the 111 bicameral differences. Absent

---

88. For an example, see *Congressional Record,* 97th Cong., 1st sess., June 4, 1981, pp. H2630–31.

89. For an example of this procedure, see *Congressional Record,* 98th Cong., 1st sess., March 22, 1983, pp. 1520–29 and S3641; and March 24, 1983, pp. H1689–95.

agreement on the 111th item, however, they report that they are unable to agree. Typical language would be "The committee of conference on the disagreeing votes of the two Houses on the amendment of the Senate to the bill (H. R. 1234) . . . having met, after full and free conference, have been unable to agree."

The procedure of the Senate is actually to vote to adopt this "report." In this instance, the conference report, as one senator explained to his colleagues, "is that the conferees are in disagreement."[90] By contrast, the House does not formally act upon a report in disagreement other than to have it read and presented to the representatives. In both chambers, however, conference floor managers may offer still additional motions to reconcile remaining bicameral disagreements by means of amendments between the houses. A 1959 Senate statement provides an example:

> Mr. President, as chairman of the conferees between the House and Senate on the airport bill, I report to the Senate that it was impossible for us to reach an agreement between the widely differing views on the bill, S. 1, as passed by the Senate and the bill as finally passed by the House of Representatives.
>
> Therefore I desire to take a new approach on the bill S. 1, since the conferees are unable to reach an accord thereon. I now move that the Senate recede and concur in the House amendment to S. 1, with an amendment in the nature of a substitute therefor.[91]

Should the Senate and then the House accept the proposal, then the legislation would be reconciled and be ready for presidential signature.

Conferees are sometimes required, for essentially technical reasons, to report in disagreement. Under the terms of the 1974 Budget Act, for example, conferees are prohibited from going either above or below the financial targets identified in the House- and Senate-passed versions of the concurrent budget resolution. When the "numbers are even slightly below or above the range," the Senate Budget Committee chairman stressed, "the conference must report in disagreement."[92] In that case, the Senate will vote to adopt the conference report "in disagreement" and then proceed to pass an amendment (as the House does next), that is not subject to scope points of order, that embodies the agreement to which the conferees had actually agreed.

Conclusions

The passage of legislation is never a foregone conclusion. Parliamentary, political, party, personal, and public complications all can influence what happens to conference reports. Last minute hitches can always derail these products as lobbyists, executive officials, staff aides, and members mobilize grass-roots and public opinion behind or in opposition to these accords. There is little doubt, however, that when conference reports

---

90. *Congressional Record*, 86th Cong., 1st sess., June 15, 1959, p. 10771.
91. Ibid.
92. *Congressional Record*, 95th Cong., 1st sess., May 13, 1977, p. S7529.

THE POSTCONFERENCE PROCESS 251

reach the floor, they are accorded a significant degree of deference. Members are far more likely to approve than disapprove these agreements.

To provide additional feel and flavor for conference committee activity, we present in the next chapter a number of case studies of conference committee politics. They are designed to highlight the unique and variable character of conference deliberations. As one House chairman put it in mid-1985, "You feel around on some things and see what you can agree on. It's not an exact science."[93]

93. *New York Times*, July 17, 1985, p. A18.

Appendix

For the reasons discussed in this chapter, conference committee reports are seldom rejected or recommitted to conference by either the House or the Senate. An examination of the fate of 2,495 conference reports over the thirty-six year span covering the eighteen Congresses from 1947 to 1982[94] has found only 28 instances when the House or Senate recommitted a report to conference, and 28 additional instances when a chamber rejected a report. These data, by Congresses, are reported in the accompanying table.

Conference Reports Recommitted and Rejected by Chamber and Congress

	House		Senate	
	Recommitted to Conference	Rejected	Recommitted to Conference	Rejected
1947–48	0	1	0	2
1949–50	0	0	0	3
1951–52	0	0	0	1
1953–54	2	2	3	1
1955–56	1	0	0	0
1957–58	2	0	0	2
1959–60	0	1	0	1
1961–62	1	2	0	0
1963–64	0	2	1	1
1965–66	3	1	0	1
1967–68	3	0	0	0
1969–70	0	0	0	0
1971–72	1	2	0	1
1973–74	3	0	1	0
1975–76	2	0	0	0
1977–78	2	1	1	1
1979–80	1	0	1	1
1981–82	0	1	0	0
	21	13	7	15

Total number of reports recommitted = 28
Total number of reports rejected = 28
Number of conference reports considered = 2,495

---

94. The tabulations reported in this Appendix were carried out by Tom Kephardt especially for this book. Appreciation is expressed to him for his analysis of the fate of 2,495 conference reports over a thirty-six-year time span.

House Budget Committee conferees, including Representative Delbert L. Latta (R, Ohio) (*far left*), meet with Senate Budget Committee members led by Senator Pete V. Domenici (R, N.M.) (*far right*) during a 1983 budget conference. The portrait is of former Senate Democratic Majority Leader Mike Mansfield. (From the *New York Times,* June 9, 1983. Photograph by George Tames. Copyright © 1983 by The New York Times Company. Reprinted by permission.)

11

Conference Politics: Nine Mini-Case Studies

In the preceding chapters of this book, we have discussed conference committee politics analytically in terms of such distinguishing devices as stages, contexts, and changes. Our examination, of course, has not been abstract; at virtually every point in our discussion we have cited insights of and examples from scholars, senators, representatives, and other close observers of or participants in congressional bicameral politics.

In this penultimate chapter (a brief conclusion follows as a final chapter), we conclude our exploration of House-Senate conference committee interactions with a series of nine mini-case studies. These accounts of conference politics vary greatly in length and complexity—as do conferences themselves. Several of the studies are brief, but in their simplicity and brevity they reflect the nature of the conferences considered. Other conference case studies—for example, those on the 1982 tax increase legislation and the 1985 Gramm-Rudman deficit reduction bill—are more detailed and complicated in their tracing of conferee moves and countermoves, negotiations, strategies and deals, and other aspects of multifacted conference interactions.

These case studies are drawn from a time span of some sixteen years, but only roughly are they representative of these years. Although the earliest conferences are from 1969 and 1972, most of the major cases studied here occurred in the early to mid-1980s, including three in 1985. Similarly, although there is great subject area diversity among the topics of the conferences—including chicory roots, children, higher education, alligators, taxes, appropriations, foreign policy, defense authorizations, and budgetary deficits—these accounts are not presented here as a perfect cross section of the enormously varied concerns of Congress.

What *is* provided in this chapter is a rich collection of snap shots of conferences in action that illuminate and illustrate general characteristics and tendencies of bicameral politics outlined in the preceding pages. The clash of institutional values and norms in the conference room, the lingering influence of the parent committee during conference, the choices available to and made by the individual conferee, the anticipation by House and Senate of the upcoming conference, the utilization and effectiveness of various strategies during conference negotiations, and the awareness of the necessity of securing the approval of both chambers of the conference's final product—all these dimensions of bicameral politics are touched upon in these accounts. The analytical examination of conference interactions contained in earlier chapters, the specific examples and observations that permeated those pages, and the self-contained mini-case studies that follow in this chapter, together provide, we trust, a diverse but cumulative set of images and insights into the complexities of bicameral politics and policymaking, as made manifest in conference committee interactions.

A. Heptanoic Acid and Needy Children

Our first mini-case study is also the earliest; it dates from the summer of 1969. Unlike the accounts that follow, this one does not deal with a single bill or legislative initiative. Rather, it discusses the intertwining of the usually quite unrelated topics of import duty on heptanoic acid, income tax surcharges, chicory root levies, and federal aid to dependent children.

The action in this account takes place on the floor of the House of Representatives and involves initial and unsuccessful attempts (because of severe time pressure) to bypass the conference stage through chamber acceptance of Senate action. This is followed by efforts, including what is described as browbeating and blackmail, to ensure favorable conference activity. These events illustrate the importance of personal stubbornness and commitment in policymaking, the effect of deadlines on policymaking, and the strong relationships that can quickly develop between seemingly unrelated measures. In this one account (all the other mini-case studies are published here for the first time), the narrative is reprinted, by permission, from an outside source, Tom Wicker of the *New York Times.*[1]

Traditionally, in any representative form of government, it is not easy to get things done. But some Americans—particularly black, poor and hungry ones—may be wondering if their own representative Government hasn't made it harder than necessary.

Here is one example of how a small but useful step had to be taken [in 1969] in the House of Representatives:

Representative Hale Boggs of Louisiana, managing things for the House Ways and Means Committee while Chairman Wilbur D. Mills was temporarily absent, told the House that he was about to ask for "unanimous consent" to take up H.R. 4229, an act to continue for a temporary period the existing suspension of duty on heptanoic acid. He needed the unanimous consent, under House rules, because both Senate and House had passed the measure but the Senate had added amendments; if any single member objected to taking up the amended measure, it would have to be referred back to the House Rules Committee.

There was no time for such a delay because the Senate amendment happened to be a rider to provide the authority for the nation's employers to go on withholding the 10 percent income tax surcharge from their employees' wages; that authority expired [in a few days] at midnight June 30 and was to be renewed for a month while Congress continued to debate whether to renew the surtax itself.

Beating a Deadline

But one member of Congress, even so, said he might object to Bogg's request. Representative Phil Burton of California, a shrewd liberal Democrat, had a deadline of

---

1. This account was written by Tom Wicker of the *New York Times* as one of his "In the Nation" columns. It was originally published in the *New York Times* on July 1, 1969, under the title "Chicory Roots and Children." Copyright © 1969 by the New York Times Company. Reprinted by permission.

his own to worry about. Unless Congress acted—again by midnight June 30—the long-delayed "freeze" on Federal funds for aiding dependent children would go into effect. That would mean the Federal Government would provide no assistance to the states for supporting more such children than were being helped by any state [eighteen months earlier] on Jan. 1, 1968.

The freeze had been voted in 1967, then delayed for one year; if it went into effect, either thousands of children would be forced off welfare rolls or the states alone would have to provide assistance to them. Meanwhile, every state was in a condition of budgetary uncertainty about how to plan its child-aid programs.

It appeared likely that Congress might merely delay the freeze again; but in the Senate, outright repeal had been voted. What Phil Burton wanted to know was what Boggs planned to do about H.R. 8644, a bill to make permanent the existing temporary suspension of duty on crude chicory roots; because, believe it or not, the Senate repeal of the freeze was contained in a rider to that measure. And unless the House agreed to accept the repeal, Burton aimed to prevent it from approving the withholding authority added to the heptanoic acid bill.

Boggs told Burton that he was opposed to the freeze, too, but that he did not know what Chairman Mills wished him to do; the ranking Republican on the Ways and Means Committee, John Byrnes of Wisconsin, told Burton he favored acting to "lift"—not repeal—the freeze, and doing so before June 30.

Legislative Tactics

But Burton held out for repeal, with as fine a mixture of metaphor as ever found expression, even in the House of Representatives. "We are not," he declared, "going to have this Sword of Damocles hanging over their head, while we contemplate, if you will pardon the expression, this legislative navel."

And they didn't. Boggs quickly found the authority to appoint a conference committee to discuss with the Senate the chicory roots bill and its welfare rider. Byrnes promised once again that he believed "the ceiling should be lifted."

Did that mean, Burton inquired, that Byrnes favored repealing the freeze outright? "That lends itself to a yes or no answer," he said pointedly. Well, said Byrnes, it meant the freeze "should be lifted for at least a year," and furthermore he did not intend to be "browbeaten or blackmailed" by Burton's threat of "creating chaos for the workers of this country and the employers of this country in making out their payroll next week."

Whereupon Burton objected to the unanimous consent request on the heptanoic acid bill. That got action; the next day the newly appointed conference committee agreed to accept the Senate's chicory roots bill, including its repeal of the welfare freeze; and the day after that the House confirmed this decision, 250 to 65. And then, in the nick of time, Burton let the House go ahead and extend the withholding authority.

Moral: Around here, it sometimes requires browbeating, blackmail, mixed metaphors and guts to feed poor children.

B. Higher Education: Personalities and Exhaustion

One important marathon conference of the early 1970s dealt with landmark higher education legislation. (This conference was cited in chapter 1 as an example of the strategy of exhaustion as a key to achieving conference agreement.)[2] This 1972 conference also resulted in one of the best informed and most carefully told insider accounts of conference committee politics. In a lengthy, detailed narrative,[3] two House committee staffers who happened also to be political scientists, Lawrence E. Gladieux and Thomas R. Wolanin, have provided an outstanding case study of events and personalities central to this eventually successful conference. Here, we present an abstract[4] of the Gladieux-Wolanin account, a mini-case study that illustrates the politics of bargaining and compromise that is central to the conference process. These events are also interesting in that they provide a view of conference committee politics at a time when conferences were otherwise closed to public view and to journalistic and scholarly study.[5]

The 1960s were marked by a significant expansion of support for higher education by the federal government. The scope of this support—who would be eligible to receive federal assistance—also increased, although more gradually. The end of the decade brought forth new questions concerning the role of the federal government in higher education. These questions centered on both the purpose and the form of federal programs at the postsecondary level. The issue was not one of great public prominence, yet to those concerned about the role of the federal government in higher education it was of high importance. This included the academic world, foundations, state agencies, and members of the federal government.

The debate among these interests over the purpose and form of federal support for higher education culminated in the Education Amendments Act of 1972, an omnibus bill that would come to be seen as a landmark measure in the area of higher education. Congressional debate over the bill initially focused on how the cost of college and graduate school should be divided between the government and the users. Subsequently, and more specifically, the key issues came to be seen as how to divide money between

---

2. As quoted in chapter 1, a key participant remembered well, even after a number of years, the conference resolution: "Finally, in one burst of energy—augmented by a large dash of 'I don't give a damn anymore. I'm dead tired and nothing is worth this kind of pain'—the conferees agreed. The final differences were reconciled, hands—now limp and numb—were shaken all around, and the conference broke up shortly after 5 A.M." (Rep. Roman L. Mazzoli [D, Ky.], "My Favorite Story," *Roll Call,* June 2, 1983, p. 5).

3. Lawrence Gladieux and Thomas R. Wolanin, "The Conference Committee," chapter 8 in their *Congress and the Colleges* (Lexington, Mass.: D. C. Heath, 1976).

4. This abstract was originally prepared by Therese A. Barry as part of her 1984 Senior Independent Studies Thesis at Lawrence University, "Conference Committees and Institutional Adaptability" and is extensively revised and published here for the first time. All facts and quoted material within this account are drawn from the fuller account of Gladieux and Wolanin cited in the preceding footnote.

5. The processes by which congressional conference committees were opened to public, journalistic, and scholarly scrutiny in the mid-1970s, and the anticipated and actual consequences of this change, are discussed in chapter 3 above.

aid to institutions and direct aid for students. Both houses of Congress wrestled with these and other questions, and each chamber passed legislation on higher education in the spring of 1972.

The Senate bill incorporated all elements of higher education assistance in one package that emphasized student aid rather than institutional aid. The main vehicle for student aid in the Senate-passed legislation was the Basic Grant, an entitlement program based on uniform national standards relating primarily to income. The House bill took a different approach and extended existing student aid programs. Its central elements were a student aid program including the middle class and a federal program to assist colleges in trouble. The emphasis in this latter program was on institutional aid. In addition, the student aid program under the House bill would treat each student on an individual basis with regard to both merit and need.

Because the language of the House and Senate legislation differed fundamentally, a conference committee was needed to work out bicameral agreement on a single higher education bill. This conference committee first met on March 15, 1972. Its basic working documents were four large, staff-prepared books that listed a total of 401 differences between the two bills.

Before we examine the specific events concerning the 1972 higher education bill conference, a brief look at the makeup of both delegations will provide insight into the agreement that finally evolved. The Senate conferees generally were united in support of their bill. The only issue Senate conferees did not agree upon was the highly contentious one of busing. The House, on the other hand, was faced with serious problems of factionalism within its delegation. The ranking minority member of the House Education and Labor Committee was Albert Quie (R, Minn.), who thereby was responsible for selecting the House Republican conferees. Quie, however, essentially favored the Basic Grant and very limited institutional aid provisions of the Senate bill. Thus, he carefully chose as conference members Republican congressmen who either favored his viewpoint or were uncommitted on these provisions. The Democratic House conferees were selected by committee chairman Carl Perkins of Kentucky and were more diverse in their outlook. Among them, John Brademas of Indiana and Frank Thompson, Jr., of New Jersey shared Quie's position in favor of Basic Grants and in general opposition to institutional aid. The remaining House Democrats, led by Edith Green (D, Ore.), favored an institutional aid program based on capitation grants and opposed the inclusion of a program such as the Basic Grant provision favored by the House Republicans and by the Senate conferees. Green and her allies had prevailed earlier during chamber passage of the House bill and in conference had ten votes. Quie and the other Republicans plus Democrats Brademas and Thompson, however, also had ten votes. Therefore, on the central substantive issues of the conference, Quie together with his Republican and Democratic supporters would need only one more vote to prevail in the House delegation. In addition, the Basic Grant proposal favored by this House conferee bloc had additional appeal because it would aid bicameral agreement; adoption of this approach would remove a major difference between the two bills and the two chambers.

Agreement in conference was also a major goal of conference chairman Carl Perkins (D, Ky.). Conference success was crucial to him and was seen in terms of two basic overriding goals: to get a bill out of conference and to have it subsequently approved by both chambers. Perkins was politically realistic in his awareness that the House would have to concede to the Senate on some of the major issues. Yet, in order to win the approval of the entire House for the conference report, it would also have to appear that House conferees had engaged in a hard, determined fight. Perkins used several techniques to attain his twin goals. First, he made effective use of his scheduling and procedural powers as conference chairman to build consensus among the House and Senate conferees. For example, he systematically moved the conference committee in sequence through the "conference books" detailing differences between the bills. This had the effect of leaving the more controversial issues—printed at the end of the volumes—to be decided last. He was further quite willing to put aside a contentious issue and move on to the next if agreement could not be easily reached. These and similar methods led to a growing sense of accomplishment in the conference and a building of momentum as agreement was reached on many relatively minor issues before the more difficult ones came up. Arriving at a consensus on the more divisive issues after so much conference progress would then seem more imperative. Perkins also ensured that important issues were fully and adequately debated. Even if there were broadly similar conference views on a major issue, Perkins used his influence to hold off on a formal agreement—especially one favoring the Senate position. In this way, the appearance was given to the House that its chamber delegation had indeed fought long and hard in conference. Chairman Perkins was primarily concerned with getting conference agreement on a bill and making sure that the bill was acceptable to the House; he was not extensively worried about its substantive issue content.

In most areas under consideration, conference agreement was reached quickly. This happened in one of two ways. When a basic consensus already existed on an approach, all that was involved was merely choosing the most appropriate language from either the House or Senate versions. Quick agreement was also reached in some areas where a few conferees felt strongly while the remainder of their colleagues were neutral. The members with intense opinions would negotiate among themselves and come up with an acceptable agreement that the whole conference would then approve. These two methods were used to settle many of the differences expeditiously and with no real problem. Much time and effort in the conference, however, involved tough bargaining on a limited subset of deeply contentious issues. It is upon these important and controversial differences that the remainder of this case study will focus.

Occupational education, community colleges, and state planning were three important issues where conference agreement proved difficult to achieve. Since these three areas were related and very complex, they were passed by when the higher education provisions were first considered in conference. Later, however, the conferees were forced to address these topics with all their complexity and interrelationships. The House bill contained a provision to assist occupational education through a program of federal grants; the Senate bill did not have such language. The Senate bill, on the other hand, offered an improvement program for community colleges. Such a program did not exist in the House bill. An even trade, of incorporating both items in the conference compromise legislation, did not seem readily feasible because different state planning provisions complicated the two issues. In the House bill, state planning would be carried out by a "broadly and equitably representative" agency. This agency would also administer the occupational education grant program and could set up a separate committee on community colleges. The Senate's measure on state planning provided for a state agency called the State Higher Education Committee to plan federally funded programs in each state. It could also apply for grants for the purpose of comprehensive planning in postsecondary education. A community college committee would be established for specific planning in this area but, under the Senate version, as part of the state overall Higher Education Committee.

The higher education associations were concerned about various aspects of the state planning issue. They favored strong state planning but, inexplicably, generally failed to follow this issue closely during conference. One exception was the chancellor of the University of Maine, Don McNeil, a leader in higher education who focused on this issue in light of problems foreseen for his state. Early in the conference, McNeil's chief administrative assistant, Aims McGuiness, distributed to the conferees the results of a study he had done that stressed how various alternatives would affect Maine. McGuiness also made personal contacts in Washington, including conversations with Congressman William Hathaway of Maine, a former member of the House Eudcation and Labor Committee. Hathaway sent a letter to the conferees advocating that states be allowed great flexibility in the administrative device to be used for planning. Thus, despite the reservations of many higher education interests, the only sustained lobbying on the state planning issue proved to be the relatively limited efforts by Chancellor McNeil and his administrative assistant.

The complexity of the planning issue made it difficult to come to an agreement on these three interwoven substantive areas. Congressman Lloyd Meeds (D, Wash.) finally proposed that the staff attempt to work out the differences between the House and Senate approaches. Meeds's suggestion was agreed to by the rest of the conferees. The staff produced a first document, which was not accepted because of many unresolved questions. A second draft had some of the previous rough spots worked out and fared much better. This staff-produced compromise document was considered in much the same way as the rest of the bill, item by item. This gave the conferees a chance to consider and amend individual provisions instead of being faced with accepting in toto a staff-produced package compromise. The final agreement managed to incorporate major aspects of both the community college program of the Senate and the House bill's federal grants to aid occupational education. In addition, state planning was handled in this manner: in order for a state to receive funds for either community colleges or occupational education, a representative planning agency would be established to designate the manner and purpose for which such funds would be spent. The agency's title would be the 1202 Commission, and it would also receive grants to plan post–high school education on a comprehensive, statewide basis. This arrangement balanced House and Senate preferences and also reflected the views of Maine more than those of the relatively inactive higher education associations. Thus, the important issues of community colleges, occupational education, and state planning were resolved in large part in response to the views of the one outside interest providing input—the staff and the chancellor of the University of Maine.

The Basic Grant program was another significant matter with which the conference had to deal. It was first considered at the third conference session. The Basic Grant provision was the pet program of Senator Claiborne Pell (D, R.I.), but there was no corresponding language in the House bill. Pell was determined to make his program part of the final conference bill, and he had the unified backing of his Senate colleagues. The House delegation was divided on the issue. Most of the House Democrats, led by Edith Green, were opposed because they thought the Basic Grant feature would diminish funds for existing programs such as the Educational Opportunity Grants (EOG), Work Study, and direct federal loans. On the other hand, House Republicans led by Quie and his Democratic allies Brademas and Thompson generally supported the Basic Grant provisions of the Senate bill. Thus, the Basic Grant plan initially had support from the full Senate delegation and from half the House side. Approval of the program depended upon the ability of the Quie-Brademas alliance to get one more vote from the House conferees. This would require assurances that the existing programs would be maintained. The Basic Grant issue, then, became a matter involving both the funding level for the grant program itself and the funding levels of the existing programs.

Even though there was general support for the Basic Grant approach in principle, agreement would not come easily. An initial proposal determining the funding levels of the Basic Grant and existing programs was offered to the Senate conferees by Representative Brademas on behalf of the House delegation. The senators rejected this House compromise plan because they were concerned it would prevent the Basic Grant program from getting the strongest start possible. The Senate conferees then offered a counterproposal that funded existing programs of Work Study at 80 percent, direct federal loans at 80 percent, and the EOG at 50 percent of existing levels. This proposal was the same proposal Brademas had earlier made to his delegation; the House members, however, had amended it to 100–100–75, which were the levels Brademas had proposed to the Senate. Following the Senate stand, the House conferees agreed, by a vote of 11 to 9, to the Senate 80–80–50 formula. The desperately needed eleventh vote came from Representative Philip Burton (D, Cal.). Brademas earlier that day had attacked the Nixon administration's antibusing legislation. Because of this position he won the gratitude and support of Burton, a strong civil rights supporter. Between the afternoon and evening conference sessions, Burton gave his conference committee proxy to Brademas instead of to Green, as he had previously done. After the conference vote, Green angrily accused Brademas of voting Burton's proxy in a manner that Burton did not support. Green also indicated that because of this, she would not sign the conference report. The carrying out of such a threat could seriously hinder the adoption of the report in the House because of Green's standing as an expert in the area of higher education policy. Although the Basic Grant and existing program funding levels had been approved, it was a narrow and uncomfortable conference victory. In this atmosphere the conferees agreed informally to allow additional amendments to be proposed at a later time. Clearly, the issue was not closed.

On April 11, conference discussion of the Basic Grant and current program issues was reopened. The level of protection of existing programs was still very much in contention. In light of the slim margin of support for the Basic Grant language among House conferees, Senator Pell told Representatives Thompson and Brademas in an informal meeting that he was willing to provide higher levels of support for the current programs. The two House Democrats readily agreed because more protection for existing programs would likely result in greater House conferee support. A larger House conference margin of victory would significantly aid the conference report on the House floor.

Besides the nagging question of levels of support for existing programs, another concern was now raised by the House parliamentarian. It regarded an earlier conference deletion of a limitation in the Basic Grant formula; the deletion struck language that specified that no grant could exceed half of the cost of attendance at the school of a student's choice. Quie had proposed deletion of this language in an amendment on March 27 that had been accepted by the conference. But with this deletion, the conference bill could face rejection in the House on the grounds that removing the limitation went beyond the scope of the legislation as passed in both houses—a clear violation of House rules. To avoid such a point of order being raised on the House floor, Quie proposed a substitute for the half-cost limitation. This substitute provided that the individual grant be $1,400 minus a family's contribution, but could not surpass a student's need. Need was determined as the total cost of attending a particular school less family contribution. Quie thought this new formula was fairer than his previous half-cost formula. Despite Quie's views, the senators opposed his new proposal because they feared it would reduce the Basic Grant program too much.

In its deliberations on the Basic Grant proposals, the conference was now left with two unresolved issues: protection for existing programs and half-cost versus half-need. As the conference continued, Brademas suggested to the House conferees that they return to the guarantee levels for existing programs of 100–100–75 percent. He also formally proposed the Quie half-need formula. Green moved an amendment that funded all the existing programs at 100 percent, only to lose on a House delegation tie vote of 10–10. The House conferees then agreed to the Brademas proposal on a voice vote and offered it to the Senate delegation. The Senators, however, refused to accept it and countered with a proposal that would decrease the protection of existing programs yearly. The House unanimously rejected this counterproposal. The Basic Grant and existing programs tangle remained. There were, however, now some tentative indications that an agreement might come about if the Senate were willing to give the House additional explicit reassurance of funding for present programs.

Because of this temporary stalemate, Chairman Perkins set the Basic Grant issues aside for a while in order to get the conference back on track. He moved on to less controversial issues until, on May 4, a final conference compromise on the Basic Grant controversy was worked out. The Senate accepted funding for current programs at the House-proposed 100–100–75 percent levels. The issue of half-cost versus half-need was also resolved by providing that if the Basic Grant program were fully funded, the half-cost limitation would be used; if the program was not fully funded, the half-need limitation would go into effect. With this complex arrangement providing the vehicle for bicameral agreement, there was broad satisfaction among the conferees. Each side had been able to gain something of what it had wanted and, despite various setbacks, one of the most central features of the higher education legislation had been adopted.

Institutional aid, an issue as important and divisive as the Basic Grant controversies, still needed to be resolved in conference. Each side again had differing approaches to aid for institutions. The Senate bill favored a "cost of instruction" approach. Under this method, the federal government would reimburse postsecondary schools for admitting students who were federally aided. The federal government would pay for the additional costs that institutions undertook in admitting these students, since tuition reimbursement alone would not cover the entire cost of education. On the other hand, the House legislation provided for "capitation grants" in which aid was based on enrollments. Under this formula, more money would be paid as the educational level of the student increased.

The question of institutional aid brought forth alliances similar to those that had emerged on the Basic Grant issue. Representatives Brademas, Quie, and their supporters favored the cost of instruction formula of the Senate bill, whereas Green and most of the House delegation stood fast for the House capitation grant approach. A preliminary conference discussion on the subject in late March brought forth a tentative consensus in favor of the Senate cost of instruction plan. Despite this seeming early agreement, House conferees Quie and Brademas were fearful that the Senate side would shift toward Green's capitation approach. Their concern that the Senate conferees might do so seemed well grounded because no senator had strong views regarding the cost of instruction method, and many thought such a compromise would be necessary to win House conferee support of the strongly backed Senate Basic Grant plan.

Eventually the course that institutional aid would take was influenced by an event outside the conference. On April 12, Representative Edith Green made a remarkable speech on the House floor in which she vehemently accused her fellow House conferees of giving in completely to the Senate side, with little regard for their parent chamber's views. She also predicted that the emerging conference legislation was unlikely to be acceptable to a majority of the House. Conference chairman Carl Perkins was angry and insulted by Green's speech and became convinced that she was determined to kill the bill that he was determined to pass. Chairman Perkins then changed his position from the relatively neutral leader of the House delegation to a conference activist helping Representatives Quie and Brademas. Previously Perkins had not taken sides among the House conferees and had been willing to see either Green's faction or the Quie-Brademas alliance emerge victorious. The addition of House committee chairman Perkins to the Quie-Brademas alignment would change the entire outcome of the conference.

Informal conference negotiations on institutional aid took place next among Representatives Quie, Brademas, Perkins, and Senator Pell. In the third week of April, a method of solving the institutional aid question was put forth by Representative Brademas. The proposal, developed by his administrative assistant James Mooney, became known as the Mooney Cocktail. It divided the funds for institutional aid three ways: (1) 45 percent of the funds would be granted based on the number of students a school enrolled who received the Basic Grant, (2) 45 percent would be distributed based on the amount of money students at an institution were getting from existing programs, and (3) the remaining 10 percent of funds would be awarded on a "per capita basis for each postgraduate student." Thus, institutional aid would consist mainly of the cost of instruction approach, with a small portion of it also granted according to the capitation method.

Representative Quie and the Senate conferees found the Brademas proposal on institutional aid to be acceptable. The only question left to be decided was how to link it to the Basic Grant program. In the Senate bill, student aid had received a higher priority than institutional aid, and no funds for the latter were allowed unless the Basic Grant program was fully funded. This was known as the Priority Amendment. Informal agreement was now reached that the Priority Amendment would apply only to the 45 percent of institutional aid that related to the Basic Grant and that institutional aid payments could be made when the Basic Grant program was funded at 50 percent.

The entire package on institutional aid was worked out informally by the Senate conferees and the Quie-Brademas House alliance. In fact, this group had by now become a House-Senate coalition of considerable power. Representatives Quie and Brademas no longer needed to worry about where they would get their eleventh House vote since House Chairman Perkins had joined their side. Green, however, was largely unaware of these informal negotiations and agreements, as were the major higher education associations, all of which favored in some manner the capitation approach. Likewise, the Nixon administration was also left out of the dealings, which took place in highly informal and discreet negotiations between individual conferees and among groups of conferees. Institutional aid was being worked out in an unofficial way parallel to the official conference proceedings, in a process that excluded those who would disagree with the cost of instruction method. These informal agreements, however, would not be brought before the conference for official approval until the final conference meeting.

The last divisive issue of the conference, one that would also be settled only at the very end, was busing. This was an issue of intense national public attention as part of the heated debate over race relations; it had reached a crisis stage by the end of 1971. The argument over busing was seen as one basically between the antibusers, whose stance was to slow the process and lessen the impact of desegregation, and the "antibusers," who wanted to maintain the role of the federal government in desegregation and supported busing as a means to accomplish desegregation ends. The House bill incorporated several antibusing amendments. This included language providing that:

1. Federal district court orders requiring busing for the purpose of integration would not go into effect until after sufficient time had elapsed for all appeals to be exhausted.
2. The federal government could not spend money appropriated for education for the purpose of promoting racial balance.
3. The federal government could not use educational funds to initiate planned racial desegregation.

Busing had been a major issue during adoption of the Senate bill as well, and the result had been the adoption by that chamber of a set of busing amendments much weaker but similar to those in the House.

Prior to the final conference session, busing was heavily debated in various informal discussions among the members of the now dominant House-Senate coalition. Congressman Green and her allies were not included. These informal sessions produced a variety of differing positions, but no clear conference consensus. Although the conferees had successfully worked their way through the difficult decisions on higher education, the discussions on busing brought home the sobering reality that the legislative honeymoon was over. As an issue embroiled in national controversy, busing had the potential of deadlocking the conference at its very conclusion and obstructing final agreement.

The final session of the conference began on May 16, 1972, at 2 P.M. The atmosphere was dominated by the unresolved busing issue. As the session began, an immediate recess was called so that the senators could caucus. Chairman Perkins met with the senators and urged them to be less rigid in their position on busing. The House chairman's pleas were not successful, for once in conference the Senate conferees refused to accept the stringent busing provisions of the House legislation.

Apparently deadlocked on busing, the conference instead took up other undecided issues more narrowly focused on higher education. The conferees approved a variety of specific measures; it took the conference, however, the rest of the afternoon and a good part of the evening to reach these agreements. As the day was ending, the conferees returned to the busing issue in a mood now emphasizing consensus and a desire for final agreement. There were twelve specific issues on busing and school desegregation with which the conference had to deal. It would be necessary to devise a package of these issues that a majority of both chambers would accept. The matter was further complicated because the House members had been instructed twice by their chamber to uphold the House position on busing. Although many of the House conferees would have personally preferred the weaker Senate position on busing, they felt unable to act on their views because of their chamber's repeated explicit instructions.

Busing proposals and counterproposals continued to be debated late that evening and into the next morning. During these long hours of conference deliberations, little ground was gained. Increasingly some conferees thought that the conference might well fail to reach final agreement. But finally, as argument, compromise, determination for success, and sheer exhaustion blurred together, the conferees began to move toward possible compromise. As 3:00 A.M. neared, only two major issues were left to be resolved. They both concerned the Broomfield Amendment to the House bill, which delayed federal court orders for the purpose of achieving racial balance until all appeals were exhausted. The Senate bill had a similar provision in the Scott-Mansfield Amendment, but it differed in that it set a finite expiration date of July 30, 1973, as the time limit for appeals. The Broomfield Amendment contained no time limit, and it also applied to court orders aimed at balancing a school district racially that involved the transfer of students within the district. The Senate provision did not apply to court orders involving the transfer of students, and the senators wanted this eliminated from the Broomfield Amendment. The House, however, insisted that no alterations of the Broomfield Amendment would be acceptable or could be considered—especially in light of House instructions.

Representative Brademas eventually came up with a solution to this dispute. He proposed to set an expiration date of January 1, 1974 (rather than July 30, 1973), and to retain the word "transfer" in the bill. This compromise would give a time limit to the Senate conferees, although one that was somewhat later than they had wanted. The House would get the provision applied to the transfer of students within a district. The House members voted 10-7 to accept the Brademas proposal, but the Senate failed to approve it in a tied 5-5 vote. The votes of two absent senators could have made a difference in this vote, but the senators holding their proxies were uncertain how their absent colleagues would have wished to have voted. As a result proxy votes for these two senators were not cast. In the very early hours that morning, the two absent senators, Richard Schweiker (R, Pa.) and Harrison Williams (D, N.J.), were roused out of bed to be asked how they wanted their proxies to be voted on the Brademas compromise. Their decisions could prolong the deadlock—or resolve the conference impasse on busing. Both Senators Schweiker and Williams gave instructions that their proxy votes be cast for the Brademas compromise; the deadlock was broken and the overall bill was saved. With the approval of the Brademas proposal, the troublesome busing issue could now be put aside. The conference seemed finally to have gotten out of the legislative woods.

The conferees next turned their attention to the remaining conference issues. Most of these were minor and presented no difficulty. The institutional aid agreement was formally considered for the first time. Discussion on it lasted no more than five minutes. The quick give and take that took place on institutional aid had been previously staged, and the conference ratified the agreement with ease. Green was silent as she realized not only that she had been defeated on this important issue, but that she had also been left out of the negotiations on matters so important to her. Several other proposals were then considered and readily disposed of. The mood of the conference was light and easy despite the extremely late hour, and virtually nothing appeared likely to keep it from concluding successfully.

It was well past 3:00 A.M. now and almost all the final issues had been resolved. The conference was winding down, and several members slipped out to go home to sleep. The number of House conferees was down to the minimum needed to maintain a quorum. Representative Ogden Reid (R, N.Y.) then left, and the House delegation no longer had a quorum. It was the vindictive Representative Green who first noticed this and quickly raised a point of order. Her wish apparently was to make one final fight with the intent of possibly rallying support for her views at a later time. Without a quorum, the conference would be unable to finish its work that morning, with possible serious problems for the emerging agreement. Fortunately, Reid's staff assistant had stayed behind, and, realizing the crisis, found Congressman Reid still in the outside hall, frantically explained the consequences of his absence, and convinced him to return. Reid reappeared just in time to reestablish the necessary quorum, and the conference was saved from last-minute collapse at the hands of Representative Green. The rest of the unfinished conference matters were taken care of quickly. As dawn neared, the exhausted conferees at long last successfully completed conference negotiations and agreed on the final conference version of the 1972 Education Amendments Act.

As it turned out, an additional meeting of the conferees was called on May 18 to reapprove the actions of the all-night conference proceedings. Chairman Perkins feared that Representative Green might still challenge the conference report based on the post-3 A.M. temporary lack of a quorum, even though a quorum had quickly and officially been reestablished. Although this move was perhaps unnecessary, Perkins wanted the House to be assured of the legitimacy of the decisions made in the conference. At this brief meeting, final approval for the conference work was secured from both House and Senate delegations, and the conference was officially over. It had taken some two months, twenty-one conference meetings, and close to eighty hours of negotiations to produce this successful conclusion.

Summary Observations

A number of important factors allowed the conference finally to reach an agreement. First, as noted earlier, the skillful use by Chairman Perkins of his procedural and scheduling powers was a factor that promoted the consensus crucial to obtaining the bill. As the conference progressed and agreements were reached, the conferees developed a sense of accomplishment and the incentive to continue the process of bicameral accommodation. Second, the conferee selection process produced a divided House delegation when Congressman Quie selected Republicans sympathetic to his views, which were compatible with the Senate's. Quie's House bloc would prove to be the key for House-Senate agreement. The third factor promoting consensus was the development of a bipartisan alliance on the House side between the House Republicans and Democrats Brademas and Thompson in support of much of the Senate position. In addition, the political skills of Representatives Quie and Brademas made this alliance possible. Finally, Congressman Green's alienation of House Chairman Perkins with her inflammatory speech on the House floor provoked Perkins to come to the aid of Representatives Quie and Brademas. This hostility was a significant development, for as Quie and Brademas gained the support of a majority of the House conferees, the views of Representative Green began to be isolated and ignored. The combination of these four major factors, then, contributed to the success of the 1972 Education Amendments Act in conference.[6]

---

6. The conference report containing the compromise version of the 1972 Education Amendments Act as painfully and painstakingly worked out in conference was subsequently approved by both houses of Congress and signed into law by President Nixon on June 23, 1972.

C. Two "Hello and Good-Bye" Conferences of 1979

Most conferences are nowhere as lengthy and complex as the 1972 higher education negotiations just examined. True, the major conference, by its very significance, usually will receive the greatest amount of journalistic and public attention—so much as to lead to the impression that conferences generally are of this character. More often, however, conferences are little-publicized proceedings of legislative technicians attempting to patch up House-Senate differences.

Among the case studies in this chapter are several examples of the major conference—for example, the 1982 Tax Increase Conference and the Gramm-Rudman Conferences of 1985. Also included are illustrations of the less prominent conference, including one account of a Typical Low-Intensity Appropriations Conference. Here we consider a special type of the less prominent conference—what we termed in chapter 7 the Hello Good-Bye conference.

The Hello and Good-Bye conference is a quite brief conference proceeding, often consisting of one session sometimes only minutes long, in which conferees meet essentially to ratify agreements or understandings previously reached through informal discussions, or just to clear up minor bicameral differences of no particular general interest. Especially when the conference is confirming understandings already worked out, the meeting may proceed as if by script, with representatives from each chamber taking turns in proposing amendments and compromise language. (Sometimes one chamber's representatives will even briefly hold out for their body's views, then "reluctantly" yield in order to establish a record of determination in fighting for their chamber's provisions.)

The hallmarks of Hello and Good-Bye conferences are their brevity and lack of controversy. Conferees are not working out significant differences between House and Senate legislation; rather they are shaking hands on adjustments previously worked out or generally acceptable and obviously necessary. Social pleasantries and personal greetings are more evident than hard bargaining and defending of preferences. Sometimes the conference is so brief that arrival greetings and best wishes upon departure seem almost a single social interaction.

In the following paragraphs, we consider two examples of Hello and Good-Bye conferences, both drawn from Capitol Hill events in 1979.[7] In one, the central issue turned out to involve alligators—Louisiana alligators, to be precise. In the other, the focus was on a more weighty matter: the creation of a new federal government department, the U.S. Department of Education.

The Endangered Species Act of 1979[8]

Legislation passed both the House and Senate in 1979 to continue federal programs designed to protect animals threatened by extinction. Existing statutory authority was

---

7. These two accounts are adapted by permission from summaries based on personal observations and interviews contained in a research paper by a Lawrence University undergraduate student: John R. Stoner, "The Congressional Conference Committee as a Center in Determining Legislative Outcomes" (1979).

8. The following five paragraphs are based on personal observation of the conference proceedings on the Endangered Species Act of 1979 by John R. Stoner.

expiring, and the House and Senate had enacted slightly differently worded bills extending the Endangered Species Act for three years.

Minor differences in language between House and Senate bills are often worked out informally without a conference when one chamber defers to the other's language. In this case, however, one key House member, Representative (now Senator) John B. Breaux (D, La.), was determined to secure a modification of the Endangered Species Act; in order to accommodate him, a conference was deemed necessary.

As soon as the conference convened, Representative Breaux expressed his concern that the act made difficult Louisiana's traditional industry of exporting alligators (or more precisely, alligator skins). It was fine to protect endangered species, but the alligator industry was an important source of jobs in some areas of Louisiana. Representative Breaux expressed his views forcibly.

The other conferees had no fixed or strong views on alligators and requested staff to propose a solution. Committee staffers huddled for a moment and came up with an ingenious compromise putting the Endangered Species Scientific Authority into the Department of the Interior and creating a new advisory commission on alligators to operate independently outside the department. The scientific authority would protect endangered species; the advisory commission would ensure that the alligator industry was not curtailed by the scientific authority.

By this administrative creativity, Louisiana's alligator industry was protected and Representative Breaux mollified. The entire conference meeting lasted about fifteen minutes, which was barely enough time to get everyone settled into the room. The conference report incorporating the changes improvised by staff in conference and otherwise reconciling House-Senate language was subsequently duly approved by House and Senate. Once the president signed it, the Endangered Species Act was renewed for the next three years.

The Department of Education Organization Act[9]

Another legislative achievement of 1979 received much greater media and political attention: the creation of a separate cabinet-level Department of Education. This administrative reorganization had long been proposed, most notably by Abraham Ribicoff while he was serving as secretary of the gargantuan Department of Health, Education and Welfare in the early 1960s. Now, a decade and a half later, Ribicoff, as a prominent U.S. senator, and more important, as chairman of the Senate Governmental Affairs Committee, was in a position to be a catalyst for this reorganization. By 1979, a set of favorable conditions for structural change seemed present. Senator Ribicoff's position now enabled him to further congressional action, many education groups had lined up behind the change, President Jimmy Carter had endorsed the creation of a separate Education Department, and there appeared to be general—but diffuse—public acceptance for the step.

9. The following account is based on John R. Stoner's personal observation of conference proceedings on the Department of Education Organization Act and interviews with staff members of the Senate Committee on Governmental Affairs and the House Committee on Government Operations.

Senator Ribicoff introduced Senate legislation establishing a Department of Education early in 1979; after predictably friendly hearings by his committee and a favorable committee report, the bill passed the Senate by a substantial 72 to 21 vote. The Senate bill was essentially a clean one, devoid of extraneous amendments.

In the House, things had not gone so smoothly. The chairman of the House Government Operations Committee, Jack Brooks (D, Tex.), was not sympathetic to the idea; in fact, legislation similar to the Senate bill barely survived in the committee and was favorably reported by it to the House floor by only a 19 to 18 vote. During House consideration, numerous amendments that altered the bill drastically were offered and accepted. Especially controversial were floor-adopted provisions encouraging school prayer and limiting school busing. Bill supporters believed that conservative opponents in the House were attempting to make the bill unpalatable in order to erode support for the legislation among liberals. Following these developments, the heavily amended bill was passed by the House, but only by the alarmingly close vote of 210 to 206. Conference compromise would be certainly necessary to resolve serious interchamber differences in bill contents; changes would also clearly be necessary in order to buttress paper-thin House support for the legislation.

The conference would not occur free of additional pressures. Requests for a conference are usually granted in the House by unanimous consent. There had been, however, objection and a rule from the House Rules Committee providing for a conference had to be introduced and formally adopted. In addition, the House had voted, by a substantial margin of 263 to 156, to instruct its conferees to insist that the House amendments be included in the conference report. Prospects for easy conference agreement on a compromise bill looked uncertain, if not bleak.

Chairman Ribicoff selected five senators (including himself) to be conferees;[10] all were strongly committed to the Senate bill and equally opposed to the House amendments. In the House, nine conferees were selected,[11] including all the members of the subcommittee that had dealt with the legislation. One reason the House delegation was so large was that the Democratic leadership was wary of possible defections and wished to have sufficient votes to ensure support for the House position.[12]

Prior to the official convening of the conference committee, the professional staffs of both the House and Senate committees met to see what could be done to facilitate agreement. The Senate committee staff members were nervous going into these preconference meetings because of the narrow 210 to 206 vote on the House floor. In light of

---

10. The Senate conferees were Senators Ribicoff, John Glenn (D, Ohio), Carl Levin (D, Mich.), Charles Percy (R, Ill.), and Jacob Javits (R, N.Y.). Formally, the two Republican conferees were not selected by Democratic Chairman Ribicoff; practically, however, he ensured that the Republican Senate conferees were in agreement with his legislation and opposed to the House amendments. (Washington interview with staff member of the Senate Committee on Governmental Affairs).

11. The House conferees were Representatives Jack Brooks (D, Tex.), Don Fuqua (D, Fla.), William Moorhead (D, Pa.), Dante Fascell (D, Fla.), Fernand St. Germain (D, R.I.), Elliott Levitas (D, Ga.), Frank Horton (R, N.J.), John Erlenborn (R, Ill.), and Arlan Stangeland (R, Minn.).

12. Washington interview with staff member of the House Committee on Government Operations.

this weak House commitment to the bill (and also taking into account that chamber's instructions to the House conferees to stand firm on the House amendments), clearly a Senate strategy of ditching the House amendments in favor of a simple, "clean" bill would not be practical. Rather, House-Senate differences would have to be worked out item by item, but with an eventual bill tending toward House preferences.[13]

During these meetings between the staffs, the two chamber-adopted versions of the legislation were read, provision by provision. The staff members jointly proceeded to identify each difference as either major or minor. In order for an issue to be classified as major, a staffer would simply indicate that it was a major concern. Everything else in disagreement between the bills was considered minor. During these lengthy daily staff meetings preceding the conference, many of the differences were quickly resolved.

As staffers turned to the more important and potentially contentious differences, the Senate staff made repeated concessions to House positions, on both substantive matters and on particularistic concerns. It was clear to those on the Senate side that, if they truly wished to get a bill—as their committee chairman Senator Ribicoff very much wanted—their bargaining position was weak. Unless the House could be bought off by a combination of substantive concessions and specific inducements, there would be little likelihood that House conferees would (or could) support a compromise bill. Further, legislation that did not reflect most House goals would not prevail on the House floor during chamber consideration of the committee report. Consequently, on item by item, the Senate staff agreed to language and provisions incorporated from the House bill or supported by the House staff. (Remember, these were all staff negotiations; the conference committee itself had yet to meet.)

In addition, the Senate and House staffs identified and worked into the compromise language a series of specific provisions of particular interest to each of the House conferees. The acknowledged (but discreetly stated) purpose was to seduce the representatives one by one, and in effect, to "buy" their votes.[14] An example of this was a specific provision concerning a junior college in Florida. This school had for some time administered the affairs of a college in the Panama Canal Zone, a relationship threatened both by the new Panama Canal Treaty and by powers conferred upon the proposed new Department of Education. Concern about this specific matter had been expressed by the congressman whose district included the junior college, Representative Don Fuqua (D, Fla.), a key House Democratic conferee. A provision was added to the bill to ensure that the junior college would be able to retain its relationship, and Representative Fuqua became a supporter of the emerging conference compromise.[15] Issue by issue, concession by concession, inducement by inducement, a consensus began to emerge on both the House and Senate sides in favor of the staff-generated compromise draft.

Finally, once the staff bill-drafting process was complete and the necessary conference votes were nailed down (or perhaps, one might say, nailed into the legislation),

13. Washington interview with staff member of the Senate Committee on Governmental Affairs.
14. Ibid.
15. Washington interview with staff member of the House Committee on Government Operations.

the conference committee on the Department of Education Organization Act itself finally met. The script had been written to ensure a successful conference,[16] and little time was required. The entire conference on this quite complex legislation took only one session of about two hours. The script was followed with little deviation, and there was no doubt regarding the outcome. The conference was, in fact, a formality; those favoring creation of the new department were now clearly in control.[17]

Following the successful conference, attention turned to the Senate where the outcome was never in doubt. Senator Ribicoff watched confidently as the Senate, acting first, approved the conference report overwhelmingly by a 69 to 22 vote. Next, the action shifted to the House, where floor support had been weak and prospects for approval of the conference report were uncertain. It was at this time that presidential support for the departmental creation became important. President Carter personally called a number of undecided representatives to ask for their support for the conference agreement. It was understood that the White House made tickets available to some representatives to see the pope at the White House during the upcoming weekend. Discussions also reportedly took place between the White House and key congressmen concerning temporary census patronage jobs that could be available to their constituents the next year.[18]

Despite presidential pressures and inducements and support by House conferees for the conference report, the vote in the House was quite close. Deliberately put in the position of acting last on the conference report so it would be in the public spotlight, the House narrowly adopted the compromise legislation on a roll call of 215 votes to 201, with the margin of victory for the conference report being attributed by both House and Senate staffers largely to intense lobbying from the White House.

With a presidential signature assured, Senator Ribicoff would finally see, after many years, the creation of a Department of Education. This creation, however, was not made in heaven, but rather was thanks to a combination of presidential favors, senatorial concessions to the House on a number of substantive matters, including most of the House amendments, and the classic remedy of adding special sweeteners for specific conferees. Legislation, in fact, is seldom written in heaven; conference compromises, however, are especially prone to be shaped in light of political realities.

16. Washington interviews with staff members of the House Committee on Government Operations and the Senate Committee on Governmental Affairs.
17. Ibid.
18. Washington interview with staff member of the House Committee on Government Operations.

D. The 1982 Tax Increase Conference

Conference committee proceedings are often focused on matters more weighty than alligators in Louisiana, junior colleges in Florida, or personality clashes and power plays between conferees. Sometimes conferences even focus on major policy questions such as taxes or—as in later case studies—defense weapon systems and deficit reduction plans. The following case study[19] deals with such a mainstream type of substantive conference, in this case bicameral negotiations dealing with tax increase legislation in 1982. This conference was *usual* in that in its concern with taxes, it was dealing with one of the perennials of political life (the other perennial concern, death, being less directly susceptible to legislative influence). The 1982 conference was also *unusual* because the conference committee found itself trying to adjust House-Senate views on a bill which the House had not considered or passed. This extraordinary situation was due to the legislative and political peculiarities of the moment, but to be fully understood requires an awareness of earlier events.

Background

In 1981, Congress enacted one of the centerpieces of the Reagan administration's economic program: a three-year tax cut titled the Economic Recovery Tax Act. The measure, skewed to benefit corporations and wealthy individuals, was intended to stimulate economic recovery by promoting savings and investment. Deficits were not expected to rise because the revival of economic growth spawned by the tax cut would generate additional revenues for the Treasury. The thrust of this approach was derived from what has been called the "supply side" theory of economics. Unfortunately for the national economy, no quick recovery followed passage of the act. Instead, unemployment soared, deficits skyrocketed, interest rates remained high, and the nation's sense of economic peril rose. At least in the short run, it appeared that the tax cut had slashed revenues too drastically during a period when recession was mandating extra outlays—for example, for unemployment benefits.

The very next year, therefore, saw an effort to correct the course. When the administration sent its Fiscal Year 1983 budget to Capitol Hill with huge projected deficits of $91.5 billion, it was subjected to sharp criticism from Republican members. "My concern with the President's budget," said Senate Budget Chairman Pete Domenici, (R, N.M.), "is that if fails to do enough to cut spending and accepts almost benignly what are malignant deficits."[20] After extensive negotiations between con-

---

19. An earlier version of the following account appeared as part of Lawrence D. Longley and Walter J. Oleszek, "The Three Contexts of Congressional Conference Committee Politics: Bicameral Politics Overviewed," paper prepared for delivery at the 1983 Annual Meeting of the American Political Science Association, Chicago, Sept. 1, 1983.

20. Dale Tate, "A Very Difficult Role: Domenici Takes on Reagan from Budget Committee Base," *Congressional Quarterly Weekly Report,* March 6, 1982, p. 509.

gressional leaders and the White House (including ultimately unsuccessful efforts to develop a bipartisan budget by a group of congressmen termed the Gang of 17), President Reagan agreed to support the fiscal plan crafted by Senator Domenici and other Republican leaders. Their budget blueprint called for revenue increases sharply at variance with the orthodoxy of supply side economics.

The president's decision precipitated sharp divisions among many of his congressional and business community allies because it reflected a move away from the tax cut approach that the president had campaigned on in 1980 and had advocated throughout 1981. Furthermore, the president would have to rely heavily for the first time in his administration on Democratic votes, particularly in the House, to pass one of the largest "revenue enhancement" packages in American history.

The multiyear tax increase was essentially fashioned in the Republican Senate, particularly by Robert Dole, chairman of the Senate Finance Committee. Despite many obstacles, such as the reluctance of the six GOP Senate Finance members up for reelection to support tax hikes, Chairman Dole put together a package of revenue raisers that made it through the Finance Committee and the Senate. Part of Senator Dole's strategy in committee was to craft a compromise package behind closed doors, excluding Finance Democrats. Explained Senator Dole, "I knew that if the Republicans couldn't produce a package, we weren't going to get a lot of help from the Democrats."[21]

Subsequently, Senator Dole's bill reached the conference stage through unconventional means and in an economic and political climate traditionally unsuited to tax hikes: a recession and an election year. Yet the tax increase did eventually become law (P.L. 97-248)—in large measure because House and Senate conferees were successful in resolving their differences. Institutional, committee, and individual factors are among the many notable and overlapping forces that affected the outcome of this controversial yet ultimately successful tax conference.

Institutional Factors

The origination clause of the Constitution (Article I, section 7), is distinctly clear in requiring that all revenue measures begin in the House: "All bills for raising revenue shall originate in the House of Representatives; but the Senate may propose or concur with amendments as on other bills." Nevertheless, on July 28, 1982, the House of Representatives voted to go directly to conference with the Senate on a tax increase measure developed solely by the Senate and never considered by either the House chamber or by the House Ways and Means Committee. The absence of any House revenue bill was the result of a deliberate decision by House party and committee leaders; as the *New York Times* reported at the time, "The House comes empty-handed [to conference] because the Democratic leadership months ago put politics above prerogative. With congressional elections coming in November, the leadership decided that

21. Pamela Fessler, "Aftertaste of Dole's Victory: Handling of Tax Bill Upsets Democrats on Finance Panel," *Congressional Quarterly Weekly Report,* July 17, 1982, p. 1705.

the Republican Senate and the Republican White House should initiate anything like a tax increase."[22]

The political concerns of House Democrats with raising taxes in an election year was quite evident; as Bill Alexander (D, Ark.), chief deputy Democratic whip, acknowledged, "I don't want my tracks on this."[23] A number of House Republicans opposed this strategy of bypassing House consideration, fearing that their party would be held to blame for tax increases initiated by the Republican Senate in an election year. One hundred Republican representatives signed a letter to President Reagan lamenting the situation: "This is potentially an explosive scenario politically, because the GOP clearly will take the blame for any tax increase passed by Congress."[24]

House Ways and Means Committee Chairman Dan Rostenkowski (D, Ill.) had initiated the controversial bypass strategy not only as a means of making political capital but also as a device for avoiding deadlock in his committee and on the House floor. Before the chairman formally proposed this unusual procedure, he insisted that some Ways and Means Republicans support the approach. "Obviously," said a Republican committee member, "the chairman didn't want a party-line vote on whether we should abdicate our constitutional responsibilities."[25] After intervention from the White House, which did not mind the Republican-controlled Senate taking the policy lead from the Democratic House, four of the twelve committee Republicans voted with Chairman Rostenkowski to request an immediate conference with the Senate. Thus, the House, in an extraordinary procedure, voted to go directly to conference with the Senate on H.R. 4961 without writing or considering a tax bill of its own. Many House Republicans objected vociferously but to no avail to what amounted to the functional equivalent of bypassing the Constitution.

Asked why the tax increase did not originate in the House, Senator Dole said, "Well, I'll be very honest, because the House didn't want to originate it. And I think the Democrats said, 'Well they control the Senate and they control the White House and if they can't pass it in the Senate why should we mess with it?'"[26] He added, ". . . You can't expect [Rostenkowski] to be the point man for the administration."[27]

There was, to be sure, technical compliance with the Constitution. The Senate attached its tax bill to an obscure House-passed revenue measure, H.R. 4961, a miscellaneous tax bill that had been adopted by the House on December 15, 1981. This measure, however, had never been acted upon by the Senate. The Senate Finance

---

22. Edward Cowan, "A Budget Conference Unlike Others," *New York Times,* August 2, 1982, sec. 2, pp. 1, 23. See also Pamela Fessler, "House Sends Tax Bill Directly to Conference," *Congressional Quarterly Weekly Report,* July 31, 1982, p. 1808; and idem, "House Members' Suit Disputes Constitutionality of '82 Tax Bill," *Congressional Quarterly Weekly Report,* Oct. 30, 1982, pp. 2761–62.

23. *Los Angeles Times,* July 29, 1982, p. 18.

24. Ibid.

25. *Wall Street Journal,* July 28, 1982, p. 3.

26. *Washington Times,* Aug. 27, 1982, p. 2A.

27. Roger H. Davidson and Walter J. Oleszek, "Changing the Guard in the U.S. Senate," *Legislative Studies Quarterly* 9, no. 4 (Nov. 1984):643.

Committee "stripped the bill of all House provisions, most of which had been included in other legislation, leaving only the bill's shell intact"[28] and used this shell as a vehicle for its tax cut proposals.

Representative John Rousselot (R, Cal.), who opposed all tax increases, twice offered privileged House resolutions to return the tax amendments to the Senate on the ground that they violated the origination clause of the Constitution. Each time the House voted to table those resolutions.[29] House Ways and Means Chairman Rostenkowski acknowledged that this "is an unusual procedural step to take . . . and, as chairman of the Committee on Ways and Means, where all revenue-raising measure must originate, I have deep personal misgivings in offering this motion" to go to conference with the Senate on H.R. 4961. But the "severe economic distress and volatile political environment at this moment, in the judgment of the Committee, dictate that we travel this route."[30]

In sum, the conference on the 1982 tax bill was certainly extraordinary in the key respect that there was no House bill at all. The Senate brought a tax bill of some 758 pages to conference while the House brought none. Further, there had been neither House committee hearings or markup nor any chamber floor debate on the revenue package. The only time the House formally considered the tax bill in any fashion was when it later debated and agreed to the conference report.

The absence of a House bill produced procedural jockeying and problems between the chambers. Overall, the lack of a House bill doubtlessly weakened the House's ability to win concessions from the Senate because it lacked bargaining chips for negotiating purposes. The House conferees argued that their conference position was indirectly reflected in tax bills previously reported from the Ways and Means Committee. But Senator Russell Long (La.), ranking Democrat and former chairman of the Finance Committee, objected to that proposition on the ground that such matters were beyond the scope of the conference committee.[31] "I don't think we have any business negotiating on something that the House hasn't enacted," he said.[32] Such a procedure, he argued, might prompt points of order in either chamber that could threaten enactment of the conference report. In the end, while there were certainly some scope violations, nevertheless the "final product looked very much like the bill the Senate approved."[33] In short, the chamber that framed the issue in this case largely framed the outcome as well.

28. Fessler, "House Members' Suit," p. 2761.

29. *Congressional Record*, 97th Cong., 2d sess., July 28 and August 19, 1982. pp. H4476, H6528. A bipartisan group of House members later brought a federal court suit challenging the constitutionality of the 1982 tax bill. See *New York Times*, August 17 and 18, 1982, pp. D17, D20. On December 16, 1982, the District Court in the District of Columbia dismissed the complaint because the House plaintiffs lacked standing and their grievance was with the House.

30. *Congressional Record*, 97th Cong., 2d sess., July 28, 1982, p. H4777.

31. *Scope* is a technical term that binds the conferees to seek compromises between the amounts or versions recommended in the House- and Senate-passed bills.

32. *Wall Street Journal*, Aug. 6, 1982, p. 3.

33. Dale Tate, "Congress Clears $98.3 Billion Tax Increase," *Congressional Quarterly Weekly Report*, Aug. 21, 1982, p. 2043.

Committee Factors

Conferees are almost always selected from the committee or committees that reported (or might have reported) the legislation. In this case, they came from the two tax-writing panels: seven from Senate Finance and eight from House Ways and Means. Practice dictates that although the formal appointing officer is the House Speaker or Senate presiding officer, in reality the conferees are named by the committee chairman.

Given strong opposition in both chambers to the tax bill, both chairmen selected their conferees carefully. Ways and Means Chairman Rostenkowski told his committee colleagues that he would be ruthless concerning who would get to be a conferee: "If you don't back me, you don't get on the bus."[34] Such conferee harmony—natural or contrived as it may be—is an advantage both to committee chairmen and to the representation of chamber views, for conferee delegations that are united have more clout in conference than those that are split on issues.

The conference process gives enormous power to House and Senate delegations, the members of which would decide which revenue provisions to retain, delete, add, or modify. As a consequence, there was enormous interest in the tax conference: "The huge Ways and Means Committee room of the House was jammed with lobbyists, assistants, and reporters as the conferees . . . agonized over each line of the Senate-passed bill. Dole presided at a 60-foot-long walnut table engraved with a giant eagle."[35] The intense interest in the tax decisions of this conference was evidenced by the presence of countless industry representatives both inside and outside the conference chamber, all of them eager to express their views on specific provisions of the legislation. (This press of lobbyists gave rise to the famous report of an aide to Senate Finance Chairman Dole: upon looking into the crowded corridors outside the conference room, the aide exclaimed, "There's wall-to-wall Guccis out there." This episode is recounted, along with other footwear humor, in chapter 3.)

Working long into the night, the conferees dealt with contentious issue after issue. For example, the Senate-passed bill provided for a doubling of the excise tax on packs of cigarettes (from 8 cents to 16 cents). Senator Dole explained to his Senate colleagues, particularly those from tobacco-growing states, that it was his wish to find other revenue raisers and to drop the cigarette tax increase, despite the Senate provision doubling the cigarette tax. Senator Dole then asked the House conferees to agree to eliminate the cigarette excise tax increase. The House conferees, however, overwhelmingly rejected that offer: "I am terribly sorry but at this juncture, the House recedes to the position of the Senate [the doubling of the tax]," replied Chairman Rostenkowski with irony. Senator Dole responded, "I can't quarrel with that decision. We thought there would be a House bill, and we could trade off a few things but there is not any House bill, and we can't trade off what we brought, and we brought the best we could."[36]

House conferees apparently calculated that they had already lost the vote of tobac-

---

34. Edward Cowan, "A Budget Conference Unlike Others," *New York Times,* Aug. 2, 1982, sec. 2, p. 23.
35. *Time,* Aug. 23, 1982, p. 7.
36. *Congressional Record,* 97th Cong., 2d sess., Aug. 16, 1982, p. S10569.

co-state members. Hence, they looked to other means of building conference and chamber support for their position. Extending unemployment benefits for jobless workers was such a provision. Neither chamber had formally adopted such a measure, but the Senate had passed a "sense of the Senate" resolution instructing its conferees to support such an extension. House conferees, too, recognized the attractiveness and value of such an extension, particularly in an election year.[37] Thus, despite earlier scope concerns, both chambers' conferees readily added an unemployment extension provision to the bill not present in the original Senate legislation. In short, House and Senate conferees adhered to conference rules in a flexible fashion as it suited them in order to create a product that would pass the House and Senate.

Individual Factors

Members who can artfully employ political events and circumstances to their advantage are likely to see their personal or chamber position upheld in conference or are at least certain to be major facilitators of conference agreement. By all accounts, Senator Dole and Representative Rostenkowski are highly skillful, seasoned politicians who can fashion agreements that will withstand the pressures of the moment. At times other conferees even urged their leaders to "meet privately to try to work out an agreement on the key issues in dispute."[38] Direct, private negotiations between the committee leaders, it was believed, would best further conference agreement.

Senator Dole was able to craft a tax increase that many commentators believed would be impossible to pass in an election year. His success ran counter to conventional wisdom concerning the impossibility of raising taxes during a recession and just prior to an election. His effort was successful for a variety of reasons. One Senate conferee highlighted several:

> [Senator Dole] did a tremendous job as chairman of the conferees. He worked constantly. I do not know how many hours the conference was in session, but we started early Friday afternoon and went all night Friday night, recessing around 9 A.M. Saturday morning. Then we came back into session at 3:30 Saturday afternoon. We then were in session until almost 3 o'clock Sunday morning. During that entire period, the distinguished Senator from Kansas, Senator Dole, had command of the situation, so to speak, and he spent full time going from one conference to another; there were a multitude of miniconferences going on simultaneously.[39]

Senator Dole also laid the groundwork for his success in conference by including in his tax package many long-time Democratic revenue reform proposals. This strategy made it more difficult for Democrats to launch partisan critiques of the legislation. Noted Representative Rostenkowski, "Let's face it. Republicans wrote a tax bill that has been

---

37. Pamela Fessler, "Tax Bill Sweetener: New Jobless Benefit Program Aids Workers in Every State," *Congressional Quarterly Weekly Report,* Sept. 4, 1982, pp. 2187–88.
38. *Los Angeles Times,* Aug. 15, 1982, pt. 1, p. 1.
39. *Congressional Record,* 97th Cong., 2d sess., Aug. 6, 1982, p. S10574.

in the bottom drawers of Democratic tax reformers for years."[40] Senator Dole pushed the measure as a "reform" that closed numerous unwarranted tax "loopholes" for corporations and wealthy individuals, hence the revenue tax increase bill's self-aggrandizing title: the Tax Equity and Fiscal Responsibility Act of 1982.

For his part, Representative Rostenkowski was cross-pressured by, among other considerations, partisan and personal concerns. On the one hand, Chairman Rostenkowski wanted to avoid having his party attacked in an election year for enacting a tax increase. On the other hand, the chairman wanted to have influence on the legislation. Explained fellow Ways and Means Democrat J. J. Pickle (Tex.), "Danny would like to have his input, so that it can be said that he, Danny Rostenkowski, had his imprint on the bill, so that he didn't let the Republicans write his tax bill. He wants to have some voice in it so historians won't say he didn't do anything on it."[41] In the end, Representative Rostenkowski announced his "active support" for the conference report, and told the press, "I'm like Colonel Bogey [in *The Bridge on the River Kwai*]. I built the bridge. I'll fight the Australians, the British *and* the Americans to save it."[42]

Other Factors

There were scores of other considerations, including additional institutional, committee, and individual factors, that shaped the conference outcome on the tax legislation. Institutionally, for instance, the tax conference was influenced and mandated by the budget reconciliation resolution to meet specified tax-raising and spending-reduction targets. Both chambers also sought to enhance the bargaining leverage of their conferees by issuing them instructions, which the conferees could, of course, feel free to disregard.

President Reagan worked behind the scenes personally to lobby members to support the final conference report. Significantly, he went on national television during prime time to mobilize national support for the tax increase. Democrats particularly had wanted the president to make this television appeal. Such a presidential commitment, they believed, would protect Democrats from charges in the upcoming election of being "taxers and spenders." The administration took other steps to woo Democrats: "The White House offered to send each supportive Democrat a letter from Reagan thanking them for their help. Democratic leaders, however, insisted on two letters from Reagan—one asking for help and then another thank-you note—to provide political insurance. The White House agreed and the first Reagan letters were delivered just before the roll call [vote on the conference report]."[43]

Congressional party leaders in both chambers exerted influence on conference negotiations and passage of the conference report. House Minority Leader Robert Michel (Ill.) faced a rebellion in Republican ranks from conservatives who vehemently opposed the tax increase. Democratic strategists, however, wanted the minority leader and the White House to persuade at least 100 of the 192 Republicans to vote for the tax

40. *Washington Post,* Aug. 3, 1982, p. A17.
41. *New York Times,* Aug. 2, 1982, p. D3.
42. *Wall Street Journal,* Aug. 16, 1982, p. 3.
43. *Los Angeles Times,* Aug. 20, 1982, pt. 1, p. 6.

bill. Some Democrats said they would wait to case their vote until they saw 100 Republican names on the electronic voting "scoreboard" above the House chamber. In the end, 103 Republicans voted for the tax increase.

Finally, interest groups influenced conference negotiations. Conferees, for example, restored tax deductions for business meals (dubbed the three-martini lunch) after intense lobbying by the Hotel and Restaurant Employees International Union. Union officials argued that without the tax deduction, business would drop and restaurant workers would lose their jobs. To the chagrin of the union, however, tax conferees also voted "to tighten up collection of taxes on tips."[44] Interestingly, conferees usually met "unofficially" behind closed doors in order to facilitate their bargaining processes. This prevented the hundreds of lobbyists from watching their deliberations and consequently freed much conference bargaining from this pressure. Interest representatives were welcome to be present (in the halls) to present their views, but the conferees seemed to believe that the best bargaining would occur when lobbyists were kept out of the conference room.

The 1982 Tax Increase conference was truly unusual, if for no other reason than the absence of a House bill. Despite this singular feature, the conference also reflected characteristics more generally common to conference committee politics. Institutional, committee, and individual factors interplayed in the course of the bicameral resolution of differing interchamber expectations. The three contexts of conference committee politics were especially highlighted in this example of bicameral politics.

---

44. *New York Times,* Aug. 15, 1982, p. 1.

E. A Typical Low-Intensity Appropriations Conference

In recounting conferences, one inevitably is drawn to those with dramatic content, such as efforts to secure a tax increase in an election year or to create landmark federal programs to assist higher education. Alternatively, one might tend toward conferences marked by colorful events, such as the use of import duty legislation as a vehicle to aid dependent children or determined efforts to preserve the alligator exporting industry of Louisiana. There is, however, another category of conference committee that is easily overlooked—the often undramatic and uncolorful business of appropriations.

The power of the purse[45] is perhaps Congress's most cherished and fundamental power; certainly decisions by Congress as to how much money will be spent for what programs and under what conditions determine the fortunes of every program and policy of government. Often these decisions are marked by enormous controversy and attention;[46] even more often, however, appropriations decisions are worked out in the conference committee through low-intensity negotiations and adjustments. Such an instance occurred in 1981 concerning appropriations for the governmental operations of the District of Columbia.[47]

Bills appropriating funds for the District of Columbia government for fiscal year 1982 passed both the House and Senate in early November 1981 with little difficulty. The legislation had originated in the House, in accord with long-standing tradition for general appropriations bills.[48] The appropriations measure was approved there by an overwhelming 299 to 105 vote and subsequently passed the Senate on a voice vote after only about thirty minutes of debate. The Senate, however, as the second-acting chamber, adopted a total of forty-two amendments to the House-passed legislation. In accord with the customary sequence of having the House act first on an appropriations conference report, the Senate requested a conference on the bill, to which the House readily agreed.

---

45. *The Power of the Purse,* the seminal study of appropriations politics by Richard F. Fenno, Jr., although published over twenty years ago, still stands as the authoritative work on the topic (Boston: Little, Brown, 1966). Chapter 12 of this volume, "The House and the Senate: The Conference Committee," pp. 616–78, provides rich insights and analyses of the role of conference committee interactions in appropriations policymaking.

46. The ongoing conference committee controversy between the House and the Senate Appropriations Committee Chairmen, Rep. Clarence Cannon (D, Mo.) and Sen. Carl Hayden (D, Ariz.), still remains part of Capitol Hill folklore. That controversy pitted the two powerful, octogenarian chairmen in a dramatic battle that involved institutional pride and prestige and that also delayed the funding of several government agencies for several months. For a discussion of this battle, see chapter 5 above.

47. The following account was written especially for this volume and is published here for the first time. The specific observations about the District of Columbia conference are based on personal observations by one of the authors at the session.

48. The custom of House originations of general appropriations bills is derived from, but not required by, Article I, sec. 7 of the Constitution. This origination clause, as discussed in the preceding case study, requires all revenue-raising measures to begin in the House. Over time, this requirement has been extended by custom also to general appropriations legislation.

NINE MINI-CASE STUDIES

The Conference Meets

The House named ten conferees (six Democrats and four Republicans) and the Senate appointed seven (four Republicans and three Democrats) for the conference on D.C. appropriations. (In fact, many of these conferees, as noted below, would not participate in the conference; they were probably included for traditional rather than effective reasons.)

All the conferees were drawn from that subcommittee of each chamber's Appropriations Committee that handles District of Columbia business. Traditionally, both the House and Senate Appropriations committees select their conferees solely from the subcommittee that reports the legislation. An important reason for this practice, which dates from the nineteenth century, is that seniority on Appropriations subcommittees (unlike subcommittees of the other standing committees of Congress) is as important as that earned on the full committee. Continuity of subcommittee service, in brief, determines who will head those units rather than a member's seniority on the full panel. Appropriations subcommittees also function somewhat like other standing full committees in regard to bill management functions. It is to the Appropriations Committees' and their chambers' advantage to name subcommittee members as conferees, for they know the most about the legislation going to conference and have the responsibility of management of the legislation both prior to and after the conference.

The conference committee had its one and only meeting in a Capitol committee room in mid-November 1981. Eight conferees were present: seven of the ten House representatives, and only one of the seven Senate conferees, Senator Alfonse D'Amato (R, N.Y.), the chairman of the District of Columbia appropriations subcommittee who also served as conference chairman. A partial group of House conferees, in short, would negotiate legislative differences with one representative of the other body, Senator D'Amato. Fewer than ten spectators observed the proceedings; most, it is safe to say, were there to monitor the session on behalf of organizations with a considerable stake in the outcome. Marion Barry, mayor of the District of Columbia, and several of his aides were among those present.

After some preliminary banter among the conferees (Representative William Natcher [D, Ky.], for instance, reminisced about the "good old days" before the fiscal crunch when there was coffee for the conferees), they got down to business. Working from spread sheets that identified the House position and the Senate position on the items in disagreement (the document had been prepared by the staffs of the respective Appropriations subcommittees), the conferees moved with dispatch to compromise their differences. In less than ninety minutes the conference was over. Never was a formal vote taken on any issue nor was a transcript kept of the proceedings. Instead, a friendly atmosphere and considerable rapport between both sides permitted each chamber to achieve substantially all its objectives. Interestingly, the few lengthy exchanges that did occur over fiscal expenditures for certain District activities were between Senator D'Amato and a fellow Republican colleague on the House side.

To reach their accords, the conferees largely employed two conventional bargaining techniques, albeit with some variations: splitting the difference and receding to one or the other chamber's position. Variations on these two themes typically involved such steps as dividing fiscal differences but also adding specific language to the joint explanatory statement or to the conference report itself that limited the District's discretion to spend certain funds. At times, one chamber would recede to the other body's position on the explicitly stated condition that its position would be sustained later on another specific item in disagreement. In some instances, however, splitting the difference or bargaining over tradeoffs was impracticable, because new information or developments clearly validated one chamber's recommendation more than the other's; in these cases, agreement was reached swiftly on that position. The values of accommodation and fair negotiation were much in evidence.

Conference Chairman D'Amato initially passed over the most controversial item in disagreement—the total amount of the federal subsidy to the District. This final matter, appropriately enough both logically and politically, was considered last. It was evident by this stage of the proceedings that everyone was committed to producing a conference accord. The House conferees decided to go along with the higher Senate figure, a full $36.6 million more than the $300 million approved by the House, in large measure because that amount was acceptable to the president and was in part dictated by necessary mandatory costs, such as cost-of-living salary increases for District employees.

On a few occasions, conferees asked Mayor Barry to clarify certain specific issues. Asking questions of executive officials and other noncongressional employees during conference committee deliberations is quite common and not a particularly recent development. As early as 1929, Representative Carl Chindblom (R, Ill.) had reported concerning a conference in which he was engaged that "when the conferees met we found that we wanted some more information from the Bureau of the Census, and we called in Doctor Stewart and Doctor Hill, of the Census Bureau. They gave us very valuable information. They were closely interrogated by the conferees."[49] Similarly, the D.C. appropriations conferees found Mayor Barry a useful source of information during their deliberations. On occasion, Mayor Barry requested that one or more of his aides respond to the more specialized inquiries of the conferees to ensure that the conference was well informed concerning its decisions.

Passage of the Conference Report

Following this brief, low-intensity, and successful conference, the conference report had to be approved by the House and the Senate. The House took up the conference report first and passed it on November 18 by a 228 to 174 vote.[50] As is common on conference reports dealing with appropriations measures, the House then considered separately the various items in disagreement (see chapter 10). One item did arouse concern because it authorized a salary increase for the District's city administrator, who had other job offers from several cities. The House floor manager for the conference

---

49. *Congressional Record,* 71st Cong., 1st sess., June 10, 1929, p. 2610.
50. *Congressional Record,* 97th Cong., 1st sess., Nov. 18, 1981, pp. H8445–53.

report pointed out the need for the District to offer competitive salaries if it was to retain qualified city managers. Other representatives stressed the necessity of maintaining the then existing pay cap for all federal employees and urged the House to insist on its disagreement to the Senate amendment that permitted a higher salary for the city manager. Members then voted to maintain the pay cap, leaving conference matters unsettled and the two chambers in disagreement.

When the Senate took up the conference report the next day, November 19, 1981,[51] it quickly adopted the report. Equally important, the Senate also receded from its salary increase amendment, finally bringing the actions of the two chambers into harmony and clearing the appropriations bill for subsequent favorable presidential action. The reconciliation of House and Senate appropriations actions concerning D.C. appropriations was now complete and had been accomplished successfully due to harmonious conference negotiations and by subsequent chamber adjustment. The conference was a low-intensity proceeding, but its success nevertheless depended on political sensitivity and accommodation.

51. *Congressional Record,* Nov. 19, 1981, pp. S13717–19.

F. The Case of the Purloined Papers: South African Sanctions in 1985

Conference politics often takes place in or around the conference committee meeting room, but this is not its only locale or the sole time of its occurence. Significant political struggles may occur during other stages of the bicameral reconciliation process, such as the selection of conferees (see in chapter 1, for example, the vehement objections of Senator William Proximire [D, Wis.] to the conferees selected for the 1970 SST conference) or during approval of the final conference report.

The following case study concerns an instance in which conference politics centered on the report approval process every bit as much as on the conference itself.[52] The reconciliation of House and Senate positions had proceeded reasonably smoothly in conference; it was during the subsequent efforts to secure Senate approval for the conference agreement that things became difficult. This postconference stage of conference politics (discussed in chapter 10) was in this case marked by two developments: a significant change in Senate Republican sentiment toward the conference report because of presidential action, and the use by opponents of approval of unusual tactics to prevent the Senate from acting.

The subject of the conference—South African sanctions—was one of the most troubling foreign policy questions of the mid-1980s; in contrast to this important and moral-laden topic, the ploy finally utilized to stymie Senate approval of 1985 sanctions legislation may strike one as technical and unusual. However, it is often the case that only by the skillful use of technical and even seemingly frivolous tactics that important, somber, and even morally significant policy questions are decided in the conference process.[53]

Background

Beginning in the fall of 1984, a combination of circumstances had led to public and congressional outcries against South Africa's official policy of apartheid, or racial separation. Press and media coverage of violent multiracial demonstrations in South Africa, frequently followed by harsh, repressive measures by the government, had incensed many Americans. Receiving national attention, too, were daily demonstrations in front of the South African Embassy in Washington, D.C., by civil rights leaders, members of Congress, and many others. During this time, South African Bishop Desmond Tutu had received extensive international attention as well as the 1984 Nobel Peace Prize for his efforts to do away with apartheid. Increasingly, many senators and representatives were disgruntled with the Reagan administration's policy of "constructive engagement" toward South Africa. Designed to promote changes in South Africa's racial policies through diplomatic channels while maintaining cordial relations with the

---

52. The following account was especially prepared for this volume and is published here for the first time.

53. A striking example of the linking of tactics based on technicalities of the conference process to significant substantive questions such as aid to dependent children was provided in the first case study of this chapter, "Heptanoic Acid and Needy Children."

South African white-only government, constructive engagement had, in the view of many, achieved only marginal results. Conditions, in short, were ripe for a new congressional initiative concerning U.S. policy toward South Africa.[54]

By mid-1985, there was strong support in both chambers of Congress for some sort of serious action against South Africa with the intent of pressuring that government into dismantling its elaborate apartheid system. Economic sanctions appeared to be the most feasible means toward this objective. Both House and Senate adopted by large margins packages of economic sanctions including, in the House, the banning of the sale of South Africa's gold coins, called Krugerrands, in the United States and the discouragement of new U.S. business investment in South Africa. The House enacted its bill in June 1985 by a 295 to 127 vote; the next month the Senate passed (80–12) somewhat similar but more limited legislation. "This issue pulls everybody together, right and left, North and South, blacks and Jews," confidently observed one Senate Democratic staff aide.[55] Everyone, however, was not together: the Reagan administration announced its opposition to both bills and threatened to veto any such legislation. Administration officials argued that sanctions legislation would be counterproductive and, by causing even more black unemployment, would hurt the very people it was supposed to help in South Africa.

The Conference Meets

In order to iron out differences between the South African measures adopted by each chamber, House and Senate conferees met on July 31, 1985, for some five hours. "From the start it was evident that a majority [of the conferees] wanted to reach agreement on a bill that could clear Congress rapidly," *Congressional Quarterly* reported. Despite this general agreement on the need to act, it was also clear that "the two sides approached the issue from opposite perspectives."[56] The Senate legislation supported U.S. involvement in South Africa for the purpose of using resulting economic and political influence to further needed change. On the other hand, the House bill stressed punitive sanctions against South Africa, including the aforementioned ban on the sale of Krugerrands in the United States and a prohibition against new investments by U.S. businesses in South Africa.

In private meetings preceding the formal convening of the conference committee, various groups of conferees assessed their positions. At one such meeting on July 30 between Senate and House Democrats, the House conferees were told that a conference bill incorporating both the Krugerrand and the new investment bans would be impossible to get through the Republican-controlled Senate, especially in light of determined presi-

---

54. For additional background and an overview of these developments, see John Felton, "Special Report: South Africa Sanctions," *Congressional Quarterly Weekly Report,* March 9, 1985, pp. 440–48. See also "U.S. Policy toward South Africa, Pro & Con," *Congressional Digest,* Oct. 1985, pp. 225–56.

55. *Los Angeles Times,* Sept. 16, 1985, p. 10.

56. John Felton, "Restive Congress Comes Close to Passing Anti-Apartheid Bill," *Congressional Quarterly Weekly Report,* Aug. 3, 1985, p. 1526.

dential opposition. Taking this advice, House Democratic conferees decided to sacrifice the House prohibition against new business investments and press only for the ban on Krugerrand sales.[57]

During the conference session the next day, House conferees formally proposed this compromise. Senator Richard G. Lugar (R, Ind.), chairman of the Foreign Relations Committee and the key Senate conference negotiator, initially resisted even this modification of the Senate bill. He argued that in light of presidential opposition and end-of-session time pressures, the only realistic conference option was to accept the Senate-passed bill without major change. Following heated discussion and an emotional personal appeal from a black member of the House delegation, Representative Parren J. Mitchell (D, Md.), Senator Lugar relented and agreed to accept the House-backed ban on Krugerrands in return for the House dropping its prohibition on new investments in South Africa. After a brief caucus, the House conferees accepted this compromise—the same deal they had unofficially agreed to the preceding day.[58] The conference completed its work in harmony, and cleared the way for what would prove to be the decisive battle: adoption by House and Senate of the conference report.

The Conference Report Considered

Even though the House was the chamber that had originally requested the conference, for strategic reasons the House acted first in considering the conference report (as noted earlier, the chamber that requests a conference customarily acts last on the report). By an overwhelming vote on August 1 of 380 to 48, it approved the conference compromise. House action, especially by such a lopsided margin, was intended to add momentum to the report's passage in the Republican-controlled Senate, where there was unease both about the conference report and over opposing the Republican president.

House adoption of the conference report occurred on the very day, August 1, that Congress was scheduled to start its long-planned five week August recess. In order to make possible Senate passage of the conference report before the break, the conference report and other official papers were quickly transmitted to the Senate. There, they were "held" at the clerk's desk in the Senate chamber, waiting to be called up for floor consideration.

Shortly after the arrival of the papers, Senator Lugar attempted to take up the conference report: "Mr. President, I submit a report of the committee of conference on H.R. 1469 (the Anti-Apartheid Act of 1985) and ask for its immediate consideration," said the Senate Foreign Relations Committee chairman. "Without objection, the Senate will proceed to the consideration of the conference report," responded the presiding officer. But objection there was, and discussion ensued. Quickly it became evident that the Senate was faced with what amounted to a filibuster by sanctions opponents, only minutes prior to the August 1 recess. In the inconclusive debate that followed, Senator Lugar abandoned his more usual mild style of speaking and, arms waving, emotionally

57. Ibid., p. 1527.
58. Ibid.

pleaded with the Senate to take up the conference report: "It is time we spoke. It is time we acted."[59] Nevertheless, the filibuster against economic sanctions together with the immediacy of the August 1 recess deadline combined to prevent Senate approval of the conference report prior to the five-week pause in legislative activity. Just before the Senate recessed, however, a cloture petition to cut off debate on the sanctions legislation was presented by the required sixteen senators. The vote to end the filibuster would occur on the day the Senate returned from its lengthy break on September 9.

The President Reconsiders as the Senate Reconvenes

During Congress's August recess, the Reagan administration came under increasing pressure to change its position on South Africa, including its announced determination to veto legislation containing economic sanctions. Republican senators stressed that there were sufficient votes in both chambers to override easily a presidential veto of congressionally passed sanctions legislation. Further, they added, the so-called fall offensive of policy actions that the White House was planning would be stymied before it got going if the president suffered a significant foreign policy defeat early in September. In the wake of growing civil strife in South Africa plus growing political strife in Congress concerning his South African policies, President Reagan reconsidered his position. Observed one Senate Republican leader, White House advisors "came to our view on South Africa because clearly the parade was getting out ahead of them."[60] The first step in the new presidential policy on South Africa would involve heading off congressional action through presidential initiative.

On the very day the Senate reconvened for business after its August break, the president issued an executive order that outlined various economic sanctions to be taken by the U.S. government against South Africa. By the time the Senate began formal floor business later in the day on September 9, numerous Republican senators who had previously urged enactment of the conference report, including conference report floor manager Lugar and Majority Leader Robert Dole, were now arguing that Reagan's executive order made further congressional action unnecessary. The president's order, they pointed out, contained essentially the same sanctions as those in the pending conference report. Further, they held, Congress ought to avoid confrontation and stand united behind the president in foreign policy. Should the executive order later prove ineffective, the Senate could again take up and pass antiapartheid legislation. Other senators, however, argued that the president's actions were not identical to the pending conference bill, and in any event it was more desirable to have enactment of sanctions by law rather than by executive order. When the Senate later that day came to a vote on the cloture motion cutting off debate on the conference report, the opponents of Senate action won. The Senate failed by seven votes (sixty were required) to close debate on the conference report.

Whereas it had been expected that the Senate would easily cut off the filibuster, pass

59. Ibid., p. 1526.
60. *Washington Post,* Sept. 16, 1985, p. A8.

the conference report, and then override the president's promised veto, Reagan's executive order had changed the political environment. The legislative battle, however, was not ended by the September 9 vote. A second cloture motion was filed that day which would require another debate-ending vote in two days' time, on September 11. (Under Senate rules, there must be an intervening period of at least a legislative day before cloture votes can occur.)

Because thirteen senators had been absent for the September 9 cloture vote, the outcome for the second vote was in doubt. Lobbyists for both sides, including the president, worked to woo supporters to their position. When the Senate voted for the second time on September 11, it again failed to invoke cloture by a 57 to 41 tally, 3 less than the 60 votes needed. Senate Democratic Leader Robert C. Bryd of West Virginia, a cloture supporter, changed his own vote from yea to nay near the end of the roll call so he could offer a motion to reconsider the vote in order to capitalize on any uncertainty. (Only a senator who is on the prevailing side or who has not voted is eligible to offer that motion.) Senator Dole, however, moved to table (or kill) Byrd's reconsideration motion, and his tabling motion carried by a 50 to 48 vote. Sanctions supporters again had fallen just short of the necessary votes, on both cloture and on reconsideration of cloture's rejection.

Despite these defeats, numerous senators made it clear that their efforts to stop the filibuster and force a vote on the conference report would not end. Press accounts reported that these senators might even attempt to attach the sanctions measure to other upcoming legislation, such as the bill to raise the national debt ceiling or a continuing resolution to provide funds for the operation of the government.[61] Both proposals were considered "must" legislation and, if enacted with the antiapartheid provisions, could conceivably present the president with a difficult choice: veto the bill and close down the government temporarily or sign the legislation and accept the unwanted sanctions legislation.

The "Papers" Disappear

Still another vote to invoke cloture was slated for September 12. This one was unusual, however, because it was directed to the motion to *proceed* to consideration of the conference report rather than to adopt the report itself. As noted in the previous chapter, conference reports in the Senate are taken up either by unanimous consent or nondebatable motion. No senator, in fact, can filibuster motions to consider conference reports.

The objective of the cloture motion obviously was not to cut off debate on a nondebatable matter; rather it sought to make the antiapartheid conference report the pending business of the Senate, which it was not at the time. The Senate majority is responsible for setting the chamber's agenda of business and, following the presidential executive order, the Republican Senate leadership now wanted to deal with other business. "We understand the seriousness of the [antiapartheid] issue," said Majority Lead-

---

61. See, for example, *Wall Street Journal*, Sept. 12, 1985, p. 37.

er Dole, "but we also understand that when we reach a point maybe we ought to move on to something else."[62] In the end, the third cloture motion attracted only 11 yea votes against 88 nays. This overwhelming negative vote occurred in large part because supporters of the conference report for tactical reasons urged their colleagues "who support the Anti-Apartheid Act . . . to vote no on cloture to demonstrate our opposition" to procedural rather than substantive cloture.[63]

Following the rejection of the third cloture motion, Democratic Leader Byrd asked (as he had done previously) if Majority Leader Dole would now order the yeas and nays on the conference report. If this was done, the report could not, under Senate precedents, be subsequently withdrawn from floor consideration. Senator Byrd inquired, "I ask the distinguished majority leader if he would be agreeable to a unanimous-consent request to let it be in order to order the yeas and nays on the conference report." Senator Dole, however, rejected this request and added ominously: "I am also advised" [that Foreign Relations Chairman Lugar] "now has the papers." The effect of Senator Lugar's action was immediately clear to Senator Byrd. Senator Lugar's possession of the conference papers, Senator Byrd bitterly pointed out, "makes it impossible now for any Senator to move to proceed to the consideration of the conference report. This is the effect of his having taken the papers."[64] Numerous senators rose to denounce the removal of the papers from the clerk's table at the front of the Senate chamber as an extraordinary and unprecedented tactic to prevent Senate consideration of a conference committee agreement.

To understand this extraordinary situation better requires two additional details. First, the House had been able to act first on the conference report because it possessed the official papers (the original House-passed bill, the Senate amendment to it, and official messages between the chambers). The Senate, however, had a duplicate set of these documents, including—most important—the conference report itself.[65] Under Senate practices, it can act on conference reports only when the Senate's copy of the agreement is before the chamber. What Senator Lugar had taken from the chamber (with the aid of Senate Majority Leader Dole)[66] was the Senate's copy of the antiapartheid accord, leaving behind at the desk of the Senate the House documents and other accompanying papers.

Second, the Senate, unlike the House, has no formal filing requirement for conference reports. This means there is no official recognition by the Senate of the receipt of conference reports. Typically what happens is that the chairman of the Senate conference delegation hands the Senate copy of a conference report to a clerk in the well of the

62. *Congressional Record*, 99th Cong., 1st sess., Sept. 12, 1985, p. S11329.
63. Ibid., p. S11327.
64. Ibid., pp. S11328–29.
65. In a key difference between the House and Senate, the conference report and accompanying joint explanatory statement are considered as part of the official papers for House purposes but not in the Senate.
66. As Senator Dole said, "I will however confess to knowing about the removal of the papers and even helping locate the papers" (*Congressional Record*, 99th Cong., 1st sess., Sept. 12, 1985, p. S11329).

Senate. These clerks act as physical custodians of the reports, insuring, for example, that they do not get misplaced. If the chairman of a Senate conference delegation wants the report back, Senate clerks have no authority to refuse such a request. A crucial issue spotlighted by this episode has to do with the question When does control over the conference report pass from the conference chair to the Senate as a whole? Based on current practices, institutional control over conference reports is established only when the Senate agrees to subject a conference agreement to a record vote on final passage.

Resolution

Many senators (especially Democratic supporters of sanctions legislation) felt that Senator Lugar's action in seizing the papers established a dangerous precedent allowing any conference chairman to deprive the other ninety-nine senators of the opportunity to vote on a conference report. Bowing to these sentiments, Lugar's coconspirator, Majority Leader Dole, suddenly announced to the Senate that the "conference report on the South Africa bill was returned to the desk." Dole asserted, however, that control of the Senate's agenda was the key issue that had precipitated the papers' removal. The whole matter, he added, "had become totally politicized," and the Senate "could best serve the interests of South Africa by turning to other business." Dole also emphasized that removal of the "conference papers was absolutely within the rules."[67]

Democratic Leader Byrd disagreed sharply with Dole's claim that the removal was sanctioned either by Senate rules or precedents. He led a three-hour "storm of protest" on the Senate floor against Lugar's action. "This is the first time I have even taken the floor in my twenty-seven years in this body to protest an action of this kind," declared Senator Byrd, "which is a pretty good indication that it is not common practice."[68] Added Senator Paul Sarbanes (D, Md.), "I would like to know of such an instance, an instance in which the Senate was acting on an issue, when in fact a significant number of Members of the Senate wished to act further on that issue, and was prevented from taking further action because a Member of the body simply walked down to the desk, took the papers and walked out with them."[69] Parliamentary inquiry was made of the Senate's presiding officer for citation of any precedents for such action; the presiding officer and the Senate parliamentarian were unable to identify any previous instance.

Despite floor suggestions that Senate rules needed amending to prohibit this sort of parliamentary situation, the heated statements made on the Senate floor on September 26, 1985, constitute to date the only restraint against the removal of conference papers from the Senate desk. For its part, the South Africa conference report remained at the desk throughout the remaining thirteen months of the Ninety-ninth Congress until adjournment in late 1986. At that time, the sanctions legislation died automatically. Still, the conference report, even while being held in limbo during this period, served a useful purpose, according to Senator Claiborne Pell (D, R.I.). He explained, "The conference

67. *Congressional Record*, 99th Cong., 1st sess., Sept. 26, 1985, p. S12220.
68. Ibid., p. S12221.
69. Ibid., p. S12219.

papers are . . . at the desk. Their very presence there constitutes a powerful reminder to the President that if he does not move forcefully enough to demonstrate America's abhorrence of apartheid, the Senate can act."[70] The next year, in the wake of continued racial unrest in South Africa, Congress did enact a South Africa Sanctions Bill, overriding the president's veto in the course of translating concern into law.

Sometimes the conference committee process has consequences beyond itself. In this case, the imminency of congressional approval of conference legislation in 1985 mandating South Africa sanctions was sufficient to lead to presidential action along similar lines. The process of ratifying the conference report was a failure initially, but statutory economic sanctions against South Africa resulted the following year.

70. Ibid., pp. S12219–20.

G. Dollars for Defense: Les Gets More Amidst 1985 House Turmoil

Our next case study of conference politics[71] also has as its central arena the floor of one of the chambers of Congress. Unlike the preceding account of South Africa sanctions, however, the key action in this instance occured on the floor of the House of Representatives and included two separate but closely linked conference committee reports. The subject matter was defense policy and programs, and among the key elements of controversy were defense procurement reforms and the level of defense spending. Also central in these controversies of 1985 was a key congressman, Representative Les Aspin (D, Wis.), installed only months before as chairman of the powerful House Armed Services Committee. Aspin's tactics and positions in and out of conference proved to be exceedingly controversial.

During much of 1985, the House of Representatives found itself tangled in seemingly endless turmoil and dissension as it considered initially a conference agreement authorizing defense expenditures for the coming year, then conference legislation appropriating funds to pay for those programs. In the course of these deliberations, votes as well as reputations were reassesed as conference compromises were closely scrutinized and in many cases roundly criticized.

Events and controversies involving the first of these conferences were crucial in setting the stage for House consideration of the next. It is important to recall that the conference process does not exist isolated from what has previously transpired. Rather, what has already gone on in related conferences can shape the context in which subsequent conferences will occur. What Woodrow Wilson once termed ''the dance of legislation'' is a sequential process in which one set of events and controversies sets the stage for the next.

Background

To the surprise of many representatives, when the Ninety-ninth Congress convened in 1985 the House Armed Services Committee had a new chairman, Les Aspin. This was particularly astonishing since as of the end of 1984, Aspin, a respected and independent-thinking defense expert, had been only the seventh-ranking Democrat on the panel. Shortly prior to the opening of the Ninety-ninth Congress, Aspin and his partisan allies skillfully engineered the ouster of the incumbent Armed Services chairman, Melvin Price (D, Ill.), who was in frail health; further, Aspin succeeded in securing his own election despite the efforts of other committee members senior to him. In large part, these victories of Aspin, which occurred in the caucus of all House Democrats, were possible because of support from caucus liberals who expected a more progressive Armed Services leadership from Aspin as chair.

In his first months as chairman of the House Armed Services Committee, Aspin

---

71. The following account was especially prepared for this volume and is published here for the first time.

became embroiled in controversy over the 1985 defense authorization conference. This controversy was rooted both in splits within Democratic ranks over broad questions of defense policy and in disagreements surrounding alleged commitments Aspin had made to win the support of liberal Democrats during the caucus fight to replace Price. These controversies eventually gave rise to innovative procedural arrangements being created in the House for consideration of issues raised by the conference report. Before addressing those complex and unusual procedures, we will highlight the deep policy differences and the personal sense of betrayal that made these procedures necessary.

During the 1980s, Democrats tended to be divided into two main camps on defense. In one were members who were concerned that their party was publicly perceived as being "soft" on defense. These Democrats, Aspin included, wanted the party to project a strong prodefense image. The other Democratic group emphasized arms control and criticized big weapons systems. Aspin understood the concerns of both camps and tried to use his considerable political talents to bridge their divergent views.

In a major, well-reported speech in April 1985, for instance, Aspin cited polls that indicated voters viewed Democrats as less likely than Republicans to keep America's defenses strong. He urged his party colleagues to propose alternative weapons programs to those they disliked and to exhibit a more sympathetic attitude toward the concerns of those serving in the armed forces. A Democratic legislator, Aspin argued, should not be the "Dr. No of the defense debate."[72]

Aspin personally had affirmed that viewpoint the previous month when he played a key role as the critical House broker in preserving continued funding for the controversial and embattled MX missle. Despite the strong and united opposition of the House Democratic leadership and almost all of his liberal Democratic colleagues and associates, Aspin backed the White House position in favor of the missile. Further, he took on the aggressive mission of marshaling House votes for MX funding. President Reagan's narrow victory (219 to 213) in the House was largely credited to Aspin's floor management zeal.

A number of liberal Democrats were angered by Aspin's role in this highly contentious matter. After all, they had voted for Aspin over Price in the expectation that he would take the lead in eliminating what they believed to be wasteful weapons systems, including the MX. Certainly, they had not anticipated his floor managing their defense. Some of these Democrats even said that Aspin had promised to vote against the MX during his caucus campaign for the military chairmanship. Democratic Representative Les AuCoin of Oregon, for one, bitterly remarked, "Aspin has used the conspicuous position we have given him to blur the distinction between the parties. We can't attack Reagan for his support for first-strike weapons when the chairman of the House Armed Services Committee is wiring the deal for him. Frankly, it burns the hell out of us."[73]

---

72. Michael R. Gordon, "Who's 'Soft' on Defense?" *National Journal*, April 27, 1985, p. 942. See also Pat Towell, "Key Players Mirror Democrats' Defense Odyssey," *Congressional Quarterly Weekly Report*, Jan. 17, 1987, pp. 105–08.

73. Pat Towell, "House Gives President the Go-Ahead on MX," *Congressional Quarterly Weekly Report*, March 30, 1985, p. 564.

The Defense Authorization Legislation

Aspin soon recovered some of his standing with the liberals (a significant, if not majority, block of the Democratic Caucus) when he successfully managed House passage on June 27, 1985, of the Fiscal 1986 Defense Authorization Bill (H.R. 1872). This important legislation limited Pentagon spending to $292.5 billion, recommended improvements in a wide variety of Pentagon procurement practices, barred tests for an antisatellite missile wanted by the administration, and addressed a variety of other defense matters, including restraining the production of chemical weapons. By comparison, the Senate bill (S. 1160), adopted on June 5, authorized $10 billion more in defense spending ($302.5 billion) than the House version, authorized antisatellite weapons testing, approved only quite modest changes in defense procurement, and recommended production of chemical weapons with "no strings" attached (the House had conditioned production on NATO approval).

The differences between the bills passed by House and Senate were enormous and could only be resolved through conference committee negotiations. The conference on the Fiscal 1986 Defense Authorization Bill first met on July 11. Given to the conferees as they convened were staff-prepared, detailed comparisons of the two bills. The analysis of differences on procurement policy questions alone ran to some ninety-one ledger-sized pages outlining thirty-six major categories of issues.[74]

The conference committee was relatively large, reflecting the importance and contentiousness of the issues at stake in the Defense Authorization Bill. The Senate was represented by all nineteen members of the Senate Armed Services Committee, headed by its chairman, Barry Goldwater (R, Ariz.). Selection of conferences on the House side was less automatic. There were heavy pressures to include among House conferees individual authors or principals interested in particular controversial amendments added to the fiscal 1986 bill during House floor debate. There was precedent for this; the preceding year, dozens of representatives had been named to the defense authorization conference to deal with one or two specific provisions. In 1985, however, Armed Services Chairman Aspin resisted such "bullet vote" conferees on the grounds that their narrow special interest would inhibit necessary conference committee horse trading. His concern was, as a close associate described it, "If you've got a guy who's a conferee on one issue, he can't trade it off."[75]

Chairman Aspin got the House delegation he sought. Only members of the Armed Services were named as conferees. (Exceptions were made in the cases of a few special provisions of the bill that House rules placed in the jurisdiction of the Intelligence and the

---

74. Pat Towell, "Pentagon's Buying Practices: Battle Lines Drawn," *Congressional Quarterly Weekly Report*, July 13, 1985, p. 1369. Procurement issues were particularly prominent in Congress at the moment because of a series of widely publicized horror stories suggesting Pentagon mismanagement of purchasing policies. Among the cases frequently cited were instances of military approval of hammers costing over $400 and specially constructed toilet seat covers costing even more. Such highly specific examples of bureaucratic shortsightedness are natural fodder for fueling extensive debate in Congress. In 1988, as reports surfaced again about major Pentagon–defense contractor procurement fraud, Congress launched a series of new inquiries into the area.

75. Ibid.

Education and Labor committees; for these specific matters, members of those respective House committees joined the Armed Services conferees.) In order to secure a House delegation with a balanced outlook on defense issues, Aspin, in selecting the twenty House conferees, agreed to reach far down the committee seniority ladder to include two prominent liberal activists on defense matters, Patricia Schroeder (D, Col.) and Nicholas Mavroules (D, Mass.). The professed purpose of this was to ensure a conference delegation prepared to defend energetically the House liberal positions during conference negotiations. Further strengthening the position of the House delegation in conference was the fact that most of the important House provisions in disagreement with the Senate had been adopted on the House floor by lopsided roll call votes.[76] It was widely expected that the House would be well represented by its conferees.

The Conference Agreement

The conference negotiations went on behind closed doors for two weeks between July 11 and 25. On July 25, conference agreement on the defense authorization bill was announced. Surprisingly, it appeared that the House had given in to the Senate on the majority of the most contentious matters in disagreement between the two chambers: dropped were the House ban on the testing of antisatellite weapons, the House requirement of NATO approval before production of new binary (chemical) munitions, and House provisions limiting the postgovernmental employment of Pentagon officials by defense contractors. The original House bill had killed some thirty-four specific weapons systems; the conference report restored twelve of the most important of them. Most astonishing to House members was the total spending level approved by the conferees. As noted earlier the House bill had authorized defense spending of $292.5 billion, the Senate bill $302.5 billion. The conference "compromise" was identical to the Senate figure: $302.5 billion was authorized for defense in Fiscal Year 1986.[77]

A number of representatives greeted the conference agreement with outrage: "This isn't a conference report," said Representative Les AuCoin. "It's a surrender document." Fellow Democrat Don Edwards (Cal.) was even terser in his assessment: "The House was skunked."[78] Adding to the initial shock was the fact that the preceding weeks of conference negotiations had occurred in secret session, thereby providing little advance word on the evolution of conference agreement. Further, the conference report and printed text of the full bill were not initially available. Even when they were finally printed five days later, on July 30, they were not easy to understand. Together, the bill and the conference report took up 180 pages of the *Congressional Record,* three columns to the page. Even the table of contents of the report was daunting: it ran to three full pages of the *Record.*[79] Much of the early House reaction to the conference report by necessity

76. Ibid.
77. Pat Towell, "Budget Dealing Derails Defense Bill in House," *Congressional Quarterly Weekly Report,* Aug. 3, 1985, p. 1532; and Ed Magnuson, "Weapons That Refuse to Die," *Time,* Aug. 12, 1985, p. 15.
78. Magnuson, "Weapons," p. 15.
79. Towell, "Budget Dealing," p. 1533.

was based on partial reports or was focused on specific provisions being omitted from the final conference legislation.

The same day that the conference report was finally available in printed form, the Senate considered the defense authorization accord. Approval there on July 30 was quick and without marked controversy; the work of the conference was approved by the Senate by a 94 to 5 vote. The House had been slated to take up the conference report the next day, but this did not happen. Opposition to House approval of the conference product was rapidly building.

On July 29 (four days after the announcement of the conference conclusion and a day prior to the availability of the printed report and the favorable Senate vote), a number of arms control lobbyists met to consider the so-called compromise bill and discuss what to do in the House. Complicating their evaluation was the fact that several House leaders on arms control, most notably Representatives Nicholas Mavroules and Charles E. Bennett (D, Fla.), had been conferees and had declared their satisfaction with the result. Nevertheless, the arms control strategists determined to oppose the conference legislation, and in a statement later that day called for the defeat of the conference report in the House.[80]

Meanwhile, House rank and file opposition to the conference-amended bill continued to grow, coming to a boil early on July 30 in the course of a heated meeting of the Democratic Caucus. There, House liberals attacked the House conferees in general and Chairman Aspin in particular for "selling out" House interests to the more prodefense Senate managers. "The positions of the House were simply not upheld. Those positions were simply sold down the river," lamented Representative George Miller (D, Cal.). "It's a matter of embarrassment for the House."[81]

What was causing House Democrats to fume was more than just institutional pride. There was also the galling fact that the conference accord increased defense expenditures from the House-approved level at the same time that the House was being forced to accept painful cuts in domestic programs. "We just cut $1 billion out of public housing for the poorest of the poor and now we're going to add $10 billion for [defense]," said Representative Charles Schumer (D, N.Y.). "Is this what Democrats stand for?"[82]

Besides institutional and policy concerns, one other factor heightened caucus outrage over the conference report—a sense on the part of some representatives of personal betrayal. References were made to allegations that Chairman Aspin, while seeking election to the Armed Services Committee the preceding January, had misled key representatives by pledging to reassess his support for the MX missile—a reassessment that was followed by his redoubled efforts on *behalf* of the MX missile in March. Perhaps

---

80. Ibid., p. 1532. The accusation that House conferees had acquiesced too easily on key issues especially rankled Representative Mavroules, perhaps the leading arms control activist on the House Committee. "Mavroules bristled at the charge," *Congressional Quarterly* reported, "insisting that he had driven the hardest possible bargain" (Towell, "Key Players Mirror Democrats' Defense Odyssey," p. 107).

81. Steve Blakely, "Conference Report under Attack," *Congressional Quarterly Weekly Report*, Sept. 7, 1985, p. 1747.

82. *Washington Post*, July 31, 1985, p. A4.

Aspin's dealings on the pending defense authorization conference, some mused, were consistent with his earlier conduct in regard to the MX missile.[83]

The caucus meeting of July 30 was friendly neither to the conference agreement nor to its chief House architect, Chairman Aspin. Nevertheless, Aspin attempted—without noteworthy success—to rally support for the conference report and in the process also to defend his performance and his personal integrity. Reflecting on this unhappy scene two days later, Aspin described the caucus mood as motivated by frustration over Senate determination on the spending level and the other conference decisions. During the caucus meeting, Aspin mused, "It was shoot-the-messenger time."[84]

Clearly this was not a fortuitous moment for the House to take up the conference report. Later that day, July 30, House Speaker Tip O'Neill (D, Mass.) announced that House consideration of the conference agreement would be postponed until after Congress returned from its traditional August recess. (This was the same 1985 recess period so central in the preceding case study of South African sanction legislation in the Senate.) This delay was intended to allow party passions to cool, for at that moment, amidst the feelings of institutional sellout and personal betrayal, there seemed a real possibility of outright House rejection of the defense conference agreement.[85]

Another consideration in the Speaker's decision was the concern of House Budget Committee Chairman William Gray (D, Penn.) that House approval of the defense accord "would undermine the House position in the volatile [budget conference] negotiations under way between House, Senate, and White House officials."[86] Approval for higher Pentagon spending as contained in the defense conference report, Gray argued, would undermine his efforts to reduce military expenditures in order to protect domestic programs.

A final step was taken prior to the recess to attempt to assuage the fury of conference report opponents. On the morning of August 1, Speaker O'Neill promised rebellious Democrats that when the House took up the Defense Authorization Bill in September, a separate vote would be held on the spending level issue—this despite procedural rules that customarily prohibit such separate votes on parts of a conference report.[87]

The House Returns to Work

When Congress reconvened in September, opposition to the conference agreement had scarcely abated. A core group of House Democrats, including Representatives Schumer, Barney Frank (Mass.), Barbara Boxer (Cal.) and Miller (Cal.), met to organize opposition to the defense conference report. Twenty-five Democrats further circulated a "Dear Colleague" letter outlining their concerns about the defense accord.

83. Towell, "Budget Dealing," p. 1533; Towell, "House Gives President the Go-Ahead on MX," p. 564.
84. Towell, "Budget Dealing," pp. 1533, 1532.
85. Ibid.
86. *Washington Times,* July 31, 1985, p. 3A; Towell, "Budget Dealing," p. 1532.
87. Towell, "Budget Dealing," p. 1532. For background on the usual indivisibility of conference reports, see chapter 10 above; for discussion of the development of this tradition, see chapter 2 above.

Armed Services Chairman Aspin was working hard, however, to head off rejection of the conference agreement. He argued, for example, that even should the House defeat the conference agreement, the Senate would still be unlikely to accept the lower House figure.[88] Moreover, a vote to cut the dollar totals, Aspin stressed, says nothing about how or where or on which programs such reductions were to be made.

To complicate matters, Democratic Senator Sam Nunn of Georgia, a respected military expert and key Senate conferee, informed Speaker O'Neill that Representative Aspin was correct in his assessment of the Senate position: even if the House reaffirmed its wish to cut military spending by $10 billion the "Senate would not reopen the issue and the authorization bill would die."[89] That message confronted Speaker O'Neill with twin problems: how to honor his commitment to liberal Democrats for a separate vote cutting defense expenditures and how to protect his party from being lambasted by President Reagan for torpedoing the Pentagon's budget, leaving the country (so the rhetoric would run) without adequate means for its own defense.

The issue of a separate vote was a thorny one procedurally because conference reports are agreed to in one up-or-down vote. At this stage of the lawmaking process, they are not open to the usual amendment procedure, such as striking the $302.5 billion figure and inserting the House-approved $292.5 billion amount. Moreover, the dollar total was an aggregate figure composed of numerous discrete spending decisions woven throughout the conference report; changing the total would also necessitate readjustments throughout the legislation.

Democratic party leaders pondered numerous ways to achieve the promised separate vote. One option would be to ask the House to reject the conference report and then request another conference with the Senate, with the explicit understanding that House conferees were now to hold absolutely firm to the $292.5 billion authorization figure. Another approach would be to request the Rules Committee to fashion a "creative" procedural special rule allowing for a separate spending level vote. A third and least satisfactory option would be to move a "sense of the House" resolution declaring that the defense appropriations bill "should correspond" with the House figure. GOP leader Bob Michel of Illinois chastised Democrats for considering these steps rather than permitting the House to vote on the defense conference report in the usual manner: "There will be a dangerous precedent set if a separate vote is demanded on this issue," he said. If the House changes the "game rules here, then they will surely be changed for other conference reports."[90]

A Procedural Bargain

By several accounts, it was Majority Leader (and as of 1987 House Speaker) Jim Wright (D, Tex.) who came up with the solution to the logjam over the defense con-

88. *Washington Times,* Sept. 6, 1985, p. 2A.
89. Towell, "House Accord May Clear Way For Vote on Defense Measure," *Congressional Quarterly Weekly Report,* Sept. 14, 1985, p. 1798.
90. *Congressional Record,* 99th Cong., 1st sess., Sept. 10, 1985, p. H7310.

ference report.[91] Democratic party leaders convinced the irate liberal Democrats to approve the conference report as issued and then use the subsequent defense *appropriations* bill to win their overall spending objective. (Authorizations bills establish a recommended level of spending while appropriations legislation actually provide the money for departments and programs.) The House leadership further suggested that the defense appropriations bill be used to restore procurement and other changes that had been contained in the House-passed version of the defense authorization bill but that had been dropped in conference. House rules usually prohibit appropriation bills from dealing with policy issues such as procurement reform, but Speaker O'Neill's influence over the Rules Committee (he names all of its Democratic members, including its chairman) would insure that a procedure would be approved by that panel for debating the defense appropriations bill while barring points of order against the inclusion of policy provisions. After some consideration, this arrangement was accepted by leading Democrats in the caucus as well as those on the House Appropriations Committee.

The Bargain is Played Out on the House Floor

On October 29, the House finally took up the defense authorization conference report, with debate on the defense appropriations bill slated for the next day. As the House started its consideration of the authorization legislation, Representative David Bonior (D, Mich.), a member of the Rules Committee, made clear that the conference report was to be considered under normal House procedure: one hour of debate and no amendments. "There had been speculation about the possibility of separate votes being taken on several of the controversial items in this conference report," he stated, but "these issues will be addressed . . . [in] the Department of Defense appropriations bill which is scheduled for floor consideration [tomorrow]."[92] To be sure, the conference accord was once again criticized and defended but in the end it passed easily by voice vote. Representative Frank wryly noted a "certain lack of fervor" in the debate, a reticence present because members now knew that the key battles would be fought in connection with the subsequent defense appropriations bill.[93]

The next day, October 30, the House took up the procedural rule regulating how the next measure, the defense appropriations bill, was to be amended. Significantly, the rule

---

91. Towell, "House Accord May Clear Way For Vote on Defense Measure," p. 1798. A later add-on to the agreement involved House consideration of a separate bill designed to clarify the intent of a provision in the defense authorization conference report dealing with reporting requirements for Pentagon contractors. This clarifying measure was brought to the floor the day before the scheduled consideration of the defense authorization accord. The ranking Republican member of the House Armed Services Committee, William Dickinson of Alabama, thought the sequence of actions unusual and inquired of Chairman Aspin, "[If the bill] does not pass, I gather that we cannot even get the conference report on the authorization bill up tomorrow." Aspin reported affirmatively (*Congressional Record,* Oct. 28, 1985, p. H9245). The clarification legislation was important to those Democrats who had been pushing for procurement reforms and was their requirement for going along with the Wright-engineered procedural bargain.

92. *Congressional Record,* Oct. 29, 1985, p. H9279.

93. Ibid., p. H9285.

from the Rules Committee disallowed scores of potential points of order against the measure, including ones based on the House rule that bars policy provisions in general appropriation bills. The military appropriations bill, as previously agreed, was to be the vehicle for addressing anew the substantive concerns of the liberal Democrats, including procurement reform, chemical weapon production, antisatellite tests in space, and defense spending levels.

Two features surrounding House consideration of the defense appropriations bill are worth noting. First, the floor manager of the bill was William Chappell of Florida, the second ranking Democrat on the Defense Appropriations Subcommittee, rather than Joseph Addabbo (D, N.Y.), the head of the panel. Addabbo had been incapacitated for several weeks because of serious illness, so Chappell took the helm. Without Addabbo's experienced leadership, Democratic liberals feared their defense spending limit and other goals might not pass the House; in light of these concerns they mobilized all their forces for a concentrated effort on the House floor.

A second factor further enhanced liberal efforts at defense expenditure limitation. There was at the moment heightened concern about soaring budgetary deficits reflected in the pending Gramm-Rudman deficit reduction plan. (See the next case study for an account of these parallel events.) Because of this, members of both parties were favorably disposed toward spending cuts generally, even in defense expenditures. Republican Representative Bill Frenzel of Minnesota spoke for many of his colleagues when he said, "My fears about the deficit swallow up all my fears about cutting the defense budget."[94]

Surprisingly, the House spent less than four hours on October 30 debating and amending the defense appropriations bill prior to its passage later that day on a 359 to 67 roll call vote. Many anticipated battles never materialized as representatives went along with most of the defense expenditure limitations and other recommendations put forth by the House Appropriations Committee and House liberals. Arms control advocates got most of what they wanted, including a ban on antisatellite tests subject to a continued Soviet moratorium, limitations on chemical weapons production, Pentagon procurement reforms, and, most important, a military spending level for Fiscal Year 1986 of $292 billion. Things were going so well at this time for the liberals that they even came close to winning significant slashes in appropriations for the MX missile![95]

Appropriations Goes to Conference

Legislative battles are not one-shot affairs, but rather long campaigns that continue in different forms and forums. Mindful of the House's appropriations actions, the Senate Defense Appropriations Subcommittee, when it subsequently took up Defense Appropriations for Fiscal 1986, deliberately approved a level of military spending exceeding the House figure by nearly $12 billion. Senate Republicans were following the conventional strategy of asking for more than they really wanted in the expectation that the final

---

94. *Washington Post*, Sept. 12, 1985, p. A10.
95. Pat Towell, "After Brief Go-Round on MX, House Votes Appropriations," *Congressional Quarterly Weekly Report*, Nov. 2, 1985, pp. 2215–21.

compromise figure arrived at in conference would thus be nearer their real wishes.[96] Senator Ted Stevens (R, Alaska), the chairman of the Defense Appropriations Subcommittee, also served notice that he strongly opposed the procurement reforms and other policy matters included by the House in the defense appropriations bill. (The Senate also has rules, usually loosely applied, prohibiting policy matters in appropriation bills.) The Senate Appropriations panel, Stevens said, "just cannot be the authorizing committee for all the items there's been a disagreement about in the [defense] authorization conference."[97] Following Senate floor confirmation of the Appropriations Subcommittee's actions, the stage was set for what would clearly be a difficult House-Senate conference.

Interestingly, the defense appropriations conference took place as a subgroup of a larger conference dealing with omnibus legislation to fund major segments of the federal government. Such comprehensive legislation, called a continuing resolution, is required whenever Congress cannot complete action on one or more of the thirteen regular appropriation bills by the start of the fiscal year, October 1. Continuing resolutions provide funding for the affected federal agencies, and in recent years have become major policy-making instruments, in part because of Congress's recurrent inability to meet budgetary timetables. In this procedure, numerous measures are bundled into one huge legislative package. With Congress still working on appropriation bills more than two months after the fiscal year had started, the continuing resolution debated in mid-December 1985 included funding for six major agencies, including the Department of Defense.

In an astonishing conference outcome, conferees from the House and Senate Appropriations committees in charge of the defense portion of the continuing resolution concluded their bicameral adjustment deliberations by agreeing to provide $14 billion more in defense expenditures than the House had approved—$2 billion above even the Senate figure! Although the conference *did* vote to accept the House's position barring antisatellite tests it also refused to accede to the House stand on procurement reforms and further accepted the Senate's position providing funding for the production of chemical weapons. When this conference settlement came to the House floor for approval just as Congress was winding down its first session of business the House reaction was both swift and hostile. To the surprise of conference leaders, the House summarily rejected the conference report. Part of the explanation for the report's defeat again involved liberal Democratic dissatisfaction with the defense compromises hammered out by the conferees, particularly concerning spending for the Pentagon. When the House had first begun almost a year earlier—at the beginning of 1985—to debate Pentagon spending, many members had believed that too much was provided to the Defense Department. Some House leaders said then, recalled Representative Barney Frank (D, Mass.), " 'Wait for the authorization.' And when the authorization came up and there was too much for defense, they said, 'Wait for the appropriation.' And when people had qualms about the appropriation, they said, 'Wait for the continuing resolution.' Well, I am tired

---

96. *Wall Street Journal,* Nov. 11, 1985, p. 50.
97. Pat Towell, "Rejecting a 'Star Wars' Study, Panel Approves Spending Bill," *Congressional Quarterly Weekly Report,* Nov. 9, 1985, p. 2330.

of waiting."[98] Besides being upset by the level of defense spending, House liberals were outraged over the deletion once again of the procurement changes. Ironically, one of Aspin's most outspoken critics, Representative AuCoin, had been a conferee on the continuing resolution. He ruefully observed that losing the procurement reforms in the continuing resolution conference "was a bitter pill to swallow, especially since I upbraided Les Aspin for losing them" in the earlier defense authorization conference.[99]

Following House rejection of the continuing resolution conference report, appropriations conferees quickly returned to the drawing board for another round of conference negotiations. Initially, only the key leaders of the defense appropriations subgroup met: Senator Stevens and Representative Addabbo (who had recovered enough to resume work), Chappell, and Joseph McDade (R, Penn.), ranking minority member of the House Defense Appropriations Subcommittee. Meanwhile, several House members and a prominent interest group, the Council for a Liveable World, obtained signatures from 140 representatives on a petition urging House conferees to drop funding for chemical weapons production. Administration lobbyists, however, were simultaneously working frantically on the opposing side to get the best deal possible for the Pentagon.[100]

In the end, a second conference report was finally agreed to in conference and subsequently was passed by both chambers. The report contained, as Addabbo phrased it, "a very delicately balanced agreement on the defense issues."[101] Conferees agreed to reduce military spending by $1.3 billion, approved funding of the production of chemical weapons, and accepted one of the four procurement reforms wanted by the House, a change that also had the approval of Senate Armed Services Chairman Barry Goldwater (R, Ariz.).[102] Senator Stevens called the final defense agreement a "product of what I consider to be the most difficult and protracted negotiations in recent years."[103]

The Continuous Dance

The legislative struggles and procedural gymnastics required to win enactment of the various 1985 defense conference reports underscore Woodrow Wilson's comment that the "dance of legislation" is seldom over. Shifts in public attitudes toward defense from high support for a military buildup at the start of the 1980s to public preference by mid-decade for a leveling off of defense expenditures probably best explains the congressional contortions needed to adopt the defense agreements. Another factor in the topsy-turvy struggle to adopt the conference reports involved divisions within the House Democratic party. Chairman Aspin tried to bridge these differences without having the structure fall on him. His explanation of the problems inherent in that effort highlights how difficult it can be to fashion winning coalitions on defense conference reports: "I would like to move the Democratic caucus to the right on defense issues and the House

98. *Congressional Record,* Dec. 16, 1985, p. H12167.
99. *Washington Post,* Dec. 17, 1985, p. A17.
100. Nadine Cohodas, "$368.2 Billion Omnibus Spending Bill Cleared," *Congressional Quarterly Weekly Report,* Dec. 21, 1985, p. 2667.
101. *Congressional Record,* Dec. 19, 1985, p. H12980.
102. Cohodas, "$368.2 Billion Omnibus Spending Bill Cleared," p. 2668.
103. *Congressional Record,* Dec. 19, 1985, p. S18136.

Armed Services Committee to the left, and it's going to be painful. Sometimes the liberals are going to be unhappy and sometimes the conservatives are going to be unhappy."[104] In an era characterized by the politics of deficit reduction, there inevitably will be many conference reports opposed by congressmen who are disgruntled by the agreements and supported by coalitions of equally unhappy members.

To be sure, many of the same defense issues would be joined the next year. What happens before shapes that which follows. For example, Senator Dan Quayle (R, Ind.), who headed the Armed Services Subcommittee on Defense Acquisition Policy, had in 1985 strongly opposed the House's approach to procurement reform, favoring instead the creation of a professional civilian acquisition corps. Early in 1986, Chairman Aspin noted that Quayle's idea would receive serious future consideration in the House, in large part because of his role in defeating the House-approved procurement changes the previous year.[105] The events of one stage of the legislative process set the players and forces determinate of the next.

Epilogue

The events of 1985 described above had an important epilogue early in 1987. In a development that surprised many, not least the central figure, the House Democratic Caucus voted 130 to 124 on January 7, 1987, to oust Representative Les Aspin as chairman of the Armed Services Committee. The possibility of a caucus challenge to Aspin had been rumored for months,[106] but Aspin had been highly confident of retaining the chairmanship as late as three weeks before the vote.[107]

The caucus's rejection of Representative Aspin was based on three frequently cited complaints: his vigorous support in March 1985 of the MX missile after having made statements to a number of representatives in January that were interpreted as pledges to oppose it; his conference stands and votes in 1985 in favor of higher defense spending; and his highly controversial efforts in 1986 on behalf of securing military aid for the Nicaraguan contras.[108] Underlying these specifics was a vague but frequently articulated

104. *Washington Post*, July 31, 1985, p. A4.
105. *Los Angeles Times*, Jan. 10, 1986, p. 18.
106. See, for example, Janet Hook and Jacqueline Calmes, "Aspin May Face Challenge at Armed Services," *Congressional Quarterly Weekly Report*, July 12, 1986, pp. 1564–65; and Leslie H. Gelb, "Aspin and Armed Services: Can the Center Hold?" *New York Times*, Aug. 13, 1986.
107. Personal discussion with Rep. Les Aspin, Milwaukee, Dec. 13, 1986. One representative, Robert J. Mrazek of New York, who was undecided until only minutes prior to the Democratic Caucus vote, commented that while he had received more than a half-dozen calls from other contenders, he had never heard from Aspin. "There was a tremendous amount of overconfidence on his side," he reported. (Jacqueline Calmes, "Aspin Ousted as Armed Services Chairman," *Congressional Quarterly Weekly Report*, Jan. 10, 1987, pp. 84, 83).
108. Calmes, "Aspin Ousted," p. 83; and Linda Greenhouse, "Aspin Loses Post on Military Panel But May Regain It," *New York Times*, Jan. 8, 1987, p. 1. An additional fact also present in the 1987 events was a lingering legacy of resentment over Aspin's leap to the Armed Services chairmanship in 1985 (at the time, he was the seventh-ranking member of the Committee). Some representatives were offended by his successful efforts to depose an elderly and ailing chairman, Melvin Price (D, Ill.); others even more strongly resented Aspin's pushing himself into the chair over the hopes of other committee members more senior to him. See Edward Walsh, "Live—and Die—by the Caucus," *Washington Post National Weekly Edition*, Jan. 19, 1987, p. 15.

feeling that Aspin as Armed Services chairman had proven to be undependable and even dishonest. As one Aspin *supporter* on the January 7 vote, Representative Barney Frank of Massachusetts, expressed it, "I admire him more than I trust him."[109]

The specific events recounted in this case study were frequently cited as evidence of the need to depose Aspin as Armed Services chairman. His actions of 1985 in connection with the Defense Authorization Bill were seen as illustrative of a more general legislative failure—"that he did not adequately represent the House in negotiations with the Senate, that he was too quick to yield to the Senate's demands in conference committee."[110]

The caucus vote on January 7, however, was not the end of the story. The decision then had been only on a yes-or-no vote on reelecting Aspin as Armed Services chairman. Following his defeat on January 7, another House Democratic Caucus meeting was scheduled for January 22 for the purpose of electing his successor. Aspin himself was among the contenders for the chairmanship on that date, along with Democratic Representatives Charles E. Bennett (Fla.), the next highest ranking member of the committee; Nicholas Mavroules (Mass.), 11th ranking on the committee and a leading liberal arms control advocate; and Marvin Leath (Tex.), 14th in seniority on the committee and the most conservative of the candidates for the chairmanship.[111] In an astonishing conclusion to these events, the House Democratic Caucus on January 22, after several roll call ballots that in turn eliminated Bennett and Mavroules, voted 133 to 116 to reinstate Aspin as Armed Services chairman.[112] (On the final vote the conservative Leath was deemed by liberals to be too much out of tune with policy concerns predominant in the Democratic Caucus.) Aspin, despite the controversies surrounding his performance as chairman in 1985 and 1986, ultimately was preferred by a majority of House Democrats as their leader and strategist on defense issues—particularly an Aspin presumably chastened by his humiliating albeit temporary dethroning two weeks earlier.

---

109. Calmes, "Aspin Ousted," p. 84.

110. Greenhouse, "Aspin Loses Post," p. 13.

111. Jacqueline Calmes, "Four Battling for Armed Services Chairmanship," *Congressional Quarterly Weekly Report*, Jan. 17, 1987, pp. 103–04; Pat Towell, "Key Players Mirror Democrats' Defense Odyssey," pp. 105–08.

112. Linda Greenhouse, "Aspin Retains Job as Unit Chairman of Armed Services," *New York Times*, Jan. 23, 1987, pp. 1, 8; Linda Greenhouse, "What Aspin Wrought," *New York Times*, Jan. 24, 1987, p. 7; and Jacqueline Calmes, "Aspin Makes Comeback at Armed Services," *Congressional Quarterly Weekly Report*, Jan. 24, 1987, pp. 139–42.

H. The Gramm-Rudman Conferences of 1985

The last of our nine case studies of conference committee politics[113] deals with the enactment of what was to date certainly one of the best known and most controversial measures of the 1980s: the Gramm-Rudman deficit reduction plan.[114] Interestingly, this legislation at first traveled a path somewhat resembling that of the 1982 tax bill (see the earlier case study "The 1982 Tax Increase Conference"). The legislation initially was sent to conference bereft of any significant subcommittee, committee, or floor consideration. Unlike the 1982 bill, however, which lacked study in the House, the 1985 legislation went to conference in October without having undergone detailed scrutiny in *either* House or Senate. The Gramm-Rudman plan was an amendment attached on short notice on the floor of the Senate to pending debt limit legislation and adopted there after relatively little debate. When the House received the debt limit bill with its Gramm-Rudman amendment, it quickly decided to pass the whole matter on to conference for consideration and evaluation. These events of 1985 indeed constitute a dramatic instance of "counting on the conference to work things out."

It is true that later, in what would prove to be a convoluted legislative process, both the House and Senate would debate and adopt versions of the Gramm-Rudman legislation in preparation for the convening of a second conference committee on the subject. What is remarkable in this case, however, is that the initial conference committee considered and drafted much of Gramm-Rudman in the manner more usually associated with House and Senate standing committees. The two chambers were disinclined or unwilling to deal with this highly disputatious legislation through the usual process of committee initiative, study, and approval followed by chamber debate and passage, and then conference committee adjustment of bicameral differences. Rather the conference committee (or at least the first Gramm-Rudman conference committee) served in effect as a standing committee in evaluating policy alternatives.

Ultimately the strain this unaccustomed role placed on the initial conference committee proved too great, and the October conference broke down and was unable to agree upon a bill. This was followed by more traditional processes: shuttling of legislation back and forth between the chambers, House and Senate adoption of chamber-preferred approaches, and—finally—reconciliation between these bills in a *second* conference. The Gramm-Rudman conferences of 1985 illustrate both exceptional and traditional roles the conference committee may play in the legislative process.

---

113. The following account was especially prepared for this volume and is published here for the first time.

114. The official name of this legislation as enacted was the Balanced Budget and Emergency Deficit Control Act of 1985 (PL 99-177). Popularly, it has been widely known as either the Gramm-Rudman plan or the Gramm-Rudman-Hollings plan (incorporating more properly the names of all three original sponsors). The former designation has predominated and for this reason as well as for ease of reference is the term we shall use. Although this shorter title somewhat slights Sen. Ernest Hollings (D, S.C.), it also appeared that he was less prominent in the legislative politics accompanying eventual adoption of the measure than were his cosponsors—and many others.

Background

Because the government regularly spends far more than it receives in taxes and other payments, Congress must periodically pass legislation to raise the statutory ceiling on the national debt. This practice enables the government to continue borrowing money to pay its bills. The ceiling is always lifted because Congress has little choice if the government is to meet various financial obligations, such as sending checks to Social Security recipients. This effort, however, regularly takes place in an atmosphere replete with political maneuvering, partisan politics, and bitter debate.

The House had become so disenchanted with the process by 1979 that it changed its rules that year to prevent direct consideration of debt raising legislation. Now, when the House passes the annual budget resolution, which sets spending, revenue, and deficit totals, it is also deemed to have passed automatically a separate debt ceiling measure. Democratic leaders had grown highly frustrated during the preceding years with the political games that members would play on the issue; representatives would customarily trade charges as to which party or administration was to blame for overspending by the government. It was to avoid these divisive, partisan scenes that House leaders successfully advocated the new process. To be sure, this new procedure would not in all cases preclude House consideration of the debt ceiling. If the Senate should choose to amend a debt measure passed automatically by the House, then the House would necessarily need to get involved in resolving bicameral differences—including questions concerning the national debt ceiling and any amendments that might have been attached in the Senate to the ceiling legislation.[115]

In October 1985, Senate Republican leaders were faced with the politically highly unpleasant task of raising the debt ceiling to over $2 trillion—twice what it had been when President Reagan took office four and one-half years earlier. Without the votes to enact the hike, Senate Republicans searched for a way out of their dilemma. The problem was compounded by growing public awareness and concern about mushrooming budgetary deficits. Senators, both Republican and Democratic, desperately wanted to vote for some means of deficit reduction rather than simply for an extension of the government's authority to borrow more money.

The Republican leaders' search ended when they backed a major deficit reduction amendment to the debt ceiling legislation. Sponsored by Senators Phil Gramm (R, Tex.), Warren Rudman (R, N.H.), and Ernest Hollings (D, S.C.),[116] the complex forty-page amendment swept onto the Senate floor without any committee hearings, prior floor debate, or even advance public warning that such a consequential amendment

---

115. Andy Plattner, "Rule Helps House Avoid Debt-Limit Fight," *Congressional Quarterly Weekly Report,* Sept. 14, 1985, p. 1788.

116. The originating and moving force behind the amendment was Sen. Phil Gramm (R. Tex.). His cosponsors well complemented Gramm's determination: "Rudman is praised for bringing a respectability, particularly on defense issues, that Gramm lacked, while Hollings gave the product a bipartisan label" (Jacqueline Calmes, "Gramm: Making Waves, Enemies and History," *Congressional Quarterly Weekly Report,* March 15, 1986, p. 614).

would be offered to the debt ceiling measure.[117] By design, the amendment, soon popularly known as the Gramm-Rudman plan, was debated in a crisis atmosphere compounded by an imminent deadline for lifting the debt ceiling. Treasury Secretary James Baker emphasized in a letter to Senate Majority Leader Robert Dole that unless the debt ceiling bill was passed "by Monday" (only days away), the government's cash balances would be "virtually exhausted . . . and the situation will deteriorate sharply thereafter."[118] Once the Treasury's cash reserves were exhausted, it was stressed, U.S. banks would have no choice but to refuse to honor U.S. government checks, including Social Security checks and federal paychecks.

Senate Democrats, thrown off balance politically and substantively by the new plan, objected strongly to "fast track" lawmaking[119] on something so complicated and momentous as a comprehensive and controversial overhaul of the federal budget process. Senate Minority Leader Robert Byrd of West Virginia described the Gramm-Rudman amendment as a "kind of bobtailed, hybrid item veto and a constitutional amendment to balance the budget, combined," and urged the Senate to take more time to attempt to understand the legislation.[120] Senator Dole replied that "it is not a requirement here to know everything about a piece of legislation" before voting on it. "In fact," he added, "it is not a requirement to know anything about it."[121]

Despite pleas from some senators for additional consideration of the Gramm-Rudman plan, Majority Leader Dole resisted with a particularly vivid football analogy: "I think we are on about the one-inch line, and somebody wants to call timeout. That is essentially what it is. We are about ready to score, and they say, 'Let's call a timeout and maybe find a way to derail this team that has come charging down the field.'" One Democrat, Joseph Biden (D, Del.), found Senator Dole's one-inch scenario disquieting. He responded that he was uncertain if the Senate was about to score from the one-inch line or was about to plunge over the one-inch line at the edge of a cliff. "I just do not know whether that one-inch line brings me six points or puts me under six feet."[122]

117. The lack of advance senatorial awareness of the Gramm-Rudman proposal should not be taken as evidence of a lack of forethought by its principal author, Sen. Phil Gramm. "It looked like it came out of nowhere," Gramm recalled later. "The truth is, a lot of preparation went into it. Two months prior to its surfacing, the majority leader and Senator Domenici [Budget Chairman Peter V. Domenici, R, N.M.] were alerted to it. I met with every element at the White House." At the time Gramm drafted the plan, it was also with the particular intention of attaching it to legislation that he correctly foresaw would be necessary in the fall to raise the debt limit. (Ibid.)

118. *Washington Post,* Oct. 3, 1985, p. A4.

119. For discussions of legislating on the "fast track," see John F. Hoadley, "Easy Riders: Gramm-Rudman-Hollings and the Legislative Fast Track," *PS* 19, no. 1 (Winter 1986):30–36; Louis Fisher, "Across-the-Board Cuts and Behind-the-Scene Fixes," *Legislative Studies Section Newsletter,* Legislative Studies Section, American Political Science Association, vol. 9, no. 2 (April 1986), pp. 58–60; and Roger H. Davidson, " 'Grambo, or First Blood, Part Two': The New Improved Budget Process," *Legislative Studies Section Newsletter,* vol. 9, no. 2 (April 1986), pp. 55–58. Fast-track legislation is discussed in chapter 3 above.

120. Fisher, "Across-the-Board Cuts," p. 59.

121. *Congressional Record,* Oct. 6, 1985, p. S12758.

122. Fisher, "Across-the-Board Cuts," p. 59.

Senate consideration of the Gramm-Rudman amendment was further characterized by advice given to one floor advocate of the plan by Majority Leader Dole: "Don't get up and explain it again. Some of us are for it."[123]

Despite efforts by some Democratic senators—particularly Gary Hart of Colorado, Daniel Patrick Moynihan of New York, and Byrd—to delay final Senate action, many other Democrats and Republicans decided to support Gramm-Rudman because of its promise to achieve a balanced federal budget within six years. The country, these senators believed, was clamoring for deficit reduction. The politics of the situation also fueled the plan's quick passage. With twenty-two Senate Republicans up for reelection in 1986 and control of the chamber at stake, Republican senators wanted to demonstrate their commitment to cutting deficits. Senate Democrats, on the other hand, were reluctant to stall action for fear of giving Republicans a campaign issue. Many senators, too, were so frustrated by past legislative-executive ineffectiveness and gridlock in reducing deficits that they supported the Gramm-Rudman amendment notwithstanding profound misgivings about its efficacy or constitutionality.

On October 9, 1985, the Senate voted 75–24 to add the budget-balancing plan to the debt ceiling bill (H.J. Res. 372), and the next day, October 10, the Senate approved the debt-increase bill along with its controversial rider by a 51–37 vote. As *Congressional Quarterly* pointed out, the highly complex and uncertain Gramm-Rudman plan had not been "subjected to committee hearings, economic or other analyses, or to the preliminary revisions of committees with expertise." Changes, some significant, had been made in the proposal in the days following its initial unveiling; these revisions, however, had been worked out in private discussions. "Both the changes and the basic plan were presented for Senate approval without material to explain their impact."[124] Senate passage of Gramm-Rudman was remarkable in a number of ways; *Congressional Quarterly* summarized this uniqueness as follows: "The Senate has approved an extraordinary budget-balancing plan, as part of an extraordinary increase in the federal debt limit, and done so in a manner that defies normal procedures for changes of such importance."[125]

Overview of Gramm-Rudman

Thus far we have not discussed in detail the substance of the deficit control legislation as it passed the Senate. In this regard, our treatment of the Gramm-Rudman plan has been similar to that of the U.S. Senate. The proposal was not considered at all there in October in terms of its specifics. Senators at that time were not voting for a clearly defined program but for a concept. But what had the Senate adopted when it approved the forty-page Gramm-Rudman amendment and sent it to the House?

The objective of the deficit control legislation was quite simple: to achieve a balanced federal budget in six years. The plan established a statutory schedule that would

123. Ibid.
124. Elizabeth Wehr, "Senate Passes Plan to Balance Federal Budget," *Congressional Quarterly Weekly Report,* Oct. 12, 1985, p. 2035.
125. Ibid.

The Pathway to Zero Deficits

Fiscal Year	Deficit Target
1986	$180* billion
1987	144
1988	108
1989	72
1990	36
1991	0

SOURCE: Joint Explanatory Statement of the Committee of Conference, December 10, 1985, p. 75.

*As later enacted into law, the FY 1986 deficit figure was $171.9 billion rather than $180 billion as proposed by the Senate; the figures for the other fiscal years remained the same.

"zero out" federal deficits by 1991. It required that a set amount ($36 billion) be chopped yearly from the previous year's allowable deficit ceiling, with the specific figures established by law for each year (see accompanying table).

To ensure that Congress and the president met the successive installment payments on the deficit, Gramm-Rudman contained an automatic deficit reduction mechanism known as sequestration. It was the core element of the whole proposal. What the sequestration mechanism would do was to change the political dynamic between the branches. Should the legislative and executive branches deadlock or be otherwise unable to cut the deficit enough, then the president would be required to make across-the-board spending cuts evenly divided between domestic and defense programs to achieve the prescribed deficit ceiling. No further action would be required of Congress. In short, inaction would produce action—a situation totally contrary to the normal course of legislative-executive politics. "Without an automatic spending cut, you don't guarantee an outcome," noted Representative Richard Gephardt (D, Mo.). "And that's what this [proposal] is all about, guaranteeing an outcome."[126]

Because of its fundamental importance, the sequestration mechanism merits further discussion. Whether it would be put into effect would depend, first, on whether Congress had met the deficit targets during its annual consideration of spending and other measures and, second, on reports prepared by three governmental agencies: the executive branch Office of Management and Budget (OMB), the Congressional Budget Office (CBO), and the General Accounting Office (GAO).

Under Gramm-Rudman, the OMB and the CBO would prepare by August 15 of each fiscal year a joint report for the GAO that estimates if—and by how much—the mandated deficit ceilings will be breached because of spending decisions by Congress together with other economic developments. If the OMB and CBO disagree on their estimates, they would be legally required to average their findings, although each agency

126. *New York Times,* Oct. 16, 1985, p. A22.

could also transmit its own analysis to the GAO. The OMB/CBO report, constituting a "snapshot" of the projected deficit for the fiscal year, would also contain proposals for program-by-program spending reductions based on complicated formulas contained in the Gramm-Rudman legislation.

The composite report would serve as the basic guide for the issuance of a GAO report by August 25 identifying the amount of potential excess deficit and specifying necessary spending reductions across each of the domestic and defense programs of the government. These reductions would be based on the aforementioned 50–50 split between defense and domestic programs, somewhat modified by other rules and requirements set forth in the Gramm-Rudman legislation. By September 1, the president would be required by law to issue a sequestration order (the GAO's report would be the equivalent of a draft order, which the president, however, could not change) that would eliminate the excess deficit. There would be a month's delay before the president's order would take effect, although during this period (September 1 to October 1) agencies would also be forbidden from spending any potentially sequestered funds.

The GAO's August report would say, in effect, "Nice job, Congress, but you didn't quite meet the deficit targets." The September period would give Congress and the president one last chance to do just that. "We will have the month of September," pointed out Senator Robert Packwood (R, Ore.), "to reorder the sequester order cuts if we don't like where they are going to fall."[127] In fact, the operative assumption and hope of those who advocated the automatic approach to spending cuts was that automatic cuts would never actually go into effect. It was anticipated that the threat that across-the-board cuts might be invoked would be so politically and substantively intolerable to Congress that this specter would compel agreement on alternate means of meeting the targeted deficit figure. Sequestration would occur, noted Senator Carl Levin (D, Mich.), only "if the President and the Congress can't agree on a better way to reduce the deficit by the specified mandatory amounts."[128]

If there was no agreement on an alternative "September" deficit reduction plan, the president's sequestration order would become fully effective on October 15. This final order would be based on a revised GAO report taking into account any early fall actions of Congress and other developments affecting the excess deficit calculation. Once the president issued the final order, its effect would be to supersede the earlier one and mandate uniform spending cuts to meet the deficit target figure.

Under Gramm-Rudman, Congress would have yet a third opportunity to pass its own deficit reductions as an alternative to across-the-board sequestration. The Act authorized the Senate Budget Committee, within two days of the issuance of the final order, to "affirm the impact of the order issued . . . in whole or in part." Legislation that modified the specific deficit reductions of the final order by making its own economies (while still achieving the overall deficit figure) would be considered under expedited congressional procedures. The last step in the sequestration cycle would occur

127. *Congressional Record*, Dec. 11, 1985, pp. S17382–83.
128. *Congressional Record*, Dec. 17, 1985, p. S17834.

when the GAO issues a November 15 compliance report that, among other things, would review the extent to which the sequestering process has comported with the balanced budget law. In summary, the sequestration timetable would be as follows:[129]

August 15	The "snapshot" of the projected deficit is taken.
August 20	The OMB and CBO jointly report to the GAO.
August 25	The GAO issues sequestration recommendations to the president, based on the findings of the OMB and CBO.
September 1	The president issues the sequestration order based on the GAO report.
October 1	The presidential order takes effect.
October 5	The OMB and CBO issue a revised report reflecting final congressional actions and changing economic conditions.
October 10	The GAO issues revised recommendations to the president.
October 15	The final presidential sequestration order, based on the revised report, is effective.
November 15	The GAO Compliance Report is issued.

Gramm-Rudman Assessed

The preceding description of the new budgetary procedures established by Gramm-Rudman may make the plan sound more technical in character than it actually was. In fact, what was central in the Gramm-Rudman approach to deficit control was an absolute statutory requirement that the government meet a yearly decreasing allowable deficit figure. Failing that, across-the-board cuts would automatically go into effect for numerous governmental programs—from operating funds for the FBI to government cancer research to military weapons purchases to federal grants to the states for education. The consequences of an across-the-board sequestration order going into effect would be devastating to many government programs widely seen as essential. As Senatory Gary Hart of Colorado wittily put it, should this actually happen, "We will cut off our nose to spite the deficit."[130]

The Gramm-Rudman plan was soundly criticized, even while support was building for it in both House and Senate. Many supporters of the proposal conceded its imperfections. In a classic admission, one of the cosponsors of the plan, Senator Warren B. Rudman (R, N.H.), was widely cited as describing his proposal as "a bad idea whose time has come."[131] Gramm-Rudman opponent Senator J. Bennett Johnson (D, La.) agreed with Rudman that the plan was far from perfect and suggested that congressional

---

129. For a full explanation of Gramm-Rudman, see the conference report printed in the *Congressional Record*, Dec. 10, 1985, pp. H11684–717. A briefer and more assessable yet comprehensive analysis of the legislation is in E. Wehr, "Congress Enacts Far-Reaching Budget Measure," *Congressional Quarterly Weekly Report*, Dec. 14, 1985, pp. 2604–11.

130. Otto Friedrich, "A Bad Idea Whose Time Has Come," *Time*, Feb. 3, 1986, p. 81.

131. Paul Taylor, "Antideficit Bill's Backers Among Its Worst Enemies," *Washington Post*, Nov. 7, 1985, p. A1; Elizabeth Wehr, "Congress Enacts Far-Reaching Budget Measure," p. 2604.

support for the legislation reminded him of "the person who writes on the bathroom mirror in lipstick, 'Stop me before I kill again.' "[132]

One of the most vivid descriptions of the Gramm-Rudman proposal came from outside Congress, in fact from overseas, in an editorial in the internationally respected British magazine *The Economist*. It concluded, "The Gramm-Rudman legislation is one of the most desperate acts ever to have come out of Washington. It is like a girl who can't say no, so she puts on a chastity belt and throws away the key."[133]

Rather less colorful but certainly comprehensive in its assessment was the judgment expressed by economist Walter Heller, President Kennedy's chief economic adviser and long-time liberal economic spokesman. Gramm-Rudman, he said, "is economically capricious, socially unfair, militarily risky, constitutionally questionable, politically irresponsible, procedurally perverse, and administratively outlandish."[134]

It was against this background of harsh substantive verdicts but also strong political support that the Gramm-Rudman plan moved from its overwhelming victory in the Republican-dominated Senate to consideration by the Democratically led House.

Gramm-Rudman Lands in the House

Following Senate passage on October 10, 1985, of the debt ceiling measure with its deficit reduction rider, Senate Majority Leader Robert Dole had anticipated fast action by the House because of the need to avoid immediate default by the federal government on its financial obligations. The Treasury Department, however, undercut Dole's expectation later that day by announcing novel, short-term financing maneuvers that would permit the government—for the moment—to pay its bills, including such political absolutes as Social Security and civil service pensions, without breaching the existing statutory debt ceiling. Those maneuvers angered Senator Dole; by these bookkeeping innovations, the Treasury Department had "pulled the plug" on efforts to achieve a speedy final passage of Gramm-Rudman and made earlier dire warnings of imminent default by the Treasury and Senate leaders appear grossly exaggerated.[135]

Democratic leaders of the House had followed Senate action on Gramm-Rudman with keen interest and had already explored ways to handle the deficit reduction bill once it landed in their laps. Majority Whip Thomas Foley (D, Wash.) took the lead by convening a small group of party colleagues to plan strategy and consider Democratic alternatives to Gramm-Rudman. Members of this group met scores of times with different Democratic factions to forge agreement on necessary modifications of the balanced budget proposal. "What began to create our coalition," said Representative Leon Panet-

---

132. "Look, Ma! No Hands!" *TIme*, Dec. 23, 1985, p. 18. Senator Johnson less vividly but perhaps even more dramatically also characterized Gramm-Rudman as "the most far-reaching, the most horrendous, the most damaging to the constitutional process and the most extreme piece of legislation" that he had ever seen considered by the Senate. Jacob V. Lamar, Jr., "Dancing Around the Deficit," *Time*, Oct. 21, 1985, p. 37.
133. "Washington Scramble," *The Economist*, Dec. 21, 1985, p. 9.
134. "Look, Ma! No Hands!" p. 18.
135. *New York Times*, Oct. 11, 1985, p. A20.

ta (D, Cal.), a key member of Foley's group, "was the reality that the votes ultimately would be there in the House to pass some form of Gramm-Rudman."[136] The Democratic goal, therefore, would be not to defeat the budget plan, but to modify it in appropriate ways.

Central in the Democratic leaders' assessments was the realization that a large number of House members, frustrated by continued political deadlock between the branches over controlling federal spending and concerned about public reaction to soaring deficits, supported the thrust of Gramm-Rudman. Many House members, however, were also critical of the Senate's "rush job" in adopting the legislation without careful study. Representative Berkley Bedell (D, Iowa) spoke for many representatives in identifying serious problems in Gramm-Rudman as originally written: "First, [the Senate's proposal] would have delayed significant deficit reductions until after the next election. Second, it would have devastated many domestic programs, but left much of the military untouched. Finally, it would have given the President too much discretion over cuts that are supposed to be equal and automatic."[137]

The Foley group, along with other Democrats, considered numerous modifications of and alternatives to the Senate-passed plan. They also remembered ruefully how then-Democratic Representative Phil Gramm had helped stampede the House in 1981 into accepting President Reagan's massive domestic spending reduction proposal. House Democrats were determined not to have a repeat performance on Gramm-Rudman. With time running out on the must debt ceiling bill, however, even with the creative financial ploys devised by the Treasury Department, there was insufficient time for the party to reach agreement on a full-blown option to Gramm-Rudman. The House Democratic response to the plan would have to await another time and a different forum.

Republican members in the House were not suffering the same indecision as Democrats. "We don't need extensive hearings on Gramm-Rudman," explained Minority Leader Robert Michel of Illinois. "What we need is old-fashioned guts."[138]

The House officially had received the measure from the Senate on October 10, the day of Senate passage. On October 11, the House voted not to consider Gramm-Rudman in any detailed manner and instead to let a conference committee work on the deficit reduction plan. The House decision sent the debt ceiling measure, together with the Gramm-Rudman amendment, directly to conference, foregoing normal House deliberation and formal approval or disapproval. The only guidance provided to House conferees came in a resolution, backed by both Democratic and Republican leaders, instructing the representatives of the House to support in conference "mechanisms for deficit reductions, including specific and mandatory budget goals for achieving a balanced budget within the next six years."[139]

These instructions constituted a broad endorsement of the concept of Gramm-Rudman without a formal approval of its specifics, and consequently enjoyed strong

---

136. Richard E. Cohen, "Balanced Budget Plan Forces House Democrats to Get Their Act Together," *National Journal*, Nov. 16, 1985, p. 2587.
137. *Congressional Record*, Dec. 12, 1985, p. E5622.
138. Lamar, "Dancing Around the Deficit," p. 37.
139. *Congressional Record*, Oct. 11, 1985, p. H8721.

House support and passed overwhelmingly, 354 to 15. Despite this seeming near unanimity, deep disagreements remained in the House (as well as in the Senate) over the details of deficit reduction legislation. These matters were delegated to the conference.

Selection of Conferees

Whenever legislation goes to conference, a major determinant of "what will happen" is "who is there." The selection of conferees is a key element of conference committee politics. The makeup of the October House-Senate conference on Gramm-Rudman was noteworthy in various respects. First, the conference was a large one, especially on the House side. In addition, the conference delegations from both House and Senate contained an unusual mix of heavyweight political talent. Finally, in an ironic twist, all three of the original sponsors (Gramm, Rudman, and Hollings) were absent—at least as official conferees.

The House contingent for the conference was indeed quite large. Forty-eight representatives—thirty-one Democrats and seventeen Republicans—were selected by House Speaker Tip O'Neill and by Republican leader Robert Michel to develop the House position on Gramm-Rudman. One reason the delegation was so large was to accommodate a number of influential, respected legislators. Six full committee chairmen were included, along with several elected party leaders from both sides and many acknowledged House budget experts such as Representative Panetta and Connie Mack (R, Fla.).

Ways and Means Chairman Dan Rostenkowski (D, Ill.) was named by the Speaker to head the forty-eight-member House delegation. Thirteen other Ways and Means members were also chosen as conferees. This was, however, to create extraordinary time and attention pressures on these key conference members. The Ways and Means Committee was under a simultaneously urgent need to complete its work on a massive rewrite of the tax system. An unanswered question at the time the balanced budget conference began was whether two legislative projects of such importance could be handled by the Ways and Means conferees without delaying action on either.

Clearly, the key House conferee would be Rostenkowski, both because of his leadership of the House conference delegation on Gramm-Rudman and because of his influential role on the pending tax legislation. In light of his strategic position, Rostenkowski was urged to extract concessions from President Reagan and other interested parties on each bill. "A number of us told Danny privately and publicly," said Representative Thomas Downey (D, N.Y.), "that he's the one holding all the cards on this, and he can tell the president unless he's reasonable on" Gramm-Rudman he will not get a tax bill.[140]

The House conferees, of course, lacked a formal counterproposal of their own; there was only the general House mandate that endorsed the overall concept of Gramm-Rudman. As a result, the goals of the House delegation, stressed conferee Panetta, would be actually quite modest—to "clean [Gramm-Rudman] up and make it as fair and as constitutional as possible."[141]

140. *Washington Times*, Oct. 16, 1985, p. 4A.
141. *Los Angeles Times*, Oct. 21, 1985, p. 10.

As for the Senate, five Republicans and four Democrats had been appointed as Senate conferees, with everyone but Carl Levin (D, Mich.) drawn from either the Finance or Budget committees.[142] Senator Robert Packwood (R, Ore.), chairman of the Senate Finance Committee, would lead the nine-member Senate conference. The task of the Senate conferees officially was relatively simple: to defend the Gramm-Rudman legislation as it had been overwhelmingly adopted by that chamber. With the House on record as favoring the deficit limitation proposal at least generally, the Senate position looked strong.

The big surprise in the selection of Senate conferees, however, was that Senators Gramm, Rudman, and Hollings were not among the nine. The official explanation was that neither Gramm nor Rudman served on the two relevant fiscal panels, while Hollings was outranked on Budget by Lawton Chiles (D, Fla.). The real reason for their absence, it was widely believed, lay in a deliberate decision by the Senate leadership not to appoint Gramm as a conferee to avoid raising the ire of House leaders and conferees. Rudman and Hollings simply got caught up in this basic decision.[143]

Senator Gramm, a highly combative congressman, had been distrusted by House leaders even back in 1981 when he was still a representative and a nominal Democrat. When the landmark Gramm-Latta spending cut bill went to conference that year, Gramm was purposefully excluded as a conferee and thus was prevented from advocating in conference his own legislation. During House floor consideration of Gramm-Rudman in late 1985, now *Republican* Senator Gramm hung around the House chamber so visibly that Republican leaders reportedly asked their Senate counterparts to help them get him off the floor. Said one prominent House Republican, "Democrats hate his guts and some Republicans have problems too." The Senate decision to leave Gramm off the Senate conference delegation on Gramm-Rudman was applauded even by one of the legislation's original sponsors, Ernest Hollings, who stated, "I think it showed good judgment on Dole's part not to include Gramm on the conference because of the known hostility House members have toward him."[144]

The Conference Begins

Amid the glare of television cameras, watchful journalists, and hordes of onlookers, the balanced budget conference began on October 16 in the cavernous House Cannon Caucus Room. Senators Gramm and Rudman, although not conferees, "con-

142. Senator Levin was apparently included as a conferee because of his role on the Senate floor in getting amendments adopted to Gramm-Rudman that limited the president's discretion in making spending cuts. He also had one other distinction: he knew the Gramm-Rudman legislation better than most senators, including at times its principal author. Minutes before one key modification was adopted on the Senate floor, for example, "Gramm explained it in a way that Levin felt was wrong. Levin and Rudman set the record straight" (Jacqueline Calmes, "Gramm: Making Waves, Enemies and History," p. 614).

143. Jonathan Fuerbringer, "Deciphering the Balanced-Budget Bill," *New York Times*, Oct. 24, 1985, p. B14. Speaker O'Neill, for example, publicly attacked Gramm for being "more responsible than anyone except Reagan for the [fiscal] mess the country was in" (Brit Hume, "Gramm Strikes Again," *New Republic*, Nov. 4, 1985, p. 11).

144. Calmes, "Gramm: Making Waves, Enemies and History," pp. 614, 615.

ducted what amounted to a pep rally for their plan [before a group of House Republicans] in an adjacent room just as the conference got under way."[145] All three sponsors were also subsequently present in the Caucus Room to observe the proceedings of the conference.

Senate Finance Chairman Robert Packwood (R, Ore.) became chairman of the conference under the tax panels' custom of alternating that position between the two chambers. Opening the discussion, Packwood stressed the wide support for Gramm-Rudman present in the Senate and urged the conferees to work together to enact a plan to reduce the deficit. House delegation leader Rostenkowski responded by highlighting three main goals of House Democrats: to insure that the legislative-executive balance of power was not upset by the ceding of new power to the president, to develop provisions that would suspend automatic cuts in the event of economic recession or slowdown, and to guarantee that defense and nondefense programs were treated fairly and equally should the sequestration process be triggered.[146]

Unspoken by Representative Rostenkowski was another goal: House Democrats wanted spending cuts to begin in 1986, before the November elections, rather than after. Suspicious because the Republican Senate had put off any cutting of programs until after the 1986 election, Speaker O'Neill viewed the deficit proposal as a "Republican incumbents' protection bill." House Democrats were determined to lower the $180 billion deficit target recommended by the Senate for 1986 (which in fact was higher than current fiscal projections) so the electorate could feel the pinch of having popular programs cut prior to the November election. If politically unpopular cuts were going to be necessary under Gramm-Rudman, they reasoned, let them initially occur at a time when the electorate could respond.

Unlike traditional conferences, in which bargaining and negotiating are immediately evident, the first several meetings of the balanced budget conference resembled more a fact-finding hearing. Conferees sought to acquire some common understanding of the plan's provisions and complexities. Because of the rush to pass Gramm-Rudman without public hearings on the legislation in either chamber, very few members of the House or Senate possessed in-depth information on how the proposal was to work. House Democrats, in particular, pushed for detailed answers about the plan from their Senate brethren from the originating chamber. The person the Senate conferees necessarily looked to for assistance was Stephen E. Bell, staff director of the Senate Budget Committee. In effect, Bell assumed a role akin to that of a "witness" at a committee hearing. As one account noted:

> At the start of the conference, [Bell] sat at the center of the staff table. Most of the tough questions posed by House Democrats, and some Republicans, were directed at Mr. Bell. He defined what was not defined. He made lists of what would be cut and what would not. To the annoyance of some of the bill's sponsors, he often told

145. *Washington Post,* Oct. 17, 1985, p. A5.
146. See Elizabeth Wehr, "Conferees Strive to Fathom Senate Budget-Balancing Plan," *Congressional Quarterly Weekly Report,* Oct. 19, 1985, pp. 2091–92; idem, "Difficult Questions Unresolved in Budget Measure Conference," *Congressional Quarterly Weekly Report,* Oct. 26, 1985, pp. 2147–48.

the lawmakers, frankly, that the bill was "silent" on certain subjects, that he really had no answer for their persistent questions.[147]

Some conferees even proposed that Bell should be "stapled" to the Gramm-Rudman legislation so he would always be available to answer questions about it.[148]

Scores of other activities occurring simultaneously with this fact-finding stage of conference deliberations influenced analysis of the plan. While the conference was underway, several standing congressional committees found the opportunity to hold public hearings on the Gramm-Rudman plan. Some of these hearings were conducted by committee chairmen who were also serving as conference participants. Representative David Obey (D, Wis.), for example, headed the Joint Economic Committee, and in that capacity chaired a committee meeting that heard criticisms of the plan from the 1985 Nobel Laureate in Economics, Franco Modigliani. The Nobel winner scathingly referred to some aspects of Gramm-Rudman as "Mickey Mousing" and sketched an alternative deficit reduction plan.[149] Another conferee, Jack Brooks (D, Tex.), chairman of the House Government Operations Committee, also conducted committee hearings during this period and heard from numerous witnesses on the impact of the Gramm-Rudman proposal. In addition, many members also offered their own ideas and interpretations of Gramm-Rudman on the floor of the House and Senate and elsewhere. House Judiciary Chairman Peter Rodino (D, N.J.), for example, sent a letter to one House conferee, Mike Synar (D, Okla.), directly challenging the plan's constitutionality.

The ongoing conference proceedings were also the object of considerable national popular and press attention. C-SPAN, the public affairs cable television channel, telecast the conference meetings live, gavel-to-gavel, and scheduled extensive additional programing dealing with the deficit reduction measure.[150] While the conference was engaged in its fact-finding labors, the national press and media were filled with comments and critiques of Gramm-Rudman. Nationally syndicated columnist and ABC commentator George F. Will, for instance, termed the proposal "government by meat cleaver."[151] Administration spokesmen such as Secretary of Defense Casper Weinberger raised the possibility that the president might invoke his commander-in-chief powers if necessary to avoid across-the-board cuts in defense. (In response, some House conferees sought to call the Attorney General, the OMB director, and even Weinberger himself to testify before the conference on this highly contentious threat.) Numerous interest groups also funneled information to selected conferees on the effect of Gramm-Rudman in their program areas. This flood of information and interpretation took place in an atmosphere of urgency. The government could shut down in part, the conference was told, if the debt raising bill to which Gramm-Rudman was attached failed to win

147. Fuerbringer, "Deciphering the Balanced-Budget Bill," p. B14. One congressman reportedly likened Bell's role at the conference to that of a "royal priest" who interprets the meaning of the entrails of the Gramm-Rudman proposal for the untutored conferees (ibid).

148. Ibid.

149. See *Congressional Record,* Oct. 22, 1985, p. E4718.

150. Kurt Sayenga, "The Full Picture: Complete Coverage of a Major Battle," *C-SPAN Update,* vol. 3, no. 42 (Oct. 28, 1985), p. 2.

151. *Washington Post,* Oct. 13, 1985, p. B7.

final congressional enactment before the short-term borrowing palliatives already invoked by the executive branch had run their course in a few days.[152]

The Conference Breaks Down

After devoting considerable attention to an overall review of Gramm-Rudman and listening to a variety of budget experts including CBO Director Rudolph Penner, the conferees buckled down to the detailed work of resolving their substantial differences. House delegation leader Rostenkowski named four bipartisan task forces from the House group, which would meet in private to identify and consider changes to the Gramm-Rudman plan.[153] Senator Packwood stressed that speedy progress in reconciling House-Senate differences was necessary and intimated that otherwise he would end the conferences and let the full House of Representatives decide on subsequent action.

As Rostenkowski's task forces translated general House concerns into specifics, the conferees found themselves grappling with at least four issues. The first concerned the impact of Gramm-Rudman on the economy, specifically, whether mandated cuts might trigger or prolong a recession. Questions concerning how to forecast economic slowdown and under what economic conditions the requirements of the act would be waived were key matters under debate.

Another topic had to do with the constitutionality of Gramm-Rudman. Two questions were prominent here: whether mandatory, across-the-board spending cuts delegated too much of Congress's constitutional power of the purse to an automatic process administered by the president, and conversely, whether this procedure violated the separation of powers by granting significant executive branch administrative responsibilities unconstitutionally to arms of Congress (the Congressional Budget Office and the General Accounting Office). A third concern involved sweeping changes that would be made by the plan in Congress's budget process. Gramm-Rudman would significantly accelerate Congress's budgetary timetable, expedite consideration of authorization and appropriation measures, expand the scope of the legislative budget resolution, and authorize new points of order (parliamentary objections) in order to help the House and Senate meet the deficit targets. All these changes were contentious proposals in both chambers, where resistance to centralized authority traditionally has been strong and in recent years has even been increasing.

Finally, the details of sequestration, such as which programs should be exempt and what discretionary authority—if any—the president should have in making the required cuts, were pervasive concerns. With selected major activities of government such as Social Security, interest on the national debt, and specified other programs exempted from cuts in the Senate-passed version, the burden of fiscal reduction was shifted onto the rest of the budget. Questions of fairness and evenhandedness of treatment of the remaining domestic and defense portions of the budget dominated the debates. An

152. See Helen Dewar, "House, Senate Split on Budget Balancing," *Washington Post*, Nov. 2, 1985, p. A7; *Washington Times*, Nov. 1, 1985, p. 1A; *Los Angeles Times*, Oct. 31, 1985, p. 14; and Gerald M. Boyd, "Reagan Aides Prod Congress on Debt," *New York Times*, Oct. 31, 1985.

153. *New York Times*, Oct. 24, 1985, p. B14.

additional element of discussion was a congressional determination that the president must be bound to adhere strictly to the sequestration order and not be able to change it unilaterally to suit his policy priorities.

As conferees continued to work on these issues, President Reagan weighed in with a public statement that charged the conference committee with "inexcusable dithering and delay."[154] To heighten the pressure, the administration reported once again that the government was running out of money to pay its obligations. Unless the conferees reached agreement on the plan by November 1, the government would most reluctantly be forced to tap into the traditionally sacrosanct Social Security Trust Fund. The Senate, too, applied pressure by adopting a resolution opposing any short-term extension of the debt ceiling alone and urging the House to come up with a comprehensive deficit reduction counterproposal. Otherwise the Senate would end the conference. The *Washington Post* reported that "unless there is a House response . . . , Packwood . . . will get the Senate to approve the legislation again and send it back to the House. That maneuver could force Democratic leaders to come up with an alternative to fend off House passage of the Senate measure without change."[155]

Much to the chagrin of Senate leaders, however, the representatives did develop a specific even if not comprehensive counterproposal. On October 30, House conferees voted 36 to 12 for a plan that would cut the deficit target for 1986 to $161 billion, a significantly deeper cut than contained in Gramm-Rudman. In a bit of one-upmanship, House conferee Jake Pickle (D, Tex.) told the Senate conferees, "We've made a bona fide offer and all you've got to do is accept it."[156] Another Democratic conferee, William Gray (Pa.), wore a button saying, "Take the Medicine Now." Senator Packwood, however, described the preferred medicine as "nonsense"; it is, he said, "an attempt to absolutely choke a new process before it gets a chance to work."[157] Amid sharp partisan and intercameral exchanges, Senator Packwood indicated that his side would refuse to consider piecemeal changes in Gramm-Rudman (the traditional approach to reconciling bicameral differences) and would only deal with a complete House package. The conference adjourned for the day with each side preparing such comprehensive plans.

The next day, October 31—which ironically also happened to be Halloween—the conference committee reconvened in the huge Room 1100 of the House Longworth Office Building, the Main Hearing Room of the Ways and Means Committee.[158] The fifty-seven conferees were supplemented by hundreds of staffers, journalists, lobbyists, and other interested persons. The crush of bodies around the double horseshoe tables reserved for the conferees was such that speakers, in responding to questions, resorted to

---

154. *Washington Times*, Oct. 29, 1985, p. 2A.
155. *Washington Post*, Oct. 29, 1985, p. A10.
156. *Washington Post*, Oct. 31, 1985, p. 3A; Jonathan Fuerbringer, "Conference on Balancing Budget Stalls," *New York Times*, Oct. 31, 1985, p. 16.
157. Edward Walsh and Helen Dewar, "Conference Panel Splits Over '86 Deficit Target," *Washington Post*, Oct. 31, 1985, p. A12; Fuerbringer, "Conference on Balancing Budget Stalls," p. 16.
158. The specifics concerning this conference meeting of October 31 are based on personal observations by one of the authors of this conference session.

identifying their locations by hand gestures and statements such as, "Senator—I'm over here." Senator Gramm looked on from a second-row seat behind the conferees and busied himself at times by passing notes to conference allies such as Senator Pete Domenici (R, N.M.).

Immediately after Senator Packwood called the conference to order, he announced that the conference would stand in recess for ten minutes. The Senate conferees would meet in a nearby office, he stated, in order to review the situation. House delegation leader Rostenkowski announced a similar meeting for a half-dozen key members of the House contingent. Each delegation met behind closed doors in order to plan chamber strategy; this political task would presumably be far easier in the seclusion of private offices than in the conference room under television lights and before the live cameras of C-SPAN and other television networks. The recess of ten mintues, as usual, stretched to many times that figure as journalists and lobbyists jockeyed for some word on what was going on behind closed doors.

Finally, the House and Senate conferees returned to the conference room. The House announced its package of changes to Gramm-Rudman while the Senate outlined its revisions of the plan. The details of the proposed amendments were not clear to everyone; questions such as, "What does this mean?" were recurrent. There were polite disagreements and considerable uncertainty concerning the effects of specific provisions. The response to a discussion as to whether the result of one item would be a $20-, $23-, or $30-billion figure was, "I'm not sure. We will work this out later."[159]

Despite confusion over such multi-billion dollar "details," the important differences between the chamber plans were evident. They were as follows:

House	*Senate*
$161 billion deficit target for 1986.	$171.9 billion deficit target for 1986.
CBO would be in charge of forecasting the excess deficit figure that would trigger sequestration.	CBO and OMB together would forecast the excess deficit figure, which would then be reviewed and certified by the GAO.
Any member could challenge the constitutionality of the act under expedited procedures. If any part of the act was declared unconstitutional, the whole act would fall.	If any part of Gramm-Rudman was declared unconstitutional, only that part would be invalid, leaving the remainder intact.
Low-income programs would be exempt from automatic cuts.	Low-income programs would be included in sequestration.[160]

Following the presentation of the two plans, the conference again paused while House and Senate conference leaders met together behind closed doors for about thirty minutes in order to discuss the proposals. Then they came back to the conference meeting room to announce that the conference negotiations were deadlocked and that the conference committee consequently stood adjourned.[161] Despite this discouraging de-

159. Ibid.
160. "The Budget Bills: A Comparison," *New York Times,* Nov. 2, 1985, p. 9.
161. Elizabeth Wer, "House Ok's Democrats' Budget-Balancing Plan," *Congressional Quarterly Weekly Report,* Nov. 2, 1985, p. 2191. See also Helen Dewar and Edward Walsh, "Budget Conference Breaks Down as U.S. Bumps Against Debt Ceiling," *Washington Post,* Nov. 1, 1985, p. A5.

velopment, conference chairman Packwood remained optimistic and noted that the two sides had agreed "to amicably disagree." Even now, Packwood suggested, the differences between the House Democratic version and Senate plan were not "irreconcilable."[162] Nevertheless, the fact remained that even with comprehensive proposals now put forth by the House and Senate delegations, conference agreement was nowhere near at hand, and the bicameral reconciliation process had broken down.

With the collapse of conference negotiations on October 31, the Reagan administration dipped into the Social Security Trust Fund to finance continued government operations. Members of both parties had vigorously sought to avoid this drastic "disinvestment" decision in order not to arouse the concern of the nation's elderly, but their reluctance proved to be of no avail. OMB Director James Miller also pointed to yet another deadline: unless agreement was reached on a deficit reduction plan by November 14, on that date the government would have to "shut down." In a sharp attack on House Democrats, Miller stated that their refusal to accept the Senate's revamped version of Gramm-Rudman threatens the nation's "international reputation and disturbs financial markets on which we depend to refinance the national debt."[163]

A Return to the Back-and Forth Amendment Approach

Following the collapse of the conference on October 31, a conference report "in disagreement" was brought to the House floor the next day, November 1. This would give the House the opportunity either to support the House conferee plan or the modified version of Gramm-Rudman offered by the Senate conference delegation. Uppermost in the minds of the House Democratic leadership was insuring party unity so that their deficit reduction plan, and not the Senate's, would be endorsed by the House. "We learned our lesson in 1981," noted Democratic Representative Panetta.[164] (That year a number of conservative Democrats—later termed Boll Weevils—joined with House Republicans to pass Reagan's sweeping tax and budget plan of that year.)

At a crucial meeting on the morning of November 1, House Speaker O'Neill appealed to his Democratic colleagues to stay together. He also met separately with the members of the Black Caucus and pledged that the programs for the poor exempted from sequestration under the House plan would be "nonnegotiable" in any subsequent conference meeting with the Senate. Additionally, by pledging not to *expand* the list of exempt domestic programs, O'Neill also was able to win the backing of conservative Democrats for the version of Gramm-Rudman drafted by House conferees.[165]

Shortly after the House convened on November 1, Ways and Means Chairman Rostenkowski formally submitted the conference report that said the House and Senate

162. Jonathan Fuerbringer, "House Showdown is Set on Budget," *New York Times,* Nov. 1, 1985, p. B7; and Helen Dewar, "House, Senate Split on Budget Balancing," *Washington Post,* Nov. 2, 1985, p. A1.
163. *Washington Times,* Oct. 31, 1985, p. 3A.
164. Dewar, "House, Senate Split on Budget Balancing," p. A6.
165. "House Democrats Unite for Balanced-Budget Vote," *Washington Post,* Nov. 2, 1985, p. A7; Jonathan Fuerbringer, "Plan to Wipe Out U.S. Deficit by '90 Passed by House," *New York Times,* Nov. 2, 1985, p. 9. See also Steven V. Roberts, "Budget Battle: Deft O'Neill Maneuver," *New York Times,* Nov. 2, 1985, p. 9.

"have been unable to agree." Procedurally, what the House now had before it were the three Senate amendments to the statutory debt ceiling bill that were still in bicameral disagreement. Two were relatively minor and quickly disposed of. The key amendment in disagreement, of course, was the Gramm-Rudman rider.

Rostenkowski offered the standard motion to have the House recede from its disagreement with the Senate language and concur with an amendment—the House Democratic alternative presented in conference the day before. Democrat Dave Obey (Wis.) then requested that the motion be divided into two parts: first, to recede, and, second, to offer the Senate amendment. Politically, the division request, which was agreed to by a wide margin, was a test vote to demonstrate broad backing for the Democratic plan. After heated debate, both motions—including the House Democratic revision of Gramm-Rudman—were approved by the House, the latter by a 249 to 180 vote. In addition, in order to buy time for a Senate response, the House passed a five-day extension of the debt ceiling bill. Then, the House deliberately adjourned for the weekend to let the Senate stew over and respond to its actions.[166]

Later the same day, November 1, the Senate debated the House moves at length before it reached a unanimous consent agreement on how to proceed. First, the Senate directed Senator Packwood to offer a complete Senate substitute to the House substitute version of the Senate-passed plan. It further ordered that the new Packwood substitute be voted on by the Senate by November 6, with floor amendments being in order until that date. Finally, the Senate enacted, with some revision, the House's five-day debt ceiling extension measure. Majority Leader Dole was somewhat skeptical about the necessity for the latter step since the government was not expected to default until November 14. Nevertheless, the extension represented a politically useful gesture toward protecting Social Security. As Senator Packwood put it during midnight Senate debate, "Everyone's frightened of the word 'Social Security.' "[167]

Concluding Senate debate shortly after one o'clock in the morning on November 2, Majority Leader Dole summed up the confusion and frustration felt by many members at the current impasse: "It's a very complicated area. Had we done nothing, nothing would have happened. Doing what we did, nothing will happen. And had we passed the House version, nothing would have happened. So that's nothing. And that's precisely what we were arguing about."[168]

During its next three sessions, the Senate sought to assist Packwood in his redrafting efforts by debating a variety of amendments to Gramm-Rudman. Senator Donald Riegle (D, Mich.), for instance, moved that the Senate endorse lowering the deficit target for 1986 from the original figure of $180 billion to $171.9 billion—the amount earlier proposed in conference by Packwood. Senator Packwood, however, opposed this chamber stand endorsing his own recommendation and successfully urged its defeat. Recounting how difficult it was to negotiate with House conferees "on the issue of what

166. Dewar, "House, Senate Split on Budget Balancing," p. A6; Fuerbringer, "Plan to Wipe Out U.S. Deficit by '90 Passed by House," pp. 1, 9.
167. Jonathan Fuerbringer, "Budget-Balancing Plan Faces New Deadline at Midmonth," *New York Times*, Nov, 3, 1985, p. 15.
168. Associated Press, "Congress Stays Stalemated," *Milwaukee Journal*, Nov. 3. 1985; Fuerbringer, "Budget-Balancing Plan Faces New Deadline at Midmonth," p. 15.

the deficit level ought to be," Senator Packwood argued that he needed not instructions but freedom to negotiate; this would give him the "strongest hand possible going into" another conference with the House.[169] On November 6, the Senate agreed by a 74 to 24 vote to Packwood's newly evolved substitute (technically a 2d-degree amendment) to the House alternative (a 1st-degree amendment) to the Gramm-Rudman plan as originally passed by the Senate in early October. [170]

After the November 6 vote, the Senate returned its modified handiwork to the House. Because of a House prohibition against 3d-degree amendments (except by unanimous consent or by a special "rule" from the Rules Committee), the House's options for dealing with the Packwood revised proposal were essentially either to agree or to disagree to it. The House took up Packwood's substitute the same day that it passed the Senate. Republicans tried without success to win House agreement for Packwood's revision of Gramm-Rudman, with Representative Mack offering a preferential motion to agree with the Senate. (At this parliamentary stage, a motion that brings the two houses together has precedence over a motion to disagree that keeps them apart.) Representative Mack's motion, however, failed in the face of House Democratic opposition. The House then adopted a motion of disagreement to Packwood's revised proposal and formally requested a further conference with the Senate. Anticipating the naming of conferees for this second conference, Minority Whip Trent Lott (Miss.) sought to have the House managers instructed to accept the Senate's position on the schedule of deficit reductions. This motion from the minority leadership, not very surprisingly, was rejected. Representative Richard Gephardt of Missouri, a leading Democratic strategist on these matters, expressed the predominant sentiment of the House (and of the majority party) on the current situation:

> The [first] conference did break up. [Representatives] came [to the House] and voted for our proposal and sent it to the other body, and in essence, now the other body has readopted Gramm-Rudman I, and has sent it back. I think the only appropriate action, in light of those actions, is to go back to conference, and this time to see if real negotiations can take place, going through the various points that are still in contention to see if they can be resolved.[171]

On November 7, the Senate agreed to a further conference with the House, and the bicameral reconciliation process on Gramm-Rudman moved into what might be termed conference committee II.

The Second Conference Begins

Several things are worth noting as the second Gramm-Rudman conference began.[172] First, both chambers had backed their rival deficit reduction plans by wide

---

169. *Congressional Record*, Nov. 5, 1985, p. S14792. See also Jonathan Fuerbringer, "Senate Retains Plan of G.O.P. to Bar Defects," *New York Times*, Nov. 5, 1985, pp. 1, 14.

170. The Packwood substitute made fifty changes in Gramm-Rudman as it had been originally enacted by the Senate. See *Congressional Record*, Nov. 6, 1985, pp. S14908–11.

171. *Washington Post*, Nov. 14, 1985, p. A9.

172. For general background information concerning the second conference, see Elizabeth Wehr, "Fiscal Crisis, Partisanship Push Budget Conferees," *Congressional Quarterly Weekly Report*, Nov. 9, 1985, pp. 2267–70.

margins. This presaged tough negotiations among conferees, who would be reluctant to compromise quickly on the major points in disagreement. These deep-seated differences themselves might require outside intervention or extraordinary and unconventional means of resolution. Senate delegation leader Packwood, for one, predicted that these problems "may have to be solved beyond conference, above conference or out of conference."[173]

Deadline pressures, too, were much in evidence with Treasury officials warning that the government would definitely run out of money to pay its bills on November 14. Another pressure point was the summit meeting between President Reagan and Soviet leader Mikhail Gorbachev, scheduled to start on November 19. Neither Congress nor the president wanted that meeting to begin with the American government in default on its debts or with huge cuts in defense spending mandated by Gramm-Rudman.[174]

Further, both chambers decided to increase the number of its conferees for the second conference. The House delegation went from an already large forty-eight members to an even larger one of fifty-three representatives, while the Senate added four to its original contingent of nine for a total of thirteen. Large delegations in and of themselves complicate the negotiating process—but, now complicating things, the Senate additions included the legislation's original authors—Senators Gramm, Rudman, and Hollings. The inclusion of Gramm, in particular, was thought likely to heighten bicameral tensions because of the widespread dislike and distrust of him by House Democrats.

Finally, the second Gramm-Rudman conference began its negotiations in the wake of a simultaneous reaffirmation by President Reagan of the Senate plan and stepped-up criticism by Defense Secretary Weinberger of the Senate plan's automatic reduction feature as applicable to defense programs. Clearly, the conferees faced an especially difficult assignment in reaching an accord that would satisfy Senate Republicans, House Democrats, and different factions in the executive branch.

When the new conference convened on November 12, House Ways and Means leader Rostenkowski became chairman of the bicameral group, replacing Senator Packwood, in accord with the tax-writing panels' custom of rotation of the conference chairmanship. In one of his first actions as chairman, Rostenkowski announced that a "miniconference" of House and Senate negotiators would take over from the full conference the job of compromise-making on Gramm-Rudman. Of immediate concern, however, was a temporary increase in the debt ceiling. There was general agreement that there should be no threat of imminent fiscal collapse hanging over the president as he went to Geneva to meet Gorbachev. After some haggling over dates, the House and Senate agreed to a continuing temporary increase in the public debt limit, providing time for the conference to try to work out bicameral accords on Gramm-Rudman.[175]

173. "Top Level Talks Called For on Plan to Cut Deficit," *New York Times*, Nov. 7, 1985, p. 9.
174. Diane Granat, "Congress Postpones Tough Budget Decisions," *Congressional Quarterly Weekly Report*, Nov. 16, 1985, p. 2343.
175. Jonathan Fuerbringer, "House Approves a One-Month Rise in Ceiling on Debt," *New York Times*, Nov. 14, 1985, pp. 1, 18; Elizabeth Wehr, "Conference Accord is Possible on Budget-Balancing Measure," *Congressional Quarterly Weekly Report*, Nov. 16, 1985, p. 2346.

The Miniconference Subdivides—and Subdivides Again

The miniconference, totaling twenty-nine House and Senate conferees, itself quickly became bogged down in intense negotiations and divisive discord. Eventually, even this group was deemed unwieldy, and an informal subgroup of five senators (Packwood, Domenici, Gramm, Rudman, and Chiles) and six representatives (Foley, Gephardt, Panetta, Aspin [D, Wis.], Obey [D, Wis.], and Lott) took the lead in exploring compromises.[176] Then each side informally designated two conferees as their chief negotiators—Packwood and Domenici for the Senate and Foley and Gephardt for the House—and gave them considerable latitude to develop agreements.[177]

From an original conference of sixty-six persons had evolved a miniconference of twenty-nine, a subgroup of that miniconference of eleven, and now an ultimate negotiating cadre of four. Progress in conference committee negotiations often requires severe limitations in the number of negotiators. That House and Senate conferees were willing to delegate real power to such small bargaining groups was crucial to the ultimately successful conference outcome— and greatly appreciated by the central negotiators. Noted Senator Packwood, "The Senate conferees were very gracious in, by and large, giving to Senator Domenici and myself broad latitude, both in negotiating conclusions, as long as we kept them advised, and in not insisting that all of them be brought into every conference."[178]

During the next several weeks, the private negotiating sessions of the central players in the second conference dragged on. Unable to reach agreement in the limited number of days left before Congress's traditional Thanksgiving break, the conferees resumed negotiations in early December during the supercharged, hectic rush-to-adjourn period. Major differences remained over such key issues as which domestic programs to include in sequestration, when the first round of cuts should occur (in March 1986 or after the November 1986 elections), and how to assuage the Reagan administration's concern about what it saw as potentially damaging reductions in defense expenditures.[179]

On December 6, a major conference "agreement in principle" was announced. Under this compromise package, Social Security, interest on the national debt, veterans' pensions, and nine low-income programs would be exempt from the automatic cutback process. Various health programs, including Medicare, would be subject to limited

---

176. *Congressional Record,* Dec. 11, 1985, p. S17381. Senator Packwood also indicated that Representative Panetta was closely involved in the negotiations. Further, the three Senate sponsors were brought into these small group sessions, "where they were particularly expert and particularly interested." See also Elizabeth Wehr, "Conference Accord is Possible on Budget-Balancing Measure," p. 2347.

177. Elizabeth Wehr, "Conferees Near Agreement on Budget Measure," *Congressional Quarterly Weekly Report,* Nov. 23, 1985, p. 2410.

178. *Congressional Record,* Dec. 11, 1985, p. S17381.

179. See Steven V. Roberts, "Road to Balanced Budget Paved with Conflict," *New York Times,* Nov. 17, 1985, p. E5; Jonathan Fuerbringer, "Budget Conferees Narrow Differences to Two Issues," *New York Times,* Nov. 22, 1985; Wehr, "Conferees Near Agreement on Budget Measures," p. 2410; Jonathan Fuerbringer, "Budget Bill Talks Reach an Impasse," *New York Times,* Dec. 6, 1985. The titles of these four articles themselves illustrate the rapidly changing nature of conference negotiations.

sequestration. Certain other programs were regulated by special rules. The remaining defense and domestic programs would each bear half the burden of automatic spending cuts.[180]

Just when this compromise was about to be accepted by the full conference, the White House expressed renewed "serious reservations" about the possible impact of Gramm-Rudman on the nation's defense. These reservations postponed for several days final conference action on the emergent agreement.[181] After intensive internal White House debate, however, President Reagan sided with Chief of Staff Donald Regan's recommendation that he endorse the conference compromise, and the presidential roadblock to conference agreement was lifted. (Probably easing presidential acceptance was the inclusion, in the carefully balanced compromise bill, of discretionary authority allowing President Reagan to exempt certain specific defense programs from sequestration in 1986 but not thereafter.) Following resolution of these uncertainties, President Reagan urged Congress to enact Gramm-Rudman and praised the absence in the measure of any tax increase.[182] The conference ended on December 10 as a majority of House and Senate conferees approved the conference report, which implemented the agreements announced on December 6. The conference committee adjourned with final successful bicameral reconciliation in sight.[183]

The Final Wrap-Up

The Senate was the chamber that had agreed to the other chamber's request for the second conference, so it fell to it to act first on the conference accord. On December 11, the day following completion of the conference, Senate Majority Leader Dole offered the necessary privileged motion to proceed to consideration of the conference report. This was agreed to without objection, as was a request to waive the reading of the exceedingly lengthy report.[184] Senator Packwood then took the Senate floor to highlight the conference compromise and to urge its adoption. Other senators followed, either lauding or criticizing the work of the conference. Besides these evaluative judgments, two procedural events of significance occurred.

First, Senator Lowell Weicker (R, Conn.), a determined opponent of Gramm-

---

180. Jonathan Fuerbringer, "Conferees Agree on a Plan to End Federal Deficits," *New York Times*, Dec. 7, 1985, pp. 1, 7; Elizabeth Wehr, "Budget Conference Leaders Agree on Key Points," *Congressional Quarterly Weekly Report*, Dec. 7, 1985, p. 2548.

181. Jonathan Fuerbringer, "Military Budget Stalls Proposal to Cut Deficit," *New York Times*, Dec. 10, 1985, pp. 1, 9.

182. See *Washington Times*, Dec. 9, 1985, p. 1A, and Dec. 11, 1985, p. 4A; *Washington Post*, Dec. 11, 1985, p. A1.

183. Jonathan Fuerbringer, "Conferees Adopt Plan to Balance U.S. Budget by '91," *New York Times*, Dec. 11, 1985, pp. 1, 15; Elizabeth Wehr, "Congress Enacts Far-Reaching Budget Measure," *Congressional Quarterly Weekly Report*, Dec. 14, 1985, p. 2605. Curiously, the final conference approval of the momentous Gramm-Rudman plan by the sixty-six conferees was by only a voice vote rather than by a formal recorded vote. Ibid.

184. Reading the conference report aloud would have been an exhausting task; it ran over thirty-three pages of small type in the *Congressional Record*. *Congressional Record*, Dec. 10, 1985, pp. H11684–717.

Rudman, raised a point of order against the report on the grounds of scope—that the conference had gone beyond the limits of legislation approved by the House and Senate. "The fact is that this conference exceeded its authority in hundreds of places," he argued.[185] The Senate presiding officer sustained Weicker's parliamentary objection, a ruling that would—if upheld—preclude Senate approval of the conference report. Anticipating this parliamentary situation, however, Senator Dole was ready with an appeal of the ruling of the chair, which carried on a Senate vote of 68 to 27. The scope objection by Senator Weicker was thus overruled by the full Senate, allowing consideration of the conference report to proceed.

A second procedural hurdle occurred later in the debate when Senator Jeremiah Denton (R, Ala.) moved that the report be recommitted to conference with instructions to the Senate conferees to protect national defense from any sequestration. This motion was, however, successfully tabled (or killed) by the Senate on a 76 to 18 vote. With these parliamentary maneuvers out of the way, the Senate turned to adopting the conference report itself. By a final roll call vote of 61 to 31, the Senate approved the conference agreement, completing its 1985 consideration of deficit reduction legislation.[186] The revised Gramm-Rudman plan's fortunes would next be determined by the House.

The House received the conference report from the Senate later that same day, December 11. Ways and Means Chairman Rostenkowski immediately called up the report under the terms of an agreement reached the day before. (Under this unanimous consent agreement, the conference report would be considered at the outset as "read" and all points of order against it would be waived.) The only significant issue of controversy during House debate, other than the expected pro and con arguments, occurred at the very beginning. It concerned the division of floor time for the one hour of debate customary in the House on conference reports.

Under House rules, if the representative of the majority party (Rostenkowski) and minority party (John Duncan of Tennessee) both support the conference report, which each did, then a member leading the opposition is automatically entitled to twenty minutes of debate. In accordance with this rule, David Obey of Wisconsin, a Democratic opponent of Gramm-Rudman, requested from the Speaker and received twenty minutes of the one-hour debate time. Duncan strenuously objected to this division of time because it meant that Democrats would control forty minutes of the one-hour debate. He proposed instead that Representative Philip Crane (R, Ill.), a Ways and Means member (which Obey was not) and likewise a foe of Gramm-Rudman, control the twenty minutes allotted to Gramm-Rudman opposition. A unanimous consent request was posed providing that Crane "have the same amount of time that the majority has and that he may control that time."[187] Objection, however, was made, and the unanimous consent request failed. Obey would control the time for opposition to Gramm-Rudman.

185. *Congressional Record*, Dec. 11, 1985, p. S17400.
186. Jonathan Fuerbringer, "Plan to Balance Federal Budget Passes in Senate," *New York Times*, Dec. 12, 1985, pp. 1, 17; Wehr, "Congress Enacts Far-Reaching Budget Measure," p. 2605.
187. *Congressional Record*, Dec. 11, 1985, p. H11875. A curious but probably not accidental consequence of the Duncan proposal was that under it Republicans would have controlled forty minutes of the one-hour debate. In light of this, it is perhaps not very surprising that there was objection to the unanimous consent request.

After this procedural flare-up, which proved of greater partisan than legislative significance, the House debated the conference report for the allotted one hour. At the conclusion of this rather brief time for consideration of the far-reaching ramifications of Gramm-Rudman, the House approved the conference report by a 271 to 154 vote at 10:15 P.M. on December 11.[188] With this vote, which followed the complementary approval earlier in the day by the Senate, congressional action on Gramm-Rudman was complete, and the legislation was sent to the White House. The next day, December 12, 1985, President Reagan signed into law the Balanced Budget and Emergency Deficit Control Act of 1985 (Public Law 99-177). Interestingly, there was no public signing ceremony with "the usual multipenned pomp and circumstance."[189] Instead, the White House contented itself with issuing a printed statement announcing presidential approval of the legislation. "No big deal," said White House spokesman Larry Speakes in discussing President Reagan's quiet signing of the bill. The absence of the usual fanfare that almost always surrounds the signing into law of consequential measures undoubtedly reflected the president's ambivalence toward the automatic spending reduction mechanism, which in the printed statement announcing his signature of the legislation he termed "constitutionally suspect."[190]

Epilogue

Within hours after the budget balancing bill became law, litigation was started in Federal District Court by one opponent of Gramm-Rudman, Representative Mike Synar (D, Okla.), seeking to have it declared unconstitutional.[191] Legal challenges to such an unconventional approach to deficit limitation had been expected and had been discussed at length during the various stages of the bill's legislative evolution.[192] The deficit

188. Wehr, "Congress Enacts Far-Reaching Budget Measure," p. 2605.

189. Francis X. Clines, "Budget-Balancing Bill is Signed in Seclusion," *New York Times,* Dec. 13, 1985, p. B8.

190. Ibid.

191. The name of the case originally was *Representative Mike Synar et al.* v. *United States.* By the time the Supreme Court decided the case in July 1986, it had become *Bowsher* v. *Synar.* (Charles Bowsher was the comptroller general, the head of the GAO, an office central in the constitutional litigation.) Representative Synar ultimately was joined by eleven other members of the House and by the National Treasury Employees Union in his efforts. Defending the constitutionality of the legislation would eventually be counsel representing the Senate, the Democratic and Republican leaders of the House, and the comptroller general. The administration, despite President Reagan's decision to sign the legislation, filed briefs urging that the automatic deficit-cutting mechanism be struck down. The grounds for the administration's position were that executive powers given by the Constitution to the president were unconstitutionally delegated by the bill to the comptroller general, an officer of the legislative branch. Stuart Taylor, Jr., "High Court Urged to Uphold New Deficit-Reducing Law," *New York Times,* March 20, 1986, p. 14.

192. One key difference between House and Senate versions of Gramm-Rudman had centered on whether a successful challenge would strike down the entire legislation or only those parts specifically ruled as unconstitutional. This dispute eventually was resolved by providing for the "severability" of the bill's various provisions. An elimination of one or more parts of the legislation would not necessarily make the entire law unconstitutional. (In fact, this is precisely what eventually resulted from 1986 Supreme Court action as discussed below: portions of the legislation were struck down, while the remaining parts were left at least nominally in effect.)

reduction measure contained even a fallback procedure in case the sequestration process was later ruled unconstitutional. The presidential statement on signing the measure had seemed even to invite such a test.

The judicial process, however, moves quite slowly (even more deliberately than the legislative process), especially concerning a case centering on such momentous questions as the proper constitutional definition of presidential and congressional powers. Two basic lines of attack were made against the law: that it unconstitutionally constrained the fiscal powers of Congress by creating a new spending limits procedure that included crucial new roles for the president and his Office of Management and Budget. (This was the argument stressed by Congressman Synar and his congressional allies.) The other grounds for challenge, a position argued by the administration, were that the Gramm-Rudman process improperly vested executive branch administrative powers in the comptroller general, essentially an officer of the legislative branch and answerable to it.

On February 7, 1986, a special three judge U.S. District and Circuit Court panel found the legislation constitutional on the first grounds but unconstitutional on the second. In a decision written by Antonin Scalia, who soon would be elevated to the U.S. Supreme Court by President Reagan, the court found that indeed Gramm-Rudman failed constitutional examination because of the role of the congressionally determined comptroller general in what are essentially executive branch responsibilities. Because of this finding the court was not strictly required to consider the constitutionality of Gramm-Rudman on the other grounds—that it improperly delegated legislative fiscal powers of Congress to the president and other governmental officials. Nevertheless, the court decided that it would be useful, in light of the certainty that the case would subsequently be considered by the Supreme Court, to rule also on the second constitutional challenge—the grounds that had originally motivated Representative Synar and his allies. In nonbinding dicta (or additional comments), the special court ruled that on these grounds the legislation adequately "passes constitutional muster."[193]

The February 7 decision by the lower Federal Court, as expected, was appealed. Under special provisions contained in the legislation, the case went in an expedited process directly to the U.S. Supreme Court. After the filing of legal briefs by various parties, special extended oral arguments were heard by the Court on Wednesday, April 23, on an occasion laden with perceived significance; the case was widely described as the Supreme Court case of the decade.[194] Debate focused both on the grounds on which Gramm-Rudman had been declared unconstitutional in the February 7 ruling, and on the additional question (ruled by the special court in the negative) of whether the Gramm-Rudman bill excessively delegated legislative powers to nonlegislative entities. Of course, the Court would not necessarily need to rule on both issues; a Supreme Court

---

193. Elizabeth Wehr, with Nadine Cohodas, "Court Rejects Gramm-Rudman-Hollings Cuts But Case Appealed," *Congressional Quarterly Weekly Report*, Feb. 8, 1986, pp. 216–17. Major excerpts from the special three-judge Court opinion may be found in "Court Opinion on Gramm-Rudman Challenge," *Congressional Quarterly Weekly Report*, Feb. 8, 1986, pp. 281–82.

194. This description presumably went back twelve years for a comparably important case, to *U.S. v. Nixon*, a 1974 court decision that sought to define the meaning of presidential Executive Privilege—and that incidentally also led within days of its announcement to the resignation in disgrace of a president.

determination of the unconstitutionality of Gramm-Rudman on either ground would be sufficient to strike down the affected provisions.

On July 7, 1986, the Supreme Court announced its decision in what had now become the case of *Bowsher* v. *Synar*.[195] In his final opinion for the court before retiring, Chief Justice Warren E. Burger held on behalf of a seven-justice majority[196] that the February 7 lower court decision was correct in invalidating Gramm-Rudman's key mechanism—the automatic sequestering of funds by means of across-the-board spending cuts. The unconstitutionality of this process, the court majority held, lay in the inclusion in it of the comptroller general (the Bowsher of the case's name) an official dependent on Congress for his tenure of office, who by the law was given the power to tell the president what spending cuts must be made. By this provision, the Court ruled, the Congress had unconstitutionally intruded into the powers of the executive branch. "The Constitution does not permit such intrusion," the Court held.[197]

The Supreme Court decision of July 7 struck down the central feature of Gramm-Rudman, its automatic sequestration of appropriated funds, but other provisions of the legislation stood, including its setting of declining deficit ceilings for each year through 1991. What had been taken out, however, constituted the core mechanism for ensuring compliance with each year's target figure. Without the automatically mandated across-the-board spending cuts mechanism, the deficit reduction legislation was transformed by the July 7 court decision from a mandatory to a voluntary process.

Under fallback language that had been included in the legislation in anticipation of possible successful constitutional challenge, estimates would still be jointly made by the Congressional Budget Office and the presidential Office of Management and Budget of the extent to which federal governmental spending would have to be reduced to meet the statutory deficit "target" for that year. But rather than the comptroller general issuing

---

195. Major excerpts from the Court opinion on *Bowsher* v. *Synar*, along with concurring and dissenting opinions, may be found in "Supreme Court's Gramm-Rudman Opinions," *Congressional Quarterly Weekly Report*, July 12, 1986, p. 1581–83. The decision and opinion of the Court in this case also controlled two companion cases: *United States Senate* v. *Synar* and *O'Neill* v. *Synar*.

196. Chief Justice Warren E. Burger was joined in his opinion for the Court by Justices William J. Brennan, Jr., Lewis F. Powell, Jr., William H. Rehnquist, and Sandra Day O'Connor. A concurring opinion written by Justice John Paul Stevens was joined in by Justice Thurgood Marshall. Separate dissents were written by Justices Byron R. White and Harry A. Blackmun.

197. Elder Witt, "Court Sees Fatal Gramm-Rudman Flaw in Power Given to Comptroller General," *Congressional Quarterly Weekly Report*, July 12, 1986, pp. 1560–61. The Court majority opinion was content to rest its determination of unconstitutionality on these grounds. The concurring opinion of Justice Stevens, joined in by Justice Marshall, found the automatic budget-cutting mechanism unconstitutional for different reasons—that Congress could not delegate its fiscal powers to an outside process or to agents. It held that "when Congress legislates, it must follow the procedures prescribed in Article I"—in other words, the regular legislative process of enactment by both chambers of identical legislation followed by presidential signature or veto.

The two dissents in the case found the unconstitutionality arguments unpersuasive. Justice White wrote that "the threat to separation of powers conjured up by the majority is wholly chimerical," and Justice Blackmun suggested that if the status of the comptroller general were a sticking point, the Court would be far wiser to modify this relatively minor matter by judicial decision than strike down a statute that "unquestionably ranks among the most important enactments of the past several decades."

mandatory spending cuts for subsequent presidential implementation, any spending cuts would now have to be worked out by congressional committees and passed as new legislation through the regular legislative process. The target deficit levels and spending cuts necessary to meet them would now be no more than suggestions dependent upon the politics of Congress for acceptance, modification, or rejection.[198]

Gramm-Rudman had started in 1985 as a radical proposal for ensuring the progressive elimination of governmental deficits by the draconian measure of compulsory across-the-board spending cuts. By July 1986, after many months of highly complex legislative maneuvering, the Gramm-Rudman plan had been formally enacted into law, but—by judicial decision—its central means of ensuring its goals had been removed. Gramm-Rudman was successful as a truly innovative idea generating sufficient political and legislative support to prevail through the difficulties of profound bicameral differences and the complexities of multiple conference committees. Following the actions of the Supreme Court in July 1986, however, insufficient means and muscle were left in the Gramm-Rudman process for it to have significant impact on the persistent problem of governmental deficits.

In response to the court action and to concerns that Gramm-Rudman as it stood was ineffectual, Congress moved reluctantly and with considerable misgivings to enact a revised (and presumably constitutional) version of the Gramm-Rudman law in September 1987. The uncertainty of congressional attitudes toward this "fix" was expressed by one senator, William L. Armstrong (R, Col.), who concluded that the measure "is not worse than doing nothing. But I am not very confident of my opinion."[199]

The revamped law, which might be termed Gramm-Rudman II, restored automatic cuts through a constitutional sequestration procedure (it directed an executive agency, the Office of Management and Budget, to issue the sequestration report that would

---

198. Despite the Supreme Court ruling striking down the sequestration process as originally structured, the Gramm-Rudman law was still left with some teeth. Early in 1987, plan cosponsor Senator Phil Gramm indicated his eagerness to use a variety of "guerrilla legislative tactics" during the coming months in order to force Congress to abide by the deficit ceiling figures specified by the law. The steps Gramm envisioned included points of order against consideration of budget proposals inconsistent with the year's maximum deficit figure, and further points of order against appropriations bills that likewise exceeded the ceiling. These parliamentary challenges were expressly provided for in the Gramm-Rudman legislation; in fact, in writing the original bill, Gramm had deliberately included these and other rules and procedures as standby enforcement provisions.

Whether these obstructionist and guerrilla warfare tactics would be successful and not counterproductive was still to be seen. Gramm-Rudman cosponsor Senator Rudman expressed some doubts: "Phil is going to stonewall it up to the end. He thinks that works. I don't play it that way because I'm not sure it will work." These uncertainties were further underscored by the plan's third cosponsor, Senator Hollings, who noted about Senator Gramm, "He loves guerrilla warfare and he loves to lose."

These views little concerned Senator Gramm. Responding to doubts as to the viability of the deficit ceiling restrictions, Gramm reportedly replied, "Tough!" and added, "The magic is that it is the law of the land. I think that getting out of that commitment is going to be a lot more difficult than they think" (Jonathan Fuerbringer, "Guerrilla Warfare and the Budget," *New York Times,* Feb. 27, 1987, p. 20).

199. Elizabeth Wehr, "Doubtful Congress Clears Gramm-Rudman Fix," *Congressional Quarterly Weekly Report,* Sept. 26, 1987, p. 2309.

trigger the across-the-board cuts) and delayed for two years—from 1991 to 1993—the timetable for eliminating the deficit.

The Gramm-Rudman deficit limits for the current budget year went into effect automatically on November 20, 1987, but in this case its provisions triggered something other than automatic spending cuts. Under the pressure of mandated 8.5 percent cuts in domestic programs and 10.5 percent cuts in defense expenditures, a congressional-administration summit task force at the last minute worked out $30 billion of "voluntary" spending cuts, an amount sufficient to negate for 1987 the Gramm-Rudman across-the-board automatic cuts. Once again, political necessities had triumphed over the more sweeping deficit reduction approach of the Gramm-Rudman plan.

Conference committees as workshops of legislation. House and Senate conferees at work during complex negotiations to reach agreement on amendments to the Clean Air Act. (From the *New York Times,* July 30, 1977. Photograph by George Tames. Copyright © 1977 by The New York Times Company. Reprinted by permission.)

12

Conference Committees and Bicameral Politics

In the preceding chapters of this book, we have outlined in some detail the bicameral politics of congressional conference committees. We stressed the centrality of bicameralism to the contemporary U.S. Congress, and the indispensable role of conference committees as the bridging mechanism facilitating (and sometimes also preventing) necessary legislative reconciliation between the House and Senate. What the Constitution has separated into two parts must also be brought into harmony on specific legislation in order for bills to be enacted finally into law. The congressional conference committee operates as that harmonizing device, and as such plays a cornerstone role in the politics of bicameralism in Congress.[1]

Throughout this study, we have supplemented our general and analytical discussions of bicameral politics with specific illustrations. These vignettes of actual conference actions and behavior were designed to illuminate the more general analysis and have provided snapshot pictures of conference politics in action. As photographic snapshots can provide only a frozen picture of one instant of action, so also our vignettes are limited by their specificity and brevity. What was needed in order to broaden our understanding of conference processes were case studies that, like movies, capture sequences of interactions and behavior among participants.

Chapter 11 of this book presented nine mini-case studies of conference politics. As

---

1. There are occasions, to be sure, when efforts will be made to avoid conferences. In mid-1988, for instance, House Minority Leader Robert H. Michel (R, Ill.) urged Speaker Jim Wright (D, Tex.) to have the House vote directly on the Senate's version of a controversial welfare bill "as a means of avoiding a long, drawn-out conference." Although Speaker Wright rejected Michel's request, attempts at conference avoidance also illustrate bicameralism in action. Julie Rovner, "Difficult Conference Likely on Welfare Bill," *Congressional Quarterly Weekly Report*, June 25, 1988, p. 1764.

CONFERENCE COMMITTEES AND BICAMERAL POLITICS   337

with actual conferences, these accounts differ greatly in their complexity, subject matter, and time of occurrence. Certainly these case studies in no way can be seen as constituting a perfect sample of bicameral interactions, but their variety doubtlessly has provided the reader with a better understanding of some of the patterns and forms that bicameral politics between House and Senate may take.

The specifics of each instance concerning such matters as conference background, strategies, negotiations, and agreements are fully recounted in chapter 11 and do not need restatement here. It would be valuable in this concluding chapter, however, to look back at the rich variety of material contained in these accounts to determine what similarities and contrasts may be found in these diverse stories. A review and comparison of these nine case studies is offered next, followed by a brief concluding restatement of some of the central themes of the book.

The Case Studies Reassessed

Our initial purpose in returning to the nine case studies previously presented is to highlight, in no more than four or five paragraphs, the central features of each controversy. Following this overview of the accounts (in the order they were told in chapter 11), we will then bring together this body of material by means of a table summarizing key recurrent patterns and noteworthy contrasts in each stage of the conference process illustrated by the case studies.

A. Heptanoic Acid and Needy Children

This first case study is somewhat of an anomaly among our accounts, for its events take place on the floor of one chamber, the House, rather than directly in the conference room. The disputes recounted in this case study involve initial efforts to avoid conference and subsequent maneuvers to ensure conference action on and chamber acceptance of an accord.

The conference stage certainly was anticipated in the House, but as something to be avoided, because of the immediacy of deadlines, on both the income tax surcharge and aid to dependent children issues. Negotiated floor agreements were the means by which bicameral agreement was sought on both issues; these floor negotiations initially were unsuccessful but finally resulted in arrangements providing for swift conference action on and chamber approval of the dependent children provision, followed by chamber acceptance of the withholding tax amendment.

Central in this account was an attempt in each instance to avoid conference, interwoven negotiations on the floor of the House on both issues, and expedited successful conference action on one provision and floor approval without a conference of the other. The legislative process does not operate in a political vacuum on a single pending proposal; often legislative and conference politics are shaped by interrelated, simultaneous events. And sometimes interwoven events even provide the means of accomplishing legislative goals—including avoiding conference or securing rapid conference action.

B. Higher Education: Personalities and Exhaustion

This far more complex case study dealt with the enactment in 1972 of major higher education legislation and was marked by unusually detailed information concerning what went on during closed conference committee negotiations. While events in the preceding account involved essentially only the pre- and postconference stages of the conference process, the key events of this case study centered most directly on actions in the conference committee itself.

The anticipation of conference was not itself a major factor influencing the content of House and Senate original bills. It was generally accepted that on legislation as multifaceted and innovative as the higher education bills, each chamber would inevitably come up with its own distinctive perspective and approach. A major conference would be necessary in any case, so the best course would be for each chamber to complete its initial work without overly excessive concern about resulting bicameral differences. The conference would be the means for subsequently working out a common approach.

The conference on the higher education legislation of 1972 was marked by a full array of political pressures and processes. The perception and anticipation of a difficult conference, for example, led Chairman Perkins to adopt a negotiation process that emphasized early agreement and fostered conference consensus. Institutional factors were present in initial House versus Senate delegation positions; as time wore on, however, the unity of House conferees broke down as Representative Quie's bloc increasingly found common cause with the Senate conferees. Committee factors were reflected in the pivotal roles in conference of Chairman Perkins of the House Education and Labor Committee and Quie, the committee's ranking minority member. Each brought to conference influence based on his leadership in the standing committee. Individual factors were forcefully manifested in the determined opportunism and opposition of Representative Green, who maneuvered at every point to impose her own policy preferences—and also to preserve her status as a House leader on education legislation. Finally, legislative creativity was quite significant in this case, for it was only through careful, extensive, and creative restructuring of legislative provisions that bicameral agreement eventually proved possible.

The postconference process played a small role in this instance (except by anticipation, reflected in the effort to clarify the presence of a conference committee quorum on the final conference votes). Overall, what was crucial in these events were factors directly related to conference bargaining: the skillful utilization by conference chairman Perkins of a negotiating process that promoted emergent conference consensus, the shift in loyalties of a number of House conferees to views compatible to Senate preferences, the development of a bipartisan alliance among House conferees in support of this shift, the extreme hostility between this House bipartisan group and another leading conferee—Representative Green—which left Green and her policy views isolated, a significant degree of conferee exhaustion, and a substantial amount of legislative creativity on the part of key participants, which made it possible for the bipartisan House majority and Senate conferees to find the means of bridging profound bicameral differences.

C. Two "Hello and Good-Bye" Conferences of 1979

These two brief accounts were included as examples of instances in which conference committees have little negotiating to do, either because there were few bicameral legislative differences or because agreements had been worked out in advance outside the formal conference meeting. In the first case, all the conference had to do was deal with a personal problem. In the latter instance, when the conference committee convened, its task was essentially one of ratifying a brokered accord. In each, the necessary task was performed swiftly.

The Endangered Species Act conference dealt with legislation that passed House and Senate in nearly identical form. In fact, the conference might well have been foregone entirely except for the determination of Representative Breaux that the legislation ensure the maintenance of Louisiana's alligator industry. In order to accommodate his forcefully expressed views, a fifteen-minute conference was held during which staff members exercised noteworthy legislative and administrative originality in resolving the problem. Following this, all shook hands on the legislation, and the conference adjourned. This Hello and Good-Bye conference provides a classic example of one purpose that a conference may perform—to assuage particularistic concerns, especially those expressed by a determined congressman.

The task facing the conference committee on *The Department of Education Organization Act* was far more daunting. The House and Senate had passed substantially different bills, and these bicameral differences had been underscored by House adoption of specific instructions to its conferees to insist on conference retention of the House amendments. Further, while the Senate had strongly supported the legislation, the House had adopted its greatly amended version on a very close vote. The prospects for reaching conference agreement on matters so disparate and in which one chamber was resolute for its position and only weakly committed to eventual passage appeared bleak.

The conference was, nevertheless, ultimately successful. This was due to two crucial factors: the decision to conduct key negotiations outside the official conference at the staff level and the willingness of staff members representing the Senate to accept House preferences on almost every key issue. In addition, a systematic process of including provisions of specific interest to particular House conferees was followed.

By the time the conference finally met, an agreement had been hammered out by these means, and the staff-generated accord was available for conference ratification. The uncertainty surrounding conference prospects was resolved, and the conference committee only had to rubber stamp the laboriously negotiated agreement.

One final hurdle, however, remained in this case—approval by the House of the conference report. Facilitating this final success was unified House conferee support for the bicameral agreement (after all, many of them now had direct political stakes in it and, further, on most points it conceded the House position), the fact that the House was acting last on the conference agreement, and the strong support given House adoption of the conference report by the president.

This conference proved to be noteworthy in that despite initial uncertain, even unfavorable prospects for success, the conference produced a compromise carefully tilted toward House preferences that was able not only to win conference committee agreement, but also to secure House and Senate ratification. Whereas the conference committee session itself was brief and confirming in character, the negotiating processes surrounding the conference committee stage were crucial in securing successful enactment of the legislation.

D. The 1982 Tax Increase Conference

The central feature of this case study involved the convening of a conference on legislation that had passed one chamber but had not been adopted—or even considered—by the other. Further, the bill at stake was a measure to increase taxes, and the chamber that had not acted was the House, which has the constitutional duty of originating all tax legislation.

How did this extraordinary situation develop? In short, it happened because such an unconventional step was mutually in the interests of House and Senate leaders. The Democratic leadership of the House was understandably loath to deal with tax-raising proposals in an election year, especially when the necessity for such measures was attributed directly to presidential and Republican actions the preceding year in pushing through Congress one of the greatest tax cuts in history. As a result, the House wished neither to initiate such a bill, nor even to consider it prior to conference. The burden of crafting this potentially unpalatable but quite necessary legislation fell upon Senate leaders, unenthusiastically backed by President Reagan. In short, the usual pattern of conference committee reconciliation between two competing proposals was, in this instance, transformed into a situation in which the conference considered and rewrote a single bill.

This is not to say that the absence of House-enacted legislation made the conference task any easier. Rather, negotiations were somewhat hampered by the conference having only one text as a point of departure, while the political necessity of a conference agreement that would be able to win adoption in both chambers remained. This was eventually accomplished by the traditional means of close bargaining between House conferees led by Ways and Means Chairman Rostenkowski and Senate representatives led by Finance Chairman Dole.

That the negotiations eventually were successful was due to such factors as unified conference delegations (especially ensured on the House side by Rostenkowski's hard-nosed conferee selection procedures), a flexible interpretation of rules whenever useful (such as on conference scope restrictions), the inclusion of provisions of great interest to each chamber as well as to a number of affected interests, behind-the-scenes as well as public presidential support for conference efforts, and the political skills of Dole and Rostenkowski. In this instance, as with the Department of Education conference just discussed, the conference committee performed impressively in transforming legislation with very weak support in one chamber (or in this instance, no demonstrated support at all in the House) into conference agreement on an extensively revamped measure capable of winning subsequent acceptance by both the House and Senate.

E. A Typical Low-Intensity Appropriations Conference

The events of this account dealt with federal funding of the government of the District of Columbia, but are representative of the large variety of minor, noncontroversial appropriations conferences that occur each year. The power of the purse is a fundamental congressional constitutional prerogative and is continually manifested in conference spending decisions concerning every area of government. Sometimes appropriations decisions are highly controversial and well publicized (as in the case of 1985 defense appropriations); at other times, as here, they are essentially routine and low intensity.

Appropriations legislation for the D.C. government had, as customary, passed the House and Senate; the House, as usual, had acted first, and the Senate had then modified the House-enacted bill by adding forty-two specific but often minor amendments. Although conceivably a conference could have been avoided by passing the legislation back and forth between the chambers, in this case (as so often) it was deemed more efficient for a small group to work out bicameral differences in a face-to-face conference.

The conference committee indeed was small—seven of the ten House-appointed conferees met for less than ninety minutes with *one* of the seven official representatives of the Senate. Accommodation and fair bargaining were values very much in evidence as conferees either split the difference in appropriated amounts or alternated in accepting each chamber's provisions. While institutional interests were nicely balanced by such means, the predominant conference mood was one of accommodation and reasonableness in evaluating the merits of each provision. The final product was generally seen as equitable and sound.

The only hitch during conference adoption of the conference report occurred in House floor objections to one specific provision in the conference agreement. When the Senate acted, it resolved that issue by accepting the House position. All this occurred in an atmosphere missing the rancor often found on more controversial matters.

Certainly this case study was one of a low-intensity issue, and this characteristic permeated every aspect of its consideration by conference and chamber. This feature allowed conference negotiations to be carried out with dispatch with an extraordinarily limited number of conferees present, and also allowed conferees to reach an agreement that, after minor adjustment, won easy approval by the House and Senate.

F. The Case of the Purloined Papers: South African Sanctions in 1985

In a number of the case studies we have discussed, the conference committee was the central mechanism facilitating bicameral compromise and the eventual success of legislative proposals. This is precisely what one might expect, for the conference committee inherently is the heart of the overall bicameral reconciliation process; what transpires there largely determines the political fortunes of bills. If it does its job well, the likelihood of success for legislation is greatly enhanced; conversely, should a conference fail to create a compromise carefully balanced among competing interests and differing cameral wishes, any resulting conference report is likely to have tough going in securing approval from both House and Senate.

The South African sanctions case study, however, constituted somewhat of an exception to these generalities. Legislation solidly backed by each chamber went to conference, and there the conferees labored conscientiously to fashion a compromise potentially agreeable to each chamber. These efforts resulted in a bipartisan-supported conference report backed by both conference delegations—a compromise seen as likely to win House and Senate ratification.

This was, however, not to be, for presidential views and actions, not the adequacy of the handiwork of the conference, were decisive in this instance in determining the fortunes of South African sanctions legislation. Before the conference, President Reagan had strongly opposed both the Senate and House bills and had threatened to veto any similar legislation finally enacted. Despite this presidential stand, the attitude prevalent in Congress was to persist in efforts at obtaining congressional passage of sanctions legislation. The president might ultimately veto the measure, it was conceded, but the task at hand was to work out bicameral differences in conference and then to enact the resulting conference compromise. A presidential veto was a problem to be faced later.

The president, however, changed the nature of the situation by his adroit maneuver of announcing sanctions against South Africa by executive order immediately prior to Senate consideration of the conference report. As a result of this action, the Republican Senate leadership switched to opposing Senate approval of the conference agreement. This new opposition was manifested in such tactics as filibustering against passage of the report and such extraordinary steps as removing the conference papers from the Senate clerk's desk. Ultimately, this opposition was successful in blocking Senate ratification of the conference compromise.

The South African sanctions legislation failed as the direct result of determined presidential intervention in the conference process. Ironically, this intervention was successful only because the sanctions ordered by the president incorporated many of the elements in the conference agreement. This case was a striking instance of a participant from outside Congress playing a decisive role in determining the outcome of conference committee negotiations. Despite the failure of congressional sanctions legislation, however, sanctions *were* imposed against South Africa—by presidential order—and these sanctions directly resulted from the congressional initiative. Further, these events of 1985 had additional consequence in 1986, when Congress enacted—over a presidential veto—statutory sanctions against South Africa.

G. *Dollars for Defense: Les Gets More Amidst 1985 House Turmoil*

As in the preceding controversy, the central action of the events in the dollars for defense case study took place on the floor of one of the chambers of Congress, in this case the House rather than the Senate. Shaping floor activity in this instance, however, were not presidential moves but hostile reactions in the House to conference agreements, first on defense authorizations, and then on defense appropriations. A lightning rod for many of these criticisms was Armed Services Chairman Les Aspin, who was seen by many representatives as having sold out House views in conference.

The conference on the defense authorizations legislation had been expected to be difficult but one in which House sentiments would be well represented. Significant differences, both quantitative and qualitative, separated the bills that cleared the House and Senate; any successful effort to bridge these gaps would require legislatively adroit skills. On the House side, its specific provisions had been adopted by particularly lopsided votes. These strongly expressed, specific preferences, backed up by strong general support in the House for controlling defense spending and securing major procurement reforms, were expected to be generally retained in the final conference product—especially because the House delegation was led by the new, youthful, and forceful Armed Services head, Representative Aspin.

It was in light of these high expectations that the conference report, when issued, was such a shock. Instead of prevailing on most matters, or even on a reasonable number, the House appeared instead to have lost in conference on almost every significant issue. The result was a Democratic floor revolt against the conference agreement, an uprising that the leadership was able to quell only by promising a second chance for the adoption of key House concerns in connection with the upcoming defense *appropriations* bill—legislation that would itself have to move through conference.

The result of this second conference, however, was scarcely more satisfactory to House liberals than the earlier authorizations conference. Again, key House-backed provisions were dropped by the conference. Again, a House floor revolt flared, which in this instance resulted in outright defeat for the appropriations conference report.

Subsequently, a revised conference agreement on defense appropriations did secure House approval, but only after extensive conference modifications of the original accord. The central arena of activity in this case was indeed the chamber, not the conference committee itself. For whatever reason, two different conference committees produced reports unacceptable to the House, and only after great turmoil and the development of a marked degree of lingering personal bitterness toward Armed Services Chairman Aspin did Congress complete its work on funding for defense.

H. The Gramm-Rudman Conferences of 1985

This final case study includes by far the most complex series of events. The Gramm-Rudman proposal was innovative and multidimensional; so also was the legislative process that led to its enactment. Necessarily (and fortunately) we will limit ourselves here to a consideration of the most significant major stages and events in its laborious passage into law.

Initially, the Gramm-Rudman plan went to conference lacking the usual detailed consideration by committee in the Senate, and absent almost all forms of House consideration. The proposal started its legislative life as a Senate floor amendment, totally bypassing all standing committees in that chamber. Following Senate passage after only limited floor consideration, the legislation went to the House, where chamber leaders took the unusual step of bypassing both committee and floor deliberation and sending

Gramm-Rudman directly to conference. (Despite the occurrence in our case studies of two instances in which conferences were called in the absence of House-passed legislation, we must again stress that such curtailing of the legislative process is indeed quite rare.)

The first Gramm-Rudman conference was marked by an unusual conference committee task: the drafting of legislation, much as is customarily done by a chamber's standing committee. Although a legislative text was available in the form of the Senate-passed bill, it had not been subjected there to any careful legislative or committee review. House conferees, for their part, had only a generally worded mandate to guide them. As a consequence, the conference spent considerable time in fact-finding and in the generation of revised, clarified language and proposals. Influencing these efforts also was a variety of external pressures, including simultaneous hearings, extensive media commentary, and strongly articulated individual, interest, and presidential evaluations of Gramm-Rudman. Further compounding the conference work was a persistent sense of time pressure as fiscal "deadlines" were repeatedly announced in draconian terms.

The initial conference committee eventually deadlocked, but resulting from its labors were proposals drafted by House and Senate conference delegations which, in the days following the conference breakdown, were shuttled back and forth between the chambers. These drafts, in fact, would be the basis for later bicameral agreement when the second conference committee convened.

The second conference was unlike the first because by then both House and Senate had given extensive and detailed attention to Gramm-Rudman, and conference-created alternative plans had been exhaustively considered and modified on the floor of each chamber. There was a real sense that a compromise plan was now ready to be worked out in the second conference. The mechanism for negotiations in this conference was that of steadily smaller and smaller informal bargaining units: the full conference committee of sixty-six members gave way to a miniconference of twenty-nine, a subgroup of eleven, and an eventual core negotiating cadre of four. It was by means of such severe limitation on conference participation in key negotiations that an agreement eventually was drafted by the second conference that was acceptable to House, Senate, and—hesitatingly—to the president.

The legislative and conference process utilized to enact Gramm-Rudman was dauntingly complex, but central to the outcome were several factors that deserve highlighting: the initial bypassing of all committee and much chamber scrutiny of the bill, the consequent use of the conference committee as a fact-gathering and mark-up institution, the inability of that first conference committee to come up with a single compromise agreeable to the representatives of House and Senate, the resort next to shuttle negotiations as versions of Gramm-Rudman went back and forth between the chambers, the eventual success of the second conference—largely due to the legislative homework that preceded it (as it did not in the first conference)—and the willingness of conference members to delegate the most sensitive negotiations to small groups of conference leaders. Whether Gramm-Rudman was "a bad idea whose time has come" (as once stated by its coauthor Senator Rudman) is a question still to be determined. It was, however, an idea whose time came only through the most skillful and innovative utilization of the conference process.

Recurrent Patterns and Noteworthy Contrasts

These nine case studies provide a rich collection of information about the processes, institutions, procedures, and behavior found in conference politics. Now we ask What recurrent patterns and noteworthy contrasts are identifiable in this set of accounts? A summary overview of the case studies is presented in the accompanying table in terms of the predominant characteristics in each instance of preconference, during the conference, and postconference activity. In addition, factors central to the eventual success or failure of the conference process are also listed for each case.

This summary table allows for a wealth of comparisons among the nine cases and their twelve conference committees (counting the defense conferences as three and the Gramm-Rudman conferences as two). In eight of the twelve conferences, for example, activities during the preconference stage were particularly significant in influencing subsequent conference actions; in seven cases (depending on interpretations), the preconference period was marked by an anticipation of a difficult conference to come.

Four of the twelve conference committees could probably be considered as actually difficult (again depending on interpretation), while four other conferences were relatively speedy and trouble-free affairs (at least the formal conference committee sessions were). Five of the twelve conference committees were quite large gatherings; on the other hand, at least one conference had quite cozy meetings. Special bargaining techniques or informal bargaining subunits were especially predominant in seven instances, while in at least two cases negotiations were carried out by the entire committee in no special pattern. An anticipation of potential problems in securing House or Senate ratification of the conference agreement was discernible in five cases, while pressures from outside Congress were especially noted in four instances. Conference committees were able to agree on a final report in eleven of the twelve conferences.

The post conference stage was marked by two instances in which the conference report was rejected by one of the chambers, and at least three additional cases in which there was considerable controversy over its adoption. Presidential influences were important in all five of these contentious ratification controversies.

Finally, the conference process resulted in conference-reported compromise legislation being approved by both House and Senate following nine of the eleven conferences that had agreed on a report. In eight of the total of nine case studies, bicameral differences eventually were resolved by means of a conference report that was approved, albeit painfully at times, by both houses of Congress; in the solitary exception, the conference report failed because many of its provisions were otherwise put into effect prior to one chamber's consideration of the conference agreement.

These nine case studies of conference committee politics have, we trust, added to an understanding of the diversity of bicameral adjustment processes and politics. Both in the fullness of their telling in chapter 11, and in the more comparative examination here,

The Case Studies Contrasted

	Characteristics of Preconference Activity	Characteristics Present During the Conference	Characteristics of Postconference Activity	Factors Central to Conference Success (or Failure)
A. Heptanoic Acid and Needy Children	House floor efforts to avoid conference on two unrelated measures leads to their interconnection.	Dependency of tax surcharge upon successful conference action on dependent children measure speeds conference action on latter.	Both linked measures are approved, one following conference, the other bypassing conference.	Success because of intertwining of unrelated legislation; skillful use of legislative rules and procedures.
B. Higher Education	Anticipation of major and difficult conference.	Negotiation process adopted that emphasizes early consensus; unity of House conferees breaks down and bipartisan and bicameral alliance formed with Senate conferees; skillful use of legislative creativity; personal impact of extreme exhaustion.	Not particularly important in this case.	Success because of skillful structuring of conference negotiating process, shift of House conferee loyalties, emergent hostility between Green and others, legislative creativity and personal exhaustion.
C₁. Endangered Species	Few chamber differences between bills; possibility that conference might not even be needed.	Need to resolve one congressman's personal problem; this speedily done by staff ingenuity; no other conference negotiations needed.	Uneventful.	Success because of lack of House-Senate differences and staff ingenuity.
C₂. Department of Education	Substantially different bills passed; strong	Agreement on concessions to House worked out in	Concern over House approval resolved by	Success because of unofficial but crucially

346

	Senate but weak House support for the legislation; House addition of many amendments; bleak conference prospects foreseen.	extensive bicameral staff meetings prior to conference; conference ratification of brokered accord carefully weighted toward House wishes; inclusion of special favors for individual House conferees; official conferees only faced with rubber-stamping agreement.	conferee support, by inclusion in conference report of most House provisions and special inducements for individual members, by the House acting last on the accord, and by strong presidential support.	important staff negotiations prior to conference, decision there to tilt conference agreement toward House and to include conferee favors, House voting last on the conference report, and presidential support for conference report.
D. Tax Increase	Tax bill goes to conference without House action; this step mutually beneficial to House and Senate leaders; careful selection of conferees—especially in House.	Conference negotiations hampered somewhat by absence of House bill; generally unified conference delegations; close bargaining between delegation chairmen carried out with skill; flexible interpretation of rules; presidential support.	Uneventful, especially with presidential support.	Success because of the work of the conference, which greatly enhanced prospects of legislative success.
E. D.C. Appropriations	Senate adds forty-two specific amendments, many minor, to House-passed bill; conference utilized as means of reconciliation.	Extremely small conference—seven House members meet with one senator in spirit of accommodation and reasonableness; traditional bargaining tools utilized of splitting the difference	House objection to one conference report provision subsequently resolved by Senate concession; otherwise uneventful.	Success because of minor initial differences; conference spirit of agreeableness and fairness; smallness of conference; traditional negotiation methods used; Senate accom-

(continued)

The Case Studies Contrasted (continued)

	Characteristics of Preconference Activity	Characteristics Present During the Conference	Characteristics of Postconference Activity	Factors Central to Conference Success (or Failure)
		and alternately including different chamber provisions; conference accord reached in only ninety minutes; lack of rancor or tension.		modation during ratification of conference report.
F. South African Sanctions	Bills strongly backed by each chamber despite presidential opposition; determination in House and Senate to complete conference and other steps of legislative process before facing likely presidential veto.	Conference agreement easier since both delegations supported some form of sanctions legislation; resulting conference report backed by almost all conferees; conference work made irrelevant through subsequent presidential action.	Easy adoption of conference report in House; failure of conference report in Senate following presidential announcement of sanctions by executive order; use of filibuster by Senate opponents together with unconventional tactics.	Failure because of presidential action that transformed the majority leadership of the Senate into conference report opponents; use of filibuster and unconventional tactics to block Senate approval; despite failure of sanctions legislation in Senate, somewhat similar actions result from president's executive order and are enacted as law by Congress the next year.

G. Dollars for Defense	Significant quantitative and qualitative differences between House and Senate defense authorizations legislation; House provisions adopted by large margins, strengthening case for their conference inclusion; conference expected to be difficult, yet House views also expected to be well represented; later expectations for defense appropriations conference shaped by events surrounding controversial authorizations conference.	Defense authorizations conference report widely perceived as heavily tilted toward Senate views; House Democratic outrage over result and actions of House conference delegation leader Aspin; later defense appropriations conference report also seen as unresponsive to House views, initially defeated in House; after modification by conference, later approved; the work of both conferences harshly denounced in House.	House Democratic revolt against approval of defense authorizations conference report; revolt contained by leadership only by urging objectors to wait for appropriations report; defense appropriations conference report likewise seen as one-sided, defeated in House; report revised by conference and later approved; postconference marked by turmoil, rancor, and bitterness, including toward Armed Services Chairman Aspin.	Both failures and successes present in case study; defense authorizations conference report initially unacceptable to House but approved after urging of leadership to wait for the appropriations report; defense appropriations report rejected at first by House, approved only after substantial conference modifications; factors central to outcomes include early anticipation that House views would be well represented, widely held perceptions that both conference reports sharply favored Senate positions, and controversies involving the actions and positions of Armed Services Chairman Aspin.

(continued)

The Case Studies Contrasted *(continued)*

	Characteristics of Preconference Activity	Characteristics Present During the Conference	Characteristics of Postconference Activity	Factors Central to Conference Success (or Failure)
H. Gramm-Rudman	The legislation in initially going to conference bypassed committee review in Senate and both committee and floor examination in House; little legislative preparation for initial conference; widespread sense that means must be found for controlling deficits; second conference preceded by extensive House and Senate consideration of drafts created by chamber delegations at first conference; continuing widespread sense that means must be found for controlling deficits.	First conference characterized by fact-finding and legislative drafting; influence during conference of external evaluations and pressures along with evident severe time constraints; House and Senate conference delegation-written plans drafted prior to conference collapse; second conference also under evidnet severe time constraints; benefits from House and Senate preparation for this conference, and by utilization of small bargaining units; presidential views somewhat vacillate on defense issue, but essentially are supportive of Gramm-Rudman.	House and Senate conferee support for report of second conference; general sentiment in both chambers that some means must be found for controlling deficits; presidential reluctance but official support for the report of the second conference.	Both failures and successes present in case study; initial conference failure to negotiate a bicameral agreement largely due to lack of legislative preparation for conference; second conference success largely due to continuing widespread sense in House and Senate that some means must be found for controlling deficits, legislative homework done prior to the second conference, and utilization in that conference of small groups for crucial negotiations.

they have provided a sense of the sequences, and sometimes also the convolutions, through which the conference process moves. The interactions between House and Senate as the two bodies enact legislation is a fascinating process to watch and to attempt to understand.

Conference Committees and Bicameral Politics

Throughout this book, we have portrayed conference committee politics not as occurring in some dusty corner at the periphery of Congress, but instead as a process central to bicameral relations between two separate components of the national legislature. As we put it in the opening pages, congressional conference committees are the central element of bicameralism and conference politics the essence of bicameral politics.

Other sections of this book have discussed legislative bicameralism as it was created for the new national Congress over two hundred years ago, how conference committees evolved over history as the vehicle for reconciling bicameral legislative differences between the two houses, and the way that conference committees influence House-Senate interactions today. Congressional bicameralism, we have argued, is a constantly changing phenomenon based both on constitutional provision and contemporary necessity.

The central forum in which congressional bicameralism is manifested is the conference committee—the only place where House and Senate members meet regularly to conduct legislative business. Conference committees, however, are more than just bicameral convening places; they are also central arenas for the development and exercise of legislative power. They provide the means by which congressmen from both chambers seek twin goals: influence over legislation and power within their chamber.[2]

Besides being power-manifesting opportunities, conference committees are also crucially important to the legislative process itself. Conference committees are major workshops for congressional lawmaking. They often determine the content of legislation, at times even generating original legislative proposals and language.[3] In short, any understanding of the dynamics of legislative policy-making requires an understanding likewise of conference committee interactions.

Central to these interactions, we have argued, are three distinct contexts within which conference committee politics occurs. Conference committees, first of all, are where the institutions of House and Senate meet (and frequently clash) in terms of such cameral differences as personalities, norms, styles, power relationships, rules, and procedures. This institutional context is supplemented by a committee context, which emphasizes committee determinants of conference behavior, and an individual context,

---

2. The staff's role in conference should also be emphasized, for House and Senate aides regularly meet in advance of bicameral negotiations to iron out problems and to take steps that will expedite the formal conference once it begins.

3. During a 1988 continuing appropriations conference, for example, Senator Carl Levin (D, Mich.) noted "forty-seven provisions in the conference report which appear to have been initiated by the conferees even though they were neither in the House nor the Senate bills" (*Congressional Record*, 100th Cong., 2nd sess., March 4, 1988, p. S2083).

which stresses the individual play of power so frequently exhibited in conference. These three contexts all operate within a larger political system that influences the speed, scope, competitive nature, and results of conference deliberations.

A final aspect of conference committees, even beyond their great significance, is that they are interesting and fun to study. Conference committee politics is indeed the epitome of legislative politics in terms of such central activities as negotiation, bargaining, and compromise. In short, in conference occur the most lively manifestations of congressional politics. Our case studies of conference committee politics, we trust, are not dry or technical in character, but rather involve real personalities engaged in complex conference interactions as they attempt to negotiate compromises that will survive the trials of the legislative process and that will also enhance their authors' political credibility and standing. There are few more lively and vibrant areas of congressional politics to examine.

Early in this study, we suggested three initial propositions: that conference committees are crucially important to policy outcomes, that they are the epitome of legislative politics, and that what we know about the dynamics of conference committees is spotty and limited. Conference committees still—today—remain among the less publicized stages of the lawmaking process. The entirety of this work itself has been an attempt to promote greater understanding and awareness of the centrality of conference committees to national policy-making and congressional politics.

Our study does not profess to provide a final or definitive analysis of conference committee politics, but rather has offered an introductory stab at analysis and understanding. Conference committee politics is as vast a topic as that suggested by the alternative term, bicameral politics. Its importance to an understanding of congressional lawmaking is great, and it behooves scholars, congressional observers, and others to come to grips with its mysteries and creative capacities.

Index

Abortion: funding for, 150–51
Amendment in disagreement, 245–46; priority of motions, 248–49. *See also* Amendment in the nature of a substitute (ANS)
Amendment in technical disagreement, 246–47
Amendment in the nature of a substitute (ANS), 234, 245–46, 249; germaneness rule and, 160–61
Amendment in true disagreement, 247–49
Amendments: germaneness rule, 49–50; as bargaining chips, 162, 163; degrees of, 325
ANS. *See* Amendment in the nature of a substitute
Anti-Apartheid Act of *1985:* case study, 286–93
Appropriation bill: compared with authorization bill, 301
"Architectural strategy." *See* Conference, meeting locations
Arter, David, 17*n*
Ashley, Thomas I., 54
Aspin, Les, 294–96, 298–99, 304–06, 343
Authorization bill: compared with appropriation bill, 301

Bach, Stanley, 21*n*, 87–88, 104
Bailey, Stephen K., 75
Baker, Howard H., 10, 22
Balanced Budget and Emergency Deficit Control Act of *1985*, 162*n;* as omnibus legislation, 5; spending limits on committees, 50; case study, 307–34, 307*n;* analysis of, 343–45, 348–49

Bargaining: in conference committees, 10–13, 192–215, 277, 284, 301–02, 338; techniques and procedures of, 135; with amendments, 163; defined, 193; features of, 194–98; theories of, 195*n;* strategies of, 208–15; timing and, 257
Basic Grant: in Education Amendments Act of *1972,* 259–65
Bell, Stephen E., 318–19
Bentsen, Lloyd, 160
Bicameral cooperation: necessity of, 103
Bicameralism: importance to conference committee, 3–5; defined, 13–19; and federalism, 14–15; national size and, 15*n;* separation of powers, 16; in state politics, 16; forms of, 18–19; inequalities in, 18–24, 19–20*n;* reconciliation in, 18–19; coequality of chambers, 20*n*, 27; English roots of, 28–29; during colonial period, 29–30; in state politics, 41–45; interinstitutional conflict, 93; U.S. Constitution on, 93; benefits of, 94; as *Federalist* theory, 97; and conference committees, 336–52
Bipartisan alliance: conference consensus and, 268
Birnbaum, Jeffrey H., 75
Bloc voting: in Bundesrat, 14
Bluffs: conference negotiation strategy, 212–15
Boggs, Hale, 256–57
Bowsher v. *Synar,* 333
Bowsher v. *United States,* 330*n*
Brademas, John, 259, 262–65, 267–68
Breaux, John B., 270

353

Britain: Parliament of, vii, 14, 17, 18–19; conference committees, 19, 28–29. *See also* British Parliament; England; House of Commons; House of Lords; Parliaments
British Parliament, vii, 14, 18–19, 20n; adaptability of, 17; conference committee origins, 28–29. *See also* House of Commons; House of Lords
Brooks, Jack, 271
Budget and Impoundment Control Act of *1974*: spending limits on committees, 50; on conference reports, 221n
Budget austerity: impact on conference agreement, 70–71
Budget: omnibus bills and, 5
Bundesrat, 18; bloc voting in, 14
Bundestag: West German upper house, 14, 18
Burton, Phil, 256–57, 262
Butler, David, 19n
Byrd, Robert C., 22, 23, 291–92
Byrnes, John, 257

Cabinet government: in England, 29
Capitol Hill staff: as nonconferee participants, 139–43; roles of, 140–42
Carmines, Edward G., 46
Carter, Jimmy, presidential influence on conference committees, 270, 273
Case studies, 253–334; Heptanoic Acid and Needy Children, 256–57, 337, 346; Education Amendments Act of *1972*, 258–68, 338, 346; Endangered Species Act of *1979*, 269–70, 339, 346; Department of Education Organization Act, 270–73, 339–40, 346–47; Tax Equity and Fiscal Responsibility Act of *1982*, 274–81, 340, 347; Low-Intensity Appropriations Conference, 282–85, 341, 347–48; Anti-Apartheid Act of *1985*, 286–93, 341–42, 348; Fiscal 1986 Defense Authorization Bill, 294–306, 342–43, 348; Balanced Budget and Emergency Deficit Control Act of *1985*, 307–34, 343–45, 348–49
Chamber-passing actions: preconference strategy, 153, 154–67
"Christmas Tree" legislation: benefits of, 159n
Civil War: conference committee development, 40n
Closed conference committee, 51–52, 297
"Closed open" conference committee, 56
Cloture rule: Senate use of, 240
Coequal bicameralism, 19–20n
Comity, 159n
Commitment strategy: increased bargaining power and, 214n
Committee caucus: limits on open conference, 58n
Committee context: of conference committees, 87–88n, 108–18, 278, 338, 350

Committee parallelism: in standing and conference committees, 110n, 110–11
Common Cause, 52, 53
Companion legislation: introduction of, 156
Compromise: in conference committees, 9, 209, 211–12
Concurrent resolutions: conference reports and, 221–22, 230
Conferees: selection of, 35–36, 40n, 65, 129, 135n, 178–86, 268, 278, 283, 296–97, 316–17, 326; limitations on, 36–38; representative types, 44; behavior with open conference, 59–60; general and special, 67; preparation for conference, 83–84n; House-Senate differences, 99n; individual goals, 119–22; roles of, 119–22; loyalties of, 122–24; instruction of, 129, 186–89, 187n; prior conference experience of, 135; personal staffs of, 140; stacking of, 183–84; House instruction rules, 188; objectives of, 194–95; dissenting from conference report, 219
Conference: frequency of, 4n; request for, 34–35; types of, 132–36; problem solving within, 133–35; considerations shaping, 154–56; traditional, 196, 340; meeting locations, 202–03; anticipation of, 338. *See also* Conference-asking; Conference committee
Conference-asking: preconference strategy, 153, 167–78; political considerations, 168–72
Conference committee: history of, vii–viii; importance of, viii, 3–5; neglect of, viii; three hallmarks of, 2; defined, 2n, 24; power of, 2n, 3, 77; bicameralism and, 3–5, 109n, 336–52; frequency of, 4n, 190–91; and omnibus legislation, 4n, 109n; as the third house of Congress, 6; composition of, 7; independence from chamber preferences, 7–8; constraints on, 8, 49–50, 117; compromise in, 9; as reconciler of differences, 9; size of, 10–11, 35–36, 66, 125, 132–33, 184–86, 316; bargaining in, 10–13, 301–02, 338; in England, 19, 28–29; evolution of, 26–45; cabinet government and, 29; during colonial period, 29–30; in early Congresses, 30–33; free versus open conference, 32, 50–61, 135n; selection of conferees, 35–36, 65, 178–86, 268, 283, 316–17, 326; during Civil War years, 40n, secret deliberations, 40n; in state legislatures, 42; in conflict resolution, 43; structural-process hypothesis of winning, 44–45; party leadership, 44n, 69–72; changing politics of, 46–72; procedures of, 47–50, 74–75; records of, 52; public access to, 54–56; external environment of, 61–72, 135–36, 344; autonomous subcommittees, 63–65; composition

INDEX

355

of, 64; subconference, 67; policymaking and, 68; politics of, 73–89, 128–32; case studies of, 75–76; who wins, 76, 77–87; members' perceptions of, 76–77; Senate dominance of, 77–87; conferee preparation for, 83–84n; committee context, 87–88n, 108–18; conference anticipation, 88; institutional context, 91–107; expectations of, 98, 128–29; House-Senate conflict in, 105–06; traditional conference, 109n, 196, 340; intercommittee relationships, 110–11; parallel membership with standing committees, 110–11, 110n; Fenno's analysis of, 117–18; individual context, 118–25; preconference process, 128–29, 153–91; official rules for, 130–31; strategies of, 130–31; unofficial rules for, 130–31; presidential influence on, 132, 143–47, 270–75, 280, 287–90, 327–28, 342; length of proceedings, 133; ex-officio members, 137; budget committees and, 139; Capitol Hill staff and, 139–43; governmental agency participants, 147–49; interest group representation, 149–51; press as participants, 151–52; impact of hearings, 157–58; alternative to, 167–78; House-Senate methods for reaching, 173–77; instruction of conferees, 188; negotiation in, 192–215, 278–79, 327, 338; multilateral features, 195–96; offer-counteroffer style, 196; pro forma, 196; subconference, 196; organization of, 198–203; chairman of, 200, 268; meeting locations, 202–03; staff participation in, 271–72; lobbyists' influence, 290; closed, 297; as de facto standing committee, 307–34; fact-finding role, 318, 344; media influence on, 319–20; brief, 269–73; avoidance of, 336n; legislative power and, 350

Conference report: floor action on, 38–39; development of, 40n; under Legislative Reorganization Act of *1970*, 49; preparation of, 131; adoption of, 131–32, 216–52, 284–93, 328–29, 339; procedural considerations, 173; privileged nature of, 227, 228, 239; House debate on, 227–38; parliamentary objections to, 231–36, 243; voting on, 236–38; defeat or recommittal of, 237–38, 244, 252; Senate debate on, 239–45; motions to dispose of, 241–43; test votes, 244; partial, 245–50; in disagreement, 249–50; House-Senate differences, 291n; control of, 292; indivisibility of, 299; Gramm-Rudman, 323–24

Conflict: bicameral institutional, 93; in conference committees, 109n, 112–14. *See also* Disagreement

Congress: conference committees in, 3–5; partisan division of, 4n; during colonial era, 14; conflict and cooperation in, 19–24; coequality of chambers, 27; free conference, 30n; divided party control of, 69–72; bicameral disagreement, 71–72

Congress and Colleges: The National Politics of Higher Education, 82

Congressional committee: selection of conferees and, 35; weakening of leadership, 62–65; impact on conferences, 66n; House-Senate power differences, 98n; differing House-Senate roles in, 112; members' perceptions, 112–14; integration and conference success, 114–16; change in values, 116; Fenno's typology of, 117–18; power of staffs, 140, 140n; hearings in, 157–58; decision making stages, 157–61; preconference process and, 157–61; markup of legislation, 158–60; reporting phase, 160–61; agency advocates, 197

Congressional Conference Committee: Seventieth to Eightieth Congresses, The (1951), 78

Congressional politics: impact on conference committees, 46–72

Congressional staff: as conference committee participants, 261, 271–72, 283

Congressmen in Committees, 77, 112, 116–18

Constitution: creation of Congress, 20; on bicameralism, 93; origination clause, 275–76, 282n, 340; congressional powers, 331

Constitutional Convention, 20, 20n, 93–97; state bicameralism, 29n

Constitutional reform: politics of, 16–17; to unicameralism, 17n

Constraints: on conference committees, 8, 49–50, 117

Continuing resolution: as policymaking instrument, 303–04

Custody of the papers, 130, 224–26; importance of, 33, 172–73, 290–91; floor action and, 225–26; and negotiating leverage, 226

D'Amato, Alfonse, 283–84
Davidson, Roger H., 63n, 65n, 66n, 69, 74, 116n
Debate: in standing committees, 161–62; on conference reports, 227–45
Decision-making: in conference committees, 117–18
Deering, Christopher J., 63n
Defeat, of conference reports, 237–38, 244
Defense authorization conference. *See* Fiscal *1986* Defense Authorization Bill
Denmark: unicameralism in, 17n
Department of Organization Act of *1979*, 270–73
Detail period: of conference negotiation process, 204n
Diagnostic stage: of conference negotiation process, 204n
Dicks, Norman D., 3

Disagreement: bicameral, 71–72; remedies to, 245–50; motion of, 325. *See also* Conflict
Dodd, Lawrence C., 46
Dole, Robert, 21, 57, 275, 276, 279, 289–92, 309, 314, 324, 328–29, 340
Domenici, Pete, 274–75

Eckhart, Dennis E., 118
Education Amendments Act of *1972:* conference on, 12; case study, 258–68; analysis of, 339–40, 346–47
Endangered Species Act of *1979:* case study, 269–70; analysis of, 339, 346
Energizer: conferee role, 120n
England: Parliament of, vii, 14, 17, 18–19; conference committee in, 19, 28–29. *See also* Britain; House of Commons; House of Lords; Parliaments
English Parliament, vii, 14, 18–19, 20n; adaptability of, 17; conference committee in, 19, 28–29; simple conference, 30n
Entrepreneurial sequence theory: of who wins conferences, 84n, 86–87n
Ervin, Sam J., 7
External environment: impact on conference committees, 61–72, 117, 135–36, 344

Fast track procedures: effect on legislation, 67–69
Federalism: and bicameralism, 14–15
Federalist Papers, 94–95
Fenno, Richard F., Jr., x, 8n, 12, 20, 24n, 76, 77, 78–80, 88, 93, 96n, 97, 98n, 99n, 100n, 109, 111n, 112, 114, 116–18, 119, 282n; on reinstruction as a bargaining tool, 193n
Ferejohn, John A., 75, 76, 81, 82, 103
Filibuster, 288–89; use of, 101n; of conference reports, 240
Fiscal *1986* Defense Authorization Bill: case study, 294–306; analysis of, 342–43, 348
Floor action: on conference reports, 38–39, 218–24, 230; sequence of, 224–26; in the Senate, 240–41
Floor leaders: in House and Senate, 101n
Floor management: of legislation, 63; preconference techniques of, 161–67
Floor manager: Senate role of, 239, 240, 245
Floor passage: preconference, 166–67
"Football huddle": limit on open conference, 58n
Formal motion: for conference report debate, 239
Formula phase: of conference negotiation process, 204n
Free conference, 30n
Froman, Lewis A., 75, 76
Fulbright, J. William, 6
Fuqua, Don, 271

Galloway, George B., 27, 34, 64n, 75
Game theory: of conference bargaining, 195n
General appropriations: amendments in technical disagreement, 246
General conferees: multiple referrals and, 67
Germaneness rule, 236, 236n: House difficulty with, ix, 49–50, 130, 160–61, 234–36; Senate lack of, 163; and Rule XX motions, 176; and points of order, 247n
Giving-and-taking: bargaining strategy, 208–15
Gladieux, Lawrence, 11–12, 75, 76, 82, 99n, 120n
Goldwater, Barry, 296
Gore, Albert, Sr., 5–6
Governmental agencies: as conference participants, 147–49
Gramm, Phil, 308, 309n, 326, 334n
Gramm-Rudman conferences. *See* Balanced Budget and Emergency Deficit Control Act
Grass-roots lobbying, 222
Great Compromise, the, 14, 15n, 93
Green, Edith, 259, 262–64, 266–68, 338
Griffith, Ernest S., 75
Gross, Bertram M., 7

Hamilton, Alexander, 94, 95n
Harmonizer: conferee role, 120n
Hatfield, Mark, 51
Hearings: committees and, 157–58
Heller, Walter, 314
"Hello and Good Bye" conferences, 57n, 133; informal meetings, 269; case studies of, 269–73; analysis of, 339–40
Heptanoic Acid and Needy Children, case study, 256–57; analysis of, 337, 346
Hollings, Ernest, 307n, 308, 317, 326, 334n
Hookup rule: in the Senate, 175n
Horn, Stephen, 108
House. *See* House of Representatives
House of Commons, 14, 18, 20n; relationship with House of Lords, 17; in English Parliament, 28–29
House of Lords, 14, 18–19, 20n; adaptability of, 17; relationship with House of Commons, 17n; in English Parliament, 28–29
House of Representatives, ix; importance of conference committees, 3–5; Rules Committee, 47–48, 48n, 243; development of subcommittees, 63–65; committee-dominated legislation, 98; political craftsmanship, 98–103; view of Senate, 100n; opportunities for conference participation, 111n; methods for reaching conference, 175–77; selection of conferees by, 178–81; instruction of conferees, 188; conference reports, 227–36, 250; obtaining a special rule, 228; size and procedural limitations, 239; and debt-raising

legislation, 308; in Defense Authorization Act, 343
House rules: on instruction of conferees, 188; on conference reports, 221, 299; and amendments, 234–36; on germaneness, 236; on appropriation bills, 301
House Rules Committee, 243; Senate difficulty with, ix; power over conference committees, 48n; special rule from, 325
House Rule X: on selection of conferees, 178n
House Rule 28: on open conference committee, 54n

Individual context: of conference committees, 118–25, 279–80, 298–99, 326, 338, 350–51; in Gramm-Rudman conference, 317
Individualism: in the Senate, 163
Informal agreements, 326–28; in Education Amendments Act of 1972, 265
Informal caucus: limit on open conferences, 56–58
Informal conference, 135
Informal meetings: limit on open conference, 61; in "Hello and Good Bye" conferences, 269
Informal negotiations: conflict resolution by, 43n; importance of, 203; conference success and, 279, 339, 344
Informal powers: conference success and, 201
Information giver: conferee role, 120n
Initiator-contributor: conferee role, 120n
Institutional context: in bicameral rivalry, 5; of conference committees, 91–107, 275–77, 298–99, 338, 350; conflict in conference, 105–06; in Gramm-Rudman conference, 318
Institutional hypothesis: of who wins conferences, 84n
Instruction of conferees, 186–89, 187n, 203n
Integration: of congressional committees, 114–16
Interest groups: influence on conferees, 59–60; omnibus bills and, 68; governmental agency representatives, 148–49; representation at conference committees, 149–51; conference-asking and, 169; lobbying by, 281
Ippolito, Dennis S., 83, 84n
Irresponsible conference. See Runaway conference

Jackson, Keith, 17n
Jay, John, 94
Jefferson, Thomas, 28n, 30n, 180n
Jefferson's Manual, 180n
Jewell, Malcolm E., 2n, 19, 42–44, 44n, 74
Joint explanatory statement: and conference report, 218–19; House rules on, 221
Jones, Charles O., 11, 23, 66n

Journalists: open conference and, 61
Judicial review: of Gramm-Rudman, 330
"Juniority": growing importance of, 5

Keefe, William J., 41, 74
Kephart, Thomas, 65n
Kozak, David C., 91

Layover rule: on conference reports, 221, 228
Legislation: introduction of, 154–56; goals of, 156
Legislative bicameralism, 13–19; forms of, 18–19
Legislative craftsmanship: of individual conferees, 120
Legislative fast track: effect on legislation, 67–69
Legislative power: bicameralism as control on, 97
Legislative reconciliation, 19, 104; through conference committees, 9; bicameralism and, 18–19
Legislative Reorganization Act of 1970, 47; on conference reports, 49
Leverage: negotiation and, 226
Levin, Carl, 317n
Lijphart, Arend, 15, 17n, 20n
Loading a bill, 128–29
Lobbying, 222–24, 298; influence on conferees, 59–60, 290; by governmental agency representatives, 148; by president, 280, lobbyist as technical expert, 150
Logrolling: conference-asking and, 170; conference negotiation strategy, 203, 209–10
Long, Russell B., 46
Longley, Lawrence D., viii, ix, x, 1, 16n, 17n, 41n
Low-Intensity Appropriations Conference: case study, 282–85; analysis of, 341, 347–48
Lowenberg, Gerhard, 14n, 15n, 18n
Lower House: in English Parliament, 28–29
Lugar, Richard, 288–89, 291–92

Madison, James, 31, 94, 95, 96n, 97
Malbin, Michael J., 75, 76
Manley, John, 1, 80, 84n, 192
Mann, Thomas E., 63n, 98n
Markup: strategies of, 158–61
Mather, Jeanie, 41
McCarthy, Eugene, 6
McCown, Ada C., 27, 74, 75
Media: influence on conference committees, 319–20
Member goals: in conference committees, 117
Mikva, Abner, 105
Mills, Wilbur, 256–57
Motioning: to avoid conference, 23. See also "Ping-pong" process

Motion to agree: in the Senate, 174
Motion to amend: in the Senate, 174
Motion to disagree: in the House, 325; in the Senate, 174–75, 174n
Motion to dispose: of conference reports, 241–43
Motion to insist on amendments: Senate amendment of House bill, 174n
Motion to perfect, 249
Motion to postpone: conference report debate, 241–43
Motion to recede and concur, 249
Motion to refer: conference report debate, 241–42
Motion to refer to committee: in the Senate, 174
Motion to table: conference report debate, 242
Multiple amendment option: in reporting stage, 161n
Multiple referral, 109n, 200n; selection of conferees, 65; of legislation to committees, 65–67; subconferences and, 67; and preconference strategy, 155–56
Murray, Alan S., 75

National Defense Authorization Act of *1987*: bargaining in conference, 10
National legislatures: state interests reflected in, 14–15
Negotiation: Senate resistance to, 102; by staff, 140–42; strategies for, 203–07; House-Senate differences, 207–08; and custody of the papers, 226; in conference committees, 278–79, 327, 338
New Zealand: unicameralism in, 17n
Nonconferees: roles of, 137–39; presence of, 138; as conference committee participants, 318–19
Norton, Philip, 17n
Nunn, Sam, 300

Obstructionist, conferee role, 120
Obtaining information, as conference negotiation strategy, 205–08
"Offer-counteroffer" conference, 196
Ogul, Morris S., 41, 74
Oleszek, Walter J., viii, ix, x, 1, 49n, 65n, 74, 75, 76, 98n
Olson, David M., 16n, 17n, 19n
Omnibus legislation, 67–69, 109n, 303; impact on conference committees, 4n; as policy instrument, 5; large conference committee and, 11; and conference committee size, 66, 132–33; strategy and, 156
Omnibus Reconciliation Act of *1981*, 67
One-hour rule: conference report debate, 227, 228n
O'Neill, Thomas P. (Tip), 22, 62, 299–300, 318, 323

O'Neill v. *Synar*, 333n
Open conference committee, 32, 50–61, 157–58n; of *1911*, 51n; consequences of, 54–61; House Rule *28*, 54n; limitations on, 56–58; interest groups and, 59–60; bargaining in, 135n; consequences of, 135n; amendments and, 163n
Opening gambits: in conference bargaining, 204–08
Organizational theory: of conference bargaining, 195n
Ornstein, Norman J., 63n, 98n

Packaging: interest groups and, 68; conference-asking and, 170–72
Packwood, Robert, 317–18, 320, 322–27, 328
Paletz, David L., 7n, 8n, 75, 76, 77, 99n
Parallelism: of conference and standing committees, 110–11, 110n
Parliamentary Act of *1911*, 18
Parliamentary Act of *1949*, 18
Parliaments: British, vii, 14, 17, 18–19, 20n, 28–29; West German, 14, 18; Danish, 17n; New Zealand, 17n; South African, 17n; Swedish, 17n; bicameral equality and, 19n
Partial conference reports, 245–50
Participatory democracy: junior legislators as conferees, 5
Partisan division: of Congress, 4n
Party leadership: and conference committees, 44n
Party loyalty, 184
Patterson, Samuel C., 2n, 14n, 15n, 18n, 19, 42–44, 44n, 74
Pell, Claiborne, 12, 262–64, 292–93
Perceptions: by conferees, 76–77; by congressional committee members, 113–14
Perkins, Carl, 12, 259–60, 263–65, 268, 338
"Ping-pong" process, 174n; and conference report approval, 11n, 23n. *See also* Motioning
Ploys: in conference negotiation, 204
Points of order, 236n; conference report debate, 231–36; in Senate conference report debate, 243; germaneness rule and, 247n; in Education Amendments Act of *1972*, 267; effects on conference report, 277; scope and, 329; as a strategy tool, 334n
Policy fragmentation: and House subcommittees, 63
Policymaking: conference committees and, 4, 68; omnibus bills and, 5
Political considerations, of conference-asking, 168–72; in selection of conferees, 181–86; conference report adoption, 218–24; lobbying, 222–24
Political facilitators: conferee role, 120, 120n
Political parties: influence on bicameral reconciliation, 19; weakening of leadership, 62–

65; divided control of Congress, 69–72; bicameral tensions within, 103n; conferee selection, 184

Political skill: importance in conference committees, 268

Politics of Finance: The House Committee on Ways and Means, The, 80, 84n

Possession of the papers. *See* Custody of the papers

Postconference process, 131–32, 216–52; of case studies, 346–50

Power: of conference committees, 2n, 3; of seniority, 2n; impact of diffusion on conference committees, 4n; committee differences in House and Senate, 98n; informal, 201

Power of the Purse, The, 78–80, 282n

Precedence: of Senate motions, 175; of House motions, 177

Precedent, 18; in conference committee action, 37; as precursor of rules, 40

Preconference process, 128–29, 153–91; bicameral differences in caucus, 99n; negotiations and conference length, 133; strategies for, 153–67; markup, 158–61; reporting phase, 160–61; case studies, 346–50

Preferential motion, 325

President: as lobbyist, 20n, 223–24; as conference committee participant, 132, 143–47, 270, 272, 274–75, 280, 287–90, 327–28, 330, 342; constitutional powers of, 330n

Press: as conference committee participants, 151–52

Pressman, Jeffrey L., 76, 87, 112

Price, David E., 77

Pro forma conference, 196

Problem solving perceptions: shared by conferees, 134–35

Procedural considerations: in conference-asking, 172–73; in conference negotiation, 204–05

Proxmire, William, 7

Proxy votes: in conference committees, 199

Psychological strategy: in conference negotiation, 205

Public choice theory, of conference bargaining, 195n

Qualitative differences: conference problem solving and, 134

Quantitative differences: conference problem solving and, 134

Quayle, Dan, 305

Quie, Albert, 259, 262–65, 268

Rayburn, Sam, 48, 62

Reagan, Ronald, 1, 326, 327–28; presidential influence on conference committees, 274–75, 280, 287–90, 342; as participant in Gramm-Rudman conferences, 321

Receding to chamber's position: bargaining technique, 284

Recommittal: of conference reports, 237–38

Recorded votes: floor management and, 166n

Reinstruction: as a bargaining tool, 193n; during conference, 203n

Repetitive games: of conference committees, 197, 197n

Reporting stage: multiple amendment option, 161n

Representative Mike Synar et al. v. United States, 330n

Ribicoff, Abraham, 270–73

Ripley, Randall B., 74

Roles: in congressional committees, 112; of individual conferees, 119–22; of nonconferee participants, 137–39, 140–42; of staffs, 142; of Senate floor manager, 142; of conference committees, 307–34

Rostenkowski, Dan, 276–79, 318, 320, 322–24, 326, 329, 340

Rudman, Warren B., 308, 313, 326, 334n

Rules: and conference committees, 198–99, 201

Rules Committee: of the House of Representatives, 47–48, 175–76, 243; special rule from, 228, 300; influence in, 301

Rule XX: House procedure for, 175–77

Rule XXII: Senate use of, 240

Runaway conference, 5–9, 36n, 181n

Rundquist, Barry S., 76, 83–87

Schelling, Thomas C., 193

Scope, 232–33, 263; markup and, 159–60; quantitative perspective of, 232–34; violations of, 243, 277, 329; defined, 277n

Seeking instructions: conference strategy of, 131

Selection of conferees. *See* Conferees, selection of

Senate, ix: importance of conference committee, 3–5; dominance in conference committee, 77–87; restraining influence of, 94, 96; comity and reciprocity in, 98; individualism in, 98–103, 112, 239; as upper house, 100n; resistance to negotiation, 102; conference participation, 111n; floor amendments in, 163; methods for reaching conference, 174–75; selection of conferees by, 180; conference reports, 239–45, 250; cloture rule, 240; points of order, 243

Senate hookup rule, 175n

Senate majority leader: floor management by, 63n; scheduling conference reports, 239

Senate rules: amendments and, 234–36; cloture, 240; on points of order, 243n; on appropriation bills, 303. *See also* Rule XXII

Seniority, 283; power of, 2n; weakening of, 62, 64, 111n; and conference committee composition, 64
Separation of powers, 20, 95, 333n; legislative bicameralism and, 16; Gramm-Rudman plan and, 320
Shepsle, Kenneth A., 110n
Shepsle-Weingast thesis: of legislative influence of congressional committees, 110n
Shuttle diplomacy: limit on open conference, 58n
Simple conference, 30n
Size: of conference committee, 10–11, 125, 132–33, 327; decision making and, 185–86
Smith, Steven S., 63n, 64n
South Africa: tricameralism in, 17n
South African Sanctions. *See* Anti-Apartheid Act of *1985*
Speaker of the House: weakened power of, 62; powers of, 177, 178n; selection of conferees, 178–80
Special conferees: multiple referrals and, 67
Special rule from the Rules Committee: House request for, 47–48, 175, 176, 300; conference report debate, 227, 228
Splitting-the-difference: conference negotiation strategy, 209, 210–11; bargaining technique, 284
Spread sheets: in conference negotiations, 142
Squeeze play: limit on open conference, 58n
Stage of disagreement, 248–49
Standing committee. *See* Congressional committee
State interests: within national legislatures, 14–15
State politics: bicameralism in, 16, 26–45, 40n; unicameralism in, 41n
Steiner, Gilbert Y., 9, 74, 76, 78
Stevens, John Paul, 333n
Stoner, John R., 269n, 270n
Strategic hypothesis: of who wins conferences, 84–87
Strategic premises: of conference committees, 117
Strategy: of conference committees, 130–31; role of staff, 142; floor action and, 225–26; of exhaustion, 258
Strom, Gerald S., 76, 83–87
Structural-process hypothesis: of who wins conferences, 44–45, 84n
Subcommittees: growth of, 5; development of, 63–65
Subconferences, 67, 196
Supersonic transport (SST) conference: conference committee independence from chamber, 7–8
Supreme Court, on Gramm-Rudman, 331–32
Suspension of the rules: House request for, 175–76; conference report debate, 227–28

Sweden: unicameralism in, 17n
Sydow, Bjorn von, 17n
Synar, Mike, 331
Systems theory: of conference bargaining, 195n

Tax Equity and Fiscal Responsibility Act of *1982*: case study, 274–81
Tax Increase Conference. *See* Tax Equity and Fiscal Responsibility Act of *1982*
Technical corrections: to conference report errors, 221–22
Test votes: on conference reports, 244
Thompson, Frank, Jr., 259, 262–63, 268
Threats: conference negotiation strategy, 212–15
Time-limitation agreements: to regulate conference report debate, 240, 243n
Timing: preconference strategy and, 154–55; of conference-asking, 168–70; in selection of conferees, 182; and conference report adoption, 218–22; and opposition to conference reports, 222
Trades: conference negotiation strategy, 209–11
Tricameralism: in South Africa, 17n
Two masters problem: for conference negotiators, 24n

Udall, Morris, 23
Unanimous consent agreement, 324; to regulate conference reports, 240, 243n
Unanimous consent request, 24, 47–48, 175, 256–57, 271, 329; minority obstruction of, 48n; in the Senate, 239
Unicameralism, 17n; settings for, 15n; resistance to, 16; in state legislatures, 41n, 42n
Unit rule: of conference decision making, 209
U.S. Congress. *See* Congress
U.S. Constitution. *See* Constitution
U.S. Senate. *See* Senate
U.S. Supreme Court. *See* Supreme Court
United States v. *Synar*, 333n
Upper house: in Bundestag, 14, 18; in English Parliament, 28–29; restraining influence of, 94; House view of Senate, 100n. *See also* Senate

Vogler, David J., 3n, 4n, 74, 76, 80, 112
von Sydow, Bjorn. *See* Sydow, Bjorn von
Voting: preconference strategy of, 165–66; test votes, 244; on conference reports, 244–45

Weingast, Barry R., 110n
West Germany: Parliament of, 14, 18
White, Byron R., 333n

Who wins: structural-process hypothesis, 44–45; in conference committees, 76, 77–87; chart summary of, 85
Wildavsky, Aaron, 214n
Willoughby, W. F., 75
Wilson, Woodrow, 97, 109

Wolanin, Thomas, 11–12, 75, 76, 82, 99n, 120n
Wordsmithing: preconference strategy and, 155
Wright, Jim, 22, 101n, 198, 300

Zartman, I. William, 204n

Augsburg College
George Sverdrup Library
Minneapolis, MN 55454

JK 1111 .L65 1989

Longley

Bicameral politics